Experimental Embryology in Aquatic Plants and Animals

NATO ASI Series

Advanced Science Institutes Series

A series presenting the results of activities sponsored by the NATO Science Committee, which aims at the dissemination of advanced scientific and technological knowledge, with a view to strengthening links between scientific communities.

The series is published by an international board of publishers in conjunction with the NATO Scientific Affairs Division

A	Life Sciences	Plenum Publishing Corporation
B	Physics	New York and London
C	Mathematical and Physical Sciences	Kluwer Academic Publishers
D	Behavioral and Social Sciences	Dordrecht, Boston, and London
E	Applied Sciences	
F	Computer and Systems Sciences	Springer-Verlag
G	Ecological Sciences	Berlin, Heidelberg, New York, London,
H	Cell Biology	Paris, and Tokyo

Recent Volumes in this Series

Series A: Life Sciences

Experimental Embryology in Aquatic Plants and Animals

Edited by

Hans-Jürg Marthy

Observatoire Océanologique de Banyuls
Centre National de la Recherche Scientifique (CNRS)
Université Pierre et Marie Curie
Banyuls-sur-Mer, France

Plenum Press
New York and London
Published in cooperation with NATO Scientific Affairs Division

Proceedings of a NATO Advanced Study Institute on
Experimental Embryology in Aquatic Plant and Animal Organisms,
held September 11–23, 1989,
in Banyuls-sur-Mer, France

QL
961
.N37
1989

The logo of the ASI shows the result of intracellular microinjections of
fluoresceinisothiocyanate–Dextran (MW 9000) into cells of an early squid
blastoderm. Whereas cells during interphase are dye-coupled into small
groups, cells in a mitotic state become uncoupled (plasmatic bridges
closed). For more details consult reference 4 of chapter 10. Logo created
by M.-J. Bodiou, Banyuls-sur-Mer.

Library of Congress Cataloging-in-Publication Data

NATO Advanced Study Institute on Experimental Embryology in Aquatic
   Plant and Animal Organisms (1989 : Banyuls-sur-Mer, France)
    Experimental embryology in aquatic plants and animals / edited by
Hans-Jürg Marthy.
       p.   cm. -- (NATO ASI series. Series A, Life sciences ; vol.
   195)
    "Proceedings of a NATO Advanced Institute on Experimental
Embryology in Aquatic Plant and Animal Organisms, held September
11-23, 1989, in Banyuls-sur-Mer, France."--CIP t.p. verso.
    Includes bibliographical references and index.
    ISBN 0-306-43678-7
    1. Embryology, Experimental--Congresses. 2. Aquatic animals-
-Congresses. 3. Aquatic plants--Embryology--Congresses.
I. Marthy, H.-J. II. Title. III. Series: NATO ASI series. Series
A, Life science ; v. 195.
QL961.N37 1989
574.92--dc20   90-43958
                                                             CIP

© 1990 Plenum Press, New York
A Division of Plenum Publishing Corporation
233 Spring Street, New York, N.Y. 10013

Printed in the United States of America

PREFACE

The NATO Advanced Study Institute on "Experimental Embryology in Aquatic Plant and Animal Organisms" was attended by more than 70 participants, including 15 invited main lecturers from 18 different countries. In accordance with the main purpose of the meeting, senior scientists, postdoctoral investigators and graduate students working in areas of descriptive and experimental embryology, classical, molecular and developmental biology, physiology and biochemistry etc., were brought together for two weeks as a community with a strong common interest in "development"; that is, the multiple phenomena and mechanisms, in molecular, cellular, genetic and organismic terms, observed in the development of aquatic organisms. Initial concern that the great variety of biological models as well as of research subjects would harm the scientific quality and coherency of the course was unnecessary. It was exactly this breadth which made the Institute worthwhile for each of the participants. Since many of the "students" were younger scientists starting a career, it was the main goal of the course to offer a concise overview of selected system models of primarily aquatic organisms and to present and discuss research carried out in the past and in progress.

Thus, each main speaker gave two in-depth lectures: one in which he presented an overview of "his" model and another dealing with current investigations. As to their contributions for this book, it was at each individual author's discretion to present his/her knowledge in the form of one manuscript or, as had been done orally, in two distinct chapters. In addition, a few participants were also invited to write short manuscripts.

The models that were presented span the range from the unicellular algae to complex vertebrate embryos. Each model has its own properties and specific value which makes it suitable for a particular type of research. For example, whereas algae or coelenterates are highly suitable for studies on cell polarity determination, ooplasmic segregation, nucleo-cyto-plasmic interactions or pattern formation phenomena, control mechanisms on oocyte maturation and fertilization events are classically best analyzed in echinoderms and ascidians. Planarians proved uniquely suitable for regeneration studies and molluscs give essential insight into compartmentalization processes in embryonic tissues. Representatives of annelids are of great interest for basic neurobiological research, and fish embryos are worthy of note for the study of cell migration *in vivo*, etc. In particular, this book contains chapters on research done on the following model systems:

Uni- and pluricellular algae by S. Berger and R. Quatrano; Coelenterates (hydroids and ctenophores) by G. Plickert and Ch. Sardet; Turbellaria (planarians) and nematodes (*Caenorhabiditis elegans*, living on a water film) by J. Bagunà and E. Schierenberg; Molluscs by J. Van den Biggelaar and H.-J. Marthy; Annelids (leeches and polychaetes) by S. Blackshaw and A. Dorresteijn; Echinoderms (starfish and urchins) by L. Meijer and R. Burke; Chordates (tunicates) by B. Dale and W. Jeffery; Vertebrates (teleost fishes) by J.P. Trinkaus and R. Fleig. It is also interesting to remember the historical and conceptual framework in which "causal embryology" is anchored (J.L. Fischer). For their high general scientific and stimulating value, the book contains finally chapters on research work done on avian eggs (G. Eichele: morphogens; P. Kucera: physiological approaches to embryogenesis; embryos' sensitivity against environmental factors). They should provide a "challenge" for encouraging similar research on and/or methodological approaches to eggs and embryos of aquatic organisms.

Twenty years have passed since Reverberi's book on "Experimental Embryology of Marine and Fresh-water Invertebrates" was published and became a standard reference book for developmental biology. It is the intention of the editor and the authors of this book that the information contained herein should not only update some of the research reported there, but by introducing new original aspects, prove to be invaluable as a contemporary reference work for research scientists, teachers and students alike.

I take the opportunity to thank the NATO Scientific Affairs Committee for having supported this ASI and, in particular, the Director of the ASI Programme Dr. L.V. da Cunha. I also want to thank the lecturers of the course and all the "students" for their great efforts in making it a real success. Thanks belong also to the Director of the Laboratoire Arago, Professor A. Guille, for hospitality. Important organizational and administrative work has been done by Mrs. N. Clara and Mr. C. Febvre. The diligent work of Mrs. U. Marthy-Stampfli, who prepared the manuscript in camera-ready form is greatly acknowledged.

Hans-Jürg Marthy

CONTENTS

SECTION I

SELECTED AQUATIC PLANT ORGANISMS

DASYCLADACEAE:

A FAMILY OF GIANT UNICELLULAR ALGAE IDEAL FOR RESEARCH

Sigrid Berger

Max-Planck-Institut für Zellbiologie
Abteilung Schweiger, Rosenhof
D-6802 Ladenburg bei Heidelberg
Federal Republic of Germany

Algae of the family Dasycladaceae belong to the most fascinating and promising objects in cell biological research. Due to their special features which are described below they have contributed fundamental knowledge to the understanding of morphogenesis, nucleo-cytoplasmic interaction, polarity and circadian rhythmicity. An immense body of literature has been generated during the more than five decades that algae of the family Dasycladaceae have been employed as research objects (for references see: Berger et al., 1987; Bonotto, 1988). Only some of the most interesting findings focusing mainly on morphogenesis and nucleo-cytoplasmic interactions will be reported here. The intent is to show the enormous potential of Dasycladaceae in cell biological research. Furthermore it might be useful for researchers working in the field of embryology to become familiar with their special features. The Dasycladaceae may be ideally suited for studies of fundamental questions in embryology, e.g. spatial and temporal organization or regulation of morphogenetic processes at the cellular level.

Dasycladaceae are a family of green algae that grow in shallow waters in the tropical and subtropical littoral zones. Three species occur in the Mediterranean sea. The algae can easily be cultured in the laboratory in an enriched sea water medium (Berger and Schweiger, 1980) or in artificial seawater (Schweiger et al., 1977). A unique culture collection which contains most of the known species of Dasycladaceae is maintained by the Max Planck Institute for Cell Biology.

All Dasycladaceae are unicellular organisms which reach an enormous size. Cells of the larger species may grow to a length of 200 mm. Under the usual culture conditions (Berger and Schweiger, 1980) the cells reach a size between 2 mm, e.g. *Acetabularia pusilla*, and 100 mm, e.g. *Acetabularia major* (Fig.1).

The various species within the family show a pronounced morphogenesis (compare Fig.1a, b, c with Fig.1d). The basic structure of all Dasycladaceae consists of a siphonous stalk

FIG.1. Four fully grown cells of different Dasycladaceae species. The gametophores of species that
belong to the genus *Acetabularia* are arranged at the
tip of the cell to form a cap-like structure. In the
genus *Batophora* the gametophores have the shape of
spheres and are attached to the upper hair whorls.
a) *Batophora oerstedii* b) *Acetabularia major* c)
Acetabularia mediterranea d) *Acetabularia pusilla*.
Bar represents in a to c: 10mm, in d: 1mm.

and a branched rhizoid. The stalk is surrounded at intervals
along its length by circularly arranged branched hairs which
are called hair whorls. In some species the older hair whorls
fall off leaving rings of scars along the stalk. Other species
keep their hair whorls over the entire length of the stalk. The
thick cell wall of the Dasycladaceae endows the cell with
rigidity, but it interferes with the exchange of materials with
the environment. Therefore, the thin-walled hairs play an
important role for the cell.

The rhizoid plays another important role. It consists of
branching projections that attach the cell to the substratum.
In nature, the cells attach to rocks, old coral reefs, shells
or other solid substrates. If the cells are kept freely
floating in culture medium the branches twist around each
other. This forms the typical skein-like rhizoid-structure of a
cell grown in laboratory culture (Berger et al., 1974).

At the end of their vegetative phase, the Dasycladaceae
develop gametophores with gametangia. The gametophores may take
the form of spheres attached to the upper hair whorls (Fig.1d).
The attachment site of these spheres is a species-specific
feature. A cap composed of sack-like rays is the typical
gametophore for all members of the genus *Acetabularia*. The
number of cap rays as well as their shape are species-specific
characteristics (Fig.1 a-c). All species form a species-
specific structure, the corona superior, above the cap rays.
Some species form another such structure, the corona inferior,
beneath the cap rays (Berger et al., 1974).

The large size and the programmed morphogenesis of a

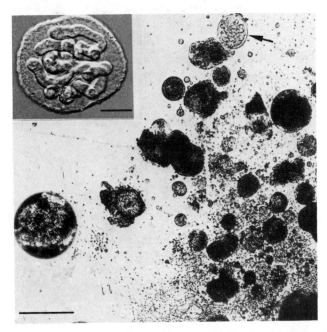

FIG.2. Cytoplasm which was squeezed out of a rhizoid from *Acetabularia mediterranea* viewed under a binocular microscope. The arrow points to the nucleus. Bar represents 200μm. The insert shows an isolated nucleus kept in buffer. Bar represents 30μm.

single cell are two of the many features that have made these algae such valuable organisms. Another unique feature of these cells is their single giant nucleus. Depending on the species, the nucleus reaches a diameter between 30 μm and 200 μm. This nucleus is predictably located in the rhizoid during the vegetative phase of the life cycle. Therefore, if the rhizoid is cut off the cell is enucleated.

The algae are extraordinary in their ability to tolerate extensive surgical manipulation. They easily survive removal of the rhizoid, the tip, or the gametophores. Fragments produced by cutting the stalk in several locations also survive (Hämmerling, 1932).

Furthermore, the giant nucleus can be isolated by squeezing the protoplasm out of the cut-off rhizoid and locating it with a binocular microscope (Fig.2). The nucleus can be kept alive in buffer for up to 24 hours (Berger et al., 1975). Such a nucleus can be subjected to different treatments as for example microinjection (Cairns et al., 1978b). It can be implanted into the original cell or into another cell which might even belong to another species (Hämmerling, 1955; Richter, 1959).

When a rhizoid is cut off to enucleate a cell the cut end remains unsealed for a short time. This enables the researcher to use the following method (Fig.3): Several cells are tied together at their tips (fifty cells is a reasonable number to form one bundle). The cells are opened and enucleated by

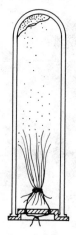

FIG.3. A bundle of Dasycladaceae cells which have been tied together at their tips and enucleated by cutting of their rhizoids. The bundle is fastened to a lid over a centrifuge tube. The cytoplasm of the cells is gently centrifuged out.

cutting off their rhizoids. The bundle is then fastened to a lid that fits onto a centrifuge tube. Cytoplasm which is free of any nuclei, nuclear debris or broken organelles can be gently centrifuged out of the open cells (Schweiger et al., 1967).

Another useful feature of the Dasycladaceae is their geological age. These algae existed as early as the ordovician which is dated back more than 500 million years. During their golden age, many genera with numerous species populated the oceans. At present, ten genera of Dasycladaceae including about 40 species exist. Each genus has arisen at distinct known times (Kamptner, 1958) (Fig.4). In their natural habitats, the Dasycladaceae acquire a calcareous coat. When the cell dies the calcinous structure is preserved and adds to the lime deposits

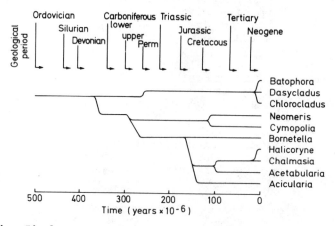

FIG.4. Phylogeny of Dasycladaceae according to a description by Kamptner (1958; from Berger et al., 1987).

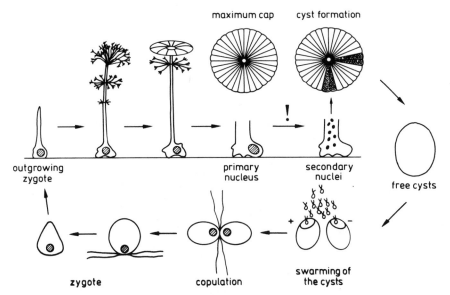

FIG.5. Life cycle of Acetabularia. The non-diffe-
rentiated zygote grows into the basic structure of
all Dasycladaceae which is composed of rhizoid, stalk
and circularly arranged hair whorls. After attaining
a certain size the cells form species-specific
gametophores. The cell is uninuclear until the gametophores are fully grown. The propagative phase
starts with meiosis of the primary nucleus followed
by many mitoses. This results in numerous secondary
nuclei which migrate up the stalk into the
gametophores where cysts are formed. The nuclei
continue to divide in the cysts. Finally many
biflagellate gametes are released. All of the gametes
from a given cyst are of the same mating type, but
both types of gametes are formed by one cell. Fusion
of two isogametes results in a zygote with four
flagellae.

of the lithosphere. Precise information about the evolution of
the genera and even of some species has been obtained by
examining structures from limestone deposits of different ages.

The life cycle of the Dasycladaceen cells (Fig.5) starts
with the formation of a zygote by fusion of two biflagellate
gametes. The zygote with its four flagellae is negatively
phototactic and swims to a dark place. There it settles and
looses the flagellae. Branches of the rhizoid and the elongate
stalk start to grow a few days later. Periods of stalk
elongation alternate with whorl formation until the stalk
reaches its full length. This length depends mainly on the
species. The species-specific gametophores are then formed. In
the case of an Acetabularia cell the gametophores take the form
of a cap. In other genera the formation of spheres at the upper
hair whorls can be observed. The vegetative phase comes to an
end with the completion of gametophore formation. Until this
time, the single nucleus which is called the "primary nucleus",
is always located in the rhizoid. Now the propagative phase
starts.

The primary nucleus undergoes meiosis followed by numerous mitoses (Koop, 1975; Liddle et al., 1976). The newly formed secondary nuclei are transported up the stalk by actin filaments and enter the gametophores. The number of secondary nuclei per gametophore is species-specific within a certain limit. Between 1 and 300 secondary nuclei might enter one gametophore.

Bundles of microtubules surround each secondary nucleus in the gametophore. They keep each nucleus in a certain position well separated from the neighboring nuclei, from the plasma membrane and the tonoplast (Menzel and Elsner-Menzel, 1989). The microtubules are also responsible for keeping chloroplasts a certain distance from each secondary nucleus. Consequently white spots form in the otherwise green cytoplasm. The "white spot" stage thus signals the arrival of secondary nuclei in the gametophores.

A thick cell wall is formed around each secondary nucleus and a certain portion of cytoplasm in the gametophore to give rise to a cyst. Numerous mitotic divisions occur in the cysts until they finally contain numerous secondary nuclei. Each nucleus together with a certain portion of cytoplasm will be surrounded by a membrane and eventually develop into a biflagellate gamete. During maturation of the cysts, the walls of the gametophores disintegrate, liberating the cysts.

The positively phototactic gametes leave the cysts through a preformed opening and swim towards the light. Gametes from a given cyst belong to the same mating type (Hämmerling, 1934a). In light, two gametes of different mating types fuse to form the negatively phototactic zygote (Hämmerling, 1934a). By this event the life cycle is completed. In laboratory culture one life cycle is completed within 4 to 6 months, depending on species and culture conditions.

Taking advantage of the special features of Dasycladaceae, Hämmerling was able to show that the information for species-specific morphogenesis is located in the cell nucleus (Hämmerling, 1934b). If one has two *Acetabularia* cells, it is easy to prepare grafts. The nucleus containing rhizoid is cut off, along with a small portion of the stalk, which is then pushed into a rhizoidless stalk of another cell (Fig.6). Hämmerling used two morphologically distinguishable species. The transplants developed the morphological characteristics of the nucleus-donor species. From this experiment it was postulated that the substances inducing morphogenesis originate in the nucleus. However, the experiment was open to criticism since cytoplasm of the rhizoid had also been transplanted. Therefore, this fundamental experiment was repeated, this time using an isolated nucleus for implantation into an enucleated cell of another species. The results were the same (Hämmerling, 1955). Since no cytoplasm had been transferred, it was concluded that chemical material must transfer the genetic information from the nucleus into the cytoplasm and to the site where morphogenesis occurs. The chemical material was called morphogenetic substances.

If a cell is cut into three fragments of approximately equal size, the basal fragment with the rhizoid is able to regenerate and form a reproductive cell. A basal fragment

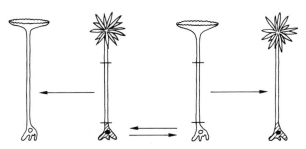

FIG.6. Effect of transplantation of a heterologous
rhizoid on morphogenesis in an anucleate basal
fragment (from Schweiger and Berger, 1979).

without the nucleus shows no growth or morphogenesis. A middle
fragment is capable of growth but morphogenesis is limited to
hair formation. An apical fragment grows and forms species-
specific gametophores which do not develop into a reproductive
structure. This means that the morphogenetic substances are
distributed in an intracellular gradient (Hämmerling, 1934b,
1936).

Rhizoids of cells at the onset of whorl formation and at
several later stages of growth before formation of gametophores
were cut off (Hämmerling, 1934b). The anucleate cells survived
and formed hair whorls. They were even able to form species-
specific gametophores. However, this was only possible for
cells that had already reached a critical stage of development
before the nucleus was removed. Since it had been shown that
the morphogenetic substances originate in the nucleus, it was
obvious from these experiments that they are released from the
nucleus long before the morphogenetic events that they direct
occur. The cell must be able to store these substances until it
is ready to use them. When later on the chemical pathways of
genetic expression were known and this knowledge was
transferred to the data obtained from experiments performed on
Dasycladaceae it was obvious that regulation of morphogenesis
does not occur at the level of transcription. Data accumulated
indicating that the morphogenetic substances are identical with
mRNA.

If mRNA is identical with the morphogenetic substances the
cell should be capable of storing it. It was shown by
radioactive labelling of *Acetabularia* cells that poly (A) RNA
is very stable if the cell looses its nucleus (Kloppstech and
Schweiger, 1982). If mRNA is identical with morphogenetic
substances the cell should not only be able to store it, it
also should be able to select and translate individual species
of the stored mRNA. In an experimental approach testing this
hypothesis poly (A) RNA from *Acetabularia mediterranea* was
isolated. Double-stranded DNA, complementary to the poly (A)
RNA from *A. mediterranea*, was then synthesized and cloned. It
was possible to demonstrate that the *A. mediterranea* cDNA
contained a high number of molecules that hybridized to poly
(A) RNA from this species, but not from six other Dasycladaceen
species. Therefore, these *A. mediterranea* clones may contain
species-specific morphogenetic information (Li-Weber and
Schweiger, 1985a).

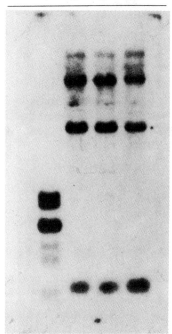

FIG.7. Hybridization after gel electrophoresis of
total RNA from different stages with cloned species-
specific cDNA probe pAM13.
Track 1: DNA marker, pBR322 digested with Alu I.
Track 2: cells of 5 mm length.
Track 3:cells at the stage of beginning cap
formation.
Track 4: cells with caps of 5 to 7 mm diameter
(from Li-Weber and Schweiger, 1985b).

RNA prepared from cells of different developmental stages
was tested for hybridization to this species-specific cDNA.
When total RNA was subjected to this analysis no significant
difference in the amount of hybridizable RNAs from different
stages of morphogenesis could be detected (Fig.7). However,
when polysomal RNA was used for hybridization a significant
increase in hybridization signals occurred during early cap
formation (Fig.8). This was also the case in anucleate cells
(Li-Weber and Schweiger, 1985b). These results suggest that the
amount of species-specific messages present in the cell is
constant but that they are preferentially translated at a
specific developmental stage, here the stage of early cap
formation. The cell must be able to select stored mRNAs for
translation at a given time. This ability does not require the
presence of a nucleus. The data also suggest that selective
translation of stored mRNAs constitutes an important regulatory
mechanism of cell differentiation and that differentiation is
controlled at the level of translation. Similar hybridization
experiments had also shown that a single cDNA probe can
hybridize to a number of electrophoretically separated RNAs
which are not degradation products of one mRNA (Li-Weber and
Schweiger, 1985b). This indicates that different mRNA species
share a common sequence. It might be that these common

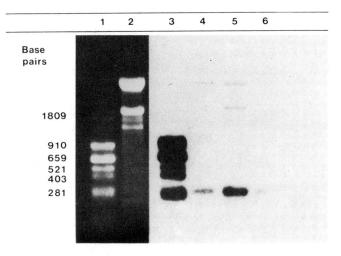

FIG.8. Hybridization after gel electrophoresis of polysomal RNA from different stages with pAM13.
Track 1,2: acridine orange staining.
Track 3 to 6: autoradiographs.
Track 1,3: DNA marker, pBR322 digested with Alu I.
Track 2: total RNA from polysomes.
Track 4: cells of 5 mm length
Track 5: cells at the stage of beginning cap formation.
Track 6: cells with caps of 5 to 7 mm diameter
(from Li-Weber and Schweiger, 1985b).

sequences identify developmental stages, so that the timing of translation of specific mRNA can be controlled.

Final verification about the nature of the morphogenetic substances is still missing. For the verification of the hypothesis that morphogenetic substances are identical with mRNA, specific mRNA should be brought into the cell where it has to induce species-specific morphogenesis.

Injection of RNA into Dasycladaceae cytoplasm might be difficult since the cells not only contain a large central vacuole, the cytoplasm is also highly vacuolized (Franke et al., 1974; Schweiger et al., 1974). Furthermore, it is not advisable to inject RNA into the cytoplasm since there is a high level of RNase activity (Schweiger, 1966). For characterization of morphogenetic substances the special features of Dasycladaceae allowed the development of an expression system: Isolated nuclei, kept alive in buffer, can be injected with RNA which is thus protected from enzymatic degradation. The injected nucleus can be implanted into a cell where it will release the injected RNA intact into the cytoplasm. The particular cell can be cultured individually and observed for morphogenesis.

It was necessary in developing this method to test whether the nucleus indeed releases injected RNA in a protected state into the cytoplasm where it can be correctly translated. As yet, only foreign RNA from viruses (TMV-RNA, mengovirus RNA) and mRNA for zein - the storage protein in maize - have been injected into *Acetabularia* nuclei. An indirect immunofluorescence technique has been used to show that the injected RNA is expressed after 3 to 5 days. Moreover, after injection of zein specific mRNA the fluorescence imaging shows circumscribed structures similar to those observed in maize endosperm (Cairns et al., 1978b 1978c; Langridge et al., 1985; Neuhaus and Schweiger, 1986).

In another set of experiments foreign DNA was injected into *Acetabularia* nuclei and shown by immunofluorescence to be translated (Cairns et al., 1978a; Neuhaus et al., 1983; Neuhaus et al., 1984; Langridge et al., 1985; Weeks et al., 1985; Brown et al., 1986). For example, the gene containing the information for neomycin-phosphotransferase II was injected. This enzyme bestows resistance to the antibiotic G 418 (geneticin). *Acetabularia* cells are not resistant to this antibiotic but the cells with the injected nucleus are. The progeny of these cells are also resistant to G 418. This shows that the injected gene is integrated correctly. By nuclear exchange experiments it could be shown that injected genes are incorporated into the nucleus and not into the organellar genome (Weeks et al., 1985; Neuhaus et al., 1986).

If one assumes that the cytoplasm is able to regulate the translation of different mRNAs, the question arises whether experiments have already been performed which can indicate a regulatory influence of the cytoplasm on different cellular activities. A body of experimental evidence exists indicating that a number of cellular activities are regulated by the cytoplasm.

Hämmerling (1939) made some very interesting observations: When he cut off the fully grown cap of an *Acetabularia* cell, cyst formation did not occur until another maximum size cap had been formed. On the other hand he was able to accelerate cyst formation by grafting a maximum size cap onto the rhizoid of a younger cell. It was later noted that the nucleus and perinuclear region of young and old cells show substantial differences in their ultrastructure (Franke et al., 1974; Berger et al., 1975). Experiments were undertaken to determine whether an influence of the cytoplasm on the nucleus could directly be visualized. A nucleus from a young cell was implanted into an anucleate old cell and *vice versa*. The ultrastructure of the nucleus and the surrounding cytoplasm adapts within days to the stage of the cytoplasm (Berger and Schweiger, 1975). This indicates that the cytoplasm is able to induce different stages of nuclear development depending on its own developmental stage.

It had been observed that anucleate Dasycladaceae cells differentiate. This requires the synthesis of specific enzymes at certain stages of development, in other words: A regulation of enzyme synthesis in the absence of the nucleus. For a number of enzymes it had been shown that their activity increases at defined stages of development - even if the nucleus was removed several weeks before (Spencer and Harris, 1964; Zetsche, 1966, 1968). This regulation clearly cannot be transcriptional since it occurs in anucleate cells. Another interesting question of regulation concerns the control of the enzymes catalyzing reactions during the course of certain nuclear events. Their regulation can easily be studied in Dasycladaceae:

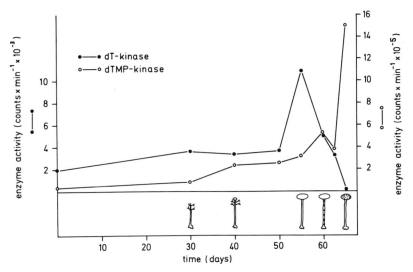

FIG.9. Schematic presentation of the development of an Acetabularia cell and the time of regulation of thymidine kinase and dTMP kinase (from Berger et al., 1987).

The diploid primary nucleus of the vegetative cell gives rise to more than 10^7 haploid secondary nuclei (Schulze, 1939). Such an enormous increase in the number of nuclei requires a very high level of DNA synthesis. This demands a large pool of DNA precursors which must be synthesized by special enzymes. Organellar DNA is not synthesized during the propagative phase (Clauss et al., 1970). Therefore, synthesis of enzymes for DNA synthesis during the propagative phase means synthesis of enzymes for nuclear DNA synthesis. The regulation of some of these enzymes has been studied in Dasycladaceae (Bannwarth et al., 1977; Bannwarth et al., 1982; de Groot and Schweiger, 1983; de Groot and Schweiger, 1985). The results of these studies show that the activities of the enzymes thymidine kinase, dCMP deaminase, dTMP kinase and ribonucleoside reductase are greatly increased during the propagative phase of the cells (Fig.9). Since the increase in activity is linked to nuclear DNA synthesis it seems reasonable to expect that it is controlled in presence of the nucleus. However, enucleation of the cell some time before the onset of the propagative phase fails to prevent the increase in enzyme activity. This result indicates that the cytoplasm even regulates metabolic events for nuclear activities.

The enzyme dTMP kinase is coded by nuclear genes. The coding site for the enzymes ribonucleoside reductase, dCMP deaminase and thymidine kinase is the chloroplast genome (de Groot and Schweiger, 1984). All these enzymes are involved in DNA synthesis during the propagative phase of the cells. Therefore, it is surprising that they are coded for by different compartments of the cell. The endosymbiont theory proposes that chloroplasts are derived from an association of cyanobacteria with predecessors of the recent eucaryotic cell. During evolution a decrease in the size of the incorporated genome occurred. The decrease resulted from the transfer of genes from the incorporated genome into the nuclear genome. An attractive hypothesis is that the enzyme dTMP kinase was originally coded for by the plastome at ancient times and during evolution it has been excised and incorporated into the nuclear genome.

The various genera of the Dasycladaceae have arisen at different times several hundred million years ago (Fig.4). Therefore, a search of the large Dasycladaceae collection was undertaken for species that still retain this gene in the plastome. The search was negative in all species of the genus *Acetabularia*. However, in *Batophora*, a genus that separated in its development from *Acetabularia* about 360 million years ago, the dTMP kinase is coded for by the plastome. *Batophora* is considered to be the most ancient genus. The result indicates that in this genus the translocation of the dTMP kinase gene has not occurred (de Groot and Schweiger, 1984).

Other results obtained from studies on Dasycladaceae support the hypothesis of gene transfer (Li-Weber et al., 1987; Tymms and Schweiger, 1985). Furthermore, a high variability in gene arrangement on the chloroplast genome has been observed in two Dasycladaceae species (Leible et al., 1989).

On the other hand, studies of the Dasycladaceae plastome have shown that some genes are highly conserved. For example, the amino acid analysis of the large subunit of the ribulose-1,5-bisphosphate carboxylase of *Acetabularia mediterranea* and *Acicularia schenckii*, two Dasycladaceae species that separated from each other about 150 million years ago, showed only 6 amino acid exchanges (Leible and Schweiger, 1986; see also Schneider et al., 1989).

The ease with which one can prepare anucleate cells and exchange nuclei between two cells has allowed experiments that have contributed to our fundamental understanding of nucleo-chloroplast interactions. The discovery that chloroplasts possess their own genetic information gave rise to the question: How autonomous are these organelles? It was not easy to answer this question since it turned out to be difficult to exclude all nuclei or nuclear debris from chloroplast preparations. If Dasycladaceae are used as research objects, the nuclei may be removed by cutting off the rhizoids of the cells. It was possible to show on isolated *Acetabularia* chloroplasts that these organelles code for their own rRNA (Berger, 1967). On the other hand NAD-dependent malate dehydrogenase isoenzymes are coded by nuclear genes even though they are located within the organelles (Schweiger et al., 1967; Rahmsdorf, 1977). This conclusion was based on the following experiments: Radioactive labelling and gel electrophoresis demonstrated a synthesis of malate dehydrogenase in anucleate cells. The isoenzyme patterns of different *Acetabularia* species were investigated. Nuclei of cells from two species which showed pronounced differences in their isoenzyme patterns were exchanged. After one week the isoenzyme patterns of the implants had changed to that of the nucleus donor cell (Fig.10). These results indicate that 1) The nucleus codes for the malate dehydrogenase. 2) The mRNA for the enzyme is very stable in anucleate cells. 3) The stored mRNA is not translated if a new nucleus is implanted.

Similar experiments demonstrated that a number of chloro-plast ribosomal proteins (Kloppstech and Schweiger, 1973) and

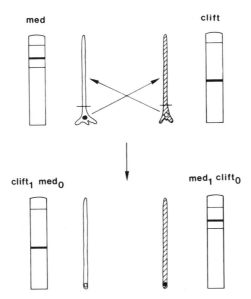

FIG.10. The effect of reciprocal nuclear transplantation on the pattern of MDH isoenzymes in two
species of Acetabularia. 1 denotes the presence and 0
denotes the absence of the nucleus of that species
(from Schweiger et al., 1967).

chloroplast membrane proteins (Apel and Schweiger, 1972, 1973)
are also coded by nuclear genes.

Results from many experiments demonstrate that multiple
interactions occur between semiautonomous chloroplast,
cytoplasmic and nuclear compartments. We have recognized
several of these interactions and gained some insight into
them. Nevertheless, the nature of the signals that are
exchanged between the interacting compartments remains unknown.
We also do not understand the mechanisms that control the
timing of these interactions. Dasycladaceae have been ideal
objects for the study of many fundamental questions in cell
biology. They are likely to continue to be valuable objects for
research in the fields of nucleocytoplasmic interactions and
differentiation.

REFERENCES

Apel, K., and Schweiger, H.G., 1972, Nuclear dependency of
        chloroplast proteins in Acetabularia, Eur.J.Biochem.,
        25:229-238.
Apel, K., and Schweiger, H.G., 1973, Sites of synthesis of
        chloroplast-membrane proteins, Eur.J.Biochem., 38:373-
        383.
Bannwarth, H., Ikehara, N., and Schweiger, H.G., 1982, Nucleo-
        cytoplasmic interactions in the regulation of thymidine
        phosphorylation in Acetabularia, Proc.R.Soc.Lond.B,
        198:177-190.
Bannwarth, H., Ikehara, N., and Schweiger, H.G., 1983,
        Deoxycytidine monophosphate deaminase in Acetabularia:
        properties and regulation in the early generative phase,

Eur.J.Cell Biol., 27:200-205.

Berger, S., 1967, RNA-synthesis in *Acetabularia*. II. RNA-synthesis in isolated chloroplasts, *Protoplasma*, 64:13-25.

Berger, S., and Schweiger, H.G., 1975, Cytoplasmic induction of changes in the ultrastructure of the *Acetabularia* nucleus and perinuclear cytoplasm, *J.Cell Sci.*, 17:517-529.

Berger, S., and Schweiger, H.G., 1980, *Acetabularia*: techniques for study of nucleo-cytoplasmic interrelationships. *In:* "Handbook of Phycological Methods. Developmental and Cytological Methods," E. Gantt, ed., Cambridge University Press, Cambridge, USA, pp. 47-57.

Berger, S., Sandakhchiev, L., and Schweiger, H.G., 1974, Fine structural and biochemical markers of Dasycladaceae, *J.Microsc.* Paris, 19:89-104.

Berger, S., Herth, W., Franke, W.W., Falk, H., Spring, H., and Schweiger, H.G., 1975, Morphology of the nucleo-cytoplasmic interactions during the development of *Acetabularia* cells. II. The generative phase, *Protoplasma*, 84:223-256.

Berger, S., Niemann, R., and Schweiger, H.G., 1975, Viability of *Acetabularia* nucleus after 24 hours in an artificial medium, *Protoplasma*, 85:115-118.

Berger, S., de Groot, E.J., Neuhaus, G., and Schweiger, M., 1987, *Acetabularia*: a giant single cell organism with valuable advantages for cell biology, *Eur.J.Cell Biol.*, 44:349-370.

Bonotto, S., 1988, Recent progress in research on *Acetabularia* and related Dasycladales. In: "Progress in Phycological Research," F.E. Round, and D. Chapman, eds, Biomedical Press, Elsevier, Amsterdam, Vol.6:59-235.

Brown, J.W.S., Wandelt, C., Feix, G., Neuhaus, G., and Schweiger, H.G., 1986, The upstream regions of zein genes: sequence analysis and expression in the unicellular green alga *Acetabularia*, *Eur.J.Cell Biol.*, 42:161-170.

Cairns, E., Doerffler, W., and Schweiger, H.G., 1978a, Expression of a DNA animal virus genome in a plant cell, *FEBS Lett.*, 96:295-297.

Cairns, E., Gschwender, H.H., Primke, M., Yamakawa, M., Traub, P., and Schweiger, H.G., 1978b, Translation of animal virus RNA in the cytoplasm of a plant cell, *Proc.Natl.Acad.Sci.USA*, 75:5557-5559.

Cairns, E., Sarkar, S., and Schweiger, H.G., 1978c, Translation of tobacco mosaic virus RNA in *Acetabularia* cell cytoplasm, *Cell Biol.Int.Rep.*, 2:573-578.

Clauss, H., Lüttke, A., Hellmann, F., and Reinert, J., 1970, Chloroplastenvermehrung in kernlosen Teilstücken von *Acetabularia mediterranea* und *Acetabularia cliftonii* und ihre Abhängigkeit von inneren Faktoren, *Protoplasma*, 69:313-329.

Franke, W.W., Berger, S., Falk, H., Spring, H., Scheer, U., Herth, W., Trendelenburg, M.F., and Schweiger, H.G., 1974, Morphology of the nucleo-cytoplasmic interactions during the development of *Acetabularia* cells, *Protoplasma*, 82:249-282.

De Groot, E.J., and Schweiger, H.G., 1983, Thymidylate kinase from *Acetabularia*. II. Regulation during the life cycle, *J.Cell Sci.*, 64:27-36.

De Groot, E.J., and Schweiger, H.G., 1984, Possible

     translocation of a gene for thymidylate kinase from the
     chloroplast to the nuclear genome during evolution,
     J.Cell Sci., 72:15-21.
De Groot, E.J., and Schweiger, H.G., 1985, Regulation of a
     ribonucleoside reductase during the early generative
     phase in *Acetabularia*, *J.Cell Sci.*, 73:1-5.
Hämmerling, J., 1931, Entwicklung und Formbildungsvermögen von
     Acetabularia mediterranea. I. Die normale Entwicklung,
     Biol.Zentralbl., 51:633-647.
Hämmerling, J., 1932, Entwicklung und Formbildungsvermögen von
     Acetabularia mediterranea. II. Das Formbildungsvermögen
     kernhaltiger und kernloser Teilstücke, *Biol.Zentralbl.*,
     52:42-61.
Hämmerling, J., 1934a, Über die Geschlechtsverhältnisse von
     Acetabularia mediterranea und *Acetabularia wettsteinii*,
     Arch.Protistenk., 83:57-97.
Hämmerling, J., 1934b, Über formbildende Substanzen bei
     Acetabularia mediterranea, ihre räumliche und zeitliche
     Verteilung und ihre Herkunft, *Roux's
     Arch.Entwicklungsmech.*, 131:1-81.
Hämmerling, J., 1936, Studien zum Polaritätsproblem, *I.-III.
     Zool.Jahrb.Abt.Allg.Zool.Physiol.Tiere*, 56:439-486.
Hämmerling, J., 1939, Über die Bedingungen der Kernteilung und
     der Zystenbildung bei *Acetabularia mediterranea*,
     Biol.Zentralbl., 59:158-193.
Hämmerling, J., 1955, Neuere Versuche über Polarität und
     Differenzierung bei *Acetabularia*, *Biol.Zentralbl.*,
     74:545-554.
Kamptner, E., 1958, Über das System und die Stammesgeschichte
     der Dasycladaceen *(Siphoneae verticillatae)*,
     Ann.Naturhist.Museum, Wien, 62:95-122.
Kloppstech, K., and Schweiger, H.G., 1973, Nuclear genome codes
     for chloroplast ribosomal proteins in *Acetabularia*. II.
     Nuclear transplantation experiments, *Exp.Cell Res.*,
     80:69-78.
Kloppstech, K., and Schweiger, H.G., 1982, Stability of
     poly(A)$^+$ RNA in nucleate and anucleate cells of
     Acetabularia, *Plant Cell Rep.*, 1:165-167.
Koop, H.-U., 1975, Über den Ort der Meiose bei *Acetabularia
     mediterranea*, *Protoplasma*, 85:109-114.
Langridge, P., Brown, J.W.S., Pintor-Toro, J.A., Feix, G.,
     Neuhaus, G., Neuhaus-Url, G., and Schweiger, H.G., 1985,
     Expression of zein genes in *Acetabularia mediterranea*,
     Eur.J.Biol., 39:257-264.
Leible, M.B., and Schweiger, H.G., 1986, Differences in amino
     acid sequence of the large subunit of ribulose-1,5-
     bisphosphate carboxylase/oxygenase from two species of
     Dasycladaceae, *Planta*, 169:575-582.
Leible, M.B., Berger, S., and Schweiger, H.G., 1989, The
     plastome of *Acetabularia mediterranea* and *Batophora
     oerstedii*: inter- and intraspecific variability and
     physical properties, *Curr.Genet.*, 15:355-361.
Liddle, L., Berger, S., and Schweiger, H.G., 1976,
     Ultrastructure during development of the nucleus of
     Batophora oerstedii (Chlorophyta; Dasycladaceae),
     J.Phycol., 12:261-272.
Li-Weber, M., and Schweiger, H.G., 1985a, Molecular cloning of
     cDNA from *Acetabularia mediterranea*: comparative studies
     with other Dasycladaceae, *Eur.J.Cell Biol.*, 38:67-72.
Li-Weber, M., and Schweiger, H.G., 1985b, Evidence for and
     mechanism of translational control during cell

differentiation in *Acetabularia*, *Eur.J.Cell Biol.*, 38:73-78.

Li-Weber, M., de Groot, E.J., and Schweiger, H.G., 1987, Sequence homology to the *Drosophila* per locus in higher plant nuclear DNA and in *Acetabularia* chloroplast DNA, *Mol.Gen.Genet.*, 209:1-7.

Li-Weber, M., Leible, M., and Schweiger, M., 1989, Difference in the location in Dasycladaceae of a DNA sequence homologous to the *Drosophila* per locus, *Plant Cell Reports*, 8:169-173.

Menzel, D., and Elsner-Menzel, C., 1989, Maintenance and dynamic changes of cytoplasmic organization controlled by cytoskeletal assemblies in *Acetabularia* (Chlorophyceae). *In:* "Algae as Experimental Systems," A.W. Coleman, L.J. Goff, and J.R. Stein-Taylor, eds, Alan R. Liss Inc., New York, pp. 71-91.

Neuhaus, G., and Schweiger, H.G., 1986, Two-way traffic between nucleus and cytoplasm: cell surgery studies on *Acetabularia*. *In:* "Nucleocytoplasmic transport," R. Peters, and M. Trendelenburg, eds, Springer-Verlag Berlin, Heidelberg, pp. 63-71.

Neuhaus, G., Neuhaus-Url, G., Schweiger, H.G., Chua, N.H., Broglie, R., Coruzzi, G., and Chu, N., 1983, Expression of higher plant genes in the green alga *Acetabularia mediterranea*, *Eur.J.Cell Biol.* 30; Suppl., 2:30.

Neuhaus, G;, Neuhaus-Url, G., Gruss, P., and Schweiger, H.G., 1984, Enhancer-controlled expression of the simian virus 40 T-antigen in the green alga *Acetabularia*, *EMBO J.*, 3:2169-2172.

Neuhaus, G., Neuhaus-Url, G., de Groot, E.J., and Schweiger, H.G., 1986, High yield and stable transformation of the unicellular green alga *Acetabularia* by microinjection of SV40 DNA and pSV2neo, *EMBO J.*, 5:1437-1444.

Rahmsdorf, U., 1977, The intracellular distribution of malate dehydrogenase isoenzymes in *Acetabularia*. *In:* "Progress in Acetabularia Research," C.L.F. Woodcock, ed., Academic Press, New York, San Francisco, pp. 47-67.

Richter, G., 1959, Die Auslösung kerninduzierter Regeneration bei gealterten kernlosen Zellteilen von *Acetabularia* und ihre Auswirkungen auf die Synthese von Ribonucleinsäure und Cytoplasmaproteinen, *Planta*, 52:554-564.

Schneider, S.U., Leible, M.B., and Yang, X.-P., 1989, Strong homology between the small subunit of ribulose-1,5-bisphosphate carboxylase/oxygenase of two species of *Acetabularia* and the occurrence of unusual codon usage, *Mol.Gen.Genet.*, 218:445-452.

Schulze, K.L., 1939, Cytologische Untersuchungen an *Acetabularia mediterranea* und *Acetabularia wettsteinii*, *Arch.Protistenk.*, 92:179-225.

Schweiger, H.G., 1966, Ribonuclease-Aktivität in *Acetabularia*, *Planta*, 68:247-255.

Schweiger, H.G., Dillard, W.L., Gibor, A., and Berger, S., 1967, RNA-synthesis in *Acetabularia*. I. RNA-synthesis in enucleated cells, *Protoplasma*, 64:1-12.

Schweiger, H.G., Master, R.W.P., and Werz, G., 1967, Nuclear control of a cytoplasmic enzyme in *Acetabularia*, *Nature*, 216:554-557.

Schweiger, H.G., and Berger, S., 1979, Nucleocytoplasmic interrelationships in *Acetabularia* and some other Dasycladaceae, *Int.Rev.Cytol.Suppl.*, 9:11-44.

Schweiger, H.G., Berger, S., Kloppstech, K., Apel, K., and

Schweiger, M., 1974, Some fine structural and biochemical features of *Acetabularia major* (Chlorophyta, Dasycladaceae) grown in the laboratory, *Phycologia*, 13:11-20.

Schweiger, H.G., Dehm, P., and Berger, S., 1977, Culture conditions for *Acetabularia. In:* "Progress in *Acetabularia* Research," C.L.F. Woodcock, ed., Academic Press New York, San Francisco, pp. 319-330.

Spencer, T., and Harris, H., 1964, Regulation of enzyme synthesis in an enucleate cell, *Biochem.J.*, 91:282-286.

Tymms, M., and Schweiger, H.G., 1985, Tandemly repeated nonribosomal DNA sequences in the chloroplast genome of an *Acetabularia mediterranea* strain, *Proc.Natl.Acad.Sci. USA*, 82:1706-1710.

Weeks, D., Brunke, K., Beerman, N., Anthony, J., Neuhaus, G., Neuhaus-Url, G., and Schweiger, H.G., 1985, Promoter regions of four coordinately regulated tubulin genes of *Chlamydomonas* and their use in construction of fused genes which are expressed in *Acetabularia, in:* "Plant Genetics," M. Freeling, ed., Alan R. Liss, New York, pp.477-490.

Zetsche, K., 1966, Regulation der UDP-Glucose 4-Epimerase-Synthese in kernhaltigen und kernlosen Acetabularien, *Biochim.Biophys.Acta*, 124:332-338.

Zetsche, K., 1968, Regulation der UDPG-Pyrophosphorylase-Aktivität in *Acetabularia*. I. Morphogenese und UDPG-Pyrophosphorylase-Synthese in kernhaltigen und kernlosen Zellen, *Z.Naturforsch.*, 23b:369-376.

ACETABULARIA:

A GIANT UNICELLULAR ORGANISM FOR STUDYING POLARITY

Sigrid Berger

Max-Planck-Institut für Zellbiologie
Abteilung Schweiger, Rosenhof
6802 Ladenburg bei Heidelberg
Federal Republic of Germany

Walter L. Dillard

Department of Zoology
University of Oklahoma
Norman, Oklahoma, USA

INTRODUCTION

To understand the biochemical and cytological basis of cell polarity is to gain insight into the process of differentiation. When organisms differentiate, modifications of morphological and functional characteristics occur at certain loci. These loci are specified relative to an axis of polarity. Polar organization of multicellular organisms directs the specialization of previously undifferentiated cells at distinct sites. It is a prerequisite for development of a specialized organism. Without a polar organization there can be no differentiation.

Although there is much to be learned from studying the differentiation of multicellular organisms, some aspects of polarity are most profitably studied in single cells. Many unicellular organisms display a high degree of morphological and physiological complexity. Differentiation in such organisms must give rise to structures that are the functional analogs of the specialized organs and structures of multicellular organisms. Furthermore, it must do so while utilizing only those resources to be found within the confines of a single plasma membrane. The small size of most single cells constitutes a barrier to their use in many applications. Small size is not a problem with giant algal cells that belong to the genus *Acetabularia* and related genera (family Dasycladaceae). The characteristics of these algae and their utilization by researchers are the subject of another monograph in this volume.

Morphologically, *Acetabularia* appears as a highly differentiated, and hence, highly polarized cell at all devel-

Experimental Embryology in Aquatic Plants and Animals
Edited by H.-J. Marthy, Plenum Press, New York, 1990

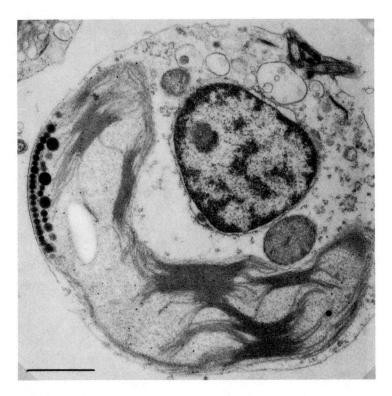

FIG.1. Section through a gamete
The gamete is polarly organized. The nucleus is always located beneath the flagellar pole while the chloroplasts are arranged at the opposite pole. A stigma in the chloroplast enables the gamete to swim towards the light. The bar represents 1 μm. (By courtesy of W. Herth, University of Heidelberg).

opmental stages. This feature, when combined with its other special advantages would seem to make this organism an ideal choice for the study of various aspects of polarity at the cellular level.

ORIGIN OF THE POLAR MORPHOLOGY

The life cycle of an *Acetabularia* cell begins with the fusion of two gametes (Fig.1). The gametes have a distinct polar organization. Each has a stigma and two flagellae at one pole. The nucleus is located near this pole, and it is possible that the location of the nucleus influences the site of origin of the flagellar pole. The polarity is preserved in the zygote.

The positive phototaxis and negative geotaxis of the gamete are reversed in the zygote. It therefore swims downward and away from the light. As a consequence, the nucleus becomes positioned towards the basal end of the developing *Acetabularia* cell. The four flagellae of the zygote are resorbed, and a rhizoid develops around the nucleus. The rhizoid extends several finger-like projections that anchor the cell to the substratum. At the same time, stalk development begins as an

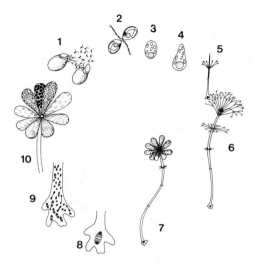

FIG.2. Life cycle of *Acetabularia*
1. Cyst germination and release of isogametes; 2.
Conjugation; 3-4 germling stage; 5-6 Whorl formation;
7. Cell with mature cap; 8. Meiosis; 9. Endomitosis
and migration of secondary nuclei; 10. Cyst formation
(from Menzel and Elsner-Menzel, 1989a).

elongation that defines the apical pole of the cell (Fig.2).
The direction of stalk growth is influenced by negative
geotactic and positive phototactic responses of the cell
(Gibor, 1977; Bonotto & Sironval, 1977).

It thus seems clear how polarity originates in
Acetabularia. The axis of polarity, and the apical and basal
poles are defined by the structure of the gamete. This primary
polarity is necessary to direct the early growth of the cell
along its axis of polarity, but it is difficult to imagine how
it alone could direct later events of differentiation such as
whorl and cap formation.

POLAR DISTRIBUTION OF MORPHOGENETIC SUBSTANCES

An apico-basal concentration gradient of morphogenetic
substances is correlated with the maintenance of polarity
(Hämmerling, 1934, 1936). This can be demonstrated by cutting
the long *Acetabularia* cell into several fragments. If the cell
is divided some time before cap formation, it can be noted that
fragments from different regions of the cell have different
morphogenetic capacities. A basal fragment which contains the
nucleus is capable of regenerating the whole cell. A basal
fragment without a nucleus shows no morphogenetic capability
unless it is specially treated. Middle fragments are capable of
growth, but their morphogenetic capability is limited to hair
formation. The apical fragment grows, forms one or two whorls,
and a cap, but it never forms a rhizoid.

Intact cells establish the gradient of morphogenetic
substances in darkness as well as in light, but the gradient is
maintained in darkness only if the nucleus is present
(Hämmerling & Hämmerling, 1959). If an enucleate cell is kept

in the dark, the concentration gradient soon disappears, resulting in a uniform distribution of the morphogenetic substances over the whole stalk. If the cell is re-illuminated, the gradient is soon re-established. However, it is possible that the re-established gradient may be reversed with the morphogenetic substances accumulating at the basal end of the stalk. When this happens, the stalk end at which growth and morphogenesis occur is also reversed. The direction of the light is an important factor in the reversal of polarity in enucleate fragments. In nucleate fragments however, the direction of light is without influence on the distribution of morphogenetic substances. Accumulation always occurs at the apical pole (Hämmerling, 1934; Hämmerling & Hämmerling, 1959).

These observations indicate that the nucleus plays an important role in the determination of polarity. This conclusion is supported by the following experiment: When the nucleus isolated from one cell is implanted into the basal enucleate fragment of another cell, a rhizoid develops at the end into which the nucleus is inserted. Stalk growth, and later cap formation occurs at the opposite pole which becomes the functional apical pole. The previous polarity has no influence (Hämmerling, 1955). These results show that the nucleus is able to reset the polarity.

Since a rhizoid is always formed in the vicinity of the nucleus, and growth and cap formation always occur at the opposite pole, it is obvious that there are two countercurrent gradients in the cell. The morphogenetic substances which are responsible for rhizoid formation have a high concentration in the vicinity of the nucleus. The morphogenetic substances for stalk, whorl and cap formation, which also originate in the nucleus, are transported to the opposite pole of the cell.

The conclusion that a gradient of chemical substances is responsible for the polar nature of morphogenesis in *Acetabularia* is a reasonable one. It would, however, be over-simplifying the problem of polarity to believe that this constitutes a complete explanation of the phenomenon. Internal heterogeneity of subcellular structures may play an important role in the uneven distribution of molecules. The cell contains a large number of membrane-enclosed organelles (Golgi vesicles, plastids, mitochondria, etc.) which constitute functional compartments within the cell. The activity and distribution of these structures should be studied to understand how they influence cell polarity.

POLAR DISTRIBUTION OF SUBCELLULAR STRUCTURES

The Primary Nucleus and Perinuclear Region

In the zygote, the nucleus is embedded in the cytoplasm and the perinuclear zone is not differentiated (Fig.3). As soon as the outgrowth of the stalk starts, a highly differentiated perinuclear region develops (Fig.4). A thin continuous layer of cytoplasm covers the nucleus. This layer is about 100 nm thick and no organelles or membrane structures are observed in it. Thin cytoplasmic strands connect the cytoplasmic layer surrounding the nucleus to the cytoplasm in the cell. The nuclear envelope has an extremely high density of pores (ca. 70

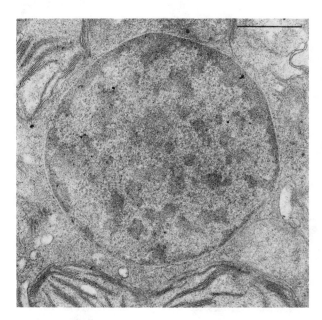

FIG.3. Section through the nucleus of a zygote
No special structures can be identified in the vicinity of the nucleus. The bar represents 1 μm (from Franke et al., 1974).

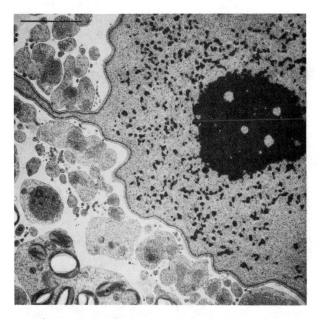

FIG.4. Section through part of the fully developed primary nucleus
The surface of the nucleus is highly invaginated, a feature that is indicative of a strong metabolic activity. The perinuclear zone is differentiated. Numerous perinuclear dense bodies can be identified in this zone. The bar represents 5 μm (from Franke et al., 1974).

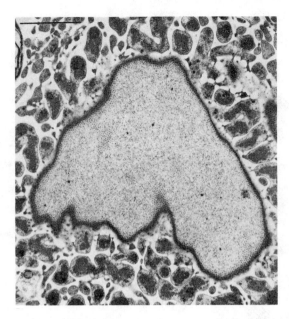

FIG.5. Section through the tip of the primary nucleus
The high number of perinuclear dense bodies
surrounding the nucleus is apparent. The bar
represents 2.5 µm (from Franke et al., 1974).

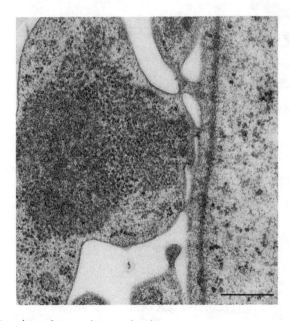

FIG.6. Perinuclear dense body
It is composed of a granular and a fibrillar
component. Densely stained large granules are
associated with the components. Polysomes are
frequently observed close to the perinuclear dense
bodies. The bar represents 0.5 µm (from Berger and
Schweiger, 1975).

- 80 pores per μm^2). The number of pore complexes per nucleus increases from ca. 2500 in the zygote nucleus to ca. 2.2 million in the fully developed nucleus (Franke et al., 1974). A large number of electron-opaque structures may be seen surrounding the nucleus. We have named these structures "perinuclear dense bodies" (Fig.5.). They are composed of fine fibrous material, dense grains and larger granules. Polysomes are frequently seen close to the dense bodies. The structure of the dense bodies is reminiscent of that of the nucleolus (Berger and Schweiger, 1975) (Fig.6). Their function is as of yet unknown, but they are known to contain RNA and protein. They have been shown by high resolution autoradiography to incorporate ^{3}H-uridine and to bind ^{3}H-actinomycin D (Tikhomirova et al., 1979). Antibodies raised against the small subunit of *Chlamydomonas* 80s ribosomes attach to them (Berger, unpublished results). Gold particles conjugated to DNase also bind to them (Berger and Schweiger, 1986). The perinuclear dense bodies may contain the chromosome fragments that have been detected outside the nucleus by staining with DAPI (4,6-Diamidino-2-phenylindole) and using epifluorescent microscopy (Shihira-Ishikawa, 1984). Perinuclear dense bodies have only been seen in close proximity to the nucleus. They disappear as the cell matures and the nucleus changes its structure and activity. It is conceivable that the nuclear pores constitute a bottleneck in the transport of ribosomes into the cytoplasm during the most active stages of cell growth and morphogenesis. The perinuclear dense bodies may be amplified rDNA genes that permit synthesis of ribosomes in the perinuclear zone.

The Tip Body

The apex of the cell, like the rhizoid has morphological and ultrastructural features that distinguish it from the rest of the cell. The most striking of these features is the structure of the growing tip (Fig.7). There is a clear cap or tip body that is devoid of chloroplasts. It consists largely of an accumulation of Golgi vesicles, endoplasmic reticulum elements and ribosomes. This would suggest that it is an area of active membrane synthesis and/or secretion. Golgi vesicles have also been implicated in cell wall synthesis (Werz, 1974). Mitochondria are less abundant in this region than in the rest of the cell.

The Chloroplasts

The stalk contains large numbers of chloroplasts (ca. 10^6 chloroplasts per cm of stalk). Although all of the chloroplasts share the same basic structure, morphologically and physiologically different populations are distinguishable (Bouloukhère, 1972). As the stalk grows, the chloroplasts develop distinctive morphologies and become distributed along an apico-basal gradient. The chloroplasts of the apical portion of the stalk are small, and rarely contain polysaccharide granules. They divide at a high rate. Chloroplasts in the middle of the stalk are larger. Division figures are not observed as frequently as in the apical region. They usually have more polysaccharide granules than the chloroplasts of the tip. Two types of chloroplasts can be distinguished in the rhizoid. Those in the vicinity of the nucleus are small and have an appearance similar to tip chloroplasts. They have well-organized membranes and form grana. Most of them have no

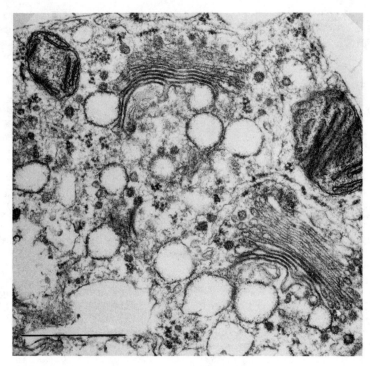

FIG.7. Section through the tip body of the cell
This region is free of chloroplasts. It contains a
high number of dictyosomes, vesicles and polysomes.
Mitochondria also appear in this region. The bar
represents 1 μm.

polysaccharide granules. If granules are present, they are very
small. The chloroplasts in the rest of the rhizoid are usually
spherical, have only a few internal membranes, and are nearly
filled with polysaccharides. Not all of the numerous
chloroplasts of an *Acetabularia* cell contain DNA (Lüttke,
1981). A higher percentage of apical chloroplasts contain DNA
than do the middle ones. Most of the chloroplasts of the
rhizoid that are not in the vicinity of the nucleus are devoid
of DNA while those close to the nucleus contain DNA.
Chloroplast transcriptional activity displays a similar
gradient (D'Emilio et al., 1979). There is an apico-basal
distribution of photosynthetic activity with the highest
activity being found in the apical chloroplasts (Issinger et
al., 1971). In addition, the subpopulations of chloroplasts may
be distinguished by differences in their relative amounts of
chlorophylls a and b, carotenoids, and saturated and
unsaturated fatty acids (Hoursiangou-Neubrun et al., 1977).

The polarized distribution of chloroplast types is
apparent in both nucleate and enucleate regenerating fragments.
There is no polarized distribution in enucleate fragments that
are not regenerating, and non-regenerating fragments are devoid
of apical-type chloroplasts.

The substantial cytoplasmic streaming that occurs in
Acetabularia would, at first glance, seem to preclude the
existence of a stable, non-random distribution of the chloro-

plast population. However, cinematographic observations have revealed that different parts of the cytoplasm stream at different rates. Some granules normally move at a high speed within the cytoplasmic strands while chloroplasts usually move much more slowly. Furthermore, chloroplasts seem to move mostly back and forth over short distances rather than migrating the entire length of the cell (Koop, personal communication).

We do not know what causes the differences in the ultra-structure of chloroplasts from different parts of the cell. Neither do we know what purpose such differences may serve. An attractive hypothesis is that the observed distribution of chloroplast types is related to the cooperation between the cell's nuclear and chloroplast genomes. The similarities of chloroplasts at the apical pole to those near the nucleus may indicate that the chloroplasts that take part in the coopera-tion move directly towards the tip of the cell. Another possibility is that such cooperation may only be possible in close proximity to the nucleus or in the tip of the cell. It seems reasonable to assume that chloroplast activity may be limited by the supply of proteins contributed by the nuclear genetic apparatus. Chloroplasts replication must be similarly limited by the rate of delivery of proteins coded by nuclear genes.

Ribosomes

The heterogeneity of the chloroplast populations and the uneven distribution of the different types of chloroplasts within the cell raise the question of whether there are other subcellular structures that exhibit intracellular gradients. Most cellular protein synthesis occurs at the tip of the cell (D'Emilio et al., 1979). The 80s ribosomes are concentrated adjacent to the nucleus and in the tip of the cell. The accumu-lation of 80s ribosomes at the tip of the cell is due to a direct transport mechanism (Kloppstech and Schweiger, 1975b). This conclusion is based on the following experiment: A growing cell was incubated in the presence of ^{3}H-uridine for 24 hours. At the end of this period the RNA that was produced in the nucleus was highly radioactive. Radioactively-labelled rRNA was released from the nucleus. Its incorporation into ribosomes and their migration through the stalk was followed. A rough estimate of the speed of migration of ribosomes from the rhizoid to the apex is 2 - 4 mm per day. Increase in cell length is only 1 - 2 mm per day. This indicates that the ribosomes are transported significantly faster than the cell increases in length. This relatively rapid transport of ribo-somes together with the extremely long half-life of ribosomes in *Acetabularia* (ca. 80 days) can account for the large accumulation of ribosomes in the tip of the cell. There is a simultaneous accumulation of ribosomes in the vicinity of the nucleus that must also be explained. It was observed that after five days, all of the labelled ribosomes were bound to membranes. It is possible that binding to membranes is a necessary preliminary step in ribosome transport. A delay between their synthesis and their attachment to membranes would cause ribosomes to accumulate in the basal part of the cell.

Poly (A) RNA also accumulates at the apical pole of the cell. It, like the ribosomes, follows a directed transport, but it is transported 5 to 10 times faster (Kloppstech and Schweiger, 1975a).

MICRO-MECHANISMS OF MORPHOGENESIS

The preceding has presented selected examples of polarity in *Acetabularia*, and its role in directing differentiation of the cell. The emphasis has been on the spatial distribution of organelles and macromolecules that convey information about the morphogenetic process. Although this information is interesting and enlightening, it does not address the important question: How does a particular distribution of "morphogenetic substances" (viz., poly (A) RNA and translation products) lead to the production of a specific shape ? This question cannot be answered at this time, but evidence is accumulating that shape is determined by the concerted action of the plasma membrane, the cortical cytoplasm and the cytoskeleton.

Cytoplasmic Streaming

There is little morphological evidence of polarity in the portion of the cell that lies between the rhizoid and the tip. However, the oriented transport of materials in this segment is clear evidence of a functional polarity. It is essentially a cylinder that is nearly filled by the large central vacuole. The cytoplasm occupies a thin layer between the vacuole and the plasma membrane. It has a heavily striated appearance because of the numerous bands of filaments that extend from the base to the apex. Subcellular organelles, vacuoles, granules, etc. are transported by the filaments. This accounts for the very active cytoplasmic streaming that can be observed during most stages of the life cycle. This tendency becomes more pronounced at the end of the vegetative stage when thousands of secondary nuclei and most of the cell's chloroplasts are transported up the stalk and into the cap rays. The net movement of chloroplasts from the stalk into the cap produces a notable lightening of the stalk. The mechanism that controls this phenomenon has not been explained. It occurs in enucleated cells that form caps despite the fact there are no secondary nuclei to transport. It does not occur in cells that do not form caps nor in those from which the cap is removed (Lüttke, 1983).

The extraordinary size and long, narrow shape of *Acetabularia* create problems of distribution. Materials produced in a given location or by a given organelle cannot be delivered to other locations in a timely manner by the mechanisms that suffice in cells of more conventional size and shape. The polar distribution of materials in *Acetabularia* is achieved by a rapid transport system that is mediated by elements of the cytoskeleton. Materials are transported by two systems of cytoplasmic filaments. "Headed streaming bands" transport small vesicles, polyphosphate granules and secondary nuclei at a rate of 3 - 11 μm/sec. Chloroplasts are transported, for the most part, by a system of thin filaments at a rate of 1 - 2 μm/sec. (Koop and Kiermayer, 1980a). Transport by both systems is blocked by cytochalasin B which specifically inhibits polymerization of actin. The headed streaming band system is also blocked by colchicine and other inhibitors of the reversible polymerization of tubulin (Koop, 1981). Thus, the thin filament system seems to be mediated by actin microfilaments while the headed streaming band system must require actin filaments and microtubules (Koop and Kiermayer, 1980b). However, Nagai and Fukui (1981) could not duplicate the inhibition by colchicine. Menzel (1986) detected actin filaments when he used an anti-actin antibody as the primary antibody in an indirect immunofluorescence technique. An anti-tubulin primary antibody did not detect the presence of microtubules in vegetative stages prior to the production of secondary nuclei. Thus, although the hypothesis that the high speed streaming is achieved by an interaction between microtubules and microfilaments is an attractive one, it has yet to be confirmed.

Nagai and Fukui (1981) used an elegantly-contrived centri-fugation/double chamber technique to show that cytoplasmic streaming is inhibited if the cortical cytoplasm is treated with cytochalasin B. It is not inhibited if only the endoplasm is treated. NEM (N-ethylmaleimide) which has been shown to inhibit actin-activated myosin ATPase, inhibits cytoplasmic streaming if the endoplasm is treated, but not if the cortical cytoplasm is treated. The authors suggest that actin filaments in the ectoplasmic striations interact with a moiety (probably myosin) in the endoplasm to produce cytoplasmic streaming. The endoplasmic organelle to which myosin may be bound (if present) is unknown. NEM inhibits by reacting with sulfhydryl groups. Since many proteins other than myosin have free sulfhydryl groups, the presumption that myosin exists in the endoplasm must be considered to be speculative.

Cyst Morphogenesis

As we have seen, the primary nucleus has a great influence on the formation of the polarity of an *Acetabularia* cell. Its position in the zygote foreshadows the orientation of the initial polar axis. It plays an important role in the polar distribution of the morphogenetic substances, of macromolecules and of subcellular organelles.

The primary nucleus divides in a special region of the rhizoid and eventually gives rise to more than 15,000 secondary nuclei (Koop and Kiermayer, 1980a). The secondary nuclei do not continue the orienting function of the primary nucleus. Instead, they migrate into the cap rays where they become nucleation centers around which cytoplasm is shaped to form cysts. They are transported in the stalk in cytoplasmic strands that contain actin filaments. Strands of microtubules are attached asymmetrically to the envelope of each secondary nucleus. When the secondary nuclei arrive in the cap, each becomes surrounded by radially-oriented microtubules. Most of the cap ray, like the stalk, is occupied by a central vacuole so that the cytoplasm and secondary nuclei are confined to a thin layer between the tonoplast and plasma membrane. The microtubules organize the secondary nuclei into a two-dimensional array in which the separation between neighboring nuclei is established and maintained (Fig.8). A cleavage ring of intertwined microtubules and actin filaments forms around the distal end of the radial microtubules. This ring delineates a cyst domain which bulges outward as the plane of the ring sinks inward (Fig.9). The plasma membrane of the cyst is formed where the surrounding microtubules end (Menzel and Elsner-Menzel, 1989a). The cleavage ring contracts, and the surface

31

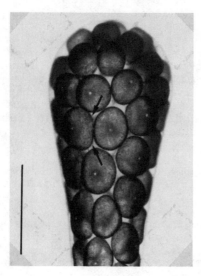

FIG.8. Secondary nuclei in a cap ray of *Acetabularia cliftoni*
Arrows show the position of the cleavage ring. The bar represents 500 μm (from Menzel and Elsner-Menzel, 1989a).

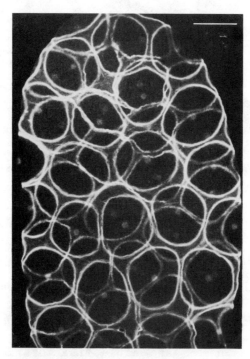

FIG.9. Immunofluorescence micrograph of a cap ray showing the distribution of actin in cleavage rings. The bar represents 250 μm (from Menzel and Elsner-Menzel, 1989a).

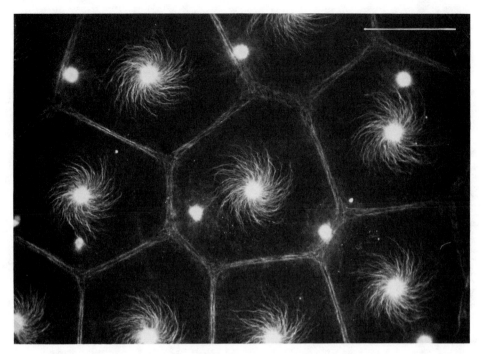

FIG.10. Secondary nuclei at a stage prior to lid formation showing counter-clockwise curving of distal microtubule ends
The bar represents 50 μm (from Menzel and Elsner-Menzel, 1989a).

area of the cyst protoplast membrane is increased by fusion with coated vesicles (Franke et al., 1977). The nucleus comes to lie in a position opposite the site of the cleavage ring. The distal ends of the radial microtubules bend to the left producing a spiral figure (Fig.10). The radial microtubules are eventually arranged into a circular band. It has been proposed that this microtubule band controls the positioning of the lid. A lid-forming apparatus develops at a site adjacent to the secondary nucleus. It is composed of a ring of rods and an amorphous layer and marks the site at which the cyst lid will develop (Neuhaus-Url and Schweiger, 1984). The lid-forming apparatus may be identical with the circular band of microtubules described above. The lid-forming apparatus may function as a boundary that restricts the passage of cellulose forming complexes (Menzel and Elsner-Menzel, 1989b). This would lead to a circular zone at the periphery of the lid from which cellulose is excluded.

After lid formation is complete, the secondary nucleus in each cyst undergoes numerous mitotic divisions so that the cysts become filled with numerous uniformly-distributed secondary nuclei. The placement of the lid is the only remnant of polarity that remains in the multinucleate cyst stage. When the gametes are formed within the cysts, the stage that is characterized by its apparent lack of polarity is completed. It comes to an end when new membranes are formed and surround each secondary nucleus and part of its surrounding cytoplasm to give rise to gametes. Gamete formation must be a shaping process similar to the one that forms the cysts, but details have not been observed.

THE INFLUENCE OF MEMBRANE-MEDIATED PHENOMENA ON POLARITY

The plasma membrane appears to play an important role in the establishment and maintenance of polarity and in processes of differentiation. Two membrane-mediated phenomena have been studied in some detail: (1) An apico-basal voltage gradient that parallels morphogenetic gradients is generated by membrane ion transport. (2) The distribution of calcium ion binding sites on the membrane surface determines the pattern of growth of whorl hairs.

Apico-basal ion and potential gradients

The results of a number of studies lead to the conclusion that normal growth and differentiation in *Acetabularia* occur only in the presence of a polar distribution of ions and electric charge. In one such study, long (12 - 18 mm) basal fragments were held in the dark for 5 - 7 days before they were enucleated. Enucleated basal fragments prepared in this manner are capable of growth and regeneration in the light. When they were placed in a cuvette that electrically isolated the apical end from the basal end (Fig.11), the fragments failed to regenerate. When an agar salt bridge was used to re-establish the electrical connection between the apical and basal ends, the capacity to regenerate was restored (Novak and Sironval, 1975).

Other studies have revealed the existence of a trans-cellular potential difference in regenerating enucleate fragments. The potential difference is oriented parallel to the long axis of the cell, and the apical pole is positive relative to the basal pole. Regeneration occurs at the positive pole. When the potential difference is clamped in the normal or reversed orientation, regeneration always occurs at the anode of the clamping circuit. If the potential is clamped at zero, less than 10% of the fragments regenerate (Novak and Bentrup, 1972).

The trans-cellular voltage gradient results from a trans-membrane potential difference that has two components: (1) a K^+ - dependent Nernst potential which is uniform along the fragment, and (2) an electrogenic Cl^- potential. The Cl^- potential is light-dependent because it results from a pump that is driven by ATP derived from photophosphorylation. The pump has been shown to be a Cl^--ATPase. If the Cl^- concentration gradient is shifted in a direction favoring pump reversal (removal of external Cl^-), ATP is synthesized (Goldfarb et al., 1984). There is a positional dependence of the Cl^- pump- viz., Cl^- is taken into the cell more rapidly at the apical pole than at the basal pole. This accounts for the trans-cellular voltage gradient (Novak and Bentrup, 1972).

Spontaneous pulses of the trans-cellular potential with a period of 10 - 25 minutes can be measured with extracellular electrodes placed at each end of the fragment. They are coincident with the period of maximum conductance in action

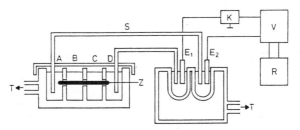

FIG.11. Apparatus to electrically isolate stalk segments and to measure continuous extracellular potential differences
A, B, C, D compartments; E1, E2 measuring electrodes; K voltage compensation; R pen recorder; S KCl/agar salt bridge; V electrometer; Z cell (from Novak and Bentrup, 1972).

potentials measured with intracellular electrodes. They arise at the presumptive regenerating pole, and may be detected several hours before there are morphological indications of regeneration (Bentrup, 1977). The tip is the invariant site of origin of action potential only in actively regenerating cells. Action potentials may originate at any location in cells that have formed caps or in those that are not regenerating. Goodwin and Pateromichelakis (1979) suggest that such "floating" hyperpolarization may be taken as a sign of developmental arrest. In other experiments (Christ-Adler and Bentrup, 1976), fragments were subjected to K^+ or Cl^- ion gradients. Regeneration occurred preferentially at the end of the fragment that was exposed to lowered K^+ or lowered Cl^- concentration. Thus, positional information seems to be conveyed in the enucleate basal fragments by the potential gradient and by the spontaneous impulses traveling from the regenerating tip (Novak and Bentrup, 1972).

The influence of calcium ions on morphogenesis

The local extracellular concentration of Ca^{++} seems to be an especially important factor in growth and morphogenesis in *Acetabularia*. Tip elongation, hair formation and cap formation are effected by experimental variation of the Ca^{++} concentration of the medium. Cap formation is most sensitive to reduced Ca^{++} concentration while tip elongation is least sensitive (Goodwin et al., 1983). The Ca^{++}, Mg^{++} ionophore A23187 reversibly inhibits whorl and cap formation, but does not effect tip growth (Goodwin and Pateromichelakis, 1979). Low concentrations of cobalt which are known to block Ca^{++} channels and to compete for Ca^{++} binding sites duplicate the effect of A23187. Whatever the action of Ca^{++} may be, it seems to be confined to the tip. Whorl and cap formation are inhibited when the apical 10% of the tip is exposed to 2 mM Ca^{++} while the basal 90% of the cell is in normal (10 mM) Ca^{++} concentration. Increasing the Ca^{++} concentration of the basal 90% to 50 mM does not counteract the tip effect.

The binding of Ca^{++} to sites near the growing tip seems to specify the location at which whorl hairs will develop.

Harrison and co-workers have shown in a series of papers that the placement of hairs in a whorl is determined by a pre-pattern that is established when Ca^{++} binds to sites on the extracellular surface of the membrane. The spacing between hair initials corresponds to a "chemical wavelength" (designated λ). An Arrhenius type plot (Ln λ vs.1/T) showed that the spacing of hair intervals behaves with regard to temperature, like a chemical rate parameter. The apparent activation energy derived from the slope of the plot was $-18 \pm 3kJ$ mol^{-1}. This value was taken as support for a mechanism in which an autocatalytic reaction is the creator of the pattern points (Harrison et al., 1981). Harrison and Hillier (1985) showed that there is a linear relationship between the spacing of hair initials and the reciprocal of the Ca^{++} concentration in the medium. Binding constants derived from these Lineweaver/Burk type plots are of the order of magnitude (K ≈ 1000) commonly associated with the binding of Ca^{++} to oxyacid anions. The binding sites might therefore be on protein side chains (e.g. on aspartic acid residues) or on phosphatidyl serine or phosphatidyl inositol in the bilayer configuration.

Changes in the Ca^{++} distribution during whorl formation were traced by using the fluorescent dye chlorotetracycline, which is believed to be specific for membrane-bound calcium. The observed changes were in good agreement with those predicted by the two-stage model of Harrison, Graham and Lakowski (1988). The model proposes that some event triggers an increase in the concentration of a substance A (the calcium binder and a catalyst for cell surface extension) which is distributed on the hemispherical growing tip. The increase in concentration (shortening of the wavelength) causes the distribution of A to shift to an annular pattern just below the growing tip (Fig.12a, 12f). This leads to tip flattening. Substance A is a reactant in a pattern-forming reaction that determines the distribution pattern of substance X. Substance X can only be formed at sites where substance A exists. Therefore, the distribution of substance A constrains the distribution of concentration maxima of substance X. A computer simulation based on the model produces a pattern that is similar to the one produced by the Ca-chlorotetracycline fluorescence (Fig.12e, 12g).

Harrison and co-workers favor a reaction diffusion mechanism in which extracellular free Ca^{++} is in equilibrium with Ca^{++} bound to sites on the membrane surface. Shape change is caused by differential growth directed by the pattern of binding sites.

Goodwin and Trainor (1985) have proposed an alternative mechanochemical mechanism in which Ca^{++} interacts with proteins that alter the viscoelastic properties of the cortical cytoplasm and the state of elements of the cytoskeleton. The plasma membrane is virtually continuous with the cortical cytoplasm since turgor pressure keeps both pressed against the cell wall. The alteration of the cortical cytoplasm applies strains to the plasma membrane and increases the activity of outwardly-directed proton pumps. External acidification weakens the cell wall which bulges out under the influence of turgor pressure and gives rise to a region of local growth.

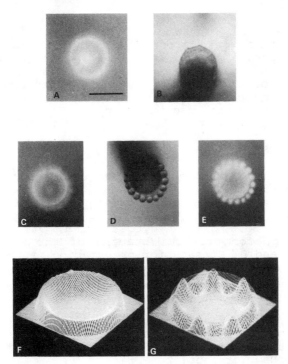

FIG.12. (A, B) Ca-CTC fluorescence and tungsten light micrographs of the same tip at a stage when the whorl pattern just emerges from the continuous annulus; (C - E) fluorescence and tungsten light micrographs of a later stage; C fluorescence micrograph focused at the base of hair initials; D, E tungsten light and fluorescence micrographs focused at the tip of the main stem; (F, G) Computer-generated planar maps based on the two-stage model; F distribution of the first-stage morphogen, A; G distribution of the second-stage morphogen, X superimposed on the pattern in F (from Harrison, Graham and Lakowski, 1988, Company of Biologists Ltd.).

The proponents of these competing models are in agreement that available data are insufficient to allow a choice to be made between them. This then, is one of the many areas in which further research promises to be especially rewarding.

Several morphological and functional manifestations of polarity have been identified during the course of this brief overview. These include the placement of the nucleus, oriented cytoplasmic streaming mediated by the cytoskeleton, polarized distribution of subcellular organelles, and apico-basal gradients of cell wall composition, electrical potential and morphogenetic capacity. The cause versus effect relationship is unclear in each of these cases. For example, is the polar distribution of subcellular organelles such as chloroplasts an expression of the polar nature of the cell or a response to it? Does the distribution of morphogenetic substances give rise to the electrical potential gradient, or does the electrical potential somehow control the distribution of macromolecules? Although these questions have been inspired by phenomena observed in *Acetabularia*, their answers have broader implications.

Acetabularia would appear to be the organism of choice with which to pursue many of the remaining questions concerning the influence of polarity on morphogenesis at the cellular level. In no other organism is the polar distribution of organelles and morphogenetic capacity so apparent or so amenable to experimental manipulation.

ACKNOWLEDGEMENTS

The authors gratefully acknowledge the assistance of the following individuals:
Prof.W. Herth for the electron micrograph of an *A. mediterranea* gamete; Drs.D. Menzel and H. Koop for clarifying fine points concerning the role of the cytoskeleton; Dr.R. Shoeman and Prof.E. Schnepf for critical reading of the manuscript, and Mrs.R. Fisher and D. Crisand for preparation of the figures.

REFERENCES

Bentrup, F.W., 1977, Electrical events during apex regeneration in *Acetabularia mediterranea, in:* "Progress in Acetabularia Research", C.L.F. Woodcock, ed., Academic Press, New York, pp. 249-254.

Berger, S., and Schweiger, H.G., 1975, The ultrastructure of the nucleocytoplasmic interface in *Acetabularia, in:* Molecular Biology of Nucleocytoplasmic Relationships," S. Puiseux-Dao, ed., Elsevier, Amsterdam, pp. 243-250.

Berger, S., and Schweiger, H.G., 1986, Perinuclear dense bodies: Characterization as DNA-containing structures using enzyme-linked gold granules, *J.Cell Sci.*, 80:1-11.

Bouloukhère, M., 1972, Différenciation spatiale et temporelle des chloroplastes d'*Acetabularia mediterranea*, *J.Microsc.*, 13:401-416.

Bonotto, S., and Sironval, C., 1977, Experimental studies on the phototropism of *Acetabularia mediterranea* and *Acetabularia crenulata, in:* "Progress in *Acetabularia* Research," C.L.F. Woodcock, ed., Academic Press, New York, pp. 241-247.

Christ-Adler, M., and Bentrup, F.W., 1976, Effect of K^+ and Cl^- ion gradients upon apex regeneration in *Acetabularia mediterranea*, *Planta*, 129:91-93.

D'Emilio, M.A., Hoursiangou-Neubrun, D., Baugnet-Mahieu, L. Gilles, J., Nuyts, G., Bossus, A., Mazza, A., and Bonotto, S., 1979, Apicobasal gradient of protein synthesis in *Acetabularia, in:* "Developmental Biology of Acetabularia," S. Bonotto, V. Kefeli and S. Puiseux-Dao, eds, Elsevier, North Holland, Amsterdam, pp. 269-282.

Franke, W.W., Berger, S., Falk, H., Spring, H., Scheer, U., Herth, W., Trendelenburg, M.F., and Schweiger, H.G., 1974, Morphology of the nucleo-cytoplasmic interactions during the development of *Acetabularia* cells. I. The vegetative phase, *Protoplasma*, 82:249-282.

Franke, W.W., Spring, H., Kartenbeck, J., and Falk, H., 1977, Cyst formation in some Dasycladacean green algae. I. Vesicle formations during coenocytotomy in *Acetabularia mediterranea*, *Eur.J.Cell Biol.*, 14:229-259.

Gibor, A., 1977, Cell elongation in *Acetabularia, in:* "Progress in Acetabularia Research," C.L.F. Woodcock, ed., Academic Press, New York, pp. 231-239.

Goldfarb, V., Sanders, D., and Gradmann, D., 1984, Reversal of
    electrogenic Cl⁻ pump in *Acetabularia* increases level
    and ^{32}P labelling of ATP, *J.Exptl.Bot.*, 35:645-658.
Goodwin, B.C., and Pateromichelakis, S., 1979, The role of
    electrical fields, ions, and the cortex in the
    morphogenesis of *Acetabularia*, *Planta*, 145:427-435.
Goodwin, B.C., Skelton, J.L., and Kirk-Bell, S.M., 1983,
    Control of regeneration and morphogenesis by divalent
    cations in *Acetabularia mediterranea*, *Planta*, 157:1-7.
Goodwin, B.C., and Trainor, L.E.H., 1985, Tip and whorl
    morphogenesis in *Acetabularia* by calcium-regulated
    strain fields, *J.Theor.Biol.*, 117:79-106.
Hämmerling, J., 1934, Über formbildende Substanzen bei
    Acetabularia mediterranea, ihre räumliche und zeitliche
    Verteilung und ihre Herkunft, *Arch.Entwicklungsmech.der
    Organismen*, 131:1-81.
Hämmerling, J., 1936, Studien zum Polaritätsproblem,
    Zool.Jahrb., 56:441-483.
Hämmerling, J., 1955, Neuere Versuche über die Polarität und
    Differenzierung bei *Acetabularia*, *Biol.Zbl.*, 74:545-554.
Hämmerling, J., and Hämmerling, C., 1959, Über Bildung und
    Ausgleich des Polaritätsgefälles bei *Acetabularia*,
    Planta, 53:522-531.
Harrison, L.G., Snell, J., Verdi, R., Vogt, D.E., Zeiss, G.D.,
    and Green, B.R., 1981, Hair morphogenesis in
    Acetabularia mediterranea: Temperature-dependent spacing
    and models of morphogen waves, *Protoplasma*, 106:211-221.
Harrison, L.G., and Hillier, N.A., 1985, Quantitative control
    of *Acetabularia* morphogenesis by extracellular calcium:
    A test of kinetic theory, *J.Theor.Biol.*, 114:177-192.
Harrison, L.G., Graham, K.T., and Lakowski, B.C., 1988, Calcium
    localization during *Acetabularia* whorl formation:
    Evidence supporting a two-stage hierarchical mechanism,
    Development, 104:255-262.
Hoursiangou-Neubrun, D., Dubacq, J.P., and Puiseux-Dao, S.,
    1977, Heterogeneity of the plastid population and
    chloroplast differentiation in *Acetabularia
    mediterranea*, in: "Progress in *Acetabularia* Research,"
    C.L.F. Woodcock, ed., Academic Press, New York, pp.
    D175-194.
Issinger, O., Mass, J., and Claus, H., 1971,
    Photosyntheseaktivität der Stielregionen von
    Acetabularia mediterranea, *Planta*, 101:360-364.
Kloppstech, K., and Schweiger, H.G., 1975a, Polyadenylated RNA
    from *Acetabularia*, *Differentiation*, 4:115-123.
Kloppstech, K., and Schweiger, H.G., 1975b, 80s robosomes in
    Acetabularia major. Distribution and transportation
    within the cell, *Protoplasma*, 83:27-40.
Koop, H., and Kiermayer, D., 1980a, Protoplasmic streaming in
    the giant unicellular green alga *Acetabularia
    mediterranea*. I. Formation of intracellular transport
    systems in the course of cell differentiation,
    Protoplasma, 102:147-166.
Koop, H., and Kiermayer, D., 1980b, Protoplasmic streaming in
    the giant unicellular green alga *Acetabularia
    mediterranea*. II. Differential sensitivity of movement
    systems to substances acting on microfilaments and
    microtubuli, *Protoplasma*, 102:295-306.
Koop, H.U., 1981, Protoplasmic streaming in *Acetabularia*,
    Protoplasma, 109:143-157.
Lüttke, A., 1981, Heterogeneity of chloroplasts in *Acetabularia*

mediterranea. Heterogeneous distribution and morphology of chloroplast DNA, *Exptl.Cell Res.*, 131:483-488.

Lüttke, A., 1983, Polarity of *Acetabularia mediterranea*: Stability in the enucleate state, *Annals of Botany*, 52:905-913.

Menzel, D., 1986, Visualization of cytoskeletal changes through the life cycle of *Acetabularia*, *Protoplasma*, 134:30-42.

Menzel, D., and Elsner-Menzel, C., 1989a, Maintenance and dynamic changes of cytoplasmic organization controlled by cytoskeletal assemblies in *Acetabularia* (Chlorophyceae), *in:* "Algae as Experimental Systems," A.W. Coleman, L.J. Goff, and J.R. Stein-Taylor, eds, Alan R. Liss inc., New York, pp. 71-91.

Menzel, D., and Elsner-Menzel, C., 1989b, Cytoskeletal rearrangements during maturation of *Acetabularia* cysts: The lid-forming apparatus, *Eur.J.Cell Biol.*, 48 (Suppl.26):75.

Nagai, R., and Fukui, S., 1981, Differential treatment of *Acetabularia* with cytochalasin B and N-ethylmaleimide with special reference to their effects on cytoplasmic streaming, *Protoplasma*, 109:79-89.

Neuhaus-Url, G., and Schweiger, H.G., 1984, The lid forming apparatus in cysts of the green alga *Acetabularia mediterranea*, *Protoplasma*, 122:120-124.

Novak, B., and Bentrup, F.W., 1972, An electrophysiological study of regeneration in *Acetabularia mediterranea*, *Planta*, 108:227-244.

Novak, B., and Sironval, C., 1975, Inhibition of regeneration of *Acetabularia mediterranea* enucleated posterior stalk segments by electrical isolation, *Plant Sci.Letters*, 5:183-188.

Shihira-Ishikawa, I., 1984, Chromosome behavior in the primary nucleus of *Acetabularia calyculus* as revealed by epifluorescent microscopy, *Protoplasma*, 122:27-34.

Tikhomirova, L.A., Zubarev, T.N., Salamakha, O.V., and Betina, M.I., 1979, The ultrastructure of the nucleus and the perinuclear zone during cell development in *Acetabularia*, *in:* "Developmental Biology of Acetabularia," S. Bonotto, V. Kefeli, and S. Puiseux-Dao, eds, Elsevier, North Holland, Amsterdam, pp. 103-113.

Werz, G., 1974, Fine-structural aspects of morphogenesis in Acetabularia, *Int.Rev.Cytology*, 38:319-367.

MODEL ALGAL SYSTEMS TO STUDY PLANT DEVELOPMENT

Ralph S. Quatrano

Department of Biology
University of North Carolina
Chapel Hill, NC 27599-3280
USA

Algal systems have been used to study the mechanism of differentiative processes and development for 100 or more years. Many of these algae, such as *Fucus* (Quatrano et al., 1979; Quatrano and Kropf, 1989; Quatrano,1990), *Acetabularia* (Berger et al., 1987), *Volvox* (Kirk, 1988, 1990) and *Chlamydomonas* (Goodenough and Adair, 1989) have provided the scientific community with amenable experimental systems to approach the most fundamental questions facing developmental biologists. This review will emphasize how these algal systems have been used to understand various developmental processes, as well as their potential for further contributions to these research areas in the next several decades. The focus will be on three main developmental processes related to the experimental embryology of aquatic plants;
I.   Gamete attraction and recognition during fertilization,
II. Hormone-mediated control of gamete formation and cell fusion,
III. Establishment of cell polarity.

GAMETE ATTRACTION AND RECOGNITION DURING FERTILIZATION

How are gametes of opposite mating types attracted to each other, and once in contact, how do they recognize each other in a species-specific manner? In the case of many aquatic algae, specialized cells for reproduction are released from the organism into the environment, thereby requiring a mechanism to attract the gametes for fusion. A highly potent pheromone, diffusing from one cell and forming a gradient to attract the opposite gamete, has evolved in a number of lower plants as a mechanism to insure proximity of gametes. The species-specific fusion event that follows appears to be based on molecular recognition at the surface of the gametes.

Fucus

Both eggs and sperm of the intertidal fucoid algae are released into the open sea upon exposure to the incoming tide.

Experimental Embryology in Aquatic Plants and Animals
Edited by H.-J. Marthy, Plenum Press, New York, 1990

Elegant work by Muller (1989) showed that eggs of the brown algae secreted sperm-attracting olefinic hydrocarbons that were highly volatile and fragrant. In the case of *Ectocarpus*, these compounds represented approximately 0.3% of the fresh weight of the eggs. With the exception of one of these attractants, fucoserraten (C_8H_{12}), all of the other characterized attractants were C-11 hydrocarbons, which included all open chains cyclopropane-, cyclopentene- or cycloheptadiene derivatives. Structure/function studies indicated that spatial arrangements of the double bonds were critical for activity (Maier et al., 1988). The attractants were active at very low concentrations (e.g. 10^{-11}M, see Boland, 1987), and when secreted from the egg, resulted in large numbers of sperm adhering to the surface of a single egg. These attractants were also shown to stimulate release of the spermatozoids from the antheridia (Müller, 1989). However, the attractants did not seem to be involved with the species-specific recognition that occurred between the eggs and sperm. For example, fucoserraten (from *F. serratus*) attracted sperm from *F. serratus* and *F. vesioculosus* with equal efficiency (see Fig. 10 in Evans et al., 1982). Hence, the function of the attractants is to bring gametes of the fucoid algae together in a species-independent manner.

What then accounts for the species-specific recognition that has been documented in these algae, and, given the large numbers of sperm that are attracted to the egg surface, why is polyspermy not prevalent among these organisms? The specific recognition between egg and sperm in the fucoid algae appeared to involve fucose- and mannose-containing glycoproteins on the surface of the egg. Evans et al (1982) found that egg membrane preparations from *F. serratus* inhibited fertilization by competing for sperm in a species-specific manner. This inhibition was destroyed by a specific fucosidase and mannosidase. Using this assay, a putative egg "receptor" was found to bind to a Conconavalin A (Con A) affinity column after detergent release from an egg membrane preparation. The glycoprotein fraction released from the column by the haptan methyl mannoside caused species-specific inhibition of egg/sperm interaction. Inhibition of the interaction caused by this fraction was sensitive to methyl mannoside competition and to a specific fucosidase. Also, when the glycoprotein fraction was preincubated with the sperm, fertilization did not occur. Preincubation with eggs had no effect on fertilization. Several bands were found after polyacrylamide gel electrophoresis (PAGE) of the glycoprotein fraction, but a glycoprotein of about 30kD was the predominant species and could correspond to the active surface component of the egg that participates in the species-specific recognition of the sperm (Evans et al., 1982). Although no specific molecules on the surface of the sperm have been implicated in species-specific recognition. Jones et al. (1988) prepared monoclonal antibodies against cell surface antigens of *F. serratus* sperm and showed some antigens highly concentrated in particular regions of the sperm (e.g.anterior flagellum), while others were found only in sperm cells (not eggs) and in sperm from the genus *Fucus* (not *Ascophyllum*). The role of these antigens detected by these antibodies in the processes of sperm motility, chemotaxis and fertilization remain to be elucidated.

The fucoid algae also appeared to have evolved a mechanism

similar to marine invertebrates to prevent polyspermy. Robinson, et al. (1981) observed a transient depolarization in egg membranes of *F. vesiculosus* and *P. fastigiata* - within 5-10 minutes after insemination. Complementing this observation, Brawley (1987) recently demonstrated that fucoid algae exhibit a "fast", sodium dependent electrical block to polyspermy, followed most likely by a "slow" block. The latter was probably in the form of cell wall formation that occurred within 10-15 minutes after fertilization (see Quatrano, 1982). At this time, both alginate and cellulose were the major components of the wall, each approximately 50% of the cell wall mass. This extracellular matrix functioned as a second or slow block to prevent further sperm from being attracted and to accelerate the release of adhering sperm. In animal eggs, an equivalent fast block (i.e. electrical) and slow block (cortical reaction-fertilization membrane) have been reported (see Jaffe and Gould, 1985).

Following the specific recognition event and fusion of the fucoid gametes, the first observable response, within minutes, was the assembly of an extracellular matrix or cell wall. The process of fertilization and fusion of wall-less gametes in higher plants was also followed by cell wall deposition, similar to what was described above for the fucoid algae. However, it was difficult to experimentally manipulate these processes in higher plants, due to the inaccessibility and lack of synchrony of the cells. Wall formation and egg activation in the Fucales could be used as a model then, to elucidate the basic mechanisms involved in these early and critical post-fertilization events (see Quatrano, 1982).

The *Fucus* cell wall within minutes after fertilization is composed only of alginate and cellulose, but by four hours and throughout early embryogenesis, the wall still remained relatively simple; about 60% alginate, and 20% each of cellulose and two sulfated glycoproteins called fucans (F1 and F3). Until about 10-12 hours after fertilization, all of these components were randomly distributed throughout the circumference of the wall. At the time of a localized wall extension to form the rhizoid (about 14 hours), however, a new fucan (F2) was locally deposited only at the tip of the elongating cell (Hogsett and Quatrano, 1978), presumably playing a role in adhesion of the zygote and later the embryo to the substratum (Crayton et al., 1974). A mosaic wall was then quite evident in the zygote when assayed by cytochemical staining (Brawley and Quatrano, 1979) or by fluorescent microscopy (Hogsett and Quatrano, 1978). This algal system offers several advantages to study wall assembly:
1) the deposition of cell wall in the zygote, occurs synchronously in a single-celled system that can develop normally in a completely defined, sterile medium (Quatrano, 1980),
2) a small number of components are found in the cell wall, 80% of which are two well-studied polysaccharides; cellulose, and the pectin-like polymer, alginate,
3) a new wall is assembled uniformly around a completely wall-less egg cell, without concomitant cell division or cell elongation, and in response to a trigger (fertilization), finally.
4) cell wall extension to form the rhizoid occurs at a predetermined site in the zygote (defined by an easily imposed external gradient such as unilateral light - see below,

ESTABLISHMENT OF CELL POLARITY), so that localized wall extension and deposition of a specific glycoprotein (F2) could be followed.

For these reasons, the fucoid algae are also attractive experimental systems to study questions related to the biosynthesis, transport, secretion and assembly of the extracellular matrix or cell wall of plant cells.

Chlamydomonas

More specific information is known of the species-specific molecules that are involved with gamete recognition in *Chlamydomonas*. The mating system in *Chlamydomonas* has been well-described; two mating types (mt) + and - recognize the opposite, morphologically identical cell-type by molecules present on the flagellar surface. Large glycoprotein complexes on the flagella surface were responsible for this mating-type, species-specific recognition. Monoclonal antibodies to flagellar extracts were obtained by a number of research groups. For example, a monoclonal antibody (mAb) to the mt⁻ agglutinin (mAb 66.3) blocked agglutinin function *in vitro* and sexual agglutination *in vivo* (Homan et al., 1988). The antigen to this mAb was found to be concentrated at the tips of the flagella after redistribution during sexual agglutination. "Tipping" or transport of patched agglutinin (Goodenough and Jurivich, 1978) was also observed artificially by treating mt⁻ gametes *in vivo* with mAb 66.3. This process of migration within the membrane was blocked by microtubule inhibitors (e.g. colchicine), but not by microfilament inhibitors (e.g. cytochalasin).

Identification of the agglutinin molecules was achieved when flagella extracts were solubilized in a non-ionic detergent (octylglucoside), and when surface molecules of gametes were labeled with ^{125}I (Adair et al., 1982). After purification by Sepharose 6B and Fractogel-75 chromatography, observation of the active fraction under the electron microscope revealed long fibers (225nm) possessing a characteristic polarity; a "head" region attached to a filament or shaft which possesses some "kinks" (Goodenough and Heuser, 1985; Goodenough and Adair, 1989). This fraction also contained large quantities of the amino acid hydroxyproline and led to the characterization of these molecules as being similar to the higher plant hydroxyproline rich glycoproteins (HRGPs). The role of this amino acid and macromolecule in the agglutination reaction was strengthened with the observations that blocking hydroxylation of proline by the inhibitor (a, a'-dipyridyl) or using the non-hydroxylatable proline analog (3,4-dehydroproline) resulted in the release of agglutinating cells (see Goodenough and Adair, 1989).

Goodenough and Heuser (1985) proposed that the HRGP properties of both the cell wall proteins and the agglutinins were similar and suggested that the agglutinins on the surface of the gametes may represent HRGP's of the wall that have come under control of the mating-type loci. This would result in one type only in the membrane of the + gamete flagella, while another is in the - gamete flagellar membrane. Gametic recognition and adhesion by these molecules on opposite flagella could occur by a mechanism similar to the recognition of wall HRGP's during wall assembly. Excellent evidence from a series of elegant papers by the group of Keith Roberts (see Hills et al., 1975) indicated that *Chlamydomonas* cell wall formation occurs by a self-assembly mechanism resulting in a crystalline array of macromolecules, undoubtedly requiring "molecular recognition". Excellent potential exists for further analysis of the specific molecular domains involved in gamete recognition in *Chlamydomonas* by use of genetic and biochemical approaches.

PHEROMONE/HORMONE MEDIATED CONTROL OF GAMETE FORMATION AND CELL FUSION

Pheromones and hormones in the algae play important roles in eliciting pathways of gamete development and cell fusion that are likely to involve a complex set of genes and intermediates that are active in the response pathway. The compounds that induce gamete development in the colonial alga *Volvox*, and cell fusion in the repair mechanism of the filamentous red alga *Griffithsia* are examples of how biologically potent molecules can elicit a specific response pathway. They also present us with examples of how one can approach and begin to elucidate the developmental processes that are common to other organisms which are less amenable to experimental manipulation.

Volvox

Asexual adult spheroids of *Volvox* contained two distinct cell types embedded in a gelatinous matrix; somatic cells (about 2,000) that were terminally differentiated to undergo senescence and programmed death with no reproductive potential, and, 16 germ cells or gonidia that retained full developmental potential. Each cell type was derived from a separate lineage from fertilization. At the sixth cleavage of the embryo, cells in the anterior end divided asymmetrically for three divisions; the larger of the two cells ceased dividing and formed the gonidial initials, while the smaller cell formed the somatic initials which divided several more times (Green and Kirk, 1982). Cells in the posterior divided to form only somatic initials. Differentiation of the somatic and gonidial cells occurred later under the appropriate cultural conditions (Kirk, 1988). Male and female asexual spheroids were indistinguishable from each other, but when exposed to a potent, species-specific pheromone or sexual inducer, the subsequent round of asexual development was modified so that the asymmetric divisions gave rise to sperm packets or eggs rather than gonidia.

The sexual inducer of *Volvox* is one of the most potent morphogens known, i.e. it is produced by sperm cells and converts asexually growing males and females to the sexual pathway of development, at the remarkably low concentration of about 10^{-17} M. However, until recently, it was difficult to obtain sufficient density of asexual males for induction as a source to begin purification of the inducer. The problem was one of autoinduction of asexually growing males. Sexual males (i.e. sperm cells) were produced spontaneously in a young culture, releasing the inducer at low population densities. This resulted in the remaining asexual males to stop growth and become sperm cells, thereby releasing their inducer into the medium. The low concentration of inducer in such cultures prevented purification by conventional means. Tschochner et al., (1987), however, found that pronase (1ug/ml of culture) completely inhibited spontaneous male sexual development, if given prior to a new round of embryogenesis. Fortunately, this treatment did not affect growth or the activity of the inducer, and resulted in high density asexual males (250,000 colonies/l) that could then be induced synchronously for the release of the inducer into the medium. Using standard techniques, Tschochner et al. (1987) then purified the inducer about 1000-fold, deglycosylated the resulting glycoprotein by hydrogen fluoride, and cleaved the 25kD protein molecule by proteases. The N-terminal amino acid sequence was determined from the resulting peptide fragments and oligonucleotides were synthesized corresponding to this sequence. The oligonucleotide (which specifically bound to an 8kb fragment on Southern analysis) was used to screen a genomic library. One clone (Ind-28) was obtained that appeared to be the gene for the inducer, based on translation of this sequence (Tschochner et al., 1987). Complete analysis of the gene is now in progress, and coupled with the ability to use genetics and a mutational approach in *Volvox* (Kirk, 1988), steps in the response pathway from inducer/receptor to gene expression/physiological response is amenable to experimental approach.

Griffithsia

Dead intercalary cells of the filamentous marine red alga *Griffithsia* were found to be replaced by either a process of regeneration or cell repair. If an intercalary cell was destroyed, the cell above regenerated a rhizoid, while the cell below regenerated an apical shoot cell, thereby expressing the apical/basal polarity of the filament and giving rise to two new identical and shorter filaments. If on the other hand, an intercalary cell was killed but not ruptured, a process of cell repair was initiated. The cell above regenerated a rhizoid as described in the regeneration pathway, but the cell below formed a shoot repair cell that elongated toward the rhizoid tip and eventually fused with the rhizoid cell. The key difference between the pathways was whether the shoot cell formed an elongating repair cell (repair pathway) or apical shoot cell (regeneration pathway). The original cell wall of the dead cell was still intact when the repair pathway was evoked, and undoubtedly served to concentrate molecules that were mediating this cell fusion event.

An elegant set of experiments were performed by Waaland (see review by Waaland, 1989) to understand the mechanism involved with the cell repair pathway. These experiments led to the identification of a species-specific morphogenetic substance, rhodomorphin, that mediated the cell fusion event. Rhodomorphin (or cell fusion hormone) was assayed by its ability to induce decapitated shoot filaments to produce repair shoot cells. Using this assay, purification of rhodomorphin was initiated. Rhodomorphin activity was identified initially as a glycoprotein because of its ability to bind specifically to the lectin Con A. Using a Con A affinity column, Watson and Waaland (1983) purified rhodomorphin activity about 40-fold. This activity was sensitive to proteinase, inactivated by short treatments at 50°C, and was associated with a macromolecule with a molecular weight of about 14kD after gel filtration.

Further purification by Watson and Waaland (1986) indicated that the glycosidic moiety had terminal alpha-D-mannosyl residues and that disulfide bridges were required for activity to be recovered after denaturation by SDS PAGE. The molecular weight of rhodomorphin activity by this procedure was between 15-17.5 kD. Assuming a molecular weight of 15kD, calculations indicated that rhodomorphin isolated after PAGE was active at about 7×10^{-14} M.

If sufficient quantities of rhodomorphin can be isolated to obtain an N-terminal amino acid sequence, the approach used to obtain the gene for the sexual inducer from *Volvox* can be followed. In both cases, if a full-length c-DNA is isolated, large quantities of the protein can be produced in pro- or eukaryotic expression systems for structural studies and for antibody production. If activity is retained in such systems, one can begin to study structure/function relationships that could lead to understanding such interesting and unknown morphogen-receptor interactions and signal-transduction pathways in algal systems.

ESTABLISHMENT OF CELL POLARITY

Zygotes and young embryos of the Fucales (*Fucus, Pelvetia*), and early cleavage stages during embryogenesis in the colonial green alga *Volvox*, provide model systems to study the basic mechanisms involved in the generation of zygotic/cell asymmetries and partitioning of localized cytoplasmic components to the resulting daughter cells, i.e. the establishment of cell polarity. The polar processes in these algae are common to many different organisms; from yeasts, amphibians, and nematodes, to vertebrates, mammals and plants. To understand how a cell establishes a polar axis and directionally transports cytoplasmic material to a predetermined site defined by the axis, is difficult to study and experimentally manipulate in most of these organisms. In contrast, eggs of the Fucales, for example, are apolar, with no apparent spatial patterning in the egg. "Polar determinants" are not localized in these eggs and rotated by directional vectors such as unilateral light, to establish the polar axis. Hence, the polar axis arises epigenetically in synchronous cultures of single-celled zygotes and is easily amenable to experimental analysis.

Fucus

Earlier studies demonstrated that the polar axis in *Fucus* can be oriented by a number of vectors (see Jaffe, 1968; Quatrano, 1978). For example, when zygotes were subjected to a gradient of light, the plane of the first cell division was always perpendicular to the light axis (see Fig. 1). The resulting cell plate divided two unequal cells; the smaller rhizoid cell on the shaded portion of the gradient, and the thallus cell on the lighted side (Fig. 1B). Polarization of the developmental axis by light was shown to have two components; axis formation and axis fixation (Quatrano, 1973). An axis formed by unilateral light at any time during the first 10 hours of development was labile and could be easily changed to a new direction by reorienting the zygote to a light pulse from a different direction. Between 10 and 12 hours, the last axis

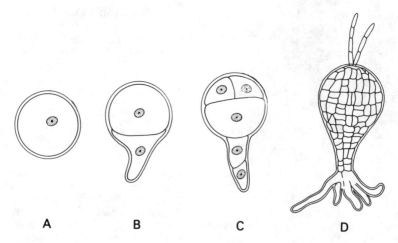

A   B   C   D

FIG 1. Diagram of early embryogenesis (A-C) and germling formation (D) in the fucoid algae. The 70-100µM symmetrical, apolar zygote (A) forms a two-celled embryo (B) composed of an elongated rhizoid cell and a spherical thallus cell. The rhizoid cell gives use to a filament of cells (C), and later to multiple rhizoids (D), which function in adhesion of the embryo to the substrate. This lineage of cells gives use to the holdfast portion of the mature plant. The thallus cell (B) produces a lineage of cells that comprise the embryo proper (C,D) and the frond portion of the mature plant.

formed was fixed in space so that other orienting vectors were not capable of forming an axis. This fixed axis was then the basis for the directional transport and asymmetric localization of cytoplasmic components that resulted in germination (i.e. expression of rhizoid and thallus polarity) of the zygote at 14 hours. The first cell division, always perpendicular to the fixed polar axis, occurred at about 20 hours, produced the rhizoid and thallus cells (Fig. 1B) which give rise to the holdfast and frond portions of the mature plant, respectively (Fig.1 C-D).

Based on recent results, it was proposed that axis fixation involved transmembrane bridges at the presumptive rhizoid pole which stabilized membrane components that were automatically localized by external gradients. The bridge was linked both to the extracellular components of the cell wall, as well as to the cytoplasmic network of microfilaments (see Quatrano, 1990). Both cell walls (Kropf et al., 1988) and microfilaments (Quatrano, 1973) were shown to be required for axis fixation. The proposed structural complex comprising this transmembrane bridge was referred to by Quatrano (1990) as the Axis Stabilizing Complex (ASC). It was proposed (Quatrano, 1978; Quatrano, 1990) that these structural components may serve:
1) to anchor Ca^{+2} or other ionic transport molecules/channels in the plasma membrane, after their asymmetric distribution in response to a directional vector, and
2) to provide "tracks" for the directional transport of particles to the site of polar growth (i.e the emerging

rhizoid) and to guide their secretion into the extracellular matrix at that point.

The asymmetric distribution of membrane components at the time of axis fixation, that were responsible for generating an endogenous electrical current, accumulated at the presumptive rhizoid site in response to a light gradient (Jaffe and Nuccitelli, 1977; Nuccitelli, 1978). However, the mechanim for redistribution is unknown. In our model, the stabilization of these components at the site determined by the gradient constituted *axis fixation*, whereas redistribution to a site determined by a gradient such as light corresponds to *axis formation*. Also, Ca^{+2} localization in membranous compartments of the zygote appeared not to be associated with axis fixation but rather with rhizoid tip growth (Kropf and Quatrano, 1987). The roles of free cytoplasmic Ca^{+2} and its localization in the zygotes, as well as the role of the endogenous electrical current in the axis fixation process have not been clearly elucidated, but other testable models have been proposed (see Brawley and Robinson, 1985).

What are the components of the ASC and how can one directly test the function of a specific ASC component in the process of axis fixation? The components of the ASC in Fucus are unknown except for the localization of actin (Kropf et al, 1989). However, it was suggested (Quatrano, 1990) that components similar to what was found in transmembrane complexes in animal cells [i.e.focal contacts or focal adhesions (see Burridge et al., 1988)], may be localized in the ASC. Rhizoid-enriched fractions of embryos obtained by cleaving embryos that were grown on screens (see Fig. 2). Extracts from these fractions could be analyzed for the presence of such components as the actin-binding proteins and the ß subunit of integrin. Also, if genes introduced into the *Fucus* zygote could be expressed, it might be possible to directly test the function of a specific gene product in the establishment of polarity. For example, if actin mRNA was newly synthesized after fertilization, one could express an antisense mRNA to actin, thereby complexing the sense mRNA and rendering it non-functional. Under such conditions, could a polar axis be fixed and expressed? Such approaches have been successfully applied in other systems including higher plants (see Weintraub, 1990). The same approach could be taken for any gene product localized in the tip, e.g. components of the ASC. Likewise, since microinjection is possible in *Fucus* (Speksnijder et al., 1989), specific antibodies to macromolecules presumed to play a role in a particular process could be introduced into the zygote and determined what effect they would have on the process in question. Dinsmore and Sloboda (1989), for example, injected affinity purified antibodies to a 62kD protein into sea urchin eggs that blocked mitosis in a stage-specific manner. Since *Fucus* is an ideal system to study the initial polarization and localization process, and techniques are now available for microinjection and application of molecular approaches in this system, a number of approaches that have been successful in other systems might be applied to *Fucus* to better understand these processes and the role of specific molecules/structures.

Once the polar axis is fixed, how are the subsequent asymmetries generated? Previous studies demonstrated that an acid-soluble sulfated fucan glycoprotein (F2) becomes localized

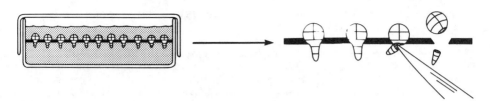

FIG 2. Zygotes of the fucoid algae can be grown on a
metal screen in such a manner so that rhizoid- and
thallus-enriched fractions can be collected after
slicing the embryo as shown in this diagram.

in the rhizoidal cell wall of the *Fucus* zygote between 10-14
hours after fertilization (Fig. 3A, see also Quatrano et al.,
1985). We used F2 as a marker of a visible asymmetry to
determine the requirements necessary for F2 localization.
Although F2 was located finally in the cell wall, it was
stored, sulfated and transported within Golgi-derived vesicles
which we called F granules. Autoradiography showed that
sulfation initially occurred in F granules that were randomly
distributed in the cytoplasm. Using pulse/chase techniques,
Brawley and Quatrano (1979) showed that these granules
containing F2 were selectively transported to the rhizoid area
(Fig.3A). In the absence of exogenous sulfate, embryos cultured
in methionine formed normal two-celled embryos (met embryos),
except that F granules were not localized (Fig. 3B) and met
embryos were not attached to the substratum (Crayton et al.,
1974). Autoradiographic evidence, as well as cytochemical
studies (Quatrano et al., 1979) on met embryos, both showed
that localization of F granules in the rhizoidal area was
dependent upon enzymatic sulfation of F2. In addition, a
cytochalasin B-sensitive structure (i.e. microfilament
networks) was required for transport of F granules, but not for
sulfation of F2 (Fig. 3C, see also Brawley and Quatrano, 1979).
Hence, these studies elucidated two essential requirements for
F granule localization; (1) sulfation of F2 within F granules,
and (2) an intact cytoskeleton (i.e actin microfilaments).
They also showed that sulfation of F2 and localization of F
granules were not required for axis fixation and polar growth,
since met embryos were morphologically similar to normal two-
celled embryos (Fig. 3B - met embryos). Furthermore, they
identified experimental conditions under which; 1) F granules
containing a sulfated F2 were either localized in the rhizoid
(Fig. 3A - normal embryos), or, randomly distributed (Fig. 3C -
cytochalasin-treated embryos), or 2) F granules were not
localized and did not contain a sulfated F2 (Fig. 3B - met
embryos).

Given these requirements for F granule localization, what
was the driving force to directionally transport F granules to
a predetermined site, once the axis was established? Jaffe and
coworkers (see Jaffe and Nuccitelli, 1977) proposed that an
endogenous electric field generated within the zygote served to
localize negatively charged polymers towards the rhizoid.
Griffing, et al.(1990) utilized the experimental conditions
described above (Fig. 3) to isolate membranes that contained F2
in order to ask, is the surface charge of the F granules
related to its ability to be directionally transported? Using
electrophoretic mobilites and pI determinations [by an

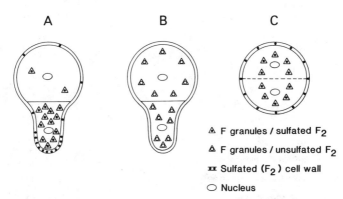

A B C

△ F granules / sulfated F_2

▲ F granules / unsulfated F_2

Ⅲ Sulfated (F_2) cell wall

○ Nucleus

FIG 3. A diagram showing the distribution of F granules and the sulfated glycoprotein F2 in normal two-celled embryos (A), met embryos (B) and embryos grown in the presence of cytochalasin B (C). These figures diagrammatically demonstrate that localization of F granules is observed only when F2 is sulfated and when an intact microfilament network is present (A).

isoelectric focusing technique (Griffing and Quatrano, 1984)] of these membranes, Griffing et al.(1990) concluded that surface charge differences of the F granules (as determined by these techniques), are not alone sufficient to account for directional transport, but are related to sulfation of F2 and the ability to secrete F2. A change in density of the F granules was associated with the ability to be directionally transported, perhaps due to the presence of a component to facilitate interactions with the cytoskeleton (see Quatrano, 1990).

In addition to the localization of F granules, we also showed that filamentous actin is localized at the tip of the elongating rhizoid. We also demonstrated that the localization of actin at this site coincided with the acquisition of a fixed polar axis (Kropf et al.,1989). How does this actin network become localized? If this actin is newly synthesized, was a specific actin mRNA localized in this region and expressed? If so, what is the mechanism of mRNA localization and stabilization? Is it newly transcribed (* in Fig. 4), or was it present as stored mRNA in the egg (+ in Fig. 4)? A diagram showing some of these possibilities is given in Figure 4 and can be used as a model to test various sources of localized mRNA in the polarization process.

The generation of zygotic asymmetry and partitioning of components to embryonic cells, including an unequal first cell division of the zygote to form two cells each with a different fate, is not unique to *Fucus*. A similar developmental pattern was observed during embryogenesis of the nematode *Caenorhabditis elegans* (see Strome, 1989; Schierenberg, 1989) and in the green alga *Volvox* (Kirk, 1988; Starr and Jaenicke, 1989), as well as during asymmetric growth or budding in yeast (Adams and Pringle, 1984). The similarity of events during embryogenesis in the nematode *C. elegans*, for example, to what has been described above for the *Fucus* system, is discussed and

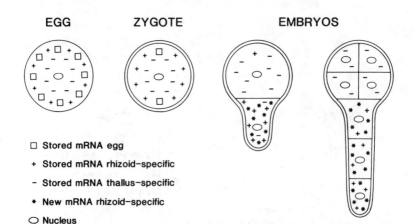

EGG   ZYGOTE   EMBRYOS

☐ Stored mRNA egg

+ Stored mRNA rhizoid-specific

- Stored mRNA thallus-specific

* New mRNA rhizoid-specific

○ Nucleus

Figure 4. Diagrams showing the hypothetical distribution of mRNA molecules and their origins during early embryogenesis in the fucoid algae. Such distributions and origins have not yet been documented but these diagrams can be used as models to determine if such patterns exist.

summarized in Quatrano (1990). Elegant studies have also been reported on the control of gene expression during regional differentiation of the sea urchin embryo (Davidson, 1989).

Volvox

As discussed above, after the sixth cleavage of the *Volvox* embryo, unequal cell divisions resulted in a partitioning of "determinants" that delineated two separate cell lineages; somatic and germ line. Unlike the *Fucus* system, factors which influenced the directionality of this unequal cell division or the cytological basis of asymmetry have yet to be identified in *Volvox*. However, the advantage of *Volvox* was that one could use a genetic approach could be used to analyze a number of very interesting developmental mutants involved with the regulation of the germ-soma switch (see Starr and Jaenicke, 1989; Kirk, 1990). One such class of mutants, the somatic regenerator (*regA*), resulted in expression of all reproductive potential in somatic cells when a lesion occurred at this locus. The protein product of the *regA+* state, then, was believed to prevent all aspects of reproduction in wild-type somatic cells. Another class of mutants, gonidialess (*gls*), continued to divide but without the asymmetric divisions, resulting in cells of equal size, all of which differentiated as somatic cells. This mutant was sterile unless carried on a *regA-* background. Molecular and cytological analysis of these and other mutants (e.g. *Lag*, *Mul*) by chromosomal walking and restriction fragment length polymorphism analysis, will likely help elucidate the role of these loci in the asymmetric division apparatus (e.g. the cytoskeleton) and in the regulatory mechanisms responsible for cellular differentiation (see Kirk, 1988, 1990; Starr and Jaenicke, 1989).

SUMMARY

The long history of experimental manipulation of the fucoid and several other algae discussed above has resulted in a considerable amount of knowledge applicable to a wide range of other developing embryo systems with respect to gamete attraction and recognition during fertilization, hormone-mediated control of gamete formation and cell fusion, and the establishment of cell polarity. I hope that in the next several decades, more interest can be generated among young scientists to use these systems to further our understanding of the procesess involved with embryo development in this group of plants. In doing so, they will also contribute to a broader elucidation of the control mechanisms operative during embryonic development in other organisms.

ACKNOWLEDGEMENTS

I thank Susan Whitfield for her excellent artwork and Nancie Welsh for her help in preparing this manuscript. The research contributions from my laboratory were supported by grants from the National Science Foundation (DCB 851152).

REFERENCES

Adair, W.S., Monk, B.C., Cohen, R., and Goodenough, U.W., 1982, Sexual agglutinins from the *Chlamydomonas* flagellar membrane, *J.Biol.Chem.*, 257:4593.
Adams, A.E.M., and Pringle, J.P., 1984, Relationship of actin and tubulin distribution to bud growth in wild-type and morphogenetic-mutant *Saccharomyces cerevisiae*, *J.Cell Biol.*, 98:934.
Berger, S., deGroot, E.J., Neuhaus, G., and Schweiger, M., 1987, Acetabularia: a giant single cell organism with valuable advantages for cell biology, *Europ.J.Cell Biol.*, 44:349.
Boland, W., 1987, Chemische Kommunikation bei der sexuellen Fortpflanzung mariner Braunalgen, *Biol.Zeit.*, 17:176.
Brawley, S.H., 1987, A sodium-dependent fast block to polyspermy occurs in eggs of fucoid algae, *Devel.Biol.*, 124:390.
Brawley S.H., and Quatrano, R.S., 1979, Sulfation of fucoidin in *Fucus* embryos. IV. Autoradiographic investigations of fucoidin sulfation and secretion during differentiation and the effect of cytochalasin treatment, *Devel.Biol.*, 73:193.
Brawley, S.H., and Robinson, K.R., 1985, Cytochalasin treatment disrupts the endogenous currents associated with cell polarization in fucoid zygotes; Studies of the role of F-actin in embryogenesis, *J.Cell Biol.*, 100:1173.
Burridge, K., Fath, K., Kelly, T., Nuckolls, G., and Turner, C., 1988, Focal adhesions: transmembrane junctions between the extracellular matrix and the cytoskeleton, *Ann Rev Cell Biol*, 4:487.
Crayton, M.A., Wilson, E., and Quatrano, R.S., 1974, Sulfation of fucoidan in Fucus embryo. II. Separation from initiation of polar growth, *Devel.Biol.*, 39:164.
Davidson, E.H., 1989, Lineage-specific gene expression and the regulative capacities of the sea urchin embryo: a

proposed mechanism, *Development*, 105:42.

Dinsmore, J.H., and Sloboda, R.D., 1989, Microinjection of antibodies to a 62kd mitotic apparatus protein arrests mitosis in dividing sea urchin embryos, *Cell*, 57:127.

Evans, L.V., Callow, J.A., and Callow, M.E., 1982, The biology and biochemistry of reproduction and early development in *Fucus*, *Prog.Phycol.Res.*, 1:67.

Goodenough, U.W., and Adair, W.S., 1989, Recognition proteins of *Chlamydomonas reinhardtii* (Chlorophyceae), *in:* "Algae as Experimental Systems," A.W. Coleman, L.J. Goff, J.R. Stein-Taylor, eds, Alan R. Liss, Inc., N.Y., p.111.

Goodenough, U.W., and Heuser, J.E., 1985, The Chlamydomonas cell wall and its constituent glycoproteins analyzed by the quick-freeze deep-etch technique, *J.Cell Biol*, 101:1550.

Goodenough, U.W., and Jurivich, D., 1978, Tipping and mating-structure activation induced in *Chlamydomonas* gametes by flagellar membrane antisera, *J.Cell Biol.*, 79:680.

Green, K.J., and Kirk, D.L, 1982, A revision of the cell lineages recently reported for *Volvox carteri* embryos, *J.Cell Biol.*, 94:741.

Griffing, L., Huber-Walchli, V., and Quatrano, R., 1990, Isolation and surface charge analysis of polar secretory vesicles from *Fucus* zygotes, *Devel.Biol.* (Submitted).

Griffing, L.R., and Quatrano, R.S., 1984, Isoelectric focusing of plant cell membranes, *Proc.Natl.Acad.Sci.USA.*, 81:4804.

Hills, G.J., Phillips, J.M., Gay, M.R., and Roberts, K.R., 1975, Self-assembly of a plant cell wall *in vitro*, *J.Mol.Biol.*, 96:431.

Hogsett, W.E., and Quatrano, R.S., 1978, Sulfation of fucoidin in *Fucus* embryos. III. Required for localization in the rhizoid wall, *J.Cell Biol.*, 78:866.

Homan, W.L., Musgrave, A., deNobel, H., Wagter, R., deWit, D., Kolk, A., and vanden Ende, H., 1988, Monoclonal antibodies directed against the sexual binding site of *Chlamydomonas* eugametos gametes, *J.Cell Biol.*, 107:177.

Jaffe, L.F., 1968, Localization in the developing *Fucus* egg and the general role of localizing currents, *Adv.Morphog.*, 7:295.

Jaffe, L.F., and Gould, M., 1985, Polyspermy-preventing mechanisms, *in:* "Biology of Fertilization," C.B. Metz and A. Monroy, eds, Academic Press, N.Y., Vol.3, p.223.

Jaffe, L.F., and Nuccitelli, R., 1977, Electrical controls of development, *Ann.Rev.Biophys.Bioeng.*, 6:445.

Jones, J.L., Callow, J.A., and Green, J.R., 1988, Monoclonal antibodies to sperm surface antigens of the brown alga *Fucus serratus* exhibit region-, gamete-, species- and genus-preferential binding, *Planta*, 176:298.

Kirk, D.L. 1988, The ontogeny and phylogeny of cellular differentiation in *Volvox*, *Trends In Genet.*, 4(2):32.

Kirk, D.L., 1990, Genetic control of reproductive cell differentiation in *Volvox*, *Recent Adv.Exp.Phycol.*, 5: (in press).

Kropf, D.L., Berge, S.K., and Quatrano, R.S., 1989, Actin localization during *Fucus* embryogenesis, *Plant Cell*, 1:191.

Kropf, D.L., Kloareg, B., and Quatrano, R.S., 1988, Cell wall is required for fixation of the embryonic axis in *Fucus* zygotes, *Science*, 239:187.

Kropf, D.L., and Quatrano, R.S., 1987, Localization of

membrane-associated calcium during development of fucoid algae using chlorotetracycline, *Planta,* 171:158.

Maier, I., Muller, D.G., and Schmid, C., 1988, Pheromone receptor specificity and threshold concentration for spermatozoid release in *Laminaria digitata,* *Naturwissen.,* 75:260.

Müller, D.G., 1989, The role of pheromones in sexual reproduction of brown algae, *in:* "Algae as Experimental Systems," A.W. Coleman, L.J. Goff, J.R. Stein-Taylor eds, Alan R. Liss, Inc.,N.Y., p.201.

Nuccitelli, R., 1978, Ooplasmic segregation and secretion in the *Pelvetia* egg is accompanied by a membrane-generated electrical current, *Devel.Biol.,* 62:13.

Quatrano, R.S., 1973, Separation of processes associated with differentiation of two-celled *Fucus* embryos, *Devel.Biol.,* 30:209.

Quatrano, R.S., 1978, Development of cell polarity, *Ann.Rev.Plant Physiol.,* 29:487.

Quatrano, R.S., Brawley, S.H., and Hogsett, W.E., 1979, The control of the polar deposition of a sulfated polysaccharide in *Fucus* zygotes, *in:* "Determinants of Spatial Organization," S. Subtelny, I.R. Konigsbert, eds, Academic Press, New York, 77-96.

Quatrano, R.S., 1980, Gamete release, fertilization, and embryogenesis in the Fucales, *in:* "Handbook of Phycological Methods: Developmental and Cytological Methods," E. Gantt, ed., Cambridge University Press, Cambridge pp 59-68.

Quatrano, R.S., 1982, Cell wall formation in *Fucus* zygotes: a model system to study the assembly and localization of wall polymers, *in:* "Cellulose and Other Natural Polymer Systems," R.M. Brown, Jr., ed.,Plenum Publishing Corp., N.Y., p.45

Quatrano, R.S., 1990, Polar axis fixation and cytoplasmic localization in *Fucus, in:* "48th Symposium of the Society for Developmental Biology," A.P. Mahowald, ed., Alan R. Liss, Inc., N.Y. (in press).

Quatrano, R.S., Griffing, L.R., Huber-Walchli, V., and Doubet, S., 1985, Cytological and biochemical requirements for the establishment of a polar cell, *J.Cell Sci.,* Suppl. 2:129.

Quatrano, R.S., and Kropf, D.L., 1989, Polarization in *Fucus* (Phaeophyceae) zygotes: Investigations of the role of calcium, microfilaments and cell wall, *in:* "Algae as Experimental Systems," A.W. Coleman, L.J. Goff , J.R. Stein-Taylor,eds, Alan R. Liss, Inc., New York, pp 111-119.

Robinson, K.R., Jaffe, L.A., and Brawley, S.H., 1981, Electrophysiological properties of fucoid algal eggs during fertilization, *J.Cell Biol.,* 91:179a.

Schierenberg, E. 1989, Cytoplasmic determination and distribution of developmental potential in the embryo of *Caenorhabditis elegans, Bioessays,* 10:99.

Speksnijder, J.E., Miller, A.L., Weisenseel, M.H., Chen, T-H., and Jaffe, L.F., 1989, Calcium buffer injections block fucoid egg development by facilitating calcium diffusion, *Proc.Natl.Acad. Sci. USA.,* 86:6607.

Starr, R.C., and Jaenicke, L., 1989, Cell differentiation in *Volvox carteri* (Chlorophyceae): the use of mutants in understanding patterns and control, *in:* "Algae as Experimental Systems," A.W. Coleman, L.J. Goff, J.R.

Stein-Taylor, eds., Alan R. Liss, Inc., New York pp 135-147.

Strome, S., 1989, Generation of cell diversity during early embryogenesis in the nematode *Caenorhabditis elegans*, Int. Rev. Cytol., 114:81.

Tschochner, H., Lottspeich, F., and Sumper, M., 1987, The sexual inducer of *Volvox carteri*: purification, chemical characterization and identification of its gene, *EMBO J.*, 6:2203.

Waaland, S.D., 1989, Cellular morphogenesis in the filamentous red alga *Griffithsia*, *in:* "Algae as Experimental Systems," A.W. Coleman, L.J. Goff, J.R. Stein-Taylor eds Alan R. Liss, Inc., N.Y., p.121.

Watson, B.A., and Waaland, S.D., 1983, Partial purification and characterization of a glycoprotein cell fusion hormone from *Griffithisia pacifica*, a red alga, *Pl.Physiol.*, 71:327.

Watson, B.A., and Waaland, S.D., 1986, Further biochemical characterization of a cell fusion hormone from the red alga, *Griffithsia pacifica*, *Pl.Cell Physiol.*, 27:1043.

Weintraub, H., 1990, Antisense RNA and DNA, *Sci.Amer.*, 262:40.

SECTION II

SELECTED AQUATIC ANIMAL ORGANISMS

EXPERIMENTAL ANALYSIS OF DEVELOPMENTAL PROCESSES

IN MARINE HYDROIDS

Günter Plickert

Zoological Institute, University Basel
Rheinsprung 9, 4051 Basel, Switzerland

INTRODUCTION

Hydroids are classical objects of developmental biologists. As early as 1740 the Swiss scientist Abraham Trembley bisected a freshwater polyp. Thus he may be regarded as the founder of experimental developmental biology because he subjected the animal to a regeneration experiment. The first experiment demonstrating what Spemann later termed the "organizer principle" was performed by Ethel Browne (1909), about 20 years earlier than the work of Mangold and Spemann. Browne observed that - upon lateral grafting of a hydra head into the gastric column of another hydra - a secondary axis was induced in the host. The stimulating ideas on the possible role of gradients in the control of developmental processes also were based on observations in Hydrozoans (Morgan, 1901, 1905, 1906; Child, 1941). More recently, experimental studies with hydrozoans have once again provided the data for further theoretical approaches on the general mechanism of development and pattern formation. For instance the, now widely used and very instructive, term "positional information" has been coined in order to describe also events occurring in the body column of a hydra (Wolpert et al., 1971, 1972, 1974).

Several properties render hydroids suitable for studies aimed at the understanding of general control mechanisms of development. They are simply constructed, consisting of only two epithelia and of only few major cell types. Among these cell types are, however, true multipotent stem cells (I-cells). Hydroids may be regarded as "permanent embryonic" since pattern formation and morphogenesis continues throughout life. Adult polyps maintain an equilibrium of cell loss and cell renewal. They represent a morphogenetic steady state. Nevertheless, excess cells are produced and arranged in a typical pattern of differentiated cells. They are excluded from the body as tiny but complete new animals. Asexual reproduction as well as the maintenance of the steady state condition depend on cells that enter the correct pathway of differentiation and assemble into the required spatial arrangement. Accordingly, the control mechanisms responsible for pattern formation and morphogenesis must be permanently active and thus can be studied at any time.

Experimental Embryology in Aquatic Plants and Animals
Edited by H.-J. Marthy, Plenum Press, New York, 1990

In addition to these autonomously ocurring processes, the formation of a specifc pattern is easily inducable as hydrozoans readily regenerate lost or removed body parts.

The aim of this review is to show in selected examples how experimental analysis of hydroid development may contribute to the general understanding of developmental processes. It must be emphasized that this overview shall not include all the experimental studies done in this field. For instance, from the extensive body of literature on experimental work with the freshwater polyp ÆSSUNØHydraÆSSNOØ only papers are mentioned in context with the subjects of this article (for overviews on different aspects of *Hydra* development see Tardent, 1978; Bode and Bode, 1984; Burnett, 1961 a,b; Lesh-Laurie, 1973, 1982; MacWilliams, 1983 a,b; Schaller et al., 1983, 1989; Webster, 1971; Wolpert et al., 1971, 1972, 1974; and others). Also excluded is the body of work on the question how the differentiated state is maintained stable in Coelenterate cells. It has been known for a long time that extensive tissue movements occur along the body column of a polyp (for overview see Tardent, 1988). By means of immunocytochemistry it has been shown that cells modify expression patterns acording to their actual axial position, e.g., in nerve cells (Koizumi and Bode, 1986; Koizumi et al., 1988). For a review on the capacity of medusa striated muscle for transdifferentiation into several other cell types (including nerve cells) see Schmid et al. (1988).

BASIC ORGANIZATION

Both metagenetic life cycle stages of the Hydroidea, polyp and medusa have a similar basic architecture. Only one axis of asymmetry exists. It matches the oral-aboral axis. The oral pole bears a mouth as the only opening of the animal. At the opposite end of the polyp stage an adhesive foot (solitary species) or a tube-like stolon (that interconnects the single polyps in colonial species) is found. In the medusa stage, the aboral pole matches the apex of the bell-shaped umbrella. The body wall of hydroids is bilayered consisting of an outer epidermis and an inner gastrodermis. The two epithelia are separated by a basal lamina, the mesogleoa. In polyps, the mesoglea generally is a thin lamella, while it forms an extensive jelly in the (outer) umbrella of medusae.

The gastrodermis consists predominantly of gland cells and digestive epitheliomuscular cells. The basal muscular processes of the latter are arranged radially and form a functional ring muscle. Neuronal cells and interstitial cells complete the spectrum of cell types in the gastrodermis.

The epidermis is constituted from epithelomuscular cells that project their processes parallel to the oral-aboral axis. Several special types of the epithelial cell occur in the ectoderm. The battery cell of the tentacle is a large epithelial cell that includes a set of different types of stinging cells. The mono-nucleated striated muscle cell from the subumbrellar swimming muscle of medusae contain cross-striated myofibrils instead of the smooth myofibrils that are usually formed in most epitheliomuscular cells. As non-epithelial cells, interstitial cells (I-cells) and their

derivatives i.e., sensory and ganglionic nerve cells, nemato-
cytes (the stinging cells of hydroids), and gland cells occur
in the epidermis. The germ cells as well derive from precursors
of I-cell morphology. They occur in both epithelial layers but
eventually mature in ectodermal gonads.

Polyp and medusa are the representatives of the two
differently shaped life cycle stages in the hydroids. In
general, a succession of asexually reproducing polyps and
sexual medusae characterizes their metagenetic life cycle.
However, species with reduced or even absent medusae as well as
species with reduced polyp stage are known (see Tardent, 1978).

The polyp basically is a hollow cylinder with two ends
that are structured differently. Apically, the mouth is located
at the centre of a conically shaped hypostome. At the border of
the so-called "head" with the gastric region a whorl of
catching tentacles extends radially from the body wall. Below
the gastric region, the diameter of the body column decreases
forming a peduncle or hydrocaulus. Most proximally, the axial
sequence of visible polyp structures is completed either on a
foot in solitary species or a stolon in colonial hydroids. The
stolon is the most basal structure and interconnects the
individual members of the colony as a gastrovascular system.
Stolons have a remarkable morphogenetic potential. They autonomously elongate at their tips, form new tips by branching and
give rise to new polyps and medusae by bud formation
(Braverman, 1971 a; Tardent, 1978).

Medusae develop asexually from polyps or polyp colonies,
or directly from planula larvae. For a description of the
budding process and the morphogenetic changes during this
process see Frey (1968) and Boelsterli (1977). Medusa formation
starts from polyp tissue and the body plan is quite similar to
that of the polyp (Tardent, 1978). Nevertheless, medusa formation is not just a rearrangement of already existing cells.
Instead, de novo differentiation is required, since medusae
contain cell types that are absent in the polyp stage (for
instance, striated muscle cells). Comparative studies of
protein patterns in polyps and medusae of *Podocorynea carnea*
showed that only 62% of all proteins found occur in both
stages, while 24% of the proteins are exclusive to the medusa
stage and 14% to the polyp stage (Bally and Schmid, 1988). In
addition, the life span of the individual animal is remarkably
different in the two stages. While senescence and death are
common features of medusa life (at least to the mature animal),
polyps appear to be somatically immortal (Tardent, 1978).

THE ACQUISITION OF POLARITY DURING EARLY DEVELOPMENT

Despite the uniformity found in the organization among
hydroids and even among the members of the entire phylum
Cnidaria, a great diversity of cleavage and gastrulation
patterns is observed during embryogenesis (see Tardent, 1978).
Cleavage can be total leading to most of all possible
arrangements of the blastomeres (except that of the spiral
type), or it can be partial as observed in the superficial
cleavage of *Eudendrium racemosum* (Mergner, 1957, 1971).
Gastrulation occurs by polar and multipolar immigration as well
as by different types of delamination. Embolic invagination

that occurs in Scyphozoa and Anthozoa has not been observed so far in Hydrozoa (Tardent, 1978).

Oocytes and eggs of hydroids are already polarized as is indicated by pigment patterns observed in *Amphisbetia* (=*Sertularia*, Teissier, 1931), for instance. The germinal vesicle or the developing female pronucleus are located excentrically just below the membrane site, where the polar bodies are shed during meiosis (Freeman and Miller, 1982; Freeman, 1987). It has been shown for *Phialidium* and *Hydractinia* that this is the only site where eggs can be fertilized (Freeman and Miller, 1982). In *Hydractinia*, this spatial restriction of possible sperm entry was correlated with a vitelline coat that covers the entire egg except the polar body site (Zürrer, 1988). Observing the development of the pigmented egg of *Amphisbetia*, Teissier (1931) referred the anterior-posterior polarity of the planula to the polar axis of the egg. At the polar body site starts the unipolar cleavage (for cleavage mechanism see Rappaport, 1969). This area of the egg develops into the posterior part of the larva. Egg polarity has been suggested to be fixed during oogenesis by egg components that cannot be dislocated by centrifugation and thus were assumed to reside in the egg cortex (e.g., Kühn, 1965). The contents of the egg of *Hydractinia* could be stratified by centrifugation. Polar cleavage of these eggs, however, did not occur in any obvious correlation to the stratification (Beckwith, 1914).

Polarization in Hydrozoan embryos was thoroughly reinvestigated by Freeman (1980, 1981 a,b, 1983). Using dye-markings he prooved that material of the egg's area of cleavage initiation is redistributed in the tissue of the the posterior planula. Thus the anterior pole of the larva - which may be regarded as the sensory pole - does not develop from that egg pole which - by the presence of polar bodies - usually is referred to as the animal pole. Moreover, gastrulation also starts at the polar body pole and not - as is usually in animal development - from the opposite pole. This could be demonstrated in the transparent embryo of *Phialidium* which gastrulates by polar ingression (Freeman, 1980, 1981 b). The experiments of Gary Freeman show clearly that the polarity of the embryo becomes fixed at the time of first cleavage. It was not already fixed in the egg cortex. Freeman carried out combined marking and centrifugation experiments. Eggs stained at the polar body site were subjected to centrifugation. If fertilized eggs were centrifuged, polar cleavage initiated preferentially in a zone where the nucleus also stratified. That the nucleus or - more likely - the associated mitotic spindle determines the cleavage site is supported by experiments using Cytochalasin B. When the first cleavage was blocked by pulse-treatment with the drug followed by centrifugation to move apart the two nuclei, two instead of only one furrow formed in the single, bi-nucleated cell at the time of the regular second cleavage. From these bi-tailed planulae develop (Freeman, 1981 a). If the site of the first cleavage in centrifuged eggs does not match the site of polar body formation, the polarity of the embryo aligns in respect to the cleavage site (Freeman, 1987). This clearly shows that only under normal conditions, where the position of the female pronucleus matches the site of polar body formation, embryo polarity and visible egg polarity correlates.

Once established, polarity becomes a property detectable in the entire embryo. Isolated fragments of the embryo retain their original polarity (Teissier, 1931: Freeman, 1981 a). In grafts with opposing polarity, however i.e., anterior blastula halfs grafted to anterior blastula halfs (or posterior halfs to posterior halfs), the polarity in the resulting embryo becomes rearranged. For instance, gastrulation starts in the bi-anterior blastula at the border of the graft. Thus material from the former anterior poles becomes lateral larval tissue. When large and small embryo fragments of different polarity are combined, then the polarity of the larger part usually dominates. Obviously, the cells of the embryo communicate in order to coordinate a common polar behavior. This is also evident after complete dissociation and reaggregation of embryonic cells. Dissociated and reaggregated blastula cells form normal planulae, provided the mass of the reaggregate does not exceed twice the normal volume of an embryo. Larger reaggregates develop multi-tailed planulae or larvae with supernumerary anterior ends. Experimentally, the resulting common polarity could be manipulated by implantation of non-dissociated, and thus polarized parts, of an embryo. The reaggregates adopt the polarity of the implant, irrespective of the origin of the graft (Freeman, 1981 a). Freeman suggests that polarity is a vector property of the tissue, due to an "element-polarity" of the single cells. In a polarized embryo, the single cells are ordered with equal polar orientation. In the disordered condition of an aggregate, re-rectification can be initiated by cells that have assembled randomly as a group of sibipolar cells. From these cells or from an implant of polarized tissue polarity is transferred in an "infectious" process to all other cells of the aggregate. The molecular mechanism of this "entrainment" - as Freeman calls it - is not known.

In contrast, polarity in Hydra was shown to be a scalar property and not vectoral (Gierer et al., 1972). Segments were cut from the body column of *Hydra*, reversed and reassembled. Thus the tissue of the single segments remained at their individual apicobasal position but with reversed polarity within the segments. Head and foot regenerated from the reassembled body column according to the polarity encoded by different apicobasal tissue levels and not - as it must be expected in the case of vector-encoded polarity - in respect to segment polarity. In reaggregates, the origin of the dissociated and reaggregated cells determines the new polarity. At least in *Hydra*, it is a quantitative difference along the body column that determines polarity and not a vectoral property of the tissue.

METAMORPHOSIS

In species with indirect development, a larva forms as the terminal stage of embryonic development. In a more or less dramatic reshaping process this transient resting stage meta-morphoses into the adult polyp or into a medusa. This chapter shall review experiments on the metamorphosis of hydroid planulae.

A great variety of natural and artificial inducers stimulate the larvae of marine invertebrates to settle and undergo metamorphosis (for general overview see Crisp, 1974, 1976; Chia and Rice, 1978; Müller, 1979; Burke, 1983; Morse, 1985). Planulae of different Hydrozoan species vary in their dependence on exogenous stimulants for metamorphosis. Larvae of *Aequorea aequorea* and *Sarsia tubulosa*, for instance, do not seem to require any external physical or chemical inducing factor (Chia and Bickell, 1978). On the other hand, habitat specialists like the colonial hydroids *Hydractinia echinata* that settles on shells populated by hermit crabs (Schijfsma, 1935), or *Proboscidactyila flavicirrata* that settles on the tube of a sabellid polychaete (Campbell, 1968 a; Donaldson, 1974 a), depend on substrate cues. In nature, the choice of the right substrate has been shown to be mediated by chemical stimuli (reviewed by Chia and Bickell, 1978).

In this respect, one of the best studied species is the polymorphic hydroid *Hydractinia echinata*. Certain marine gram-negative bacteria of the genus *Alteromaonas* have been identified as the natural inducer (Müller, 1969, 1973 a,b; Spindler and Müller, 1972). The activity of the bacterial factor was attributed to lipophilic compounds (Wittmann, 1977). Based on a Michaelis-Menten saturation kinetics of the dose-response it was proposed that the larval response to the inducer involves an enzyme or a carrier-system. The primary effect of the inducer was attributed to a stimulation of the Na^+/K^+-ATPase since metamorphosis induction could be prevented by Ouabain, a specific inhibitor of this enzyme (Müller and Buchal, 1973). Monovalent cations such as Cs^+, Li^+, Rb^+, and K^+ were shown to induce metamorphosis in *Hydractinia echinata* (Spindler and Müller, 1972; Müller and Buchal, 1973. The most effective one, Cs^+, has been successfully employed to induce metamorphosis also in *Halocordyle disticha* (Archer and Thomas, 1984) and *Phialidium gregarium* (Freeman, 1981 b), a species in which metamorphosis can also be induced by bacteria (Thomas et al., 1987). Reduction of the Mg^{2+}-level promotes or even induces metamorphsis (Ludewig, unpublished work, Müller, 1985; Berking, 1988 a; Schwoerer-Böhning et al., 1990). Recent studies suggest that metamorphosis induction involves intracellular signal transduction via activation of Kinase C, since metamorphosis could be induced by tumor-promoting phorbol esters (most effectively with 12-o-tetradecanoylphorbol 13-acetate, Müller, 1985), or by 1,2-dioctanoyl-*sn*-glycerol (Leitz and Müller, 1987).

Berking (1988 a) shows that externally applied ammonia also induces metamorphosis in *Hydractinia*. Several substances shown to induce metamorphosis were argued to increase the internal level of produced ammonia. These substances include Cs^+, Rb^+, Ba^{2+}, Sr^{2+}, and tetraethylammonium (which may hinder the efflux of NH_4^+ via K^+-channels), Li^+ and amiloride (which may inhibit the export via a Na^+/H^+-antiporter). Stimulation of Kinase C also reduces the efflux of ammonia via K^+-channels. Ammonia and some other compounds including methylamine and ethanolamine are argued to cause metamorphosis through their ability to accept methyl-groups, thus leading to a low level of internal S-adenosyl-methionine. Compounds that may function as donors of methyl-groups consistently stabilize the larval state (Berking, 1986 a,b, 1987, 1988 a).

It is not known how hydroid planulae receive and transmit external stimuli of metamorphosis. Many of the inducers could be expected to be functional in provoking membrane depolarization and thus in generating conducted signals as proposed by Freeman. Transduction could be nervous, neuroid, or mediated by compounds released from cells (Chia and Bickell, 1978). Nerve cells have been described in planulae of several hydroid species, e.g., in *Phialidium gregarium* (Thomas at al., 1987, *Halocordyle disticha* = *Pennaria tiarella* (Martin and Thomas, 1977, 1981), *Mitrocomella polydiademata* (Martin et al., 1983), and *Hydractinia echinata* (Weis et al., 1985; Plickert et al., 1988, Plickert 1989). Both types, neurosensory cells as well as ganglionic cells occur.

In *Hydractinia*, occasionally metamorphosis stops while the transformation of larva tissue into adult tissue is still incomplete (Spindler and Müller, 1972; Plickert, 1987; Berking, 1987). Such animals are composed of a non-metamorphosed posterior larva tail and of basal stolons that derive from anterior parts of the planula. This may indicate that the process of transformation starts at the anterior pole and progresses into posterior direction. Isolation experiments show that in *Hydractinia* the capacity to receive and/or to respond to an inducing stimulus decreases from anterior to posterior (Müller et al., 1976; Schwoerer-Böhning et al., 1990). For *Hydractinia* it has been reported that sensory cells occur exclusively in middle and posterior parts of the planula (Weis et al., 1985). In *Phialidium gregarium* sensory cells occur in lateral as well as in anterior parts of the larva (Thomas et al., 1987). By means of immunocytochemistry, Plickert (1989) demonstrates in contrast to the results of Weis et al. that part of the nervous system in planulae of *Hydractinia* is centralized to the anterior pole. Neurosensory cell bodies that contain neuropeptide with the carboxyterminus Arg-Phe-amide occur exclusively in the anterior third of the larva. This nerve cell population comprises only about 10 % of all nerve cells found in mature planulae (Plickert et al., 1988). Neuropeptide containig processes are found to penetrate the anteriormost ectoderm to form a conspicious sensory structure. On the other hand, processes of these cells extend also to the posterior parts of the larva, This suggests a possible role also in signal transduction. Since these sensory cells disappear during metamorphosis we can attribute them with a function in larval life, for example in metamorphosis. Neurosensory cells that disappear soon after initiation of metamorphosis are known to occur also in *Mitrocomella polydiademata* (Martin et al., 1983). Sensory cells with immunoreactivity to Phe-Met-Arg-Phe-amide (FMRF-amide) -like peptides were also observed in planulae of other hydroids, e.g. *Halocordyle disticha* (Martin, 1989) but not with such a distinct arrangement in relation to the anterior pole of the larva as in *Hydractinia*. In the polyp stage of hydroids and other Coelenterates, FMRF-amide immunoreactive sensory and ganglionic nerve cells are generally found with a maximum density in the head region (Grimmelikhuijzen, 1985; Grimmelikhuijzen and Graff, 1985).

From experiments of Schwoerer-Böhning et al. (1990) it appears that signal transmission in *Hydractinia* from the anterior part of the larva (that receives the stimulus) to the posterior part (that by itself cannot receive most natural and artificial stimuli but respond to the signal from the anterior pole) is a slow process. Sectioning experiments showed that the internally transmitted signal requires at least one hour to reach (or to irreveribly stimulate) the posterior quarter of the larva. This indicates that the internal signal transduction does not occur by means of nervous or epithelial conduction which would be expected to be much faster. Moreover, the authors showed that metamorphosis induction could be transferred from a previously stimulated anterior planula part to a grafted non-stimulated posterior part. Thus tissue was induced to undergo metamorphosis in the absence of any treatment that could achieve the generation of a conducted depolarization.

For a correct interpretation of these results one has to consider that the internally transduced signal can be by-passed by several means. So far known, only depletion of the Mg^{2+}-concentration can induce metamorphosis in *isolated* tails of larvae (Schwoerer-Böhning et al., 1990). However, in intact planulae several compounds were shown to induce partial metamorphosis, affecting exclusively the posterior larva. Animals that remained larva in the anterior part but transformed to polyp heads in the posterior part developed. Compounds that cause such partial transformation are Li^+ (Spindler and Müller, 1972), ammonia, tetraethylammonium, and methylamine (Berking 1988a). It must be expected that these substances interfere with the internally transmitted signal. One possible mechanism involving ammonia in a key role been suggested by Berking (1988 a, see above).

Metamorphosis may involve neurochemical signalling. Planulae of *Halocordyle disticha* are stimulated to undergo metamorphosis by different catecholamines. Catecholamines are contained in ganglion cells of this species (Edwards et al., 1987) whereas neurosensory cells contain a FMRF-amide neuropeptide (Martin, 1989). Based on these findings Edwards et al. suggest that by action of the primary trigger (bacteria) FMRF-amide might be released from the sensory cells. Subsequently the peptide causes release of catecholamines from the ganglionic cells as the crucial step of metamorphosis induction. However, in Phialidium gregarium, metamorphosis does not depend on ganglionic cells since larvae deprived of these cells were capable to undergo successful metamorphosis (Thomas et al., 1987). In *Hydractinia* there is evidence for an endogenous signal compound (Schwoerer-Bîhning et al., 1990). RF-amide neurosensory cells are located at the anterior larva pole (Plickert, 1989) where the metamorphosis stimulus is apparently received. However, the internal signal may be different from that in *Halocordyle* since here catecholamines do not stimulate metamorphosis (Edwards et al., 1987). The finding that Mg^{2+}-free sea water induces metamorphosis (Ludewig, unpublished work; Müller, 1985; Schwoerer-Böhning et al., 1990) may indicate that neurotransmitters are also involved in the metamorphosis of *Hydractinia*. Mg^{2+} blocks the release of neurotransmitters that occur also in Coelenterates (Spencer, 1982). Reducing the Mg^{2+}-level could perhaps initiate a release of metamorphosis promoting substances.

The adult hydroid planula represents a resting stage. Proliferative activity and processes of cell differentiation have ceased almost completely in mature larvae (Plickert et al., 1988). Most planulae are similarly drop-shaped with two discernable ends, a blunt anterior and a tapered posterior end (Tardent, 1978). Although not obvious, a clear longitudinal organization does indeed exist in the larvas. On the cellular level, a characteristic spatial distribution of different cell types is observed along the anterior-posterior axis but also according to the inner (=entodermal)/outer (epidermal) organization (for review see Tardent, 1978). During metamorphosis a new pattern emerges. Much more detailed structures like a hypostome, tentacles, or stolons develop for the first time. Since metamorphosis is a rapid event (e.g., in *Hydractinia* it only lasts about one day), it may be argued that part of the adult polyp pattern is already preformed in the larva. Experimental data indicate that this is - in part - true. Planulae of *Hydractinia echinata* contain embryonically transcribed poly (A)-rich RNA that is utilized during metamorphosis (Eiben, 1982). Cells that leave the cell cycle late in embryonic development of *Hydractinia echinata* become comitted to differentiate into a type of nematocyte that is used in the catching tentacle of the postmetamorphic polyp stage (Kroiher, 1989; Plickert et al., 1988). The most compelling evidence for the existance of somehow predetermined polyp structures in a larva is derived from experiments in which segments of planulae were investigated for their capacity to form polyp structures (Schwoerer-Böhning et al., 1990). From isolated terminal ends of the larva only the corresponding polyp parts develop as isolated structures i.e., polyp heads form from the tip of the planula tail and stolons derive from the anteriormost planula fragment. However, the same study shows that pattern formation during metamorpohosis is not just the realization of an already existent prepattern. Middle pieces of planulae deprived of their terminal parts are capable to develop into complete primary polyps. This indicates that de novo pattern formation occurs during metamorphosis. Supporting evidence for this was obtained by experimental approaches using artificial (Müller et al., 1977; Müller, 1984) or endogenous compounds (Müller et al., 1977; Berking, 1984, 1986 a,b, 1987; Plickert, 1987, 1989) that interferred with pattern formation during metamorphosis. Neuropharmaka, retinoic acid and ions like Cs^+ were shown to alter proportions of polyp structures along the oral/aboral axis (Müller et al., 1977;, Müller 1984). Endogenous compounds that may function as methyl donors in transmethylation pathways (Berking, 1986 b) caused over-sizing of the gastric region or the stolon region when applied during early metamorphosis (Berking, 1986 a, 1987). A yet unidentified low-molecular weight factor from colonial hydroids caused severe overproportioning of the head region on the expense of basal body parts (Plickert, 1987, 1990). The factor was shown to stimulate nerve cell differentiation in hydroids (Plickert, 1989, 1990). Obviously, metamorphosis realizes partially predetermined structures. The fact that the shape of the developing polyp can be dramatically altered during metamorphosis indicates that substantial parts of the adult pattern are first formed during this process.

CONTROL OF POLYP BUDDING AND BRANCHING IN HYDROID COLONIES

A hydroid colony expands by elongation and branching of the tube-like stolons and by asexual budding of new polyps on these stolons. Colony form and growth have been described for hydroids by Kühn (1910, 1914), for *Campanularia* by Crowell (1957), Crowell and Wyttenbach (1957), Brock (1974); for *Cordylophora* by Fulton (1961, 1963); for *Tubularia* by Mackie (1966); for *Podocoryne carnea* by Braverman (1963,1974) and Braverman and Schrandt (1966), for Clytia johnstoni by Hale (1973 a,b,, 1974); for *Hydractinia echinata* by Hauenschild (1954) and McFadden et al. (1984). Mechanisms of epithelial morphogenesis in hydroid development have been studied by Beloussov (1973) Beloussov et al. (1972, 1980, 1989). Stolon elongation and branching have been investigated in studies by Braverman (1971 a), Campbell (1968 b), Crowell (1957, 1974), Crowell and Wyttenbach (1957), Crowell et al. 1965, Donaldson (1973, 1974b), Hale (1960, 1964), Overton (1963), Suddith (1974), Wyttenbach (1968, 1969, 1973, 1974), Wyttenbach et al. (1965, 1973), Petriconi and Plickert (1974), Plickert (1978, 1980), Müller et al. (1987), and others.

For the solitary *Hydra* it has been suggested that morphogenetic gradients emerging from the terminal ends control the positioning of new polyp buds (Hyman, 1928; Burnett, 1961b; Webster and Hamilton, 1972; Shostak, 1974). In young, and therefore short, animals inhibition emanating from the terminals extends over the entire body column and prevents the formation of a new axis. By growth of the animal, the tissue of the budding area escapes from the reach of inhibition and is allowed to form a bud (see Bode and Bode, 1984). However, studies on the the low-budding-rate mutant L4 of *Hydra magnipapillata* (Sugiyama and Fujisawa, 1979) have shown that the high level of head inhibition in this strain (Takano and Sugiyama, 1983) is not the cause for the deficiency in budding. A special diet has been shown to alter the budding rate (Takano, 1984; Takano and Sugiyama, 1985) but not the level of inhibition (Takano and Sugiyama, 1985).

Consistently, in colonial hydroids budding is controlled by existing hydranths. Removal of hydranths from a colony causes an increase in new bud formation from the remaining stolons (Braverman, 1971 b). Budding has been analysed in colonies that have been deprived of hydranths in one half and that have been left intact in the other part. A prompt stimulation of budding occurs during days one and two after polyp excision in the experimental half. With a delay of one further day, polyp removal stimulates bud formation to twice the normal rate also in the control part of the colony. Even though Braverman suggests a local control mechanism for budding, the above mentioned results indicate also a long range control by factors probably distributed throughout the entire colony (see below). Experiments by Hale (1974) in Clytia johnstoni indicate an inhibitory field controlling new polyp formation on stolons. Interpolyp distances are quite regular in this species. Thus, the position where a new bud will appear can be predicted precisely. Hale transplants hydranths into the vicinity of the expected budding site and shows that existing hydranths prevent budding within a distance of up to 300 Êm. An inhibitory field has been found to control polyp spacing in the colonial hydroid *Eirene viridula* (Plickert et al., 1987). Model

colonies consisting of only one hydranth and one or two stolons
have been used to study factors affecting the distance at which
a new hydrant will appear. The positioning of the bud is
determined by inhibition emanating from the head of the polyp:
removal of the entire polyp or at least the polyp head causes a
decrease in the distance. Already young buds exert inhibition
onto the surrounding tissue. Inhibition seems to be mediated by
a diffusable hydrophilic compound. This factor apparently is
tranmitted through the stolon tissue. But it also leaks into
the surrounding sea water since interpolyp distances are
strongly affected by culture conditions. Distances depend on
volume and the degree of agitation of the culture medium.
Inhibition can be transferred to other colonies by means of
conditioned medium. Distances are strongly influenced by the
polyp density in the entire colony. This has been observed even
in stolons far remote from the crowded central parts. A
mechanism which could explain this result and also the data of
Braverman (1971 b) is based on the idea that the inhibitor also
leaks into the gastrocoelic fluid. By peristaltic pumping of
the stolon tubes and the interconnected hydranths this fluid
and thus the inhibitor is distributed in the entire colony.
From the gastric cavity the inhibitor can be expected to react
back on spacing control in the tissue. Experimental support for
this idea comes from the observation that cutting, and thus
opening the stolon tubes, stimulates bud formation. In respect
to this "leaky" behavior of the inhibitor, in *Eirene viridula*
transfer of inhibition is likely to occur by intercellular
spreading. Experiments in *Hydra* using antibodies to gap
junction protein showed that transfer of inhibition could be
disturbed by the antibody and thus is likely to occur by
diffusion via gap junctions (Fraser et al 1987, 1988).

Several observations indicate that marine hydroids
generally may use a "leaky" inhibitor to control morphogenesis.
Some species are known to be very difficult to keep in
laboratory culture, in particular thecate species. The polyps
tend to regress or to degenerate when kept in closed systems of
even large volume tanks or aquaria but do very well in running
sea water. Presumably these species depend on large volumes of
sea water to avoid self-inhibition.

Numerous species show a pronounced adaptation to water
currents in colony form (see Riedl, 1983; Svoboda, 1976;
Petriconi and Plickert, 1980). Fan-shaped colonies are always
oriented perpendicular to the main direction of currents. It
may be asssumed that in a growing upright a branch or a new
polyp is positioned at a site where the inhibitor concentration
is lowest around the circumference. Provided that inhibitor can
escape from the tissue to the sea water, a current acting on
the stem should increase convection and thus removal of the
inhibitor. Due to the laws of hydromechanics, current velocity
is greatest at two sites of the stem that are located in a
plane perpendicular to the direction of the current. At these
lateral sites convection and thus depletion of inhibitor would
be slightly greater than anywhere around the circumference of
the stem. Side branches or new polyps form exactly in these
positions.

In several hydroids we can observe the phenomenon of
autonomous hydranth regression. Hydranths of apparently healthy
colonies maintain their shape for a couple of days, then

degenerate by loosing typical morphology and are resorbed by the stolon system. Some days later they reappear as regenerates. This has been reported from naturally occuring material of, e.g., *Obelia*, *Campanularia*, *Clytia* and other species (Hammett, 1946; Crowell, 1953; Brock, 1974, 1979; Hale, 1973 a, and others). This behavior may indicate oscillations in the concentration of endogenous inhibitor due to unsufficient removal of the factor. If the local concentration in a hydranth exceeds a threshold this individual regresses including its inhibitor-producing head. Since the local source of inhibition is obliterated the local inhibitory level decreases to subcritical values. Subsequently, regeneration is allowed to occur.

Considerable efforts were made to isolate substances that may control polyp morphogenesis during regeneration and budding. Factors that inhibited regeneration were isolated and characterized from *Tubularia* (Rose and Rose, 1941; Tardent, 1955; Tardent and Eyman, 1958; Tweedell, 1958 a,b; Beloussov and Geleg, 1960; Powers; 1961; Rose, 1963, 1966, 1967, 1970 a,b; Rose and Powers, 1966; Akin and Akin, 1967) and other colonial hydroids (Müller, 1969; Plickert, 1987). From *Hydra* inhibitors were isolated and partially purified by Lenhoff and Loomis (1957), Lenique and Lundblad (1966 a,b), Davis (1967), Schaller et al. (1979), Schmidt and Schaller (1976), Berking (1977). Most of the activities were studied concerning their effect on regeneration. Berking has shown that inhibitor I from *Hydra* interferes with budding in *Hydra* (Berking, 1977; Berking and Gierer, 1977). Polyp inhibiting factor found in *Eirene viridula*, *Hydractinia echinata*, and *Eudendrium species* increases interpolyp distances dose dependently in *Eirene viridula* (Plickert, 1987). Several compounds isolated from *Hydractinia echinata* (Berking, 1986 a,b, 1987, 1988 b) act as inhibitors during metamorphosis, some of them possibly by transferring methyl groups to intracellular targets (Berking, 1986 b). One of these compounds, homarine, increases polyp distances in *Eirene viridula* (Berking, 1986 b); homarine and trigonelline inhibited polyp formation in *Hydractinia echinata* (Berking, 1987).

Work on the description and isolation of factors that stimulate budding, or formation of polyp head structures has been done by Lesh-Laurie and Burnett (1964, 1966), Lentz (1965), Lenique and Lundblad (1966 a, b), Müller (1969), Müller and Meier-Menge (1980), Schaller (1973), Schaller and Bodenmüller (1981), Plickert (1987). The chemical structure has been determined only of the head activator from *Hydra*. It is an undecapeptide with the primary sequence pGlu-Pro-Pro-Gly-Gly-Ser-Lys-Val-Ile-Leu-Phe. The biological activity of these factors has been assayed primarily by their capability to induce supernumerary head structures such as tentacles, by the effect on polarity, and by the ability to accelerate budding. Proportion altering factor from colonial hydroids decreases distances by which newly forming polyp buds appear (Plickert, 1987). A similar effect is achieved by sinefungine which inhibits transfer of methyl groups in transmethylation pathways (Berking, 1986 b).

Hydroid colonies grow by elongation and branching of stolons and by the formation of new polyp individuals on the stolons. Branch formation is initiated by the morphogenesis of a new stolon tip that subsequently starts to produce new stolon (Plickert, 1978). Naturally, such tips develop autonomously from the stolon keeping a certain distance to already existing tips. Tips also form by induction. Whenever an existing stolon tip encounters the lateral tissue of another stolon, a tip develops at the site of contact. Subsequently, both tips, the inducing one as well as the induced one fuse, forming an anastomosis (Müller, 1964; Braverman, 1971 a).

Factors affecting branching of the stolon have been studied experimentally (Petriconi and Plickert, 1974; Plickert, 1978, 1980; Müller and El Shershaby, 1981; Müller and Plickert, 1982; Müller et al., 1987). Stolons of *Eirene viridula* form branches preferentially towards the main direction of water currents that affect a colony (Petriconi and Plickert, 1974; Plickert, 1978). An local increase in mechanical pressure on the stolon tissue has been shown to initiate branch formation at just this site (Plickert, 1978, 1980; Müller et al., 1987) indicating a possible mechanism by which water currents cause positive rheotropism. With increasing effectiveness, also local tissue lesions, local application of positive electrical current and injection of cAMP cause branching (Müller and El Shershaby, 1981). It has been assumed that tip induction during anastomosis is based also on diffusing effector molecules that act over intervening sea water (Braverman, 1971 a). That tips are effective in tip induction even in heterospecific encounters and over distances of up to 100 Êm has been shown by Müller et al., (1987).

The development of new (lateral) tips is controlled by an inhibitory field emanating from existing stolon tips. Such a field can be traced by induction experiments. By means of mechanical stimulation tips can by induced anywhere in the stolon except in close vicinity (< 400 um) to existing tips. Mutual inhibition has been observed between two stimulation sites if they are placed closer than 250 um to each other (Plickert, 1980). When the distance between the two stimuli is decreased to 200 um, a branch forms predominantly at only one of the two stimulation sites. The response at the other site is inhibited. A further decrease of the distance to 150 um results in only one branch that appears between the two stimulation sites. This behavior has been successfully simulated in theoretical models on biological pattern formation. Such models are based on reaction-diffusion kinetics of a short ranged activator and a long-ranged inhibitor (Meinhardt, 1982) or, used local and cooperative tension forces that affect the state of polarization of epithelial cells (Belintsev et al., 1987).

The inhibitory field of the stolon tip was analyzed quantitatively by comparing relative inhibitory levels at the two ends of isolated stolon fragments (Müller and Plickert, 1982). Inhibitory levels were found to decrease with increasing distance from the tip. In the species studied, *Eirene viridula*, *Hydractinia echinata*, and *Leuckartiara nobilis*, the gradient field extends proximally for about 400-700 um. After removal of the stolon tip, inhibition decays very rapidly with a half life of 0.5 hours. Though regeneration of tip morphology is a rapid process (6 hours), the restoration of original inhibitory levels needs 8-24 hours. The frequency of autonomous or regenerative tip formation depends strongly on culture condidtions: The branching frequency is low in colonies that are cultured in crowded dishes (Plickert et al., 1987); a dramatic increase in branch formation occurs after exchange of the conditioned culture medium to fresh sea water (Müller et al., 1987). Conditioned medium inhibits tip regeneration while agitation of the medium favours tip regeneration. This indicates that an inhibitory molecule is released from the tissue into the culture medium. The size of this heat-stable and hydrophilic compound is about or less 500 dalton (Müller et al., 1987).

In sum, both morphogenetic processes that start from stolon tissue, polyp formation as well as tip formation, appear to be controlled by a lateral inhibition mechanism. Molecules apparently involved in this control escape from the tissue and remain stable enough to react onto the tissue. Stolon tips not only emanate inhibition but as well have activating properties.

ACKNOWLEDGEMENTS

I wish to thank S. Berking, F. Vollrath and V. Schmid for critical reading of the manuscript. Thanks also to C. Baader and M. Kroiher for help and support.

REFERENCES

Akin, G.C., Akin, J.R., 1967, The effect of trypsin on regeneration inhibitors in Tubularia, *Biol.Bull.*, 133:82.

Archer, W., and Thomas, M.B., 1984, An SEM study of morphological changes during metamorphosis in *Pennaria tiarella*, Proc.Southeast Electron Microsc.,Soc., 7:21.

Bally, A., and Schmid, V., 1988, The jellyfish and its polyp: a comparative study of gene expression monitored by the protein patterns, using two-dimensional gels with double-label autoradiography, *Cell Diff.*, 23:93.

Beckwith, C.J., 1914, The genesis of the plasma-structure in the egg of *Hydractinia echinata*, *J.Morph.*, 25:189.

Belintsev, B.N., Beloussov, L.V., and Zaraisky, A.G., 1987, Model of pattern formation in epithelial morphogenesis, *J.theor.Biol.*, 129:369.

Beloussov, L.V., 1973, Growth and morphogenesis of some marine Hydrozoa according to histological data and time-lapse studies, *in*, "Recent trends in research in Coelenterate Biology," Publ. Seto Mar.Biol.Lab., 20:315.

Beloussov, L.V., and Geleg, S., 1960, Chemical regulation of the morphogenesis of hydroid polyps, *Dokl.Akad.Nauk.*, *USSR.*,130:165.

Beloussov, L.V., Badenko, L.A., Katchurin, A.L., and Kurilo, L.F., 1972, Cell movements in morphogenesis of hydroid polyps, *J.Embryol.exp.Morph.*, 27:317.

Beloussov, L.V., Badenko, L.A., and Labas, J.A., 1980, Growth rhythms and species-specific shape in Thecaphora hydroids *in*, "Developmental and Cellular Biology of Coelenterates," P. Tardent, and R. Tardent, ed., Elsevier/North-Holland, Biomedical Press, Amsterdam, New York, Oxford, 175.

Beloussov, L.V., Labas, J.A., Kazakova, N.I., and Zaraisky, A.G., 1989, Cytophysiology of growth pulsations in hydroid polyps, *J.Exp.Zool.*, 249:258.

Berking, S., 1977, Bud formation in Hydra. Inhibition by an endogenous morphogen, *Wilhelm Roux's Archives*, 181:215.

Berking, S., 1984, Metamorphosis of *Hydractinia echinata*. Insights into pattern formation of hydroids, *Roux's Arch.Dev.Biol.*, 193:370.

Berking, S., 1986a, Is homarine a morphogen in the marine hydroid Hydractinia?, *Roux's Arch.Dev.Biol.*, 95:33.

Berking, S., 1986b, Transmethylation and control of pattern formation, *Differentiation*, 32:10.

Berking, S., 1987, Homarine (N-methylpicolinic acid) and trigonelline (N-methylnicotinic acid) appear to be involved in pattern control in a marine hydroid, *Development*, 99:211.

Berking, S., 1988a, Ammonia, tetraethylammonium, barium and amiloride induce metamorphosis in the marine hydroid Hydractinia, *Roux's Arch.Dev.Biol.*, 197:1.

Berking, S., 1988b, Taurine found to stabilize the larval state is released upon induction of metamorphosis in the hydrozoan Hydractinia, *Roux's Arch.Dev.Biol.*, 197:321.

Berking, S., and Gierer, A., 1977, Analysis of early stages of budding in Hydra by means of an endogenous inhibitor, *Wilhelm Roux's Archives*, 182:117.

Bode, P.M., and Bode, H.R., 1984, Patterning in Hydra *in*, "Pattern formation," G.M. Malacinski and S.V. Bryant, ed., Macmillan Press, New York, I:213.

Boelsterli, U., 1977, An electronenmicroscopic study of early developmental stages, myogenesis, oogenesis and cnidogenesis in the anthomedusa, *Podocoryne carnea* M. Sars, *J.Morphol.*, 154:259.

Braverman, M., 1963, Studies on hydroid differentiation. II. Colony growth and the initiation of sexuality, *J.Embryol.exp.Morph.*, 11:239.

Braverman, M., 1971a, Studies on hydroid differentiation. VII. The hydrozoan stolon, *J.Morphol.*,135:131.

Braverman, M., 1971b, Studies on hydroid differentiation. IV. Regulation of hydranth formation in *Podocoryne carnea* , *J.exp.Zool.*, 176:361.

Braverman, M., 1974, The cellular basis of colony form in *Podocoryne carnea*, *Am.Zool.*, 14:673.

Braverman, M., and Schrandt, R., 1966, Colony development of a polymorphic hydroid as a problem of pattern formation, *Symp.Zool.Soc.*, London, 16:169.

Brock, M.A., 1974, Growth, developmental, and longevity rhythms in *Campanularia flexuosa*, *Am.Zool.*, 14:757.

Brock, M.A., 1979, Differential sensitivity to temperature steps in the circannual rhythm of hydranth longevity in the marine cnidarian *Campanularia flexuosa*, *Comp.Biochem.Physiol.A.Comp.Physiol.*, 64:381.

Browne, E., 1909, The production of new hydranths in hydra by the insertion of smaller grafts, *J.exp.Zool.*, 7:1.

Burke, R.D., 1983, The induction of metamorphosis of marine invertebrate larvae: stimulus and response, *Can.J.Zool.*, 61:1701.

Burnett, A.L., 1961a, The growth process in Hydra, *J.Exp. Zool.*, 146:21.

Burnett, A.L., 1961b, Growth factors in the tissue of Hydra, *in*, "The Biology of Hydra," H.M. Lenhoff and W.F. Loomis, ed., Univ.Miami Press, Coral Gables, 425.

Campbell, R.D., 1968a, Colony growth and pattern in the two-tentacled hydroid, *Proboscidactyla flavicirrata*, *Biol.Bull.*, 135:96.

Campbell, R.D., 1968b, Holdfast movement in the hydroid
    Corymorpha palma. Mechanism of elongation, *Biol.Bull.*,
    134:26.
Chia, F.S., and Rice, M.E., 1978, "Settlement and Metamorphosis
    of Marine Invertebrate Larvae," Elsevier, New York.
Chia, F.S., and Bickell, L., 1978, Mechanisms of larval
    settlement and the induction of settlement and
    metamorphosis: a review, *in*, F.S. Chia and M.E. Rice,
    ed., "Settlement and Metamorphosis of Marine
    Invertebrate Larvae," Elsevier, New York.
Child, C.M., 1941, "Patterns and Problems of Development",
    University of Chicago Press, Chicago,
Crisp, D., 1974, Factors influencing the settling of marine
    invertebrate larvae, *in*, "Chemoreception in marine
    organisms," P.T. Grant and A.M. Mackie, ed., Academic
    Press, New York,177.
Crisp, D., 1976, Settlement responses in marine organisms *in*,
    "Adaptations to environment: essays on the physiology of
    marine animals," R.C. Newell, ed., Butterworths, London,
    83.
Crowell, S., 1953, The regression, replacement cycle of
    hydranths of Obelia and Campanularia, *Physiol.Zool.*,
    26:319.
Crowell, S., 1957, Differential responses of growth zones to
    nutritive level, age, and temperature in the colonial
    hydroid Campanularia, *J.exp.Zool.*, 134:63.
Crowell, S., 1974, Morphogenetic events associated with stolon
    elongation in colonial hydroids, *Am.Zool.*, 14:665.
Crowell, S., and Wyttenbach, C.R., 1957, Factors affecting
    terminal growth in the hydroid Campanularia, *Biol.Bull.*,
    113:233.
Crowell, S., Wyttenbach, C.R., and Suddith, R., 1965, Evidence
    against the concept of growth zones in hydroids,
    Biol.Bull., 129:403.
Davis, L.V., 1967, The source and identity of a regeneration-
    inhibiting factor in hydroid polyps, *J.exp.Zool.*,
    164:187.
Donaldson, S., 1973, Hydroid elongation - evidence of a distal
    locomotory organ in *Proboscidactyla flavicirrata*,
    Experientia, 29:1157.
Donaldson, S., 1974a, Larval settlement of a symbiotic hydroid:
    specificity and nematocyst responses in planulae of
    Proboscidactyla flavicirrata, *Biol Bull.*,147:573.
Donaldson, S., 1974b, Terminal motility in elongating stolons
    of *Proboscidactyla flavicirrata*, *Am.Zool.*, 14:735.
Edwards, N.C., Thomas, M.B., Long, B.A., and Amyotte, S.J.,
    1987, Catecholamines induce metamorphosis in the
    hydrozoan *Halocordyle disticha* but not in *Hydractinia
    echinata*, *Roux's Arch.Dev.Biol.* 196:381.
Eiben, R., 1982, Storage of embryonically transcribed
    poly(A)RNA and its utilization during metamorphosis of
    the hydroid *Hydractinia echinata*, *Wilhelm Roux's
    Archives*, 191:270.
Fraser, S.E., Green, C.R., Bode, H., and Gilula, N.B., 1987,
    Selective disruption of gap junctional communication
    interferes with a patterning process in Hydra, Science,
    327:49.
Fraser, S.E., Green, C.R., Bode, H.R., Bode, P.M., and Gilula,
    N.B., 1988, A perturbation analysis of the role of gap
    junctional communication in developmental patterning,
    in, "Modern Cell Biology, Gap Junctions," International

Conference, Pacific Grove, California, USA, July, 6-10,
E.L. Herzberg and R.G. Johnson, ed., Alan R. Liss, Inc.,
New York, 512.

Freeman, G., 1980, The role of cleavage in the establishment of
the anterior-posterior axis of the hydrozoan embryo, in,
"Developmental and Cellular Biology of Coelenterates,"
P. Tardent and R. Tardent, ed., Elsevier/North-Holland
Biomedical Press, Amsterdam, New York, Oxford, 97.

Freeman, G., 1981a, The cleavage initiation site establishes
the posterior pole of the hydrozoan embryo, Wilhelm
Roux's Archives, 190:123.

Freeman, G., 1981b, The role of polarity in the development of
the hydrozoan planula larva, Wilhelm Roux's Archives,
190:168.

Freeman, G., 1983, Experimental studies on embryogenesis in
hydrozoans (Trachylina and Siphonophora) with direct
development, Biol.Bull., 165:591.

Freeman, G., 1987, The role of oocyte maturation in the
ontogeny of the fertilization site in the hydrozoan
Hydractinia echinata, Roux's Arch.Dev.Biol., 196:83.

Freeman, G., and Miller, R.L., 1982, Hydrozoan eggs can only be
fertilized at the site of polar body formation, Dev.
Biol., 94:142.

Frey, J., 1968, Entwicklungsleistungen der Medusenknospen und
Medusen von Podocoryne carnea M. Sars nach Isolation und
Dissoziation, Wilhelm Roux's Archives, 160:428.

Fulton, C., 1961, The development of Cordylophora, in, "The
Biology of Hydra and some other Coelenterates," H.M.
Lenhoff and W.F. Loomis, ed., Univ. of Miami, Coral
Gables, 287.

Fulton, C., 1963, The development of a hydroid colony, Dev.
Biol., 6:333.

Gierer, A., Berking, S., Bode, H., David, C.N., Flick, K.,
Hansmannn, G., Schaller, H.C., and Trenkner, E., 1972,
Regeneration of Hydra from reaggregated cells, Nature,
New Biology, 239:98.

Grimmelikhuijzen, C.J.P., 1985, Antisera to the sequence Arg-
Phe-amide visualise neuronal centralisations in hydroid
polyps, Cell Tissue Res., 241:171.

Grimmelikhuijzen, C.J.P., and Graff, D., 1985, Arg-Phe-amide-
like peptides in the primitive nervous systems of
coelenterates, Peptides, 6, Suppl 3:477.

Hale, L.J., 1960, Contractility and hydroplasmic movements in
the hydroid Clytia johnstoni, Quart.J.Microscop.Sci.,
101:339.

Hale, L.J., 1964, Cell movements, cell division and growth in
the hydroid Clytia johnstoni, J.Embryol.exp.Morph.,
12:517.

Hale, L.J., 1973a, The pattern of growth of Clytia johnstoni,
J.Embryol.exp.Morph., 29:283.

Hale, L.J., 1973b, Morphogenetic properties of the parts of the
colony of Clytia johnstoni, J.Embryol.exp.Morph.,30:773.

Hale, L.J., 1974, The morphogenetic properties of the node in
Clytia johnstoni, J.Embryol.exp.Morph., 31:527.

Hammet, F.S., 1946, Correlations between the hydranth
components of Obelia colony populations, Growth, 10:331.

Hauenschild, C., 1954, Genetische und entwicklungsphysiolo-
gische Untersuchungen über Intersexualität und
Gewebeverträglichkeit bei Hydractinia echinata Flem.
Hydroz. Bougainvill., Wilhelm Roux's Archiv für
Entwicklungsmechanik, 147:1.

Hyman, L., 1928, Miscellaneous observations on Hydra, with special reference to reproduction, *Biol.Bull.*, 54:65.

Koizumi, O., and Bode, H.R., 1986, Plasticity in the nervous system of adult hydra. I. The position-dependent expression of FMRFamide-like immunoreactivity, *Dev.Biol.*, 116:407.

Koizumi, O. ,Heimfeld, S., and Bode, H.R., 1988, Plasticity in the nervous system of adult hydra. II. Conversion of ganglion cells in the body column to sensory cells in the hypostome, *Dev.Biol.*, 129:358.

Kroiher, M., 1989, Zelluläre Grundlagen der Muster- und Gestaltbildung im Zuge der Embryogenese und Metamorphose von *Hydractinia echinata* - Wirkung eines endogenen Faktors, Doctoral dissertation, University of Heidelberg, Heidelberg, FRG.

Kühn, A., 1910, Sprosswachstum und Polypenknospung bei den Thecaphoren, *Zool.Jahrb.Anat.Ontogen.*, 28:387.

Kühn, A., 1914, Entwicklungsgeschichte und Verwandtschafts- beziehungen der Hydrozoen. 1. Teil. Die Hydroiden, *Ergebn.Fortschr.Zool.*, 4:1.

Kühn, A., 1965, "Vorlesungen über Entwicklungsbiologie," Springer, Berlin Göttingen Heidelberg, 2. Auflage.

Leitz, T., and Müller, W.A., 1987, Evidence for the involvement of PI-signaling and diacylglycerol second messengers in the initiation of metamorphosis in the hydroid *Hydractinia echinata* Fleming, *Dev.Biol.*, 121:82.

Lennhoff, H.M., and Loomis, W.F., 1957, The control of clonal growth of hydra by self-inhibition of tentacle differentiation, *Anat.Rec.*, 127:429.

Lenicque, R. M., and Lundblad, M., 1966a, Promoters and inhibitors of development during regeneration of the hypostome and tentacles of *Clava squamata*, *Acta Zool.*, 47:185.

Lenicque, R.M., and Lundblad, M., 1966b, Promoters and inhibitors of development during regeneration of the hypostome and tentacles of *Hydra littoralis*, *Acta Zool.*, 47:277.

Lentz, T.L., 1965, Hydra, induction of supernumerary heads by isolated neurosecretory granules, *Science*, New York,150:633.

Lesh-Laurie, G.E., 1973, Expression and maintenance of organismic polarity, *in*, "Biology of Hydra," A. Burnett, ed., Academic Press, New York,144.

Lesh-Laurie, G.E., 1982, Hydra *in*, "Developmental Biology of Freshwater Invertebrates," F.W. Harrison and R.R. Cowden, ed., Alan R. Liss Inc., New York, 69.

Lesh-Laurie, G.E., and Burnett, A.L., 1964, Some biological and biochemical properties of the polarizing factor in hydra, *Nature*, 204:492.

Lesh-Laurie, G.E., and Burnett, A.L., 1966, An analysis of the chemical of polarized form in hydra, *J.Exp.Zool.*,163:55.

Mackie, G.O., 1966, Growth of the hydroid Tubularia in culture, *in*, "The Cnidaria and their evolution," W.J. Rees, ed., Academic Press, New York, London, 397.

MacWilliams, H.K., 1983a, Hydra transplantation phenomena and the mechanism of Hydra head regeneration. I. Properties of the head inhibition, *Dev.Biol.*, 96:217.

MacWilliams, H.K., 1983b, Hydra transplantation phenomena and the mechanism of hydra head regeneration. II. Properties of the head activation, *Dev.Biol.*, 96:239.

McFadden, C.S., Mc Farland, M.J., and Buss, L.W., 1984, Biology of Hydractiniid hydroids. I. Colony ontogeny in *Hydractinia echinata, Biol.Bull.*, 166:54.

Martin, V.J. 1989, Development of nerve cells in hydrozoan planulae: II. Examination of sensory cell differentiation using electron microscopy and immunocytochemistry, *Biol. Bull.*, Woods Hole, 175:65.

Martin, V.J., and Thomas, M.B., 1977, A fine-structural study of embryonic and larval development in the gymnoblastic hydroid *Pennaria tiarella Biol.Bull.*, 153:198.

Martin, V.J., and Thomas, M.B., 1981, The origin of the nervous system in *Pennaria tiarella*, as revealed by treatment with colchicine, *Biol.Bull.*, 160:303.

Martin, V.J., Chia, F., and Koss, R., 1983, A fine-structural study of metamorphosis of the hydrozoan *Mitrocomella polydiademata, J.Morphol.*, 176:261.

Meinhardt, H., 1982, "Models of Biological Pattern Formation," Academic Press, New York, Oxford.

Mergner, H., 1957, Die Ei- und Embryonalentwicklung von *Eudendrium racemosum* Cavolini, *Zool.Jahrb.Abt.Anat. Ontog.Tiere*, 76:63.

Merger, H., 1971, Cnidaria, *in*, "Experimental embryology of marine and fresh-water invertebrates," G. Reverberi, ed., North-Holland Publ. Co, Amsterdam, London, 1.

Morgan, T.H., 1901, Regeneration in Tubularia, *Roux´s Arch. Entw.Mechn.Org.*, 11:346.

Morgan, T.H., 1905, Polarity considered as a phenomenon of gradation of materials, *J.Exp.Zool.*, 2:495.

Morgan, T.H., 1906, Hydranth formation and polarity in Tubularia, *J.Exp.Zool.*, 3:501.

Morse, D.E., 1985, Neurotransmitter-mimetic inducers of larval settlement and metamorphosis, *Bull.mar.Sci.*, 37:697.

Müller, W.A., 1964, Experimentelle Untersuchungen über Stockentwicklung, Polypendifferenzierung und Sexualchimären bei *Hydractinia echinata, Wilhelm Roux's Archiv*, 155:181.

Müller, W.A., 1969, Auslösung der Metamorphose durch Bakterien bei den Larven von *Hydractinia echinata, Zool.Jahrb. Anat.Ontog.*, 86:84.

Müller, W.A., 1973a, Induction of metamorphosis by bacteria and ions in the planulae of *Hydractinia echinata*; an approach to the mode of action *in*: Publ.Seto.Mar.Biol. Lab. 20 Proc. Second Int. Symp. Cnidaria, 195.

Müller, W.A., 1973b, Metamorphose-Induktion bei Planulalarven. I. Der bakterielle Induktor, *Wilhelm Roux's Archives*, 173:107.

Müller, W.A., 1979, Release and control of metamorphosis of lower invertebrates, *in*, "Ontogenese und Phylogenese," R. Siewing, ed., Erlanger Symp. 1977, Parey, Hamburg, Berlin, Fortschritte in der Zoolog Systematik und Evolutionsforschung, 160:165.

Müller, W.A., 1984, Retinoids and pattern formation in a hydroid, *J.Embryol.exp.Morph.*, 81:253.

Müller, W.A., 1985, Tumor-promoting phorbol esters induce metamorphosis and multiple head formation in the hydroid Hydractinia, *Differentiation*, 29:216.

Müller, W.A., and Buchal, G., 1973, Metamorphose-Induktion bei Planulalarven. II. Induktion durch monovalente Kationen, *Wilhelm Roux's Archives*, 173:122.

Müller, W.A., and El-Shershaby, E., 1981, Electrical current and cAMP induce lateral branching in the stolon of hydroids, *Dev.Biol.*, 87:24.

Müller, W.A., and Meier-Menge, H.M., 1980, Polarity reversal in Hydractinia by head activators and neurotransmitters, and comparative studies in Hydra *in:* "Developmental and Cellular Biology of Coelenterates," P. Tardent and R. Tardent, ed., Elsevier/North Holland Biomedical Press, Amsterdam, New York, Oxford, 383.

Müller, W.A., and Plickert, G., 1982, Quantitative analysis of an inhibitory gradient field in the hydrozoan stolo, *Wilhelm Roux's Archives*, 191:56.

Müller, W.A., Hauch, A., and Plickert, G., 1987, Morphogenetic Factors in Hydroids. I. Stolon tip activation and inhibition, *J.exp.Zool.*, 243:111.

Müller, W.A., Wieker,F., and Eiben, R., 1976, Larval adhesion, releasing stimuli and metamorphosis *in:* "Coelenterate Ecology and Behavior," G.O. Mackies, ed., Plenum Press, New York, London, 339.

Müller, W.A., Mitze, A., Wickhorst, J.P., and Meier-Menge, H.M., 1977, Polar morphogenesis in early hydroid development. Action of cesium, of neurotransmitters and of an intrinsic head activator on pattern formation, *Wilhelm Roux's Archives*,182:311.

Overton, J., 1963, Intercellular connections in the outgrowing stolon of Cordylophora, *J.Cell.Biol.*, 17:661.

Petriconi, V., and Plickert, G., 1974, Zum Einfluß der Strömung auf die Entwicklung von Hydrorhizastöcken, *Verh.Dtsch. Zool.Ges.*, 1974, 107:111.

Plickert, G., 1978, Ursachen des strömungsabhängigen Stock-wachstums von *Eirene viridula* (Thecata, Campanulinidae) - Untersuchungen zur Differenzierung des terminalen Stolons, Doctoral dissertation, University of Bochum, Bochum, FRG.

Plickert, G., 1980, Mechanically induced stolon branching in *Eirene viridula* (Thecata, Campanulinidae), *in:* "Developmental and Cellular Biology of Coelenterates," P. Tardent and R. Tardent, ed., Elsevier/North-Holland Biomedical Press, Amsterdam, New York, Oxford.

Plickert, G., 1987, Low-molecular-weight factors from colonial hydroids affect pattern formation, *Wilhelm Roux's Arch.Dev.Biol.*, 196:248.

Plickert, G., 1989, Proportion-altering factor (PAF) stimulates nerve cell formation in *Hydractinia echinata*, *Cell.Diff.Dev.*, 26:19.

Plickert, G., 1990, A low-molecular weight factor from colonial hydroids affects body proportioning and cell differentiation *in:* "Proc. 5th Int. Congress on Coelenterate Biology," Supplement, Hydrobiol. Dev. Hydrobiol.," in press.

Plickert, G., Heringer, A., and Hiller, B., 1987, Analysis of spacing in a periodic pattern, *Dev.Biol.*, 120:399.

Plickert, G., Kroiher, M., and Munck, A., 1988, Cell proliferation and early differentiation during embryonic development and metamorphosis of *Hydractinia echinata*, *Development*,103:795.

Powers, J.A.,1961, Effects of distal and proximal hydranth extracts and stem extracts from adult Tubularia on the regeneration of proximal ridge regions, *Biol.Bull., Woods Hole*, 121.

Rappaport, R., 1969, Division of isolated furrows and furrow fragments ininvertebrate eggs, *Exp.Cell.Res.*, 56:87.

Riedl, R., 1983, "Fauna und Flora des Mittelmeeres," 3. Auflage, Paul Parey, Hamburg, Berlin.

Rose, S.M., 1963, Polarized control of regional structure in Tubularia, *Dev.Biol.*, 7:488.

Rose, S.M., 1966, Polarized inhibitory control of regional differentiation during regeneration in Tubularia, II. Separation of active materials by electrophoresis, *Growth*, 30:429.

Rose, S.M., 1967, Polarized inhibitory control of regional differentiation during regeneration in Tubularia, III. The effect of grafts across sea water-agar bridges in electric fields, *Growth*, 31:149.

Rose, S.M., 1970a, Differentiation during regeneration caused by migration of repressors in bioelectric fields, *Am.Zool.*,10:91.

Rose, S.M., 1970b, Restoration of regenerative ability in ligated stems of Tubularia in an electrical field, *Biol. Bull.*, 138:344.

Rose, S.M., and Powers, J.A., 1966, Polarized inhibitory control of regional differentiation during regeneration in Tubularia, I. The effect of extracts from distal and proximal regions, *Growth*, 30:419.

Rose, S.M., and Rose, F.C., 1941, The role of a cut surface in Tubularia regeneration, *Physiol.Zool.*, 14:328.

Schaller, H.C., 1973, Isolation and characterisation of a low-molecular-weight substance activating head and bud formation in Hydra, *J.Embryol.Exp.Morphol.*, 29:27.

Schaller, H.C., and Bodenmüller H., 1981, Isolation and aminoacid sequence of a morphogenetic peptide from Hydra, *Proc.Natl.Acad.Sci.USA*, 78:7000.

Schaller, H.C., Schmidt T., and Grimmelikhuijzen, C.J.P., 1979, Separation and specificity of action of four morphogens from Hydra, *Wilhelm Roux's Archives*, 186:139.

Schaller, H.C., Grimmelikhuijzen, C.J.P., and Schmidt, T., 1983, Isolation of substances controlling morphogenesis in hydra *in:* "Hydra Research Methods," H. M. Lenhoff, ed., Plenum Press, New York, London.

Schaller, H.C., Hoffmeister, S.A.H., and Dübel, S.,1989, Role of the neuropeptide head activator for growth and development in hydra and mammals, *Development, Supplement*, 99.

Schijfsma, K., 1935, Observations on *Hydractinia echinata* (Fleming) and *Eupagurus bernhardus* (L.), *Arch Neederland.Zool.*, 1:261.

Schmidt, T., Schaller, H.C., 1976, Evidence for a foot-inhibiting substance in hydra, *Cell Differentiation*, 5:151.

Schwoerer-Böhning, B., Kroiher, M., and Müller,W.A., 1990, Signal transmission and covert prepattern in the metamorphosis of *Hydractinia echinata* (Hydrozoa), *Roux's Arch.Dev.Biol.*, in press,

Schmid, V., Alder, H., Plickert, G., and Weber, C., 1988,Transdifferentiation from striated muscle of medusae in vitro *in:*, "Regulatory mechanisms in developmental processes," G. Eguchi, T.S. Okada, and L. Saxen, Elsevier Scientific Publishers, Ireland, Ltd, 137.

Shostak, S., 1974, Bipolar inhibitory gradients´ influence on the budding region of Hydra viridis, *Am.Zool.*, 14:619.

Spencer, A.N., 1982, The physiology of a coelenterate neuromuscular synapse, *J.Comp.Physiol.*, 148:353.

Spindler, K.D., and Müller, W.A., 1972, Induction of metamorphosis by bacteria and by a lithium-pulse in the

larvae of *Hydractinia echinata Wilhelm Roux's Arch*,
169:271.

Suddith, R.L., 1974, Cell proliferation in the terminal regions
of the internodes and stolons of the colonial hydroid
Campanularia flexuosa, Am.Zool.,14:45.

Sugiyama, T., and Fujisawa, T., 1979, Genetic analysis of
developmental mechanisms in hydra, VII. Statistical
analysis of developmental, morphological characters and
cellular compositions, *Dev.Growth Diff.*, 21:361.

Svoboda, A., 1976, The orientation of Aglaophenia fans to
current in laboratory conditions (Hydrozoa,
Coelenterata) *in:* "Coelenterate Ecology and Behavior,"
G.O. Mackie, ed., Plenum Press, New York, London, 41.

Takano, J., and Sugiyama, T., 1983, Genetic analysis of
developmental mechanisms in hydra, VIII. Head-activation
and head-inhibition potentials of a slow-budding strain
(L4), *J.Embryol.exp.Morph.*, 78:141.

Takano, J., and Sugiyama, T., 1984, Genetic analysis of
developmental mechanisms in Hydra, IX. Effect of food on
development of a slow-budding strain (L4), *Dev.Biol.*,
103:96.

Takano, J., and Sugiyama, T., 1985, Genetic analysis of
developmental mechanisms in hydra, XVI. Effect of food
on budding and developmental gradients in a mutant
strain L4, *J.Embryol.exp.Morph.*, 90:123.

Tardent, P., 1955, Zum Nachweis eines regenerationshemmenden
Stoffes im Hydranth von Tubularia, *Rev.Suisse Zool.*,
62:289.

Tardent, P., 1978, Coelenterata, Cnidaria, *in:* "Morphogenese
der Tiere," F.Seidel, ed., VEB Gustav Fischer, Jena.

Tardent, P., 1988, "Hydra," Naturforschende Gesellschaft,
Zürich, Orell Füssli, Zürich, Switzerland.

Tardent, P., and Eymann, H., 1958, Some chemical and physical
properties of the regeneration inhibitor of Tubularia,
Acta Embryol.Morph.Exp., 1:280.

Teissier, G., 1931, étude expérimentale du dévéloppement de
quelques hydraires, *Ann.Sci.Nat.Ser.Bot.Zool.*, 14:5.

Thomas, M.B., Freeman, G., and Martin, V.J., 1987, The
embryonic origin of neurosensory cells and the role of
nerve cells in metamorphosis in *Phialidium gregarium*
(Cnidaria, Hydrozoa), *Int.J.Invert.Reprod.Dev.*, 11:265.

Trembley, A., 1744, Mémoires pour servir à l'histoire d'un
genre de polypes d'eau douce, a bras en forme de cornes,
Jean and Herman, Verbeek, Leiden.

Tweedel, K.S., 1958a, Inhibitors of regeneration in Tubularia,
Biol.Bull., 114:255.

Tweedel, K.S., 1958b, A bacteria-free inhibitor of regeneration
in Tubularia, *Biol.Bull.*, 115:369.

Webster, G., 1971, Morphogenesis and pattern formation in
hydroids, *Biol.Rev.*, 46:1.

Webster, G., and Hamilton, S., 1966, Budding in Hydra. the role
of cell multiplication and cell movements in bud
initiation, *J.Embryol.Exp.Morphol.*, 16:91.

Weis, V.M., Keene, D.R., and Buss, L.W., 1985, Biology of
Hydractiniid hydroids, 4. Ultrastructure of the planula
of *Hydractinia echinata, Biol.Bull.*, 168:403.

Wittmann, W., 1977, Auslösung der Metamorphose bei Hydractinia
durch Bakterien: Isolierung und Charakterisierung der
Bakterien und der auslösenden Substanz, Doctoral
dissertation, Tech. University Braunschweig,
Braunschweig, FRG.

Wolpert, L., Clarke, M.R., and Hornbruch, A., 1972, Positional
        signalling along Hydra, *Nature*, 239:101.
Wolpert, L., Hicklin, J., and Hornbruch, A., 1971, Positional
        information and pattern regulation in regeneration in
        Hydra, *Symp.Soc.Exp.Biol.*, 25:391.
Wolpert, L., Hornbruch, A., and Clarke, M.R., 1974, Positional
        information and positional signalling in Hydra,
        Am.Zool., 14:647.
Wyttenbach, C.R., 1968, The dynamics of stolon elongation in
        the hydroid *Campanularia flexuosa*, *J.Exp.Zool.*, 167:333.
Wyttenbach, C.R., 1969, Genetic variations in the mode of
        stolon growth in the hydroid *Campanularia flexuosa*,
        Biol.Bull., 137:547.
Wyttenbach, C.R., 1973, The role of hydroplasmic pressure in
        stolonic growth movements in the hydroid Bougainvillia,
        J.exp.Zool., 186:79.
Wyttenbach, C.R., 1974, Cell movements associated with terminal
        growth in colonial hydroids, *Am.Zool.*, 14:699.
Wyttenbach, C.R., Crowell,S., and Suddith, R.L., 1965, The
        cyclic elongation of stolons and uprights in the hydroid
        Campanularia, *Biol.Bull.*, 129:429.
Wyttenbach, C.R., Crowell, S., and Suddith, R.L., 1973,
        Variations in the mode of stolon growth among different
        genera of colonial hydroids, and their evolutionary
        implications, *J.Morph.*, 139:363.
Zürrer, D., 1988, Untersuchungen zur Befruchtung bei
        Hydractinia echinata Flem. (Hydrozoa, Cnidaria),
        Doctoral dissertation, University of Zürich, Zürich,
        Switzerland.

REPRODUCTION AND DEVELOPMENT IN CTENOPHORES

Christian Sardet, Danièle Carré, Christian Rouvière

URA 671 C.N.R.S.
Biologie Cellulaire Marine
Université Pierre et Marie Curie
Station Zoologique
Villefranche-sur-mer, F-06230

THE BODY PLAN OF CTENOPHORES

Most ctenophores (also called comb jellies) are gelatinous zooplancton exclusively marine that are characterized by 8 meridional ciliated comb rows (ctenes) disposed around a unique oral-aboral axis.

This axis is established during the early cleavage period. The ctenophore embryo hatches as a cydippid larvae with the same general features as the adult. The animals are biradially symmetrical. One plane of symmetry is defined by the tentacles (tentacular plane) or their rudiments, the other perpendicular to the first, by the stomodeum (sagittal or stomodeal or pharyngeal plane (Fig.1 b)(see ref.1,2,3,4,5).

A schematic representation of the ctenophores body plan is represented in Figure 1. The animal is made of two layered body wall sandwiching a thick mesoglea that has amoebocytes and smooth muscle fibers. Nerves and photocytes are present under the comb rows. In the drawing the positions of the comb plates, the pharynx (or stomodeum), tentacles and gonads are represented.

Early in the larval stages, two structures are easily identified (see Fig.2): the 8 rows of comb plates and the apical organ including a statolith used as a gravity sensing organ (Fig.1c).

SPECIATION, ECOLOGY AND REPRODUCTION OF CTENOPHORES

Ctenophores, a small phylum with only about 100 species are usually divided into 2 main classes: those having tentacles (class tentaculata: 6 orders) and those lacking tentacles (class nuda: 1 order: Beroïda)(2,4,5,).

The genus most studied in the laboratory are found in

Experimental Embryology in Aquatic Plants and Animals
Edited by H.-J. Marthy, Plenum Press, New York, 1990

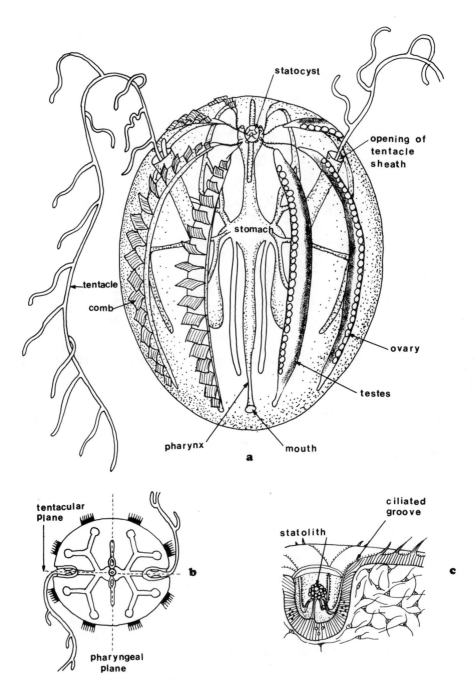

FIG.1. Body plan of a ctenophore (*Pleurobrachia*)
redrawn from Pearse and Buchsbaum and Dunlap Pianka.
a) The animal is tilted toward the viewer to show the
sensory pole. On the left comb plates but not gonads
are shown. On the right gonads but not comb plates
are shown. b) Section perpendicular to the oral-
aboral axis. c) Detail of the apical organ.

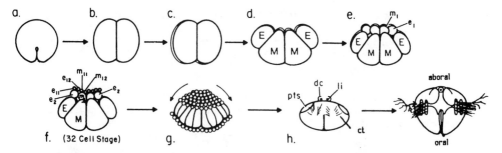

FIG.2. Normal development in ctenophores (redrawn from Martindale). a) The initiation of first unipolar cleavage. b,c,) The plane of first cleavage coïncides with the pharyngeal (or sagittal) plane, the second plane of cleavage to the tentacular plane. d) At the eight cell stage the embryo consists of four M (Middle) and four E (End) macromeres. e,f) The macromeres give rise to a set of micromeres at the aboral pole (m1, e1 at the 16 cell stage and m2 and e2 at the 32 cell stage). g) The micromeres divide several times, then macromeres divide budding off a second generation of micromere at the oral pole. Gastrulation by epiboly follows. h) Beating ctenes (ct) can be seen 10 hrs after first cleavage. They beat in a coordinated fashion 3-4 hrs later. The mesoglea starts to swell, the presumptive tentacle sheets (pts) invaginate, the entodermal canal system develops and the formation of the apical organ becomes completed. i) The apical organ is completed; the lithocytes (li) of each quadrant are suspended under the dome cilia (dc).

inshore waters and catch prey with their tentacles studded with sticky colloblast cells (*Pleurobrachia*, *Bolinopsis*, *Mnemiopsis*...) or engulf their prey. They are carnivorous, eating other ctenophores or soft bodied plancton. In particular the Beroidae are equipped with an extraordinarily extensible mouth lined with giant macrocilia (6).

Except for a few sessile species (Platyctida), most ctenophores follow currents and move within, mouth forward with the help of their rows of comb plates made of connected cilia that beat synchronously. Some deep sea ctenophores (as Ocyropsis) also move through contractions of well developed oral muscular lobes.

Their ecology is poorly understood mostly because they are difficult to sample and it is hard to make exact predictions about their occurrence and abundance throughout the year (7). In the bay of Villefranche-sur-mer several genus can generally be found from February through June (*Pleurobrachia*, *Cestus*, *Bolinopsis*, *Beroe*, *Leucothea*).

Most ctenophores are hermaphrodites, however recently two oceanic species (*Ocyropsis crystallina* and *maculata*) have been described as dioecious (8).

It is also interesting to note that most ctenophores have an early reproductive period (paedogenesis): 8-15 day old larvae are able to make viable gonads (9). These larval gonads regress, thereafter until the reproductive adult stage. This dual larval-adult period of reproduction is called dissogony. In addition ctenophores have remarkable abilities to regenerate missing parts (10).

Further information on the speciation, ecology, nutrition and reproduction of ctenophores can be found in several reviews worth consulting (2,4,5,7).

REFERENCES TO CTENOPHORE DEVELOPMENT

At the turn of the century, the study of the development of the remarkably transparent eggs of ctenophores attracted some of the most prestigious biologists: Kowalewsky (11), Agassiz (12), Metschnikoff (13), Chun (14), and Ziegler (15) provided accurate descriptions of normal development (Fig.2).

Experimental manipulations of the embryos by Yatsu (16, 17), Driesch and Morgan (18) and Fischel (19) were important in establishing the concept of mosaic development (i.e. that developmental potential is restricted to parts of the egg or cleavage embryo (see Davidson (20)).

In the last 30 years the establishment of cell lineages and the role of cell divisions in the localization of the developmental potential were critically examined essentially by Reverberi and Freeman and their colleagues on *Beroe*, *Bolinopsis*, *Pleurobrachia* and *Mnemiopsis* (21,22,23,24,25). The work up to the 1970's has been well reviewed by Reverberi (1). Freeman has also reexamined his work and others in an interesting review (27). The key experiments and their major conclusions are schematized in Fig.3. We will examine briefly oogenesis, spawning and fertilization in ctenophores and the role played by the site of sperm entry in axis formation.

OOGENESIS, SPERMATOGENESIS

The gametes are probably from endodermal origin and occur along the eight meridional canals beneath the comb rows (see Fig.1). Except in dioecious species, in each canal, ovaries face the tentacular or sagittal planes while testis face the interadial planes.

The eggs develop rapidly (1 or 2 days in *Pleurobrachia* and *Beroe*) from clusters of germ cells that form a syncytium. Three groups of nurse cells, surrounding the small oocyte, sequentially transfer to it their central cytoplasm (endo-plasm), their subcortical constituents and cortical cytoplasm (ectoplasm) through cytoplasmic bridges (2).

Spermatogenesis has been examined in *Beroe* by Franc (28). The spherical head of the mature sperm possesses particular features of yet unknown function (sub-membranous densities, centriolar vesicle, accessory nuclear body).

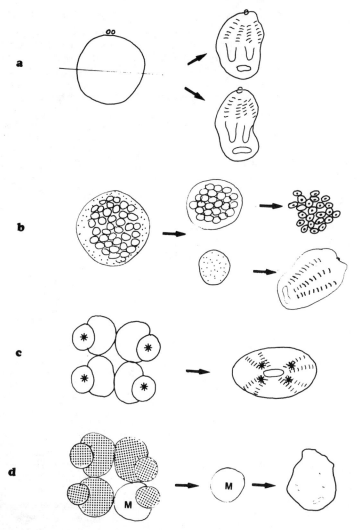

FIG.3. Three types of important experiments (redrawn from Reverberi, Yatsu). a) Fragments of eggs before fertilization yield small but quite normal larvae. b) Centrifugation experiments show that the cortical peripheral layer only develop into a ciliated larvae. c) External micromeres labelled with small chalk particles (crosses) will give comb plates. d) An isolate M blastomere yields a larva without ciliated plates.

SPAWNING

Spawning in the laboratory is generally induced after a dark period (24-72 hours for *Beroe*) by exposure to bright light. In some species gametes are shed after being placed in the dark (2).

On an average, in captivity, adult animals lay 50-2000 eggs depending on the species and produce gametes every 1-2 days for 1-2 weeks when properly fed and when water is often changed. First sperm, then eggs, are emitted in bursts through gonopores in the epidermis above the gonads. In many species, eggs are held loosely in a string of gelatinous material that is apparently secreted by gland cells in the oviduct. The strings of eggs are easily broken by gentle pipetting.

The eggs are exceptionally transparent and generally autofluorescent (blue, green). Their sizes vary from 100-200µm (*Pleurobrachia*, *Bolinopsis*, *Mnemiopsis*) up to 1000µm (*Beroe ovata*). They can be easily micromanipulated and develop rapidly into larvae with clearly identifiable structures (comb plates, apical organ) or properties (light emission by photocytes).

FERTILIZATION AND POLYSPERMY

Self-fertilization seems to occur in many hermaphrodite ctenophores kept in isolation in finger bowls. However, there is very little information on the timing, localization of the fertilizing sperm or the extent of polyspermy which is known to occur in several species.

In recent years we have examined spawning, fertilization and polyspermy in *Beroe ovata* (29). The egg is undergoing the first meiotic division as it is released in a cloud of the animal's own sperm, or in a mixture of sperm, if several animals are kept together. The first polar body remains on the surface while the second polar body formation takes place (~'1hr'). A vitelline membrane and a jelly coat elevate and harden upon exposure to sea water. They change into a more refractile and resistant layer upon fertilization. In Beroe, these envelops are clearly involved in the control of self-fertilization. Eggs of freshly collected animals kept in isolation will not be fertilized by the sperm shed by the same animal. However, manual removal of the egg envelops with micro-needles will allow one to several of the animal's own sperm to enter the egg even after meiosis has been completed. This block to self-fertilization is not absolute. It will be overcome with time, some eggs still getting fertilized after several hours.

The block to self-fertilization does not seem to exist in a minority of animals and decreases as animals are kept in captivity. We suspect that in the situations when self-fertilization occurs lesions are created easily by repeated pipetting thus weakening envelops or that the vitelline membrane is progressively changed due to the animal's confinement.

In practice, these recent observations allow for the first time to study fertilization in a ctenophore. Due to the size (1 mm), clarity of the egg, use of simple labelling techniques of nuclei, mitochondria, microfilaments and microtubules, we could make the following self-fertilization observations (Fig.4 and Sardet, Carré in preparation):
-from 1 to 20-30 spermatozoa can enter the egg during or even after meiosis and normal larvae can be obtained with a high degree of polyspermy.
-spermatozoa can enter anywhere on the egg surface and over several minutes, indicating that there is no fast block to polyspermy.
-the single or several sperm that enter remain within 10-

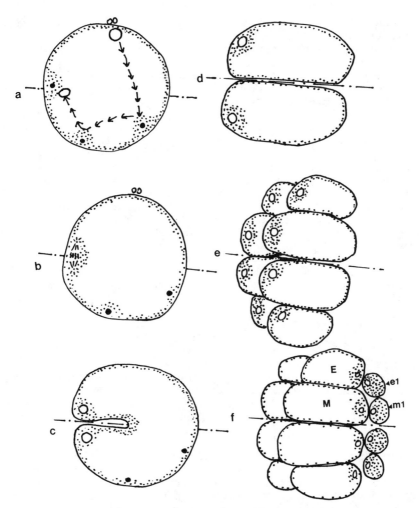

FIG.4. Fertilization and ooplasmic segregation in *Beroe ovata*. a) In case of non self polyspermy, the female pronucleus migrates successively to 3 sperm surrounded by a zone of cortical differentiation (accumulation of mitochondria and other organelles). b,c,d,e) The unipolar cleavages lead to the formation of 2,4,8 cells with a thickened cortical zone around the nuclei. f) Micromere formation with an accumulation of cortex material in the micromeres (e1, m1).

20μm of their entry site and stay in the egg cortex causing a localized contraction-relaxation of the egg surface that lasts 2-3 minutes.

-a patch of microvilli and a finely granular thickened layer constituted of mitochondria and autofluorescent vesicles are formed around each male nucleus during the completion of meiosis and the early migration of the female pronucleus.

-localized exocytosis contributes to the constitution of a fertilization network that is the most visible hallmark of fertilization as well as the cortical plaques of mitochondria that form around each sperm pronucleus.

The second phase of fertilization (the movement and fusion

of pronuclei) is particularly remarkable in *Beroe ovata* for several reasons:
    -sperm and egg pronuclei as well as the major part of the egg cytoplasm remain cortical at all stages.
    -the male pronucleus or pronuclei remain in fixed position in the cortex.
    -the female pronucleus migrates just beneath the plasma membrane over long distances in straight line at a speed of 0,5 µm/sec and, if going to the antipode of the meiotic pole, where it originates, it can be observed migrating for an hour.

    We have found that 2 situations can occur:
    -the female pronucleus can enter the differentiated cortical zone and fuse with the sperm nucleus.
    -alternatively the female pronucleus can reorient at the edge of the differentiated cortical zone and migrate in a straight line toward another sperm or even several other sperms.

    We have indirect evidence that this behavior of the female pronucleus is associated with the choice between the animal's own sperm or sperm from other individuals.

    Immunofluorescent localization of microfilaments, microtubules and perfusion of drugs that perturb the cytoskeleton all indicate that microtubules are involved in the directed movements of the female pronucleus. Asters are formed near each sperm pronucleus and grow to giant sizes. Surprisingly, the female pronucleus has extensive connections with the network of endoplasmic reticulum lamellae that are the main constituent of the cortical cytoplasm with microtubules (Sardet and Carré in preparation).

    The fusion of pronuclei and mitosis can be observed in great detail as they take place just beneath the plasma membrane. During mitosis the cortical differentiated zone disappears around supernumary sperm nuclei. It persists around the forming karyomeres and daughter nuclei that are quickly separated by an unipolar cleavage furrow that progresses to the antipode of the original successfull sperm entry site carrying the organelles that cause the ectoplasmic thickening with it.

FERTILIZATION AND AXIS FORMATION IN CTENOPHORES

    In the 1971's, Reverberi assumed the oral-aboral axis of the ctenophore larvae and adult was related to the animal vegetal axis of the egg. Marking experiments, blastomere deletions and isolations showed that the first and second cleavage planes corresponded to the sagittal and tentacular planes respectively. Furthermore, Freeman (26) experimenting on *Bolinopsis* and *Pleurobrachia* saw that in a significant proportion of the embryos, the position of the polar bodies (animal or meiotic pole) and the site of first cleavage did not coïncide. He deduced from centrifugation experiments and serial histological sections that in fact the location of the first mitotic apparatus and the oral pole of the larva was not related to the animal pole of the egg (3,26).

    We re-examined the relative position of the animal pole and site of cleavage in *Beroe*. In many cases, they did not

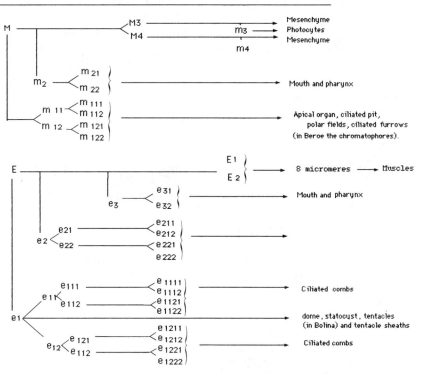

Stage of development (number of cells)

8 16 32 48 56 60 80 92 96 128   Territories

FIG.5. Cell lineage of the egg of the Ctenophores
from Reverberi and Ortolani, Freeman and Reynolds.

correspond (29). This suggested that Reverberi's original
observations were probably due to the fact that, in his
experiments, the large *Beroe* eggs were most likely exposed to
abundant sperm at the animal pole and fertilized there, when
extruded from the gonopore (1).

We further showed that, because sperm nuclei do not move
appreciably in the cortex of *Beroe*, the location of pronuclear
fusion and of the mitotic apparatus is in fact the site of
sperm entry. We hypothesize that in *Beroe* and perhaps in all
ctenophores:
　　-the unique oral aboral axis is determined by the site of
sperm entry.
　　-the axis can be set anywhere on the egg surface as sperm
enters randomly in laboratory condition.

Since Yatsu demonstrated in 1911 (16) that one could
obtain normal miniature larvae by fertilizing egg fragments
(see Fig.3a), it therefore appears that the ctenophore embryo
is ideally suited to study how a developmental axis is set up
by the fertilizing sperm in an egg where developmental
potential is apparently not prelocalized during oogenesis.

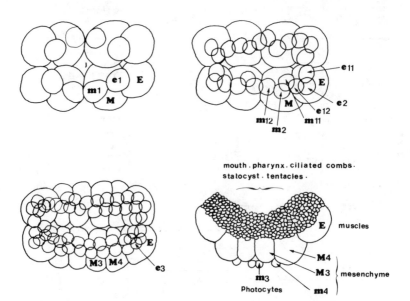

FIG.6. Position of the blastomeres in Ctenophore embryos (see Fig.5 for their lineages)(redrawn from Freeman).

CLEAVAGES AND OOPLASMIC SEGREGATION

The marking experiments of Ortolani, Reverberi and Farfaglio led to the establishment of the major cell lineages (21,23). These were largely confirmed and carried further by Freeman and Reynolds in their elegant studies of the origin of comb plates and photocytes (3,24,25). We have summarized their findings (Fig.5,6).

We have examined early cleavages in *Beroe ovata* and the segregation of the naturally fluorescent cortical cytoplasm (concentrated in small vesicles) or of the mitochondria (revealed by the vital dye Rhodamine 123). We can summarize our observations as follows (see Fig.4).
    -The cortex originally differentiated around each sperm entry site (accumulation of mitochondria and naturally fluorescent vesicles) remains differentiated only around the mitotic apparatus.
    -During the first 3 cleavages the cortex remains differentiated around the nuclei that stay close to the original cleavage initiation sites (sperm entry site-future oral pole). During each unipolar cleavage, a part of the differentiated cortex seems to be dragged by the furrow to the opposite pole.
    -The major event in the segregation of the cortically differentiated zone takes place during the fourth cleavage divisions where micromeres are formed at the antipode of the original sperm entry site and first cleavage furrow initiation site. During the fourth cleavage, nuclei migrate to the opposite pole still surrounded by a cortically differentiated zone enriched in mitochondria and small autofluorescent vesicles. The micromeres are then formed by a peristaltic contraction

wave that squeezes the internal content of the macromeres to leave a cortically enriched small blastomere (micromere).

-Our preliminary experiments show that there are large portions of the blastomere cortex that are differentiated (smooth and microvillated regions, microfilament poor or rich regions etc.). We do not know yet where these regions occur and by what mechanisms they are progressively segregated.

REFERENCES

1. G. Reverberi, Ctenophores, *in:* "Experimental Embryology of Marine and Fresh-water Invertebrates," *North-Holland Publ.*, Amsterdam (1971).
2. H. Dunlap, Ctenophora *in:* "Reproduction in Marine Invertebrates," Giese, and Pearse ed., Acad.Press. New York, (1974).
3. G. Freeman, The establishment of the oral-aboral axis in the ctenophore embryo, *J.Embryol.Exp.Morphol.*, 42:237 (1974).
4. M. Strathmann, "Reproduction and Development of Marine Invertebrates of the North Pacific Coast," University Washington Press (1987).
5. G.R. Harbison, On the classification and evolution of ctenophora *in:* "The origin and relationship of lower invertebrates," S. Conway Morris, J.D. George, R. Gilson, and H.M. Platt, ed., Clarendon Press, London (1985).
6. S. Tamm, Motility and mechanosensitivity of macrocilia in the Ctenophore *Beroe*, *Nature*, 305:430 (1983).
7. M.R. Reeve, and M.A. Walter, Nutritional ecology of ctenophores. A review of recent research, *Adv.Mar.Biol.*, 15:249 (1978).
8. G.R. Harbison, and R. Miller, Not all ctenophores are hermaphrodites. Studies on the systematics, distribution, sexuality and development of two species of Ocyropsis, *Mar.Biol.*, 90:413 (1986).
9. M.Q. Martindale, Larval reproduction of the ctenophore *Mnemiopsis mccradyi* (order Lobata), *Mar.Biol.*, 94:409 (1987).
10. M.Q. Martindale, The ontogeny and maintenance of adult symmetry properties in the ctenophore *Mnemiopsis mccradyi*, *Dev.Biol.*, 118:356 (1986).
11. A. Kowalewsky, Entwicklungsgeschichte der Rippenquallen, *Mém.Acad.Imp.Sci*.St;Pétersbourg, sér.710:1 (1866).
12. A. Agassiz, Embryology of Ctenophorae, *Mem.Amer.Acad.Arts Sci.*, 10:357 (1874).
13. E. Metchnikoff, Vergleichend-embryologische Studien, 4. Über die Gastrulation und Mesodermbildung der Ctenophoren, *Z.Wiss.Zool.*, 42:24, 42:648 (1885).
14. C. Chun, Die Ctenophoren des Golfes von Neapel, Fauna Flora Golfes Neapel, 1:1 (1880).
15. H.E. Ziegler, Experimentelle Studien über die Zellteilung, III, Die Furchungszellen von *Beroë ovata*, *Arch.Entwicklungsmech.Organ*, 7:34 (1898).
16. N. Yatsu, Observations and experiments of the ctenophore egg, *Annot.Zool.Japon*, 7:333 (1911).
17. N. Yatsu, Observations and experiments on the ctenophore egg, *Annot.Zool.Japon*, 8:5 (1912).
18. H. Driesch, and T.H.Morgan, Zur Analysis der ersten Entwicklungsstadien des Ctenophoreneies, *Arch.Entwicklungsmech.Organ*, 2:204 (1895).

19. A. Fischel, Experimentelle Untersuchungen am Ctenophorenei, I.*Arch.Entwicklungsmech.Organ*, 6:109 (1897).
20. E.H. Davidson, "Gene activity in early development," Acad.Press., New York (1986).
21. G. Reverberi, and G. Ortolani, On the origin of ciliated plates and of the mesoderm in the ctenophores, *Acta Embryol.Morphol.Exp.*, 6:175 (1986).
22. G. Reverberi, and G. Ortolani, The development of the ctenophore's egg, *Riv.Biol.*, Lisbon 58:113 (1965).
23. G. Farfaglio, Experiments on the formation of the ciliated plates in ctenophores, *Acta Embryol.Morphol.Exp.*, 6:191 (1963).
24. G. Freeman, and G.T. Reynolds, The segregation of developmental potential during early cleavage stages in the ctenophore *Mnemiopsis leidyi*, *Biol.Bull.*, 143:461 (1972).
25. G. Freeman, and G.T. Reynolds, The development of bioluminescence in the ctenophore *Mnemiopsis leidyi*, *Dev.Biol.*, 31:61 (1973).
26. G. Freeman, The effects of altering the position of cleavage planes on the process of localization of developmental potential in ctenophore, *Dev.Biol.*, 51(2):332 (1976).
27. G. Freeman, The multiple roles which cell division can play in the localization of developmental potential, *in:* "Determinants of Spatial organization," S.Subtelny and I.R.Konigsberg, ed., Acad.Press, New York (1979).
28. J.M. Franc, Etude ultrastructurale de la spermatogenèse du cténaire *Beroe ovata*, *J.Ultrastruct.Res.*, 42:255 (1973).
29. D. Carré, and C. Sardet, Fertilization and early development in *Beroe ovata*, *Dev.Biol.*, 105:188 (1984).

DESCRIPTIVE AND EXPERIMENTAL EMBRYOLOGY OF THE TURBELLARIA:

PRESENT KNOWLEDGE, OPEN QUESTIONS AND FUTURE TRENDS

Jaume Baguñà[1] and Barbara C. Boyer[2]
1
Departament de Genètica, Facultat de Biologia
Universitat de Barcelona
Diagonal 645, 08028 Barcelona, Spain
2
Department of Biological Sciences
Union College, Schenectady
New York 12308, USA
and the Marine Biological Laboratory
Woods Hole, MA, USA

GENERAL INTRODUCTION

Basic morphological characteristics

The Turbellaria are acoelomate, triploblastic, unsegmented and bilaterally symmetrical animals, with distinct antero-posterior polarity expressed in head, trunk and tail regions that are not markedly distinguishable. With the exception of the Acoela, which have a solid mass of digestive tissue, the Turbellaria are characterized by a pharynx and a blind gut (no anus). Circulatory and respiratory organs are absent, and excretory organs consist of protonephridia. A solid mass of tissue, called mesenchyme or parenchyma fills the space between the cellular, monoestratified, ciliated epidermis and the gut and surrounds the internal organs. It consists of several non proliferating differentiated cell types and a particular class of undifferentiated mitotic cells usually called neoblasts (for a quantitative analysis of cell types, see Baguña and Romero, 1981; Romero, 1987).

The nervous system of primitive turbellarians comprises a simple subepithelial nerve net plus three or four pairs of longitudinal cords and a slight concentration of cell bodies near the anterior end. In more advanced forms, there is tendency towards reduction in the number of pairs of cords and increased prominence of the ventral pair, accompanied by an increase in the mass of the brain. Paired or multiple cephalic sensory elements, located primarily at the anterior end, also are abundant.

Most turbellarians are hermaphrodites with cross fertilization following copulation and deposit egg capsules from which one or more ciliated hatchlings emerge, grow, and

Experimental Embryology in Aquatic Plants and Animals
Edited by H.-J. Marthy, Plenum Press, New York, 1990

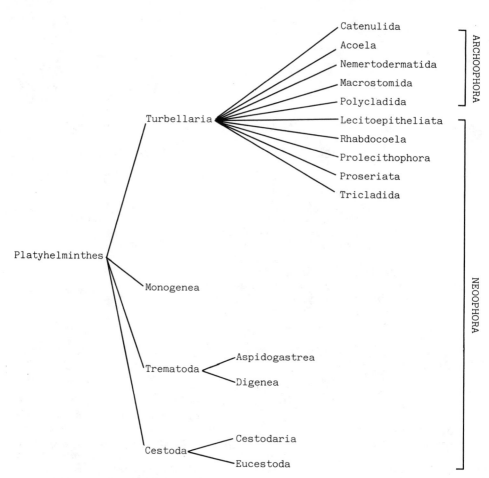

FIG.1. Classification of the phylum Platyhelminthes
with specification of turbellarian orders (from
Barnes et al. 1988, slightly modified).

differentiate to adults. Others have asexual reproduction and
some are parthenogenetic. Reproductive systems are often very
complex, consisting of many testes, that usually produce
biflagellate sperm and many ovaries that produce entolecithal
eggs or a pair of ovaries with many separate vitellaria. The
latter produce yolk cells, so that the egg is ectolecithal (see
below).

   The Turbellaria are soft bodied organisms, often dorso-
ventrally flattened, ranging in size from a few millimeters
(those found in interstitial habitats) to the giant land
turbellarians, that may be more than 50 cm long. They are
common animals found widely distributed in lakes, ponds, and
the sea where they occupy bottom habitats. Although most are
predators and may also feed on carrion, some are herbivores
feeding on benthic microflora. Some species are commensal or
parasitic, but most are free-living.

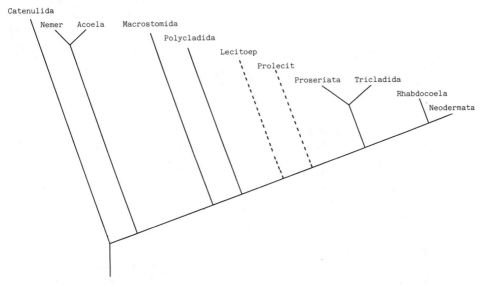

FIG.2. Diagram of the phylogenetic relationship in the Platyhelminthes, namely in Turbellaria. Based on Ehlers (1985) and Ax (1987), albeit in a simplified form. Broken lines mean uncertain position. Nemer: Nemertodermatida; Lecitoep: Lecitoepitheliata; Prolecit: Prolecithophorata.

Taxonomy and Phylogeny

Is Turbellaria a valid taxon ? Turbellaria (a name coined by Ehrenberg, 1831), comprises the so-called free-living flatworms, and is one of the four taxonomic classes of the phylum Platyhelminthes (Barnes, 1968; Kaestner, 1984; Barnes et al., 1988). Distinguishing features are a free-living life style and a body covered by a multiciliated epidermis. The class Turbellaria, which presently consists of 10 orders, has been divided into two supraorders: Archoophora (comprising five orders; see Fig.1), with homocellular female gonads, entolecithal eggs, and spiral cleavage, and Neoophora (including five orders; Fig.1) with heterocellular female gonads and yolk cells, ectolecithal eggs, and development departing markedly from the spiral pattern. For general overviews of the Turbellaria see Hyman (1951), De Beauchamp (1961), and Crezée (1982).

From ultrastructural studies and cladistic analysis, Ehlers (1984, 1985, 1986; see also Ax, 1987) has recently expressed serious doubts as to the validity of Turbellaria and Archoophora as taxonomic entities, arguing that their distinctive features are plesiomorphies (*sensu* Hennig, 1966), and that no autoapomorphy exists to define either taxon as a monophylum. This means that Turbellaria and Archoophora are paraphyletic groups; that is, artificial assemblages of plathelminthes that do not have stem species in common. Therefore, they can no longer be used in a phylogenetic system of the Platyhelminthes.

Despite Ehlers' and Ax's arguments appear to us to be sound and well founded, more studies are clearly needed. Moreover, the name Turbellaria is still entrenched in all zoological textbooks, and time, rationality and persuasion will be needed in the coming years for a new phylogenetic scheme to become acceptable. Therefore, however artificial, the name Turbellaria will be used in this review to mean all known free-living forms of the phylum Platyhelminthes.

Internal phylogeny

Modern schemes of turbellarian phylogeny stem from the work of Karling (1974). Recent proposals of Hendelberg (1986), Smith et al. (1986), and primarily of Ehlers (1984, 1985), have removed doubts concerning the relationship of the most primitive groups. A consensus phylogenetic diagram, which mainly follows Ehlers' proposal (Ehlers, 1985) is depicted in Figure 2.

As far as embryonic development is concerned, it is of interest to point out that, however artificial, Archoophora groups together the more primitive taxons which have an unmodified spiral type of cleavage. Neoophora, representing a true monophyletic taxon (Ax, 1987), comprises the more advanced turbellarians, including parasitic groups (Neodermata, Ehlers, 1984), with a very modified type of development.

THE IMPORTANCE OF TURBELLARIA IN EVOLUTION AND DEVELOPMENT

Turbellaria: a key group in animal phylogeny

A controversy over the origin of Platyhelminthes (namely turbellarians), either as derived from non-bilaterian taxa (Protista, Cnidaria, Ctenofora,..) or as reduced coelomates (e.g. from annelids) has lasted from more than a century. As pointed out by Ax (1987), most of the arguments presented by the supporters of either theory are empirically untestable speculations and the presumed homologies are unproven. This impasse has been particularly unfortunate since a final answer to this longstanding question would either confirm the turbellarians as a key group in metazoan evolution or relegate them to a blind-end position as offshoots of a particular group of coelomates.

In moderm phylogentic reconstructions, however, the Platy-helminthes or the Plathelmintomorpha a taxon comprising Platyhelminthes and Gnathostomulida; Ax, 1987) appears as a true monophyletic sister group of the Eubilateria; that is, they are a primitive group, not a recent derivation from any coelomate ancestor (Ax, 1987). This conclusion is backed by molecular data. Sequences of the 5S ribosomal RNA show that the divergence of some freshwater triclads *(Dugesia (D) japonica)* is very old, occurring between protists and all the rest of the metazoan phyla (including Porifera and Cnidaria) (Hori et al., 1988). Moreover, sequences of the phyletically more reliable 18S ribosomal RNA subunit show clearly that the Platyhelminthes occupy a very ancient position in the evolution of the Metazoa

(Field et al., 1988). Comparison of recent date from sequences of several plathelminthes (including three parasitic species) with a large number of animal and protist sequences suggest that: 1) Platyhelminthes is a monophyletic group since all the species studied clearly branch together, 2) Platyhelminthes is the true sister group of the Eubilateria (Ax, 1987), and both are derived from a stem species common to the two groups alone; and 3) Platyhelminthes can not be considered to be a simplified group derived from any coelomate ancestor (Riutort, Field, Raff and Baguñà, unpublished data).

Turbellaria: a key group in animal development

Because of the key phyletic position of the Platy-helminthes, knowledge of their embryonic development (primarily the Turbellaria) is crucial to understand how certain innovations in development and evolution (e.g. bilateral symmetry, antero-posterior organization, cephalization among others) have appeared and been transformed during ontogeny and evolution in the major spiralian groups (Nemertea, Annelida, Mollusca, Sipuncula, Echiura,..). To us, this is a primary reason for fostering the study of embryonic development in this largely neglected group of organisms.

HISTORICAL BACKGROUND

Despite the key position of the Turbellaria within the animal kingdom and its clear relationship to the major spiralian groups, knowledge of embryonic development in this group is scanty, and largely restricted to descriptive work. Currently experimental data are available for only a few species of acoels, polyclads and freshwater triclads.

Descriptive studies

General descriptions of the embryonic development of several turbellarian orders date back to the middle of the last century. The best known works, however, were produced in the latter part of the 19th and the early 20th centuries (see Dawydoff, 1928; Hyman, 1951, and De Beauchamp, 1961, for historical references and a comparative analysis of the groups).Compared to this early flush of work, modern accounts (from 1950s on), though excellent, are comparatively scarce. However, the works of Bogomolov (1960), Steinböck (1966), Ax and Dörjes (1966), Apelt (1969) and Henley (1974) an Acoela; Seiler-Aspang (1957) on Macrostomida; Kato (1940, 1968), Anderson (1977) and Teshirogi et al. (1981) on Polycladida; Reisinger et al. 1974) for Lecitoepitheliata; Giesa (1966), and Reisinger et al. (1974) on Proseriata; and Seiler-Aspang (1958) and Le Moigne (1963) on Tricladida, must be mentioned, as well as the general reviews of Skaer (1971) and Benazzi and Gremigni (1982) on freshwater triclads. In contrast, some orders such as Rhabdocoela, though studied in the past, have not been recently reviewed and, as far as we know, no data are available for Nemertodermatida, Catenulida and Prolecitophora.

At the cellular level, cell lineages, primarily of early development, are known only for acoels and polyclads, which have entolecithal, usually transparent eggs that are easy to culture and handle. Noteworthy are the works of Steinböck

(1966) and Apelt (1969) on acoels, and the early studies of Surface (1907) and Kato (1940), and later works by Anderson (1977) and Teshirogi et al. (1981) on polyclads.

Comparative analysis of embryonic development within the Turbellaria and with other spiralians have received little attention, though the recent works by Costello and Henley (1976), Ivanova-Kasas (1982), Thomas (1986), Ax (1987) and Boyer et al. (1988) are highly relevant in this context. Moreover, comparative analysis of sperm morphology (Hendelberg, 1974, 1986) and the ultrastructure of the female gonads in the Turbellaria (Gremigni, 1988) provide information on phylogenetic relationships within the group.

Experimental studies

Experimental studies of turbellarians have received much less attention than descriptive studies; only three orders, Tricladida (primarily freshwater species), Acoela and Polycladida, have being examined to some extent. There are considerable technical difficulties in working with embryos of fresh water triclads and all neoophoran orders because the eggs are surrounded by many yolk cells and are laid in cocoons with opaque and tough shells. Moreover, culture methods that allow normal development of early embryos after removal from the cocoon have not been devised. Therefore it is not surprising that most experimental work on triclads, (excellently reviewed by Skaer 1971), has been limited to perturbations of early embryos using centrifugation and ionizing radiation techniques. The results, though interesting, do not provide relevant information concerning the most pressing questions of early development such as cell lineages, establishment of body axes, and determinative (topographical and histotypical) phenomena.

Polyclads, and to a lesser extent acoels, with ento-lecithal eggs, have been recently studied by Boyer and associates in a very interesting series of experiments (Boyer, 1986, 1987, 1988; Boyer et al., 1988). Analyzing the effects of deletion/separation of blastomeres and removal of vegetal egg cytoplasm on late embryos and Muller's larvae, she concluded that cytoplasm determinants controlling right/left and dorso/ventral axes, as well as eye and lobe formation are localized in eggs and early embryos of polyclads. However, they appear to be located primarily in the animal hemisphere of the egg, to segregate independently of cleavage planes, and no single blastomere corresponding to the D cell of higher spiralians exists (see below). These characteristics are unlike those demonstrated by most spiralians and are interpreted to reflect an early stage in the evolution of this supraphylum grouping of organisms (Boyer, 1988).

Compared to the other invertebrate groups, knowledge of embryonic development in turbellarians clearly lags behind. There are several reasons for this neglect. First, cell lineages have not been confirmed using the new macromolecular tracers that have been employed successfully in such diverse groups as leeches (Weisblat et al., 1984), sea urchins (Cameron et al., 1987) and amphibians (Smith et al., 1885). Moreover, other lineage markers such as lectins have not been used and policlonal and monoclonal antibodies have not been produced. Second, molecular data (e.g. rates of RNA and protein synthesis, temporal and spatial variation in protein patterns; detection of regional or cell lineage antigens using monoclonal antibodies,..) are, as far as we know, not available for any turbellarian group. Finally, techniques of molecular genetics, namely the use of genomic, cDNA and expression libraries, have not been used to any extent.

In this review, a brief comparative sketch of the embryonic development of four turbellarian orders, the archoophoran Polycladida and Acoela and the neoophoran Rhabdocoela and Tricladida, highlighting their common trends and major differences, will be presented. In addition, the parallels with other spiralian groups, as well as the future trends necessary to foster the knowledge of development in this neglected group of organisms will be discussed.

EMBRYONIC DEVELOPMENT IN TURBELLARIA. DESCRIPTIVE DATA

Embryonic development in the Turbellaria clearly is influenced by the homocellular or heterocellular condition of the female gonad. The archoophoran level of organization, though ill defined taxonomically, is the primitive plesiomorph character, not only in Platyhelminthes, but in the entire animal kingdom (Ax, 1987; Gremigni, 1988). These organisms have simple female gonads consisting of ovaries that produce entolecithal eggs containing yolk (Fig.3 a). The neoophoran condition is an autoapomorphic character derived from the homocellular, entolecithal condition. In this group, the female gonads are complex; consisting of ovarians that produce alecithal (or nearly so) eggs and vitellaria with numerous yolk cells (Fig.3 b).

After fertilization, the eggs of both archoophorans and neoophorans are encased within protective capsules that, in the latter case, contain yolk cells. In archoophorans, which lack vitelline cells, the eggs, though not very large (100-200 μm), have substantial amounts of yolk (heterolecithal eggs) and are covered by a transparent egg shell membrane formed by the exocitosis and coalescence of electron-dense granules present in the periphery of the unfertilized egg (Fig.3 c). In neoophorans the eggs (single or multiple) are small (30-40 μm) and are packaged with numerous yolk cells within the eggshell (or cocoon) which is formed by the extrusion and coalescence of shell granules that are primarily present in yolk cells (Gremigni, 1988) (Fig.3 d, 3e). The main function of yolk cells in neoophorans is to serve as nutritive substratum for the embryo (or embryos) during middle and late development. For further comparative information on oogenesis and vitellogenesis see Thomas (1986) and Gremigni (1988). Detailed accounts of different modalities of copulation and fertilization, as well as on the early stages of polar body formation are considered in Apelt (1969) for acoels, Teshirogi et al. (1981) and Boyer et al. (1988) for polyclads, Giesa (1966) for proseriates, and Benazzi and Gremigni (1982) for freshwater triclads.

Polyclads

Although polyclads have some features considered advanced with respect to other turbellarians, their archoophoran condition and mode of cleavage are clearly plesiomorphic

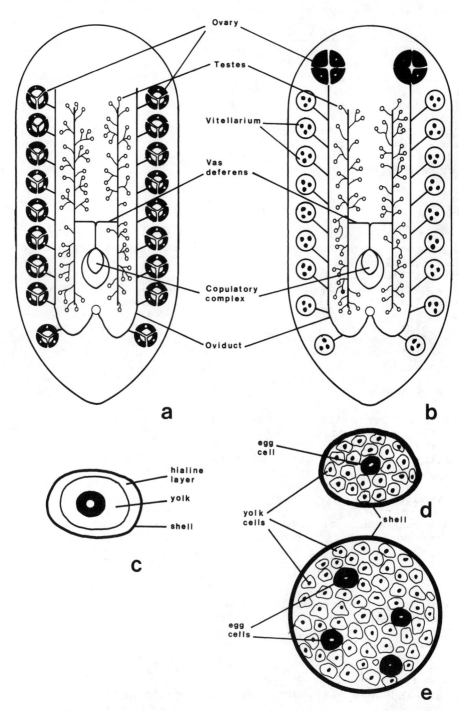

FIG.3. Reproductive system and eggs in Archoophora
(a, c) and Neoophora (b, d, e). For more details, see
text.

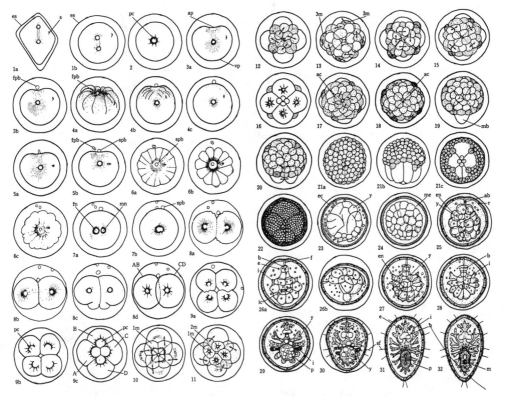

FIG.4. Diagrammatic representation of the main stages of embryonic development in *Notoplana humilis* (after Teshirogi et al., 1981). Abbreviations: ab, aboral organs; ap, animal pole; b, brain; e, eye; ec, ectoderm; en, endoderm; es, egg shell; f, frontal organ; fn, female nucleus; fpb, first polar body; i, intestine; m, mouth; mb, mesoblast; me, mesenchyme; mn, male nucleus; p, pharynx; r, rhabdite; s, spermatozoan; sf, sensory filament; spb, second polar body; vp, vegetal pole; y, yolk.

characters (Ax, 1987). A brief sketch of their development, based on the sequence obtained by Teshirogi et al. (1981) in *Notoplana humilis* will be presented (Fig.4).

Cleavage in polyclads is of the spiral determinate type, being homoquadratic or slightly heteroquadratic, and leads to an unequal coeloblastula or to a stereoblastula. In some species, differences in blastomere size are apparent at the two-cell stage, with CD being larger than AB. At the four-cell stage and later on, the D blastomere and its descendants may be larger than the other blastomeres. After initial cleavage (Fig.4:8 a-13), three quartets of micromeres (1m, 2m, 3m) are given off, occupying the animal hemisphere (Fig.4:15). The macromeres then divide to form a fourth quartet (4m) of large micromeres (4a-4d) and four small macromeres (4A-4D), that lie at the vegetal pole (Fig.4:16). It is important to point out that traces of the rosette and the cross, distinctive of higher spiralians forms (annelids and molluscs) are sometimes seen at the animal pole.

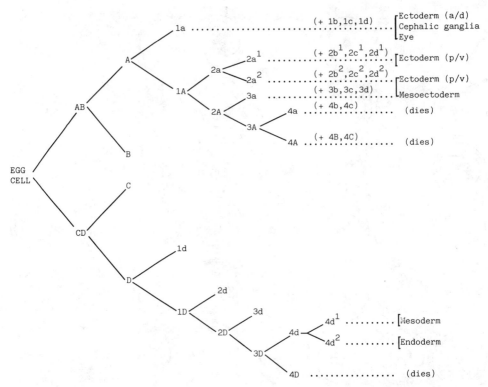

FIG.5. Diagram of the lineage of a polyclad. The designations represent names of individual cells (see Fig.4). For the sake of clarity, the descendants of blastomeres B and C have been omitted. Drawn from descriptions given in Dawydoff (1928), Hyman (1951) and Teshirogi et al. (1981).

Gastrulation occurs primarily by epiboly (Fig.4:21 b-22). After division of the 4d blastomere, micromeres from the first three quartets migrate towards the vegetal pole over the surface of large fourth quartet micromeres (4a-4c) and the descendants of 4d. The later will proliferate to produce the endoderm ($4d^1$) and the mesoderm ($4d^2$). Later, the ectoderm, at or near the site of blastopore formation, invaginates to form the mouth and pharynx. They then connect to the endoderm which subsequently hollows out forming the gastric cavity. Meanwhile, the large micromeres (4a-4c) and the small macromeres (4A-4D) disintegrate and the yolk droplets fuse into large globules.

Definitive body axes in polyclads are established by a gradual shift of the animal-vegetal axis. The animal pole, bearing the frontal gland, moves forward and becomes the anterior end where the brain forms from an invagination of the ectoderm. Meanwhile, the mouth region shifts backwards adopting a ventro-caudal position. Later on, the embryo flattens and in the Acotylea it develops directly into a small worm that, after rupturing the egg capsule, will grow to the adult size. In Cotylea and some Acotylea, a transitory pelagic larvae forms (Müller's larva; Götte's larva) before being transformed into an adult (for further references see Ruppert, 1978).

The early lineage in polyclads is summarized in Figure 5. Although some uncertainties still remain, several points merit consideration. First, as in most spiralians, the first quartet of micromeres apparently gives to all the cephalic (head) structures as opposed to the rest of the body ("trunk"). Second, in contrast to other spiralians, the ectoderm of the body wall is not entirely derived from the 2d micromere (the first somatoblast) but from several micromeres of the second and third quartets. Third, blastomere $4d^2$, considered homologous to the 4d micromere (second somatoblast) of higher spiralians, gives rise by a teloblastic process, to short and transient mesodermal bands that soon disperse. This may foreshadow the teloblastic process of germinal band and mesoderm formation in higher spiralians, namely annelids. Finally, in contrast to other archoophorans (e.g. Catenulata, Macrostomida), whose macromeres and fourth quartet of micromeres (4a-4c) produce the endoderm and endodermal derivatives, in polyclads these cells are resorbed and used as nutritive cells by the embryo.

Acoels

The development of acoels is of the spiral determinate type and is similar to that of polyclads except that the egg has only one meridional cleavage forming blastomeres A and B (or AB and CD), before giving off the usual four sets of micromeres. The latter, consisting of two cells each, are termed duets instead of quartets.

Gastrulation is primarily by epiboly and produces a stereogastrula. The internal mass comprises cells 4A, 4B, 4a and 4b, that will give the mesoendoderm (or inner parenchyma), jointly with derivatives of the second and third quartets that form the mesoectoderm (outer or peripheral parenchyma). When the blastopore closes, cells remaining at the surface separate forming the epidermis.

The cell lineage of acoels is depicted in Figure 6, and can be summarized as follows. The first duet of micromeres gives rise to antero-dorsal (cephalic) epidermis and the nervous system; the second, and probably the third duet, form the mesoectoderm that produces the postero-ventral ("trunk"/tail) epidermis and the outer parenchyma. Finally, the fourth duet and macromeres form the inner parenchyma that is considered to be a sort of mesoendoderm with digestive functions.

Neoophora

The evolution of the ectolecithal egg with numerous separate yolk cells has greatly modified embryonic development in neoophorans. In some orders, cleavage is highly modified as compared to the spiral quartet or duet forms of polyclads, acoels and other archoophoran orders. This is particularly true in triclads, prolecitophorates, and some proseriates where the phenomenon of "Blastomeren-Anarchie" occurs. Here, eggs cleave and the resulting blastomeres disperse and become isolated by yolk cells. Later, these scattered blastomeres aggregate to form a solid blastema from which the embryo, and later on the adult, develops.

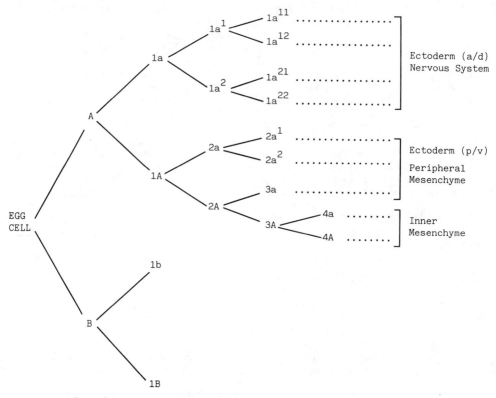

FIG.6. Diagram of the early cell lineage of an acoel. For the sake of clarity, the descendants of blastomere B have been omitted. Drawn after descriptions given in Hyman (1951) and Apelt (1969).

In some orders (e.g. Lecitoepitheliata, Rhabdocoela, and some Proseriata) traces of spiral cleavage still remain, though the pattern is not clearly fixed and becomes random at later stages. This means that the phenomenon of blastomere dispersal is not an obligate condition of ectolecithy.

Rhabdocoels

Since no modern account exists on the embryonic development of rhabdocoels, we must rely on the description given by Bresslau (1904) of *Mesostoma ehrenbergii* and *Bothromesostoma personatum*, and by Ball (1916) for *Paravortex gemellipara*, as reviewed by Hyman (1951) and Henley (1974). In this review, we follow the description of *Mesostoma ehrenbergii* which is depicted, slightly modified, in Figure 7.

The egg, surrounded by 50-100 yolk cells (Fig.7 a) divides unequally forming a mass of blastomeres that remains in the center of the yolk-cell mass (Fig.7 b). Some peripheral yolk cells flatten to surround the remaining blastomeres (Fig.7 c) and form the so-called yolk mantle, hull membrane or embryonic ectoderm (a term in neophoran development describing a cellular layer which occurs beneath the eggshell and encloses the blastomeres and the yolk cells). Later, the mass of blastomeres moves to one side of the yolk mass (Fig.7 d); this

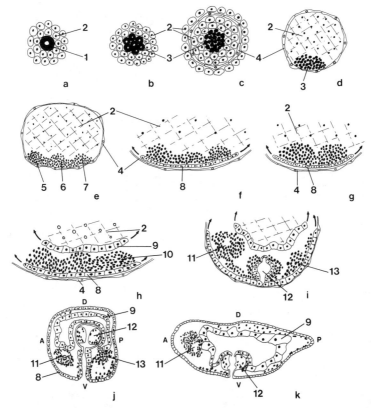

FIG.7. Development of rhabdocoels. a, b: early
cleavage; c: formation of embryonic ectoderm; d:
anlage formation; e: antero-posterior determination
of primordia; f: formation of the definitive ectoderm
(sagittal view); g: formation of the definitive
ectoderm (transversal view); h: formation of the
definitive endoderm; i: dorsal epidermal spreading;
j: body wall completed. (Redrawn, partially, from
Bresslau, 1904, and Hyman, 1951). 1, egg cell; 2,
yolk cells; 3, mass of blastomeres; 4, embryonic
ectoderm (hull membrane); 5, anterior anlage; 6,
middle (pharyngeal) anlage; 7, posterior anlage; 8,
definitive ectoderm; 9, definitive endoderm; 10,
definitive mesoderm; 11, brain ganglia; 12, pharynx;
13, genital (posterior) anlage; A, anterior; D,
dorsal; P, posterior; V, ventral. Arrows indicate the
direction of epidermal spreading.

side will become the future ventral side of the embryo while
the other half, occupied by yolk cells, will be dorsal. The
mass of blastomeres, now called the embryonic anlage or
blastema, proliferates actively, and often is divided
bilaterally along a line that will mark the sagittal plane
(Fig.7 g). The blastema becomes divided anterioposteriorly into
three masses: the anterior or brain anlage, the middle or
pharyngeal anlage, and the posterior or genital anlage (Fig.7
e). The brain anlage coincides with the animal pole, whereas
the pharynx and genital anlage are meridional.

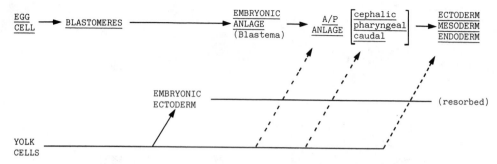

FIG.8. Diagram of the cell lineage and the topological (topographical) and histotypical determinations in rhabdocoels. Underlined, components from which the embryo originates. Broken lines indicate passage of yolk cells into embryonic structures.

Late development involves the segregation of germ layers within the anlage, starting peripherally with the separation of the definitive ectoderm (Fig.7 f,g), and later by the definitive endoderm (Fig.7 h); between them, the rest of cells can be considered mesodermal and will give rise, in conjunction with some ectodermal cells, to the brain, pharyngeal and copulatory primordia, as well as to mesenchymal derivatives. Subsequently, epidermal cells from the ventral side spread laterally and dorsally along the inner surface of the embryonic ectoderm (hull membrane) to enclose the large, yolky blastomeres present in the dorsal half of the embryo (Fig.7 i,j). Internally, a similar, albeit more imperfect, randon spreading process occur dorsally at the level of the definitive endoderm.

The anterior (cephalic) anlage develops into the paired cerebral ganglia, from which the longitudinal nerve cords grow out posteriorly, as well as into pigment and retinal cells of the eyes. The middle (pharyngeal) anlage will form the musculature, gland cells and parenchyma of the pharynx. In contrast, the epithelia of the pharynx, pharyngeal cavity and oesophagus arise from an epidermal invagination that later hollows out. The posterior (caudal) anlage forms the posterior end of the worm and the genital system. Parenchyma and subepidermal and parenchymal musculature come from cells of the three anlage.

A general sketch that summarizes cell and tissue lineages in rhabdocoels is depicted in Figure 8.

Triclads

The development of triclads, though seeming to differ from that in other turbellarians to the extent that comparisons are meaningless (Thomas, 1986), nevertheless it is similar to that of rhabdocoels. A general diagram of the main stages is presented in Figure 9.

Briefly, 20-40 egg cells are deposited within the cocoon with tens or hundreds or thousands vitelline (yolk) cells. The egg divides but blastomeres disperse without becoming attached to each other ("blastomeren-anarchie") (Fig.9 a, b). Sub-

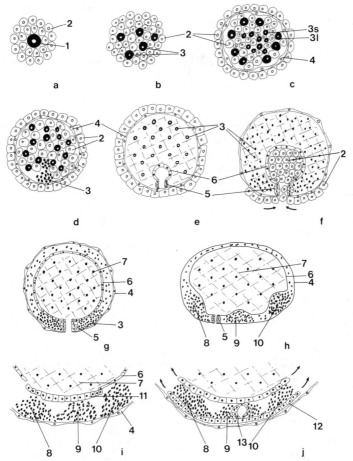

FIG.9. Development of triclads. a, b: early cleavage;
c: formation of embryonic ectoderm; d: aggregation of
small blastomeres at the future ventral side; e:
development of the embryonic pharynx and intestine;
f: embryo beginning to ingest yolk cells; g:
ingestion of yolk cells completed and formation of
the embryonic anlage at the ventral side; h:
anteroposterior determination of primordia; i:
formation of the definitive endoderm; j: formation of
the definitive ectoderm and dorsal spreading
(arrows). 1, egg-cell; 2, yolk cells; 3, blastomeres;
3 l, large blastomeres; 3 s, small blastomeres; 4,
embryonic ectoderm; 5, embryonic pharynx; 6, embryonic intestine; 7, mass of yolk cells; 8, anterior
(brain) anlage; 9, middle (pharyngeal) anlage; 10,
posterior (genital) anlage; 11, definitive endoderm;
12, definitive ectoderm; 13, definitive pharynx.
Arrows indicate the direction of epidermal spreading.

sequently, some peripheral blastomeres flatten and form the
embryonic (provisional) ectoderm, enclosing the remaining
blastomeres and thousands of yolk cells (Fig.9c; stage 1 of Le
Moigne, 1963). The smallest blastomeres then aggregate at a
point in contact with the inner side of the embryonic ectoderm

(Fig.9 d); from them, a transient embryonic pharynx and a transient embryonic intestine form (Fig.9 e; stage 2 of Le Moigne, 1963). These transient structures are developmental innovations of triclads and have no homologues in other turbellarians. The main function of the embryonic pharynx and intestine is to swallow and keep the remaining yolk cells around the embryo to be used later as food.

The process of swallowing yolk cells, which lasts 4 days, results in a hollow spherical embryo with an inner embryonic intestine full of yolk cells, a transient embryonic pharynx, and an outer embryonic ectoderm. Between these two layers, the remaining blastomeres have increased in number by proliferation and aggregate at the ventral side near the embryonic pharynx (Fig.9 g; stage 3 of Le Moigne, 1963) forming the embryonic anlage or blastema. The later stages of development in triclads are similar to those seen in rhabdocoels. The blastema segregates bilaterally into two masses and anteroposteriorly into three anlage or primordia whose fate is essentially the same as in rhabdocoels (Fig.9 h).

Segregation of germ layers starts peripherally with formation of the definitive endoderm that, simultaneously with the degeneration of the embryonic intestine, spreads over the yolk cells located in the dorsal side of the embryo (Fig.9 i). The rest of the embryonic anlage segregate later into definitive ectoderm and mesoderm (mesenchyme).After the definitive ectoderm forms (Fig.9 j), the embryonic pharynx degenerates, and a new, definitive, pharynx appears within the pharyngeal anlage (stage 4 of Le Moigne, 1963). Meanwhile, the ectoderm spreads laterally and dorsally until it encloses the embryo dorsally.

The remaining cells of the embryonic anlage give rise to mesodermal elements such as the subepidermal and parenchymal muscles, gland cells, and other parenchymal cells and, eventually, to the reproductive system. Some cells remain as undifferentiated neoblasts. These cells, which are the only mitotic cell type known in the adult (Baguñà, 1981; Ehlers, 1985) are pluripotent stem-cells that give rise to most differentiated cell types during the continuous daily cell renewal in these organisms. Further details of later stages of embryogenesis (stages 5 to 7 of Le Moigne, 1963) can be found in Le Moigne (1963), Skaer (1971) and Benazzi and Gremigni (1982).

A general scheme summarizing cell and tissue lineages in triclads is shown in Figure 10.

EXPERIMENTAL EMBRYOLOGY OF THE TURBELLARIA

The entolecithal Turbellaria (Archoophora) are generally recognized as being very primitive, occupying a phylogenetic position at the base of the protostome line, and are the most primitive animals with bilateral symmetry. However, given the evolutionary position of this group and the critical role that developmental studies play in revealing evolutionary relationships, turbellarian embryos have been the subject of surprisingly few experimental studies. Among these few are the developmental analyses of the acoel *Neohildia* and the polyclad

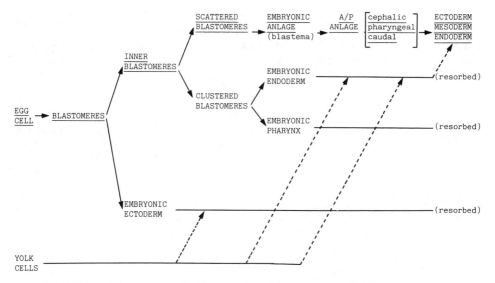

FIG.10. Diagram of the cell lineage and the topological (topographical) and histotypical determinations
in freshwater triclads. Underlined, components from
which the embryo proper originates. Broken line
indicates the passage of yolk cells into embryonic
structures.

Hoploplana by Boyer (1971, 1986, 1987, 1988, 1989). The embryos
of both species have spiral cleavage, a protostome
characteristic.

The Acoela, which may be one of the most primitive
turbellarian orders, have spiral cleavage in which duets of
micromeres are formed, rather than the quartets of the more
typical spiralian pattern. When blastomeres were deleted from
embryos of *Neohildia* during the early cleavage stages (two-cell
stage through the third duet), development was normal except in
the absence of both macromeres. The aberrant animal from the
latter experiments were ciliated spheres with a central cavity
and lacked any differentiated structures, indicating that the
macromeres are necessary for normal morphological and
histological development. The results also suggest an inductive
interaction between the micromeres and macromeres (Boyer,
1971). This study was the first to demonstrate regulative
development in a spiralian embryo.

Since early embryonic determination (mosaicism) is
probably specialized and derived from the indeterminate type of
development, it seems unlikely that the acoel ancestor was
mosaic and this feature was lost in present day acoels. The
regulative capacity of the acoel embryo then suggests that
spiral cleavage preceded mosaicism in evolution and only later
did this very precise cleavage pattern become associated with
early programming of the cell's fate.

The polyclad Turbellaria, another archoophoran order, have
quartet spiral cleavage that is very similar to the cleavage
pattern of the higher Spiralia such as annelids and molluscs.
The polyclads, therefore, may provide a link between the

regulative development of the acoels and the more typical determinative development of the higher groups. The early embryonic stages of the polyclad *Hoploplana inquilina* have been the subject of experimental studies to examine the nature of embryonic determination in this group.

Experiments carried out on two- and four-cell stage embryos have established that early development of *Hoploplana* is determinative (Boyer, 1986, 1987). When blastomeres were deleted or isolated at the two-cell stage, characteristic "half larvae" were produced that were abnormal in body shape and in the development of lobes and eyes. Less anomalous "three-quarter larvae" resulted when one blastomere was deleted at the four-cell stage, but they still were underdeveloped in one quadrant and often exhibited eye abnormalities, with almost three quarters of the larvae being one-eyed (68%) or eyeless (3%). It is hypothesized that eye development is a consequence of specific and discrete localization of both an eye precursor and an inducer that segregate independently of cleavage planes, and that cell interactions are involved in development of the normal two eyes.

Deletion of any of the blastomeres at four cells frequently produced abnormal or missing ventrolateral lobes but these were significantly more common when A or C rather than B or D was deleted. This suggests that A and C are more likely to receive determinants for right/left symmetry than B or D and conversely B and D have a tendency to form the dorsoventral axis. However no specific deficiency is consistently related to the absence of a particular blastomere. Thus, while cytoplasmic determinants clearly have been localized by the four-cell stage, these localizations appear to be independent of cleavage planes.

Though cytoplasmic localization are characteristic of the polyclad embryo in early cleavage stages, the time and mechanism of establishment of the embryonic axes of symmetry remains unclear. In molluscan embryos two different mechanisms are involved. Gastropods with unequal cleavage not only exhibit early cell determination, but definitely establish the axes of symmetry by the four-cell stage through an intracellular mechanism involving localization of cytoplasmic determinants in the large D cell. In gastropods with equal cleavage, however, the first quartet cells collectively play a crucial role in symmetry determination by inducing the central macromere to become the D quadrant mesentoblast mother cell (3D) after formation of the third quartet. Moreover in three different species of equally cleaving gastropods, isolated blastomeres from two-cell embryos have been shown to give rise to complete larvae. (See Davidson, 1986 for review of determination of embryonic symmetry in molluscs.) The *Hoploplana inquilina* embryo at the four-cell stage has two equal sized A and C blastomeres and two equal sized but larger B and D blastomeres that are determined, but there is no blastomere corresponding to the morphogenetically significant D macromere. Therefore this embryo does not appear to fit either gastropod model. Because the ancestral flatworms probably were the first animals to evolve bilateral symmetry, understanding the mechanism of determination of embryonic symmetry in this group is particularly significant.

Experiments on eight-cell embryos of *Hoploplana inquilina* have revealed specific contributions made by the first quartet micromeres and the macromeres and their role in establishing bilateral symmetry (Boyer, 1989; Boyer and Wallace, 1989). As more micromeres or macromeres were deleted at this stage, the larvae became progressively more abnormal, including reduction in the number of eyes, abnormality in lobe development and disturbance of symmetry. Deletion of three of four micromeres produced larvae with almost perfectly spherical morphology, abnormally large size, and very aberrant tissue development. Such larvae were classified as "swollen". When one macromere was deleted, the majority of embryos were bilaterally symmetrical. However less than one-quarter were when two macromeres were removed and deletion of three or four macromeres produced almost 100% radially symmetrical "swollen" larvae. Moreover, macromere deletions often resulted in the formation of supernumerary eyes. (When all four macromeres were deleted, 77% of the larvae had three or more eyes).

These results indicate that *Hoploplana* embryo does not develop axes of bilateral symmetry when more than two micromeres or more than one macromere are deleted and provide evidence that macromere/micromere interactions are involved in the determination of embryonic symmetry, in which the B or D quadrant is more likely to become dorsal than A or C. They also suggest the presence of an inhibitor of eye formation in the vegetal region that is more likely to be localized in the 1B or 1D cell than in 1A or 1C.

Thus, while cytoplasmic localizations characterize the early cleavage stages of *Hoploplana*, with partial embryos forming deficient larvae, the experiments on first quartet embryos suggest that the mechanism of determination of the embryonic axes of symmetry may be similar to that of the equally cleaving gastropod molluscs, in which positional relationships and interactions among blastomeres are crucial in establishing developmental pathways. The polyclads, therefore, might serve as an appropriate model for an ancestral form that gave rise to the two different developmental pathways characterizing present day higher Spiralia.

Demonstration of mosaicism in polyclads raises questions as to the time and site of localization of cytoplasmic determinants. Scanning electron microscopic examination of the zygotes and early cleavage stages of *Hoploplana* has revealed pronounced shape changes and alterations of surface morphology during the maturation divisions which may be related to the localization process. During first polar body extrusion, large blebs appear on the surface, primarily in the animal hemisphere, and one quadrant is characteristically smoother than the others. Second polar body formation again is accompanied be cycle of asymmetric surface blebbing, though it is less pronounced (Boyer et al., 1988). Preliminary study of four- and eight-cell embryos suggests that the surface of one of the macromeres is smoother than that of the other three (Boyer and Wallace, 1989). These asymmetric shape changes during meiosis and early development may correlate with a primitive form of morphogenetic segregation and beginning quadrant specialization foreshadowing the more definitive cytoplasmic localization characteristics of the higher spiralian groups.

Though blebbing is primarily an animal hemisphere phenomenon that may involve the localization of morphogenetic determinants, it is not clear that the episodic nature or the regionalization of the surface changes are related to the localization process. One approach to these problems is to remove portions of the vegetal region during the maturation divisions and examine the effects on development. Whether these experiments were done before the first blebbing cycle, between cycles, or after the second cycle, approximately two thirds of the larvae were completely normal (Boyer, 1988). These results provide further evidence that the localization of cytoplasmic determinants which perhaps is reflected in the blebbing, occurs primarily in the animal hemisphere, unlike in the higher spiralians were cytoplasmic determinants are localized in the vegetal region. They also indicate that the sequestering of any determinants in the vegetal hemisphere, such as an inhibitor of eye development, probably are not occurring during meiosis.

The uniformity of cleavage pattern and cell lineage among the widely diverse groups belonging to the Spiralia provides strong evidence of descent from a common ancestor, probably a flatworm. In contrast to the acoel, which are regulative, experimental analysis of the *Hoploplana* embryo indicates that the blastomeres are determined by two cell stage and development, therefore, is fundamentally mosaic. This suggests that early embryonic determination and quartet spiral cleavage are always associated and probably represent a primitive, strongly conserved evolutionary condition. However the lack of consistent blastomere localization patterns between *Hoploplana* embryos and the absence of a morphogenetically significant cell corresponding to the D macromere of higher Spiralia, indicate that the developmental pattern is less rigid than in higher forms. In summary, the regulative nature of acoel development associated with duet cleavage and the relatively loose mosaicism of the polyclads, suggest that determinative development became associated with spiral cleavage in the quartet pattern during the evolutionary history of the Turbellaria and subsequently became a permanent feature of the protostome line.

COMPARATIVE EMBRYOLOGY OF TURBELLARIA. MAIN FEATURES AND OPEN QUESTIONS

Early mode of cleavage: spiral quartet or duets ? Its bearing on mosaic versus regulative development

Although all turbellarians with entolecithal eggs have spiral cleavage, there are two basic patterns of cleavage: 1) quartet cleavage, similar to that of most higher spiralians; and 2) duet cleavage, characterized so far only in Acoela. This raises the question of whether the duet system in acoels represents a primitive stem pattern of spiral cleavage or is a derived character that arose secondarily in this particular group.

If embryonic determination (mosaicism) is considered to be a specialized character derived from indeterminate (regulative) development, the primitiveness of the duet mode of cleavage is supported by the regulative capacity of the acoel embryo (Boyer, 1971). This would suggest that spiral cleavage preceded mosaicism in evolution and that only later on this type of cleavage became associated with the early programming of cell fate, as in higher spiralians. The relatively loose mosaicism of polyclads could then be considered an intermediate stage between the regulative development of acoels and the more rigid determination of the higher spiralians.

The apparent simplicity of this hypothesis is not supported by some of the data on acoel morphology and phylogenetic reconstruction theory. First, as pointed out by Ax (1987), the quartet mode is very widespread in many Eubilateria whereas duets have only been described in Acoela; therefore, if spiral duets were the primitive mode of spiral cleavage the quartet mode would have arisen by convergence several times, a very unparsimonious explanation (*sensu* Hennig, 1966). Second, recent studies have changed the traditional view of considering acoels a very primitive group. Indeed, some features of this group previously considered as primitive (e.g. lack of true gut and protonephridia, interconnection of ciliary rootlets and presence of additional rootlets in the epidermis) are now thought to be advanced derived features (Ehlers, 1985). Third, all neoophorans retaining spiral cleavage also have the quartet mode with unequal sized blastomeres as in polyclads and higher spiralians.

An alternative, more parsimonious view proposes that the ancestors of acoels had regulative development and quartet spiral cleavage, and that the duet pattern is derived. This transition to duet cleavage may have occured once, simply by suppression of one meridional early cleavage, probably the second. In this view, quartet spiral cleavage and regulative (as opposed to mosaic) development represent the primitive condition in Platyhelminthes and all Eubilateria, and gave rise first to the loose mosaicism of polyclads and subsequently to strict mosaicism associated with the unequal cleavage of higher spiralians. The duet cleavage pattern of acoels, retaining the primitive regulative type of development is considered to be a derived secondary modification that arose very early in the evolution of the Turbellaria.

A final answer to these questions of quartet *vs* duet spiral cleavage and regulative *vs* mosaic development awaits further studies. In particular descriptive and experimental analyses of development in other turbellarian orders such as Nemertodermatida and Macrostomida, as well as of the sister group of Platyhelminthes, the Gnathostomulida, are necessary. Moreover, the introduction of techniques of molecular taxonomy (namely the sequencing of 18S and 28S ribosomal genes) in investigations of restricted key groups should provide essential information.

Early cleavage: equal or unequal ?

Whereas CD and D blastomeres in spiral cleavage embryos (e.g. annelids and molluscs) generally are larger than the other blastomeres, it is still uncertain if unequal or equal cleavage can be considered as primitive. AB and CD blastomeres are known to differ in size in some polyclad species (e.g. *Pseudostylochus* sp, and *Notoplana*, Teshirogi et al., 1981; *Hoploplana*, Boyer, 1987) though these differences are very small and not constant (embryos of the same species have either equal or unequal blastomeres); besides, other species have homoquadratic cleavage. Similarly, A and B cells of acoels are usually equal in size. In contrast, unequal cleavage and different sized blastomeres have been reported in several neoophoran species that retain spiral cleavage in early development. In the lecitoepitheliate *Xenoprorhyncus steinboecki*, the D macromere is the largest (Reisinger et al. 1974), whereas in the rhabdocoel *Paravortex gemellipara* (Ball, 1916) and in the proseriate *Monocelis fusca* Giesa (1966), CD and D blastomeres are clearly larger than AB and C blastomeres respectively. These results led Thomas (1986) to suggest that unequal cleavage is primitive and that homoquadratic (equal) cleavage in polyclads is a derived character.

The instances of equal cleavage in polyclads and acoels associated with loose mosaicism and a regulative development respectively, in conjunction with studies on higher spiralians in which early determination is associated with unequal cleavage and polar lobes (and later determination in forms with equal cleavage), suggest, instead, that equal cleavage is the primitive condition and that unequal cleavage evolved later associated to an early pattern of cell determination, this being a more parsimonious explanation. If this is so, the presence of unequal cleavage in neoophoran orders retaining spiral cleavage should be considered as derived from archoophoran forms with slight heteroquadratic cleavages. Further studies are needed, namely in Macrostomida, to trace this presumed connection.

Ectoteloblasts do not exist in Turbellaria

Whereas in most higher spiralians, the 2d blastomere (called the first somatoblast in polychaetes and the ectoteloblast in oligochaetes and hirudineans) gives rise to most of the noncephalic ("trunk") epidermis, in archoophoran turbellarians, noncephalic epidermis originates from several second and third quartet micromeres. The basis for this fundamental difference is unknown and deserves immediate further investigation.

Do the Turbellaria form typical mesodermal bands ?

In most Spiralia, the 4d blastomere, also called second somatoblast (or mesoteloblast in the Hirudinea) forms most mesodermal derivatives. In annelids, this cell is known to sink into the anterior end of the embryo, dividing first bilaterally and later teloblastically to give rise to a rostro-caudal bandlet composed of several blast cells that, after a series of stereotyped divisions, form the mesodermal area of the germinal band. Within mesodermal bands, coelomic cavities arise by a schizocoelic process.

In polyclads, the 4d cell or mesoblast sinks into the interior of the embryo during gastrulation. Later, it divides into $4d^1$ and $4d^2$ cells; the latter forms the endoderm and the former divides bilaterally and, through a teloblastic-like mode of division, gives rise to short mesodermal band that soon disperses and forms several elements of the parenchyma. In the lecitoepitheliate *Xenoprorhyncus steinboecki*, the 4d mesoblast divides bilaterally and gives rise to short uniserial mesodermal bands which soon disintegrate into mesenchymal cells, that can no longer be traced. Neither polyclads nor lecitoepitheliates form coelomic cavities within these transitory mesodermal bands.

Can mesodermal bands of turbellarians, however rare and transient, be considered true mesodermal bands ? And if so, do they represent a primitive state of mesoderm formation or a simplified derived state paralleling true mesoderm band formation in higher spiralians ? Although a clear answer can not presently be given, it is most parsimonious to think that the primitive teloblastic mode of proliferation and the loose arrangement of blastic cells in the Turbellaria represent the primitive state of mesoderm formation in spiralians. Moreover, this suggests, in turn, that turbellarians are true acoelomate organisms and not "reduced" coelomates that lost the coelomic cavities secondarily. However, cell lineage studies using macromolecular tracers clearly are needed to follow the fate of these cells compared to similar lineages worked out for blast cells in other spiralians, particularly in leeches (Weisblat, 1984) and oligochaetes (Shimizu, 1982), as well as to ascertain their determinate of regulative nature.

Establishment of the embryo body plan. Similarities and differences within Turbellaria

Comparison of Figure 4 (archoophoran polyclads) with Figure 7 and 9 (the neoophoran rabdocoels and triclads) in conjunction with a survey of the literature leaves little doubt, both as to the unity of neoophorans with regard to body plan as well as to the great differences between neoophorans and archoophorans.

If differences in the embryological origin of the embryonic ectoderm (hull membrane) are set aside (see Thomas, 1986, for a thorough discussion on the diverse origin of the hull membrane), the unity of neoophorans stems from the similar pattern of middle-late development that may be staged into four main periods: 1) aggregation of blastomeres to form the embryonic anlage or blastema; 2) bilateral and anteroposterior determination (segregation) of the embryonic anlage into the primordia of brain (anterior), pharynx (middle) and genital organs (posterior); 3) histotypical determination (segregation) of the germ layers (namely the definitive ectoderm and endoderm) from the peripheral cells of all primordia, and 4) dorsal spreading of the definitive ectoderm to close over the yolk cells and form the definitive body wall.

Although neoophoran development bears little resemblance to the development of polyclads (see Fig.11), another archo-ophoran group, the Macrostomida, shows transitional forms leading towards neoophoran development. *Macrostomum appendi-culatum* studied by Seiler-Aspang (1957), forms a sort of transitory embryonic ectoderm (or hull membrane) from the macromeres, followed by the formation of an embryonic anlage or blastema along the future ventral surface of the embryo from which the three anteroposterior primordia segregate, as in neoophorans (Fig.11 b). Moreover, the neoophoran lecitoepi-theliate *Xenoprorhynchus steinboecki* (Reisinger et al., 1974), during early cleavage bears a close resemblance to the spiral pattern of polyclads and other archoophorans but in middle-late development follows a process similar to that seen in

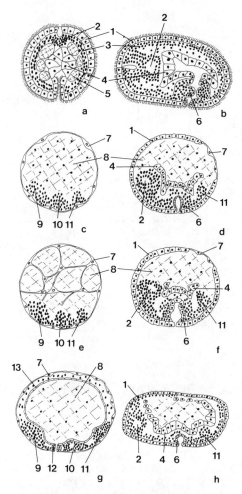

FIG.11. Generalized comparative schemes of late developmental stages in polyclads (a, shortly after
epiboly; b, before hatching); macrostomids (c, after
primordia formation; d, near completion of epidermal
spreading); rhabdocoels (e, after primordia formation; f, near dorsal closure by epidermal spreading);
and triclads (g, after primordia formation; h, after
epidermal spreading and body wall formation). 1,
definitive ectoderm (epidermis); 2, brain anlage; 3,
mesoderm; 4, definitive endoderm; 5, yolk globules;
6, definitive pharynx; 7, embryonic ectoderm (hull
membrane); 8, yolk contained within blastomeres (c,
d) or into yolk cells (e–h); 9, anterior (brain)
anlage; 10, middle (pharyngeal) anlage; 11, posterior
(genital) anlage; 12, embryonic pharynx; 13,
embryonic intestine. (b, c and d, modified from
Thomas, 1986; a, e, f, g and h, modified from Hyman,
1951).

Macrostomum. This has led Thomas (1986) to consider that
development in *Macrostomum* may represent a form of
preadaptation to ectolecithy and, therefore that the most
important differences in development occur not between
Archoophora and Neophora, but between the former and some

species of Macrostomida. These embryonic similarities agree with the phylogenetic schemes proposed by Karling (1974) and Ehlers (1985) (see Figure 2), based primarily on morphological features in adults. They suggest, however, a more central role for the macrostomids with regard to the origin of Neoophora, and closer relationship between Prolecitophorata, Proseriata and Tricladida on one hand, and fundamental differences between this latter group and the Rhabdocoela on the other.

The formation of body axes in neoophorans, as well as in macrostomids, seems to occur basically within the embryonic anlage formed by the aggregation and proliferation of blastomers at the ventral side of the future embryo. Within this mass of cells, bilateral and anteroposterior anlagen are later determined, though the actual mechanism (or mechanisms) are completely unknown. How can this process be compared to body axis formation in archoophorans, namely polyclads ? In the latter, definitive body axes arise from the shifting of the animal pole towards an anterior position, while the vegetal pole (indicated by the pharynx) occupies a ventro-caudal position (Fig.11 a, b). It is in this late stage that polyclads appear strikingly similar to neoophorans (Fig.11 c-j), the main difference being that whereas polyclad embryos are already delimited, due to gastrulation, by the definitive body wall or ectoderm, the ectoderm in neoophorans has just segregated from peripheral cells of the blastema and starts spreading dorsally to close the embryo.

This difference has led several authors (Ball, 1916; Giesa, 1966; Reisinger et al., 1974; Thomas, 1986) to consider the process of epibolic gastrulation in polyclads to be homologous to the period spanning from hull membrane formation to epidermal dorsal spreading in neoophorans. However, only the second would constitute gastrulation in the classical sense of positioning germ layers in the embryo. If this homology is accepted, some difficulties arise, the primary one being that the so-called blastopore in neoophorans (formed by epidermal spreading) occurs on the dorsal side of the embryo, whereas in polyclads it is formed on the ventral surface where mouth opening and pharynx formation occur.

To overcome this difficulty, Thomas (1986) considers that dorsal location of the blastopore in neoophorans is simply due to the fact that epidermal epiboly in this group is delayed with regard to establishment of body axes, whereas in polyclads the converse is true, that is, gastrulation occurs before establishment of the organ anlagen and body axes. Since definitive body axes in polyclads are established by an anterior (90°) shift in the animal-vegetal axis after gastrulation (see Fig.4), a similar shift must occur before cleavage in neoophorans (probably due to a rearrangement in ooplasmic determinants within the egg) to explain the occurrence of the blastopore in a dorsal position.

This hypothesis, however ingenious is open to criticism. First, as Dawydoff (1928) pointed out, the embryonic ectoderm or hull membrane is a transient, embryonic structure of diverse embryological origin (either from macromeres, micromeres or yolk cells; see Thomas, 1986) that under any circumstance can not be related to the definitive germ layers. Moreover, it is not involved in the process of gastrulation.Instead, formation of the hull membrane seems, at least functionally, to be homologous to the development of other types of provisional embryonic structures such as the provisional epithelium of leeches derived from the expanding micromeres (Ho and Weisblat, 1987) and similar structures found in oligochaetes (Shimizu, 1982). Second, the so-called epibolic gastrulation by dorsal spreading of epidermal cells in neoophorans is strikingly similar to some processes found in diverse phyla. These include the dorsal closure by the definitive ectoderm in leeches (Weisblat et al., 1984) and in insects (e.g. *Drosophila*, Campos-Ortega and Hartenstein, 1985) both of which occur in yolk-rich embryos after gastrulation. This similarity supports the idea that epidermal spreading in neoophorans is not related to gastrulation and, hence, that the point of closure of the epidermis can not be considered a blastopore. Third, in organisms such as neoophorans with cells (blastomeres) remaining scattered during considerable periods in early development, it is rather difficult conceive of axial shifting of determinants within the egg as reponsible for axial body determination. And last, but not least, no evidence has been produced so far to substantiate any of the proposals suggested by Thomas (1986), namely the shift of the animal-vegetal body axis in neoophorans and, especially, the presence and axial shift of ooplasmic determinants.

The main difficulty seems to lie in defining when gastrulation begins and when the gastrula stage is attained in neoophorans. If gastrulation is defined as the laying down of the classical germ layers (ectoderm, mesoderm and endoderm), the stage of segregation (separation) of ectoderm or endoderm *versus* the other cells in the anlagen (Figs.7 f-i and Fig.9 i, j for rhabdocoels and triclads respectively) is the one that fits best. In this case the gastrula stage is attained when the three germ layers are clearly separated from each other (Figs.7 and 9 j respectively), that is, well before epidermal spreading starts and considerably later than formation of hull membranes.

If this view is accepted, the problem posed by the appearance of a dorsal "blastopore" disappears, as this structure does not fit the definition. Instead, as happens even in polyclads, the mouth opening and the epithelium of the pharynx will appear later on by invagination of the definitive ectoderm. However, the actual mechanisms operating during segregation of the germ layers in neoophorans, probably involving complex phenomena of cell-cell interaction and establishment of new positional cues, is one of the main problems posed by development in the Turbellaria and certainly merits further study in.

Early determination in turbellarian development: topological (territorial) or histotypical ?

One of the traditional dogmas of classical embryology states that determination (segregation) of germ layers (usually a consequence of gastrulation) is one of the early, if not the earliest, determinative events in animal development. Recent molecular and genetic data, gathered in several systems (see Gardner and Lawrence, 1985, for general references), in conjunction with redescription of cell lineages using new tracer methods, have cast serious doubts on this traditional wisdom. First, it has been clearly shown in several systems

Table 1. COMPARISON OF CELL LINEAGES BETWEEN POLYCLADS AND HIGHER SPIRALIANS

Blastomeres	Phylum			
	Platyhelminthes (Polycladida)	Nemertea	Annelida	Mollusca
1st quartet (1m)	Epidermis (a/d) Nervous system (cephalic)	Epidermis (a) Nervous system (cephalic) Stomodeum	Epidermis (a) Nervous system (cephalic) Prototroche	Epidermis (a) Nervous system (cephalic)
2nd quartet (2m)	Epidermis (p/v) Nervous system ('trunk')	Epidermis (p) Nervous system ('trunk')	Epidermis (p) Neurotroche	Epidermis (p) Mesenchyme Nervous system
3rd quartet (3m)	Epidermis (p) Mesenchyme	Proctodeum Mesenchyme	Mesenchyme	Epidermis (p) Mesenchyme
4th quartet (4m)	$4d \nearrow 4d^1$ Mesoderm $\searrow 4d^2$ Endoderm	$4d \rightarrow$ Mesodermal bands	$4d \rightarrow$ Mesodermal bands	$4d \rightarrow$ Mesodermal bands
MACROMERES	(disintegrate and resorbed)	Endoderm	Endoderm	Endoderm

Side labels: HEAD, 'TRUNK' (right); MICROMERES, SOMEROMERES (left)

[1]
Summarized from Surface, 1907; Hyman, 1951; Kato, 1968; Shimizu, 1982; and Weisblat et al, 1984.

Abbreviations: a, anterior; p, posterior; a/d, antero-dorsal; p/v, postero-ventral

that cells from a particular germ layer can give rise to cells traditionally considered to belong to a different one. Second, the use of molecular probes to detect expression of developmental and cell lineage products (or genes) during early development, have shown them to be restricted to topological defined areas (e.g. head *vs* tail, alternate segments, etc,...) rather than to particular germ layers. Finally, cell lineage studies indicate that particular blastomeres give rise to topologically restricted areas of the embryo, from which descendants of more than one germ layer originate. In particular, the first quartet of micromeres in spiralian embryos has been shown repeatedly to form mainly cephalic structures with ectodermal and mesodermal descendants.

It is instructive in this context to compare cell lineages between polyclads and higher spiralians. Table 1 summarizes the main results, and illustrates a particular point worthy of discussion. As occurs in higher spiralians, the first quartet of micromeres gives rise to most cephalic structures, as opposed to "trunk" (body) structures that are formed from the rest of the blastomeres. However, the question of whether head determination is due to the existence of particular determinants present in the animal pole (or animal hemisphere) of the egg, or to cell-cell interactions between first quartet micromeres and macromeres, as indicated by Boyer (1989) and Boyer and Wallace (1989) in polyclads remains unresolved. This important problem merits further study using new techniques of cell lineage, experimental embryology and, if available, molecular probes of topographical restricted products.

It is in neoophorans, however, that the dichotomy topological *vs* histotypical determination becomes more evident. Germ layers arise here "de novo" from a mass of cells (blastema anlage) that earlier on had segregated topologically into three antero-posterior masses. This topological process seems formally equivalent to the presumed head/trunk determination in archoophorans and other spiralians. With regard to particular mechanisms, no specific model can be advanced, though cell-cell interactions as well as positional cues may be involved. In this case, however, no particular cues from the embryo as a whole, and even less from the oocyte, can be envisioned. Instead, the embryonic anlage or blastema self-organizes, probably through cellular interactions or through antero-posterior and dorso-ventral cues that, whatever they may turn out to be , must develop anew.

Development and regeneration

The process of topological determination (segregation) during development in neoophorans bears a striking parallelism with the well studied process of regeneration in turbellaria, mainly in the neoophoran freshwater triclads. Indeed, the main stages, general morphology, and cellular details of formation of the brain ganglia and, most especially, the pharynx during embryonic development in rhabdocoela (see Hyman, (1951) and in the proseriate *Monocelis fusca* (Giesa, 1966; see in particular his Figs. 40 A-D and 41 A-E) are strikingly similar to the stage of brain and pharynx formation during regeneration in freshwater triclads (Baguñà, 1973).

Like development in neoophoran embryos, regeneration involves the agregation of undifferentiated cells (called neoblasts in the adult) near the wound due to mixed processes of cell proliferation and cell migration (Saló and Baguñà, 1984, 1989) followed by early determination of different regions (head, pharynx,..) along the antero-posterior axis, and later on by histotypical differentiation of tissues and organs (for general references, see Baguñà et al., 1988). Although much data has accumulated in the last 20 years, the main mechanisms involved in topological an histotypical determination during regeneration are almost unknown. Again, it is thought that cell-cell interactions and, if any, the establishment of new positional cues, must be key events in the process.

Given the similarities between both processes, the difficulties of working with neoophoran embryos, and the easier handling and better knowledge of regeneration in freshwater triclads, the advances in the knowledge of the later would

Table 2.   NEW APPROACHES TO FOSTER THE KNOWLEDGE OF EMBRYONIC
           DEVELOPMENT IN TURBELLARIA

1) Introduction of new techniques of cell lineage
(macromolecular tracers, genetic markers, retro-viruses,
embryonic chimaeres..) to get a complete description of
cell lineages in suitable turbellarian groups, namely
Acoela and Polycladida.

2) Use of molecular probes (monoclonal antibodies, lectins,
gene probes,..) to detect determinants of a) embryonic
axial polarity, and b) topographical and histotypical
segregations in early development.

3) To undertake a careful screening, namely within Acoela
and Polycladida, to find the best available species
fulfilling most of the criteria needen to start a genetic
analysis of development. In the meantime, the construction
of genomic libraries from suitable species of turbellarians
and their screening using probes of developmentally
regulated genes (e.g. the "homeo-box" and several cellular
proto-oncogenes from *Drosophila* and other organisms), may
be highly rewarding.

contribute in the future to a better understanding of the
similar processes taking place within neoophoran embryos.

FUTURE TRENDS

Table 2 summarizes the main trends needed to stimulate the
knowledge of the embryonic development and their mechanisms in
Turbellaria.

First and foremost, new methods of cell lineage, namely
the introduction of macromolecular tracers (e.g. horseradish
peroxidase, fluorescence dextrans, lucifer yellow dextran,..)
into blastomeres are needed to follow cell lineages from early
to late embryos and adults. This will be essential to validate,
modify and extend the lineages worked out by early authors as
well as to obtain a wealth of new data unattainable using the
classical methods. As regards suitable groups to work with,
acoels and polyclads seem to be the groups of choice, though
"transitional" groups between archoophorans and neoophorans
such as Macrostomida and those neoophorans retaining spiral
cleavage must not be neglected.

Besides macromolecular markers, other more sophisticated
lineage techniques such as retroviral insertion of marker
(reporter) genes, easy to detect (e.g. β-galactosidase), may be
useful namely in neoophorans, where classical and recent
lineage methods are difficult to use. Moreover, the development
of "in vitro" culture of neoophoran embryos jointly with
suitable cell markers (chromosomal, ploidy, biochemical,..) may
enable to make chimaeric embryos and introduce them as a new
powerful technique of analysis.

A second set of methods use molecular probes to detect the
differential expression of genes and/or their products as
markers of embryonic axial polarity, topographical and

histotypical segregations, and cell differentiation. How may these molecular markers be obtained ? At the molecular level, the most promising technique, already employed successfully in different groups of organisms, will be to use cDNA libraries, obtained from mRNAs of either different stages of development or different regions of the embryo, and screen them for differentially expressed products. A different approach consists in raising monoclonal antibodies to detect stage-specific, and region and cell-specific antigens and study their cellular location and expression. Also useful, though less informative, is the study of the stage-specific and region and cell-specific changes in the protein pattern by two-dimensional (2-D) electrophoresis. Once detected and isolated, and when specific antibodies are raised against them, these specific polypeptides could serve as temporal and spatial markers of the embryonic develoment. Finally, growth factors and their inhibitors, as well as specific antibodies against them can be used to study the role of these factors in the control of cell proliferation (see Baguñà et al., 1988, for a similar approach in regenerating freshwater triclads), cell-cell interactions and inductive phenomena during development.

The third approach, the genetic analysis of development, represents the best way to get a full understanding of the mechanisms by which embryonic development is controlled. Essentially, it consists in obtaining mutations that affect development to trace from their phenotypic effects the hypothetic role of the wild type gene. *Drosophila*, later on the nematode *Caenorhabditis elegans*, and more recently the plant *Arabidopsis thaliana,* have become commonplace names associated with the genetic control of development.

What are the prospects of undertaking a mutagenesis program in turbellarians aimed at obtaining mutants that affects the process of development ? For fast and reliable genetic analysis, organisms must be small, easy to culture and handle, with external development and transparent eggs, short-lived, with several generations per year, and having as many offsprings as possible and a small genome. Moreover, methods to detect and recover individuals bearing induced mutations should be devised and tested. As far as we know, such a program has not been tried so for in any turbellarian. Leaving aside neoophorans, some archoophorans can be considered to be good candidates, namely some acoels, polyclads and macrostomids. They are small, easy to culture and handle, with external development within transparent egg capsules, have a reasonably low number of chromosomes (2n = 6 for most macrostomids; 2n = 6 to 12, in some acoels), and though data of genome sizes are not available for most species, recent data obtained from the bigger and more complex freshwater triclads (e.g. 8.0 X 10^8 base pairs for haploid genome in *Dugesia (S) polychroa*; Prats, Romero and Baguñà, unpublished data), suggest that their genomes would be rather small. On the negative side, turbellarians are, with two or three exceptions, hermaphrodites, and no males are known. Since hermaphrodites alone are of little use for genetic analysis because they offer no means for recombining genes between individuals, this represents a major drawback for genetic analysis in turbellarians. However some methods can be devised to suppress female development and turn some organisms into functional males (Schierenberg, personal communication).

Meanwhile, and until the best available species of turbellarian that, while being amenable to developmental studies also have most of the criteria required to make classical genetics feasible is found, an alternative approach, successfully employed in several groups of organisms, must be tried. This is to screen genomic and cDNA libraries of suitable turbellarians for homologous sequences to the homeobox of *Drosophila* and other organisms, as well as for sequences homologous to proto-oncogenes and several growth factors know to play a key role in embryonic development. Although sequences as such have not been found yet in turbellarians, probably due to the phyletic distance between Platyhelminthes and other Eubilateria (Field et al., 1988; Riutort, Field, Raff and Baguñà, unpublished data), more sophisticated techniques of gene screening will uncover them in the near future. If this, in conjunction with classical genetic analysis, will turn out to be attainable, turbellarians may become, after *Drosophila* and *Caenorhabditis elegans*, a new key organism in Developmental Biology and Developmental Genetics, with the additional bonus of their privileged phyletic position.

ACKNOWLEDGEMENTS

We are most grateful to Dr. Maria Ribas and colleagues in the Departament de Genètica (Barcelona) for preparation of figures and for typing the manuscript. This work was supported by grants from Comisión Asesora de Investigación Científica y Técnica (CAICYT; PB85-0094) to J.B., and by Research Corporation grants, NSF grant DCB-8817760 and the Union College Faculty Research Fund to B.C.B.

REFERENCES

Anderson, D.T., 1977, The embryonic and larval development of the turbellarian *Notoplana australis* (Schmarde, 1859) (Polycladida; Leptoplanidae), *Aust.J.Mar.Freshwater Res.*, 28:303-310.

Apelt, G., 1969, Fortpflanzungsbiologie, Entwicklungszyklen und vergleichende Frühentwicklung acoeler Turbellarien, *Mar.Biol.*, 4:267-325.

Ax, P., 1987, "The Phylogenetic System," John Wiley & Sons, Chichester.

Ax, P., and Dörjes, J., 1966, *Oligochoerus limnophilus* nov. spec., ein kaspisches Faunenelement als erster Süsswasservertreter der Turbellaria Acoela in Flüssen, Mitteleuropas, *Int.Rev.ges.Hydrobiol.*, 57:15-144.

Baguñà, J., 1973, Estudios citotaxonómicos, ecológicos e histofisiologia de la regulación morfogenética durante el crecimiento y la regeneración de la raza asexuada de la planaria *Dugesia mediterranea* n. sp. Ph. D. Thesis, University of Barcelona.

Baguñà, J., 1981, Planarian neoblast, *Nature*, 290:14-15.

Baguñà, J., and Romero, R., 1981, Quantitative analysis of cell types during growth, degrowth and regeneration in the planarians *Dugesia(S)mediterranea* and *Dugesia(G)tigrina*, *Hydrobiologia*, 84:181-194.

Baguñà, J., Saló, E., Collet, J., Auladell, M.C., and Ribas, M., 1988, Cellular, molecular and genetic approaches to regeneration and pattern formation in planarians,

    Fortschr.Zool., 36:65-78.
Ball, S.C., 1916, The development of *Paravortex gemellipara*
    (Graffilla gemellipara Linton), *J.Morphol.*, 27:453-558.
Barnes, R.D., 1968, "Invertebrate Zoology," Saunders,
    Philadelphia.
Barnes, R.S.K., Calow, P., and Olive, P.J.W., 1988, "The
    Invertebrates: a new synthesis," Blackwell, Oxford.
Beauchamp, P. de, 1961, Classe des Turbellariés: Turbellaria
    (Ehrenberg,1831), *in:* "Traité de Zoologie," Vol.4, 1:35-
    212, Masson, Paris.
Benazzi, M., and Gremigni, V., 1982, Developmental biology of
    triclad turbellarians (Planaria), *in:* "Developmental
    Biology of Freshwater Invertebrates," pp 151-211,
    Harrison, F.H., and Cowden, R.R., eds Alan R. Liss, New
    York.
Bogomolov, S.I., 1960, The development of *Convoluta* in
    connection with the morphology of the turbellarians,
    Trudy Obshch.Estest.Kazan.Gos.Univ., 63:155-208 (in
    Russian).
Boyer, B.C., 1971, Regulative development in a spiralian embryo
    as shown by cell deletion experiments on the acoel
    Childia, *J.Exp.Zool.*, 176:97-106.
Boyer, B.C., 1986, Determinative development in the polyclad
    turbellarian *Hoploplana inquilina*,
    Int.J.Invertebr.Reprod.and Develpt., 9:243-251.
Boyer, B.C., 1987, Development of *in vitro* fertilized embryos
    of the polyclad flatworm *Hoploplana inquilina* following
    blastomere separation and deletion, *Roux's.Archiv
    Dev.Biol.*, 196:158-164.
Boyer, B.C., 1988, The effects if removing vegetal cytoplasm
    during the maturation divisions on the development of
    Hoploplana inquilina (Turbellaria, Polycladida),
    Fortschr.Zool., 36:277-282.
Boyer, B.C., 1989, The role of the first quartet micromeres in
    the development of the polyclad *Hoploplana inquilina*,
    Biol.Bull., (in press).
Boyer, B.C., Arnold, J.M., and Landolfa, M., 1988, Origins of
    mosaic development.: Zygote surface differentiation
    during meiosis in the polyclad flatworm *Hoploplana*,
    Int.J.Invertebr.Reprod. and Develpt., 13:157-170.
Boyer, B.C., and Wallace, G.A., 1989, Early cleavage and the
    role of the macromeres in the development of the poyclad
    flatworm *Hoploplana*, *Biol.Bull.* (in press).
Bresslau, E., 1904, Beiträge zur Entwicklungsgeschichte der
    Turbellarien. I. Die Entwicklung der Rhabdocölen und
    Alloiocölen, *Z.wiss.Zool.*, 76:213-332.
Cameron, R.A., Hough-Evans, B.R., Britten, R.J., and Davidson,
    E.H., 1987, Lineage and fate of each blastomere of the
    eight-cell sea urchin embryo, *Genes.Dev.*, 1:75-84.
Campos-Ortega, J.A., and Hartenstein, V., 1985, "The Embryonic
    Development of *Drosophila melanogaster*," Springer-
    Verlag, Berlin.
Costello, D.P., and Henley, C., 1976, Spiralian development: a
    perspective, *Amer.Zool.*, 16:277-291.
Crezée, M., 1982, Turbellaria, *in:* "Synopsis and Classification
    of Living Organisms," Parker, S.P. ed. McGraw-Hill, New
    York, 1:718-740.
Davidson, E.H., 1986, "Gene Activity in Early Development,"
    Academic Press, New York.
Dawydoff, C., 1928, "Traité d'Embryologie Comparée des
    Invertébrés," Masson, Paris.

Ehlers, U., 1984, Phylogenetisches System der Plathelminthes, *Verh.Naturwiss.Ver.Hamburg* (N.F.), 27:291-294.

Ehlers, U., 1985, "Das Phylogenetische System der Plathelminthes," G. Fischer, Stuttgart.

Ehlers, U., 1986, Comments on a phylogenetic system of the Platyhelminthes, *Hydrobiologia*, 132:1-12.

Field, K.G., Olsen, G.J., Lane, D.J., Giovannoni, S.J., Ghiselin, M.T., Raff, E.C., Pace, N.R., and Raff, R.A., 1988, Molecular phylogeny of the animal kingdom, *Science*, 239:748-753.

Gardner, R.L., and Lawrence, P.A. eds, 1986, "Single Cell Marking and Cell Lineage in Animal Development," The Royal Society, London.

Giesa, S., 1966, Die Embryonalentwicklung von *Monocelis fusca* Oersted (Turbellaria, Proseriata), *Z.Morphol.Okol.Tiere*, 57:137-230.

Gremigni, V., 1988, A comparative ultrastructural study of homocellular and heterocellular female gonads in free-living Platyhelminthes-Turbellaria, *Fortschr.Zool.*, 36:245-261.

Hendelberg, J., 1974, Spermiogenesis, sperm morphology, and biology of fertilization in the Turbellaria, *in:* "Biology of the Turbellaria," Riser, N.W., and Morse, M.P. eds, McGraw-Hill, New York, 148-164

Hendelberg, J., 1986, The phylogenetic significance of sperm morphology in the Platyhelminthes, *Hydrobiologia*, 132:53-58.

Henley, C., 1974, Platyhelminthes (Turbellaria), *in:* "Reproduction of Marine Invertebrates," Vol 1, Giese, A.C., and Pearse, J.S. eds., Acad.Press, New York, 267-343.

Henning, W., 1966, "Phylogenetic Systematics," University of Illinois Press, Chicago.

Ho, R.K., and Weisblat, D.A., 1987, A provisional epithelium in leech embryo: cellular origins and influence on a developmental equivalence group, *Dev.Biol.*, 120:520-534.

Hori, H.A., Muto, A., Osawa, S., Takai, M., Lue, K.Y., and Kawakatsu, M., 1988, Evolution of Turbellaria as deduced from 5S ribosomal RNA sequences, *Fortschr.Zool.*, 36:163-168.

Hyman, L.H., "The Invertebrates: Platyhelminthes and Rhynchocoela," Vol. II, McGraw-Hill, New York.

Ivanova-Kasas, O.M., 1982, Phylogenetic significance of spiral cleavage, *in:* "Evolutionary Embryology," Plenum Press (translated from *Biologiya Morya*, 5:3-14, in russian).

Kaestner, A., 1984, "Lehrbuch der Speziellen Zoologie," Vol.I. G. Fischer, Stuttgart.

Karling, T.G., 1974, On the anatomy and affinities of the turbellarian orders, *in:* "Biology of the Turbellaria," Riser, N.W., and Morse, M.P. eds, McGraw-Hill, New York.

Kato, K., 1940, On the development of some Japanese polyclads, *Japan.J.Zool.*, 8:537-573.

Kato, K., 1968, Platyhelminthes (Class Turbellaria), *in:* "Invertebrate Embryology," Kume, M., and Dan, K., eds, Nolit, Belgrade.

Le Moigne, A., 1963, Etude du développement embryonnaire de *Polycelis nigra* (Turbellarié, Triclade), *Bull.Soc.Zool.Fr.*, 88:403-422.

Reisinger, E., Cichocki, J., Erlach, R., and Szyskowitz, T., 1974, Ontogenetische Studien an Turbellarien: ein Beitrag zur Evolution der Dotterverarbeitung im ektolecithalen Ei. I. Teil, *Z.zool.Syst.Evolut.-forsch.*, 12:161-195.

Romero, R., 1987, Anàlisi cel.lular quantitativa del creixement i de la reproducció a diferentes espècies de planàries, Ph. D. Thesis, University of Barcelona.

Saló, E., and Baguñà, J., 1984, Regeneration and pattern formation in planarians. I. The pattern of mitosis in anterior and posterior regeneration in *Dugesia(G)tigrana*, and a new proposal for blastema formation, *J.Embryol.exp.Morph.*, 83:63-80.

Saló, E., and Baguñà, J., 1989, Regeneration and pattern formation in planarians. II. Local origin and role of cell movements in blastema formation, *Development*, 107:69-76.

Seiler-Aspang, F., 1957, Die Entwicklung von *Macrostomum appendiculatum* (Fabricius), *Zool.Jb.Anat.*, 76:311-330.

Seiler-Aspang, F., 1958, Entwicklungsgeschichtliche Studien an Paludicolen Tricladen, *W.Roux's Arch.*, 150:425-480.

Shimizu, T., 1982, Development in the freshwater oligochaete *Tubifex*, *in*: "Developmental Biology of Freshwater Invertebrates," Harrison, F.H., and Cowden, R.R. eds, Alan R. Liss, New York, pp 283-316.

Skaer, R.J., 1971, Planarians, *in*: "Experimental Embryology of Marine and Freshwater Invertebrates," Reverberi, G. ed., North-Holland, Amsterdam, pp 104-125.

Smith, J.P.S., Tyler, S., and Rieger, R.M., 1986, Is the Turbellaria polyphyletic ?, *Hydrobiologia*, 132:13-21.

Smith, J.C., Dale, L., and Slack, J.M.W., 1985, Cell lineage labels and region-specific markers in the analysis of inductive interactions, *J.Embryol.exp.Morph.*, 89; Supplement: 317-331.

Steinböck, O., 1966, Die Hofsteniiden (Turbellaria Acoela). Grundsätzliches zur Evolution der Turbellarien, *Z.zool.Syst.Evolut.-forsch*, 4:58-195.

Surface, F.M., 1907, The early development of a polyclad, *Planocera inquilina*, *Proc.Acad.nat.Sci.Philad.*, 59:514-559.

Teshirogi, W., Ishida, S., and Jatani, K., 1981, On the early development of some Japanese polyclads, *Rep.Fukaura.Mar.Biol.Lab.*, 9:2-31 (in japanese).

Thomas, M.B., 1986, Embryology of the Turbellaria and its phylogenetic significance, *Hydrobiologia*, 132:105-115.

Weisblat, D.A., Kim, S.Y., and Stent, G.S., 1984, Embryonic origins of cells in the leech *Helobdella triserialis*, *Dev.Biol.*, 104:65-85.

GROWTH, DEGROWTH AND REGENERATION AS DEVELOPMENTAL PHENOMENA IN

ADULT FRESHWATER PLANARIANS

Jaume Baguñà, Rafael Romero, Emili Saló, Joan
Collet, Carme Auladell, Maria Ribas, Marta
Riutort, Jordi García-Fernàndez, Ferràn Burgaya
and David Bueno

Departament de Genètica, Facultat de Biologia
Universitat de Barcelona
Diagonal 645, 08028 Barcelona, Spain

GENERAL INTRODUCTION

Morphological background

Freshwater planarians are Platyhelminthes belonging to the class Turbellaria, order Seriata, suborder Tricladida, infraorder Paludicola. The term Tricladida (or triclads) refers to the three main branches into which their digestive system are divided; Paludicola means members are inhabitants of freshwater habitats. Freshwater planarians are the best known planarians due to there easy culture and ease of handling under laboratory conditions and, because they have been, and still are, the most widely used turbellarian in experimental research, particularly with regards to regeneration (see Brønsted, 1969, and Gremigni, 1988, for general references).

Externally, freshwater planarians are soft bodied bilaterally symmetrical, dorso-ventrally flattened organisms, ranging in size from 4-5 millimeters to the large forms like some dendrocoelids (e.g. *Bdellocephala punctata*) that may be 40 mm long. They are common animals widely distributed in lakes, ponds and rivers throughout the world. Most freshwater planarians are some shade of grey or brown, but there are some unpigmented species (mainly dendrocoelids). Internally, they are characterized, like the rest of turbellarians, by being tripoblastic, acoelomates, and unsegmented and by the lack of circulatory, respiratory and skeletal structures. The digestive system is formed by a pharynx and a blind gut lacking an anus. A solid mass of tissue, called mesenchyme or parenchyma, fills the space between the cellular monostratified ciliated epidermis and the gut and surrounds the internal organs. The parenchyma consists of several non proliferating differentiated cell types and a particular class of undifferentiated mitotic cells usually called neoblasts (Baguñà, 1981; Ehlers, 1985).

Experimental Embryology in Aquatic Plants and Animals
Edited by H.-J. Marthy, Plenum Press, New York, 1990

Freshwater planarians have asexual, sexual, and mixed (sexual/asexual, usually seasonal) modalities of reproduction. Asexual reproduction occurs by transverse fission and forms two new individuals which regenerate the missing parts. Sexually reproducing species are hermaphrodites with cross fertilization; following copulation, they deposit egg capsules from which several hatchlings, looking like miniature adults, emerge, ready to feed and grow. The reproductive system is usually very complex, consisting of many testes and a pair of antero-dorsally located ovaries with many separate vitellaria. Eggs are ectolecithal. The copulatory apparatus is very complex and has been largely used to establish the extant classification of freshwater planarians.

Further information on planarian anatomy, collecting techniques, preparation and classification of freshwater planarians can be found in Ball and Reynoldson (1981), Benazzi and Gremigni (1982) and Cowden (1982).

Taxonomy and phyletic position

Triclads, along with rhabdocoels, are considered the most advanced members of the turbellarian neoophorans (Ehlers, 1985). According to Ball (1974; see also Ball and Reynoldson, 1981) triclads may be divided into two broad groups of uncertain taxonomical entity: a) the Haploneura, comprising the aquatic forms in which the ventral longitudinal nerve cords lie at or very near the submuscular nerve plexus; and b) the Diploneura, containing the terrestrial forms where the ventral nerve cords lie, outside the submuscular nerve plexus, in a parenchymal nerve net. The Haploneura are, in turn, divided into the infraorders Maricola, or marine triclads, and Paludicola, or freshwater planarians. This classification, mainly ecological, though not as well founded as was previously thought, also has a morphological basis which still makes it useful, although several exceptions occur (Ball, 1981).

The Paludicola or freshwater planarians are characterized by the location, anterior to the penis, of the bursa copulatrix, by the absence of precerebral intestinal diverticula and because vitellaria extend usually behind the ovaries. They are currently divided into three families: the Dugesiidae, the Planariidae and the Dendrocoeliidae, comprising altogether some 40 genera and over 300 species. Type genera are *Dugesia*, *Planaria* and *Dendrocoelum*, and type species, well known as subjects of many regenerative and ecological experiments are *Dugesia(D)gonocephala*, *Dugesia(S)lugubris*, *Polycelis nigra*, *Polycelis felina* and *Dendrocoelum lacteum*, among others.

The extant classification of Tricladida is depicted in Figure 1, and a tentative phylogeny of the group that incorporates the uncertainties exposed by Ball (1981), i.e. a possible independent origin of each infraorder from marine proseriate ancestors and a diphyletic origin for Paludicola, is shown in Figure 2.

DEVELOPMENTAL PHENOMENA IN ADULT FRESHWATER PLANARIANS

In most animal groups, adult size and form remain within strict, though slightly variable, limits. Freshwater planarians

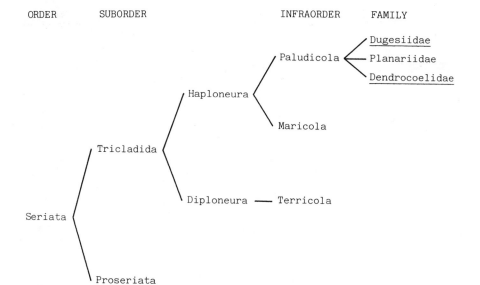

ORDER   SUBORDER   INFRAORDER   FAMILY

FIG.1. Classification of the order Seriata with specification of Tricladida infraorders and families of Paludicola. Underlined, families that furnished most of the data referred to in this paper.

are characterized by two phenomena which are clearly exceptions to this rule, i.e.: growth/degrowth and regeneration. Before an in depth discussion of each phenomenon is given, a brief sketch, in cellular terms, of freshwater planarians is needed.

Knowledge accrued to date allows us to consider the planarians to be composed of two cell populations or compartments: 1) a functional one, made by 12-14 non proliferating differentiated cell types (approx. 75-80% of the total number of cells) that are continuously replaced during the life-time of the individual, and 2) a proliferative compartment formed by a single, morphologically identifiable, population of toti-potent stem-cells (approx. 20-30% of total cells), also called neoblasts, which give rise, by differentiation to all differen-tiated functional cell types, while maintaining its own density by cell proliferation (Lange, 1968, 1983; Baguñà, 1981; Baguñà and Romero, 1981). When temperature and food are kept at the optimum (which varies for different species) planarians remain in steady-state since a balance between the number of cells (neoblasts) produced by proliferation and the number of cells lost from the functional compartment exists (Romero, 1987; Romero and Baguñà, 1988).

As a whole, planarians behave like most permanent renewing populations described in higher organisms (e.g. blood, testis, and stratified squamous epithelia in mammals), characterized by rapid and continous cell turnover in which the terminally differentiated cells have a short lifespan and are replaced through proliferation and differentiation of a distinct sub-population of cells, the stem cells.

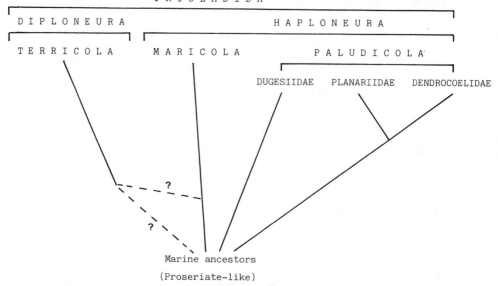

FIG.2. Diagram of the phylogenetic relationships in the Tricladida. Based on Ball (1981), slightly modified. Broken lines mean uncertain relationships.

Growth and degrowth

General data. After hatching and when maintained under conditions of plentiful food, freshwater planarians increase in length at rates which vary with temperature until a final steady-state is attained that is species-specific (Calow, 1981). In early studies, growth rates were measured in terms of body volume (Abeloos, 1930) and body length (Reynoldson, 1966); however, as this characterization of triclad size was found to introduce significant errors, a better measure, plan area (in mm^2) was introduced (Calow, 1977, 1981). It was found that, in common with most animals, triclads have sigmoidal growth curves with an exponential phase followed by a decelerating phase, before a steady-state size is reached. The coefficient of exponential growth was found to be species-specific and temperature-dependent.

Compared to other animals, planarians show a greater plasticity both in the growth of individuals and in final size. In common with other phyla (cnidarians, nemertines, and some annelids, molluscs and ascidians; see Calow, 1978, for general references) most planarians can withstand long periods of starvation, and during this time may shrink from an adult size to, and sometimes beyond, the initial size at hatching. Thus, specimens of *Dugesia (S) mediterranea* 16 mm in length decreased to less than 1 mm before disintegrating (Baguñà, 1973); similar findings have been reported by other authors (see Ball and Reynoldson, 1981, for general references).

More surprisingly, when food is given to shrunken individuals, they grow again to adult size. This process may alternate back and forth for long periods without apparent impairment of the individual or to its future maturing and breeding capacities. A detailed study of shrinkage in individuals of several species showed that the rate of degrowth was a negative exponential, tracking a continuously decelerating curve (Calow, 1978). Moreover, since shrunken adults resemble juveniles in both appearance and physiological characteristics, it was suggested (Child, 1915) that starvation not only caused worms to decrease in size but also in age; that is, degrowth results in reverse of the life-cycle or, in other words, the rejuvenation of the individual.

The cellular basis of growth and degrowth

The process of degrowth in freshwater planarians has been studied, mainly descriptively, at the tissue and organ levels. Until recently, this process was thought to be due to the regression and resorption of certain organs following a characteristic progression (Bowen et al., 1982). First, food reserves disappeared from the gastrodermis and parenchyma and, later on, reproductive cells, testis, copulatory organs and ovaries, reversing the order of the first appearance of these structures during growth. Although other structures such as gastrodermis, the nervous system and musculature were clearly also reduced in volume, no quantitative estimates of their reduction were obtained.

When growth and degrowth are studied in cellular terms, both processes appear highly coupled to the rates of proliferation and cell loss and to their mutual balance as influenced by food availability, temperature, body size, and the genetic characteristics of the species, races or populations (Baguñà and Romero, 1981; Romero, 1987). The cellular approach to growth and degrowth in planarians considers both processes as resulting from the differences between cells born by cell division (expressed in number of new cells.10^3 cells^{-1}/day^{-1}) and cells lost by death and apoptosis (expressed in number of cells lost.10^3 cells^{-1}/day^{-1}). Hence, growth and degrowth rates can be considered, under any environmental circumstances, in terms of cell turnover rates.

To obtain such data two basic techniques were used. First, the total number of cells and the percentage of each cell type in individuals of given lengths and plan areas were estimated using a maceration technique that dissociates whole organisms into single cells (Baguñà and Romero, 1981). Second, a stathmokinetic method (based on metaphase blockage by colchicine at given time intervals) was devised to estimate the daily number of cells produced in organisms of different length under different conditions of feeding and temperature. At weekly intervals, plan area (in mm^2) was measured in all individuals and the average total number of cells per individual deduced; from them, the rate of growth or degrowth (K_G/K_{DG}), expressed in cells gained or lost (10^3 cells^{-1}/day^{-1}), was estimated. The number of cells born during this interval, that is the cell birth rate (K_B, expressed as cells born ([10^3 cells^{-1}/day^{-1}])) was estimated following stathmokinetics after colchicine blockage. The rate of cell loss (K_L) was obtained as the difference between growth/degrowth rates (K_G/K_{DG}) and cell birth rate (K_B), and expressed as number of cells lost [10^3 cells^{-1}/day^{-1}].

133

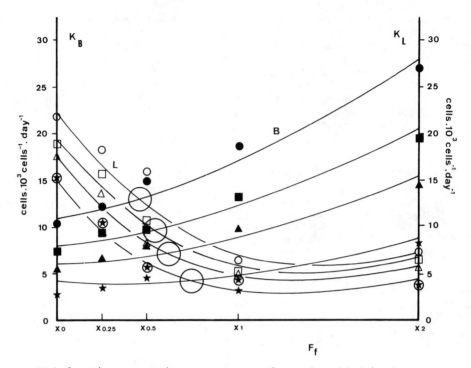

FIG.3. Diagrammatic representation of cell birth rate
(KB; filled symbols) and cell loss rate (KL; open
symbols) at different frequences of feeding (Ff; x2,
feeding 'ad libitum' twice a week; x1, once a week;
x0.5, once every two weeks; 0.25, once a month; x0,
starved) for 3mm (circles), 5mm (squares), 7mm
(triangles) and 11mm (stars) long organisms of the
planarian *Dugesia(G)tigrina* kept at 12°C. Large
circles indicate, for each body length, the cross-
points between KB and KL values where 'steady-state'
body size holds if the corresponding frequence of
feeding (Ff) is maintained. To the left of each
cross-point, degrowth occurs; to the right, growth
holds. Note that during starvation (Ff = x0) KB is
maintained at a basal level and, similarly, a basal
level of KL occurs even at optimal feeding regimes
(Ff = x1 and x2). Based on Romero (1987).

The main results obtained can be summarized as follows.
First, growth/degrowth in planarians is due mainly to cell
hyperplasia and not to cell hypertrophy, the latter only
accounting for a 15-20% of the increase/decrease in the total
body volume. Second, the total number of cells of different
cell types varies enormously (often more than an order of
magnitude) during growth whereas their percentages show
positive or negative allometries depending on cell type (Table
1); these tendencies are reversed during degrowth. Third, cell
birth rate (KB) is, as expected, directly proportional to
temperature and frequence of feeding (Ff), though the specific
growth rate decreases with increasing body length. Moreover,
and contrary to expectations, cell proliferation is maintained
during degrowth by starvation. Fourth, the rate of cell loss
(KL) is directly proportional to temperature and inversely

proportional to the frequence of feeding, it follows an exponential negative curve with body size and, interestingly, it is maintained at a basal rate even in optimal conditions of temperature and food availability. Fifth, K_B and K_L define, for given lengths, temperatures, and frequency of feeding, the conditions where growth or degrowth occur (Figure 3), and the maximal and minimal sizes attainable. Finally, the maximal and minimal rates of K_B and K_L set the limits of cell proliferation and cell loss for a given species; these limits are higher for asexual and sexual perennial species than for sexual annual species (Romero, 1987; Romero and Baguñà, 1988).

Altogether, these results suggest that, in similarity with other simple freshwater organisms, namely coelenterates (Bode et al., 1986), freshwater planarians are organisms in a continuous state of cell turnover. Even in steady state conditions, a continuous rate of cell proliferation matched by an equivalent rate of cell loss occurs (Figure 3). Taking into consideration that neoblasts are the only proliferative cells (and that differentiated cells do not divide), it would suggest that most (if not all) the cells lost, are the differentiated type. Indeed, ultrastructural studies during the growth and degrowth of intact organisms clearly showed the presence of numerous lysing of dead differentiated cells (Bowen et al., 1982).

Implications for pattern formation phenomena

Body and tissue allometries. Growth and degrowth bring about clear changes in body and tissue proportions. The percentage, by volume, of the nervous system, pharynx, and neoblasts to total body volume decreases during growth and, conversely, increases again during degrowth. However, the gastrodermis and parenchyma, as a whole, increase as the organism becomes longer and decrease when it is starved (Baguñà, 1973). These observations are in basic agreement with those obtained from quantitative cellular analyses of growth and degrowth (see Table 1).

Interestingly, the changes in the proportion of tissues and organs can also be deduced from changes of percentage along the antero-posterior axis during growth and degrowth (Baguñà, 1973). If body length is divided into 10% intervals along the antero-posterior axis (1,2,...10; head to tail), brain ganglia, mainly located in the 2nd and 3rd intervals in small organisms (3-5mm in length), are anteriorly displaced to the 1st and 2nd intervals in longer individuals. Similarly, the pharynx, located in a middle-caudal position (6th, 7th and 8th intervals) is displaced anteriorwards (5th and 6th intervals) in longer animals. The gastrodermis, having an overall positive allometry during growth shows a peculiar gradual increase within the anterior intervals. As regards neoblasts, their percentage is maintained, with minor variations, along the antero-posterior axis; the main ones show slight increases in the most anterior and posterior intervals and a relative depletion at intermediate levels, as the animal grows in length.

The regularity of the overall allometric changes and the associated variation in the antero-posterior percentages, jointly with their reversal during degrowth, suggest that

Table 1. Distribution (in percentage) of cell types in standard individuals of *Dugesia(G)tigrina* of different body length[a]

	Body length (mm)			
Cell type[b]	3	5	7	11
Neoblast	36	34	32	28
Nerve	24.5	23	22	20
Epidermal	15	13	11.5	10
Fixed parenchyma	5	8	11.5	15
Acidophilic	3	3	3	4
Basophilic	2	2.5	3	3.5
Pigment	1	1.5	1.5	2
Muscle	1	1.5	1.5	2
Intestinal	2	3	4	5
Goblet (granular)	0.5	0.5	1	1
'Unclassified'	10	10	10	10

[a] For the sake of clarity values have been rounded and standard deviations (with ranges not higher than 10% of the average value) ommitted. Taken from Romero, 1987.

[b] For a detailed description, see Baguñà and Romero (1987).

overall body and tissue proportioning mechanisms should operate during both processes. Since the allometric and antero-posterior changes are a reflection of changes in the whole body and the antero-posterior percentages of different cell types, it follows that the differential production of differentiated cell types from neoblasts along the antero-posterior axis will show an inverse, complementary, behaviour during growth and degrowth. Unfortunately, neither the body proportioning mechanism nor how differentiated cell types are differentially produced along the antero-posterior axis in planarians is presently known, though substances similar to the "proportion activating factor" (PAF) described in cnidarians (see Plickert, this volume) could hypothetically exist.

Changes in the number of periodic (iterated) structures. Although freshwater planarians are non segmented organisms, some structures, such as the small ganglia, commisures, and lateral nerves along the longitudinal nerve cords as well as the gastrodermal diverticula, appear serially repeated. Growth and degrowth are known to bring about changes in the number of these structures (Baguñà, 1973), though a thorough quantitative analysis has not been carried out. The main problem posed is by what mechanism can such iterated structures increase or decrease in number during growth and degrowth.

The small ganglia found at the cross-point between the longitudinal nerve cords, transverse commisures and lateral nerves (see Baguñà and Ballester, 1978, for a general description) are formed by a few scattered neurons and by bundles of longitudinal and transversally interconnected nerve fibers. The number of such ganglia and the associated commisures and lateral nerves, increase during growth and decrease during degrowth. To explain it, two main mechanisms can be envisaged. First, new ganglia can be thought to appear when the distance between neighbouring ganglia exceeds a critical value. The location of the new ganglia would then be at or near the mid point of the 'old' ganglia. A second mechanism may consist of the splitting or 'segmentation' of an existing ganglion into two neighbour masses followed by the growth of interconnecting nerve bundles and the spreading out of transversal commisures and lateral nerves. The problems posed by degrowth are even more difficult to tackle. Here we need to explain how actual ganglia, commisures and lateral nerves along the shrinking nerve cords disappear in order to 'accommodate' their decreasing number in a progressively reducing body size. As regards to particular mechanisms, either the coalescence ('fusion') of close ganglia or the random loss of some ganglia can be suggested, though no evidence has been obtained to back either mechanism.

The changes in number of gut diverticula during growth and degrowth, though similar in form to those seen within the nervous system, present some peculiar problems, namely with regards to mechanisms. During embryonic development, gut diverticula in freshwater planarians stem from one anterior and two posterior branches. During postembryonic growth, the number of diverticula increase and each diverticulum branches extensively, often anastomising with lateral branches of neighbouring diverticula. Although the number of diverticula was once thought to have considerable importance as a species diagnostic feature (see Ball and Reynoldson, 1981, for a critical assessment), it is no longer considered such. Nevertheless, for a given species, their number and complexity increases during growth and decreases during starvation.

The genesis of new diverticula in growing organisms has not been studied in detail; hence only tentative mechanisms can be suggested. The most simplistic sees it as arising from the bulging or evagination of the intestinal epithelium due to local mechanical deformations, when a critical distance between the bases of neighbour diverticula is exceeded. A second mechanism considers that the diverticula arise by differentiation from a separate cluster of neoblasts that, later on, will connect to the main branch or diverticulum by further growth and/or elongation (migration). The location of this presumed cluster can be either close to the intestinal epithelium or within the parenchyma filling the space between two neighbouring diverticula. In either case, the initial clustering of neoblasts and the further recruitment of cells is thought to occur when the concentration of an inhibitory molecule produced by gastrodermal cells falls below a certain critical value, as has been shown to occur in several branch forming systems (Meinhardt, 1982). It is worth noting that during embryonic development, gut diverticula do not arise by bulging (evagination) from the simple, saccular, embryonic endodermal epithelium but from the clustering of undifferentiated embryonic cells that later connect to the former, through differential growth and migration (Le Moigne, 1963).

Regeneration

General data. When a planarian is cut, the wound epithelium rapidly contracts and a thin film of epidermal cells from the stretched old epidermis covers it in less than one hour (Baguñà et al., 1988). Wound epithelium does not proliferate (Morita and Best, 1974). Below the wound epithelium, groups of undifferentiated cells aggregate to form a few layers of cells. These cells grow by addition of new undifferentiated cells, formed by cell division in the underlying parenchyma which has spread to the wound area. After one day of regeneration, this accumulation of undifferentiated cells is externally visible due to its unpigmented character, and is called the regenerative blastema. In subsequent days, the blastema grows exponentially, and is clearly visible after 2-3 days of regeneration. Several studies have shown that despite growing in size and cell number, blastema cells do not divide (Morita and Best, 1984; Saló and Baguñà, 1984). From this, it has been suggested that blastema grow by the continuous entrance of undifferentiated cells, produced by cell division in the old stump (postblastema), to the base of the blastema. Using chromosomal and ploidy markers (Saló and Baguñà, 1989) it has been shown that cells forming the blastema are of local origin; that is, cells originally placed farther than 500μm from the wound boundary are barely represented in 3- and 5-days old blastemata. Moreover, the number of cells produced by mitosis within a 200-300μm postblastema area around the wound accounts for the increasing number of blastema cells (Saló and Baguñà, 1989). After 4-6 days of regeneration, new structures are differentiated within the blastema and postblastema areas. The lost structural pattern is thus restored and the initial body proportions finally acquired after 3-4 weeks of regeneration.

The main problems encountered in planarian regeneration are: 1) the origin of blastema cells, namely whether they originate from pre-existing undifferentiated cells (neoblasts) or by dedifferentiation of differentiated functional cells, and how their proliferation is controlled in both blastema and postblastema; and 2) how the lost pattern of structures is reset within the blastema and postblastema and, more specifically, when, where and how it happens.

General reviews dealing with the "hot points" of planarian regeneration have recently been published (Gremigni, 1988; Baguñà et al., 1988), and should be consulted for further details.

The origin of blastema cells. In most regenerating systems, blastema cells arise by dedifferentiation of functional tissue cells. In planarians, though, it is still debatable whether dedifferentiated cells or a population of undifferentiated cells, the neoblasts, are the main source of blastema cells. In the last 50 years, this issue has been polarized into what is called the 'neoblast *versus* dedifferentiation' controversy, between the so-called 'neoblast theory' and the 'dedifferentiation theory' (Slack, 1980; Baguñà, 1981).

Recent general reviews on the processes of regeneration in planarians hold that both theories are open to criticism as most of the experimental data drawn to support them are incomplete and no definitive test or experiment has yet been devised (Gremigni, 1988; Baguñà et al., 1988). However incomplete, two recent experiments supporting each theory are worth mentioning. Using a strain of the species *Dugesia(S)polychroa* that is a naturally occurring mosaic: the somatic cells are triploid, the male germ cells diploid, and the female germ cells hexaploid; Gremigni and co-workers (Gremigni and Miceli, 1980; see Gremigni, 1988, for a general summary) showed that regeneration from a cut surface through the gonadal region gave rise to blastemata and regenerates that contained mainly triploid cells but also diploid and/or hexaploid cells from which somatic cells (e.g. pharyngeal muscle cells) originated. This suggested that dedifferentiation and transdifferentiation (and hence, metaplasia), however limited, occurred during planarian regeneration.

These results suggested that blastema cells in planarians arise through similar mechanisms (e.g. dedifferentiation) as in most regenerating organisms. This lead to a call, the description of a general universal mechanism to explain the recruitment of undifferentiated blastema cells in the Animal Kingdom (Slack, 1980). This view, however, was criticised on the grounds that Gremigni's experiments did not demonstrate the occurrence of dedifferentiation and metaplasia but, at most, suggested the existence of determination (or transdeter-mination) (Baguñà, 1981), because the germ cells shown to transdetermine were not differentiated cells but premeiotic undifferentiated cells undistinguishable from neoblasts. In his recent review of planarian regeneration, Gremigni (1988) takes an intermediate view assuming that both neoblasts and dedifferentiated cells take part in blastema formation. More specifically, he stresses three main points: 1) blastema formation and subsequent regeneration are mainly due to undifferentiated cells or neoblasts; 2) a small percentage of germ cells can participate in blastema formation, being thus pluripotent again; and 3) a similar process of 'dedifferen-tiation'-dedetermination may also occur in other somatic cell types.

A different approach has made use of specific nuclear (chromosomal and ploidy) and cytoplasmic (fluorescent latex beads) markers (Saló and Baguñà, 1985), jointly with the separation and purification of neoblasts and differentiated cells and testing their regenerative and stem cell capabilities when introduced, separately, into the parenchyma of irradiated hosts which had neither functional neoblasts nor mitotic activity. The results obtained (Baguñà et al., 1989b) have shown that when purified neoblasts are introduced into the host, mitotic activity resumes leading, in a fair percentage of cases to long survival and blastema formation. On the other hand, injection of differentiated cells never gave mitotic recovery nor blastema formation. From these results it was concluded that the ease of recovery and regeneration of irradiated hosts was proportional to the number of neoblasts introduced and that, at least under the experimental conditions employed, differentiated cells were not able to rescue the host nor make it regenerate. Taking into account that neoblasts are the only planarian cells known to divide, these results clearly suggested that these cells (or at least a subpopulation of them) are totipotent (or pluripotent) stem cells in the intact organism and the main source of blastema cells in regenerating organisms.

However interesting, these experiments do not rule out the existence of cell dedifferentiation during planarian regeneration. Indeed, a definite proof of the exclusive (or even a main) role of neoblasts in planarians should be based on marking differentially, and permanently, neoblasts and differentiated cells and tracing, in both intact and regenerating organisms, the lineage of these cells. New labelling methods such as neoblast-specific monoclonal antibodies (Romero, Burgaya, Bueno and Baguñà, work in progress) and the introduction of gene markers (e.g. the gene of β-galactosidase) into neoblasts by retroviral transfection are presently being tried.

The control of cell proliferation in the blastema and postblastema. The temporal mitotic pattern in most regenerating planarian species studied so far, show a first mitotic maximum during the first hours of regeneration (2-12 hours), a second and higher maximum at 2-4 days, and a relative minimum in between (Saló and Baguñà, 1984). Spatially, the highest mitotic density is found initially in stump regions near the wound (0-300µm) and later on, is slightly displaced to more proximal regions. No mitoses are seen within the blastema despite the number of blastema cells which increase steadily during regeneration (Saló and Baguñà, 1989). This apparent paradox can be explained after considering that high levels of cell proliferation within the postblastema drive cells towards the wound area to form the blastema; there, and due probably to high cell density and/or close cell packing, cellular proliferation is inhibited.

Altogether, these results raise several questions. How are cells near the wound area stimulated to enter into mitosis? Which kind of factors or substances are responsable for such an increase? Which type of tissues or organs produce them, and which are the molecular mechanisms through which neoblasts respond? To answer these questions, two main approaches have been employed. The first was aimed at finding, either from total body or tissue extracts, or cell conditioned media, the natural activators or inhibitors of cell proliferation for intact and regenerating organisms. This approach has been used in several systems, being particularly successful in coelenterates, namely in hydras (Schaller et al., 1979) in which several low molecular weight activators and inhibitors have been isolated and purified. The second approach lies in testing on intact and regenerating organisms, stimulatory or inhibitory, several growth factors and mitogenic substances isolated and characterized from heterologous species, namely from mammals.

The attempts to isolate natural substances from planarian extracts have met with very limited success (Lender, 1974; Steele and Lange, 1977; Friedel and Webb, 1979; Saló and Baguñà, unpublished data). Actually, no activator or inhibitor has been fully isolated, and let alone characterized. The second approach, instead, seems more promising. The neurotransmitters serotonin, noradrenaline and dopamine, as well as

Table 2. Effects of neuropepetides and growth factors on cell proliferation in intact planarians[a]

Substance	Symbol	Mitogenic[b] effect	Activity range[c] (in M)	Tissular localization[d]
Substance P	SP	A	$10^{-7} - 10^{-10}$	Nervous system
Substance K	SK	A	$10^{-7} - 10^{-10}$	NT
Hydra head activator	HA	A	$10^{-8} - 10^{-9}$	Nervous system; pharynx(?)
Bradykinin	--	A	$10^{-6} - 10^{-7}$	NT
Bombesin	--	n.e	-------	NT
Met-Enkephalin	--	I	$10^{-5} - 10^{-6}$	Nervous system
FMRF-amide	--	n.e	-------	Nervous system,
FR-amide	--	n.e	-------	Nervous system
Epidermal Growth Factor	EGF	A	$10^{-6} - 10^{-8}$	Nervous system
Fibroblast Growth Factor	FGF	A	$10^{-6} - 10^{-8}$	NT
Growth Hormone Releasing Factor	GRF	A	$10^{-7} - 10^{-8}$	Nervous system

a   Substances were added to planarian saline (PS; Saló, 1984), organisms incubated for 12-24 hours, and mitosis counted. For each substance and concentration, ten organisms were used (for further details, see Saló and Baguñà, 1986).

b   A: activation; I: inhibition; n.e: no effect

c   Molar ranges giving activation or inhibition values over 25% of control values

d   as shown using immunocytochemical methods with mammalian antisera. NT: not tested.

cyclic AMP and calcium ions, were found to activate at low concentrations (10^{-5}-10^{-6}M) the rate of regeneration and the mitotic rate in regenerating organisms and in cultured planarian cells, respectively (Franquinet, 1979; Martelly, 1983). A greater effect was subsequently found for some neuropeptides and growth factors isolated from mammalian tissues. The tachykinin substance P (SP) was the first neuropeptide shown to activate, at nanomolar concentrations (10^{-7}-10^{-10}M), mitotic activity in planarians (Saló and Baguñà, 1986). Later, other neuropeptides such as hydra head activator (HA), bradykinin, substance K (SK), as well as the epidermal growth factor (EGF) were also shown to be mitogenic in intact planarians (Baguñà et al., 1988). Further studies have increased the list of activators and inhibitors that is summarized in Table 2. Immunocytochemical studies using mammalian antisera against some of these factors, detect immunoreactivity (IR) primarily within the central and peripheral nervous system (Burgaya, Bueno, Sumoy, Romero and Baguñà, submitted). This agrees with the postulated mitogenic action, through neurosecretory products, on the nervous system suggested earlier (see Brønsted, 1969, and Baguñà, 1976, for general references). Recent studies aimed to localize which types of cells bear receptors for the EGF, SP and SK-like substances have met with little success as only a faint reaction by the EGF receptor has been detected in neoblasts (Burgaya, Romero and Baguñà, unpublished data).

The specific role of some of these substances, namely substance P, has been tested using SP analogues such as spantide, as well as by inhibiting SP release through Met-enkephalin, activating SP release by capsaicine, and by adding antibodies for SP to culture media with intact and regenerating planarians. The results obtained (Baguñà et al., 1989a) fully agree with a very specific mitogenic action of SP that can be, at first, made extensive to the other mitogenic substances found so far.

Altogether, these results suggest the following scenario during regeneration in planarians. After being cut, stored neuropeptides, growth factors and neurotransmitters are released in high amounts from severed nerve fibers to the extracellular space. There, they induce undifferentiated cells (neoblasts) to divide. This may explain the sudden increase in mitotic activity seen shortly after cutting, provided these substances act preferentially on G2 arrested neoblasts. Substance P (10^{-8}M) added to cultures of intact planarians activates the mitotic index as early as 1 hour after application (Baguñà, 1986). Interestingly, hydra head activator (HA), bearing a limited homology to SP, stimulates cellular proliferation 2 hours after application on hydra cells and on the neural cell line NH15-CA2, whereas it does not stimulate DNA synthesis (Schaller et al., 1989); that is, it functions as a control signal in the G2/M transition and not in the G1/S transition.

After the first mitotic peak, a transient decrease ensues to be followed by a second, higher and long-lasting, mitotic maximum at 2-4 days of regeneration. Several lines of evidence suggest that this second peak is due to cell entering mitosis after going through the S phase, an event known to start at 10-12 hours of regeneration and reach a maximum between 16-24 hours (Martelly, 1983). Whereas, the transient decrease in mitosis is probably due to depletion of mitogenic substances after the sudden release during the early stages of regeneration, the second mitotic maximum may result, tentatively, from new synthesis and release of mitogenic factors by the newly determined nerve cells (an event occuring from the second day of regeneration). These mitogens may act either at the G2/M transition like SP and HA, at the G1/S transition, or in both. Currently, work is in progress to test the temporal specificity of other mitogens namely EGF and FGF (fibroblast growth factor).

Pattern formation in planarians. Facts and uncertainties. Despite decades of intense research, pattern formation in planarians is the least understood aspect of planarian regeneration. The most accepted model, proposed by the French School (see Wolff, 1962, for general references), features pattern formation as a disto-proximal sequence of inductions and inhibitions mediated by specific molecular factors. Twenty five years after being proposed, many aspects of the model are still uncertain and open to criticism, and none of the postulated activators or inhibitors have ever been isolated.

In most animal systems, pattern formation is characterized by the sequential or simultaneous determination of groups of cells which are to become particular regions, organs and tissues of the final organism or regenerant. The main uncertainties lie in how groups of cells to be (or already) determined are defined and in which period of time or stage this event occurs. Last but not least, how are both of these characteristics achieved at the genetic level (e.g. which genes control it) is the ultimate, and main, unsolved question.

In planarians, grafting procedures successfully employed to estimate determination of head structures in hydra (McWilliams, 1983), suggest that head determination in anteriorly regenerants is a very early event (3-12 hours at 24°C, 6-24 hours at 17°C) whereas determination of the pharynx occurs slightly later (12-36 hours), both happening within a narrow strip of tissue (0-500μm) below the wound when the blastema has not been formed or is barely visible (Saló, 1984). Moreover, the ability of blastemal structures to inhibit the regeneration of head structures when transplanted to a host regenerating organism increases rapidly (20 to 32 hours old blastemas), long before overt differentiation starts. As regards to the spatial laying down of particular structures, head ganglia appear within the blastema itself or at the junction blastema-postblastema, whereas other structures such as the pharynx are entirely patterned within the postblastema area.

These results support a tentative model that sees pattern formation set first morphallactically within a narrow strip of tissue below the wound during the first day of regeneration, and later amplified and refined by epimorphosis (Saló, 1984; Saló and Baguñà, 1984, 1989). Indeed, irradiated (X-rays) planarians, having no mitotic activity and an ever decreasing number of neoblasts, form after cutting, a small (down to 15-20% of normal size) and transient blastema that, before disintegration, differentiates all the missing structures albeit on a smaller scale. This rapid, and probably sequential, determination of the lost structures can be thought to be driven either by cell-cell interactions or by transient gradients of morphogenetic substances induced at or near the wound area. The former modality may accomodate the old disto-proximal inductive model of Wolff and Dubois (see Wolff, 1962, for references) provided it occurs within the first 48 hours of regeneration.

Despite the fact that epimorphosis and morphallaxis have been traditionally considered as antagonic, excluding, modalities of regeneration, they may not be as different as was once thought, as no clear opperational differences between them occur during normal regeneration (García-Bellido, personal communication). Indeed, both seem to lead to a sequential deployment of structures with (epimorphosis) or without (morphallaxis) the concourse of cell proliferation.

CELLULAR, MOLECULAR AND GENETIC APPROACHES TO GROWTH, DEGROWTH AND REGENERATION IN PLANARIANS

New approaches to solving the main problems posed by the process of regeneration, problems shared to some extent by growth and degrowth processes, have been recently reviewed (Baguñà et al., 1988). Generally speaking, the main problems focus on methods to label and follow particular cells (and their descendants), to assess their role in blastema formation, pattern formation, and body repatterning, and to detect and characterize the genes that play a central role in both processes. The final aim is to chart the programs of growth/degrowth and regeneration in cellular and genetic terms.

Cell labelling and clonal analysis

Since freshwater planarians seem to be impervious to exogenous labelled DNA precursors, alternative methods to score and follow particular cells, namely using chromosomal and ploidy markers (see Saló and Baguñà, 1985, 1989; and also Gremigni, 1988, for general references) in chimaeric and mosaic organisms have been tried. Although such markers, already employed to estimate the spreading of cells in intact planarians and in regions near to and far from the wound of regenerating organisms, have several advantages over RNA/protein labelling and other markers used such as pigmentation, they are only scorable in mitotic cells (chromosomal markers) or are difficult to detect (ploidy markers).

The application of extrinsic markers, such as vital dyes and, more recently, fluoresceine-lysine dextrans (FLDx) or horse-radish peroxidase (HRP), introduced by microinjection or iontophoresis, either directly into particular cells or marking single or groups of cells before incorporating into chimaeras, are currently used techniques to label cells and establish their lineage. Although such techniques have been extremely successful in the analysis of cell lineages in embryos of several animal groups, notably in leeches (Weisblat et al., 1984), molluscs (Serras and van den Biggelaar, 1987), and amphibians (Smith et al., 1985), their application to planarians face two main difficulties. First, the main cell type in the study of cell lineage, the neoblasts, are small cells (mean diameter, 5-10µm) bearing a very scant rim of cytoplasm; therefore, even when problems associated with impalement and introduction of the label are overcome, the amount of tracer taken up by these cells is too limited to make lineage feasible. Second, the requirement for an applied cell marker to be cell-localized (e.g. to label a neoblast within a particular area of the blastema or postblastema), conflicts with the need for a simple and efficient means of delivering the marker to the required cell, a problem very difficult to solve for a tissue like the blastema and postblastema made of a solid mass of very small cells. Moreover, applied markers are only suitable for relatively short time studies because they are rapidly diluted by cell division.

The use of chimaeras may circumvent some of these problems. Single cells, or groups of cells (e.g. neoblasts) can be marked, either by fluorescent nuclear markers such as Hoechst 33258 or DAPI, or microinjected with FLDx or HRP before being introduced by microinjection into unirradiated or irradiated hosts (see Baguñà et al., 1989b, for cell microinjection into whole organisms). These markers, notably DAPI, have been shown to be cell-autonomous in hydras (Bode et al., 1986) lasting up to one month. However, up to now, no results have been reported on the use of such markers in planarians. In chimaeric planarians, the main difficulties in the application of such markers lie in the presumed heterogeneity of neoblasts (see below) with cells in different stages of determination and differentiation that would produce clones, highly diverse and difficult to analyze. Moreover, microinjection of cells is random and introduced cells tend to occur in large clusters or aggregates, a situation not occuring in normal intact organisms.

Needless to say, the best cell marker should be stable (that is, stably inherited by all descendants of the marked cell) and produced with the slightest manipulation of the organism (ideally within the same individual and not through cell transplantation). Two recently developed methods, both based on the introduction of heterologous marker genes into the genome of transfected cells, should be worth trying in planarians. First, retroviral vector-mediated gene transfer of histochemical markers, such as the β-galactosidase (β-lac) gene, can be introduced by microinjection to blastema or postblastema areas or, using a packing cell line, into isolated neoblasts before being introduced into unirradiated or irradiated hosts, regenerating or not. The resulting β-lac activity permits histochemical identification of clones containing the integrated vector (see Price, 1987, for a general discussion and a review of recent applications). Since only dividing cells seem able to integrate the virus, this technique looks particularly useful for planarians as only neoblasts would be labelled.

The second approach uses electroporation as a way to introduce recombinant plasmids bearing marker genes (e.g. β-lac) either into whole organisms or isolated cells (neoblasts). Though the method is cleaner and faster than the former one, it has one main drawback: most cells, not only neoblasts, will be labelled. Moreover, it remains to be seen whether these sequences remain stable within the cells or, as in recent reports on electroporated hydras (Bosch, unpublished data), they are slowly but steadily being lost.

Table 3. Qualitative and quantitative differences in the patern of polypeptides along the antero-posterior axis in the planarian *Dugesia (G) tigrina* as shown by two-dimensional electrophoresis

Polypeptide	Isoelectric point (pI)	Molecular weight (x10^3)	Body region[a]					
			1	2	3	4	5	PHX
PO	9.1	22	-	++	+++	+	-	++++
P1	7.9	40	++	-	-	-	++	+
P2	7.9	42	+++	+++	+++	-	++	++
P3	7.6	26	+	++	+++	++	++	++++
P4	7.7	35	-	-	++	+++	+++	-
P5	7.5	45	-	++	+++	+++	-	+++
P6	8.3	30	+++	+++	+++	-	+++	+
P7	6.9	28	-	++	+	+	++	+
P8	5.9	56	+	++	+++	+	-	-
P9	5.6	31	+	+	++	++	-	-
P10	6.0	60	+++	+	+	+	+	-
P11	5.7	72	+++	-	-	-	-	-
P12	4.8	28	++	++	+++	+	+++	-
P13	6.6	33	+++	+++	+++	+++	+++	-
P14	5.2	62	+	++	++	++	+++	++++
P15	6.5	68	-	+	+	+	-	+++

a 1, head region; 2, prepharyngeal region; 3, pharyngeal region (except the pharynx); 4, postpharyngeal region; 5, tail region; PHX, pharynx. - : not detectable; + : present at very low concentration; ++ : moderate concentration; +++ : abundant; ++++ : very abundant.

Table 4. Summary of the main qualitative and quantitative differences in the pattern of polypeptides during anterior regeneration in the planarian Dugesia(G) tigrina a

Polypeptide	Isoelectric point (pI)	Molecular weight (x10^3)	Time of regeneration (hours and days)							
			0h	4h	12h	1d	2d	3d	5d	9d
4B1	5.3	23.5	+	++	++++	+++	+++	++	++	+
4B2	6.8	52.0	+	++	++++	++	++	++	+	+
4B3	5.0	18.0	+	+++	++++	+++	++	+	+	+
4B4	4.7	38.5	-	+	+++	++++	++++	+++	+++	+
4R1	6.3	21.5	+	++	+++	++	++	+	+	+
8B1	7.5	45.0	+	+	+++	+++	++	++	++	+
8B2	8.3	79.0	++	++	+++	+++	+++	+++	+++	++
8B3	5.7	63.0	+	+	+++	++	++	++	++	+
7B1	5.5	15.0	++++	++	++	++	++	++	+++	++++
7B2	6.6	76.0	++++	++	++	++	++	++	+++	++++
7B3	5.7	72.0	++++	+	-	+	+	+	+++	++++

a For symbols, see legend of Table 3.

147

If any of these approaches turn out to be feasible in planarians, specific questions about cell lineage (such as the division history of each neoblast at different regenerative stages, the kind of cell types and tissues to which they will give rise, the number of divisions before final differentiation is achieved), about the equivalence of neoblasts along the main axis of the blastema, about the existence of dedifferentiation, and about the equivalence between neoblasts and blastema cells could be answered. Moreover, these markers could also shed light on important questions such as the directionality of migration of neoblasts to the base of the blastema.

Molecular markers of determination and differentiation

To establish how the lost pattern is first reset and how new structures and organs appear during regeneration, as well as during growth and degrowth, molecular markers of the early stages of cell differentiation are clearly needed. This would allow visualisation of the pattern before morphogenesis and overt differentiation takes place during regeneration, as well as the detection of the appearance of new primordia of iterated structures (e.g. new ganglia along the longitudinal nerve cords, new gut diverticula) during growth and their fading during degrowth.

How can be obtained these molecular markers? Some of the potential techniques and experiments have recently been listed and discussed (Baguñà et al., 1988). First, two-dimensional (2-D) electrophoresis of protein extracts from: a) purified neoblasts and differentiated cells; b) different body regions along the antero-posterior (a-p) axis of intact organisms; and c) blastema and postblastema at different stages of regeneration have been recently carried out (Collet and Baguñà, unpublished data). The main results are summarized in Tables 3 and 4. Out of 800 polypeptides detected, only 7 are neoblast-specific and 8 are specific for differentiated cells, whereas a group of 24-30 polypeptides show considerable quantitative variation between both groups of cells. The rest (95% of all polypeptides) are common to both. The study of regional differences along the a-p axis (Table 3) yielded some interesting regional markers for the head region, namely the P11, and some for the pharynx (P0, P5 and P15), whereas others are specific for tail (P1) and middle areas of the body (P0, P5, P8 and P15). As regards the changes seen during regeneration (Table 4), two main groups of polypeptides are detected: those, that are barely represented in the intact organism and which increase in concentration shortly after cutting with their maxima during the first day of regeneration (B1-4; 4R1, 8B1-3); and a second group, clearly abundant in the intact organism, which show a decrease in concentration to almost non detectable levels during the first days after cutting, and increase later on (5-9 days of regeneration). The first group may hold, at least in part, the pleyade of substances which are involved, directly or not, in early reparative processes, cell activation (Moraczewski et al., 1987), cell proliferation and early pattern formation; the second group, contain potential markers of territorial and cellular differentiation. Although the nature of none of these substances is at present known, current methods to isolate and purify some of the most interesting polypeptides from 2-D gels and, from them, deduce the amino acid sequence to make synthetic oligonucleotides and screen cDNA libraries should be worth trying in the near future.

The second approach to detect markers of early territorial determination makes use of monoclonal antibodies (mAbs). This approach, successfully applied in several adult and embryonic systems, is currently being tried in planarians (Romero, Bueno, Burgaya and Baguñà, work in progress). Up to now, several mAbs showing cell type specificity and regional specificity have been obtained and are presently being characterized. Some of these mAbs may be extremely useful as markers of cell determination and differentiation in the early stages of regional determination during regeneration, as well as unveiling the appearance and fading of iterated structures during growth and degrowth. Again, once the most interesting mAbs are characterized, they can be used to detect, either by western blotting, antigen microsequentation, oligonucleotide synthesis and cDNA library screening or, more directly through expression libraries, the genes codifying regional or temporally interesting products.

Finally, the third approach makes use of differential cDNA libraries obtained from spatially or temporally restricted populations of mRNAs to isolate those specific of a restricted area, a group of cells, or a critical period of regeneration. This technique, successfully applied in a considerable number of embryonic and adult systems, has not been tried so far in planarians.

The genetic approach

Before the advent of molecular biology and molecular genetic techniques, and even today, most information on how embryonic development is controlled comes from classical genetic analysis: induction of mutations that affect development and trace, from their phenotypic effects, the hypothetical role of the normal gene. From this, a wealth of mutants that affect early pattern formation, mainly in *Drosophila*, and more recently in the nematode *Caenorhabditis elegans* and in the plant *Arabidopsis thaliana*, have been described, their genes detected and mapped, and their possible roles inferred.

The prospects of undertaking such a program in planarians or, broadly speaking, in any free-living turbellarian, have recently been discussed (Baguñà et al., 1988; see also Baguñà and Boyer, this volume), and are actually rather bleak. Instead, recent developments in molecular genetic screening may be particularly useful for organisms, such as planarians which are difficult to study at the genetic level.

Since the discovery in 1984 of the homeobox, a 180 base pair long stretch of DNA present in many of the so-called homeotic genes of *Drosophila* (genes that play a key role in early patterning during development), a thorough search was undertaken in many organisms to find in their genomes homologous sequences to the homeobox. The rationale behind this approach, lies in that finding of a homologous stretch of DNA in the genome of an organism would indicate the presence of a gene that could play a similar role in pattern formation during development or regeneration. Although scores of homeoboxes have been actually found in several animal groups, spanning from

A

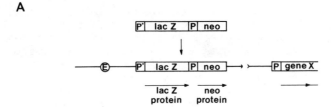

B

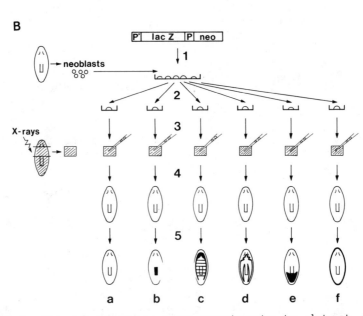

a   b   c   d   e   f

FIG.4. Use of reporter gene constructs to detect cis-acting regulatory elements of genes expressed in specific patterns in planarians. A) Mechanism of activation of lac Z reporter gene constructs. The bacterial β-galactosidase (lac Z) gene with its own translational initiation site is linked to a minimal promotor (P*). Integration close to an enhancer (E) element of an active host gene X can cause transcription and translation of the lac Z gene (from Rossant and Joyner, 1989, slightly modified). B) Identifying differentially spatially regulated genes in planarians using reporter gene integrations in neoblasts. 1, electroporation of marker genes into isolated neoblasts and selection for neomycin resistance; 2, clonal growth of resistent neoblast lines; 3, injection of clonal neoblasts into pre-pharyngeal pieces of irradiated hosts; 4, rescue of hosts by repopulating neoblasts and regeneration; 5, staining with X-gal to identify differential territorial activation of genes. a, no activation; b, activation within pharyngeal tissues; c, activation within nervous tissue; d, activation within the gastrodermis; e, activation at the posterior parenchyma; f, activation within the epidermis.

nematodes and annelids through echinoderms to most arthropods (namely insects) and vertebrates, no sequence as such has been found yet in planarians (García, Baguñà and Saló, unpublished data). For us, the main reason for this apparent failure could be due to an insufficient degree of homology between the probes tried (namely from *Drosophila*) and the presumed homeoboxes of planarians given the enormous phyletic distance known to exist between planarians (and platyhelminthes as a whole) and the rest of Eubilateria (Field et al., 1988; Riutort, Field, Raff and Baguñà, unpublished data).

A recently developed approach that can overcome this lack of homology is to screen cDNA planarian libraries with degenerate oligonucleotide probes of the most conserved motif (helix 3) of the homeobox. This method has been applied to detect scores of homeoboxes (up to 40) in the genome of the nematode *C. elegans* (Bürglin et al., 1989), as well as to identify the hydra homologue of the *src*-oncogene from vertebrates (Bosch, unpublished data) despite the enormous phyletic distance between vertebrates and coelenterates.

The second approach to detect genes playing key roles in both development and regeneration is based on the introduction of reporter gene constructs to identify regions of the genome transcriptionally active in a temporally and spatially restricted manner. This method, developed for *Drosophila* (O'Kane and Gehring, 1987) and already applied in the mouse (Gossler et al., 1989) is depicted, as applied to planarians, in Figure 4. Here, the presence of neoblasts, which bear a striking similarity to the ES (pluripotent stem) cells of the mouse, as the cellular targets, has the major advantage over a possible transgenic event of screening a large number of integration events and studying those that activate lac Z in interesting patterns. From these events, it would be possible to identify and clone the host (e.g. 'X', see Fig.4) gene from the flanking genomic DNA, this providing a new source of genes active in specific patterns during regeneration as well as during growth and degrowth.

However suggestive and worth trying, some elements of this approach as applied to planarians are still not available. Although neoblasts have been isolated and enriched to a reasonable extent (Baguñà et al., 1989b; Auladell, unpublished data) and kept in culture for a short while (up to 2 weeks), clonal growth of isolated single neoblasts have not been attained. On the other hand, though morphologically alike, neoblasts are a heterogeneous class of cells (see below) with true stem-cells (those having the capacity to give all differentiated cell types) being a small percentage of total neoblasts; hence, even if feasible, many integration events will be lost. Moreover, though some constructs have been introduced and kept stable via electroporation or via transposing elements in several groups of organisms, there is no hint that such an approach may similarly work in planarians. Despite these difficulties, this approach appears as a fruitful new way to detect pattern genes in planarians; hence, future work must be directed to solve the technical points mentioned above.

OPEN QUESTIONS

1) *Growth, degrowth and regeneration: do they have a common cellular basis ?*

Several arguments strongly support the idea that growth/degrowth and regeneration rely on the same type of cells: the neoblasts. First, during growth/degrowth as well as during regeneration, neoblasts are the only cells able to divide. Second, the best available ultrastructural and experimental evidence (Morita and Best, 1984; Baguñà et al., 1989b) clearly indicate that blastema cells and neoblasts are alike, the former originating from the later. Third, injection of purified neoblasts into unirradiated hosts of the same species leads to resumed mitotic activity, blastema formation and extended or complete survival of the host, whereas, injected differentiated cells never do so. Moreover, similar rescue experiments done between the asexual and sexual races of the planarian *Dugesia(S)mediterranea* showed that the introduction of neoblasts from one race into irradiated hosts of the other and viceversa gave, besides a reciprocal rescue, the 'transformation' of the host race into individuals of the donor race able to grow, degrow and regenerate (Baguñà et al., 1989b).

Although the arguments mentioned above present good evidence for a common cellular basis for both processes, some alternatives are still likely. Thus, it can be argued that blastema and postblastema cells appearing after neoblast injection arise by dedifferentiation of differentiated cells produced from injected neoblasts and not directly from the latter. This argument can also be extended to intact organisms if neoblasts are considered as transient proliferating cells arising continuously by dedifferentiation from some or all differentiated cells. As already mentioned, a clear solution to this important problem must be based on marking differentially, and permanently, neoblasts and differentiated cells and tracing, in both intact and regenerating organisms, the lineage of these cells.

2) *Neoblasts: a heterogeneous bag of cells*

Neoblasts have been traditionally described as a toti-potent or pluripotent class of undifferentiated stem cells, morphologically alike. Although most of the evidence reported so far fits this description, it is also more than probable that under the label "neoblasts", a rather diverse collection of cells in different stages of determination and differen-tiation exist.

In the best studied cell-renewing systems of mammals: haemopoiesis, the intestinal epithelium and the epidermis, undifferentiated stem-cells are divided at least into two main classes: 1) true stem-cells with unlimited capacity of self-renewal, potential for asymmetric division, and irreversible differentiation to a range of terminal differentiated cell types; and 2) transit amplifying, or progenitor, populations with a more limited capacity of self-renewal. In the epidermis, only about 10% of the basal keratinocytes constitute the true stem cell population, whereas 50% of the basal cells, with capacity to divide, may constitute a transit amplifying (progenitor) population, and the remaining 40% of basal cells are presumably post-mitotic and commited to terminal differentiation (see Hall and Watt, 1989, for a general review). In the haemopoietic system, less than 0.4% of the total population of haemopoietic cells can be considered as stem-cells.

In planarians, cells morphologically defined as neoblasts amount to 20-30% of cells depending on body size, temperature and nutritional conditions (Baguñà and Romero, 1981). This percentage clearly exceeds the number of true stem-cells expected in any renewing system. Considering that a substantial number of 'morphological' neoblasts could be post-mitotic determined cells, in the early stages of differentiation into post-mitotic differentiated cell types, the actual number of true stem-cells must be considerably lower. Indeed, continuous blockage of cell division by colchicine leads to an accumulation in the number of metaphases never exceeding 30-40% of the total number of neoblasts; hence, more than 50% of total neoblasts should be post-mitotic (Baguñà, 1973). Moreover, blockage of the G1→S transition by hydroxyurea showed that 80-90% of dividing neoblasts are blocked after one day of incubation; instead, 10% of dividing neoblasts are in the G2 period where they can last for up to 5 days (Saló and Baguñà, 1984). Morphometric and functional analyses of purified neoblasts (Auladell and Baguñà, unpublished data) indicates the presence of a subpopulation of big G2 cells, with low nucleocytoplasmic ratio, RNA concentration and mitochondrial activity, that comprises 3-5% of total neoblasts. In common with other stem-cells described for several renewing systems having similar characteristics, it can be speculated that this subpopulation of neoblasts constitutes the true-stem cells in planarians.

What are the prospects of demonstrating this subpopulation of cells are the true-stem cells in planarians? The approach followed to find similar cells in the haemopoietic system in mammals, has been to characterize these populations through monoclonal antibodies and clonogenic assays. Recently (Spangrude et al., 1989) a group of cells (labelled as Thy-1[10] lin- Sca-1+, with reference to the presence or absence of particular surface markers detected by monoclonal antibodies) have been enriched by magnetic separation and flow cytometry and shown, by clonogenic assays and by radioprotection of lethally irradiated animals, to give all the haematopoietic cell lineages; hence; they are the main candidates to be the true stem-cells of the haemapoietic system. However, the specific Sca-1 (stem-cell) antigen is expressed in cells other than haematopoietic stem-cells, such as all endothelial cells and some mature lymphoid cells. On the other hand, and despite much effort, no specific molecular markers for intestinal stem-cells and epidermal stem-cells have so far been reported (Hall and Watt, 1989). Altogether, this suggests that the detection of stem-cells by the use of specific antigens is (however interesting and worth trying), a bit misleading because antigens as such may not exist. Instead, it can be speculated, that in common with the findings in early embryogenesis in *Drosophila* and *Caenorhabditis elegans*, that a particular determined state could be based on particular combinations of regulatory gene products more than on the presence/absence of unique, specific, gene products.

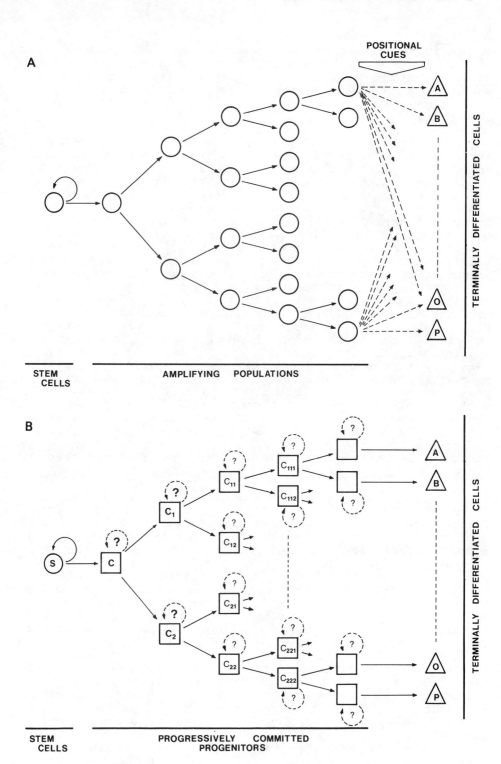

FIG.5. Hypothetical cell lineage models of cell
renewal in planarians. A, Simple amplifying model
without lineage determination and with stochastic
differentiation of potentially equivalent cells to
any of the terminally differentiated cell types (A,
B,..., P; triangles) through different positional

According to this view, the prospects of obtaining, in high purity, the subpopulation of true stem-cell neoblasts would rely more on the development of clonal assay systems to demonstrate the developmental potential of each neoblast than on the detection of specific antigens through monoclonal antibodies, though the later approach should be also actively pursued.

3) *To what extent does involve all cell types; or, are there permanent cells ?*

Degrowth in planarians results from the progressive and steady decrease in the absolute number of cells of all differentiated cell types. It has also been shown (see Fig.3) that even during this process, cell proliferation (KB), cell differentiation, and cell loss (KL), that is cell turnover, goes on unabated (Romero, 1987; Romero and Baguñà, 1988). However, within a particular cell type (e.g. epithelial, nerve, muscle cells,..), it is uncertain whether all cells are transient or whether particular cells remain during the lifetime of the individual (permanent cells).

Whereas in some cell lineages (e.g. those making the gonads, the vitellaria and the copulatory apparatus, among others) all cells disappear during degrowth to be formed anew during growth, it remains to be seen if all the neurons of the central and peripheral nervous system turn over, or if a few of them remain during the lifetime of the individual as a sort of basic scafolding or guideposts to maintain the 'structural memory' of the system. Besides its intrinsic interest, this problem has also a bearing on the problem of organismal ageing, or the presumed lack of it in asexual populations.

4) *The control of cell lineage in planarians: extrinsic or intrinsic ?*

Figure 5 depicts, from several possible alternatives, two extreme models of cell lineage as applied to planarians. The first (Fig.5A) sees cell determination and differentiation arising from a population of pluripotent or totipotent stem cells *via* a transit amplifying, or progenitor, populations that have a more limited capacity for self renewal. The differentiation of the last progenitor cells produced by cell proliferation is considered to be under the control of

---

cues. B, Amplifying model of progressively committed progenitors with a finite but uncertain (broken circles and question marks) self-renewing capacity giving rise to specific differentiated cell types (A, B,..., P; triangles). S represent the self-renewing stem cell or true neoblast; C represent neoblasts committed to certain lineages but still exhibiting some degree of pluripotentiality. Subindexes indicate the progressive commitment of cells to specific lineages and sublineages (e.g. ectodermal *vs* meso-endodermal; epidermal *vs* nerve,...). Empty squares represent uni-committed progenitor cells that will differentiate to a specific terminally differentiated cell type.

positional cues that may vary quantitatively along the body axes (antero-posterior, dorso-ventral,..) or qualitatively at or near particular organs and tissues of the organism. Following this view, cells in the amplifying populations are potentially equivalent, and the differential production of terminally differentiated cells along the body axes would be mainly due to external influences.

The second model (Fig.5B), introduces internal commitment, *via* an invariant sequence of cell divisions which produces cells progressively committed to specific lineages, as a means to generate a particular differentiated cell type out of several possible cell types. In this case, lineage is the sole, or main, determinant of the specific cell types produced. From this view, progenitor cells can not be considered equivalent, and the differential production of cell types along the body axes of the organism is more difficult to explain as similar numbers of them will be produced everywhere. Nevertheless, some mechanisms can be suggested (e.g.' selective cell migration or cell death, local proliferation of uni-committed progenitor cells,..) to account for these positional differences.

Data available so far in planarians, are of no help in choosing either model or in suggesting an alternative one. This is due mainly to the lack of cell lineage studies using labelled precursors and to the failure to keep long term *in vitro* cultures of neoblasts to analyze the fate of their individual progeny. Whereas the first model agrees basically with the fact that neoblasts from any body region give rise, during regeneration, to any structure or region of the body, the second model introduces a self-consistent internal order seen in other developmental, regenerative and cell renewal systems (see Hall and Watt, 1989, for a general discussion).

The study of mitotic activity in the freshwater planarian *Dugesia(S)mediterranea* shows that over 90% of daughter cells at anaphase and telophase are clearly unequal in size; in the larger cells despiralizing of the chromatin occurs sooner than in the smaller (Baguñà, 1973). In most developmental systems, asymmetric divisions are known to give cells with different developmental outcomes. Although such observation in planarians can not be taken as evidence of different fates for sister cells, it suggests that a fair percentage of commitment may occur during cell proliferation linked to an internal programme independent of external cues or due to cell-cell interactions with neighbour cells.

In the long run, however, it is highly probable that a mixed model embracing some sort of internal cell commitment lineage jointly with the action of specific positional cues (long diffusion signals and/or cell-cell interactions) enhancing or inhibiting the production of particular committed cells in specific regions of the body, will be uncovered. To this aim, and besides introducing modern labelling techniques to follow 'in vivo' the fate of single neoblasts, there is clear need for molecular markers to distinguish stem from transit cells (if, indeed, these markers exist), as well as the development of cell culture models to study the determinants of asymmetry at the level of individual mitoses (e.g. to analyze the differential effects of mitogenic neuropeptides and growth factors on the production of terminal differentiated cell types).

5) *The importance of neoblasts in the senescence/immortality problem*

Both sexual and asexual reproduction must involve a kind of rejuvenation if their products are not to continue ageing from where the parents left off. In sexual reproduction, it has been suggested that germinal cells, produced early on during development in most animal systems, either are kept in a latent state with their DNA free of errors (perhaps through a special kind of repair mechanism), or avoid cell ageing from generation to generation through genetic assortment during meiosis.

In asexual reproducing organisms, it is generally admitted that some rejuvenation must exist; otherwise, species depending on it would ultimately die out. However, how these organisms escape from ageing is one of the main unsolved problems in biology. Several species of freshwater planarians (triclads), as well as others belonging to several turbellarian orders (e.g. rhabdocoels), reproduce indefinitely (or at least it seems so) by binary fission. Therefore, it could be expected that each fission product would be rejuvenated to a similar extent. That this is not necessarily so was demonstrated by Sonneborn (1930) in a series of classical experiments on the asexual rhabdocoel *Stenostomum incaudatum*. It was found that lineages derived from successive heads soon ceased to divide and died out, whereas lineages derived from tails continued to divide and showed apparent immortality. These differences can be explained by the extent to which remaining tissues turn over and are replaced after fission. Indeed, tails become fairly reorganized making brain ganglia and pharynx anew, whereas heads retain the 'old' brain, specialized head structures and the pharynx. Although experiments as such have not been performed in freshwater triclads, it can be anticipated that the outcome would be rather similar. If this were so, the ageing of lineages retaining the old head could be explained by the presence of some permanent cells (e.g. some particular neurons) serving as a sort of scaffold or positional memory of the system. Moreover, this also would explain why asexual races are 'immortal' whereas organisms belonging to sexually reproducing species, having no binary fission, however longlived (21 years for *Dugesia(D)etrusca*, Lange, 1968) ultimately die.

Since asexually reproducing planarians are, at the level of some of its products, immortality, and since neoblasts are the only cell type known to divide and give rise to all differentiated cell types, it follows that in such organisms, these cells can also be qualified as immortal. From this, it follows that the knowledge of how neoblast proliferation is controlled and how its rate varies as related to body size and age may be of importance to understand the relationship between cell proliferation, cell ageing and immortalization. Recent findings linking growth factors, membrane receptors and oncogenes may be of relevance to the problem posed by immortalization in asexual reproducing organisms.

In most organisms, a decline in proliferative capacity ensues with age, both *in vivo* and *in vitro*. However, immortalized cells escape from such a decline, and it has been suggested that oncogenes may play a role on it. If this were so, it can be speculated that neoblasts (or, at least, some of them, namely the true stem cells or true neoblasts) could be immortal due to the constitutive expression of activated cellular oncogenes. It would be then highly interesting to study: 1) if cellular oncogenes do occur in planarian cells (namely in neoblasts) and how its activity varies during regeneration and asexual reproduction; and 2) how mitogenic neuropeptides, growth factors and their receptors vary in concentration and activity during both processes, and how they interact with the presumed oncogenes.

Moreover, sexually reproducing species of freshwater planarians have life-spans going from the semelparous ('annual') species which reproduce once and die (e.g. *Dendrocoelum lacteum*) to the iteroparous ('perennial') species that reproduce yearly and live several years (e.g. *Dugesia (D) gonocephala; Dugesia (S) mediterranea*). It has been suggested that ageing and death of semelparous species are due to a higher investment in reproduction than in somatic cell turnover (Calow, 1981), whereas a longer life in iteroparous species is due to a converse strategy. That is, turnover of somatic tissues is slowed down in semelparous as compared to iteroparous species, thus leading to the ageing and death of the former and to longer survival in the later. These observations can be linked to a model which provides a general mechanism for ageing (see Calow, 1978, 1981, for general references). According to this model, the age-state (vitality) of the tissues is supposed to be proportional to the density of damage within them, this being generated continuously by errors, thermal noise, etc,.. but being also continuously repaired. As repair is expensive in resources (building blocks and power) and is manifested in the turnover of cells and molecules in organisms (even in those not growing), vitality (and its converse, senescence) would depend on the difference between density of damage and capacity of repair. In semelparous species, repair (measured as cell turnover) is much reduced as most energy goes to reproduction (Romero, 1987; Romero and Baguñà, 1988; Dawson, Calow, Romero and Baguñà, unpublished data); therefore, these species age rapidly and die. In iteroparous species, somatic repair is slightly slowed down; therefore, ageing is also slowed down and organisms die after several years. Finally, asexual species, forming neither gametes nor reproductive tissues, may maintain a cell turnover that eliminates all damage produced and thus are potentially immortal, even though, the known ageing and death of lineages retaining the old head in asexual *Stenostomum* clearly indicates that only those parts having a complete and continuous cell turnover do not age.

The key issue of this problem is to know how the true stem cells or true neoblasts are kept immortal and (probably) free of errors: by special mechanisms of cellular and molecular repair, by the maintenance of a very small percentage of cells free of errors, by the constitutive activation of some cellular oncogenes, or through the combined action on any of these mechanisms?

ACKNOWLEDGEMENTS

This work was supported by grants from Comisión Asesora de Investigación Científica y Técnica (CAYCIT; 1108/81 and PB85/0094) and Fondo de Investigaciones Sanitarias (FISS; 87/1533 and 88/0988) to JB.

REFERENCES

Abeloos, M., 1930, Recherches expérimentales sur la croissance et la régénération chez les planaires, Bull.Biol.Fr.et Belg., 64:1-140.

Baguñà, J., 1973, Estudios citotaxonómicos, ecológicos e histofisiología de la regulación morfogenética durante el crecimiento y la regeneración de la raza asexuada de la planaria Dugesia mediterranea n.sp. Ph. D. Thesis, Universitat de Barcelona.

Baguñà, J., 1976, Mitosis in the intact and regenerating planarian Dugesia mediterranea n.sp. I. Mitotic studies during growth, feeding and starvation, J.Exp.Zool., 195:53-64.

Baguñà, J., 1981, Planarian neoblast, Nature, (London), 290:14-15.

Baguñà, J., 1986, Efecte de neuropèptids i factors de creixement sobre la proliferació cel.lular a planàries, in: "Biologia del Desenvolupament," Societat Catalana de Biologia ed., Barcelona, Vol.4, pp 71-78.

Baguñà, J., and Ballester, R., 1978, The nervous system in planarians: peripheral and gastrodermal plexuses, pharynx innervation, and the relationship between central nervous system structure and the acoelomate organization, J.Morphol., 155:237-252.

Baguñà, J., and Romero, R., 1981, Quantitative analysis of cell types during growth, degrowth and regeneration in the planarians Dugesia(S)mediterranea and Dugesie(G)tigrina, Hydrobiologia, 84:181-194.

Baguñà, J., Saló, E., Collet, J., Auladell, M.C., and Ribas, M., 1988, Cellular, molecular and genetic approaches to regeneration and pattern formation in planarians, Fortschr.Zool., 36:65-78.

Baguñà, J., Saló, E., and Romero, R., 1989a, Effects of activators and antagonists of the neuropeptides substance P and substance K on cell proliferation in planarians, Int.J.Dev.Biol., 33:261-264.

Baguñà, J., Saló, E., and Auladell, C., 1989b, Regeneration and pattern formation in planarians. III. Evidence that neoblasts are totipotent stem cells and the source of blastema cells, Development, 107:77-86.

Baguñà, J., and Boyer, B.C., 1990, Descriptive and experimental embryology of the Turbellaria. Present knowledge, open questions and future trends, in: "Experimental Embryology in Aquatic Plants and Animals", Marthy, H.J., ed., Plenum Press, New York.

Ball, I.R., 1974, A contribution to the phylogeny and biogeography of the freshwater triclads (Platyhelminthes Turbellaria), in: "Biology of the Turbellaria," N.W. Riser, and M.P. Morse, eds, McGraw-Hill, New York, pp 339-401.

Ball, I.R., 1981, The phyletic status of the Paludicola, Hydrobiologia, 84:7-12.

Ball, I.R., and Reynoldson, T.B., 1981, "British Planarians," *Synopses Br.Fauna* (N.S.) No 19:1-141.

Benazzi, M., and Gremigni, V., 1982, Developmental biology of triclad turbellarians (Planaria), *in:* "Developmental Biology of Freshwater Invertebrates," F.H. Harrison and R.R. Cowden, eds, Alan R. Liss, New York, pp 151-211.

Bode, H.R., Dunne, J., Heimfeld, S., Huang, L., Javois, L., Koizumi, O., Westerfield, J., and Yaross, M., 1986, Transdifferentiation occurs continuously in adult hydra, *Curr.Topics.devl.Biol.*, 20:257-280.

Bode, P.M., Awad, T.A., Koizumi, O., Nakashima, Y., Grimmelikhuijzen, C.J.P., and Bode, H.R., Development of the two-part pattern during regeneration of the head in hydra, *Development*, 102:223-235.

Bowen, I.D., den Hollander, J.E., and Lewis, G.H.J., 1982, Cell death and acid phosphatase activity in the regenerating planarian *Polycelis tenuis* Iijima, *Differentiation*, 21:160-167.

Brønsted, H.V., 1969, "Planarian Regeneration," Pergamon Press, London.

Bürglin, T.R., Finney, M., Coulson, A., and Ruvkun, G., 1989, *Caenorhabditis elegans* has scores of homeobox genes, *Nature* (London), 341:239-243.

Calow, P., 1977, The joint effects of temperature and starvation on the metabolism of triclads, *Oikos*, 29:87-92.

Calow, P., 1978, "Life Cycles," Chapman and Hall, London.

Calow, P., 1981, Growth in lower invertebrates, *Comp.Anim.Nutr.*, 4:53-76.

Child, C.M., 1915, "Senescence and Rejuvenescence," University of Chicago Press, Chicago.

Cowden, R.R., 1982, Supplement: collection, maintenance and manipulation of planarians, *in:* "Developmental Biology of Freshwater Invertebrates," F.H. Harrison and R.R. Cowden, eds, Alan R. Liss, New York, pp 213-220.

Ehlers, U., 1985, "Das Phylogenetische System der Plathelminthes," G. Fischer, Stuttgart.

Field, K.G., Olsen, G.J., Lane, D.J., Giovannoni, S.J., Ghiselin, M.T., Raff, E.C., Pace, N.R., and Raff, R.A., 1988; Molecular phylogeny of the animal kingdom, *Science*, 239:748-753.

Franquinet, R., 1979, Rôle de la sérotonine et des catecholamines dans la régénération de la planaire *Polycelis tenuis*, *J.Embryol.Exp.Morph.*, 51:85-95.

Friedel, T., and Webb, R.A., 1979, Stimulation of mitosis in *Dugesia tigrina* by a neurosecretory fraction, *Can.J.Zool.*, 57:1818-1819.

Gossler, A., Joyner, A.L., Rossant, J., and Skarnes, W.C., 1989, Mouse embryonic stem cells and reporter constructs to detect developmentally regulated genes, *Science*, 244:463-465.

Gremigni, V., and Miceli, C., 1980, Cytophotometric evidence for cell 'transdifferentiation' in planarian regeneration, *Wilhelm Roux's Arch.devl.Biol.*, 188:107-113.

Gremigni, V., 1988, Planarian regeneration: an overview of some cellular mechanisms, *Zool.Sci.*, 5:1153-1163.

Hall, P.A., and Watt, F.M., 1989, Stem cells: the generation and maintenance of cellular diversity, *Development*, 106:619-633.

Lange, C.S., 1968, A possible explanation in cellular terms of the physiological ageing of the planarians, *Exp.Gerontol.*, 3:219-230.

Lange, C.S., 1983, Stem cells in planarians, *in:* "Stem Cells," C.S. Potten, ed., Churchill Livingstone, Edinburgh, pp 29-66.

Le Moigne, A., 1963, Etude du développement embryonnaire de *Polycelis nigra* (Turbellarié, Triclade), *Bull.Soc.Zool.Fr.*, 88:403-422.

Lender, T., 1974, The role of neurosecretion in freshwater planarians, *in:* "Biology of the Turbellaria," N.W. Riser and M.P. Morse, eds, McGraw-Hill, New York, pp 460-475.

MacWilliams, H.K., 1983, *Hydra* transplantation phenomena and the mechanism of *Hydra* head regeneration. II. Properties of the head activation, *Devl.Biol.*, 96:239-257.

Martelly, I., 1983, Effets du calcium sur la synthèse d'ARN et d'ADN de cellules de planaires cultivées *in vitro*, *C.R.Acad.Sc.Paris*, 297:9-12.

Meinhardt, H., 1982, "Models of Biological Pattern Formation," Academic Press, London.

Moraczewsky, J., Martelly, I., Franquinet, R., and Castagna, M., 1987, Protein kinase C activity during planarian regeneration, *Comp.Biochem.Physiol.*, 87B:703-707.

Morita, M., and Best, J.B., 1974, Electron microscopic studies of planarian regeneration. II. Changes in epidermis during regeneration, *J.Exp.Zool.*, 187:345-374.

Morita, M., and Best, J.B., 1984, Electron microscopic studies of planarian regeneration. IV. Cell division of neoblasts in *Dugesia dorotocephala*, *J.Exp.Zool.*, 229:425-436.

O'Kane, C.J., and Gehring, W.J., 1987, Detection *in situ* of genomic regulatory elements in *Drosophila*, *Proc.Natl.Acad.Sci.*, 84:9123-9127.

Plickert, G., 1990, Experimental analysis of developmental processes in marine Hydroids.(this volume)

Price, J., 1987, Retrovirus and the study of cell lineage, *Development*, 101:409-419.

Reynoldson, T.B., 1966, Preliminary laboratory experiments on recruitment and mortality in triclad populations, *Vehr.Int.Ver.Limnol.*, 16:1621-1631.

Romero, R., 1987, Anàlisi cel.lular quantitativa del creixement i de la reproducció a diferentes espècies de planàries, Ph.D. Thesis, Universitat de Barcelona.

Romero, R., and Baguñà, J., 1988, Quantitative cellular analysis of life-cycle strategies of iteroparous and semelparous triclads, *Fortschr.Zool.*, 36:283-289.

Rossant, J., and Joyner, A.L., 1989, Towards a molecular-genetic analysis of mammalian development, *TIG*, 5:277-283.

Saló, E., 1984, Formació del blastema i re-especificació del patró durant la regeneració de les planàries *Dugesia(S)mediterranea* i *Dugesia(G)tigrina*, Ph.D. Thesis, Universitat de Barcelona.

Saló, E., and Baguñà, J., 1984, Regeneration and pattern formation in planarians. I. The pattern of mitosis in anterior and posterior regeneration in *Dugesia(G)tigrina*, and a new proposal for blastema formation, *J.Embryol.exp.Morph.*, 83:63-80.

Saló, E., and Baguñà, J., 1985, Cell movement in intact and regenerating planarians. Quantitation using chromosomal, nuclear and cytoplasmic markers, *J.Embryol.exp.Morph.*, 89:57-70.

Saló, E., and Baguñà, J., 1986, Stimulation of cellular proliferation and differentiation in the intact and regenerating planarian *Dugesia (G) tigrina* by the neuropeptide substance P, *J.Exp.Zool.*, 237:129-135.

Saló, E., and Baguñà, J., 1989, Regeneration and pattern formation in planarians. II. Local origin and role of cell movements in blastema formation, *Development*, 107:69-76.

Schaller, H.C., Schmidt, T., and Grimmelikhuijzen, C.J.P., 1979, Separation and specificity of four morphogens from *Hydra*, *Wilhelm Roux's Arch.devl.Biol.*, 186:139-149.

Schaller, H.C., Druffel-Augustin, S., and Dübel, S., 1989, Head activator acts as an autocrine growth factor for NH15-CA2 cells in the G2/mitosis transition, *EMBO J.*, 8:3311-3318.

Serras, F., and van den Biggelaar, J.A.M., 1987, Is a mosaic embryo also a mosaic of communication compartments? *Devl.Biol.*, 120:132-138.

Slack, J.M.W., 1980, The source of cells for regeneration, *Nature* (London), 288:760.

Smith, J.C., Dale, L., and Slack, J.M.W., 1985, Cell lineage labels and region-specific markers in the analysis of inductive interactions, *J.Embryol.exp.Morph.*, 89, Supplement:317-331.

Sonneborn, T.M., 1930, Genetic studies on *Stenostomum incaudatum* n.sp. I. The nature and origin of differences in individuals formed during vegetative reproduction, *J.Exp.Zool.*, 57:57-108.

Spangrude, G.J., Heimfeld, S., and Weissman, I.L., 1988, Purification and characterization of mouse hematopoietic stem cells, *Science*, 241:58-62.

Steele, V.E., and Lange, C.S., 1977, Characterization of an organ-specific differentiator substance in the planarian *Dugesia etrusca*, *J.Embryol.Exp.Morph.*, 37:159-172.

Weisblat, D.A., Kim, S.Y., and Stent, G.S., 1984, Embryonic origins of cells in the leech *Helobdella triserialis*, *Devl.Biol.*, 104:65-85.

Wolff, E., 1962, Recent researches on the regeneration of planaria, *in:* "Regeneration," D. Rudnick, ed., The Ronald Press, New York, pp 53-84.

GENEALOGY, GEOMETRY AND GENES:

EXPERIMENTAL EMBRYOLOGY OF *CAENORHABDITIS ELEGANS*

Einhard Schierenberg

Zoologisches Institut der Universität Köln
Weyertal 119, 5000 Köln
Federal Republic of Germany

I. INTRODUCTORY REMARKS

The free-living nematode *Caenorhabditis elegans* is a small and unpretentious organism. It may thrive unnoticed in the cabbage patch in your backyard or the flower pot on your balcony. In their natural habitat soil nematods live in a thin film of water. In the laboratory *C. elegans* dwells on Petri dishes in the liquid film on the top of an agar layer, but can also be grown in liquid culture (e.g. Rothstein and Coppens, 1977). As in other nematodes the liquid-filled body cavity (pseudocoelom) functions as a hydroskeleton. When the worm dries out, the hydroskeleton collapses and the animal inevitably dies. In a loose sense *C. elegans* may therefore be considered as a kind of aquatic animal. Because of this and because *C. elegans* is particularly well suited to the study of certain aspects of development, the following chapter is included in this book on Experimental Embryology of Aquatic Organisms. The intention of this contribution is to serve as an introduction and as a reference source rather than as a complete summary of present knowledge in the field. As indicated by the title, the review will focus on embryonic cell lineages, pattern formation in the embryo and the analysis of mutants affecting early development.

II. NEMATODES AS CLASSICAL OBJECTS FOR THE STUDY OF
     EMBRYOGENESIS

More than 100 years ago scientists realized the suitability of nematode embryos for developmental studies. Several notable developmental discoveries were made in nematodes, particularly in the then most popular species *Parascaris equorum* (formerly: *Ascaris megalocephala*). These include: significance of meiosis (van Beneden, 1883), early separation of soma and germline (Boveri, 1887), individuality of chromosomes (van Beneden and Neyt, 1887; Boveri, 1888, 1909), determinative cleavage (zur Strassen, 1896; Boveri, 1899), cytoplasmic determination of cells (Boveri, 1910), eutely (Martini, 1909). *Ascaris* has the advantage that

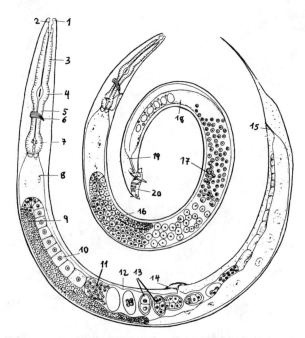

FIG.1. The nematode *Caenorhabditis elegans*
1-15: Hermaphrodite, 16-20: Male.
1. One of six lips. 2. Mouth cavity 3-5. 7. Pharynx.
6. Nerve ring. 8. Intestine. 9. Oogonia. 10. Oocyte.
11. Sperm. 12. Uterus. 13. Cleaving eggs. 14. Vulva.
15. Anus. 16. Spermatogonia. 17. Sperm. 18. Vas
deferens. 19. Cloaca. 20. Copulatory bursa. (Modified
after Meglitsch, 1967).

thousands of fertilized but uncleaved eggs can be obtained from
a single individual. Development starts outside the mother at
room temperature, can be accelerated by increasing temperature
and interrupted anytime for longer periods by transferring eggs
into the cold. After Boveris death (1915), interest in
nematodes as developmental models declined. The new field of
genetics made other systems (like *Drosophila*) more attractive
than the parasitic *Ascaris*.

III. HOW TO BECOME A MODEL ORGANISM

Half a century later nematodes came back on stage when
molecular biologists began to seek for new challenges after it
was "widely realized that nearly all the 'classical' problems
in molecular biology have either been solved or will be solved
in the next decade" (Brenner, 1963). With the idea in mind that
the problems of cellular development should be analyzed in a
manner analogous to molecular genetics of bacteria, Brenner
looked for an organism with a simple structure, short life
cycle and amenable genetics that was easy and cheap to culture
in large numbers in the laboratory. In a proposal to the
Medical Research Council in 1963 he wrote: "We think we have a
good candidate in the form of a small worm..." (Fig.1). During
the next decade he established the methods for isolating and
mapping structural and behavioral mutants (Fig.2), and
localized about a hundred genes on the six linkage groups. When

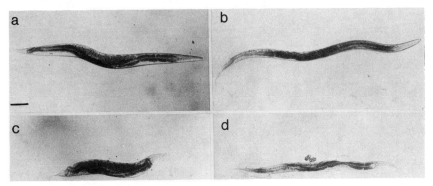

FIG.2. Structural Mutants of *C. elegans*
a) Wildtype, b) Long-2, c) Dumpy-11, d) Blister-2

he published his pioneering work on the genetics of *C. elegans* (Brenner, 1974) he provided a sound basis which others could take as a starting point. Particularly in the U.S. new laboratories took up the task of isolating and analyzing mutants (mainly researchers who had previously spent some time with Brenner in Cambridge). Over the years the numbers of laboratories working with *C. elegans* constantly increased. In a kind of a self-amplifying process the accumulating new data lured more and more scientists to join the "*C. elegans* community". Besides the attractiveness of the subject, the boost given by Brenner, and the scientific progress achieved by those working with the new system, obviously additional factors contributed to the rapid establishement of *C. elegans* as a model system. Introductory courses were given for newcomers, a *C. elegans* newsletter ("Worm Breeders Gazette") was launched, biennial international symposia on *C.elegans* have regularly taken place since 1977, and a *C. elegans* Genetics Center was established. Last but not least all members of the "*C. elegans* community" gained by the spirit of frankness and cooperation present from the very beginning. Today *C. elegans* is - together with *Drosophila* - genetically the best understood metazoan system. It is the only organism in which cell lineages have been completely traced from fertilization to adulthood (Sulston and Horvitz, 1977; Deppe et al., 1978; Kimble and Hirsh, 1979; Sulston et al., 1980; Sulston et al., 1983) and where a complete description of cellular anatomy is available including the wiring diagram of the nervous system (White et al., 1986). Molecular cloning of interesting genes is in progress and an ordered cosmid library of genomic DNA fragments providing a physical map of the genome is nearly complete (Coulson et al., 1986 and personal communication). More recently other fields of research, like aging and pharmacology have started to take advantage of the nematode system. We can expect *C. elegans* to continue to play a distinctive role in further elucidation of developmental control mechanisms.

IV. GENEALOGY: EMBRYOGENESIS CELL-BY-CELL

At 25°C embryogenesis of *C. elegans* takes only about 12 h

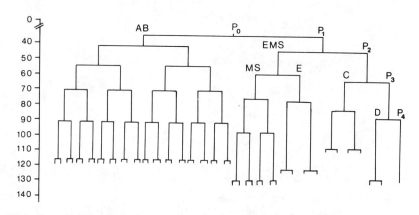

FIG.3. Early lineage tree of the *C. elegans* embryo
The zygote P_0 cleaves into the somatic founder cell AB
(predominantly producing neuronal and hypodermal
cells) and the germline cell P_1. After the equal
division of AB (into two AB cells) P_1 cleaves
unequally into a somatic cell EMS and a new germline
cell P_2. After equal and synchronous division of both
AB cells, EMS cleaves unequally into two different
somatic founder cells, MS (predominantly contributing
to pharynx and body muscle) and E (generating the
complete gut). P_2 divides unequally into the somatic
founder cell C (contributing predominantly to body
muscle and hypodermis) and P_3, a new germline cell.
After all cells have doubled in the sequence AB, MS
and E, C, P_3 divides unequally to generate a somatic
founder cell D (producing body muscle cells) and the
primordial germ cell P_4. Note that while MS and E
enter mitosis nearly synchronously, the descendants
of E express longer cell cycle periods compared to
those in the MS cell lineage. Scale at the left gives
time in minutes after fertilization. From Schierenberg, 1988.

from fertilization to hatching. It can be subdivided into two
parts. A proliferation phase (lasting about 5 1/2 hours   at
25°C) during which nearly all cells of the hatching worm are
produced, and a morphogenesis phase (about 6 1/2 h) in which
the layers of cells gradually arrange to form a worm. As the
embryo can develop outside the mother under the microscope and
because the eggshell is completely transparent, cleavage and
spatial arrangement of cells can be readily observed with
Nomarski optics (Sulston et al., 1983). For assessment of cell
differentiation electronmicroscopy, antibody staining, and
other techniques have complemented light microscopical data.

From Egg to Animal

Typical for nematode embryogenesis is the presence of an
identifiable germline from the very beginning. The zygote P_0
can be regarded as the first germline cell. It cleaves to give
rise to a somatic cell AB and a new germline cell P_1. In a
further series of unequal cleavages in the germline with a
spindle orientation along the anterior-posterior (a-p) axis of
the cell, 5 somatic founder cells (AB, MS, E, C, D) and the
primordial germcell P_4 are generated (Figs.3 and 4). Each
founder cell establishes a cell lineage. From each lineage a

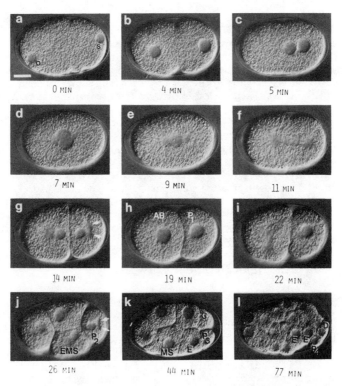

FIG.4. Early embryogenesis of C. elegans at 23°C±2°C
a) Fertilized egg about 45 min. after fertilization.
Pronuclei from egg (o) and sperm (s) have formed at
opposite poles (relative time: 0 min.). b) Pronuclei
have started to approach each other, a temporary
constriction (pseudocleavage) has formed. c)
Pronuclei have met more towards the posterior pole.
d) Pronuclei have rotated through 90°. e) Pronuclei
have fused and first mitosis has started. f) Typical
for unequal cleavage of the zygote is the translocation of the posterior aster towards the pole;
beginning of cytokinesis. g) Early 2-cell stage. Note
flat centriolar region in P1 (*arrows*). h) Late 2-cell
stage. i) AB has entered mitosis; orientation of the
cleavage spindle is transverse. j) The 4-cell stage;
typical for the germline cell P2 is a flattened
centriolar region (*arrows*). k) The 8-cell stage. l)
The 26-cell stage. With the immigration of the two
gut precursor cells (E) gastrulation has started.
Orientation, anterior to the *left*, dorsal at the *top*.
Bar, 10μm. From Schierenberg, 1988.

fixed number of cells arises. The members of a lineage
initially cleave in synchrony (becoming somewhat less so in
later cell stages) with cell cycle periods different from those
in other lineages (Fig.3). Cell cycles are short, the shortest
taking only 10 minutes. The primordial germcell P4 is already
present by the 24-cell stage (one hour after the onset of
cleavage), when gastrulation starts with the immigration of the
two gut precursor cells (Fig.4l). During further progression of
gastrulation, the two daughters of P4 follow them, and then the

4 descendants of the D cell (muscle precursors) rearrange and come to lie left and right of the germline cells. One group of the C cells (muscle precursors) travel around the posterior pole and are also translocated interiorly while the more anterior C cells (precursors for hypodermis and neurons) remain outside and cover the posterior-dorsal surface. At the same time the MS cells (predominantly precursors for pharynx and body muscles) located in an anterior ventral position, sink inwards. Towards the end of gastrulation most of the embryo's surface is covered by AB cells. They spread along both sides ventrally and eventually meet at the ventral midline. Most AB cells also take up position in the interior and contribute to the nervous system and the pharynx, while the remainder forms that part of the hypodermis not generated by C cells. The morphogenesis phase starts with a ventral indentation ("lima bean stage"). Without gross rearrangement of cells and with only a few additional cleavages a worm gradually develops by elongation of the embryo.

Two Types of Cleavage in the Early Embryo

Two basically different types of cell division are found in the nematode embryo, germline-like (unequal, stemcell-like, with a-p spindle orientation) and soma-like (equal, proliferative, with variable spindle orientation). The germline cells P_1 - P_3 (Fig.3 and 4) can be viewed as cells which possess a visible polarity absent in somatic cells. The most dramatic indication of this a-p polarity is the behavior of germline-specific cytoplasmic structures (P granules), which segregate in a microfilament-dependent manner to one pole prior to the onset of mitosis (Strome and Wood, 1983). The primordial germcell P_4 does not express a visible polarity, however. It cleaves equally (last embryonic cleavage in the germline), both daughter cells receive approximately equal amounts of P granules, and the descendants of both cells differentiate likewise into eggs and sperm. It is an unsolved question whether a hidden polarity remains in the germline and is transferred from one generation to the next or whether polarity is definitely lost in the primordial germcell and newly established prior to or in conjunction with fertilization of the egg.

In order to determine where in the embryo the germline-like cleavage potential (GLCP) is located, fragments of cytoplasm together with surrounding cell membrane were removed from germline cells (Schierenberg, 1988). About half of the fragments removed from the posterior pole of a 1-cell embryo cleave like a complete zygote. The other half first performs an equal cleavage, but both daughter blastomeres behave like germline cells (Fig.6). From these and other results it has been deduced that GLCP is a non-nuclear property, is normally localized in the posterior region of the zygote, and depending on its concentration and segregation controls the type of cleavage a fragment performs. In the germline cell P_2 a reversal of cleavage polarity takes place such that the new germline cell comes to lie anterior to its somatic sister in contrast to the previous germline cleavages (Schierenberg, 1987). This and other observations, led to the conclusion that at least certain aspects of polarity are newly established during the cell cycle in the germline.

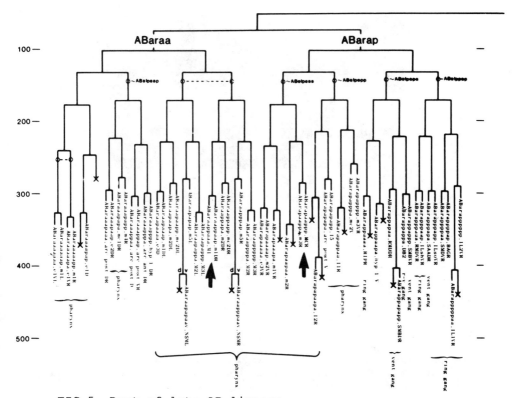

FIG.5. Part of late AB-lineage
With each division, daughter cells receive a lower
case letter, which indicates its position relative to
its sister in addition to the name of the mother. At
the end of the lineage each cell receive an
abbreviated name indicating its fate (e.g. NSMR,
right neurosecretory motorneuron). "x" indicates
programmed cell death. o-----o or o~ mark lineage
branches which generate bilaterally symmetric
structures. Arrows mark sister cell pairs one of
which differentiates into a muscle cell, the other
into a neuron (Modified after Sulston et al., 1983).

Germ Layers and Cell Fate

The strict correlation of position in the lineage tree and
cell fate postulated by classical researchers has been
confirmed as a general rule. However, more detailed investi
gation has uncovered a considerable number of deviations from
this rule (Sulston et al., 1983). At several points in the
lineage the last embryonic division gives rise to two
completely different daughters, one of which will differentiate
into a neuron, the other into a muscle cell (Fig.5). Assuming
cell-autonomous development (see below), this means that cells
can retain the differentiation potential for more than one cell
type until the very end of the cleavage program. If one
associates individual lineages (or parts of it) with different
germlayers (based on their behavior during gastrulation), this
would imply that neurons can develop from embryonic mesoderm
and muscle cells from ectoderm. The classification into

169

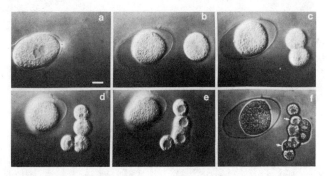

FIG.6. Cleavage of posterior fragment
a) With a laser microbeam a hole is punctured in the
eggshell at the posterior pole of a 1-cell embryo. b)
A posterior fragment is extruded together with both
pronuclei and the centrosomes. c) The fragment
cleaves equally.d) Both daughter cells cleave
unequally. e) All four cells are in interphase. f)
After the two larger central cells have divided
equally, the two smaller peripheral blastomeres have
performed an unequal cleavage. Arrows, smaller
germline-like cells. Bar, 10µm.

different germlayers must therefore be seen primarily as a
formal anatomical description and may not be associated with a
restriction in developmental capacity.

Programmed Cell Death

As part of the normal developmental program 113 specific
cells die within a few hours in the embryo *C. elegans* (Fig.5).
Some of these cells apppear to perform only a transient
function and may therefore be discarded afterwards. Most of
them, however, die soon after their birth and no function has
been attributed to them. One possible interpretation of this
phenomenon is that the repeated use of lineage subprograms
(sublineages) is an economical way to construct the lineage
tree. In the course of evolution the same lineage routine may
have been used in different regions of the embryo and modified
according to local requirements to include elimination of
unnecessary cells. Most cell deaths appear to be suicides
because they are not be prevented by killing neighboring cells
or in mutants where the normally occuring phagocytosis of dead
cells does not take place. In a few cases, however, cell death
is obviously murder because it does not take place after prior
ablation of adjacent cells (Horvitz et al., 1982; Hedgecock et
al., 1983). Programmed cell death is not a necessary part of
development. Mutants have been described in which no cell
deaths are observed. Surprisingly, these mutants look and
behave normally (Ellis and Horvitz, 1986).

V. GEOMETRY: PATTERNS IN TIME, SPACE, AND DIFFERENTIATION

Cell Cycle Periods and Positioning of Cells

Timing of developmental events appears to play a crucial
role in the nematode embryo. Each cell lineage established by

the unequal cleavages in the germline is characterized by specific cell cycle periods (Fig.3). This leads to a fixed order of cleaving cell groups and a reproducible spatial arrangement of cells relative to their neighbors. Thus, cells can be identified by their position. This makes it unnecessary during lineage analysis to start from the beginning whenever a new individual is examined. Analysis of mutants (see next paragraph) and laser-induced retardation of cell cycle periods in specific lineages led to the conclusion that proper spatial arrangement of cells depends on correct cell cycle timing. Experiments in which cytoplasm was removed from early blastomeres or was transferred between adjacent cells demonstrate that the different cell cycle periods are due to differential segregation of cytoplasmic components. Alteration in size or ploidy of cells only causes marginal effects (Schierenberg and Wood, 1985).

Establishment of Bilateral Symmetry, Functional Decisions, and Visible Differentiation

The hatching worm is higly bilateral symmetric. This is reached by symmetry formation within individual lineages. In the MS, C, and D lineages the first cleavage separates left from right precursors. In the MS and C lineages the second division goes along with a functional decision: the anterior daughters of both MS cells predominantly contribute to the pharynx, the posterior daughters predominantly produce muscle cells. This point becomes even more obvious in the C lineage where the second division generates two anterior C cells (not sisters) which produce ectodermal tissue (hypodermis and neurons) and two posterior C cells which contribute exclusively to the body wall muscle (Sulston et al., 1983).

The question whether a minimal number of replication rounds of DNA is a prerequisite for visible cell differentiation was addressed by Edgar and McGhee (1988). They never found expression of gut-specific markers in 4-cell embryos in which DNA synthesis had been blocked with Aphidicolin. If they added the drug at the 8-cell stage (when the founder cell for the gut is present; see Fig.4) visible gut differentiation was always observed. From this they concluded that a short period of DNA synthesis is required in the first cell cycle after the gut has been clonally established.

Mosaic Development and Intercellular Regulation

Experiments in which blastomeres have been destroyed with a laser microbeam (Sulston et al., 1983) or cultured in isolation (Laufer et al., 1980) suggest that the differentiation program of the embryo works in an essentially cell autonomous fashion. However, the ablation experiments are not completely conclusive, because it cannot be excluded that interaction can still proceed after irradiation. Recently, a few examples have been described which show that, in contrast to the classical assumption, cell-cell interaction takes place during early nematode embryogenesis (Priess and Thomson, 1987; Schierenberg, 1987). This means that here as in many other systems the early phase of development includes aspects of regulative and mosaic cell behavior.

VI. GENES: GENETIC DISSECTION OF DEVELOPMENT

One of the most powerful strategies with which one can identify the processes involved in determination and differentiation of a cell, is the isolation and characterization of mutants which affect single steps within that pathway. In *C. elegans* (like in other suitable systems), the genetic approach has been most successful in trying to better understand development (for review, see Wood, 1988). As a convenient procedure for identifying genes essential for early embryogenesis, temperature-sensitive mutants have been isolated which develop normally at a permissive temperature (16°C) but arrest at the non-permissive temperature (25°C). With simple genetic tests, it can be determined whether expression of a gene identified by mutation is required in the mother, the father or the embryo (Fig.7). A considerable number of mutants affecting postembryonic development has been described, leading to models of how the control mechanisms for cellular specification may work (e.g. Sternberg and Horvitz, 1989). In contrast, the variety of mutants found to affect specific steps in early embryogenesis is rather limited. One reason for this may be that - as in other systems - early embryogenesis is essentially controlled by maternal gene products. The number of visible mutant phenotypes reflecting abnormal segregation of these maternal gene products may be limited in the nematode. Here we want to look briefly at three different types of maternal-effect mutants in which cellular behavior is altered in the young embryo.

In one class of mutants, cell cycle periods in certain cell lineages are either retarded or accelerated. These embryos show early defects in cellular positioning which are not compensated during further development (Schierenberg et al., 1980). Such mutants arrest as 'monsters' with several hundred cells and with various signs of cellular differentiation but without ever having entered a proper morphogenesis phase. Based on this and other data, it has been suggested that correct timing of cell divisions is necessary for proper cellular positioning. Further analysis of such mutants may help us to better understand how the length of the cell cycle is controlled, and to what extent spatial patterning of cells in the early embryo is due to differential cell cycle timing.

Another type of mutants does not express the typical polarity along the anterior-posterior axis (Kemphues et al., 1988). This is accompanied by loss of the dichotomy between germline and soma; all cells cleave equally like somatic cells. Germline granules are not segregated into specific cells but become randomly distributed. At the arrest stage these embryos possess about 50% more cells than the wildtype, suggesting that both (equal-sized) daughters of the zygote express characteristics of AB cells (which in normal embryos produce about two thirds of all embryonic cells). However signs of differentiation typical for other cell lineages are also detectable in these embryos. Further analysis of such mutants may help us to identify the mechanism by which polarity is established in the embryo, and to correlate polarity with cellular determination.

Very recently mutants have been described in which germline cells express prolonged cell cycle periods. The germline

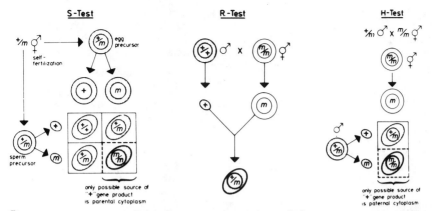

FIG.7. Progeny tests for mode of gene expression Genotypic configurations are indicated in the nuclei: m, mutant allele, +, wildtype allele. Possible interpretations and the assignments to classes of gene expression are given under each scheme. (From Isnenghi et al., 1983)

cells affected apparently loose or never acquire their identity. Instead they behave like their somatic daughter cells (Schnabel and Schnabel, 1989). This finding is explained with a model of cellular determination involving a cytoplasmic clock. These mutants provide a promising basis for identifying the mechanism of how cell fate is specified in the early embryo.

VII. CLOSING REMARKS

The case of *C. elegans* constitutes a good example for the progress that can be achieved by the concerted effort of many scientists working on one suitable model system. Today the nematode is probably the best understood multicellular organism in terms of anatomy, genetics, development, and behavior. In spite of this, our understanding of the processes controlling early embryogenesis is still rudimentary. The analysis of mutants alone may not be sufficient to unravel the underlying mechanisms. As only a small number of different mutant classes affecting early embryogenesis has been identified so far, we have to look for additional approaches to complement our present knowledge. A number of questions have been successfully attacked by direct manipulation of embryos (e.g. Laufer et al., 1980; Priess and Thomson, 1987; Schierenberg, 1987, 1988).

In another project we have begun to compare early development in different free-living nematode species (Skiba and Schierenberg, unpublished results). We observe differences in the pattern of early embryogenesis, in particular with respect to the expression of polarity, the sequence of events and cellular pattern formation. Our findings provide further support for the notion that in the development of the embryo of *C. elegans* timing is of central importance. This appears not only to be true for correct positioning but also for functional determination of cells (Schierenberg, 1985; Schnabel and

Schnabel, 1989). One task for the near future is to elucidate in more detail the role and the mechanisms of timing and to compare them to other systems, like *Drosophila*, where arrangement in space plays a primary role for cellular determination in the young embryo.

ACKNOWLEDGEMENTS

Thanks go to Paul Hardy for comments on of the manuscript. Work from my laboratory reported here was supported by grants from the Deutsche Forschungsgemeinschaft.

REFERENCES

Boveri, T., 1887, Über die Differenzierung der Zellkerne während der Furchung de Eies von *Ascaris megalocephala*, *Anat.Anz.*, 2:668

Boveri, T., 1888, Zellstudien II. Die Befruchtung und Teilung des Eies von *Ascaris megalocephala*, *Jena.Zeitschr.Naturw.*, 22:685.

Boveri, T.,1909, Die Blastomerenkerne von *Ascaris megalocephala* und die Theorie der Chromosomenindividualität, *Arch.Zellforsch.*, 3:181.

Boveri, T., 1910, Die Potenzen der *Ascaris*-Blastomeren bei abgeänderter Furchung, *in:* Festschrift für R. Hertwig: 133, Fischer, Jena.

Brenner, S., 1963, Letter to Max Perutz, reprinted *in:* "The nematode *Caenorhabditis elegans*," W.B. Wood ed., Cold Spring Harbor Laboratory, Cold Spring Harbor (1988).

Brenner, S., 1974, The genetics of *Caenorhabditis elegans*, *Genetics*, 77:71.

Coulson, A., Sulston, J., Brenner, S., and Karn, J., 1986, Towards a physical map of the genome of the nematode *Caenorhabditis elegans*, *Proc.Nat.Acad.Sci.*, 83:7821.

Deppe, U., Schierenberg, E., Cole, T., Krieg, C., Schmitt, D., Yoder, B., and von Ehrenstein, G., Cell lineages of the embryo of the nematode *Caenorhabditis elegans*, *Proc.Nat.Acad.Sci.*, 75:376.

Edgar, L.G., and McGhee, J.D., 1988, DNA synthesis and the control of embryonic gene expression in *Caenorhabditis elegans*, *Cell*, 53:589.

Ellis, H.M., and Horvitz, H.R., 1986, Genetic control of programmed cell death in the nematode *Caenorhabditis elegans*, *Cell*, 44:817.

Hedgecock, E.M., Sulston, J.E., and Thomson, J.N., 1983, Mutations affecting programmed cell deaths in the nematode *Caenorhabditis elegans*, *Science*, 200:1277.

Horvitz, H.R., Ellis, H.M., and Sternberg, P.W., 1982, Programmed cell death in nematode development, *Neurosci.Comment*, 1:56.

Isnenghi, E., Cassada, R., Smith, K., Denich, K., and von Ehrenstein, G., 1983, Maternal effects and temperature-sensitive period of mutations affecting embryogenesis in *Caenorhabditis elegans*, *Dev.Biol.*, 98:465.

Kemphues, K.J., Priess, J.R., Morton, D.G., and Cheng, N., 1988, Identification of genes required for cytoplasmic localization in early *C. elgans* embryos, *Cell*, 52:311.

Kimble, J., and Hirsh, D., 1979, The postembryonic cell
    lineages of the hermaphrodite and male gonads in
    Caenorhabditis elegans, Dev.Biol., 70:396.
Laufer, J.S., Bazzicalupo, P., and Wood, W.B., 1980,
    Segregation of developmental potential in early embryos
    of Caenorhabditis elegans, Cell, 19:569.
Martini, E., 1909, Über Eutelie und Neotenie,
    Verh.dt.zool.Ges.,19:292.
Meglitsch, P.A., 1967, "Invertebrate Zoology," Oxford
    University Press, Oxford.
Priess, J.R., and Thomson, J.N., Cellular interactions in early
    C. elegans embryos, Cell, 48:241.
Rothstein, M., and Coppens, M., 1978, Nutritional factors and
    conditions for the axenic culture of free-living
    nematodes, Comp.Biochem.Physiol., 61B:99.
Schierenberg, E., 1985, Cell determination during early
    development of the nematode Caenorhabditis elegans, Cold
    Spring Harbor Symp.Quant.Biol., 50:59.
Schierenberg, E., 1987, Reversal of cellular polarity and early
    cell-cell interaction in the embryo of Caenorhabditis
    elegans, Dev.Biol., 122:452.
Schierenberg, E., 1988, Localization and segregation of
    lineage-specific cleavage potential in embryos of
    Caenorhabditis elegans, Roux's Arch.Dev.Biol., 197:282.
Schierenberg, E., Miwa, J., and Ehrenstein, G., 1980, Cell
    lineages and development of temperature-sensitive
    embryonic arrest mutants in Caenorhabditis elegans,
    Dev.Biol., 76:141.
Schierenberg, E., and Wood, W.B., 1985, Control of cell-cycle
    timing in early embryos of Caenorhabditis elegans,
    Dev.Biol., 107:337.
Schnabel, R., and Schnabel, H., 1989, Early determination in
    the C. elegans embryo: A gene, cib-1, required to
    specify a set of stem-cell-like blastomeres,
    Development, (in press).
Sulston, J.E., and Horvitz, H.R., 1977, Post-embryonic cell
    lineages of the nematode Caenorhabditis elegans,
    Dev.Biol., 56:110.
Sulston, J.E., Albertson, D.G., and Thomson, J.N., 1980, The
    Caenorhabditis elegans male: Postembryonic development
    of non-gonadal structures, Dev.Biol., 78:542.
Sulston, J.E., Schierenberg, E.; White, J., and Thomson, N.,
    1983, The embryonic cell lineages of the nematode
    Caenorhabditis elegans, Dev.Biol., 100:64.
Sternberg, P.W., and Horvitz, H.R., 1989, The combined action
    of two intercellular signaling pathways specifies three
    cell fates during vulval induction in C. elegans, Cell,
    58:679.
Strome, S., and Wood, W.B., 1983, Generation of asymmetry and
    segregation of germ-line granules in early C. elegans
    embryos, Cell, 35:15.
van Beneden, E., 1883, Recherches sur la maturation de l'oeuf,
    la fécondation et la division cellulaire, Gand et
    Leipzig, Paris
van Beneden, E., and Neyt, A., 1887, Nouvelle recherches sur la
    fécondation et la division mitosique chez l'Ascaride
    megalocephale, Bull.Acad.Roy.Sci.Belg., 7:215.
White, J.G., Southgate, E., Thomson, J.N., and Brenner, S.,
    1986, The structure of the nervous system of the
    nematode Caenorhabditis elegans,
    Phil.Trans.Roy.Soc.Lond., 314:1.

Wood, W.B., ed., "The nematode *Caenorhabditis elegans*," Cold
    Spring Harbor Laboratory, Cold Spring Harbor (1988).
zur Strassen, O., 1896, Embryonalentwicklung der *Ascaris
    megalocephala*, *Arch.Entw.Mech.*, 3:27.

GAP JUNCTIONAL COMMUNICATION AND CELL CYCLE DURATION IN THE

EARLY MOLLUSCAN EMBRYO

Jo A.M. Van den Biggelaar and Florenci Serras

Department of Experimental Zoology
University of Utrecht
The Netherlands

1.INTRODUCTION

The most remarkable aspect of the early molluscan deve-lopment is the extremely regular succession and pattern of cleavages. Without any variance the embryos of the same species exactly reproduce the same cell pattern. Initially, all blastomeres are in phase, and divide synchronously. After a species specific number of simultaneous division cycles, the cells in the different lineages become out of phase and an in time and space well defined program of cell divisions is executed. In this chapter the possible influence of inter-cellular communication on the duration of the cell cycle in early molluscan development will be discussed. Although extra-cellular factors may also influence progress through the cell cycle, these will be left out of consideration.

Somatic cells do not divide synchronously, but at random. In syncytia mitoses are synchronous (Mitchison, 1971). In its typical form the cell cycle of a somatic cell can be subdivided into four phases: the presynthetic or postmitotic G1 phase, the S phase in which the DNA is reduplicated, the postsynthetic or premitotic G2 phase, and the mitotic or M phase. In eukaryotic cells the duration of (S + G2 + M) is relatively constant (Prescott, 1976). This period is mostly regarded as the chromosome or nuclear cycle. Variation in the duration of the cell cycle is mainly restricted to the postmitotic phase. During the G1 phase the decision is made to divide or not to divide, to remain quiescent or not. Exogenous or endogenous stimulation occurs in the postmitotic phase and appears to depend upon a probabilistic event. Therefore, this period may be subdivided into a Go phase, which in fact does not make part of the cell cycle, and the G1 phase, which is the period after which the decision to divide has been made. The Go phase is the period at which a cell can execute its somatic functions. In actively dividing somatic tissues the cell cycles may vary from about 8-30 hours (Lloyd et al., 1982). In embryonic cells, the cell cycles are short. For instance, in the mollusc *Patella vulgata* the first division cycles are as short as 30 minutes (van den Biggelaar, 1977a). In most embryonic systems the cell cycle is almost exclusively restricted to the S and M phase, eventually lengthened by a short G2 phase, whereas the G1 phase is usually lacking. As the DNA is not available for transcription during the S and M phase, the embryonic genome is scarcely available for gene expression during the early development. The degree to which the genome can come into play, increases with the degree to which the duration of the cell cycle is extended. The striking differences between the duration and the composition of the cell cycle of a somatic and an embryonic cell may be related with the absence of growth in the embryonic cell. It may be expected that, sooner or later after the specification of the developmental programs of the various lineages, changes in the durations and compositions of the cell cycles will occur, eventually followed by cell cycle arrest, if specialised cell functions are executed. In the pond snail *Lymnaea stagnalis* it has been found indeed that at the 8-cell stage, the cell cycles get out of phase (van den Biggelaar, 1971a, b) and early differentiating cells stop dividing. Comparable results have recently been obtained from an analysis of the duration and composition of the cell cycles in the leech *Helobdella triserialis* (Bissen and Weisblat, 1989). These observations are in accordance with Agrell's view that:"An early centre of low mitotic activity may be a centre of early differentiation" (Agrell, 1964, p 62).

From cell deletion experiments it is known that in molluscs the invariant succession of cleavages is a pre-requisite for normal development (Morill et al., 1973. Normal embryos are only obtained if a blastomere of a 2-cell stage divides as a whole embryo, and thus repeats the whole cleavage pattern. If the cell divides as if still part of the whole embryo, development will be abnormal. Similarly, alterations in the duration of the cell cycle, followed by an abnormal succession of the cleavages, lead to abnormal development (van den Biggelaar, 1977b). These observations indicate that the factors which determine the duration of the cell cycles, and consequently the cell patterns thus formed, have a great morphogenetic significance. Therefore, it is important that in a variety of developmental systems, renewed attention is paid to the regulation of the cell cycle during embryonic development (Swenson et al., 1989).

2.CELL PROLIFERATION AND JUNCTIONAL COMMUNICATION IN SOMATIC CELLS

In somatic cells cell proliferation strongly depends upon the influence of exogenous growth factors (James and Brandshaw, 1984; Baserga, 1985) and upon the endogenous synthesis of cell cycle regulating factors (Edmunds, 1988). Moreover, the regu-lation of cell proliferation is not determined at the cellular level, but at the level of the cell population. This means that an individual cell cannot independently change its mitotic rate without a concomitant reduction of the intercellular communi-cation with the other cells of the population. It also means that the effects of a mitotic stimulus to a single cell are extended to the whole population of cells. The regulation of cell proliferation, at least partly, depends upon intercellular junctional communication (Loewenstein, 1979; Larsen, 1983; Sheridan, 1987; Pitts et al., 1988). As cells in different tissues have different regimes of proliferation it appears evident that junctional communications between heterotypic cells are less common than between homotypic. From this point of view it is interesting to study the development of the pattern of junctional communications during early development, and to analyse whether and when the regulation of the cell cycles may be influenced by junctional communication.

3.CELL CYCLE CONTROL IN EMBRYONIC CELLS

3.1. *Endogenous Determination of the Duration of the Cell Cycle in Embryonic Cells*

In contrast to the somatic cell, during the early cleavages the embryonic cell is almost completely independent of exogenous influences, and primarily depends upon endogenous cytoplasmic factors. This is nicely demonstrated by the cleavage pattern of molluscan species in which part of the ooplasm is temporarily set apart in the form of a polar lobe at the first two cleavages. Of the four cell lines A-D, mainly the D is enriched with the contents of the polar lobe. As a result, the cleavage pattern and cleavage rhythm in the D line deviate from those in the other three lines (Guerrier et al., 1978; van Dongen and Geilenkirchen, 1974). The two daughter cells of the first somatoblast 2d pass through a series of unequal divisions, at each cleavage a small cell is alternately split of in animal or vegetal direction. In the A, B and C quadrant the second quartet cells do not show this typical alternation of unequal cleavages. At the fifth cleavage the micromere 1d[1] divides ahead of its counterparts in the other quadrants; at the sixth cleavage the macromere 3D divides before the other three macromeres. All these differences fail to occur after deletion of the polar lobe (van Dongen and Geilenkirchen, 1975). If the polar lobe content is artificially segregated into two of the four quadrants, then the division rhythm and the division pattern in both quadrants replicates pattern and rhythm of the D line in a normal embryo (Guerrier et al., 1978). Apparently, the cleavage pattern and the succession of the early cell divisions are predominantly determined by the segregation of specific domains of the ooplasm in the different cell lineages.

3.2. *Exogenous Regulation of the Cell Cycle and Intercellular Communication between Embryonic Cells*

Regulation of the cell cycle during the early cleavages is mainly under endogenous control. Exogenous agents like growth factors are not expected to play a role. Similarly, growth control by the formation, presence or absence of extracellular matrices (Hay, 1982) will be of little importance during the early cleavages. The discussion on exogenous influences upon the duration of the cell cycle control will be concentrated on intercellular communication via gap junctions.

3.2.1. *Electron Microscopical Evidence for the Presence of Gap Junctions*

The presence of gap junctions during the early development has been analysed in two species: *Patella vulgata* and *Lymnaea stagnalis*.

In *Lymnaea* gap junctional plaques have been found from the 4-cell stage (Dohmen and van de Mast, 1978). If no gap junctions have been observed prior to the 4-cell stage, this does not necessarily mean that they are absent. It may indicate that they are less frequent than at later stages. Considerably larger gap junctions are present between the blastomeres of the 8-, 16- and 24-cell embryos (Dorresteijn et al., 1981). No differences have been observed in the structure of the junctions at the different stages. As during the 24-cell stage the cleavage cavity disappears, new and additional cell contacts are formed between the animal and vegetal cells. Also in the newly formed common cell borders, gap junctions have been observed, especially between the central macromere 3D and the animal cells. No indications for the absence of gap junctions between adjacent cells have been obtained.

In a preliminary study the presence of gap junctions has also been analyzed in *Patella vulgata* (Dorresteijn et al., 1982).Junctional contacts can be observed as early as the 2-cell stage. The number and size of gap junctional plaques increase at the 32-cell stage. As in most molluscs, also in *Patella* after the fifth cleavage, a reorganization of the cell contacts takes place, as a result of which the animal micromeres come into close contact with one of the four vegetal macromeres. Up to the 16-cell stage the embryo of *Patella* does not have a cleavage cavity. The blastomeres form a compact aggregation of cells. The packing of the cells is such that at the 16-cell stage the two equatorial tiers of micromeres $1a^2$-$1d^2$ and 2a-2d meet each other centrally and form a barrier between the four animal cells $1a^1$-$1d^1$ and the four vegetal macromeres 2A-2D (van den Biggelaar, 1977a). Prior to the fifth cleavage this barrier disappears simultaneously with the secretion of extracellular material in the form of glycoconjugates (Kühtreiber et al., 1986). These glycoconjugates resemble hyaluronic acid and it may be assumed that they cause a swelling of the intercellular clefts and finally the formation of a blastocoelic cavity (Kühtreiber and van Dongen, 1989); this breaks the equatorial barrier beween the animal micromeres and the vegetal macromeres.At the same time a basal lamina like extracellular layer appears at the central tips of the animal micromeres. Then the macromeres protrude into the blastocoel and finally come into touch with this basal lamina. This contact is only maintained with one of the four macromeres, 3D, the stem cell of the mesentoblast 4d. The other three macromeres are displaced into a more vegetal position. It is not unlikely that the ECM plays a role in the adhesion between the micromeres and macromeres, followed by the development of gap junctions. The data on the presence of gap junctions between the animal micromeres and vegetal macromeres are not yet conclusive. In contrast with the embryo of *Lymnaea*, Dorresteijn et al. (1982) did not observe gap junctions in the newly formed common cell borders between the animal micromeres and the central 3D macromere in the *Patella* embryo. In a later study (Krul, personal communication), however, membrane appositions which resemble gap junctions have been found between 3D and the animal micromeres. Therefore, also in *Patella* it may be assumed that, once cells have contact, they will share gap junctional channels. In a comparable way it has been shown that cell adhesion molecules play a role in the formation of gap junctions between sponge cells (Loewenstein, 1967) and between neurectodermal cells (Keane et al., 1988).

3.2.2. *Electrical and Dye-coupling*

Electrical and dye-coupling experiments are necessary in order to demonstrate that gap junctions are functional. Both types of experiments have been performed at various stages in the development of *Lymnaea* and *Patella*. In *Lymnaea* dye-coupling can be observed from the late 4-cell stage (van den Biggelaar and Serras, 1988), corresponding with the moments from which the presence of gap junctions has been demonstrated at the electronmicroscopical level. Up to the early 48-cell stage no blastomeres are excluded from dye-coupling (Serras and van den Biggelaar, 1987) and the embryo is an uninterrupted communication unit.

In *Patella* gap junctions are present from the 2-cell stage. From the same moment electrical coupling but not dye-coupling can be observed. Dye-coupling occurs from the 32-cell stage (de Laat et al., 1980; Dorresteijn et al., 1983; Serras et al., 1988). This change in junctional coupling takes place during the interval between the fifth and the sixth cleavage. Up to the early 64-cell stage, no restrictions in dye-coupling have been observed, and the embryo forms an uninterrupted communication unit.

4. CORRELATION BETWEEN CHANGES IN CELL CONTACTS AND CHANGES IN THE DURATION OF THE CELL CYCLES

Demonstrating that gap junctions are present, and that they allow the passage of electrical currents and dyes is one thing. Quite another thing is to answer the question whether junctional communication influences the duration and composition of the cell cycles of the coupled cells. The answer can only be given as soon as data are available on the correlation between changes in the pattern of intercellular contacts and changes in the duration of the cell cycles of the involved cells. Changes of that kind occur during normal development.

4.1. *Changes in Cell Contacts and Cell Cycle Durations in Relation with the Induction of the Stem Cell of the Mesentoblast*

In *Lymnaea* as well as in *Patella* a remarkable change in the duration of cell cycles in relation with a change in the pattern of cell contacts, occurs during the interval between the fifth and the sixth cleavage. As described before, then one out of the four initially equivalent macromeres at the vegetal pole attains a central position and, as a consequence, it is the only macromere which makes long lasting contacts with the overlying cells of the animal pole. In *Lymnaea*, this contact is associated with a considerable shortening of the cell cycle of the 3D macromere, and a lengthening of the cell cycles of the micromeres $1d^1$, $1c^2$, and $1d^2$, with which the contacts are maintained longer than with the corresponding animal cells ($1a^1$, $1b^1$, $1c^1$; $1a^2$ and $1b^2$). The cell cycle of 3D is about 200 minutes, whereas the macromeres 3A-3C will divide about 90 minutes later (van den Biggelaar, 1971b). The cell cycles of

$1a^1$, $1b^1$ and $1c^1$ are 300 minutes and of $1d^1$ 330 minutes; in $1a^2$ and $1b^2$ they are 340, and in $1c^2$ and $1d^2$ 400 minutes. As we are looking for indications that intercelluar contacts are important for the regulation of the duration of the cell cycles, it is important to stress that the micromeres which divide in advance of their counterparts appear to loose their contact with 3D long before the first quartet cells which have a delay. The micromeres $1a^1$-$1d^1$ synchronously reduplicate their DNA. The S phase in the micromeres $1a^2$-$1d^2$ is much longer, but also these cells synchronously reduplicate their DNA (van den Biggelaar, 1971b). This indicates that in both groups of micromeres the differences in duration of the cell cycles are only expressed in the duration of the G2 phases. The shortening of the cell cycle of 3D is similarly restrictet to a change in the duration of the G2 phase. Apparently, cellular interactions influence the transition from G2 to M. At this moment there is only circumstantial evidence that the cellular interactions are mediated by junctional communication. As mentioned before, gap junctions have been observed between the central macromere and the animal micromeres. Experiments have been performed in which at different stages cells have been loaded with Lucifer Yellow. At the 24-cell stage all blastomeres are dye-coupled. However, it cannot be distinguished whether the dye spreads directly via the intercellular channels between 3D and the animal micromeres and vice versa, or indirectly from the animal micromeres to the vegetal, centrally located 3D macromere via the intermediate equatorial cells along the surface of the embryo, or the other way around.

In *Patella* a comparable change in the cell pattern, associated with a change in the duration of the cell cycle, occurs during the interval between the fifth and sixth cleavage. After five synchronous and short (30 minutes) division cycles, the embryo reaches the 32-cell stage. At the sixth cleavage the blastomeres in the different tiers along the animal-vegetal axis still divide synchronously, but between the tiers synchrony is lost and the duration of the cell cycle is extensively increased. There is only one exception to the rule that cells within a tier divide simultaneously: at the vegetal pole the macromere 3D shows a significant division delay (about 18 minutes) in comparison with 3A-3C. In the animal hemisphere no asynchronies have been observed, as well as no differences in the duration of the contacts of the animal cells with the central 3D, as has been observed in *Lymnaea*. The division delay of 3D is associated with its unique contact with the animal micromeres. It should be stressed that, here we have a second clear example of a correlation between changes in cell contact and a concomitant change in the duration of the cell cycle. Just as has been described for *Lymnaea*, this contact induced change in the duration of the cell cycle adumbrates the determination of 3D to develop the stem cell (denominated as 4d or M) of the mesodermal bands, whereas the other macromeres only develop endoderm. Apparently, the first effect of the induction of 3D to develop the M-lineage is or is accompanied by a change in the duration of the cell cycle. In *Lymnaea* this induction was followed by a considerable shortening of the cell cycle of 3D, whereas in *Patella* it is lengthened. At a later moment we will discuss whether the shortening of the cycle of 3D in *Lymnaea* and the lengthening of the cycle in *Patella*, both might be the result of junctional communication.

4.2. *Coincidence between Cell Cycle Arrest of the Trochoblasts and Restrictions in Junctional Communication*

A second remarkable change in the duration of the cell cycle is demonstrated by the larval cells, especially the primary prototroch cells. After the 48-cell stage in *Lymnaea* and the 64-cell stage in *Patella* these cells do not divide any more and differentiate into ciliated cells, whereas cell proliferation in the surrounding cells is continued. Above we have postulated that, when in a population of cells, a particular cell stops dividing, whereas neighbouring cells continue to proliferate, this will be associated with a reduction in junctional communication. If in *Patella* directly after the last division and shortly before ciliation of the trochoblasts one of them is injected with Lucifer Yellow, dye spreads to all surrounding cells. About 20 minutes later, when the embryo has reached the 72-cell stage, dye-spread cannot longer be observed, neither to sister cells, nor to other cells, electrical-coupling appears to be maintained at a low level (Serras et al., 1990). Also in the embryo of *Lymnaea* after the last division of the primary trochoblasts, at the transition of the 24- to the 48-cell stage, the trochoblasts are dye-coupled with all neighbouring cells, whereas shortly later neither dye-spread can be observed from a trochoblast to any of the other cells, nor dye-transfer from any of the other cells to a trochoblast (Serras and van den Biggelaar, 1987; Serras et al., 1990). These results are in accordance with the assumption that cell cycle arrest in an individual cell is incompatible with unrestricted junctional coupling with actively dividing cells, but the electrical coupling also indicates that this is not incompatible with free intercellular diffusion of ions. This result also sheds new light on the older observations of Wilson (1904) on the development of isolated blastomeres of the *Patella* embryo. Wilson observed that the cell cycle arrest of the trochoblasts is independent of cellular contacts. Just as in the normal embryo isolated primary trochoblasts divide only twice, and then differentiate into ciliated cells. This result has been confirmed by Janssen-Dommerholt et al. (1983). In both papers the observations have only been discussed in relation with the mosaic character of molluscan development. However, one may assume that also in the normal embryo their cleavage arrest and early differentiation into ciliated cells will be associated with a strong reduction in the physiological cell contacts of the trochoblasts with surrounding cells. It would be interesting to inhibit the reduction of junctional communication in order to see if cell division and differentiation of the trochoblasts will change.

An additional aspect of the cell cycle arrest of the trochoblasts is their early differentiation into ciliated cells. It is known that ciliated cells do not divide. This has led to the assumption that mitotic activity and ciliation mutually exclude each other as the cellular centrioles or microtubule organizing centres cannot be involved simultaneously with the development of cilia and the formation of the mitotic apparatus (Lloyd et al., 1982). Lengthening of the cell cycle or cell arrest is a prerequisite for the expression of characteristic features of cell differentiation. This is in accordance with the observed relation between changes in the duration of the cell cycle at midblastula transition in *Xenopus*

(Newport and Kirschner, 1982) after the twelfth cleavage. From that moment transcription proceeds rapidly. In sea urchins "after the tenth cleavage, the cleavage rate declines and mitotic stages are rare" (Okazaki, 1975). At that time cilia develop. In *Drosophila* nuclear transcription is first seen during the interval between the tenth and eleventh nuclear division, the first cycle with a notable G2 (10 min.); especially after the fourteenth cycle the G2 phase is extended to 60 minutes. This moment coincides with cellularization, after which the cells divide asynchronously, and the maternally dominated part of embryogenesis is followed by the period which is dominated by the activity of the embryonic genome (Edgar and O'Farrell, 1989). In *Xenopus* it has been observed that if the cell cycle is lengthened artificially, this prematurely initiates transcription and cell motility (Kimelman et al., 1987). In *Lymnaea* we have shown that an experimental lengthening of the early cell cycles is accompanied by a premature formation of nucleoli and intracellular relocalization of ooplasmic components (van den Biggelaar, 1977b).

4.3. *The Effect of Cell Dissociation on the Duration of the Cell Cycles*

Almost no data are available on the effect of the dissociation of embryonic cells on the rate of cell division. If during the early cleavages cells cyclically produce a proliferation stimulating factor sufficiently enough to trigger their own progress through the cell cycle, as presumed for somatic cells, and if the synthesis of this factor in adjacent and junctionally coupled cells is out of phase, it may be expected that junctionally communicating cells will mutually slow down their progress through the cell cycle. Dissociation of the embryo into isolated cells might result in a shortening of the cell cycles. The effect of changes in cell contacts on the duration of the cell cycles can be derived from the results of dissociation experiments in *Patella* (van den Biggelaar and Guerrier, 1979; Janssen-Dommerholt et al., 1983). In the normal embryo the blastomeres divide synchronously up to the fifth cleavage. Up till that moment the junctional communication is limited to electrical coupling, whereas dye-coupling only occurs shortly after the fifth cleavage. Like *in vivo* the blastomeres of 16-cell embryos divide synchronously and almost simultaneously with the blastomeres in the control embryos. It may be assumed that the production of a mitogenic factor or the degradation of an inhibitor in all blastomeres occurs in phase. The transition of the 32-cell stage into the 64-cell stage is not reached by a simultaneous division of all blastomeres. Along the animal-vegetal egg axis the cells in the successive tiers divide synchronously, but the tiers are out of phase. Apparently from the 32-cell stage the synthesis of the stimulator or the degradation of the inhibitor is no longer in phase throughout the embryo. If the assumption that junctional communication between heterophasic cells will result in a mutual change of the progress through the cell cycle, will be true, it may be expected that in dissociated embryos the sixth division of the blastomeres will be less asynchronous than in the normal embryo. The following preliminary result has been obtained: during normal development the difference between the first and last dividing cells is about 50 minutes, this diference was only 20 minutes in the dissociated embryo (van den Biggelaar and Guerrier, 1979). This result indicates that from the fifth cleavage the duration of the cell cycles partially depends upon cell contacts.

5. A MODEL FOR THE POSSIBLE ROLE OF GAP JUNCTIONAL COMMUNICATION IN THE REGULATION OF CELL CYCLE DURATION IN EARLY MOLLUSCAN DEVELOPMENT

Of all the possible roles that have been attributed to gap junctional communication, a role in the regulation of cell proliferation, thus in the regulation of the cell cycle, is by far the most supported and best documented (for references the reader is referred to recent reviews on gap junctions and cell-to-cell communication, De Mello, 1987; Hertzberg and Johnson, 1988). The way in which junctional communication may be involved with the intercellular regulation of the cell cycle is most evident in somatic cells, and this does probably not differ from its role during the early cleavages. Therefore, we want to start with a discussion about gap junctions and regulation of the cell cycle in somatic cells.

In somatic cells cell proliferation is stimulated by endogenous and exogenous factors, and one may ask whether stimulation of one cell will not automatically influence adjacent cells. For instance, if cell proliferation is stimulated by growth factors, only those cells will be activated and pass from the quiescent to the G1 phase, which are provided with the appropriate receptors. The effect of growth factors is activation of the second messenger system, part of which are small molecular weight substances that can easily pass through gap junctions. If the activated cells are junctionally coupled with other cells, the proliferative signal will be transferred to the neighbouring cells (Pitts et al., 1988): the activation of a single cell may either lead to the activation of a population of cells, or vice versa the dilution of the signal may annihilate the effects of growth factor stimulation and the activated cell will remain in the quiescent G0 phase. Another example for the significance of junctional communication in the regulation of proliferation in a multicellular system are co-cultures of normal and transformed cells (Yamasazki, 1988). Yamasaki assumed that in transformed cells a gene is altered, as a consequence of which the normal control of cell proliferation is disturbed and the cells ceaselessly divide; the expression of the gene is under control of intercellular communication with normal cells, because these normal cells provide diffusible factors which suppress the expression of the malignant phenotype, or vice versa, the cell cycle promoting factor in the transformed cell is diluted into the population of normal cells and cannot reach the critical level in order to trigger mitosis. Also in this case, progress through the cell cycle is not controlled on the level of the single cell but on the level of the population cells.

In the above examples the intercellular regulation of the cell cycle is related to the transition G0/G1. The inhibition of the G2/M transition in the mammalian oocyte similarly demonstrates the significance of intercellular communication for the control of cell cycle on the level of the transition G2/M (Moor and Osborn, 1982). This cell cycle arrest depends upon the junctional contact betwen the surrounding follicle cells and the oocyte. It appears that the changes in junctional communication do not directly involve the junctions between the cumulus cells and the oocyte, but presumably those between the granulosa cells and the cumulus cells (Salustri and Siracusa, 1983; Moor et al, 1981; Larsen et al., 1986, 1987; Racowsky et al., 1989).

The above examples clearly demonstrate a role of junctional communication in the regulation of cell proliferation and progress through the cell cycle. Little is known about the effect of junctional communication on the duration of the cell cycle phases in heterophasic cells. The possible involvement of gap junctions in the control of cell proliferation in somatic cells has mainly been focused on the G0/G1 phase (Sheridan, 1987). Junctional communication during S-phase is probably limited to metabolic cooperation. Junctional coupling would not be of particular interest in the regulation of the progress through G2; as progress through M phase is controlled by the concentration of a number of small molecules, it might be advantageous for a cell to reduce junctional coupling during mitosis (Sheridan, 1987). Our results on embryonic cells, however, indicate that cell contacts have noticeable effects on the duration of the G2 phase.

To our knowledge, it is not known whether phase shifting will occur when heterophasic cells become junctionally coupled. In this respect it is interesting to refer to phase shifting in a heterophasic heterokaryon. If two cells in a different phase of the cell cycle are fused, there appears to be a specific hierarchy of phases. M phase dominates, a nucleus in M forces a G1, S or G2 nucleus to enter precociously the M phase. If one of the cells is in S and the other in G1, the latter passes into S. Even more interesting are the observations of Schierenberg and Wood (1985). The authors have fused blastomeres from cell lines with different cell cycle rhythms in the embryo of *Caenorhabditis elegans*. It appeared that addition of cytoplasm of a faster dividing cell line could accelerate the cell cycle of a slowly dividing lineage, whereas addition of cytoplasm of a slowly dividing lineage could lengthen the cell cycle of faster dividing recipient cell. These effects were long term effects and were obtained when both, the donor and the recipient cell were in interphase. The short term effects are somewhat different if the cells are heterophasic. The time at which a recipient cell will enter mitosis can be altered independent of the division rate of the donor cell, but depends on its position in the cell cycle. If the donor cell had just started mitosis, its cytoplasm will delay the transition to M in the recipient cell. This result is in contrast with the M Phase dominance in somatic cells, where after fusion of a cell in mitosis with a cell in whatever of the other phases forces the second cell to enter mitosis. If the donor is in late interphase and the recipient cell in early interphase, the latter is prematurely triggered to enter M. In our discussion it is important that from these results it can be concluded that a cytoplasmic factor present in a cell in M phase can influence the progression to the M phase of an other cell. Unfortunately, the authors only made a distinction between M and interphase, and did not subdivide the interphase in G1, S and G2. It would be interesting to know whether the effect of the cytoplasmic factor might pass junctional channels.

In the absence of a G1 phase during the early cleavage stages, the most important transition point in the regulation of the cell cycle appears to be the transition between G2 and M. Changes in the duration of the cell cycle in *Helobdella* (Bissen and Weisblat, 1989), in *Drosophila* (Edgar and Schubiger, 1986; Edgar and O'Farrell, 1989, *Caenorhabditis* (Edgar and McGhee, 1988) and *Lymnaea* (van den Biggelaar, 1971b) mainly concern the duration of the G2 phase. The early cell cycles usually lack a G1 phase. When the cell divisions become out of phase, the S and G2 phases are lengthened (van den Biggelaar, 1971b; Bissen and Weisblat, 1989).

From dye-coupling experiments in *Lymnaea* (van den Biggelaar and Serras, 1988; Serras and van den Biggelaar, 1987) and *Patella* (Dorresteijn et al., 1983; Serras et al., 1990) it is known that up to and inclusive the sixth cleavage cycle, the embryo is one dye-coupling unit. So all cells are coupled with the surrounding cells. If in such a system junctional communication plays a role in the determination of the cycle duration, all cells will mutually influence each other and it will be difficult to determine how far the duration of the cell cycles in the different cell lines is determined by endogenous factors and how far by exogenous factors, for instance by gap junctional communication. Up to the fifth cleavage the embryos of *Patella* and *Lymnaea* are radially symmetrical; this means that in each of the four quadrants there is the same succession of cells along the animal-vegetal axis, and in each quadrant every blastomere is surrounded by the same number of equivalent cells. As soon as the cell pattern becomes asymmetrical and a number of equivalent cells no loger have the same number of comparable cell contacts, it will be possible to notice whether additional contacts are accompanied by additional alterations in the duration of the cell cycle.It should be realized that in the following discussion changes in the duration of the cell cycle in relation with changes in cell contacts only refer to the effect of additional contacts. Initially, the embryo is radially symmetrical; in each quadrant there is the same succession of blastomeres with the same number of comparable cells as neighbours. Therefore, if the durations of the cell cycles of the blastomeres partly depend upon the communication with adjacent cells, in each quadrant each blastomere will be influenced in the same way as its counterparts in the other three quadrants. As the cells do not shift and maintain existing contacts on the periphery of the embryo, new and additional contacts are limited to contacts inside of the embryo.

In the description of the dependence of the duration of the cell cycle on intercellular contacts in *Lymnaea* (van den Biggelaar, 1971b) it has been shown that changes in the contacts between cells are primarily expressed in changes in the duration of the G2 phase, thus the determination of the transition from G2 to M. A remarkable difference has been pointed out in the effect of the changes in cell contact during the induction of the stem cell of the mesentoblast (3D) during the interval beween the fifth and the sixth cleavage in *Lymnaea stagnalis* and *Patella vulgata*. In *Lymnaea* the division cycle of 3D is about 200 minutes, whereas the corresponding macromeres have a division cycle of 290 minutes, this shortening of the cell cycle of 3D is due to a corresponding shortening of the G2 phase. The animal cells of which the duration of the contact with 3D is longer than of the corresponding first quartet cells, show a significant lengthened cell cycle which is also limited to a lengthening of the G2 phase (van den Biggelaar, 1971b). During the contact period the central macromere passes from G2 to M, whereas the animal cells are partly in S, but predominantly in G2. In *Patella* the 3D cell shows a cleavage cycle of 148 minutes, whereas the macromeres 3A-3C have a division cycle of 130 minutes. No differences in the duration of the cell cycles of equivalent cells at the animal pole can be observed. In *Patella* the composition of the cell cycle has not been determined, but from cytological observations it is known that during the period of contact between the animal micromeres and the central 3D macromere, the former go through mitosis, whereas the macromere does not. This implies that the micromeres probably pass from G2 to M, from M to S and eventually from S to G2. The acceleration of the cell cycle of 3D and the retardation of specific cells at the animal pole in *Lymnaea*, on the one hand, and the retardation of the cell cycle of 3D, and the absence of differences in the duration of the cell cycle of equivalent micromeres at the animal pole in *Patella*, on the other hand, appear to be a regular aspect of the induction of the stem cell of the mesentoblast in molluscs. From the older literature on cell lineage in molluscan embryos it can be derived that an acceleration of 3D and a retardation of animal cells occurs in those species in which after the fourth cleavage the macromeres and second quartet cells divide, whereas the animal micromeres skip one division. The embryo then passes a 24-cell stage. In those species in which all blastomeres divide synchronously and a 32-cell stage is reached after the fifth cleavage, the stem cell of the mesentoblast is retarded, whereas no difference in the cell cycle can be observed in the cells of the animal hemisphere. In the 24-cell embryos the central macromere 3D comes into touch with at least 8 animal cells (van den Biggelaar, 1971b) which have passed one cell cycle less than the 3D. In the 32-cell embryos, the central macromere 3D comes into touch with about 20 animal cells which are one cell cycle ahead of 3D. The embryo of *Physa* passes a comparable 24-cell stage and similar changes occur in the succession of cleavages (Wierzejski, 1905). In *Crepidula* Conklin (1897) describes a 24-cell stage accompanied by similar changes in the cell cycles of 3D and the animal cells. Boring (1989) also observed a precocious division of 3D and a division asynchrony in the first quartet cells in the opisthobranch mollusc *Haminoea*. Species with a 32-cell stage like *Trochus* (Robert, 1902) and *Haliotis* (personal observation) follow the same pattern as *Patella*.

The observed acceleration or retardation of the cell cycle in a specific group of cells can be explained in two ways, which do not necessarily exclude each other. In the first explanation it is assumed that phase shifting occurs as the result of junctional communication between heterophasic cells, with the additional assumption that when cells which go through mitosis while junctionally coupled with cells that in the same period do not enter mitosis, the latter will be delayed in their G2/M transition. This resembles the retardation of an interphase nucleus after cell fusion with a cell in mitosis in *Caenorhabditis* (Schierenberg and Wood, 1985). In this way 3D is retarded in *Patella*, whereas in *Lymnaea* the animal cells are delayed by their contact with 3D during its mitosis. If this explanation will be true it remains to be explained why in the case of *Lymnaea* 3D divides in advance of the other three macromeres without being different from them before the contact with the animal micromeres. The second explanation does not focus on the phase differences between the contacting cells, but on the difference in the number of cell divisions that the contacting cells have passed. The additional assumption that has to be made in this case is that cells produce a small molecular weight substance that positively or negatively influences progress through the mitotic cycle, that the rate at which this product is synthesized is different in the various cell lines, and in the case of a positive influence this progressively diminishes after each cell division, whereas in the case of the synthesis of an inhibitor, this would increase after each cell cycle. In the *Patella* embryo this would explain why 3D is delayed in comparison with 3A, 3B and 3D. The animal cells which only make contact with 3D are one cell cycle ahead of 3D, and might have left or synthesize less cell cycle stimulating factors. If they come into touch with 3D, in which more is left or which produces more, these might diffuse to the animal cells; as a great number (16) of animal cells are in contact with 3D this will loose a significant amount of the stimulator, and become retarded, whereas the net acceleration of the micromeres will be negligable. In *Lymnaea* the central 3D is two cell cycles ahead of the eight animal cells with which it makes additional contacts; this means that in 3D the synthesis of the activator or the inhibitor will be much less or much higher, respectively, whereas in the micromeres the opposite situation exists. Then, from a number of cells activator will flow to a single macromere, or inhibitor can flow from 3D to a number of cells with the observed significant acceleration of 3D and the relative slight retardation of the micromeres as a result.

Although the above speculations are in accordance with the observed changes in cell cycle duration, we still do not have any definitive evidence for the intercellular junctional transfer of any specific proliferation signal. The regular division pattern and the mutual changes in the duration of the cell cycle that follow changes in cell contacts in early molluscan development are promising enough to stimulate further studies on the possible role of gap junctions in the regulation of cell proliferation during embryonic development.

6. REFERENCES

Agrell, I., 1964, Natural division syncrony and mitotic gradients in metazoan tissues. *In:* "Synchrony in cell division and growth," E. Zeuthen, ed., Interscience Publishers, New York.
Baserga, R., 1985, "The biology of cell reproduction," Harvard Univ.Press.
Bissen, S.T., and Weisblat, D.A., 1989, The durations and compositions of the cell cycles in embryos of the leech *Helobdella triserialis*, Development, 105:105.
Conklin, E.G., 1897, The embryology of Crepidula, J.Morphol., 13:1.
De Laat, S.W., Tertoolen, L.G.J., Dorresteijn, A.W.C., and van den Biggelaar, J.A.M., Intercellular communication patterns are involved in cell determination in early molluscan development, *Nature*, 287:546.

De Mello, W.C., 1987, "Cell-to-cell communication," Plenum Press, New York.

Dohmen, M.R., and Van de Mast, J.M.A., 1978, Electron microscopical study of RNA-containing cytoplasmic localizations and intercellular contacts in early cleavage stages of eggs of *Lymnaea stagnalis* (Gastropoda, Pulmonata), *Proc.Kon.Ned.Akad.Wetens* Serie C 81:403.

Dorresteijn, A.W.C., van den Biggelaar, J.A.M., Bluemink, J.G., and Hage, W.J., 1981, Electron microscopical investigations of the intercellular contacts during the early cleavage stages of *Lymnaea stagnalis* (Mollusca, Gastropoda), *W.Roux's Arch.Dev.Biol., 190:215.*

Dorresteijn, A.W.C., Bilinsky, S.M., vand den Biggelaar, J.A.M., and Bluemink, J.G., 1982, The presence of gap junctions during early *Patella* embryogenesis: an electron microscopical study, *Dev.Biol.*, 91:397.

Dorresteijn, A.W.C., Wagemaker, H.A., de Laat, S.W., and van den Biggelaar, J.A.M., 1983, Dye coupling between blastomeres in early embryos of *Patella vulgata* (Mollusca, Gastropoda): its relevance for cell determination, *W.Roux's Arch.Dev.Biol.*, 192:262.

Edgar, B.A., and McGhee, J.D., 1988, DNA synthesis and the control of embryonic gene expression in *C. elegans*, *Cell*, 53:589.

Edgar, B.A., and Schubiger, G.,1986, Parameters controlling transcriptional activation during early *Drosophila* development, *Cell*, 44:871.

Edgar, B.A., and O'Farrell, 1989, Genetic control of cell division patterns in the *Drosophila* embryo, *Cell*, 57:177.

Edmunds, L.N., 1988, "Cellular and molecular basis of biological clocks," Springer Verlag, New York, Berlin.

Guerrier, P., van den Biggelaar, J.A.M., van Dongen, C.A.M., and Verdonk, N.H., 1978, Significance of the polar lobe for the determination of dorsoventral polarity in *Dentalium vulgare* (da Costa), *Dev.Biol.*, 63:233.

Hay, E.D., 1982, "Cell biology of extracellular matrix," Plenum Press, New York, London.

Hertzberg, E.L., and Johnson, R.G., 1988, Modern Cell Biology, vol.7, "Gap Junctions," A.Liss, New York.

James, R., and Brandshaw, R.A., 1984, Polypeptide growth factors, *Ann.Rev.Biochem.*, 53:259.

Janssen-Dommerholt, C., van Wijk, R., and Geilenkirchen, W.L.M., 1983, Restriction of developmental potential and trochoblast ciliation in *Patella* embryos, *J.Embryol.exp.Morph.*, 74:69.

Keane, R.W., Mehta, P.R., Rose, B., Honig, L.S., Loewenstein, W.R., and Rutishauser, U., 1988, Neural differentiation, NCAM-mediated adhesion, and gap junctional communication in neurectoderm. A study *in vitro*, *J.Cell Biol.*, 106:1307.

Kimelman, D., Kirschner, M., and Scherson, T., 1987, The events of the midblastula transition in *Xenopus* are regulated by changes in the cell cycle, *Cell*, 48:399.

Kühtreiber, W.M., and van Dongen, C.A.M., 1989, Microinjection of lectins, hyaluronidase, and hyaluronate fragments interferes with cleavage delay and mesoderm induction in embryos of *Patella vulgata*, *Dev.Biol.*, 132:436.

Kühtreiber, W.M., Dorresteijn, A.W.C., van de Bent, J., van Dongen, C.A.M., and van den Biggelaar, J.A.M., 1986, The presence of an extracellular matrix between cells involved in the determination of the mesoderm bands in embryos of *Patella vulgata* (Mollusca, Gastropoda), *W.Roux's Arch.Dev.Biol.*, 195:265.

Larsen, W.J., 1983, Biological implications of gap junction structure, distribution and composition: a review, *Tissue and Cell*, 15:645.

Larsen, W.J., Wert, S.E., and Brunner, G.D., 1986, A dramatic loss of cumulus gap junctions is correlated with germinal vesicle breakdown in rat oocytes, *Dev.Biol.*,113:517.

Larsen, W.J., Wert, S.E., and Brunner, G.D., 1987, Differential modulation of rat follicle gap junction populations at ovulation, *Dev.Biol.*, 122:61.

Lloyd, D., Poole, R.K., and Edwards, S.W., 1982, "The cell division cycle. Temporal organization and control of cellular growth and reproduction," Acad.Press, New York.

Loewenstein, W.R., 1967, On the genesis of cellular communication, *Dev.Biol.*, 15:503.

Loewenstein, W.R., 1979, Junctional intercellular communication and the control of growth, *Biochim.Biophys.Acta*, 560:1.

Mitchison, J.M., 1971, "The biology of the cell cycle," Cambr.Univ.Press.

Moor, R.M., Osborne, J.C., Cran, D.G., and Walters, D.F., 1981, Selective effect of gonadotropins on cell coupling, nuclear maturation and protein synthesis in mammalian oocytes, *J.Embryol.exp.Morphol.*, 61:347.

Moor, R.M., and Osborn, J.C., 1982, The functional integration of cells in ovarian follicles, in: "The functional integration of cells in animal tissues," J.E. Pitts and M.E. Finbow, eds, Cambridge University Press.

Morrill, J.B., Blair, C.A., and Larsen, W., 1973, Regulative development in the pulmonate gastropod, *Lymnaea palustris*, as determined by blastomere deletion, *J.exp.Zool.*, 183:47.

Newport, J., and Kirschner, M., 1982, A major developmental transition in early *Xenopus* embryos. II. Control of the onset of transcription, *Cell*, 30:687.

Okazaki, K., 1975, Normal development to metamorphosis. *In:* "The sea urchin embryo," G. Czihak, ed., Springer Verlag, Berlin.

Pitts, J.D., Kam, E., and Morgan, D., 1988, The role of junctional communication in cellular growth control and tumorigenesis. *In:* Modern Cell Biology 7, "Gap Junctions," E.L. Hertzberg and R.G. Johnson, eds, Alan Liss, New York.

Prescott, D.M., 1976, "Reproduction of eukaryotic cells," Acad.Press, New York.

Racowsky, C., Baldwin, K.V., Larabell, C.A., DeMarais, A.A., and Kazilek, C.J., 1989, Down-regulation of membrana granulosa cell gap junctions is correlated with irreversible commitment to resume meiosis in golden Syrian hamster oocytes, *Eur.J.Cell Biol.*, 49:244.

Robert, A., 1902, Recherches sur le développement des troques, *Arch.Zool.exp.gén.*, 10:269.

Salustri, A., and Siracusa, G., 1983, Metabolic coupling, cumulus expansion and meiotic resumption in mouse cumuli oophori cultured *in vitro* in the presence of FSH ordcAMP, or stimulated *in vivo* by hCH, *J.Reprod.Fertil.*, 68:335.

Schierenberg, E., and Wood, W.B., 1985, Control of cell cycle timing in early embryos of *Caenorhabditis elegans*, *Dev.Biol.*, 107:337.

Serras, F., and van den Biggelaar, J.A.M., 1987, Is a mosaic embryo also a mosaic of communication compartments ? *Dev.Biol.*, 120:132.

Serras, F., Dictus, W.J.A.G., and van den Biggelaar, J.A.M., 1990, Changes in junctional communication associated with cell cycle arrest and differentiation of trochoblasts of *Patella vulgata*, *Dev.Biol.*, in press.

Sheridan, J.D., 1987, Cell communication and growth. *In:* "Cell-to-cell communication," W.C. De Mello, ed., Plenum Press, New York.

Swenson, K.I., Westendorf, J.M., Hunt, T., and Ruderman, J.V., 1989, Cyclins and regulation of the cell cycle in early embryos. *In:* "Molecular Biology of Fertilization," G. Schatten and H. Schatten, eds, Acad.Press, New York.

van den Biggelaar, J.A.M., 1971a, Timing of the phases of the cell cycle with tritiated Thymidine and Feulgen cytophotometry during the period of synchronous division in *Lymnaea*, *J.Embryol.exp.Morphol.*, 26:351.

van den Biggelaar, J.A.M., 1971b, Timing of the phases of the cell cycle during the period of asynchronous division up to the 49-cell stage in *Lymnaea*, *J.Embryol.exp.Morphol.*, 26:367.

van den Biggelaar, J.A.M., 1977a, Development of dorsoventral polarity and mesentoblast determination in *Patella vulgata*, J.Morphol., 154:157.

van den Biggelaar, J.A.M., 1977b, Significance of cellular interactions for the differentiation of the macromeres prior to the formation of the mesentoblast in *Lymnaea stagnalis*, *Proc.Kon.Ned.Akad.Wetensch.* Amsterdam, Series D, 80:1.

van den Biggelaar, J.A.M., and Guerrier, P., 1979, Dorsoventral polarity and mesentoblast determination as concomittant results of cellular interactions in the mollusc *Patella vulgata*, *Dev.Biol.*, 68:462.

van den Biggelaar, J.A.M., and Serras, F., 1988, Determinative decisions and dye-coupling changes in the molluscan embryo. In: Modern Cell Biology, vol.7, "Gap Junctions," E.L. Hertzberg and R.G. Johnson, eds, Alan Liss, New York.

van Dongen, C.A.M., and Geilenkirchen, W.L.M., 1974, The development of *Dentalium* with special reference to the significance of the polar lobe. I, II, III. Division chronology and development of the cell pattern in *Dentalium dentale* (Scphopoda), *Proc.Kon.ned.Akad.Wetensch.* Ser.C, 78:57.

van Dongen, C.A.M., and Geilenkirchen, W.L.M., 1975, The development of *Dentalium* with special reference to the significance of the polar lobe. IV. Division chronology and development of the cell pattern in lobeless embryos of *Dentalium dentale* after removal of the polar lobe at first cleavage, *Proc.Kon.ned.Akad.Wetensch., Amsterdam*, Ser.C, 78:358.

Wierzejski, A., 1905, Embryologie von *Physa fontinalis*, *Z.wiss.Zool.*, 83:502.

Wilson, E.B., 1904, Experimental studies in germinal localization, *J.exp.Zool.*, 1:197.

Yamasaki, H., 1988, Role of gap junctional intercellular communication in malignant cell transformation. *In:* "Gap Junctions," Modern Cell Biology, vol.7, E.L. Hertzberg and R.G. Johnson, eds, Alan Liss, New York.

IN VITRO PREPARATION OF THE EARLY SQUID BLASTODERM

Hans-Jürg Marthy[1], Luigia Santella[2] and Brian Dale[2]
1
Laboratoire Arago, UA 117 du CNRS
Université P.et M. Curie
66650 Banyuls-sur-mer, France
2
Stazione Zoologica di Napoli
Villa Comunale
80121 Naples, Italy

PRACTICAL CUES

The early squid embryo (*Loligo vulgaris*) presents a "bi-dimensional" blastoderm architecture as well as cell structural and physiological properties, which makes it worthwhile for studies on individual cell migration *in vivo* and *in situ* and cell-to-cell communication devices (Marthy 1982, 1985; Segmüller and Marthy 1989; Marthy and Dale 1989). However, whereas the size of the egg, its translucency and the dimension of the blastoderm (egg: 2,2 x 1,5 mm in size; blastoderm: 0,5 - 1,5 mm in diameter, during the preorgano-genetic stages) are well appreciated when working on living material, the shape of the egg (a hen's egg form), on which the blastoderm expands from its narrow pole over the egg surface, is less advantageous. In fact, the more the blastoderm grows towards the equatorial egg region; the less the strong curvature of the egg allows a simultaneous precise focusing on the central and the peripheral zones of the blastoderm (from an "on top" view). For an optimum observation of the blastoderm and/or manipulations on it (e.g. microsurgery, intracellular microinjection), a totally "flat" blastoderm is needed. This preparation can be achieved in principal by three techniques of which the latest will be described in more detail in this paper:

1) An egg is placed, the blastoderm pole up, into a seawater filled small Petri-dish. By sucking off the water with a pipette, a thin cover glass, placed on the water surface above the egg, progressively flattens the egg by pressure. This method only can be used for observation; for example for recording the cleavage process. The chorion has not to be removed.

2) An egg, without the chorion, is placed as described into a Petri-dish (into a hole in the agar bottom). With fine

Experimental Embryology in Aquatic Plants and Animals
Edited by H.-J. Marthy, Plenum Press, New York, 1990

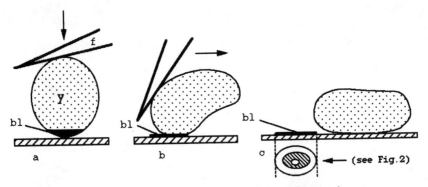

FIG.1. For legend see text; bl: blastoderm;
f: forceps; y: yolk.

needles the ectoderm can now be separated from the
mesentoderm and the underlying yolk syncytium. The
mesentoderm can also be removed without damaging the yolk
syncytium. Thus both germ layers can be isolated and placed
on a suitable artificial substrate such as plastic or glass.
This method has proved to be very useful for characterizing
the germ layers and the various cellular and acellular
structures of squid embryos at preorganogenetic stages
(Marthy 1982, 1985). The technique is rather delicate
however and time consuming. The preparation of an intact
blastoderm is only possible with great patience and
practice.

3) The third method is rapid and simple. It allows the preparation of an intact and flat blastoderm and has already proved
useful for intracellular microinjections (Marthy and Dale,
1989). It may be termed "the stripping method" and shall be
described in more detail.

The stripping method

As is necessary for any type of direct manipulation on the
egg, the egg jelly and the chorion have first to be removed by
watch maker forceps (e.g. Marthy 1970). Then the egg is placed
into a Petri-dish and again with forceps the vitelline
membrane, closely attached to the egg surface, is removed. The
blastoderm can then be stripped from its natural substrate, the
yolk syncytium and "stuck" onto a suitable artificial
substrate such as the bottom of a new Petri-dish, a plastic
sheet, a cover glass or a collodion membrane etc. Figure 1
illustrates the essential steps of this blastoderm detaching
technique. The egg, that is, the pre-organogenetic embryo, is
placed, upside down on the artificial substrate (a). The whole
blastoderm has to be in contact with the substrate and it may
be necessary therefore to apply slight pressure with the
forceps on the egg. In this position, the egg is held for 5 - 7
minutes and the blastoderm, with its outer surface, will firmly
adhere to the support. Now, the yolk mass, surrounded by the
yolk syncytium (below the blastoderm) and the egg cortex (egg
surface not yet cellulated) can be separated from the
blastoderm by pushing with forceps (b). The intact and flat
blastoderm (c) is directly accessible, from its internal face,

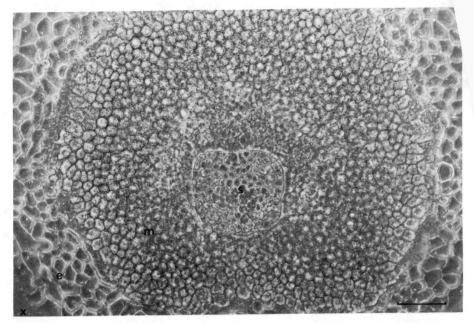

FIG.2. Blastoderm of a squid embryo, at a preorgano-
genetic stage, attached by its outer cell layer, the
ectoderm (e) to a plastic substrate (x) View on its
inner face; on top: ring of mesentodermal cells (m);
centre: ectodermal shell field (s). Scale bar: 10 μm.

for observation and micromanipulations (Fig.2). The yolk mass
is sucked off with a pipette.

As already stated, this method of in *vitro* preparation of
the early squid blastoderm is simple and does not need
particular training. The possibilities however for investigation and application should not be underestimated. So far, we
have applied it successfully in the following cases:
Intracellular microinjections of vital dyes for studying cell
communication phenomena in the preorganogenetic squid embryo
(Marthy and Dale 1989) and blastoderm preparations for Scanning
Electron Microscopy studies.

In conclusion, it appears that the blastoderm-stripping-
technique can be used, for example, in the following research
approaches:
- intracellular microinjections already successfully done;
- vital staining of cells (nuclear and/or plasmatic components;
- culturing in *vitro* of the blastoderm in the absence of yolk
but in the presence of a nutritive medium;
- recording of cell behaviour by microcinematography and video
microscopy;
- marking of cell surface structures or of interdermal
matrices;
- structural analysis of cells and tissues as seen from their
inner surfaces;
- quantitative analysis of the blastoderm composition;
- rapid separation of the germ layers and of individual
cell/groups for molecular or biochemical analyses.

., 1970, Aufzucht von Embryonen und
/onalfragmenten, ausserhalb des Chorions, von *Loligo*
aris, mit speziellen Bemerkungen zum Auftreten von
celdeformationen, *Ann.Embryol.Morph.*, 3:3-19.

.-J., 1982, The cephalopod egg, a suitable material
r cell and tissue interaction studies. *In*: Embryonic
evelopment, Part B. Cellular Aspects (eds. M.M. Burger
and R. Weber), Progress in Clinical and Biological
Research, Vol. 85, Allan R. Lyss, New York, 223-233.

, H.-J., 1985, Morphological bases for cell-to-cell and
cell-to-substrate interaction studies in cephalopod
embryos. *In*: Cellular and Molecular Control of Direct
Cell Interactions (ed. H.-J. Marthy), NATO ASI Series,
Series A: Life Sciences, Vol. 99, Plenum Press, New York
and London, 159-197.

rthy, H.-J., and Dale, B., 1989, Dye-coupling in the early
squid embryo, *Roux's Arch.Dev.Biol.*, 198:211-218.

egmüller, M., and Marthy, H.-J., 1989, Individual migration of
mesentodermal cells in the early embryo of the squid
Loligo vulgaris: *in vivo* recordings combined with
observations with TEM and SEM, *Int.J.Dev.Biol.*, 33:287-
296.

ON THE ESTABLISHMENT OF POLARITY IN POLYCHAETE EGGS

Adriaan W.C. Dorresteijn and Bernhard Kluge

Zoologisches Institut der Universität Mainz
Saarstrasse 21
D-6500 Mainz, F.R.G.

INTRODUCTION

The study of Spiralian development began about a hundred years ago when Whitman (1878) published a description of the development of the leech, *Clepsine marginata*. Subsequently, Spiralian development became popular because the developmental fate of each individual blastomere can be determined precisely from the cell lineage. About the turn of the century several extensive papers describing the cell lineages of various molluscs (e.g. Blochmann, 1881, 1883; Kofoid, 1895; Conklin, 1897; Wierzejski 1905) and annelids (e.g. Wilson, 1892; Mead, 1897; Woltereck, 1904) appeared. From these studies it became clear that the general principles of mollusc and annelid development (and to a much lesser degree polyclad development; see Wilson, 1898) are identical. In annelid and mollusc embryos the first, second and third quartets of micromeres contribute to the ectoderm, the micromere of the fourth quartet within the dorsal quadrant is the stem cell for the mesoderm, and the macromeres together with the other micromeres of the fourth quartet form the entoderm. The invariant cleavage pattern as well as the apparant early determination of the blastomeres led to the assumption that the spiralian egg is a developmental mosaic. This means that the determination of blastomeres is governed by qualitative differences in cytoplasmic factors which are localized in specific regions of the ooplasm and correctly distributed by the cleavages. Due to these factors blastomeres would develop and differentiate autonomously. This theory of a strict mosaic development was supported by blastomere isolation experiments (Wilson, 1904a,b). The results of these experiments showed that isolated blastomeres develop as if they were still part of the whole embryo. This was, however, proven for larval cells only. Wilson demonstrated that a presumptive trochoblast cell when reared, became ciliated. Regarding this observation Wilson wrote:

"and if such be the case with one such specific germ area, we have strong ground to infer that it is also so with others. In such cases as these it is evident that the factors of cleavage run so accurately parallel to those of

Experimental Embryology in Aquatic Plants and Animals
Edited by H.-J. Marthy, Plenum Press, New York, 1990

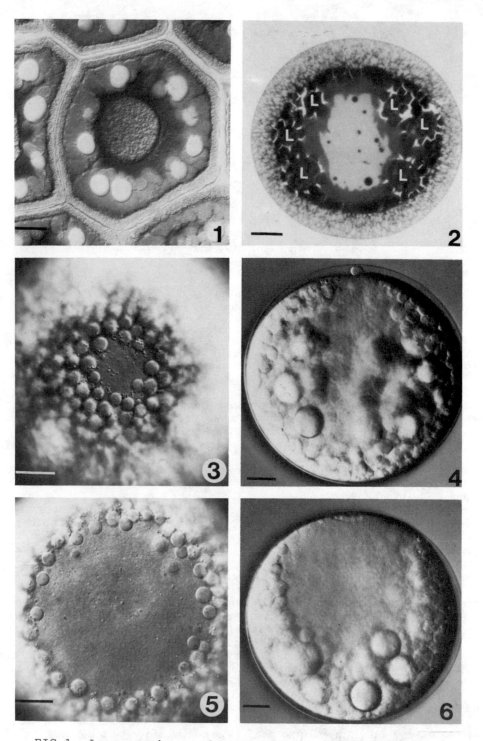

FIG.1. Large numbers of polygonous oocytes fill the coelomic cavity of the epitokous female. Note the absence of somatic cells around the oocytes. Bouin fixation. Scale bar = 20 μm.

FIG.2. The freshly shed, still unfertilized egg is an ellipsoid and its nucleus has a columnar appearance.

differentiation that they must be referred to a common determinative cause, and may be treated as practically identical".

If this holds true, it would mean that blastomere fate is irrevocably fixed as soon as it formed. To support this idea of mosaic development one has to assume the presence of several determinants or morphogens that guide the development of blastomeres toward a particular fate. Indeed, there is experimental evidence for such morphogens in polar lobes of some molluscs and polychaetes. Yet, the presence of morphogens need not be the common cause for the diversification of all blastomeres in spiralians. In fact, we know very few parameters that could be determinitive for the development of polarity and the determination of blastomeres. If one considers the complexity of pattern formation in *Drosophila* (Sander et al., 1985; Nüsslein-Volhard et al., 1987), it becomes necessary to reinvestigate the early development of spiralians and other invertebrates using high resolution techniques such as molecular biological probes. This would allow us to compare pattern formation in dipterans with other classes of invertebrates. The first step in this direction is to re-evaluate descriptive and experimental work done on such embryos in the past.

SEGREGATION, CLEAVAGE AND DETERMINATION

Among the genera of polychaetes we can discern three modes of early development (for review see Dorresteijn and Fischer, 1988). In *Pomatoceros*, many other serpulids and some of the hesionids and polynoids that have small eggs (< 70μm), first and second cleavage are equal (von Drasche 1884, Groepler, 1985). Thus, the four founder cells of the embryonic quadrants are the same size, and predicting their developmental fate, i.e., the acquisition of dorsal, lateral or ventral potencies,

---

The cytoplasmic components are arranged in concentric shells: the yolk-free cytoplasm directly surrounding the nucleus, the yolk components (lipid droplets (L) and protein yolk granules) and the numerous cortical granules forming the peripheral layers. Glutaraldehyde-Osmium fixation. Scale bar = 20 μm.

FIG.3. Animal view of the small circular area that is cleared from yolk components. Here, the first meiotic spindle attaches to the cortex. DIC. Scale bar = 20 μm.

FIG.4. Optical section in the egg axis showing the first polar body. DIC. Scale bar = 20 μm.

FIG.5. View at the animal pole of an egg at the moment of dissolution of the zygote nucleus. The animal yolk-free area has expanded markedly. DIC. Scale bar = 20 μm.

FIG.6. Optical section in the egg axis shortly before first cleavage. The yolk lies in a cup-shaped fashion predominantly in the vegetal hemisphere. DIC. Scale bar = 20 μm

seems impossible. This suggests that such embryos remain radially symmetrical for several cleavage cycles, as is the case in the equally cleaving molluscan embryos of *Lymnaea* and *Patella* (van den Biggelaar, 1976, 1977). Unfortunately, most papers on the development of equally cleaving polychaetes are descriptive, and experiments demonstrating the equivalence (or non-equivalence) of the four quadrants in such embryos are lacking.

A second cleavage mode is characterized by the formation of an anucleate vegetal cytoplasmic protrusion, the polar lobe, at first and second cleavage. Although first cleavage is essentially equal, the fusion of the polar lobe with one of the blastomeres introduces a qualitative and, depending on the size of the polar lobe, quantitative difference between the daughter blastomeres. This leads to the formation of a "small" AB- and a "large" CD-cell. At the late 2-cell stage only CD will form a second polar lobe, showing that the property to form a polar lobe is transferred by either the cytoplasm or the cortex of the lobe itself. Experiments with *Sabellaria alveolata* by Hatt (1932) and Speksnijder and Dohmen (1983) indicate that the cause for the qualitative differences between the blastomeres of the 2-cell stage becomes localized at the vegetal pole during the period of meiotic divisions. Guerrier (1970) compressed the eggs of *Sabellaria* prior to polar lobe formation. In such cases first cleavage bisects the egg in two equal parts. Both parts contain the vegetal cytoplasm and the cortex predestined for polar lobe formation. The outcome of this experiment is that both blastomeres show CD type development, resulting in the duplication of a dorsal quadrant, and leading to double-embryos. We will discuss the generation of duplicated structures later in this chapter. Other experiments were performed by Render (1983) on early embryos of *Sabellaria cementarium*. Consistent with Hatts' (1932) results, her experimental data clearly show that the quality localized in the first polar lobe is different from that of the second polar lobe. Removal of the first polar lobe results in larvae that lack the posttrochal region and the apical tuft. Removal of the second polar lobe produces larvae lacking the posttrochal region but possessing en apical tuft. Since blastomere isolation experiments at the 4-cell stage show that the C-quadrant derivatives form an apical tuft only, it was proposed that the second polar lobe contains an inhibitor for apical tuft formation. This "inhibitory substance" prevents apical tuft formation in D-quadrant derived cells of the apical organ. This shows that second polar lobe changes the properties of the D-quadrant, thus distinguishing it from its sister blastomere, C. Although the formation of such a transient larval structure as the apical tuft may be mediated by the polar lobe, the main contribution of the lobe to the adult body plan is the introduction of dorsoventral polarity, which is inevitably linked to the formation of the mesentoblast by the dorsal quadrant.

In *Chaetopterus variopedatus* the polar lobe seems to lack a role in the determination of dorsoventral polarity. The inequality between the AB- and CD-blastomere is only in part a result of the fusion of the polar lobe with one of the blastomeres. The main cause for this inequality is the spindle shift during first cleavage. After removal of the polar lobe (Henry, 1986), the development of dorsoventral polarity is

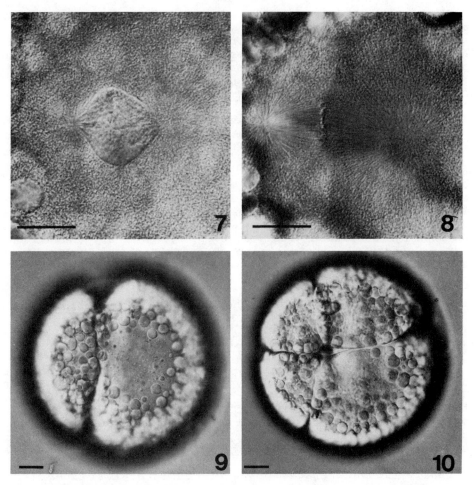

FIG.7. Optical section below the animal pole showing
the zygote nucleus. The asters at opposite sides are
unequal in size. Glycerol-acetic acid fixation. DIC.
Scale bar = 20 μm.

FIG.8. The metaphase spindle of first cleavage is
asymmetric and has moved into an excentric position,
the smaller aster lying in the periphery of the yolk-
free area. Glycerol-acetic acid fixation. DIC. Scale
bar = 20 μm.

FIG.9. Two-cell stage showing the unequal size of the
blastomeres (to the left: AB; to the right: CD). DIC.
Scale bar = 20 μm.

FIG.10. Four-cell stage showing the founder cells for
the embryonic quadrants. DIC. Scale bar = 20 μm.

unaffected. The lobeless larvae, however, do not possess
functional photocytes. By removing part of the vegetal and, as
a control, lateral cytoplasm of the CD blastomere Henry showed
that determinants for dorsoventral polarity are localized in
the vegetal region of CD. Early observations by Lillie (1906)

indicate that ooplasmic segregation in *Chaetopterus* sorts out a peripheral layer of ectoplasm with an asymmetric localization of cytoplasmic components. Unfertilized, but artificially activated eggs show the same sorting during ooplasmic segregation. Lillie (1902) showed that such activated eggs "differentiate" without cleavage and form cilia at their surface. In contrast, cytoplasmic sorting does, but cilia formation does not occur in activated eggs of *Platynereis* (Spek, 1930; Kluge and Dorresteijn, unpublished observations). However, activated eggs of *Podarke* and *Amphitrite* (Treadwell, 1902; Scott, 1906: cited in Wilson, 1925) show bands of cilia that resemble the ciliation of trochophore larvae. This suggests that at least the factors for ciliation become operative within a particular area of the cortex even if the cleavage process is eliminated. If this is true for determinants controlling cilia formation, other determinants, e.g. dorsoventral determinants, may also be localized in the cortex. *In situ* hybridization with poly(U)-probes (Jeffery and Wilson, 1983; Jeffery, 1985; Swalla et al., 1985) shows that mRNA is preferentially located in the cortex of the *Chaetopterus* egg. It was also shown that this localization involves binding of the mRNA to a detergent resistant cytoskeletal domain. However, it remains to be shown that the determinant for dorsoventral polarity in the vegetal region of the CD blastomere (see Henry, 1986) is a (D-quadrant specific) mRNA and bound to the cortical cytoskeletal domain.

A third mode of polychaete development is unequal cleavage due to spindle shift. This type of development is found in Nereids and several other polychaetes with large eggs (ranging from 100-300µm). As a result of the unilateral movement of the spindle with a slight inclination to the equatorial plane, the cleavage plane deviates from the meridional plane. After cytokinesis the two cell stage is composed of a small AB- and a large CD-blastomere. Costello (1945) isolated the blastomeres of early cleavage stages of *Nereis limbata*. His experiments demonstrate that the developmental potential of AB differs from that of CD. Similar differences were found between blastomeres at later stages. These differences concern the formation of prototrochal and anal pigment, the differentiation of trochophore eye spots, and the development of an apical tuft. None of these differences among the isolates concern the formation of mesoderm as a characteristic for dorsal developmental potential. This suggests that the development of dorsoventral polarity in nereid embryos may involve mechanisms other than the allocation of determinants into cell lines. Obviously the other mechanisms are not operative in isolates. Since the descriptive work on the cell lineage of *Nereis* by Wilson (1892) and the experimental work done by Costello (1945, 1948), very little data have been gathered on the development of polarity during embryogenesis of nereids. In our laboratory we are investigating the determinative processes leading to dorsoventral polarity in a small nereid, *Platynereis dumerilii*.

DEVELOPMENT OF POLARITY IN PLATYNEREIS

Platynereis dumerilii can be collected on the mediterranean and atlantic coasts of Europe, and is readily cultured in the laboratory (Hauenschild and Fischer, 1969). Although the source of germ cell precursors is not yet clear, the longest

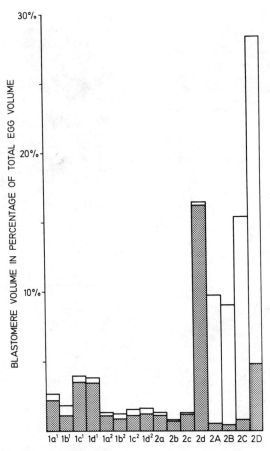

FIG.11. Histogram with the morphometric data of the
16-cell stage. The data were collected by planimetric
analysis of serially sectioned embryos. The height of
each column represents the blastomere volume and the
dotted area its contents of yolk-free cytoplasm.

period of gametogenesis occurs in a free-floating state as
solitary cells. As a sign of sexual maturation the animals
undergo epitokous metamorphosis, which is especially clear in
the male. By this time the entire coelom is loaded with
uniform-sized gametes. The oocytes of the female appear polygonous, as a result of their abundance in the narrow body
cavity (Fig.1).

Immediately after shedding of the female gamete the
unfertilized oocyte appears as an ellipsoid, with a shorter
axis corresponding to the future animal-vegetal axis. The cytoplasmic components (cortical granules, lipid droplets, yolk
granules) are located in distinct concentric shells that
surround a central plug of clear cytoplasm containing the large
oocyte nucleus (Fig.2). At the onset of fertilization a
dramatic reorganization of the egg takes place. During the
cortical reaction (the first 20 minutes), i.e., the exocytosis
of the cortical granules that contain the egg jelly, the close
apposition of the lipid and yolk granules is lost, and the egg
becomes spherical. A subsequent phase of ooplasmic segregation

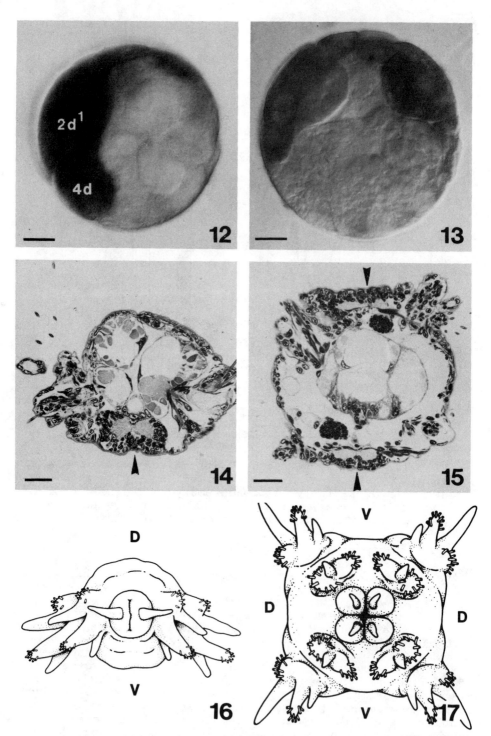

FIG.12. Gallocyanin-staining of an embryo after the
formation of the second somatoblast, i.e., the
mesentoblast 4d (31-cell stage). The yolk-free cytoplasm of the two somatoblasts, that mark the dorsal
side, stains intensely. Zenker's fluid fixation.
Scale bar = 20 μm.

involves the migration of the lipid and yolk granules. This process is easy to monitor by conventional light microscopy. Approximately 30 minutes after fertilization a small circular area (approximately 35μm) at the site of the future animal pole is cleared from yolk components. Here, the first meiotic spindle attaches to the cortex. The diameter of this yolk-free area remains more or less constant during meiosis, the first and second polar body forming 55 and 75 minutes after fertilization respectively (Fig.3,4). The mechanism of this first sign of cytoplasmic rearrangement, foreshadowing the animal pole, can be assayed by the application of drugs that affect the cytoskeleton. The process appears to be unaffected by cytochalasin B in concentrations ranging up to 10μg/ml. Drugs that affect the microtubular system, such as nocodazol and taxol, prevent the formation of the yolk free area at the animal pole at a concentration of 5μg/ml. As a consequence, meiosis is inhibited and the eggs do not cleave. However, after two hours of development, the yolk granules show the spontaneous tendency to aggregate in the periphery of the egg in an apolar fashion. The absence of the meiotic spindle at the animal pole in these experiments and the obvious apolar segregation of the yolk suggest that the spindle may be essential

---

FIG.13. Gallocyanin-staining of an embryo at a comparable cleavage stage as shown in Fig.12. This embryo was centrifuged before first cleavage. As a result of centrifugation the yolk-free cytoplasm was partitioned equally between the blastomeres of the 2-cell stage. Two dorsal quadrants, each with two yolk-free somatoblasts, can be identified in diametrical position. Zenker's fluid fixation. Scale bar = 20 μm.

FIG.14. Cross-section in the second segment of a 3-segmented young worm showing the ventral nerve cord (arrowhead) and the setal sacs of the lateral parapodia. Scale bar = 20 μm.

FIG.15. Cross-section in the second segment of a 3-segmented young worm that developed from an embryo after equalization of first cleavage by cytochalasin B treatment. The ventral nerve cord (arrowheads) and the parapodia are duplicated. Scale bar = 20 μm.

FIG.16. Drawing of the trunk of a normal 3-segmented young worm. Posterior view. SEM pictures were used as source, but for clarity the bristles in the drawing have been omitted. Note that each parapodium has a clear dorsoventral polarity. D= dorsal; V= ventral.

FIG.17. Drawing of the duplicated trunk of a 3-segmented young worm, whose first cleavage was equalized by cytochalasin B treatment. Posterior view. Note the presence of four rows of parapodia along the trunk. Just like in normal young worms, each parapodium shows a clear dorsoventral polarity, allowing to distinguish dorsal and ventral sides of such duplicates in the external view. D= dorsal; V= ventral.

for establishment of animal-vegetal polarity, possibly by interacting with the cortex.

The diameter of the yolk-free area at the animal pole expands during the 20 minutes following meiosis. During this second phase of ooplasmic segregation yolk moves towards the vegetal pole along the periphery of the egg, the clear yolk-free cytoplasm accumulating at the animal pole. Ooplasmic segregation stops as soon as the zygote nucleus dissolves, approximately 95 minutes after fertilization. By that time a large area of the animal hemisphere is free of yolk (Fig.5,6). The sorting out after the formation of the second polar body can be stopped by cytochalasin B at a concentration of 10µg/ml and impaired by application of nocadozol (5µg/ml) and taxol (5-20µg/ml). The initial polarity, however, is maintained even in eggs treated continuously with cytochalasin B.

During normal development the two asters of the first cleavage spindle are unequal in size even before dissolution of the zygote nucleus (Lillie, 1912). The cleavage spindle is shifted to an asymmetrical position, with the smaller aster approaching the egg cortex (Fig.7,8). As a result of this spindle shift, the first cleavage is unequal, producing a small AB- (27% egg volume) and a large CD-cell (73% egg volume)(Fig.9). The clear cytoplasm allocated at the animal pole, however, is partitioned disproportionately with respect to the blastomere volumes. The CD-cell contains 80% of the total mass of clear cytoplasm, the AB-cell only 20%. The cleavage program of CD differs from AB. During the interphase between first and second cleavage, a drastic cytoplasmic sorting takes place in CD only, in which the mass of yolk rotates around the axis perpendicular to the cleavage plane. Second cleavage is equal in AB, and the cytoplasmic components are partitioned equally between the daughter blastomeres. The cleavage programs of A and B are identical. Second cleavage in CD is unequal, and the clear cytoplasm is shifted largely into the D blastomere (Fig.10). The cleavage program within the D quadrant differs distinctly from the other quadrants. This becomes apparent at third cleavage when the first quartet of micromeres is being formed. The A-,B- and C-quadrant form a micromere that represents 25% of the initial blastomere volume. The blastomere 1d is just as large as 1c and represents only 10% of the initial blastomere volume of D. At fourth cleavage a particularly large micromere 2d - the first somatoblast- is being formed. The 2d cell contains the bulk of the clear cytoplasm (Fig.11). The remaining clear cytoplasm in 2D is reserved for the formation of 4d - the second somatoblast or mesentoblast - at sixth cleavage. As a result, the clear cytoplasm is predominantly located in 2 cells in the future posttrochal region; these cells are located in the dorsal median (Fig.12).

We have found that a large absolute quantity of clear cytoplasm correlates positively with short cell cycles in various tiers of blastomeres. Cells, rich in clear cytoplasm, proliferate at a much higher rate than other blastomeres. The most rapidly proliferating cells are the first somatoblast 2d, which forms a large part of the posttrochal ectoderm, the setal sacs and the ventral nerve cord, and the mesentoblast 4d, which contributes two small entoderm cells and the mesodermal germ bands. The only exception to the described correlation is the interval between 4th and 5th cleavage. Then, the cell cycles are elongated in the various tiers of blastomeres. After this interval the trochoblasts cleave synchronously, although they are descendents of cells that were previously asynchronous. This suggests, that cell-cell interactions between 4th and 5th cleavage play a role in blastomere determination.

Equalization of first cleavage by cytochalasin B (Dorresteijn et al., 1987) or centrifugation changes the program of both daughter blastomeres into CD-like development (Fig.13). The young worms from such experiments show duplications within the posttrochal region, i.e., the setal sacs and the nerve cord (compare Figs.14-17). This means that the stem cell for these structures, 2d, must have been duplicated. Since the trunk of such monsters is otherwise harmonious in structure, harmony must be due to a changed developmental fate of cell lines other than D quadrant derivatives. Thus, on the one hand determination in the *Platynereis* embryo depends upon segregation and cytoplasmic diversification, but on the other hand it also seems capable of regulation and dependent upon cell-cell interactions.

ACKNOWLEDGEMENTS

Our research is supported by a grant (Do 339/1-1) from the Deutsche Forschungsgemeinschaft, Bonn, F.R.G. The authors wish to thank Dr.A. Fischer and Dr.W.R. Jeffery for reading the manuskript and helpful comments. For the artwork we gratefully acknowledge the help of J. Jacobi and K.Rehbinder. The reproduction of figures 14-17 was permitted by Springer Verlag, Heidelberg.

REFERENCES

Blochmann, F., 1881, Über die Entwicklung der *Neritina fluviatilis* Müll., *Z.Wiss.Zool.*, 36:125-174.
Blochmann, F., 1883, Beiträge zur Kenntnis der Entwicklung der Gastropoden, *Z.Wiss.Zool.*, 38:392-410.
Conklin, E.G., 1897, The embryology of *Crepidula*, *J.Morphol.*, 13:1-226.
Costello, D.P., 1945, Experimental studies of germinal localization in *Nereis*. I. The development of isolated blastomeres, *J.Exp.Zool.*, 100:19-66.
Costello, D.P., 1948, Ooplasmic segregation in relation to differentiation, *Ann.N.Y.Acad.Sci.*, 49:663-683.
Dorresteijn, A.W.C., and Fischer, A., 1988, The process of early development, *in:* "Microfauna Marina Vol 4: The Ultrastructure of Polychaetae," W.Westheide, and C.O.Hermans, eds., Gustav Fischer Verlag, Stuttgart-New York, pp 335-352.
Dorresteijn, A.W.C., Bornewasser, H., and Fischer, A., 1987, A correlative study of experimentally changed first cleavage and Janus development in the trunk of *Platynereis dumerilii* (Annelida, Polychaeta), *Roux's Arch.Dev.Biol.*, 196:51-58.
Groepler, W., 1985, Die Entwicklung bei *Pomatoceros triqueter* L. (Polychaeta, Serpulidae) vom befruchteten Ei bis zur schwimmenden Blastula, *Zool.Beitr.N.F.*, 29:157-172.
Guerrier, P., 1970, Les caractères de la segmentation et la détermination de la polarité dorsoventrale dans le

développement de quelques Spiralia. II. *Sabellaria
alveolata* (Annélide polychète), *J.Embr.Exp.Morphol.*,
23:639-665.
Hatt, P., 1932, Essais expérimentaux sur les localisations
germinales dans l'oeuf d'une annélide (*Sabellaria
alveolata* L.), *Arch.Anat.Micr.*, 28:81-98.
Hauenschild ,C., and Fischer, A., 1969, *Platynereis dumerilii*.
Mikroskopische Anatomie, Fortpflanzung, Entwicklung.
Grosses Zoologisches Praktikum 10b. Gustav Fischer
Verlag, Stuttgart.
Henry, J.J., 1986, The role of unequal cleavage and the polar
lobe in the segregation of developmental potential
during first cleavage in the embryo of *Chaetopterus
variopedatus*, *Roux's Arch.Dev.Biol.*, 196:103-116.
Jeffery, W.R., 1985, The spatial distribution of maternal mRNA
is determined by a cortical cytoskeletal domain in
Chaetopterus eggs, *Dev.Biol.*, 110:217-229.
Jeffery, W.R., and Wilson, L.J., 1983, Localization of
messenger RNA in the cortex of *Chaetopterus* eggs and
early embryos, *J.Embryol.Exp.Morphol.*, 75:225-239.
Kofoid, C.A., 1895, On the early development of *Limax*,
Bull.Museum Comp.Zool., 27:35-118.
Lillie, F.R., 1902, Differentiation without cleavage in the egg
of the annelid *Chaetopterus pergamentaceus*, *W.Roux's
Arch.Entw.Mech.*, 14:447-499.
Lillie, F.R., 1906, Observations and experiments concerning the
elementary phenomena of embryonic development in
Chaetopterus, *J.Exp.Zool.*, 3:153-269.
Lillie, F.R., 1912, Studies of fertilization in *Nereis*. III.
The morphology of the normal fertilization of *Nereis*,
J.Exp.Zool., 12:413-427.
Mead, A.D., 1897, The early development of marine annelids,
J.Morphol., 13:227-326.
Nüsslein-Volhard, C., Frohnhöfer, H.G., and Lehmann, R., 1987,
Determination of anteroposterior polarity in
Drosophila, *Science*, 238:1675-1681.
Render, J.A., 1983, The second polar lobe of the *Sabellaria
cementarium* embryo plays an inhibitory role in apical
tuft formation, *Roux's Arch.Dev.Biol.*, 192:120-129.
Sander, K., Gutzeit, H.O., and Jaeckle, H., 1985, Insect
embryogenesis: Morphology, physiology, genetical and
molecular aspects, *in*: "Comprehensive Insect
Physiology, Biochemistry and Pharmacology. Vol 1.
Embryogenesis and Reproduction," G.A. Kerkut and L.I.
Gilbert, eds., Pergamon Press, Oxford, pp 319-385.
Spek, J., 1930, Zustandsänderungen der Plasmakolloide bei
Befruchtung und Entwicklung des Nereis-Eies,
Protoplasma 9:370-427.
Speksnijder, J.E., and Dohmen, M.R., 1983, Local surface
modulation correlated with ooplasmic segregation in
eggs of *Sabellaria alveolata* (Annelida, Polychaeta),
Roux's Arch.Dev.Biol., 192:248-255.
Swalla, B.J., Moon, R.T., and Jeffery, W.R., 1985,
Developmental significance of a cortical cytoskeletal
domain in *Chaetopterus* eggs, *Dev.Biol.*, 111:434-450.
van den Biggelaar, J.A.M., 1976, Development of dorsoventral
polarity preceding the formation of the mesentoblast in
Lymnaea stagnalis, *Proc.K.Ned.Akad.Wet*, C 79:112-126.
van den Biggelaar, J.A.M., 1977, Development of dorsoventral
polarity and mesentoblast determination in *Patella
vulgata*, *J.Morphol.*, 154:157-186.

von Drasche, R.,1884, Beiträge zur Entwicklung der Polychaeten. I. Entwicklung von *Pomatoceros triqueter* L., published privately, Vienna, pp 1-10.

Whitman, C.O., 1878, The embryology of *Clepsine*, *Quart.J.Micr.Sci.*, 18:215-315.

Wierzejski, A., 1905, Embryologie von *Physa fontinalis* L., *Z.Wiss.Zool.*, 83:502-706.

Wilson, E.B., 1892, The cell-lineage of *Nereis*. A contribution to the cytogeny of the annelid body, *J.Morphol.*, 6:361-480.

Wilson, E.B., 1898, Considerations on cell-lineage and ancestral reminiscence, *Ann.N.Y.Acad.Sci.*, 11:1-27.

Wilson, E.B., 1904a, Experimental studies on germinal localization. I. The germ-regions in the egg of *Dentalium*, *J.Exp.Zool.*, 1:1-72.

Wilson, E.B., 1904b, Experimental studies on germinal localization. II. Experiments on the cleavage-mosaic in *Patella* and *Dentalium*, *J.Exp.Zool.*, 1:197-268.

Wilson, E.B., 1925, The Cell in Development and Heredity. Third edition with corrections, The MacMillan Company, New York.

Woltereck, R., 1904, Beiträge zur praktischen Analyse der *Polygordius* - Entwicklung nach dem Nordsee- und dem Mittelmeer-Typus, *W.Roux's Arch.Entw.Mech.Org.*, 18:377-403.

EXPERIMENTAL EMBRYOLOGY IN LEECHES: CELLULAR AND MOLECULAR

APPROACHES

Susanna Blackshaw

Department of Cell Biology
School of Biological Sciences
University of Glasgow
G12 8QQ
Scotland

INTRODUCTION

Among the annelids, glossiphoniid leeches, and in particular *Helobdella triserialis*, have become a favorite preparation
for modern experimental embryology, and are currently used both
for cellular and molecular genetic studies of development. The
principal adventages of *Helobdella* as a model organism accrue
from the large cells and well defined lineages, important
experimental advantages lacking in animal species such as
Drosophila. The eggs of glossiphoniid leeches are relatively
large and the yolk of the egg is the major nutrient source for
the developing embryo, enabling embryos to be cultured
separately from the parent in a simple salt solution.
Development from egg to adult is direct with no intervening
trochophore or metamorphosis seen in polychaet annelids. The
early embryos comprise large cells that are individually
identifiable and accessible to experimental manipulation. Their
suitability as experimental material was recognised by Charles
Whitman in the 1890's (Whitman, 1878). On the basis of his
observations in the light microscope on the early cleavage of a
glossiphoniid leech egg, Whitman first stated the idea that
each identified cell in the early embryo is developmentally
distinct and that each identified blastomere and the clone of
its descendant cells plays a specific predestined role in later
development. In the 1970's, new techniques for lineage analysis
by intracellular injection of tracers were developed using
leeches. This has enabled the construction of detailed lineages
for identified cells of the early embryo. Subsequent
experimental work has been concerned with: the role of
cytoplasmic determinants, the relative roles of cell ancestry
and cell interactions in determining developmental fate, and
the control of cell cycle in embryonic cells. Recently,
Helobdella has also been used for molecular genetic studies of
development. Highly conserved homeoboxes from *Drosophila* genes
have been used to identify genes in *Helobdella* that may be
important for regulating development.

Experimental Embryology in Aquatic Plants and Animals
Edited by H.-J. Marthy, Plenum Press, New York, 1990

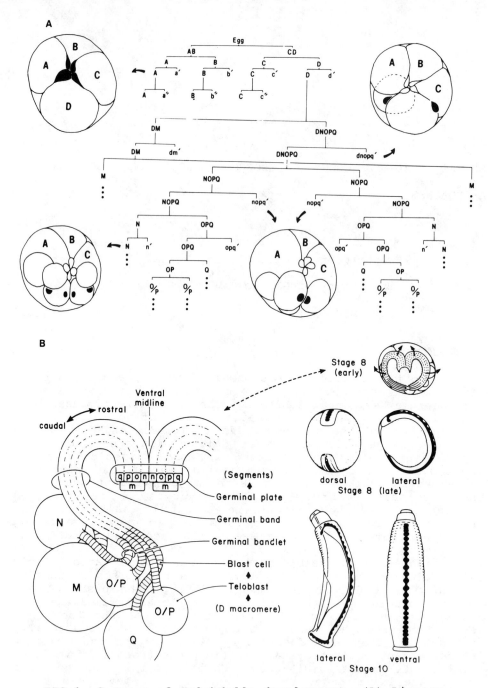

FIG.1. Summary of *Helobdella* development. (A) Lineage tree showing the early divisions, including the generation of micromeres; four embryos are depicted as well, showing the positions of the blastomeres at four different stages (indicated by arrows) and the most recently born micromeres for each stage (in black). (B) Left. Drawing showing the relationship of the teloblasts and the blast cell bandlets which coalesce to form the germinal band and germinal plate. Note that sister O/P teloblasts generate

OUTLINE OF EMBRYOGENESIS IN GLOSSIPHONIID LEECHES

Early development of glossiphoniid leeches has been described by several authors (Whitman, 1878; Weisblat et al., 1978, 1980; Fernandez, 1980; Fernandez and Stent, 1980; Weisblat, 1981; Fernandez and Olea, 1982; Stent, et al., 1982; Blackshaw, 1987, 1988; Wedeen, et al., 1989). Development of *Helobdella triserialis* has been divided into 11 stages based on cell divisions, migrations and cell differentiation (Stent et al., 1982; Fig.1). Fertilization occurs internally and development is then arrested until the eggs are laid. A distinct feature of development in the leech is the formation during the first stages of development of a germinal plate from which the ectoderm and mesoderm derived tissues of the adult arise. During developmental stages 1-6 the eggs undergo a highly determinate sequence of embryonic cleavages, following the typical spiral pattern of annelids (Anderson, 1973). At first cleavage most of the teloplasm passes into the larger of the two daughter cells (CD). The second cleavage gives rise to 4 macromeres (A,B,C,D) and the teloplasm passes into blastomere D (see later). Each of the 4 macromeres then cleaves unequally to produce a quartet of smaller cells or micromeres surmounting the blastomeres (8-cell embryo). Three of the macromeres (A,B,C) generate additional micromeres and then eventually become incorporated into the gut, where they are digested during late development and consequently contribute little to the definitive tissues of the leech (Weisblat et al., 1984). By contrast, the fourth macromere, D, undergoes further cleavages, giving rise to 5 bilateral pairs of embryonic stem cells, the M, N, O/P, O/P, and Q teloblasts, plus other micromeres. During developmental stage 7 left and right germinal bands form: each teloblast undergoes a series of several dozen unequal divisions producing primary blast cells in columns (the m,n,o,p,q bandlets). The 5 bandlets on either side of the midline merge to form left and right germinal bands (Fig. 1b). During stage 8 the two bands migrate over the surface of the embryo and coalesce rostrocaudally along the future ventral midline to form a sheet of cells called the germinal plate. During stages 9-11 the embryo gradually changes from spherical to cylindrical in shape, and the segmental tissues arise by differentiation of blast cell clones. The germinal plate lengthens, broadens and thickens due to the proliferation of blast cells and expands over the surface of the embryo. Eventually the leading edges of the expanding germinal plate meet and fuse along the dorsal midline (stage 10) enclosing the tubular body of the leech. The embryos hatch from the vitelline membrane during stage 9 and attach themselves to the underside of the parent. By stage 11,

---

bandlets which are distinguished as o and p on the basis of their relative positions in the germinal band. The blast cells derived from the sister O/P teloblasts interact in a position-dependent, hierarchical manner and thus constitute a developmental equivalence group. Right. Representation of embryos at later stages of development. The definitive progeny of teloblasts injected with lineage tracers are identified in stage 10 embryos, which have almost the complete complement of adult structures (from Ho & Weisblat, 1987).

the final stage of embryogenesis, the yolk supply is exhausted, the gut has matured and the anterior and posterior suckers developed and functional. The juvenile leeches are carried to their first few meals by the parent.

LOCALISATION OF CYTOPLASMIC DETERMINANTS

The idea that segregation of cytoplasmic determinants to different cells in the early embryo helps establish distinct cell populations is supported by experiments in both vertebrates and invertebrates (reviewed in Davidson, 1976). In several species of glossiphoniid leeches, as in many annelids, reorganisation of the cytoplasm occurs prior to first cleavage to generate distinct animal and vegetal domains of yolk-deficient cytoplasm called teloplasm. Both domains are inherited by cell CD at first cleavage and segregate to cell D at second cleavage. By labelling mitochondria with rhodamine 123 it was shown that the two pools of teloplasm do not remain separate but mix shortly before third cleavage, after which the mixture is split into the cells DN and DNOPQ, the mesodermal and ectodermal precursors (Holton et al., 1989). This finding argues against the idea that distinct mesodermal and ectodermal determinants are localised within animal and vegetal teloplasms respectively.

Early attempts to examine the role of teloplasm in *Glossiphonia* (Schliep, 1914) by centrifugation to redistribute cytoplasm failed because the centrifuged embryos stopped cleaving. In more recent work on *Helobdella* (Astrow et al., 1987) low speed centrifugation caused the teloplasm present in cell CD and normally inherited by cell D to be redistributed to cells C and D at the second cleavage. When the cytoplasm was redistributed roughly equally between cells C and D, both cells cleaved to make teloblasts, a pattern of division normally only associated with cell D. The degree of centrifugation needed to induce such changes in cleavage pattern redistributed the non-yolk associated proteins, normally found in higher quantities in cell D, between the two cells. Thus the results of these experiments support the idea that the fates of C and D are influenced by the distribution of cytoplasmic components.

CELL LINEAGE STUDIES

The first study of developmental cell lineage was carried out in a glossiphoniid leech by direct observation of dividing cells (Whitman, 1878). Direct observation as a technique for lineage analysis in leeches is however limited and in order to construct detailed cell pedigrees at later developmental stages different techniques are needed.

Techniques for studying cell lineage by intracellular injection of tracer molecules were first developed using *Helobdella* embryos (Weisblat et al., 1978) and have since been used for lineage analysis in other invertebrates and most classes of vertebrates (e.g.Balakier and Pedersen, 1982; Nishida and Satoh, 1983; Kimmel and Warga, 1986). The first intracellular lineage tracer used was horseradish peroxidase, the enzyme previously used so successfully for intracellular labelling of neurones (Muller and McMahan, 1976). Subsequently,

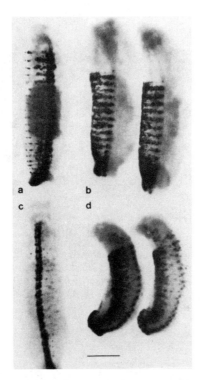

FIG.2. Segmentally iterated contributions of the
ectodermal teloblasts to nervous system and
epidermis. Labeling pattern of whole-mounted stage 10
Helobdella embryos in which one teloblast has been
injected with HRP at stage 7. Since prior to
injection the teloblast has already produced some
blast cells, the frontmost body segments are
unlabeled. All labeled cell bodies lie on the same
side of the embryo as the injected teloblast.
Anterior is up; scale bar 200 microns. (a) Right O/P
teloblast injected; O pattern obtained. Labeled cell
processes can be seen to project frontward through
the connective nerves from the anteriormost labeled
ganglion. (b) right O/P teloblast injected (in 2
replicate embryos); P pattern obtained. (c) Left N
teloblast injected. (d) Right Q teloblast injected
(in 2 replicate embryos). (a-c): ventral views; (d)
lateral views. Ventral midline of embryo is marked by
apparent right edge of labeling pattern in (a), (b),
and (d) and by apparent left edge in (c). In (d),
leading edge of expanding germinal plate is marked by
apparent left edge of labeling pattern. (From
Weisblat, Kim & Stent, 1984).

improved fluorescent tracers were introduced (Weisblat et al.,
1980; Gimlich and Braun, 1985; Ho and Weisblat, 1987). The
tracer is injected into a chosen cell at an early stage of
embryogenesis. The injected embryos continue their normal
development, in the course of which the tracer is passed on to
the descendants of the injected cell. The distribution of the
tracer and hence of the progeny of a particular cell can then
be observed at a chosen later stage of development. For the

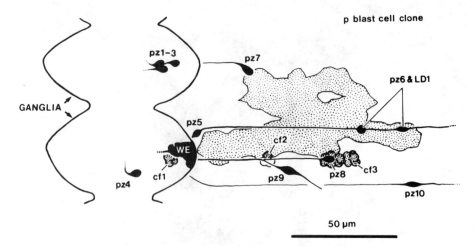

FIG.3. Camera lucida drawing showing the set of descendant pattern elements that comprise the p blast cell clone in a typical midbody segments of a stage 10 leech embryo. Cells located within the epidermis are stippled, and all other cells are showm in black. The p clone includes one cluster of three identified ganglionic neurons (pz1-pz3); a separate wedge-shaped neuron cluster (WE) located in the next posterior ganglion; a single ganglionic neuron (pz4) which is present in only one half of the clones examined at this stage; seven uniquely identified peripheral neurons (pz5-pz10 and LD1); epidermal specialisations known as cell florets 1 and 3 (cf1 and cf3) as well as a portion of cell floret 2 (cf2); and a single, large patch of squamous epidermis. The axonal trajectories of the peripheral neurons have been included, but those of the central neurons have not (from Shankland, 1987c).

experiments, selected teloblasts are injected with lineage tracer during developmental stages 6-7 at varying times after the onset of blast cell production, and the pattern of labelled descendants observed at stage 10, by which time segmental structures are well differentiated. These experiments show that in leech development cell fates are highly predictable. Each of the 5 teloblasts gives rise to a characteristic and segmentally repeated pattern of descendants, the M,N,O,P and Q cell lines (Weisblat et al., 1984). So for example, if an N teloblast on one side of an embryo is injected with lineage tracer at an early stage of development, the embryo at stage 10 shows a pattern of labelled cells (designated the N pattern) that is repeated in each segment on that side of the leech and that is characteristic of the N teloblast (Fig.2). The N cell line, like all other cell lines, gives rise to both neural and non-neural cells - thus cell lines are not specialised for the production of a particular cell type. However individual cells such as identified neurones of the adult nervous system identified cell clusters invariably arise from a particular cell line (Zackson, 1984; Kramer and Weisblat, 1985; Weisblat and Shankland, 1985; Stuart et al., 1987; Shankland, 1987a, b, c; Braun and Stent, 1989a, b; Bissen and Weisblat, 1989; Figs. 3, 4, 5).

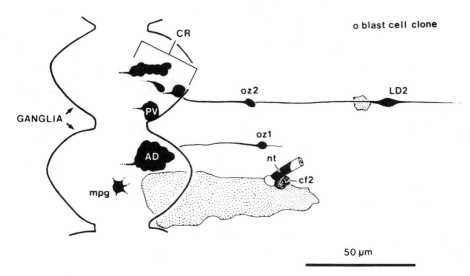

FIG.4. Camera lucida drawing showing the set of
desendant pattern elements that comprise the o blast
cell clone in a typical midbody segment of the stage
10 leech embryo. Cells located within the epidermis
are stippled and all other cells are shown in black.
The o clone icludes three separate clusters of
central neurons (CR, crescent; PV, postero-ventral;
AD, antero-dorsal); the medial packet glia (mpg);
three identified peripheral neurons (oz1, oz2 and
LD2); the outermost portion of the nephridial tubule
(nt); a portion of the epidermal specialization known
as cell floret 2 (cf2); and two other discrete
patches of epidermis. The axonal trajectories of the
peripheral neurons are included, but those of the
central neurons have been left out   (from Shankland,
1987b).

SEGMENTATION IN LEECH DEVELOPMENT: CELL LINEAGE GOVERNS THE FORMATION OF THE METAMERIC BODY SEGMENTS

When a teloblast is injected with lineage tracer after it
has begun making blast cells, the blast cells already born do
not contain the label and a boundary is seen between anterior
unlabelled segments containing progeny of blast cells born
before the injection, and posterior labelled segments born
after the injection (Fig.2). By examining such boundaries generated in all 5 teloblast cell lines it is possible to
establish the relationship between blast cell clones and
segments (Weisblat and Shankland, 1985; Price and Wedeen,
1988). Such boundary analyses show that there are 7 basic
classes of primary blast cells. In the m,o, and p bandlets each
primary blast cell makes one hemi-segment's worth of progeny,
and each undergoes a stereotyped and characteristic sequence
of mitoses in generating the segmental complement (Zackson,
1974). By contrast, in the n and q bandlets, two primary blast
cells are needed to generate one hemi-segment's worth of
progeny (Fig.6). Each of the two primary n and q blast cells

217

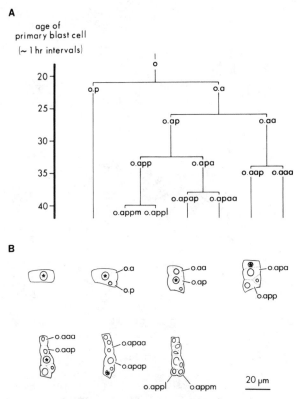

FIG.5. Descendant lineage of the primary o blast cell. (A) genealogy depicting the first six o blast cell divisions. (B) camera lucida tracings of the primary o blast cell clone following each of these divisions, arranged in 2 rows that read from left to right. In each tracing * marks the cell that will divide next, and the daughters of that division are designated by name in the next clone to the right. All clones were viewed from the future ventral surface of the right germinal band, so that the medial daughter of a transverse division will lie to the right. (From Shankland, 1987b).

has a different definitive fate. So for example, in the N cell line, one primary blast cell generates ganglionic neurones and epidermal cells primarily in the anterior portion of the segment, while the primary blast cell just behind it generates a small set of peripheral neurones, a glial cell and posterior ganglionic neurones (Bissen and Weisblat, 1987). Similarly, the 2 q blast cells have different definitive fates. In addition to the differences in definitive fates of the 2 n and 2 q blast cells, alternate blast cells in the n and q bandlets show differences in the timing and symmetry of their first mitoses (Zackson, 1984). Thus in contrast to the m,o, and p bandlets, each of which comprises a single class of blast cell, the n and q bandlets comprise two distinct classes of blast cells produced in exact alternation (called nf and ns, qf and qs) making a total of 7 classes of primary blast cells.

The boundary analyses also show that there is no simple

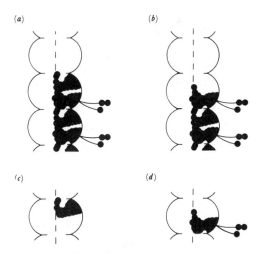

FIG.6. Two primary n blast cells generate one
segmental complement for the N cell line. Anterior is
up, the ventral midline is indicated by a dashed line
trhough the centre of the segmental ganglia and the
representation is that of an animal which has been
opened along the dorsal midline and laid out flat.
(a) and (b) schematic drawing of the boundaries
between labelled and unlabelled segments in stage 10
embryos obtained after injection of N teloblasts
early in stage 7. Three complete segments are shown.
Two classes of boundary are seen. In (a) all cells in
the N kinship group are stained in the first labeled
segment, including three peripheral neurons and a
small patch of epidermis which lies just ventral to
the ganglion and is thus not shown. In (b) only the
cells in the posterior half of the first labelled
segments are stained, including the peripheral
neurons. The inferred contributions of the first
labelled blast cell in these two classes are shown in
(c) and (d), respectively (from Weisblat &
Shankland, 1985).

relationship between primary blast cell clones and morphologically defined segments of the leech. Although in the M, O
and P cell lines each primary blast cell makes one segmental
complement, the individual clone derived from an m, o and p
primary blast cell extends longitudinally across parts of two
or more segments and interdigitates with cells of adjacent
clones from the same line. Thus segmental boundaries are not
coincident with clonal boundaries.

BOTH POSITIONAL INFORMATION AND CELL ANCESTRY ARE IMPORTANT IN
DETERMINING THE DEVELOPMENTAL FATE OF A CELL

The detailed characterisations of the lineages of
individual precursor cells have shown that leech embryonic
development is highly determinate in that many elements of the
mature body pattern such as uniquely identifiable cells or
cellular arrays consistently arise from particular precursor
cells. This suggests that a cell's ancestral lineage plays a

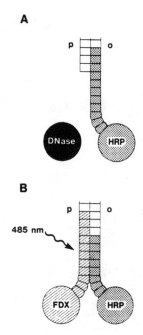

A

B

FIG.7. To study the development interaction between the O and P cell lines the generative O teloblast was injected with HRP and the ipsilateral p bandlet eliminated by either of two methods. (A) In one set of experiments the generative P teloblast was ablated by DNase injection, thereby ensuring that the more posterior o blast cells do not come into contact with the p bandlet. Times of injection were routinely staggered so that the first few HRP-labeled of blast cells lie anterior to this point. (B) in a second series of experiments the generative P teloblast was injected with FDX and its fluorescently labeled blast cell progeny photoablated by brief exposure to intense 485nm illumination. In this way the o blast cells can be deprived of their p blast cell neigbours at various times after they enter the band. Times of ijection were routinely staggered so that the first HPR-labelled o blast cells would be unable to interact with any of the more anterior, unlabeled blast cells (from Shankland & Weisblat, 1984).

major role in determining its adult identity. Consistent with this idea, if certain cells are ablated in early development to alter the relationship of neighbouring cells, no regulation occurs and specific tissues derived from the ablated cells are missing from the adult (Blair, 1982, 1983; Blair and Weisblat, 1982; Zackson, 1984). So for example, on deletion of the N teloblast in the early embryo, no regulation occurs and specific serotonin neurones are absent from the ventral nerve cord. Similarly, no regulation occurs on deletion of M or Q teloblasts.

By contrast, for other blastomeres there is a dramatic change in developmental fate when a neighbouring bandlet is ablated (Shankland and Weisblat, 1984). While ablation of the O

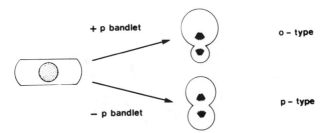

FIG.8. At its first division the o blast cell has the potential to manifest either of two geometrically distinct types of cleavage, with the choice being determined by the presence or absence of the adjoining p bandlet. If the p bandlet is present and intact, the o blast cell will undergo the highly asymmetric o-type cleavage. On the contrary, if the p bandlet has been damaged or is missing, neighboring o blast cells will undergo the more symmetric p-type cleavage (from Shankland, 1987a).

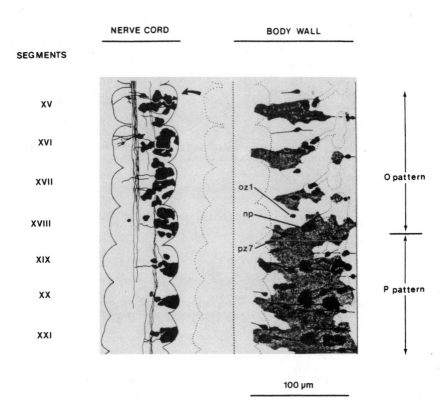

FIG.9. Camera lucida tracing or a stage 10 embryo in which the HRP-labeled o bandlet changed fate along the body's length in response to P teloblast ablation. In the anterior segments, where the p bandlet was present, the o bandlet gave rise to a normal O pattern of descentants. However the pattern of labeled tissue changes posteriorly to include all of the cellular elements seen in a normal P pattern. np, nephridiopore; oz1, pz7, peripheral neurons (from Shankland & Weisblat, 1984).

221

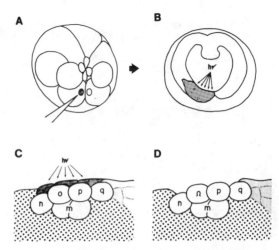

FIG.10. Diagram outlining the procedure of experiments to ablate portions of the provisional epithelium. (A) A micromere is injected with a photosensitizing lineage tracer, in this case fluorescein dextran. (B) The embryo develops to stage 8 at which time the labeled progeny from the micromere are ablated by laser irradiation at the fluorescein adsorption maximum. (C) A cross-sectional view to show the relative positions of the provisional epithelium and the blast cell bandlets. (D) The effects of the ablation are then followed in the O and/or the P blast cells which contain the nonphotosensitive lineage tracer, BFD. The nominal o blandlet is now designated as Ω to emphasize its altered fate (from Ho & Weisblat, 1987).

teloblast has little effect on development of the P cell line, if P is ablated, the prospective o blast cells forsake their normal O pathway and take on the P fate (Figs. 7,8,9). Thus the o bandlet has the potential to follow either of two alternative developmental pathways. During normal development the o blast cells interact with the adjoining column of p blast cells and become committed to the O developmental pathway as a result of this interaction.

The o and p bandlets lie at the surface of the embryo beneath the squamous epithelium of a transient embryonic covering called the provisional integument. This is derived from micromeres produced during the early cleavage divisions (Fig. 1a). Experiments have shown that this provisional epithelium provides positional clues for the underlying o and p blast cells. Thus photoablation of selected portions of the provisional epithelium interferes with the normal determinative interactions within the O/P equivalence group so that o blast cells and some of their progeny express P fates even in the presence of the p bandlet (Figs. 10,11). This suggests that it is the epithelium that is responsible for the generation and/or reception of signals by which the o and p blast cell normally determine their fate (Ho and Weisblat, 1987).

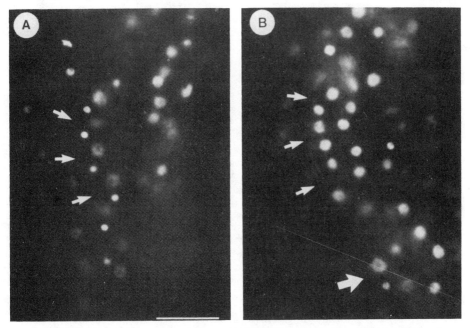

FIG.11. Epithelial ablation affects the symmetry of blast cell mitoses in the o bandlet. Embryos stained with the fluorescent DNA stain Hoechst 33258 and photographed in an area of the left germinal band where the primary o and p cells have already undergone their first mitoses. Only portions of the o and p bandlets are visible. The o bandlet lies to the left in each panel. Small arrows point to daughter cell pairs arising from o blast cell divisions in normal (A) and photoablated embryos (B). (A) in the normal embryo, each o blast cell has divided into one larger cell and a smaller cell with compact nucleus. (B) The o blast cells affected by photoablation have undergone an essentially equal mitosis like that of the adjacent p blast cells. Large arrow at bottom points to a younger blast cell that has resumed the normal pattern of o blast cell division, presumably due to wound healing in the overlying epithelium. Anterior is up, medial to the right, scale bar = 25 microns (from Ho & Weisblat, 1987).

GAP JUNCTIONAL COMMUNICATION DURING EMBRYOGENESIS

It has often been proposed that interactions between cells during early development are mediated through gap junctions which permit the cell to cell transfer of ions or small messenger molecules. Consistent with this idea has been the demonstration in a variety of systems of temporally and/or spatially specific loss of coupling between cells as they take on different developmental fates (eg Blackshaw and Warner, 1976; Warner and Lawrence, 1977; reviewed in Fraser, 1985; Warner, 1984). Dye coupling is known to be present between cells in *Helobdella* at early cleavage stages (Weisblat et al., 1978) and fine structural work has shown gap junctions to be present at later stages (6 and early stage 7) in the

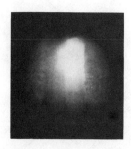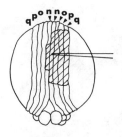

FIG.12. Dye coupling between cells during embryo-genesis in *Theromyzon tessulatum*. The photograph on the left is a whole mount of a mid stage 8 embryo in which left and right germinal bands have coalesced to form the germinal plate. Lucifer Yellow was injected into a cell in the n bandlet on the right and the embryo photographed 10 minutes later by which time dye had spread into cells of all bandlets on the same side. There is also clear evidence of spread across the midline into cells of the n bandlet on the contralateral side (unpublished results of S. Astrow & S. Blackshaw).

glossiphoniid *Theromyzon rude* (Fernandez and Stent, 1980). Junctional communication during embryogenesis in *Theromyzon tessulatum* has been studied by paired intracellular voltage recording from identified teloblasts and blast cells, and by intracellular iontophoresis of Lucifer Yellow (Astrow and Blackshaw, unpublished). These experiments show that extensive dye and electrical coupling persists throughout embryogenesis between cells of different developmental fates. Low resistance intercellular pathways are present between cells within bandlets, from bandlet to bandlet, between bandlet cells and their teloblast of origin, and between bandlet cells and the macromeres over which they move. Thus extensive coupling is present during stages in which fate determining interactions take place between O and p blast cells. Coupling is retained throughout stage 8 (Fig. 12), and is established between cells in left and right germinal bands as they coalesce to form the germinal plate during stage 9. At later stages there is some evidence of restriction of dye transfer, both across the midline of the germinal plate and between ectodermal and mesodermal cell layers.

CELL CYCLES IN LEECH EMBRYOS ARE CHARACTERISTIC OF CELL TYPE

As in most organisms, during the development of glossiphoniid leeches there is an early period of relatively fast, fairly synchronous cell divisions followed by a period of slower asynchronous cell divisions (Whitman, 1878; Fernandez, 1980; Wordeman, 1983; Zackson, 1984). The lengths and compositions of mitotic cell cycles in identified cells in *Helobdella* embryos have been analysed by incorporation of bromodeoxyuridine triphosphate (a thymidine analogue detectable by a specific antibody) to identify cells in S phase (DNA synthesis), and by use of a DNA specific stain to identify cells in the same embryo in mitosis (M phase) or non-

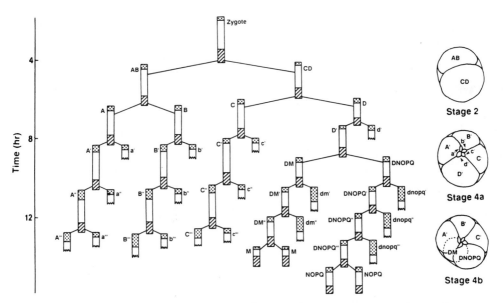

FIG.13. Cell cycles of cells during stages 1 through
4 of *Helobdella* development. The cell lineage tree
presents the divisions as well as the composition of
the cell cycle of each cell. Each vertical bar
represents the cell cycle of an identified cell; S
phase is shown in stippling, G2 phase in white, M
phase in diagonal stripes. Time was measured from the
time of egg deposition. The sloping horizontal lines
represent cytokinesis. Note that nascent large
blastomeres entered S phase before cytokinesis was
completed. Since the complete cell cycle of the
micromeres and macromeres A'''- C''' are not known,
their bars end in jagged lines. On the right are
schematic drawings of embryos at representative
stages, with each cell identified. Approximate
diameter of an embryo is 400 microns (from Bissen &
Weisblat, 1989).

replicative interphase (G1 or G2 phase), (Bissen and Weisblat,
1989). These experiments show that the stereotyped cell
lineages of leech embryos are mirrored by highly reproducible
stereotyped cell cycles. These are composed of S, G2 and M
phases from the very beginning (Fig. 13). Thus *Helobdella* is
different from other invertebrates such as *Drosophila* and
Caenorhabditis, and from *Xenopus*, whose early rapid cell cycles
are composed of S and M phases only (Graham and Morgan, 1966;
Foe and Alberts, 1983; Edgar and Schubiger, 1986; Edgar and
McGhee, 1988). Rather the cell cycles of the early leech embryo
are similar in composition to the first several cycles of
mouse, sea urchin and snail embryos (Dalq and Pasteels, 1955;
Hinegardner et al., 1964; Van den Bigelaar, 1971) which also
have G2 phases of significant duration.

In leech embryos there is a dramatic transition from the
shorter cell cycles of the early blastomeres to the much longer
cell cycles of the primary blast cells (Fig.14). This is due to
a 10 to 40 fold increase in the length of time spent in the G2

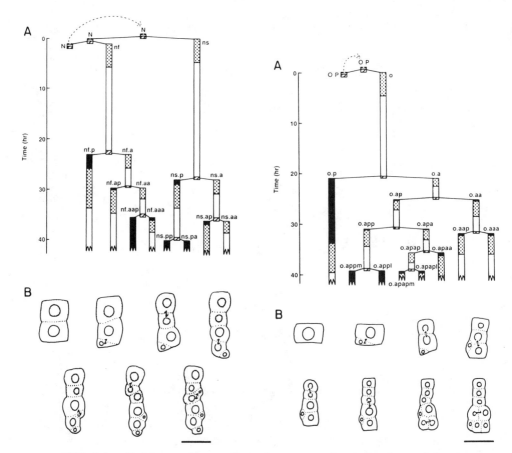

FIG.14. Cell cycles of primary and secondary blast
cells. (A) cell lineage trees present the divisions
and cell cycles of each class of blast cell. Each
vertical bar represents the cell cycle of an
identified cell; G_1 phase is shown in black, S phase
in stippling, G_2 phase in white and M phase in
diagonal stripes. Cells whose cell cycles are not
known in entirety have bars ending with jagged lines.
Time is measured from the birth of each class of
primary blast cell; in the left panel, which shows
cell cycles of ns and nf blast cells, time is
measured from the birth of the ns blast cell. The
time scale is consequently shifted by one hour for
the nf blast cell and its progeny. a, anterior; p,
posterior; l, lateral; m, medial; d, deep; s, superficial. (B) Schematic drawings of the primary blast
cell clones after each division, arranged in two rows
that read from left to right. The daughters of the
most recent division are indicated by the double
arrow. The clones are drawn as viewed in the left
germinal band; anterior is up, lateral (which refers
to the future position of the cell in the germinal
plate) is to the right. Scale bar, 20 microns. Left
panel: cell cycles of ns and nf blast cells. The 3
divisions of the nf blast cells and the first
division of the ns blast cells have been previously
described by Zackson, 1984; the next 2 divisions of
the ns blast cells are newly described. A total of 25

phase of the cell cycle, with a smaller increase in the length of their S phases. M phase remains relatively constant and G1 phases are acquired only later in the blast cell cycles.

Studies of the control of cell cycle in cultured mammalian cells and in yeast have shown that cell cycle length is largely regulated during the prereplicative G1 phase (Prescott, 1976; Pardee, 1974). Less is known about how the durations of embryonic cell cycles are regulated. Current studies in *Helobdella* are using the tools of reverse genetics to isolate leech genes whose homologues in other organisms have been shown to control the progression of the cell cycle.

MOLECULAR GENETIC STUDIES OF DEVELOPMENT: THE ROLE OF HOMEOBOX GENES IN LEECH DEVELOPMENT

Leeches are also being used for studies of the genetic control of development. The advantages and disadvantages of *Helobdella* as an organism for genetic studies of development are discussed in Wedeen et al., 1989. In brief, animal species that are particularly suitable for classic genetic analyses, such as *Drosophila* and *Caenorhabditis* have a relatively short life cycle, are easy to culture, have a small genome and many mutant strains. *Helobdella* shares some of these advantages: its genome size is quite small, close in size to that of *Drosophila*, and it is easy to culture. Its life cycle however (10 weeks from egg to adult) is considerably longer than that of *Drosophila* (14 days) or *C. elegans* (65 hours at 20 degrees C); and there are no known mutant strains. Consequently classical genetic studies will not be useful for the identification of genes controlling development. An alternative approach has been to take advantage of molecular genetic advances in other species. Highly conserved homeoboxes from 12 different *Drosophila* genes have been used to estimate the number and diversity of homeo-box containing genes in *Helobdella*. Thus, genomic Southern blot analysis carried out on restricted *Helobdella* and *Drosophila* DNA's suggest that there are between 16 and 18 homeobox-containing genes in *Helobdella* (Wedeen et al., 1989), slightly fewer than in *Drosophila* (Gehring, 1987; Scott et al., 1989).

Expression of a homologue to the *Drosophila* gene engrailed (*en*) has been studied in *Helobdella* (Weisblat et al., 1988; Patel et al., 1989). In *Drosophila en* is expressed in the posterior compartment of every segment and is required for cells in this portion to assume their normal identities (Kornberg, 1981; Kornberg et al., 1985; DiNardo et al., 1985). In *Helobdella* the en homologue is expressed in a single bandlet in the stage 7 embryo, segmentally repeating in a single large cell in the late stage 8 embryo, and in many neurones of the head ganglia in stage 9-10 embryos. Thus, as in *Drosophila*,

---

n bandlets were examined. In (B) ns blast cell clones are presented in stippling and nf blast cell clones in white. Right panel: cell cycles of o blast cells. The first 3 divisions have been described by Shankland (1987a); the division of the cell o. apap is newly described. A total of 35 o bandlets were examined (from Bissen & Weisblat, 1989).

expression is seen early in development in a subset of segmental founder cells, and later in development in a subset of differentiating neurones. Results with *en* thus indicate that analysing expression patterns of evolutionarily conserved genes that are putative regulators of development will be useful in studying leech development.

The major advantage of using *Helobdella* for molecular genetic studies of development lies in its potential for detailed developmental studies. Since the embryos contain large robust cells that can be individually microinjected it should be possible not only to study expression of homeobox containing genes by using antibodies to protein products of genes, but also to microinject antibodies into chosen cells in the early embryo to test the function of the *Helobdella* genes.

REFERENCES

Anderson, D.T., 1973, Embryology and phylogeny in annelids and arthropods, Pergamon Press, Oxford.

Astrow, S., Holton, B. and Weisblat, D.A., 1987, Centrifugation redistributes factors determining cleavage patterns in leech embryos, *Dev.Biol.*, 120: 270-283.

Balakier, H., and Pedersen, R.A., 1982, Allocation of cells to inner cell mass and trophectoderm lineages in preimplantation mouse embryo, *Dev.Biol.*, 90:352-362.

Bissen, S.T., and Weisblat, D.A., 1987, Early differences between alternate blast cells in leech embryo, *J.Neurobiol.*, 18 (3):251-269.

Bissen, S.T., and Weisblat, D.A., 1989, The durations and compositions of cell cycles in embryos of the leech, *Helobdella triserialis*, *Development*, 106:105-118.

Blackshaw, S.E., 1987, Organisation and development of the peripheral nervous system in annelids, *in:* "Nervous systems in Invertebrates," ed M.Ali, NATO-ASI series, Plenum Press, New York.

Blackshaw, S.E., 1988, Cell lineages and the development of identified neurones in the leech, *in:* "The making of the nervous system," Eds.J.G. Parnavelas, C.D.Stern and R.V.Stirling, Oxford University Press, 22-51.

Blackshaw, S.E., and Warner, A.E., 1976, Low resistance junctions between mesoderm cells during development of trunk muscles, *J.Physiol.*, 255:209-230.

Blair, S.S., 1982, Interactions between mesoderm and ectoderm in segment formation in the embryo of a glossiphoniid leech, *Dev.Biol.*, 89:389-396.

Blair, S.S., 1983, Blastomere ablation and the developmental origin of identified monoamine-containing neurones in the leech, *Dev.Biol.*, 95:65-72.

Blair, S.S., and Weisblat, D.A., 1982, Ectodermal interactions during neurogenesis in the glossiphoniid leech *Helobdella triserialis*, *Dev.Biol.*, 91:64-72.

Dalcq, A., and Pasteels, J., 1955, Determination photometrique de la teneur relative en DNA des noyaux dans les oeufs en segmentation du rat et de la souris, *Expl.Cell Res.* Suppl., 3:72-97.

Davidson, E.H., 1976, Gene activity in early development, 3rd Ed.Academic Press Inc.London Ltd.

DiNardo, S., Kuner, J., Theis, J., and O'Farrell, P., 1985, Development of embryonic pattern in *D.melanogaster* as

revealed by accumulation of the nuclear engrailed
protein, *Cell*, 43:59-69.

Edgar, B.A., and Schubiger,G., 1986, Parameters controlling
transcriptional activation during early *Drosophila*
development, *Cell*, 44:871-877.

Edgar, B.A., and McGhee, J.D., 1988, DNA synthesis and the
control of embryonic gene expression in *C. elegans*,
Cell, 53:589-599.

Fernandez, J., 1980, Embryonic development of the glossiphoniid
leech *Theromyzon rude:* characterisation of developmental
stages, *Dev.Biol.*, 76:245-262.

Fernandez, J., and Olea, N., 1982, Embryonic development of
glossiphoniid leeches, *in:* "Developmental biology of
freshwater invertebrates," Eds. F.W.Harrison and
R.C.Cowden, Liss, New York, 317-361.

Fernandez, J., and Stent, G.S., 1980, Embryonic development of
the glossiphoniid leech *Theromyzon rude* : structure and
development of the germinal bands, *Dev.Biol.*, 78:407-
434.

Foe, V.E., and Alberts, B.M., 1983, Studies of nuclear and
cytoplasmic behaviour during the 5 mitotic cycles that
precede gastrulation in *Drosophila* embryogenesis, *J.Cell
Sci.*, 61:31-70.

Fraser, S.E., 1985, Gap junctions and cell interactions during
development, *TINS*, 79:3-4.

Gehring,W.J., 1987, Homeoboxes in the study of development,
Science, 236:1245-1252.

Gimlich, R.L., and Braun, J., 1985, Improved fluorescent
compounds for tracing cell lineage, *Dev.Biol.*, 109:509-
514.

Graham, C.F., and Morgan, R.W., 1966, Changes in the cell cycle
during early amphibian development, *Dev.Biol.*, 14:439-
460.

Hinegardner, R.T., Rao, B., and Feldman, D.E., 1964, The DNA
synthetic period during early development of the sea
urchin egg, *Exptl.Cell Res.*, 36:53-61.

Ho, R.K., and Weisblat, D.A., 1987, A provisional epithelium in
leech embryo: cellular origins and influence on a
developmental equivalence group, *Dev.Biol.*, 120:520-534.

Holton, B., Astrow, S.H., and Weisblat, D.A., 1989, Animal and
vegetal teloplasms mix in the early embryo of the leech
Helobdella triserialis, *Dev.Biol.*, 131:182-188.

Kimmel, C.B., and Warga, R.M., 1986, Tissue specific cell
lineages originate in the gastrula of the zebrafish,
Science, 231: 365-368.

Kornberg, T., 1981, Engrailed: A gene controlling compartment
and segment formation in *Drosophila*, *PNAS* 78: 1095-1099.

Kornberg, T., Siden, I., O'Farrell, P., and Simon, M., 1985,
The engrailed locus of *Drosophila*: *In situ* localisation
of transcripts reveals compartment specific expression,
Cell, 40:45-53.

Muller, K.J., and McMahan, U.J., 1976, The shapes of sensory
and motor neurones and the distribution of their
synapses in ganglia of the leech: a study using
intracellular injection of horseradish peroxidase,
Proc.R.Soc.B., 194:481-499.

Nishida, H., and Satoh, N., 1983, Cell lineage analysis in
ascidian embryos by intracellular injection of a tracer
enzyme. I. Up to the 8 cell stage, *Dev.Biol.*, 99:382-
394.

Pardee, A.B., 1974, A constriction point for control of normal animal cell proliferation, *P.N.A.S.*, 71:1286-1290.

Patel, N.H., Martin-Blanco, E., Coleman, K.G., Poole, S.J., Ellis, M.C.,Kornberg, T.B., and Goodman, C.S., 1989, Expression of *engrailed* Proteins in Arthropods, Annelids, and Chordates, *Cell* (in press).

Prescott, D.M., 1976, The cell cycle and the control of cellular reproduction, *Adv.Genet*, 18:99-177.

Schliep, W., 1914, Die Entwicklung zentrifugierter Eier von *Clepsine sexoculata*, *Zool.Jahrb.Abt.Ontog.Tiere*, 37: 236-253.

Scott, M.P., Tamkun, J.W., and Hartzell, G.W., III 1989, The structure and function of the homeodomain, BBA Reviews on Cancer (in press).

Shankland, M., and Weisblat, D.A., 1984, Stepwise commitment of blast cell fates during the positional specification of the O and P cell lines in the leech embryo, *Dev.Biol.*, 106:326-342.

Shankland, M., 1987a, Determination of cleavage pattern in embryonic blast cells of the leech, *Dev.Biol.*, 120:494-498.

Shankland,M., 1987b, Differentiation of the O and P cell lines in the embryo of the leech. I. Sequential commitment of blast cell lineages, *Dev.Biol.*, 123:85-96.

Shankland, M., 1987c, Differentiation of the O and P cell lines in the embryo of the leech. II. Genealogical relationship of descendant pattern elements in alternative developmental pathways, *Dev.Biol.*, 123:97-107.

Stent, G.S., Weisblat, D.A., Blair, S.S., and Zackson, S.L., 1982, Cell lineage in the development of the leech nervous system, *in:*"Neuronal Development," Ed.N.Spitzer, Plenum Press, New York, 1-44. *Adv.Physiol.*, 10:87-123.

Van den Bigelaar, J.A.M., 1971, Timing of the phases of the cell cycle during the period of asynchronous division up to the 49-cell stage in *Lymnaea*, *JEEM*, 26:367-391.

Warner, A.E., 1984, Physiological approaches to early development, *Recent Adv.Physiol.*, 10:87-123.

Warner, A.E., and Lawrence, P.A., 1982, Permeability of gap junctions at the segmental border in insect epidermis, *Cell* 28:243-252.

Wedeen, C.J., Price, D.J., and Weisblat, D.A., 1989, Analysis of the life cycle, genome, and homeobox genes of the leech, *Helobdella triserialis*, *in:* "Cellular and Molecular Biology of Pattern Formation," Oxford University Press Inc., (in press).

Weisblat, D.A., 1981, Development of the nervous system. *In:* "Neurobiology of the leech," Eds.K.J.Muller, J.G. Nicholls and G.S. Stent, Cold Spring Harbor Publications, New York, 173-196.

Weisblat, D.A., Sawyer, R., and Stent, G.S., 1978, Cell lineage analysis by intracellular injection of a tracer enzyme, *Science*, 202:1295-1298.

Weisblat, D.A., Zackson, S.S., Blair, S.S., and Young, J.D., 1980, Cell lineage analysis by intracellular injection of fluorescent tracers, *Science*, 209:1538-1541.

Weisblat, D.A., and Shankland, M., 1985, Cell lineage and segmentation in the leech, *Phil.Trans.R.Soc.Lond.*,B. 312:39-56.

Weisblat, D.A., Price, D.J., and Wedeen, C.J., 1988, Segmentation in leech development, *Development* 104, Supplement, 161-168.

Whitman, C.O., 1878, The embryology of Clepsine,
        Q.J.Micros.Sci., 18:215-315.
Wordeman, L., 1982, Kinetics of primary blast cell production
        in the embryo of the leech *Helobdella triserialis*,
        Honors Thesis, Department of Molecular Biology,
        University of California, Berkeley.
Zackson, S.L., 1984, Cell lineage, cell-cell interactions and
        segment formation in the ectoderm of a glossiphoniid
        leech embryo, *Dev.Biol.*, 104:143-160.

PRACTICAL APPROACHES TO THE STUDY OF NERVOUS SYSTEM DEVELOPMENT

IN HIRUDINID LEECHES

Susanna Blackshaw

Department of Cell Biology
School of Biological Sciences
University of Glasgow
G12 8QQ Scotland

INTRODUCTION

Cellular and molecular genetic studies of development use glossiphoniid leeches because their embryos contain large identifiable cells (Blackshaw, this volume). However, most neurobiological research has been done on a different species, the medicinal leech, *Hirudo medicinalis* (Retzius, 1891; Muller et al., 1981). As a result of work done in a number of laboratories over the past 30 years, individual neurones or glia in *Hirudo* have been extensively characterised in terms of their physiology, their transmitter chemistry, their synaptic relations and their behavioural roles. Because the endpoint of development, the adult nervous system, is so well defined, it is possible to ask detailed questions about its development in terms of individual cells. Unlike leeches of the family of Glossiphoniidae, *Hirudo* lays small non-yolky eggs into a hard cocoon and these develop into an embryo that has transient specialisations for feeding on the albumen supplied in the cocoon fluid (Sawyer, 1986). For these reasons *Hirudo* embryos are not as well suited to studies of early cleavage stages. The non-yolky eggs do however offer advantages for studies of neural development since the more transparent nature of the later embryos means that developing neurones can be visualised in whole mounts of the germinal plate. Adult leeches are widely available from commercial suppliers and easy to maintain, and a number of laboratories have established breeding colonies to provide embryos for studies of neural development. This chapter outlines embryogenesis in hirudinid leeches and reviews techniques that have been used successfully to study normal development of identified cells as well as procedures used to manipulate some aspects of development.

MAINTENANCE, BREEDING AND EMBRYO CULTURE

Commercial suppliers of adult *Hirudo medicinalis* include the following: in the UK, Biopharm (UK) Ltd., Bryngelen House, 2 Bryngwili Road, Hendy, Dyfed, SA 4 IXB; Blades Biological,

Experimental Embryology in Aquatic Plants and Animals
Edited by H.-J. Marthy, Plenum Press, New York, 1990

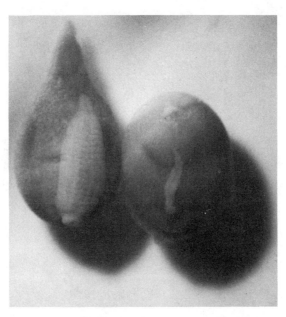

FIG.1. The cryptolarva of *Hirudo medicinalis* removed from the hard cocoon.

Scarletts Oast, Furnace Lane, Cowden, Edenbridge, Kent; in France, Ricarimpex, Bordeaux; West Germany, Blutegel Import und Versand, Reckungshausen-sud; in the USA, Biopharm (USA) Ltd, 701 East Bay Street, BTC Box 1212, Charleston, S.C.29403. Adult leeches are easily maintained in the laboratory in copper free water. To obtain embryos leeches are kept at room temperature (22-24 degrees C) and fed defibrinated bovine or rabbit blood. In this laboratory heparinised blood is loaded into short lengths of intestine normally used for sausage manufacture and obtained from a local butcher. In some laboratories leeches are individually isolated for a period of 2-4 weeks before mating (e.g. Fernandez & Stent, 1982; Gao & Macagno, 1987). Gravid leeches can be recognised by a yellow/orange coloration of the skin in segments 6 and 7 (sex segments) and are removed to plastic boxes filled with moist sphagnum moss. Eggs are laid into cocoons 2-3 cm long and staged according to days of development at 22-24 degrees C. A gravid leech lays several cocoons each containing 5-25 eggs in the viscous cocoon fluid referred to as albumin. If boxes are checked daily, new cocoons can be recognised by a white frothy covering and removed to a moist petri dish in an incubator at 22-24 degrees centigrade.

OUTLINE OF EMBRYOGENESIS

    Early development of hirudinid leeches has been described by a number of authors (Brandes, 1901; Shumkina, 1951, a-d; Fernandez & Stent, 1982; reviewed in Sawyer, 1986). The following brief summary is based on Fernandez & Stent (1982) and concentrates on aspects relevant to development of the nervous system. The initial cleavages ressemble those of *Helobdella* (see Chapter 12, this volume) and result in the production of 4 pairs of ectodermal teloblasts and one pair of mesodermal teloblasts from the D macromere. The cleavage period

234

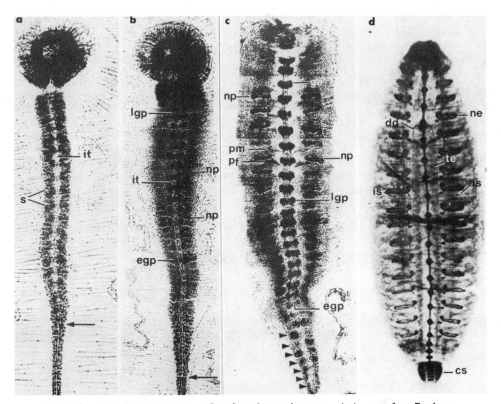

FIG.2. Whole mounts of Hirudo embryos (a) early 7-day
(b) late 7-day (c) late 9-day (d) 11-day embryo. In
(b) the anterior sector of the germinal plate
includes 20 segments, of which 12 have formed
nephridial primordia (np). Late ganglionic primordia
(lpg) lie to the front of early ganglionic primofdia
(epg). The arrows mark the border between the two
sectors of the germinal plate.it, interprimordial
tissue; s, somites. In (c) the arrow points to the
degenerating ribbon part of the germinal plate. The
anterior sector of the germinal plate includes 32
body segments (the last 7 are marked by arrow heads)
that are at different stages of development. Since
development of the germinal plate occurs in a
rostrocaudal sequence, the most advanced body
segments lie at the front of the germinal plate. The
developing nerve cord consists of 12 ganglia (ga) and
10 late (lpg) and 10 early (epg) ganglionic
primordia. The primordia of the female (pf) and of
the male (mf) genitalia, as well as the 17 pairs of
nephridial primordia (np) are seen. In (d)
intersegmental septa (is) extend from the middle of
the ganglia to the lateral edge of the germinel
plate. Thus ganglia present an intersegmental
distribution, whereas developing nephridia (ne) and
testes (te) are distributed segmentally. The paired
deferential ducts (d) have begun to grow caudalward
from the primordium of the male genitalia. The
incipient caudal sucker (cs) includes 7 ganglia.Scale
bars: (a, b) 0,2mm (c) 0,4mm (d) 1mm   (from Fernandez
& Stent, 1982).

235

ends by about 2 days of development when formation of the early larva begins. Cells of the micromere cap give rise to the larval envelope and mouth. Albumin from the cocoon fluid is ingested via the larval mouth up to day 9 of development during which time the germinal plate is forming. Left and right germinal bands arise by repeated divisions of the teloblasts and extend along either side of the larva. Coalescence of left and right bands along the ventral midline is complete by 5 days of development (Figs. 1 & 2). Segmentation of the germinal plate begins on day 6 of development when the primordia of the frontmost ganglia of the ventral nerve cord can be distinguished, and formation of somites from the mesoderm has begun at the head end. By day 7 about half the final number of ganglia are apparent; by day 11, when segmentation of the germinal plate tissue is complete, the first four ganglia have fused to form the suboesophageal ganglion; all 21 ganglia of the future ventral nerve cord are apparent and separated by connectives, and the last 7 ganglia form an elongated mass of neural tissue that corresponds to the caudal ganglion. As in *Helobdella* (Weisblat et al., 1984), the supraoesophageal ganglion is not derived from the germinal plate. In *Hirudo* it arises from a mass of cells in front of the larval mouth. During days 5-18 the lateral edges of the germinal plate continue to expand: they meet and fuse along the dorsal midline around day 18-20. The embryos spend a further 8-10 days within the cocoon and hatch as miniature adults around day 30. From 7 to 10 days of development embryos can be removed from the cocoon and cultured separately in sterile dilute Instant Ocean (600 mg/L).

TECHNIQUES AND PROCEDURES

1. *Describing normal development*

a) Intracellular labelling of embryonic cells

A number of laboratories have used intracellular dye injection to study the morphology of cells within the developing ventral nerve cord (Blackshaw et al., 1984; Wallace, 1984; Glover & Mason, 1986; Macagno et al., 1986; Jellies et al., 1987; Loer et al., 1987; Gao & Macagno, 1987, 1988) or body wall (Jellies & Kristan, 1988; Blackshaw, unpublished). For the experiments embryos are pinned onto a Sylgard coated slide. To overcome problems of movement of embryos during intracellular injection embryos can be anaesthetised using 8% ethanol in leech Ringer (Muller et al., 1981), or fixed briefly with paraformaldehyde (1% in phosphate buffered saline for 30 seconds). Cells can be visualised using a compound microscope with DIC optics and a x40 water immersion lens. Access to cells under the limited working distance of objectives can be improved by bending the electrode tip with a heated Nichrome wire (Gao & Macagno, 1987). Both Lucifer Yellow and horseradish peroxidase have been used successfully to label embryonic cells. Typical proceedures are as follows: for Lucifer Yellow injection, electrodes are filled with a 3-5% solution of the dye in either distilled water or 0.1% LiCl, and the dye iontophoresed using hyperpolarising pulses (200ms, 2Hz, 1-8nA for 1-10mins: Gao & Macagno, 1987) or constant hyperpolarising current (0.2-1nA for 1-3mins: Jellies & Kristan, 1988). For horseradish peroxidase injection electrodes are filled with 4-

5% in 10mM Hepes at pH 7.9 and iontophoresed using depolarising pulses 200ms long at 2Hz, 1-8nA for 1-8mins (Gao & Macagno, 1987), or filled with a 3% solution of the enzyme in 0.2M KCl containing 2% Fast Green dye and injected by applying pressure to the back of the electrode (Jellies & Kristan, 1988). Some laboratories find Lucifer Yellow easier to use and the success of the injection can be monitored in the live preparation using epifluorescence optics. Following injection the preparations are processed using standard techniques developed for adult leech neurones (Muller et al., 1981). Two additional dyes that fluoresce at different wavelengths have been used in conjunction with Lucifer Yellow to label cells in the embryonic body wall (Jellies & Kristan, 1988). Sulforhodamine 101 (Molecular Probes, Junction City, Oregon) is a red-fluorescent molecule, prepared as a 2% aqueous solution and visualised using a rhodamine filter set. 8-hydroxy-1,3,6-pyrenetri-sulphonic acid, trisodium salt (Eastman Kodak, Rochester, NY) is a blue fluorescent molecule prepared as a 3% aqueous solution. Both can be iontophoresed using hyperpolarising current as for Lucifer Yellow. Neither dye is fixable and preparations must be photographed within one hour of filling since the dyes diffuse out of the cells within 12-24 hours. By using multiple exposures on colour film through different sets the relationships between different cells in the same preparations can be directly examined.

b) Immunohistochemistry

Embryonic cells can be visualised due to expression of antigens recognized by monoclonal antibodies raised against adult leech nerve cords (Johansen et al., 1985; Macagno et al., 1983; Stewart et al., 1985; Zipser & McKay, 1981; Zipser, 1982, Zipser et el., 1989; Cole et al., 1989). For example, develop-ing muscle cells in the embryonic body wall have been visualised using monoclonal antibody Lan 3-14 that recognises an unidentified antigen associated with adult muscle cells (Zipser & McKay, 1981; Jellies & Kristan, 1988). For the experiments embryos are fixed overnight (cold) in 4% para-formaldehyde in 0.1M phosphate buffer (pH 7.4), rinsed several times in PBS and then incubated in primary antibody overnight at RT. After rinsing in PBS embryos are incubated with a secondary antibody, goat anti-mouse IgG (Cappel Worthington Biochemicals, Malvern, PA) conjugated to either rhodamine or fluorescein. Expression of monoclonal antibody Laz1-1 has been used to map cell death during gangliogenesis (Stewart et al., 1987). Laz1-1 in the adult nerve cord labels between 20 and 35 cells in each segmental ganglion, including identified mechanosensory and motor neurones, via an unidentified antigen. In embryos between 7 and 12 days of development, the antigen is additionally expressed by a pair of cells of unknown function in each ganglion, named bipolar cells, that appear and subsequently degenerate. In this study double labelling with Lucifer Yellow injected intracellularly and with Laz1-1 was used to study the morphology of the transiently appearing bipolar cells.

Commercially available antibodies to serotonin have been used to visualise 5-HT immunoreactivity and hence projections of serotonin-containing Retzius cells in embryos (Jellies et al., 1987; Loer & Kristan, 1989; see also 2a below).

c) Non-specific staining

Non-specific staining with toluidine blue (the poor man's antibody) or Evans blue has been used to visualise developing ganglia and body wall muscle (Fernandez & Stent, 1982; Jellies & Kristan, 1988). Fixed tissue can be stained as a whole mount with Evans Blue (Sigma, 2% in PBS) or as sections with toluidine blue (1% in buffer), destained in 70% alcohol, dehydrated in graded ethanol and mounted in Permount.

d) Molecular genetic techniques

Several homeobox genes in *Hirudo medicinalis* have been isolated on the basis of sequence homology to *Drosophila* homeobox genes of the *Antennapedia* class (Wysocka-Diller & Macagno, 1989). In these experiments, *in situ* hybridisation with probes generated from these genes is used on whole mounts of embryos at various stages. This gives information on where and when homeobox genes are expressed in the developing central nervous system and how this relates to differentiation of identified cell types (see also Chapter x, this volume).

2. *Perturbing normal development*

A number of techniques are available to manipulate aspects of development

a) Selective cell ablation

Both mechanical and photoablation techniques have been used successfully to delete chosen cells during development (Gao & Macagno, 1988; Jellies & Kristan, 1988; Loer & Kristan, 1989). The effects of these perturbations are then examined by visualising remaining cells using techniques described above.

Mechanical ablations have been performed on embryos 9-10 days old by Gao & Macagno (1987). Embryos were anaesthetised with 9% ethanol in sterile leech Ringer containing 15mM Mg (Muller et al/, 1981) on ice and placed on a Sylgard coated slide in which a groove had been cut with a razor blade. Fire-polished glass probes were used to rotate the embryo in the groove until its ventral surface was uppermost and the segmental ganglia could be seen under the dissecting microscope. A fine pin held by forceps was used to mechanically ablate cells. Such lesions can be confined to a single glial packet and cause the loss of between 5 and 30 neurones. After the operation embryos are transfered to sterile Ringer for 10 minutes before being returned to sterile artificial sea water.

Mechanical ablation of Retzius cells was used by Loer & Kristan (1989). In these experiments a hand-held microelectrode was passed 10-15 times through the central region of the ganglion where the Retzius cells are located. The success of the ablation technique was tested by using anti-serotonin antibodies to show the absence of 5-HT immunoreactive somata in ablated ganglia.

Photoablation allows killing of individual cells after filling them with fluorescent dye (Miller & Selverston, 1979).Anaesthetised embryos are viewed in transmitted light, a chosen cell identified visually, impaled and filled with

Lucifer Yellow as above (1a) or with 5(6)-carboxyfluorescein (6% in 0.4M KOH, Sigma). The preparation is then exposed to UV light for a few minutes to kill the cell. Operated embryos are then allowed to develop for a chosen time before assessing the effect of the ablation as above. The photoablation technique requires cuts in the body wall to expose the chosen neurone for microinjection, and extended viewing time with transmitted and epifluorescent light, and for these reasons is more likely to damage or kill embryos. Mechanical ablation on the other hand, although less specific than photoablation, is very rapid and a larger fraction of embryos survive the operation.

b) Target organ ablation; homotopic or ectopic transplantations (Baptista & Macagno, 1988; Loer & Kristan, 1989)

To assess the role of target tissue in the development of axonal projections by identified neurones, techniques have been developed for ablating or transplanting chosen peripheral tissue. Genitalia have been ablated successfully in 9, 10, 15, 20 and 25 day old embryos. Embryos are anaesthetised in 8% ethanol in sterile artificial spring water and genitalia removed by cutting a small piece of skin containing the primordia with sharp scissors and forceps. Wounds heal rapidly, skin openings appear closed after a few hours and muscle connective tissue grows smoothly through the area. For transplantation, skin containing the primordia is removed and placed in an opening of appropriate size made in the skin of a host embryo, or in skin of a different segment in the same embryo. To help transplanted tissue adhere, a piece of glass coverslip was pressed onto the transplant for about an hour. Using these techniques, transplants are incorporated and contribute apparently normal tissue.

c) Cutting embryonic nerve roots (Gao & Macagno, 1988)

Techniques used successfully for lesionning segmental nerves in adult animals (Van Essen & Jansen, 1977; Bannatyne et al., 1989) have been adapted for use in embryos. Operations have been performed on embryos at 11, 14 and 30 days. Embryos are anaesthetised and manipulated as in a, b, above and a sharp Minuten pin held by forceps used to open the skin covering connectives or peripheral roots, which are then cut using sharp pins or forceps. Older embryos are stretched and held down with fine pins placed at both ends and sharpened scissors used to open the skin and cut roots. After surgery embryos are returned to sterile artificial sea-water. Operated animals have been maintained for up to 5 months (during which time they were fed 5 times) before being used to map projection patterns of damaged neurones.

REFERENCES

Bannatyne, B.A., Blackshaw, S.E., and McGregor, M., 1989, New growth elicited in adult leech mechanosensory neurones by peripheral axon damage, *J.exp.Biol.*, 143:419-434.
Baptista, C.A., and Macagno, E.R., 1988, Modulation of the pattern of axonal projections of a leech motor neuron by ablation or transplantation of its target, *Neuron*, 1:949-962.
Blackshaw, S.E., 1990, Experimental embryology in leeches: cellular and molecular approaches. This volume.

Blackshaw, S.E., Parnas, I., and Thompson, S.W.N., 1984, Changes in the central arborisation of primary afferent neurones during development of the leech nervous system, *J.Physiol.*, 353, 47p.

Brandes, G., 1901, Die Begattung der Hirudineen, *ABl. Naturf.Ges.Halle*, 22:373-382.

Cole, R.N., Morell, R.J., and Zipser, B., 1989, Glial processes, identified through their glial-specific 130KD surface glycoprotein, are juxtaposed to sites of neurogenesis in the leech germinal plate, *GLIA* 2:446-457.

Fernandez, J., and Stent, G.S., 1982, Embryonic development of the hirudinid leech *Hirudo medicinalis:* structure, development and segmentation of the germinal plate, *J.Embryol.exp.Morphol.*, 72:71-96.

Gao, W.-Q., and Macagno, E.R., 1987a, Extension and retraction of axonal projections by some developing neurons in the leech depend upon the existence of neighbouring homologues. I. The HA cells, *J.Neurobiol.*, 18:43-59.

Gao, W.-Q., and Macagno, E.R., 1987b, Extension and retraction of axonal projections by some developing neurons in the leech depend upon the existence of neighbouring homologues. II. The AP and AE neurons, *J.Neurobiol.*, 18:295-313.

Gao, W.-Q., and Macagno, E.R., 1988, Axon extension and retraction by leech neurons: severing early projections to peripheral targets prevents normal retraction of other projections, *Neuron*, 1:269-277.

Glover, J.C., and Mason, A., 1986, Morphogenesis of an identified leech neuron: segmental specification of axon outgrowth, *Dev.Biol.*, 115:256-260.

Jellies, J., Loer, C.M., and Kristan, W.B., 1987, Morphological changes in leech Retzius neurons after target contact during embryogenesis, *J.Neurosci.*, 7:2618-2629.

Jellies, J., and Kristan, W.B., 1988, Embryonic assembly of a complex muscle is directed by a single identified cell in the medicinal leech, *J.Neurosci.*, 8:3317-3326.

Johansen, J., Thompson, I., Stewart, R.R., and McKay, R.G., 1985, Expression of surface antigens recognized by the monoclonal antibody Lan 3-2 during embryonic development in the leech, *Brain Research*, 343:1-7.

Loer, C.M., Jellies, J., and Kristan, W.B., 1987, Segment-specific morphogenesis of leech Retzius neurons requires particular peripheral targets, *J.Neurosci.*, 7:2630-2638.

Loer, C.M., and Kristan, W.B., 1989a, Peripheral target choice by homologous neurons during embryogenesis of the medicinal leech. I. Segment-specific preferences of Retzius cells, *J.Neurosci.*, 9:513-527.

Loer, C.M., and Kristan, W.B., 1989b, Peripheral target choice by homologous neurons during embryogenesis of the medicinal leech. II. Innervation of ectopic reproductive tissue by non-reproductive Retzius cells, *J.Neurosci.*, 9:528-538.

Macagno, E.R., Stewart, R.R., and Zipser, B., 1983, The expression of antigens by embryonic neurons and glia in segmental ganglia of the leech *Haemopis marmorata*, *J.Neurosci.*, 3:1D746-1759.

Macagno, E.R., Peinado, A., and Stewart, R.R., 1986, Segmental differentiation in the leech nervous system: specific phenotypic changes associated with ectopic targets, *PNAS*, 83:2746-2750.

Macagno, E.R., and Stewart, R.R., 1987, Cell death during
    gangliogenesis in the leech: competition leading to the
    death of PMS neurons has both random and nonrandom
    components, *J.Neurosci.*, 7:1911-1918.
Miller, J.P., and Selverston, A.I., 1979, Rapid killing of
    single neurons by irradiation of intracellularly
    injected dye, *Science*, 206:702-704.
Muller, K.J., Nicholls, J.G., and Stent, G.S., 1981,
    Neurobiology of the leech, Cold Spring Harbor
    Publications.
Retzius, G., 1891, Zur Kenntnis des zentralen Nervensystems der
    Würmer, *Biologische Untersuchungen*, Neue Folge, II, 1-
    28, Samson and Wallen, Stockholm.
Sawyer, R.T., 1986, Leech Biology and Behaviour, Vol.I.
    Anatomy, Physiology and Behaviour, Clarendon Press,
    Oxford.
Shumkina, O.B., 1951a, Cleavage of the egg in the medicinal
    leech (in Russian), *Dokl.Akad.Nauk SSSR*, 77:353-356.
Shumkina, O.B., 1951b, Development and metamorphosis of *Hirudo
    medicinalis* (in Russian) *Dokl.Akad.Nauk SSSR*, 77:761-
    764.
Shumkina, O.B., 1951c, Germ band and the head primordium of the
    medicinal leech (in Russian), *Dokl.Akad.Nauk SSSR*,
    77:821-824.
Shumkina, O.B., 1951d, Periods of intracocoon development of
    the medicinal leech (in Russian), *Dokl.Akad.Nauk SSSR*,
    77:1259-1262.
Stewart, R.R., Macagno, E.R., and Zipser, B., 1985, The
    embryonic development of peripheral neurons in the body
    wall of the leech *Haemopis marmorata*, *Brain Research*,
    332:150-157.
Stewart, R.R., Gao, W.-Q., Peinado, A., Zipser, B., and
    Macagno, E.R., 1987, Cell death during gangliogenesis in
    the leech: bipolar cells appear ane then degenerate in
    all ganglia, *J.Neurosci.*, 7:1919-1927.
Van Essen, D.C., and Jansen, J., 1977, The specificity of
    reinnervation by identified sensory and motor neurons in
    the leech, *J.comp.Neurol.*, 171:433-454.
Wallace, B.G., 1984, Selective loss of neurites during
    differentiation of cells in the leech central nervous
    system, *J.comp.Neurol.*, 228:149-153.
Weisblat, D.A., Kim, S.Y., and Stent, G.S., 1984, Embryonic
    origins of cells in the leech *Helobdella triserialis*,
    Dev.Biol., 104:65-85.
Wysocka-Diller, J.W., and Macagno, E.R., 1989, The leech
    homeobox gene LOX2 is expressed embryonically in
    posterior segmental ganglia of *Hirudo medicinalis*,
    Neuroscience Abstracts, 15:101.
Zipser, B., 1982, Complete distribution patterns of neurons
    with characteristic antigens in the leech central
    nervous system, *J.Neurosci.*, 2:1453-1464.
Zipser, B., and McKay, R., 1981, Monoclonal antibodies
    distinguish identifiable neurons in the leech, *Nature*,
    289:549-554.
Zipser, B., Morell, R., and Bajt, M.L., 1989, Defasciculation
    as a neuronal pathfinding strategy: involvement of a
    specific glycoprotein, *Neuron* 3:621-630.

STARFISH OOCYTES AND SEA URCHIN EGGS AS MODELS TO STUDY THE

INTRACELLULAR MECHANISMS CONTROLLING THE CELL DIVISION CYCLE

Laurent Meijer

CNRS
Station Biologique
29682 Roscoff cédex - France

The cell division cycle is composed of two major phases, S (DNA synthesis) and M (mitosis-meiosis), interspaced by gap periods (G_1, before S, and G_2, before M). The initiation of the S and M phases constitute the two major control points of the cell cycle. These last few years have seen major progress in the understanding of the intracellular factors that regulate the G_2/M transition of both meiotic and mitotic divisions. In this paper I will review these recent advances, putting the emphasis on the contribution of starfish and sea urchin gametes to this important field of cell biology.

1. STARFISH OOCYTE MEIOTIC DIVISIONS

Starfish oocytes are naturally arrested at the first prophase of meiosis (end of G_2), characterized by a large nucleus, called germinal vesicle (Fig.1). At the time of spawning, a neurohormonal mechanism is switched on which induces the resumption of meiotic divisions (or maturation) and the release of fertilizable oocytes (review in Meijer and Guerrier, 1984). Briefly, the radial nerves release a peptidic " Gonad-Stimulating Substance" (GSS) which stimulates the follicle cells surrounding the oocyte to liberate a second hormone, 1-methyladenine (1-MeAde). This hormone triggers a series of biochemical, biophysical and morphological events in the oocytes which lead to nuclear envelope breakdown (or germinal vesicle breakdown, GVBD) within 20 minutes, first polar body emission (1 hr), second polar body and formation of a female pronucleus (2 hrs). This mechanism can be easily reproduced *in vitro* by the simple addition of 1-MeAde to a suspension of follicle cells-deprived oocytes (for methods, see Meijer et al., 1984). The very high synchrony, and the speed of response of starfish oocytes has allowed a detailed investigation of the biochemical events underlying oocyte maturation and, in particular, the transition from G_2 to M of the first meiotic division. It now appears that 1-MeAde acts on oocyte plasma membrane receptors (Yoshikuni et al., 1988), through G-proteins (Shilling et al., 1989) and that it induces a decrease of cAMP concentration (Meijer and Zarutskie, 1987)

Experimental Embryology in Aquatic Plants and Animals
Edited by H.-J. Marthy, Plenum Press, New York, 1990

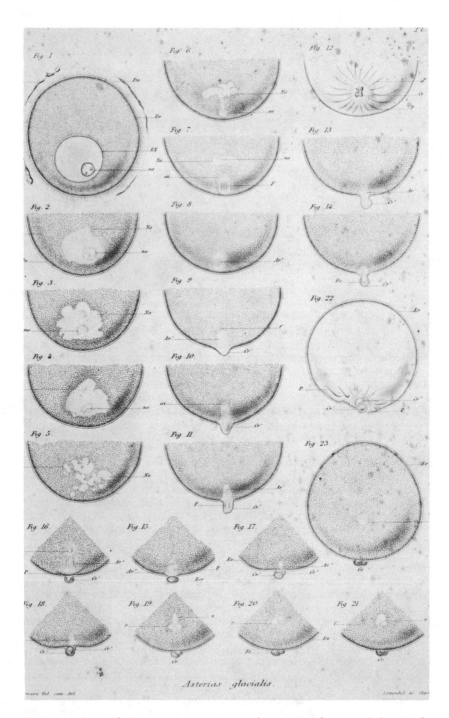

FIG.1. Starfish oocyte maturation as pictured by Fol
(1879). 1) the immature oocyte surrounded by a thin
layer of follicle cells and containing a proeminent
germinal vesicle; 2-6) nuclear envelope breakdown and
fading of the nucleus; 7-14) first meiotic division
and release of the first polar body; 15-18) second
meiotic division and emission of the second polar
body; 23) fully mature egg with female pronucleus.

which is only part of the intracellular mechanism leading to GVBD (Meijer et al., 1989). 1-MeAde triggers a major burst of protein phosphorylation (Guerrier et al., 1977; Mazzei and Guerrier, 1982; Dorée et al., 1983; review in Pondaven et al., 1987) due to the activation of several protein kinases (see further in the text) and it triggers the appearance of an intracellular "Maturation (or M phase)-Promoting Factor" (MPF). This factor triggers GVBD and meiotic divisions when microinjected into prophase-arrested, non-stimulated oocytes (Kishimoto and Kanatani, 1976).

2. SEA URCHIN EGG MITOTIC DIVISIONS

In contrast to starfish, sea urchin oocytes undergo meiotic divisions very discretely in the gonad and they are stored in the ovary as fully fertilizable eggs, arrested at the end of the second meiotic division, characterized by a small female pronucleus. These cells can be easily prepared as a suspension of interphase eggs and the simple addition of sperm triggers a major cellular activation involving numerous pathways. After gamete fusion, the male and female pronuclei fuse and DNA synthesis is initiated (S phase) with 30-40 minutes post-fertilization. By 80 min., the eggs undergo nuclear envelope breakdown and enter the M phase; soon after the cells undergo the first mitotic cleavage (Fig.2) rapidly followed by a series of successive and highly synchronized mitosis. Although investigated for more than a century the sequence of biochemical events underlying the mitotic events are largely unknown; nevertheless, as in meiotic starfish oocytes, protein phosphorylation appears to play a key role in controlling the transient appearance of a M-phase-Promoting Factor and the mitotic divisions (review in Pondaven et al., 1977; Meijer and Pondaven, 1988).

3. INTRACELLULAR CONTROL OF THE G2/M TRANSITION OF THE CELL CYCLE

Three rather independent approaches have provided im-portant progress in the understanding of the intracellular factors that regulate the G2/M transition of cell division: yeast cell division cycle mutants, M-phase promoting factor (MPF) and M-phase-specific protein kinases.

3.1. *Cell division cycle mutants in yeast*

The genetic approach to cell division cycle regulation has led to the isolation of a variety of cdc mutants, in *Saccharomyces cerevisiae* (Hartwell, 1974) and *Schizosaccharo-myces pombe* (Nurse et al., 1976), in which the G2/M transition is perturbed (review in Beach et al., 1988; Lee and Nurse, 1988; Lohka, 1989). These studies have identified the *cdc2/CDC28* gene as the central element triggering entry into M phase. This gene encodes a 34 Kd protein kinase present in all actively dividing eukaryotic cells investigated so far, including yeast, *Physarum*, starfish, sea urchin, *Xenopus* and human cells (Reed et al., 1985; Arion et al., 1988; Arion and Meijer, 1989; Dunphy et al., 1988; Gautier et al., 1988; Labbé et al., 1988, 1989; Meijer et al., 1989; Shipley and Sauer, 1989; Westendorf et al., 1989). The p34cdc2 protein associates

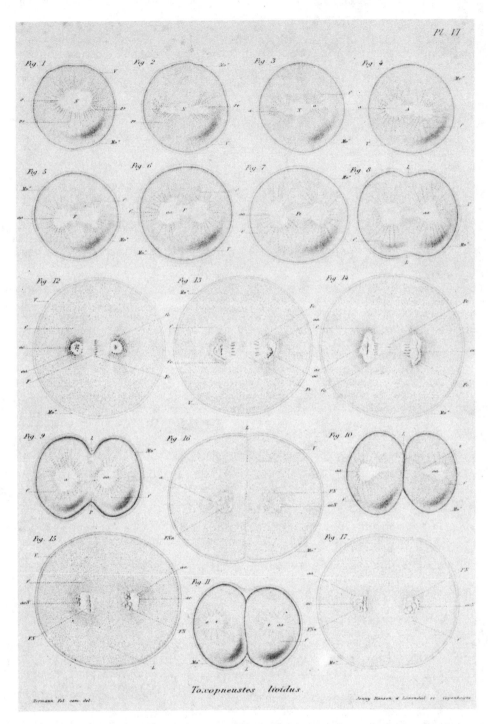

FIG.2. Sea urchin egg mitosis as pictured by Fol (1879). 1-7) spindle formation; 8-11) first cleavage; 12) metaphase; 13) anaphase; 14) telophase; 15-17) reformation of the nuclear envelope.

specifically and stoechiometrically with two other proteins. One, of 13 Kd, is the product of the $suc1^+$ gene present in yeast (Brizuela et al., 1987) and higher eukaryotes (Draetta et al., 1987; Draetta and Beach, 1988). The other, of 58-62 Kd, is the product of the yeast $cdc13^+$ gene (Booher and Beach, 1987, 1988; Booher et al., 1989). This protein displays a strong sequence homology with cyclins, a class of proteins showing a striking cell cycle oscillation of their abundance in phase with the cell cycle. Identified in various marine invertebrates, in *Xenopus* cleaving embryos and in human Hela cells (Rosenthal et al., 1980; Evans et al., 1983; Swenson et al., 1986; Pines and Hunt, 1987; Standart et al., 1987; Meijer et al., 1989; Westendorf et al., 1989; Minshull et al., 1989; Murray et al., 1989; Murray and Kirschner, 1989; Pines and Hunter, 1989), cyclins show maximal accumulation at each M phase. This pattern is due to a continuous synthesis by a complete proteolysis at the end of each metaphase. Cyclins interact physically with p34[cdc2] in clam (Draetta et al., 1989; Westendorf et al., 1989), sea urchin eggs (Meijer et al., 1989), starfish oocytes (Pondaven et al., 1990) and in human Hela cells (Pines and Hunter, 1989); the p62 protein that associates with p34[cdc2] in human cells may actually belong to the cyclin family (Draetta and Beach, 1988; Draetta et al., 1989; Brizuela et al., 1989).

At least three other genes interact with cdc2 in the regulation of mitosis:
-*wee 1*, a 112 Kd protein kinase, negatively controls cdc2 (Russell and Nurse, 1987a)
-*nim 1*, a 50 Kd protein kinase, is a negative regulator of wee 1 and thus an indirect positive regulator of cdc2 (Russel and Nurse, 1987b).
-*cdc 25*, a 67 Kd protein, has a positive effect on cdc2 activation (Russel and Nurse, 1986).

3.2. *M-phase Promoting Factor*

A second approach to the intracellular mechanisms controlling cell division has arisen from cell fusion and microinjection experiments: an intracellular meiosis- or mitosis-inducing factor appears transiently in the cytoplasm of cells undergoing the G2/M transition. When transfered into a non-dividing cell this factor triggers entry in mitosis or meiosis (reviews in Adlakha and Rao, 1987; Kishimoto, 1988; Lohka, 1989). This "M-phase-Promoting Factor" (or "Maturation Promoting Factor") (MPF) has been demonstrated in meiotic (maturing) oocytes of many species: coelenterates (Freeman and Ridgway, 1988), molluscs (Kishimoto et al., 1984), starfish (Kishimoto and Kanatani, 1976), amphibians (Detlaff et al., 1964; Masui and Markert, 1971) and mammals (Balakier, 1978; Kishimoto et al., 1984; Sorensen et al., 1985). MPF has been found in mitotic cells such as yeast cdc mutants (Weintraub et al., 1982; Tachibana et al., 1987), *Physarum* (Adlakha et al., 1988), cleaving blastomeres of starfish (Kishimoto et al., 1982) and amphibians (Wasserman and Smith, 1978; Gerhart et al., 1984), numerous mammalian cultured cells synchronized at M phase such as Hela, CHO, V79 (Rao and Johnson, 1970; Sunkara et al., 1979; Nelkin et al., 1980; Kishimoto et al., 1982). The most interesting property of MPF is its complete lack of species-specificity: MPF from any dividing cell, at the G2/M transition, will trigger entry into M phase when transfered into any G_2-arrested cell. MPF thus appears as an universal intracellular inducer of cell division at the G_2/M transition level. It controls nuclear envelope disassembly, chromosome condensation and spindle formation.

The purification of MPF has proven to be difficult because of its lability (Wu and Gerhart, 1980; Adlakha et al., 1985; Kishimoto and Kondo, 1986; Nguyen-Gia et al., 1986). The most extensive purification of MPF shows that it is composed of at least two major proteins (32 and 45 Kd) (Lohka et al., 1988). p34^{cdc2} has recently been identified as one of the components of this factor (Dunphy et al., 1988; Gautier et al., 1988; Labbé et al., 1989) and there are some indications that the other component, p45, may represent a proteolytic fragment of cyclin. Two types of arguments demonstrate the fundamental role of cyclins in MPF activity: microinjection of cyclin mRNA into *Xenopus* oocytes triggers the G_2/M transition (Swenson et al., 1986; Pines and Hunt, 1987; Westendorf et al., 1989); translation of cyclin mRNA is necessary and sufficient for extracts of activated *Xenopus* eggs to enter mitosis (Minshull et al., 1989; Murray et al., 1989; Murray and Kirschner, 1989).

Several arguments demonstrate the close link between protein phosphorylation and MPF activity: stabilization of MPF activity by phosphatase inhibitors (Wu and Gerhart, 1980) which potentiate or even trigger oocyte maturation (Hermann et al., 1984; Pondaven and Meijer, 1986; Le Goascogne et al., 1987); inhibition of MPF action by microinjected phosphatases (Hermann et al., 1984; Meijer et al., 1986); presence of kinase activities in partially purified MPF (Maller et al., 1977; Wu and Gerhart, 1980; Halleck et al., 1984).

3.3. *M-phase-specific protein kinases*

Investigation of the enzymes that undergo a cell cycle-regulated variation in activity has led to the discovery of a "growth-associated histone kinase" ("M-phase-specific histone kinase","kinase M") (reviews in Hohmann, 1983; Matthews and Huebner, 1985; Wu et al., 1986). This protein kinase is transiently activated at the G_2/M transition in all dividing cells investigated so far: mitotic *Physarum* (Bradbury et al., 1974a; Hardie et al., 1976) mitotic sea urchin eggs (Meijer and Pondaven, 1988; Pelech et al., 1989; Arion and Meijer, 1989; Meijer et al., 1989), meiotic starfish oocytes (Picard et al., 1985; Sano, 1985; Meijer et al., 1987; Pelech et al., 1987; Arion et al., 1988; Labbé et al., 1988, 1989; Pondaven et el., 1990), meiotic amphibian oocytes (Cicirelli et al., 1988; Labbé et al., 1988), chinese hamster fibroblasts (Woodford and Pardee, 1986) and ovary cells (Lake and Salzmann, 1972), C6 rat glioma cells and Erlich ascites tumor cells (Schlepper and Knippers, 1975), mouse plasmacytoma (Quirin-Stricker and Schmidt, 1981; Quirin-Stricker, 1984), Novikoff hepatoma cells (Zeilig and Langan, 1980). Although its natural substrate is unknown it preferentially phosphorylates histone H1 *in vitro* at "mitosis-specific" sites (Langan, 1978). These sites are also phosphorylated *in vivo* at the time of chromosome condensation during early metaphase (review in Wu et al., 1986). This histone H1 kinase (H1K) requires magnesium, uses both ATP and GTP and is independent of cyclic nucleotides, calcium-calmodulin, calcium-diacylglycerol, polyamines (Woodford and Pardee, 1986; Pelech et al., 1987; Cicirelli et al., 1988).

However, maximal recovery of its activity requires the presence of phophatase inhibitors, suggesting that H_1K activation is controlled by phosphorylation or by a phosphorylated modulator (Pelech et al., 1987; Cicirelli et al., 1988; Arion and Meijer, 1989). Despite a variety of experimental conditions H_1K activation is undissociable from the triggering of cell division (Meijer et al, 1987; Meijer and Pondaven, 1988). It has been directly implicated in the induction of mitosis in *Physarum* (Bradbury et al., 1974b; Inglis et al., 1976) and in chromatin condensation (Matsumoto et al., 1980; Mueller et al., 1985; review in Wu et al., 1986).

Because of their high synchrony, meiotic starfish oocytes and mitotic sea urchin eggs provide particularly good models to study this M-phase specific H_1K and its regulation. 1-MeAde (starfish) and the fertilizing sperm (sea urchin) both trigger a strong activation of H_1K (Sano, 1985; Meijer et al., 1987; Pelech et al., 1987; Pondaven et al., 1987; Pelech et al., 1988; Arion and Meijer, 1989; Labbé et al., 1989; Meijer et al., 1989; Pondaven et al., 1990). One subunit of the starfish oocyte H_1K has been identified as a 34 Kd protein homolog to $p34^{cdc2}$ (Arion et al., 1988; Labbé et al., 1988, 1989; Meijer et al., 1989). Very recently we have shown that cyclin constitutes a second component of the sea urchin egg H_1K (Meijer et al., 1989). Using p13-sepharose affinity chromatography H_1K can now be rapidly purified to near homogeneity (Labbé et al., 1989b; Pondaven et al., 1990): it clearly contains equimolar amounts of $p34^{cdc2}$ and cyclin.

The mechanism of H_1K activation as the cell enters the M phase is starting to be understood. In starfish oocytes this process does not require any protein synthesis (Pelech et al., 1987) and $p34^{cdc2}$ and cyclin already form an inactive complex in the G2-arrested oocyte. 1-MeAde triggers a rapid dephosphorylation of $p34^{cdc2}$ simultaneously with a rapid phosphorylation of cyclin (Pondaven et al., 1990). In sea urchin eggs, protein synthesis is required for the activation of H_1K (Meijer and Pondaven, 1988; Arion and Meijer, 1989). $p34^{cdc2}$ is present throughout the cell cycle, but cyclin needs to be synthesized before each division (Meijer et al., 1989). It appears that a phosphorylated form of $p34^{cdc2}$ associates with a dephosphorylated cyclin during the G2 phase; soon after, as the cell enters M phase, $p34^{cdc2}$ gets dephosphorylated, cyclin becomes phosphorylated and H_1K is activated. A similar $p34^{cdc2}$ dephosphorylation has been observed during H_1K activation in *Xenopus* oocytes (Dunphy and Newport, 1989; Gautier et al., 1989) and in mammalian cells (Morla et al., 1989).

Active M-phase-specific H_1K is thus constituted of dephosphorylated $p34^{cdc2}$ and phosphorylated cyclin in an equimolar ratio. Because they share many properties, including H_1 kinase activity, a $p34^{cdc2}$ subunit, possibly a cyclin subunit and a transient appearance at the G2/M transition, MPF and M-phase-specific H_1K many well represent the same entity.

By their natural synchrony, their speed of division, their large size and transparency, the large amounts by which they can be obtained, starfish oocytes and sea urchin eggs have significantly contributed to the understanding of the general intracellular mechanisms controlling cell division. This honours the early researchers who, more than a century ago, had already foreseen the potentialities of these models and started their study (Hertwig, 1876; Selenka, 1879; Fol, 1877, 1879).

ACKNOWLEDGEMENTS

Many thanks are due to Nicole Guyard for typing the manuscript and to the fishermen of the "Station Biologique de Roscoff" for providing sea urchins and starfish to numerous researchers on the cell cycle. This work was supported by grants from the "Association pour la Recherche sur le Cancer" (ARC 6268) and INSERM 891012.

REFERENCES

Adlakha, R.C., and Rao, P.N., 1986, Molecular mechanisms of the chromosome condensation and decondensation cycle in mammalian cells, *Bio Essays* 5, 100-105.

Adlakha, R.C., Shipley, G.L., Zhao, J.Y., Jones, K.B., Wright, F.A., Rao, P.N., and Sauer, H.W., 1988, Amphibian oocyte maturation induced by extracts of *Physarum polycephalum* in mitosis, *J.Cell Biol.* 106:1445-1452.

Adlakha, R.C.,Wright, D.A., Sahasrabuddhe, C.G., Davis, F.M., Prashad, N., Bigo, H., and Rao, P.N., 1985, Partial purification and characterization of mitotic factors from Hela cells, *Exp.Cell Res.*, 160:471-482.

Arion, D., and Meijer, L., 1989, M-phase specific protein kinase from mitotic sea urchin eggs: cyclic activation depends on protein synthesis and phosphorylation but does not require DNA or RNA synthesis, *Exp.Cell Res.*, 183:361-375.

Arion, D;, Meijer, L., Brizuela, L., and Beach, D., 1988, *cdc2* is a component of the M-phase specific histone H1 kinase:evidence for identity with MPF, *Cell*, 55:371-378.

Balakier, M., 1978, Induction of maturation in small oocytes from sexually immature mice by fusion with meiotic or mitotic cells, *Exp.Cell Res.*, 112:137-141.

Beach, D., Basilico, C., and Newport, J., 1988, eds, Cell cycle control in eukaryotes, *Curr.Comm.Mol.Biol.*, Cold Spring Harbor.

Booher, R., Alfa, C.E., Hyams, J.S., and Beach, D.H., 1989, The fission yeast cdc2/cdc13/suc 1 protein kinase: regulation of catalytic activity and nuclear localization, *Cell*, 58:485-497.

Booher, R., and Beach, D.H., 1987, Interaction between *cdc13* [+] and *cdc2* [+] in the control of mitosis in fission yeast; dissociation of the G1 and G2 roles of the *cdc2* [+] protein kinase, *EMBO J.*, 6:3441-3447.

Booher, R., and Beach, D.H., 1988, Involvement of *cdc13* [+] in mitotic control in *Schizosaccharomyces pombe*: possible interaction of the gene product with microtubules, *EMBO J.*, 7:2321-2327.

Bradbury, E.M., Inglis, R.J., and Matthews, H.R., 1974a, Control of cell division by very lysine rich histone (f1) phosporylation, *Nature*, 247:257-261.

Bradbury, E.M., Inglis, R.J., Matthews, H.R., and Langan, T.A., 1974b, Molecular basis of control of mitotic cell division in eukaryotes, *Nature*, 249:553-556.

Brizuela, L., Draetta, G., and Beach, D., 1987, p13[suc1] acts in

the fission yeast cell division cycle as a component of
the p34^{cdc2} protein kinase, *EMBO J.*, 6:3507-3514.
Cicirelli, M.F., Pelech, S.L., and Krebs, E.G., 1988,
    Activation of multiple protein kinases during the burst
    in protein phosphorylation that precedes the first
    meiotic cell division in *Xenopus* oocutes, *J.Biol.Chem.*,
    263:2009-2019.
Detlaff, T.A., Nikitina, L.A., and Stroeva, O.G., 1964, The
    role of the germinal vesicle in oocyte maturation in
    anurans as revealed by the removal and transplantation
    of nuclei, *J.Embryol.exp.Morphol.*, 12:851-873.
Dorée, M., Peaucellier, G., and Picard, A., 1983, Activity of
    the maturation promoting factor and the extent of
    protein phosphorylation oscillate simultaneously during
    meiotic maturation of starfish oocytes, *Dev.Biol.*,
    99:489-501.
Draetta, G;, and Beach, D., 1988, Activation of cdc2 protein
    kinase during mitosis in human cells: cell cycle-
    dependent phosphorylation and subunit rearrangement,
    Cell, 54:17-26.
Draetta, G., Brizuela, L., Potashkin, J;, and Beach, D., 1987,
    Identification of p34 and p13, human homologs of the
    cell cycle regulators of fission yeast encoded by cdc2$^+$
    and suc1$^+$., *Cell*, 50:319-325.
Dunphy, X.G., Brizuela, L., Beach, D., and Newport, J., 1988,
    The *Xenopus* homolog of cdc2 is a component of MPF, a
    cytoplasmic regulator of mitosis, *Cell*, 54:423-431.
Dunphy, W.G., and Newport, J., 1989, Fission yeast p13 blocks
    mitotic activation and tyrosine dephosphorylation of the
    Xenopus cdc2 protein kinase, *Cell*, 58:181-191.
Evans, T., Rosenthal, E.T., Youngblom, J., Distel, D., and
    Hunt, T., 1983, Cyclin: a protein specified by maternal
    mRNA in sea urchin eggs that is destroyed at each
    cleavage division, *Cell*, 33:389-396.
Fol, H., 1877, Sur le premier développement d'une étoile de
    mer, *C.R.Acad.Sci.Paris*, 84:357-360.
Fol, H., 1879, Recherche sur la fécondation et le commencement
    de l'hénogénie chez divers animaux, *Mémoires Soc.Phys.et
    Hist.Nat. de Genève*, 26:89-397.
Freeman, G., and Ridgway, E.B., 1988, The role of cAMP in
    oocyte maturation and the role of the germinal contents
    in mediating maturation and subsequent developmental
    events in hydrozoans, *Roux's Arch.Dev.Biol.*, 197:197-
    211.
Gautier, J., Matsuka, T., Nurse, P., and Maller, J., 1989,
    Dephosphorylation and activation of *Xenopus* p34^{cdc2}
    protein kinase during the cell cycle, *Nature*, 339:626-
    629.
Gautier, J., Norbury, C., Lohka, M., Nurse, P., and Maller, J.,
    1989, Purified maturation-promoting factor contains the
    product of a *Xenopus* homolog of the fission yeast cell
    cycle control gene cdc2$^+$, *Cell*, 54:433-439.
Gerhart, J., Wu, M., and Kirschner, M., 1984, Cell cycle
    dynamics of an M-phase-specific cytoplasmic factor in
    Xenopus laevis oocytes and eggs, *J.Cell Biol.*, 98:1247-
    1255.
Guerrier, P., Moreau, M., and Dorée, M., 1977, Hormonal control
    of meiosis in starfish: stimulation of protein
    phosphorylation induced by 1-methyladenine, *Mol.Cell
    Endocrinol.*, 7:137-150.
Halleck, M.S., Lumley-Sapanski, K., Reed, J.A., Iyer, A.P.,

Mastro, A.M., and Schlegel, R.A., 1984, Characterization of protein kinases in mitotic and meiotic cell extracts, *FEBS Lett.*, 167:193-198

Hardie, D.G., Matthews, H.R., and Bradbury, E.M., 1976, Cell-cycle dependence of two nuclear histone kinase enzyme activities, *Eur.J.Biochem.*, 66:37-42.

Hartwell, L.H., 1974, *Saccharomyces cerevisiae* cell cycle, *Bacteriol.Rev.*, 38:164-198.

Hermann, J., Mulner, O., Bellé, R., Marot, J., Tso, J., and Ozon, R., 1984, *In vivo* effects of microinjected alkaline phosphatase and its low molecular weight substrates on the first meiotic cell division in *Xenopus laevis* oocytes, *Proc.Nat.Acad.Sci.USA*, 81:5150-5154.

Hertwig, O., 1876, Beiträge zur Kenntnis der Bildung, Befruchtung und Theilung des thierischen Eies, *Morphol.Jahrbuch*, 1:347-434.

Hohmann, P., 1983, Phosphorylation of H_1 histones, *Mol.Cell Biochem.*, 57:81-92.

Inglis, R.J., Langan, T.A., Matthews, H.R., Hardie, D.G., and Bradbury, E.M., 1976, Advance of mitosis by histone phosphokinase, *Exp.Cell Res.*, 97:418-425.

Kishimoto, T., 1988, Regulation of metaphase by a maturation-promoting factor, *Dev.Growth and Differ.*, 30:105-115.

Kishimoto, T., and Kanatani, H., 1976, Cytoplasmic factor responsible for germinal vesicle breakdown and meiotic maturation in starfish oocytes, *Nature*, 260:321-322.

Kishimoto, T., and Kondo, H., 1986, Extraction and preliminary characterization of maturation-promoting factor from starfish oocytes, *Exp.Cell Res.*, 163:445-452.

Kishimoto, T., Kuriyama, R., Kondo, H., and Kanatani, H., 1982, Generality of the action of various maturation-promoting factors, *Exp.Cell Res.*, 137:121-126.

Kishimoto, T., Yamazaki, K., Kato, Y., Koide, S.S., and Kanatani, H., 1984, Induction of starfish oocyte maturation-promoting factor of mouse and surf clam oocytes, *J.Exp.Zool.*, 231:293-295.

Labbé, J.C., Lee, M.G., Nurse, P., Picard, A., and Dorée, M., 1988, Activation at M-phase of a protein kinase encoded by a starfish homologue of the cell cycle control gene $cdc2^+$, *Nature*, 335:251-254.

Labbé, J.C., Picard, A., Karsenti, E., and Dorée, M., 1988, An M-phase specific protein kinase of *Xenopus* oocytes: partial purification and possible mechanism of its periodic activation, *Dev.Biol.*, 127:157-169.

Labbé, J.C., Picard, A., Peaucellier, G., Cavadore, J.C., Nurse, P., and Dorée, M., 1989, Purification of MPF from starfish: identification as the H_1 histone kinase $p34^{cdc2}$ and a possible mechanism for its periodic activation, *Cell*, 57:253-263.

Lake, R.S., and Salzman, N.P., 1972, Occurrence and properties of a chromatin-associated F1-histone phosphokinase in mitotic chinese hamster cells, *Biochemistry*, 11:4817-4825.

Langan, T.A., 1978, *Methods*, Cell Biol., 19:127-142.

Lee, M., and Nurse, P., 1988, Cell cycle control genes in fission yeast and mammalian cells, *Trends in Genetics*, 4:287-290.

Le Goascogne, C., Sananes, N., Gouezou, M., and Baulieu, E.E., 1987, Alkaline phosphatase activity in the membrane of *Xenopus laevis* oocytes: effects of steroids, insulin and inhibitors during meiosis reinitiation, *Dev.Biol.*, 119:511-519.

Lohka, M., 1989, Mitotic control by metaphase-promoting factor and cdc proteins, *J.Cell Sci.*, 92:131-135.

Lohka, M., Hayes, M.L., and Maller, J.L., 1988, Purification of maturation-promoting factor, an intracellular regulator of early mitotic events, *Proc.Nat.Acad.Sci.USA*, 85:3009-3013.

Maller, J.L., Wu, M., and Gerhart, J.C., 1977, Changes in protein phosphorylation accompanying maturation of *Xenopus laevis* oocytes, *Dev.Biol.*, 58:295-312.

Masui, Y., and Markert, C., 1971, Cytoplasmic control of nuclear behaviour during meiotic maturation of frog oocytes, *J.Exp.Zool.*, 177:129-146.

Matthews, H.E., and Huebner, V.D., 1985, Nuclear protein kinases, *Mol.Cell Biochem.*, 59:81-89.

Matsumoto, Y.I., Yasuda, H., Mita, S., Marunouchi, T., and Yamada, M.A., 1980, Evidence for the involvement of H1 histone phosphorylation in chromosome condensation, *Nature*, 284:181-184.

Mazzei, G., and Guerrier, P., 1982, Changes in the pattern of protein phosphorylation during meiosis reinitiation in starfish oocytes, *Dev.Biol.*, 91:246-256.

Meijer, L., Arion, D., Goldsteyn, R., Pines, J., Brizuela, L., Hunt, T., 1989, Cyclin is a component of the sea urchin egg M-phase specific histone H1 kinase, *EMBO J.*, 8:2275-2282.

Meijer, L., Dostmann, W., Genieser, H.G., Butt, E., and Jastorff, B., 1989b, Starfish oocyte maturation: evidence for a cyclic AMP-dependent inhibitory pathway, *Dev.Biol.*, 133:58-66.

Meijer, L., and Guerrier, P., 1984, Maturation and fertlization in starfish oocytes, *Int.Rev.Cytol.*, 86:129-196.

Meijer, L., Pelech, S.L., and Krebs, E.G., 1987, Differential regulation of histone H1 and ribosomal S6 kinases during sea star oocyte maturation, *Biochemistry*, 26:7968-7974.

Meijer, L., and Pondaven, P., 1988, Cyclic activation of histone H1 kinase during sea urchin egg mitotic divisions, *Exp.Cell Res.*, 174:116-129.

Meijer, L., Pondaven, P., Tung, H.Y.L., Cohen, P., and Wallace, R.W., 1986, Protein phosphorylation and oocyte maturation. II. Inhibition of starfish oocyte maturation by intracellular microinjection of protein phosphatases-1 and 2A and alkaline phosphatase, *Exp.Cell Res.*, 163:489-499.

Meijer, L., and Zarutskie, P., 1987, Starfish oocyte maturation: 1-methyladenine triggers a drop of cAMP concentration related to the hormone-dependent period, *Dev.Biol.*, 121:306-315.

Minshull, J., Blow, J.J., and Hunt, T., 1989, Translation of cyclin mRNA is necessary for extracts of activated *Xenopus* eggs to enter mitosis, *Cell*, 56:947-956.

Morla, A.O., Draetta, G., Beach, D., and Wang, J.Y.L., 1989, Reversible tyrosine phosphorylation of *cdc2*: dephosphorylation accompanies activation during entry into mitosis, *Cell*, 58:193-203.

Mueller, R.D., Yasuda, H., and Bradbury, E.M., 1985, Phosphorylation of histone H1 through the cell cycle of *Physarum polycephalum*. 24 sites of phosphorylation at metaphase, *J.Biol.Chem.*, 260:5081-5186.

Murray, A.W., and Kirschner, M.W., 1989, Cyclin synthesis

drives the early embryonic cell cycle, *Nature*, 339:275-280.

Murray, A.W., Solomon, M.J., and Kirschner, M.W., 1989, The role of cyclin synthesis and degradation in the control of maturation promoting factor activity, *Nature*, 339:280-286.

Nelkin, B., Nichols, C., and Vogelstein, B., 1980, Protein factor(s) from mitotic CHO cells induce meiotic maturation in *Xenopus laevis* oocytes, *FEBS Lett.*, 109:233-238.

Nguyen-Gia, P., Bomsel, M., Labrousse, J.P., Gallien, C.L., and Weintraub, H., 1986, Partial purification of the maturation-promoting factor MPF from unfertilized eggs of *Xenopus laevis*, *Eur.J.Biochem.*, 161:771-777.

Nurse, P., Thuriaux, P., and Nasmyth, K.A., 1976, Genetic control of the division cycle of the fission yeast *Schizosaccharomyces pombe*, *Molec.Gen.Genet.*, 146:167-178.

Pelech, S.L., Meijer, L., and Krebs, E.G., 1987, Characterization of maturation-activated histone H_1 and ribosomal S6 kinases in sea star oocytes, *Biochemistry*, 26:7960-7968.

Pelech, S.L., Tombes, R.M., Meijer, L., and Krebs, E.G., 1988, Activation of myelin basic protein kinases during echinoderm oocyte maturation and egg fertilization, *Dev.Biol.*, 130:28-36.

Picard, A., Peaucellier, G., Le Bouffant, F., Le Peuch, C., and Dorée, M., 1985, Role of protein synthesis and proteases in production and inactivation of maturation-promoting activity during meiotic maturation of starfish oocytes, *Dev.Biol.*, 109:311-320.

Pines, J., and Hunt, T., 1987, Molecular cloning and characterization of the mRNA for cyclin from sea urchin eggs, *EMBO J.*, 6:2987-2995.

Pondaven, P., and Meijer, L., 1986, Protein phosphorylation and oocyte maturation. I. Induction of starfish oocyte maturation by intracellular microinjection of a phosphatase inhibitor, α-naphthylphosphatase, *Exp.Cell Res.*, 163:477-488.

Pondaven, P., Meijer, L., and Beach, D., 1990, Activation of M-phase specific histone H_1 kinase by modification of the phosphorylation of its $p34^{cdc2}$ and cyclin components, *Genes and Develop.*, in press.

Pondaven, P., Meijer, L., and Pelech, S.L., 1987, Protein phosphorylation in starfish oocyte meiotic divisions and sea urchin egg mitotic divisions, *Adv.Protein phosphatases*, 4:229-251.

Quirin-Stricker, C., 1984, Histone H_1 kinase from mouse plasmacytoma. Further characterization and molecular structure, *Eur.J.Biochem.*, 142:317-322.

Quirin-Stricker, C., and Schmidt, M., 1981, Purification and characterization of a specific histone H_1 kinase from mouse plasmacytoma, *Eur.J.Biochem.*, 118:168-172.

Reed, S.I., Hadwiger, J.A., and Lorincz, A.T., 1985, Protein kinase activity associated with the product of the yeast cell division cycle gene CDC28, *Proc.Nat.Acad.Sci.USA*, 82:4055-4059.

Sano, K., 1985, Calcium- and cyclic AMP-independent, labile protein kinase appearing during starfish oocyte maturation: its extraction and partial characterization, *Dev.Growth Differ.*, 27:263-275.

Schlepper, J., and Knippers, R., 1975, Nuclear protein kinases from murine cell, *Eur.J.Biochem.*, 60:206-220.

Selenka, E., 1879, *Z.Wiss.Zool.*, 33:39-55.

Shilling, F., Chiba, K., Hoshi, M., Kishimoto, T., and Jaffe, L.A., 1989, Pertussis toxin inhibits 1-methyladenine-induced maturation in starfish oocytes, *Dev.Biol.*, 133:605-608.

Shipley, G.L., and Sauer, H.W., 1989, Evidence for a homolog of the yeast cell cycle regulatory gene product $cdc2^+$ in *Physarum polycephalum*, *Eur.J.Cell Biol.*, 48:95-103.

Simanis, V., and Nurse, P., 1986, The cell cycle control gene $cdc2^+$ in fission yeast encodes a protein kinase potentially regulated by phosphorylation, *Cell*, 45:261-268.

Sorensen, R.A., Cyert, M.S., and Petersen, R.A., 1985, Active maturation-promoting factor is present in mature mouse oocytes, *J.Cell Biol.*, 100:1637-1640.

Standart, N., Minshull, J., Pines, J., and Hunt, T., 1987, Cyclin synthesis, modification and destruction during meiotic maturation of the starfish oocyte, *Dev.Biol.*, 124:248-258.

Sunkara, P.S., Wright, D.A., and Rao, P.N., 1979, Mitotic factors from mammalian cells induce germinal vesicle breakdown and chromosome condensation in amphibian oocytes, *Proc.Nat.Acad.Sci.USA*, 76:2799-2802.

Swenson, K.I., Farrell, K.M. and Ruderman, J.V., 1986, The clam embryo protein cyclin A induces entry into M-phase and the resumption of meiosis in *Xenopus* oocytes, *Cell*, 47:861-870.

Tachibana, K., Yanagishima, N., and Kishimoto, T., 1987, Preliminary characterization of maturation-promoting factor from yeast *Saccharomyces cerevisiae*, *J.Cell Sci.*, 88:273-281.

Wasserman, W.J., and Smith, D.L., 1978, The cyclic behavior of a cytoplasmic factor controlling nuclear membrane breakdown, *J.Cell Biol.*n 78:R15-R22.

Weintraub, H., Buscaglia, M., Ferrez, M., Weiller, S., Boulet, A., Fabre, F., and Baulieu, E.E., 1982, Mise en évidence d'une activité "MPF" chez *Saccharomyces cerevisiae*, *C.R.Acad.Sci.Paris*, 295:787-790.

Westendorf, J.M., Swenson, K.I., and Ruderman, J.V., 1989, The role of cyclin B meiosis I., *J.Cell Biol.*, 108:1431-1444.

Woodford, T.A., and Pardee, A.B., 1986, Histone H1 kinase in exponential and synchronous populations of chinese hamster fibroblast, *J.Biol.chem.*, 261:4669-4676.

Wu, M., and Gerhart, J., 1980, Partial purification and characterization of the maturation-promoting factor from eggs of *Xenopus laevis*, *Dev.Biol.*, 79:465-477.

Wu, R.S., Panusz, H.T., Hatch, C.L., and Bonner, W.H., 1986, Histones and their modifications, *CRC Crit.Rev.Biochem.*, 20:201-263.

Yoshikuni, M., Ishikawa, K., Isobe, M., Goto, T., and Nagahama, Y., 1988, Characterization of 1-methyladenine binding in starfish oocyte cortices, *Proc.Nat.Acad.Sci.USA*, 85:1874-1877.

Zeilig, C.E., and Langan, T.A., 1980, *Biochem.Biophys.Res.Commun.*, 95:1372-1379.

MORPHOGENESIS IN THE SEA URCHIN EMBRYO:

MECHANISM OF GASTRULATION

Robert D. Burke

Dept. of Biology
University of Victoria
Victoria, B.C., Canada, V8W 2Y2

INTRODUCTION

We are fortunate in having a number of thorough reviews on the subject of the development of sea urchin embryos. Reverberi (1971), Horstadius (1973), Guidice (1973; 1986), Stearns (1974) and Czihak (1975) are comprehensive reviews examining the processes of cellular differentiation and morphogenesis. Davidson (1986) contains a detailed examination of the mechanisms underlying gene expression in early development. Davidson (1989) reconciles several classical theories of morphogenetic gradients with more recent theories on differential gene expression. Wilt (1987) examines several aspects of determination and morphogenesis. Reviews of the development of form in sea urchin embryos include Dan (1960) and Wolpert and Gustafson (1963, 1967). Harkey (1983) and Solursh (1986) should be consulted for accounts of the differentiation of micromeres and the development of mesenchyme. Ettensohn (1984) reviews in detail the process of gastrulation.

The objective of this paper is to review the mechanisms proposed to account for gastrulation in sea urchins. The review will examine the initial phase of gastrulation archenteron elongation and review a number of reports that indicate gastrulation is dependent upon proper development of components of the extracellular matrix. The data we have at hand and some new experiments permit a new proposal of a mechanism to account for the initial phase of gastrulation and provide some insights into possible roles for the extracellular matrix.

For many developmental biologists, their most vivid image of gastrulation is from their observations of sea urchin embryos. In the small, clear embryo the neat infolding of the vegetal plate and its subsequent elongation into a tube can be clearly seen. Despite the tantalizing clarity and apparent simplicity of gastrulation, we have no comprehensive explanation for the cellular mechanisms that bring about gastrulation in sea urchins. However, because sea urchin embryos are excellent for morphogenetic studies and have proven amenable to molecular studies there is currently a great deal of interest

Experimental Embryology in Aquatic Plants and Animals
Edited by H.-J. Marthy, Plenum Press, New York, 1990

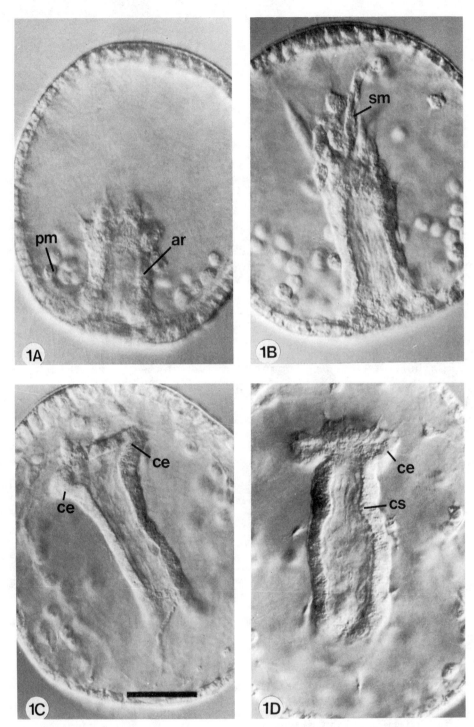

FIG.1. A series of light micrographs with Nomarski differential interference contrast optics showing the phases of gastrulation in embryos of the sea urchin, *Strongylocentrotus purpuratus*. a) the initial phase of gastrulation during which the rudiment of the archenteron (ar) is displaced into the blastocoel

in establishing the morphogenetic mechanisms underlying gastrulation.

In most species of sea urchin, the fertilized egg cleaves
to form an aggregate of blastomeres that then become organized
into a hollow ball of cells. The blastomeres develop cilia, and
hatch from the fertilization envelope to become free swimming
embryos. The vegetal plate usually becomes apparent as a
slightly thickened region of the embryo from which primary
mesenchyme migrate into the blastocoel.(Fig.1) After the
release of mesenchyme, the thickening of the vegetal plate
again becomes apparent and the putative archenteron is
displaced inwardly. Initially the archenteron is a relatively
short, squat cylinder, which is about a quarter of its final
length. This short tube has at its tip cells from which extend
numerous, filopodial projections. These cells, termed secondary
mesenchyme extend their processes to the blastocoelar wall. The
archenteron elongates until it spans the blastocoel, usually
contacting the putative stomodeum at a point on the blastoderm
near the edge of the apical plate. Early observations by Dan
and Okazaki (1956) and Gustafson and Kinnander (1956) showed
that the initial phase of gastrulation, which they termed
primary invagination, is distinct from the second phase during
which the archenteron elongates. Gustafson and Kinnander
plotted the length of the archenteron against time and showed
the transition between the two phases is marked by an
inflection point in the graph, indicating a change in the rate
of movement of the archenteron. Recently, mechanisms have been
proposed that appear to account for the secondary elongation of
the archenteron. However, the means by which the initial phase
of gastrulation takes place remains mysterious.

INITIAL PHASE OF GASTRULATION

A variety of mechanisms have been proposed to account for
the invagination of the vegetal plate in sea urchin embryos.
One early proposal suggested that there is a contraction of the
vegetal hyaline layer to cause the buckling of the vegetal
plate (Lewis, 1947). This proposal has received little
attention. Although the hyaline layer is a complex component of
the extracellular matrix with a variety of structural roles and
it is necessary for gastrulation, it seems unlikely that it is
able to produce the sort of active contraction necessary.

Another early proposal held that the initial phase of
gastrulation results from the firm attachment of the blastomeres to the outer hyaline layer and a subsequent reduction in
the volume of the blastocoel (Dan, 1960). These two events,
acting together would intuitively produce a wrinkling, or

(pm, primary mesenchyme) b) the elongation phase of
gastrulation during which the secondary mesenchyme
cells (sm) are apparent at the tip of the archenteron
c) the completion of gastrulation prior to formation
of the mouth d) further development of the
archenteron into the functional gut involves
formation of the sphincters (cs, cardiac sphincter)
and the development of the coeloms (ce). Bar = 20 µm

buckling of the blastoderm. The decrease in blastocoelar volume was presumed to be based on a change in the solute concentration and a resulting decrease in osmotic pressure. Dan and Okazaki (1956) had shown from measurements of individual embryos throughout the course of gastrulation that there was no apparent decrease in the volume of the blastocoel. There have been a variety of demonstrations that by changing the solute concentration of the sea water surrounding embryos, they can be made to swell and gastrulation inhibited or the archenteron forced to evert to form an exogastrula (Moore, 1941; Dan and Okazaki, 1956; Dan, 1960). But it was a series of experiments described some years earlier that are primarily responsible for rejection of the osmotic hypothesis. Moore and Burt (1939) showed by cutting embryos in half that the locus of forces responsible for gastrulation reside within the vegetal half of the embryo. Ettensohn (1984) has repeated and expanded these experiments with embryos of another species of sea urchin and confirmed that vegetal plates isolated prior to gastrulation have an autonomous capacity to undergo the initial phase of gastrulation. Clearly with the blastocoel opened it would be unlikely that osmotically induced changes in the volume of the blastocoel are likely to be the principal cause of the initial phase of gastrulation.

Using a variety of measurements Nislow and Morill (1988) proposed that localized growth in the vegetal plate produces the force causing the inward buckling of the archenteron. In *Lytechinus variegatus* there is apparently an increase in the number of cells in the embryo coincident with gastrulation. Measurements of dissociated cells indicate that mean cell volume remains about the same during gastrulation. From auto-radiographs following pulses of labelled thymidine incorporation and Feulgen stained preparations to calculate regional mitotic indices, Nislow and Morrill concluded that there were significantly more cells dividing in the vegetal regions than in apical regions at this stage. These observations suggest that there may be localized proliferations of cells in the vegetal regions, and as these are thought not to be typical cleavage divisions (daughter cells regain the volume of the parent cells rather than reducing in volume) there is growth in the region of the vegetal plate. Presumably if the blastula is constrained to retain its size, this increase in the surface area of the blastoderm would produce a force which could result in the inward buckling of the vegetal plate.

There are a variety of attractive aspects to this hypothesis, but there are several observations which are inconsistent with the mechanism proposed by Nislow and Morrill (1988). Stephens et al. (1986) have reported that treatment of embryos with aphidicolin, an inhibitor of DNA polymerase α specially blocks DNA synthesis and cell division but appears to have no effect on morphogenesis. Treatment of embryos prior to the thickening of the vegetal plate (before release of primary mesenchyme) will arrest development prior to gastrulation, but treatment after the thickening of the vegetal plate results in a normal looking embryo with about 1/3 of the cells in the control embryos. These observations are interpreted to indicate that morphogenesis, including gastrulation, occurs independently of cell divisions.

Agrell (1953) using Feulgen stain was the first to report

a gradient of mitotic activity along the animal-vegetal axis of the embryo. The findings of Nislow and Morrill (1988) are in agreement with these findings. Intuitively one might expect such an uneven distribution of cell division as macromeres have to divide more times than the mesomeres to achieve the minimum cell volume typical of the pluteus. In my laboratory we have utilized lineage tracing techniques to determine the timings of the late cell divisions of *S. purpuratus* embryos and do not find higher rates of cell division in the vegetal regions prior to gastrulation. In embryos in which mesomeres or macromeres were injected with horseradish peroxidase at the 16 cell stage, the number of mesomere progeny increase by a factor of 2.1 times between hatching and the initiation of gastrulation. Similarly there are 1.8 times as many macromere progeny during this same interval. Thus both mesomeres and macromere progeny go through about 1 cell cycle during this interval. The problem with the mitotic index data lies in the difficulty of obtaining data from which mitotic indices can be calculated when there are small numbers of cells dividing and the interval of time is less than a complete cell cycle. Although the hypothesis that localized growth in the vegetal plate cannot be completely discounted, it remains for it to be unequivocally demonstrated as a mechanism involved in the initial phase of gastrulation.

Perhaps the best known hypothesis to account for the inward movement of the vegetal plate is that put forward by Gustafson and Wolpert (1963, 1967). Their general model, derived from observations in sea urchins, has formed the basis for a number of morphogenetic mechanisms in a variety of organisms. Wolpert and Gustafson proposed that changes in the form of cellular sheets, such as the blastoderm, could be accounted for by changes in the adhesion between cells and between cells and supporting membranes (e.g. the hyaline layer). The changes in adhesion between cells and changes in the tension within cellular membranes would bring about changes in cellular shape. Thus, as cells changed from cuboidal to wedge-shaped, the sheet of cells would develop a curve. Autonomously controlled changes in cell shape has become an important model for explaining morphogenetic movements in a variety of organisms. This model predicts that there will be associated with the initial phase of gastrulation a change in shape of the blastomeres. Wolpert and Gustafson suggested that the blastomeres of the vegetal plate, which are initially cuboidal in shape, decrease their contacts and become more rounded. This results in an increase in the surface area of the vegetal plate and, provided it is fixed at it's periphery, the plate will buckle. Ettensohn (1984) has examined serial sections of *Lytechinus pictus* embryos and found that these predicted changes in cell shape do not occur. In this species there is only a 12% decrease in the height of the cells of the archenteron, whereas the theory predicts a decrease of about 50% is necessary to accomplish the change in surface area associated with the invaginating archenteron.

A model similar to that described by Wolpert and Gustafson in that it involves changes in cell shape is the apical constriction model. Rhumbler (1902) noted that if cells in an epithelial sheet become more constricted at one end, the sheet will curve. There have been a number of demonstrations in a variety of tissues of such apical constrictions facilitating morphogenetic processes. Typically arrays of actin filaments

261

are associated with cells undergoing apical constriction, and it is thought that they are directly involved with producing the contractile force. Ettensohn (1984) has reported ultra-structural studies of cells within the vegetal plate during gastrulation and describes what may be actin filaments in the apical regions of these cells. Treatment with the cytochalasin B and D have general deleterious effects on the cells and appear not to be useful in establishing the role of contractile actin in gastrulation. It should be noted that actin is a common constituent of most cells and apical arrays associated with cell junctions as are reported by Ettensohn (1984) are found in most epithelial cells, whether they are constricting or not. As well, there appear not to be substantial constrictions in the apical ends of the vegetal plate cells. As for several of the other putative mechanisms suggested to be involved in the initial phase of gastrulation, apical constriction remains a potential explanation, but convincing support for the hypothesis is wanting.

In studies recently undertaken in my laboratory, the movements of clones of blastomeres during gastrulation were traced by injecting the marker horseradish peroxidase into blastomeres.(Fig.2) In experiments in which a macromere is injected at the 16 cells stage and embryos allowed to develop to the mesenchyme blastula before being fixed and processed, the progeny of the macromere can be identified. In such embryos the macromere derived clones of cells occupy exactly one quarter of the vegetal hemisphere of the embryo. The cells form a neat triangle with the upper boundary of the clone half way between the vegetal and animal poles. In embryos in which a mesomere was injected, and the embryo fixed as a mesenchyme blastula, the clone of cells occupies one eighth of the animal hemisphere of the embryo. The cells again form a neat triangle with the lower boundary of the clone at the equator of the embryo. In embryos in which a macromere was injected and the embryo fixed after the primary phase of gastrulation, the clone of cells can be seen to have moved vegetally. The tip of the triangle of cells is within the blastocoel and the upper boundary is shifted to a position about midway between the equator and the vegetal pole. Clones derived from progeny of mesomeres in embryos fixed after the initial phase of gastrulation are triangular in outline, with the tip at the animal pole and the lower boundary shifted to midway between the equator and the vegetal pole. The movement of macromere derived clones suggests that one of the mechanisms involved in the initial phase of gastrulation is involution, or the concerted movement of cells within an epithelium toward the vegetal pole. Such a movement would produce a compressive force within the blastoderm, which would cause the buckling of the epithelium. The movements of these cells are implied by the fate maps developed from blastomere marking experiments of early workers (Horstadius, 1973). The movements are also consistent with the simple observation that up to 32 primary mesenchyme cells migrate out of the vegetal pole, yet no vacant space is left.

These observations of the size and shape of clones relate to the other mechanisms hypothesized to account for the initial phase of gastrulation. As the size of the clones derived from mesomeres and macromeres retain their proportions, it is unlikely that there are enhanced rates of cellular prolife-

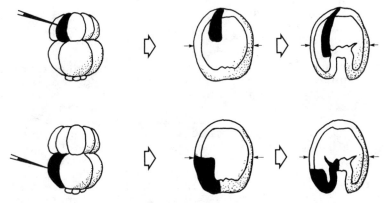

FIG.2. Sketch to show the outline of the blastomere injection experiments. By injecting an inert marker into a macromere or mesomere the position, size and shape of the clone of cells derived from the blastomere can be determined. The size and shapes of the clones suggests that there is no differential growth of cellular rearrangement during gastrulation. The position of the clones suggests that involution is the process by which the archenteron rudiment is displaced into the blastocoel.

ration in the vegetal regions of the embryos as suggested by Nislow and Morrill (1988). The retention of the triangular shape of the clones also suggests that differential rates of growth can be discounted as a mechanism underlying the initial phase of gastrulation. The mechanisms proposed by Gustafson and Wolpert (1963, 1967) and the apical constriction models (Ettensohn, 1984) are based upon epithelia fixed in position. These models propose the cells situated at the vegetal pole undergo changes in shape resulting in the folding of the epithelium. As stated, these models are insufficient to explain the net movement of blastomeres which occurs coincident with the initial phase of gastrulation.

SECONDARY ELONGATION

Following the initial invagination of the presumptive archenteron, there is a distinct phase during which it elongates and crosses the blastocoel to contact the future mouth. Throughout this phase there are numerous secondary mesenchyme cells at the tip of the archenteron which extend long filopodia. Many of the descriptions of this process suggest that the filopodia appear to be playing a role in the movement of the archenteron (Dan and Okazaki, 1956; Gustafson and Kinnander, 1956). The impression is in part created by what are described as cones of attachment, where the filopodia contact the blastodermal cells and appear to deform their basal ends into small cones, as though there were pulling. The contention that they provide the motive force for the extension of the archenteron has been supported by the observation that the archenteron fails to elongate or will retract if the filopodia break, or disappear either naturally or as a result of treatment with reduced calcium, hypertonic sea water, or general proteases (Dan and Okazaki, 1956; Gustafson, 1964).

Spiegel and Burger (1982) have injected proteases and lectins into the blastocoel and found that these treatments cause release of the filopodial attachments and subsequent regression of the archenteron. Tilney and Gibbins (1969) examined thin sections of the filopodia and report the presence of arrays of 5 nm filaments. This is about the size of cytoplasmic actin filaments and it is suggested that this observation supports the hypothesis that the filopodia are contractile and are involved in the elongation of the archenteron. Tilney and Gibbins (1969) also report that the elongation of the archenteron can be inhibited by exposing the embryos to colchicine, or hydrostatic pressure. Hydrostatic pressure disrupts microtubules and microfilaments (actin) found within the filopodia and colchicine disrupts microtubules. It has since been shown by Hardin (1987) that colchicine, which is known to affect other cellular processes is not acting specifically in this case. Treatment with nocodazole, another microtubule inhibitor has no effect on gastrulation. Thus, microtubules, which were suggested to be involved in the extension of filopodia (Gibbins and Tilney, 1969) appear not to be essential for gastrulation. Whereas the contractile activity of the filopodia, which is presumed to be based on actin, still seems to have a role in elongation.

Hardin and Cheng (1986) noted that filopodial contraction can not be the complete explanation for archenteron elongation. They point out that in exogastrulae, in which the filopodia do not have the opportunity to attach and contract, the archenteron is capable of autonomous elongation. As well, in computer models filopodial contraction alone would produce deformation not seen in life unless it is assumed that the archenteron is less stiff than the blastoderm. Hardin (1988) has done a series of experiments in which the secondary mesenchyme at the tip of the archenteron were ablated with laser microsurgery. When the cells are ablated at the onset of elongation, the archenteron continues to advance at its normal rate but stops at the 2/3 gastrula stage. If the secondary mesenchyme cells are ablated at the 2/3 gastrula stage further elongation is inhibited. Hardin (1988) suggests that the tension apparently produced by the filopodia is only important to the final stages of archenteron elongation.

The mechanism that has been proposed to account for the first part of archenteron elongation is cell rearrangement. Ettensohn (1985) prepared serial cross sections of *L.pictus* embryos and reported that the number of cells around the circumference of the archenteron is reduced from 20 to 25 to about 10 cells during the elongation phase. Hardin and Cheng (1986) have made similar observations on *S. purpuratus* embryos. These authors have proposed that these changes could be accounted for by active rearrangement of the cells. Thus a short cylinder with a large diameter is transformed to a long cylinder with a smaller diameter by the cells exchanging neighbors. Such a mechanism has previously been demonstrated to be involved in other similar morphogenetic processes, notably the elongation of insect imaginal discs (Fristrom, 1976).

A model of archenteron elongation has developed which appears to be consistent with reported observations (Hardin, 1988). This model proposes that the elongation of the archenteron results from an initial phase that is the result of cell rearrangement. This is followed by a phase during which the elongation is completed by active contraction on the filopodia of the cells at the tip of the archenteron.

ROLE OF THE EXTRACELLULAR MATRIX

As the sea urchin embryo develops, it acquires an elaborate extracellular matrix. This matrix in the blastula is associated with the apical and basal surfaces of the blastomeres. The apical surface of the cells is overlain with the hyaline layer, a heterogeneous complex of glycoproteins arranged in several distinct layers (reviewed by Spiegel et al., 1989). The basal surfaces of the cells have been known for some time to rest upon a thin basal lamina (Endo and Uno, 1960; Wolpert and Mercer, 1963). More recent studies have shown that there is an elaborate matrix of proteins and glycoproteins that radiate from the basal lamina and fill the blastocoel (Spiegel et al., 1989). It is probably useful to consider both the hyaline layer and the blastocoelar ECM as being analogous structures with similar functions (Dan, 1960; Spiegel et al., 1989).

The hyaline layer has been suggested to play a role in several of the hypothesized mechanisms underlying aspects of gastrulation. The hyaline contraction model of Lewis (1947) and the differential adhesion models of Wolpert and Gustafson (1963, 1967) are two examples where the hyaline layer plays a central role. It is recurrent in the literature that blastomeres adhere to the hyaline layer. This idea stems from the experiments of Herbst (1900) in which the hyaline layer was dissolved with low calcium sea water resulting in a loss of integrity of the embryo. Dan (1960) showed that there were apical microvilli on the blastomeres embedded in the hyaline layer and suggested that these served an anchoring function. More recently it has been shown that dissociated blastomeres do adhere to hyalin, a major component of the hyaline layer (Fink and McClay, 1985). As well, echinonectin, a substrate adhesion molecule which binds dissociated blastomeres, has been identified as a component of the hyaline layer (Alliegro et al., 1988).

Citkowitz (1971) provided some experimental results that support a role for the hyaline layer in gastrulation. In her experiments the hyaline layer was removed by treating embryos with pronase, a general proteinase. Treatment prior to the initiation of gastrulation, inhibited it completely in *S. purpuratus*. She concluded that an intact layer was essential to morphogenesis. Adelson and Humphreys (1988) reported that treating embryos with a monoclonal antibody against hyalin halts development at the stage at which the antibody is added. Monovalent fragments of the antibody (Fab fragments) also interfere with morphogenesis. In control experiments using another antibody to hyalin, embryos were unaffected. Adelson and Humphreys (1988) suggest that there are specific regions of the hyalin molecule that are involved in cell adhesion. Blocking these sites with antibodies is thought to be the basis for interference in processes involving epithelial folding, including gastrulation.

One component of the hyaline layer, the apical lamina, is

a complex of glycoproteins composed of 180, 140 and 110 k molecules (Hall and Vacquier, 1982). Monoclonal antibodies to the apical lamina glycoproteins indicate that they are released from granules after fertilization, synthesized throughout development, and is localized to the inner zone of the hyaline layer (Myers, Burke and Tamboline, submitted). These antibodies appear to interfere specifically with gastrulation in embryos grown in these antibodies (Myers, Burke and Tamboline, submitted). Cross linking of the apical lamina with these antibodies delays the initial phase of gastrulation and results in the formation of exogastrulae. In embryos treated with the antibodies the hyaline layer overlying the vegetal plate remains intact, whereas it releases from vegetal plate cells and is disrupted in untreated embryos. We propose that the antibody cross-links the apical lamina and interferes with the release of blastomeres from the hyaline layer inhibiting the initial phase of gastrulation.

There is experimental evidence indicating that the hyaline layer provides a substrate to which the cells adhere (Fink and McClay, 1985). As antibodies to the apical lamina interfere with the disruption of the layer and with the initial phase of gastrulations, it appears that the release of the vegetal plate from the hyaline layer is an integral part of the process of gastrulation. To further examine this proposal we have under-taken preliminary studies to determine if endogenous proteases are responsible for release of the vegetal plate. Embryos were grown in the presence of peptides which bind to certain classes of proteases and block their activity. We have found that the initial phase of gastrulation is blocked by antipain, a serine and thiol protease inhibitor. We also have data that indicates extracts of concentrated cultures of embryos contain proteases and that there are at least three distinct antipain sensitive proteases released from embryos. These proteases appear to be developmentally regulated in that their secretion begins coin-cident with the initiation of gastrulation.

The role of the hyaline layer in gastrulation is not completely clear, but it seems reasonable that it forms a substrate from which the vegetal plate cells must release for the initial phase of gastrulation to take place. It is also possible that the hyaline layer has additional roles suggested by the experiments in which antibodies to hyalin block further morphogenesis. Given that ECM components have been shown to have roles in cell shape, cell migration, control of cell growth and differentiation (Hay, 1981), the full scope of the contribution of the hyaline layer to gastrulation remains to be seen.

The blastocoelar ECM has been shown by several methods to be comprised of a variety of sulfated macromolecules including heparin-like material (Kinoshita, 1971); dermatan sulfate (Yamagata and Okazaki, 1974; Oguri and Yamagata, 1980) sulfated glycans (Akasaka and Terayama, 1980) and sulfated glycoproteins (Heifetz and Lennarz, 1979). Other typical ECM components have been localized to the blastocoel. These include: types I, III and IV collagen (Glolob et al. 1974; Pucci-Minafra et al., 1972; Gould and Benson, 1978, Wessel et al., 1984), fibronectin and laminin (Spiegel et al., 1980, 1983; DeSimone et al., 1985; McCarthy et al., 1987). There are several experimental studies, based largely on inhibitors, that indicate perturbations of the

normal development of this ECM will interfere with gastrulation.

Embryos grown in sea water devoid of sulfate ions fail to
develop mesenchyme that migrates normally, and fail to gastru-
late (Herbst, 1904). This manipulation is thought to princi-
pally affect the formation of sulfated glycans within the
blastocoel (Karp and Solursh, 1974), but there are also
indications that there are additional effects (Gezelius, 1976).
The effects of this treatment on mesenchyme migration has been
studied in some detail, but much less is known about how such a
treatment inhibits gastrulation (Solursh, 1986; Lane and
Solursh, 1988). Tunicamycin is an inhibitor of one of the
initial steps in the formation of N-glycosidically linked
oligosaccharides of glycoproteins (Lennarz, 1983). In sea
urchin embryos treatment with tunicamycin inhibits migration of
primary mesenchyme and gastrulation (Schneider et al., 1978).
Another class of inhibitors, β-xylosides and derivatives of β-
xylose are thought to substitute as a substrate for the xylose
linkage of glycosaminoglycans (GAG) to core proteins (Solursh,
1986). This interferes with the proper formation of
proteoglycans containing xylose linked GAG's, such as
chondroitan sulfate, heparin sulfate and dermatan sulfate.
Treatment of sea urchin embryos with β-D-xylopyranosides
interferes with the migration of primary mesenchyme within the
blastocoel and inhibits gastrulation (Kinoshita and Saiga,
1979; Akasaka et al., 1980). For all these treatments, sulphate
deprivation, tunicamycin and β-D-xylopyranosides, it has been
shown that there are effects on the composition and
organization of the blastocoelar ECM (Akasaka et al., 1980).

Collagen is an important component of the ECM and several
types of collagen have been demonstrated within the blastocoel
(Wessel et al., 1984; Wessel and McClay, 1987). Apparently
collagen is stored in vesicles within the egg and fertilization
initiates their migration and ultimate deposition within the
blastocoel as it forms. There are also some indications that
collagens are synthesized de novo by mesenchyme (Venkatesan et
al., 1986; Wilt, 1987). Experiments with inhibitors to collagen
synthesis have been shown to inhibit gastrulation (Wessel and
McClay, 1987; Butler et al., 1987). Treatment with β-amino-
proprionitrile (βAPN), an inhibitor of collagen crosslinking,
inhibits some aspects of mesenchyme migration, and arrests
embryos at an early stage of the initial phase of gastrulation.
Mizoguchi and Yasumasu (1982) report that in embryos in which
morphogenesis is blocked by sulfate deprivation, gastrulation
can be induced by treatment with ascorbate or α-ketoglutarate,
activators of protocollagen proline hydroxylase. They present
some evidence that these treatments stimulate protocollagen
hydroxylation, a step essential to the formation of collagen
fibers.

There are no mechanistic explanations which account for
these various observations that indicate that an intact blastocoelar ECM is essential to gastrulation. One possibility is
that the treatments, which also interfere with mesenchyme
ingression, block gastrulation by interfering with the release
of mesenchyme which usually precedes. Such a proposal is
discounted by reports of gastrulation in embryos in which
primary mesenchyme migration has not occurred (Kinnander and
Gustafson, 1960; Ettensohn, 1984). As well, there are species

in which primary mesenchyme release normally follows the initiation of gastrulation (Schroeder, 1981). Another possible mechanism is that the normal development of the blastocoelar ECM provides an inductive signal for the differentiation of endoderm. Without this signal, the cells that are to invaginate do not begin expression of the necessary gene products which facilitate their movement. Wessel and McClay (1987) have observed that Endo 1, a cell surface epitope normally expressed by endodermal cells can not be detected in embryos in which gastrulation is blocked by βAPN. This marker is expressed after the removal of βAPN. It is not possible to sort out cause and effect in this case, as Endo 1 expression may also be dependent upon the movements of cells which normally occur during gastrulation. The putative role of ECM components in mediating cell movements raises the possible explanation that the initial phase of gastrulation is dependent upon the presence of blastocoelar ECM components as substrates for cell movements. However, we must know more about the means by which the putative endodermal cells move during the initial phase of gastrulation, to provide a more detailed hypothesis for the role of the ECM in such movements.

SUMMARY

     I propose that there are three basic morphogenetic mechanisms underlying gastrulation in sea urchins. The initial phase of gastrulation is suggested to be based upon the concerted movement of macromere derived blastomeres towards the vegetal pole. This produces a compressive force within the blastoderm. The movements of these cells have associated with them increased pulsatile activity (Kinnander and Gustafson, 1960) and utilizes the basal lamina and hyaline layer as substrates. Proteases either secreted by or at the surface of vegetal plate cells release the cells from the hyaline layer, which results in an inward buckling of the vegetal plate. Once the initial phase of gastrulation is completed, the two mechanisms proposed by Ettensohn (1985) and Hardin (1988) come into play. The cells of the archenteron rearrange to achieve the initial stages of elongation and the secondary mesenchyme at the tip of the archenteron extend filopodia which contract to guide the tip of the archenteron to the presumptive stomodeum.

     Several aspects of these hypothesis remain tentative. The movements of the macromere derived cells toward the vegetal pole is demonstrated by marking experiments, but direct imaging of the movements should be possible. The mechanism by which the vegetal plate cells move requires elucidation. Although the cells are highly pulsatile, it is not clear if they employ mechanisms such as cortical tractoring, which has been proposed to account for movements of cells in the urodele notoplate (Jacobson et al., 1986). Alternatively, microvilli and basal processes, which have been suggested to have a structural role may be dynamic structures, which are extended and retracted facilitating movements requiring apical and basal ECM components as substrates. A detailed examination of the role of proteases in gastrulation may show how these are produced and their action localized. The rearrangement of cells in insect imaginal discs has been shown to have associated with it the release of proteases (Pino-Heiss and Schubinger, 1989) and similar mechanisms may be involved in archenteron elongation. In addition to the proteases associated with the initiation of gastrulation, we have also observed proteases released from sea urchin embryos coincident with the late stages of gastrulation but it is not clear they are involved with cellular rearrangements.

As always, a great deal remains to be learned about gastrulation in sea urchins. However, current interest in the morphogenetic processes and the development of the tools of molecular biology provide an opportunity for studies of sea urchin embryos to make further contributions to our understanding of how the fertilized egg transforms itself into a fully functional individual.

ACKNOWLEDGEMENTS

The studies in my laboratory on sea urchin gastrulation have been supported by an Operating Grant from the Medical Research Council of Canada. I am grateful to Robert Myers and Colin Tamboline for thoughtful discussions of sea urchin gastrulation.

REFERENCES

1. D.L. Adelson, and T. Humphreys, Sea urchin morphogenesis and cell-hyalin adhesion are perturbed by a monoclonal antibody specific for hyalin, *Development*, 104:391-402 (1988).
2. I. Agrell, A mitotic gradient in the sea urchin embryo during gastrulation, *Arkiv.Zool.*, 6:213-217 (1953).
3. K. Akasaka, and H. Terayama, General pattern, $^{35}SO_4$ incorporation and intracellular localization of glycans in developing sea urchin *(Anthocidaris)* embryos, *Dev.Growth Differ.*, 22:749-762 (1980).
4. K. Akasaka, S. Amemiya, and H. Terayama, Scanning electron microscopical study of the inside of sea urchin embryos *(Pseudocentrotus depressus)*. Effects of Aryl B-xyloside, Tunicamycin and deprivation of sulfate ions, *Exp.Cell Res.*, 129:1-13 (1980).
5. M.C. Alliegro, C.A. Ettensohn, C.A. Burdsal, H.P. Erickson, and D.R. McClay, Echinonectin: a new embryonic substrate adhesion protein, *J.Cell Biol.*, 107:2319-2327 1988).
6. E. Butler, J. Hardin, and S. Benson, The role of lysyl oxidase and collagen crosslinking during sea urchin development, *Exp.Cell Res.*, 173:174-182 (1987).
7. E. Citkowitz, The hyaline layer: its isolation and role in echinoderm development, *Dev.Biol.*, 24:348-362 (1971).
8. G. Czihak, The Sea Urchin Embryo: Biochemistry and Morphogenesis, 1st ed. Springer-Verlag, Berlin (1975).
9. K. Dan, Cyto-embryology of echinoderms and amphibia, *Int.Rev.Cytol.*, 9:321-367 (1960).
10. K. Dan, and K. Okazaki, Cyto-embryological studies of sea urchins III. Role of the secondary mesenchyme in the formation of the primitive gut in sea urchin larvae, *Biol.Bull.*, 110:29-42 (1956).
11. E.H. Davidson, Gene Activity in Early Development, 2nd ed. Academic Press, Orlando (1986).
12. E.H. Davidson, Lineage-specific gene expression and the

regulative capacities of the sea urchin embryo: a proposed mechanism, *Development*, 105:421-445 (1989).

13. D.W. Desimone, E. Spiegel, and M. Spiegel, The biochemical identification of fibronectin in the sea urchin embryo, *Biochem.Biophys.Res.Commun.*, 133:183-188 (1985).

14. Y. Endo, and N. Uno, Intercellular bridges in sea urchin blastula, *Zool.Mag.*, 69:8 (1960).

15. C.A. Ettensohn, Primary invagination of the vegetal plate during sea urchin gastrulation, *Am.Zool.*, 24:571-588 (1984).

16. C.A. Ettensohn, Gastrulation in the sea urchin is accompanied by rearrangement of invaginating epithelial cells, *Dev.Biol.*, 112:383-390 (1985).

17. R.D. Fink, and D.R. McClay, Three cell recognition changes accompany the ingression of sea urchin primary mesenchyme cells, *Dev.Biol.*, 107:66-74 (1985).

18. D. Fristrom, The mechanism of evagination of imaginal discs of *Drosophila melanogaster*.3. Evidence for cell rearrangement, *Dev.Biol.*, 54:163-171 (1976).

19. G. Gezelius, Effect of sulphate deficiency on the RNA synthesis of the sea urchin larvae, *Zoon*, 4:43-46 (1976).

20. G. Giudice, Developmental Biology of the Sea Urchin Embryo, 1st ed.Academic Press, New York (1973).

21. G. Giudice, The Sea Urchin Embryo, Springer-Verlag, Berlin (1986).

22. R. Golob, C.J. Chetsanga, P. Doty, The onset of collagen synthesis in sea urchin embryos, *Biochim.Biophys.Acta* , 349:135-141 (1974).

23. D. Gould, and S.C. Benson, Selective inhibition of collagen synthesis in sea urchin embryos by a low concentration of actinomycin D., *Exp.Cell Res.* 112:73-78 (1978).

24. T. Gustafson, and H. Kinnander, Micro aquaria for time-lapse cinematographic studies of morphogenesis in swimming larvae and observations on gastrulation, *Exp.Cell Res.*, 11:36-51 (1956).

25. T. Gustafson, and L. Wolpert, The cellular basis of morphogenesis and sea urchin development, *Int.Rev.Cytol.*, 15:139-214 (1963).

26. T. Gustafson, and L. Wolpert, Cellular movement and contact in sea urchin morphogenesis, *Bio.Rev.*, 42:442-498 (1967).

27. H.G. Hall, and V.D. Vacquier, The apical lamina of the sea urchin embryo: major glycoprotein associated with the hyaline layer, *Dev.Biol*, 89:168-178 (1982).

28. J.D Hardin, The role of secondary mesenchyme cells during sea urchin gastrulation studied by laser ablation, *Development*, 103:317-324 (1988).

29. J.D. Hardin, Archenteron elongation in the sea urchin is a microtubule-independent process, *Dev.Biol.*, 121:253-262 (1987).

30. J.D. Hardin, and L.Y. Cheng, The mechanisms and mechanics of archenteron elongation during sea urchin gastrulation, *Dev.Biol.*, 115:490-501 (1986).

31. M.A. Harkey, Determination and differentiation of micromeres in the sea urchin embryo. *In*: Time, Space, and Pattern in Embryonic Development, W.R. Jeffery, and R.A. Raff, editors, Allan R. Liss, New York, 131-155 (1983).

32. E.D. Hay, Cell biology of the extracellular matrix, 1st ed. Plenum Press, New York (1981).

33. A. Heifetz, and W.J. Lennarz, Biosynthesis of N-glycosidically linked glycoproteins during gastrulation of sea urchin embryos, *J.Biol.Chem.*, 254:6119-6127 (1979).

34. C. Herbst, Über das Auseinandergehen bei Furchungs- und Gewebezellen in Kalkfreiem Medium, *Roux's Arch.Entwicklungsmech.Org.*, 9:424-463 (1900).

35. C. Herbst, Über die zur Entwicklung der Seeigellarven notwendigen anorganischen Stoffe, ihre Rolle und Vertretbarkeit. II. Teil. Die Rolle der notwendigen anorganischen Stoffe, *Roux's Arch.Entwicklungsmech.Org.*, 17:306-520 (1904).

36. S. Horstadius, Experimental Embryology of Echinoderms, Clarendon Press, Oxford (1973).

37. A.G. Jacobson, G.F. Oster, G.M. Odell, and L.Y. Cheng, Neurulation and the cortical tractor model for epthelial folding, *J.Embryol.Exp.Morphol.*, 96:241-256 (1986).

38. G.C. Karp, and M. Solursh, Acid mucopolysaccharide metabolism, in the cell surface, and primary mesenchyme cell activity in the sea urchin embryo, *Dev.Biol.*, 41:110-123 (1974).

39. H. Kinnander, and T. Gustafson, Further studies on the cellular basis of gastrulation in the sea urchin larva, *Exp.Cell Res.*, 19:278-290 (1960).

40. S. Kinoshita, Heparin as a possible initiator of genomic RNA synthesis in early development of sea urchin embryos, *Exp.Cell Res.*, 64:403-411 (1971).

41. S. Kinoshita, and H. Saiga, The role of proteoglycan in the development of sea urchins I. Abnormal development of sea urchin embryos caused by the disturbance of proteoglycan synthesis, *Exp.Cell Res.*, 123:229-236 (1979).

42. M.C. Lane, and M. Solursh, Dependence of sea urchin primary mesenchyme cell migration on xyloside- and sulfate-sensitive cell surface-associated components, *Dev.Biol.*, 127:78-87 (1988).

43. W.J. Lennarz, Glycoprotein synthesis and embryonic development, *Crit.Rev.Biochem.*, 14:257-272 (1983).

44. W.H. Lewis, Mechanics of invagination, *Anat.Rec.*, 97:139-156 (1947).

45. R.A. McCarthy, K. Beck, and M.M. Burger, Laminin is structurally conserved in the sea urchin basal lamina, *EMBO, J* 6:1587-1593 (1987).

46. H. Mizoguchi, and I. Yasumasu, Archenteron formation induced by ascorbate and α-ketoglutarate in sea urchin embryos kept in $SO_4{}^{2-}$free artificial sea water, *Dev.Biol.*, 93:119-125 (1982).

47. A.R. Moore, Osmotic and structural properties of the blastocoelar wall in *Dendraster excentricus*, *J.exp.Zool.*, 84:73-79 (1940).

48. A.R. Moore, and A.S. Burt, On the locus and nature of the forces causing gastrulation in the embryos of *Dendraster excentricus*, *J.exp.Zool.*, 82:159-171 (1939).

49. C. Nislow, and J.B. Morrill, Regional cell division during sea urchin gastrulation contributes to archenteron formation and is correlated with the establishment of larval symmetry, *Dev.Growth Differ.*, 30:483-499 (1988).

50. K. Oguri, and T. Yamagata, Appearance of proteoglycan in developing sea urchin embryos, *Biochim.Biophys.Acta*, 541:385-395 (1980).

51. S. Pino-Heiss, and G. Schubinger, Extracellular protease production by *Drosophila* imaginal discs, *Dev.Biol.*, 132:282-291 (1989).

52. I. Pucci-Minafra, C. Casano, and C. Larosa, Collagen synthesis and spicule formation in sea urchin embryos, *Cell Differ.*, 1:157-165 (1972).

53. G. Reverberi, Experimental Embryology of Marine and Freshwater Invertebrates, North Holland Publishers, Amsterdam, (1971).

54. E.G. Schneider, H.T. Nguyen, and W.J. Lennarz, The effects of tunicamycin, an inhibitor of protein glycosylation on embryonic development in the sea urchin, *J.Biol.Chem.* 253:2348-2355 (1978).

55. T.E. Schroeder, Development of a "primitive" sea urchin *(Eucidaris tribuloides)*: Irregularities in the hyaline layer, micromeres, and primary mesenchyme, *Biol.Bull.*, 161:141-151 (1981).

56. M. Solursh, Migration of sea urchin primary mesenchyme cells. *In* Developmental Biology: A Comprehensive Synthesis, Vol.II.L.W. Browder, editor, Plenum Press, New York, 391-431 (1986).

57. E. Spiegel, M.M. Burger, and M. Spiegel, Fibronectin in the developing sea urchin embryo, *J.Cell Biol.*, 87:309-313 (1980).

58. E. Spiegel, L. Howard, and M. Spiegel, Extracellular matrix of sea urchin and other marine invertebrate embryos, *J.Morphol.*, 199:71-92 (1989).

59. M. Spiegel, and M.M. Burger, Cell adhesion during gastrulation, *Exp.Cell Res.*, 139:377-382 (1982).

60. L.W. Stearns, Sea Urchin Development: Cellular and Molecular Aspects, 1st ed. Dowden, Hutchinson and Ross, Stroudsburg, Pennsylvania (1974).

61. L. Stephens, J. Hardin, R. Keller, and F. Wilt, The effects of aphidicolin on morphogenesis and differentiation in the sea urchin embryo, *Dev.Biol.*, 118:64-69 (1986).

62. L.G. Tilney, and J.R. Gibbins, Microtubules and filaments in the filopodia of the secondary mesenchyme cells of *Arbacia punctulata* and *Echinarachnius parma*, *J.Cell Sci.*, 5:195-210 (1969).

63. M. Venkatesan, F. DePablo, G. Vogelli, and R.T. Simpson, Structure and developmentally regulated expression of a *Strongylocentrotus purpuratus* collagen gene, *Proc.Nat.Acad.Sci.U.S.A.*, 83:3351-3355 (1986).

64. G.M. Wessel, and D.R. McClay, Gastrulation in the sea urchin embryo requires the deposition of crosslinked collagen within the extracellular matrix, *Dev.Biol.*, 121:149-165 (1987).

65. G.M. Wessel, R.B. Marchase, and D.R. McClay, Ontogeny of the basal lamina in the sea urchin embryo, *Dev.Biol.*, 103:235-245 (1984).

66. F.H. Wilt, Determination and Morphogenesis in the sea urchin, *Development*, 100:559-575 (1987).

67. L. Wolpert, and E.H. Mercer, An electronmicroscope study fo the development of the blastula of the sea urchin embryo and its radial polarity, *Exp.Cell Res.*, 30:280-300 (1963).

68. T. Yamagata, and K. Okazaki, Occurence of a dermatan sulfate isomer in sea urchin larvae, *Biochim.Biophys.Acta*, 372:469-473 (1974).

FERTILIZATION IN AQUATIC ANIMALS

Brian Dale

Stazione Zoologica
Villa Comunale
80121, Napoli
Italy

GENERAL INTRODUCTION

Over the past 20 years much progress has been made in improving conditions for the culture of mammalian gametes. In fact, many laboratories worldwide routinely maintain human gametes and embryos *in vitro* and experiments on human fertilization are now feasible. Although sperm-egg interaction relies on the species-specific complementary matching of surface receptors on the two gametes, the physiological mechanisms of egg activation in a wide variety of species appear to adhere to a few unifying concepts (see general reviews by Dale, 1983; Hartmann, 1983; Metz and Monroy, 1985). Gametes from aquatic animals have been a favoured material for over a century and despite the recent surge of interest in mammals, they remain to be advantageous models, not only for the study of the fertilization process in its own right, but also as models for a wide variety of basic problems in cell biology.

In this review paper three particularly common aquatic models, the sea urchin, the frog and the ascidian will be discussed. Perhaps the greatest advantage of using aquatic animals is the availability of the adults themselves and their prolific production of gametes. In the laboratory little attention has to be made to temperature - marine invertebrate gametes may be used at 10-22°C - and sterile conditions are not absolutely essential for many experiments. The gametes themselves are often robust and amenable to microdissection and microinjection.

Eggs are metabolically repressed cells arrested at a particular stage of the meiotic cycle (see Monroy and Moscona, 1979; Dale, 1983). The signal for metabolic activation and for the progression of meiosis usually comes from the fertilizing spermatozoon. This means that the experimentalist has a large population of synchronous cells under his control with which to study many aspects of biochemistry related to metabolism and the cell cycle. Form and function of the cell cytoskeleton may

Experimental Embryology in Aquatic Plants and Animals
Edited by H.-J. Marthy, Plenum Press, New York, 1990

be studied easily in what are often large and transparent cells. Since most somatic cells in culture are transformed cells, studies on the mitotic apparatus and chromosomes may be more meaningful in eggs and embryos. Problems related to cell recognition and cell-cell interaction can be posed using gametes as a model and of course exocytosis and membrane fusion in general may be studied with ease.

THE FORM OF GAMETES

If we look through the animal kingdom we may note a considerable variation in the form of gametes. Most sea urchin eggs vary from 60-120um diameter, ascidian eggs vary from 100-200um in most cases, and of course frog eggs are much larger, being about 1500um in diameter. The most obvious characteristic of eggs is the fact that they are surrounded by several layers of accessory cells and structures. The inner most layer is usually a glycoprotein sheet called the vitelline membrane in echinoderms and frogs, the chorion in ascidians and the zona pellucida in mammals. Outside this a variety of structures may be found; a thick jelly-layer in echinoderms and frogs, and follicle cells in mammals and ascidians. The spermatozoa must recognize and interact with these structures to successfully penetrate the egg. Spermatozoa are typically long polarized cells with a head region of 1-3um diameter. Considering the head consists mainly of DNA, mitochondria and enzymes in the acrosomal region, there remains little space for other components. Aquatic eggs are triggered into an explosive sequence of activation events within seconds of interacting with the fertilizing spermatozoon which, considering that the spermatozoon is about one millionth the volume of the egg, makes it a remarkable process.

HOW DOES A SPERMATOZOON ACTIVATE AN EGG ?

At the turn of the century it was commonly held that egg activation was triggered by a component of the sperm that enters the egg cytoplasm (Robertson, 1912; Loeb, 1913).In other later models for triggering, the effect of the spermatozoon on the external surface of the egg was emphasized (Lillie, 1922; Mazia et al., 1975). To date, both hypotheses are still in contrast and, in fact, the problem is a popular arguement for debate (see Dale, 1987 for a review, Dale et al., 1978, 1985 and Kline et al., 1988).

To answer the question how a spermatozoon activates an egg, the first step is to observe and record chronologically the activation events in the egg and then attempt to correlate these changes with stages in sperm-egg interaction. The morphological changes occurring in eggs at activation are now classical and probably familiar to all. The cortical reaction in regulative eggs has been studied for decades. Moser (1939) was one of the first to describe the breakdown of small granules in the cortex of sea urchin eggs at activation, and suggested this to underly the subsequent elevation of the fertilization membrane.

The granules, of about 1um diameter, fuse to the plasma membrane releasing their contents into the perivitelline space and thus inducing the elevation and hardening of the vitelline membrane. The granules around the point of sperm-egg fusion are first to exocytose and then a wave of exocytosis spreads around the egg surface taking about 10secs at 25°C. This elegant reaction has been the object of countless studies and review papers (see for example, Schuel, 1978; Vacquier, 1981; Hartmann, 1983; Metz and Monroy, 1985). In addition to the cortical reaction, both regulative eggs and mosaic eggs undergo surface contractions at activation. This contraction in ascidian eggs is again a propagative event, and will be dealt with later (see Reverberi, 1971 for older references and Dale, 1989 for more recent bibliography).

Both morphological events may also be triggered by a wide variety of chemical and physical agents such as temperature extremes, alcohol, ionophores etc., which means they are auto-catalytic responses of the egg to an intracellular messenger that may be mobilized in one of several ways. This makes it difficult to identify the primary events induced by the spermatozoon from those occurring autocatalytically. The first obvious direct response of the egg to the spermatozoon and a response not caused by chemical agents is the formation of the fertilization cone. Within seconds of attachment to the egg surface the successful fertilizing spermatozoon stops gyrating around its point of attachment and stiffens perpendicular to the surface (Epel et al., 1977, Dale and De Santis, 1981, Schatten and Hulser, 1983). Shortly afterwards the egg surface protrudes outwards engulfing the sperm head and then the cortical reaction starts. Since Wilson described the fertilization cone in 1895, it has been the subject of innumerous morphological studies (Runnström and Monné, 1945; Runnström, 1963; Franklin, 1965; Longo, 1978; Tilney and Jaffe, 1980; Dale et al., 1981; Dale and Santella, 1985).

It is becoming increasingly evident that many cellular processes are triggered and regulated by changes in intra-cellular ions (see Boynton et al., 1982). Changes in the concentration of intracellular ions may result from the release of ions from internal stores or from alterations in the permeability of the plasma membrane: both of these mechanisms appear to be involved in the early events of fertilization. It was known for some time that in the sea urchin the first indication of egg activation was a depolarization of the plasma membrane (Steinhardt et al., 1971; Ito and Yoshioka, 1973; Jaffe, 1976, and Chambers and de Armendi, 1979). Closer observation showed the depolarization to be biphasic. The initial phase of the depolarization was shown to be composed of discrete events, each spermatozoon that entered the egg inducing a small, 1-2mV, step-like depolarization (Fig.1, Dale et al., 1978; De Felice and Dale, 1979).

Voltage clamp studies also demonstrated this sperm induced electrical event in the sea urchin (Lynn and Chambers, 1984), and a comparable event has been identified both in the ascidian (Dale et al., 1983) and in the anuran *Discoglossus pictus* (Talevi et al., 1985). This small step-like electrical event lasts about 5-10 seconds at room temperature, when the second larger depolarization is triggered. The delay between the two corresponds more or less to what has been described in sea urchins as the latent period (see Ginsberg, 1988 for a review), during which time there is no obvious morphological change.

275

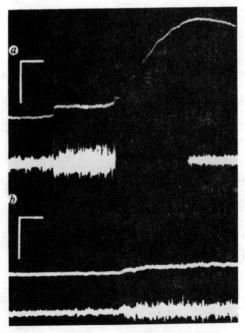

FIG.1. a) Intracellular recording from a sea urchin
egg following insemination at 25°C. The bell shaped
depolarization occurs at about the time of the
cortical reaction and is preceded by some 10sec by a
step depolarization. The lower trace shows the
increase in voltage noise at the step event. Vertical
bar represents 12mV; the horizontal bar 5 sec. b) The
step event at 5°C.

Shortly after the fertilization potential in the sea urchin
(Eisen, 1984) and in the ascidian (Brownlee and Dale, 1989)
there is a massive release of Ca from intracellular stores that
causes an increase in cytosolic Ca from 100nM to 10uM. Within
minutes the Ca returns to resting values. In the sea urchin the
cortical reaction occurs at about the same time as the
fertilization potential, whereas in the ascidian the Ca wave
starts to propagate 5-10 seconds after the initiation of the
fertilization potential and the contraction starts some 50 sec.
later (Brownlee and Dale, 1989).

In the following sections we shall see how various aquatic
animal models have contributed to answer some of the outstanding questions in fertilization.

WHAT IS THE PRIMARY ELECTRICAL EVENT ?

Owing to the rapid succession of change in the egg during
activation it is difficult to distinguish individual events. To
partially overcome this problem we selected the sea urchin
germinal vesicle stage oocyte. These cells may be fertilized,
however since they are immature they do not give rise to the
cortical reaction or other autocatalytic events seen in the
egg. When an oocyte is fertilized not all of the spermatozoa

are capable of penetrating the cell or of producing a fertilization cone. Over a thousend spermatozoa may attach to the oocyte, but usually not more than 10 enter as demonstrated by the formation of fertilization cones and histological sections. If we record electrically from oocytes, successful spermatozoa give rise to an electrical depolarization and conductance increase and induce a fertilization cone some 50 sec later (Dale and Santella, 1985). Other sperm were not capable of inducing either an electrical event or a cone, whilst a third category induced a step depolarization that after several seconds spontaneously reversed. These sperm also did not enter or induce the formation of a fertilization cone. These experiments raised the possibility that the step depolarization was in fact the direct result of sperm-egg fusion, the conductance increase being due to the appearance of sperm channels in the newly formed syncytium. The ATPase inhibitor Quercetin does not prevent sperm from attaching to sea urchin eggs and undergoing the acrosome reaction, however it does prevent incorporation, probably by blocking fusion of the gametes (Eckberg and Perotti, 1983); a similar effect is observed in Mg free sea water (Sano et al., 1980). In the presence of Quercetin, or in Mg free sea water, spermatozoa attached to oocytes but were not able to induce any electrical or morphological change in the oocyte. The effect however was reversible. To further test the hypothesis ideally one would like to remove an attached spermatozoon following fusion and observe the resulting electrical change. As an alternative experiment it is possible to add a spermicide to oocytes following the step event with the intent of destroying the relatively small spermatozoon before affecting the much larger egg cell. In such experiments the potential is anulled to pre-insemination values (Dale and Santella, 1985).

In a subsequent approach, Longo and colleagues (Longo et al., 1986) voltage clamped eggs, fertilized them and then serially sectioned them to locate the fertilizing spermatozoon. The authors first detected gamete fusion at 5 sec after the step depolarization. Chambers and McCulloh (1987) took the work further using the electrical measurement of capacitance to time sperm-egg fusion, thereby reducing the time delay inherent in the fixation of biological material. Since, in biological membranes capacitance is positively correlated with surface area, an increase in capacitance at the depolarization indicated gamete fusion.

WHAT HAPPENS DURING THE LATENT PERIOD ?

In most animals there is a time delay from the moment the spermatozoon attaches to the egg surface until cortical exocytosis. This period varies from animal to animal (see review by Ginsberg, 1988) and electrophysiological recording has shown that a step depolarization marks the beginning of this period. Rothschild and Swann (1952) suggested that a fast propagated change traverses the egg surface during the latent period, however since that date there has been no evidence of such. The sea urchin egg is a useful model to study the latent period for two reasons; one because the latent period is relatively long and is temperature dependent (Ginsberg, 1988 and Dale and De Santis, 1981), and second because the cortical reaction may be reversibly interrupted by a mild heat shock

(Allen and Hagström, 1955; Hagström and Runnström, 1959). Partially fertilized eggs may be re-fertilized showing there has been no functional alteration to the "unactivated surface" and, in fact, such eggs give rise to normal step depolarizations indicating additional fusions (Dale et al., 1989). It is not clear why several sperm interact with the virgin surface. Studies at the electron microscope reveal that the unactivated cortex in partially fertilized eggs is unchanged at least at the organelle level with respect to the unfertilized egg. Using the fluorescent indicator for polymerized actin, NBD-phallacidin, it can be seen that cortical polymerization also propagates around the egg in a wave at about the time of cortical exocytosis. Since, raising the level of intracellular Ca, by micro-injection of Ca-CaEGTA buffers triggers exocytosis (Hamaguchi and Hiramoto, 1981) it is possible that the wave of Ca release has also been interrupted by the heat shock and therefore it also progresses around the egg surface at about the time of cortical exocytosis, and in any event after the latent period (Dale et al., 1989).

WHAT TRIGGERS THE SECOND PHASE OF THE FERTILIZATION POTENTIAL ?

The channels underlying the generation of the large second depolarization phase, and possibly also the first, are now known to be large non specific ion channels (see later). To distinguish between the possibilities that they are gated directly by a messenger released from the sperm or via a second messenger, generated by the egg cytoplasm, the anuran *Discoglossus pictus* was selected. The sperm entry site in this frog is a pre-determined specialized area called the animal dimple (Hibbard, 1928). *Discoglossus* eggs as other frog eggs may be activated by pricking with a steel needle. At fertilization, the spermatozoon initiates a large regenerative depolarization that is Cl⁻ dependent (Talevi et al., 1985); pricking elicits a comparable response. When eggs were pricked outside the dimple area a wave of contraction was seen to spread from the puncture site to the antipode, and furthermore the activation potential was not generated until the wave reached the dimple. This experiment suggested that the channels underlying the depolarization are found in the dimple and that they are gated by a second messenger liberated in the egg cytoplasm that spreads around the egg with the contraction wave. In a subsequent paper it was shown that when the jelly plug over the dimple was experimentally displaced laterally the spermatozoa interacted with the sides of the dimple rather than the centre. In these cases the spermatozoa were unable to elicit a fertilization potential, but generated small step depolarizations, which together with histological sections indicated gamete fusion had occurred (Talevi and Campanella, 1988).

MECHANISM OF FERTILIZATION IN ASCIDIANS: CORRELATION OF THE EARLY TRIGGER EVENTS AND MEMBRANE BIOPHYSICS

In ascidians, spermatozoa are maintained in the testis in a quiescent state. Many factors may be responsible for this metabolic suppression, such as physical restraint, pH and low oxygen tension of the seminal fluid. In the Japanese tunicates *Ciona savigny* and *C. intestinalis* experiments suggest that motility is suppressed by a high K$^+$ concentration in the seminal fluid (Morisawa and Morisawa, 1985). A transmembrane exchange of K$^+$ and Ca^{2+} at spawning may lead to an increased production of cAMP that directly triggers sperm motility. Once released and motile the spermatozoa must contact the spawned eggs. For decades it has been assumed that sperm-egg interaction depends upon a random collision of gametes, however evidence is accumulating for the existence of chemotactic factors. Miller (1975) in a series of very convincing experiments has assigned a chemotactic role to the follicle cells of *Ciona intestinalis* eggs, while many researchers from Reverberi's Laboratory in Palermo maintain that eggs release factors into the sea water that have the capacity to stimulate spermatozoa into activity (see Review by Reverberi, 1971).

The primary event of fertilization is the species-specific recognition and binding of spermatozoa and eggs. It has been shown in ascidians that the chorion is the structure responsible for these processes (Rosati and DeSantis, 1978; Rosati et al., 1978) and that specific sites or sperm receptors are to be found on this glycoprotein sheet. Binding has been suggested to be mediated by the interaction of fucosidase on the sperm head and fucosyl sites on the vitelline coat (Hoshi et al., 1985). Once bound, the ascidian spermatozoon undergoes a number of changes described as sperm activation. First, the single mitochondrion swells and is displaced along the head towards the tail (Lambert and Epel, 1979; De Santis et al., 1983; Casazza et al., 1984), possibly by a mechanism involving actin and myosin (Lambert and Lambert, 1984). Second, the spermatozoon generates an excess of heat that does not correlate with oxygen consumption and may result from an alteration to its metabolism (Elia et al., 1983), linked to the mitochondrial movement. Extracellular Ca^{2+} is required for binding in *Ciona* gametes and an influx or release of Ca^{2+} from cytoplasmic stores in the spermatozoon is a pre-requisite for sperm activation (Casazza et al., 1984).

The last event of sperm activation is the acrosome reaction. Despite a decade of contention it is now generally accepted that ascidian spermatozoa, in particular those of *Ciona intestinalis* possess an acrosome (Rosati and De Santis, 1978; Elia et al., 1983; Franzen, 1976; Villa, 1975; Kubo et al., 1978; Woollacott, 1977; Honegger, 1986; Lambert, 1982; Villa and Tripepi, 1983; Fukumoto, 1984; Cloney, 1980; De Santis et al., 1980; Cotelli et al., 1980; Rosati et al., 1985). The head of *Ciona intestinalis* spermatozoa is elongated with a wedge-shaped tip and a single mitochondrion, laterally placed to the nucleus. In sagittal and transverse sections through the head a flattened vesicle of 200nm length, 180 nm width and 40 nm height may be observed, which is the acrosome. The outer membrane of the acrosome is in close contact with the plasmalemma, while a gap between the acrosomal inner membrane and the nuclear membrane corresponds to the sub-acrosomal space of other animals. Electron-dense material fills the acrosomal vesicle, while the sub-acrosomal space appears to be empty. Although we cannot be exactly certain when the acrosome reaction occurs, spermatozoa of *Ciona* attached to the chorion present an altered acrosomal region (Rosati and De Santis, 1978; Fukumoto, 1984; De Santis et al., 1980). This was found not to be the case (McNatty et al., 1979) in *Phallusia* spermatozoa (Honegger, 1986). What is of interest is the fact that not all spermatozoa attached to the chorion undergo the acrosome reaction and penetrate this investment (Honegger, 1986), suggesting that a precise molecular match between receptors on the chorion and those on the sperm surface is required for this reaction (Dale and Monroy, 1981).

In many animals, lysins are closely associated with the acrosome. These lysins are released at some stage of fertilization to act upon the investment allowing the spermatozoon to penetrate. At present, in *Ciona* we do not know whether presumptive lysins are bound to the plasmalemma or contained within the acrosome. A second fundamental function of the acrosome reaction is to expose a region of sperm membrane that is capable of fusing with the egg plasma membrane. Once through the chorion into the peri-vitelline space the successful spermatozoon makes its way to the egg surface. Conklin was the first to describe sperm entry into ascidian eggs and according to his classical paper (Conklin, 1905) the fertilizing spermatozoon enters an arc of 30° at the vegetal pole. The process of sperm-egg fusion is by no means understood. Most eggs appear to have preferential entry sites, however it is also clear that spermatozoa may enter other areas of the egg under certain experimental conditions. For example, the unfertilized egg of *Ciona* may be cut into two segments, one originating from the animal hemisphere, the second from the vegetal hemisphere. Both segments may be inseminated and give rise to normal larvae (Ortolani, 1958; Dalcq, 1932). Polyspermy is extremely rare in ascidian eggs and nude eggs challenged by hundreds of active spermatozoa are invariably monospermic. Dispermy may occur in aged nude eggs and then the two spermatozoa usually enter the vegetal hemisphere (Conklin, 1905). Much will be gained from the study of sperm entry sites in ascidian eggs, and the simple technique of egg dissection will certainly be instrumental.

Morphological Events During Egg Activation

The first indication that an ascidian egg has been successfully fertilized is a rapid modification of its shape. At about 2 minutes after insemination a constriction appears at the animal pole, which slowly traverses the egg reaching the vegetal pole after 30 seconds to 2 minutes. The egg appears dumbbell-shaped when the constriction reaches the equator and pear-shaped when at the vegetal hemisphere (Sawada and Osanai, 1981). After the contraction wave has traversed the egg a clear cytoplasmic bulge can often be observed at the vegetal pole. Before expulsion of the 1st polar body, at about 10 minutes after insemination, the egg assumes a spherical shape (Reverberi, 1971; Sawada and Osanai, 1981).

Conklin (1905) was one of the first to comment on movements of the egg cortex at fertilization, noting a displacement of the test cells. Ortolani (1955, 1957, 1973) took this observation further by placing chalk granules on the surface of unfertilized eggs. The chalk granules attach firmly to the surface and were rapidly displaced at fertilization (Ortolani, 1955). Granules at the animal hemisphere spread out suggesting an expansion of the cortex, while those at the vegetal hemisphere accumulated indicating a contraction of the surface. Furthermore, these movements were modified by pretreating the eggs with trypsin, suggesting that surface proteins are invol-

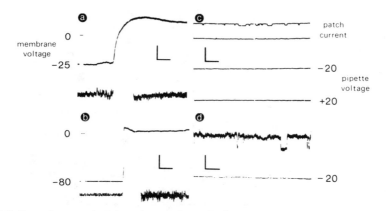

FIG.2. (a and b) show fertilization potentials in ascidian eggs. Note the small event in (a), (c) and (d) show currents from single fertilization channels.

ved in cortical contraction. Cortical contraction is inhibited in the presence of cytochalasin B (Sawada and Osanai, 1981; Zalokar, 1974; Reverberi, 1975), implicating microfilaments as the motive force, but not by colchicine (Zalokar, 1974), which blocks microtubule function.

The surface of unfertilized nude ascidian eggs is relatively smooth with no (Rosati et al., 1977), or few, microvilli (Sawada and Osanai, 1981). Ascidian eggs do not have cortical granules, nor any comparable organelle, although numerous small vesicles are present in the cortex (Rosati et al., 1977). Mitochondria are abundant and densely packed in the sub-cortical region, as are yolk granules, whereas the cytoplasm generally is rich in smooth endoplasmic reticulum and occasional Golgi complexes are found (Rosati et al., 1977). In longitudinal sections of unfertilized eggs the mitochondria appear as a layer in the sub-cortical region, except for a region at the animal pole (Sawada and Osanai, 1981). At fertilization, it appears that many of the vesicles present in the cortex fuse with the plasma membrane, since at 5-10 minutes after insemination the number of vesicles decrease (Rosati et al., 1977). The surface becomes smoother as the cortical contraction wave passes over the egg, and the sub-cortical mitochondria and granules are transported to the vegetal pole (Sawada and Osanai, 1981; Mancuso, 1964). This movement of organelles is termed cytoplasmic segregation.

Electrical Events

Since the egg plasma membrane is distributed between the membranes of the blastomeres it is not surprising that many ion channels, typical of differentiated tissues, are found in the unfertilized egg. The unfertilized ascidian egg membrane has been the focus of numerous biophysical studies, which have characterized voltage-gated Na, Ca and K channels (Miyazaki et al., 1974; Okamoto et al., 1976; Ohmori and Yoshii, 1977; Ohmori 1978, 1980, 1981; Takahashi and Yoshii, 1978; Fukushima, 1981, 1982; Kozuka and Takahashi, 1982; Hirano and Takahashi, 1984; Hirano et al., 1984). Of relevance to early differentiation is the topographical distribution of these channels in

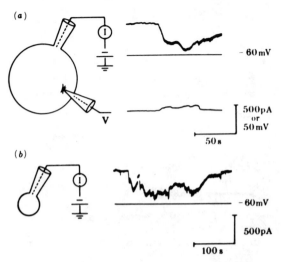

FIG.3. Whole-cell fertilization currents in an intact
egg (a), and an egg fragment with a surface area
approximately 10% of the egg (b). Note the similarity
in amplitude.

the zygote and this will be dealt with later. As far as
fertilization itself is concerned, a new population of ion
channels, the "fertilization channels", appear in the membrane.
Seconds after insemination in *Ciona intestinalis* a small step
depolarization may be measured followed some 5-7 seconds later
by a much larger overshooting depolarization. The potential
remains at a positive value for several minutes and then
gradually returns to its original value (Dale et al., 1983).
Subsequent studies, using the patch clamp technique, showed
that these fertilization channels are large with a single
channel conductance of 400 pS (Fig.2, Dale and De Felice,
1984). Since their reversal potential was around 0 mV, it was
suggested that these channels were not ion specific. Whole-cell
currents were shown to peak near -30 mV and approach zero near
0 mV (De Felice and Kell, 1987), supporting the preliminary
observations on these channels. Knowing the total conductance
change at fertilization, the single channel conductance and the
probability of a channel being open, it was possible to
estimate that the fertilizing spermatozoon opens between 200 to
2000 fertilization channels.

By cutting unfertilized eggs into fragments and insemi-
nating each fragment it was found that fertilization channel
precursors and voltage gated ion channels are uniformly
distributed around the ascidian egg surface (Talevi and Dale,
1986; De Felice et al.,1986; Dale and Talevi, 1989). Since
fertilization currents were similar in whole eggs or fragments,
irrespective of their size and global origin, it was concluded
that the fertilizing spermatozoon opens a fixed number of
fertilization channels limited to an area around its point of
entry (Fig.3, De Felice et al., 1986). The spermatozoon enters
the intact egg at the vegetal pole (Conklin, 1905) and creates
a localized ion current (De Felice et al., 1986) that might
regulate movements of the cytoskeleton involved in cytoplasmic
segregation. Studies on the gating mechanism of fertilization

282

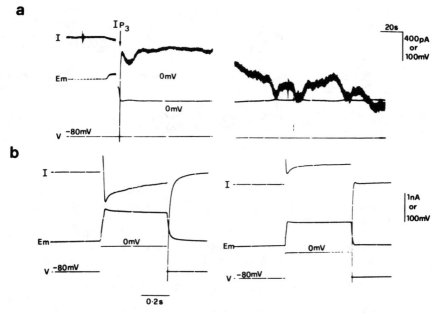

FIG.4. a) Whole cell current in an ascidian egg following micro-injection with 10uM IP3. Note the fertilization like current. b) Voltage induced currents in ascidian eggs before (left) and after (right) micro-injection of IP3.

channels have shown that intracellular Ca^{2+} is not involved (Dale, 1987), whereas inositol-triphosphate is a putative second messenger (Fig.4). It is possible that IP_3 or other intermediates in phosphoinositide metabolism are contained in the spermatozoon and delivered to the egg cytoplasm following gamete fusion.

Within 2 minutes of insemination there is a large transient increase in intracellular Ca^{2+} that starts at the animal pole and sweeps across the egg in 10 seconds to the vegetal pole (Speksnijder et al., 1986; Speksnijder et al., 1987; Brownlee and Dale, 1989). Intracellular Ca^{2+} remain high for about 5-10 minutes, and then slowly return to its resting level before expulsion of the 1st polar body. Measurements with the fluorescent indicator Fura-2 show that Ca^{2+} increases from a resting level of 100 nM to 10 μM, a 100 fold increase. Although this elevated Ca does not gate fertilization channels it appears to be involved in the mechanism of cortical contraction (Sawada and Osanai, 1981; Dale, 1989; Brownlee and Dale, 1989).

Metabolic Events

To date there is little information on the mechanism of metabolic de-repression in ascidian eggs. In many species the primary signal from the spermatozoon is transduced to the egg via an increase in intracellular pH. This appears not to be the case in ascidian eggs. Using ion-selective intracellular micro-electrodes it has been shown that the pH of unfertilized eggs ranges from 7.2 to 7.5 and that there is no variation in this value at least in the first 10·minutes of activation (Russo et al., 1989). Unfertilized ascidian eggs are metabolically repressed with a relatively low respiratory activity. At fertilization activity increases considerably (Tyler and Humason, 1937; Minganti, 1957; Runnström, 1930; Lentini, 1961), however the molecular basis for this increase and the trigger mechanisms are unknown. Finally, DNA synthesis in *Ascidia malaca* eggs is initiated after the expulsion of the second polar body, some 30 minutes after fertilization (Ortolani et al., 1975), and appears to be triggered by a cytoplasmic factor.

REFERENCES

Allen, R., and Hagström, B., 1955, Interruption of the cortical reaction by heat, *Exp.Cell Res.*, 9:157.
Bevan, S., O'Dell, D., and Ortolani, G., 1977, Experimental activation of ascidian eggs, *Cell Diff.*, 6:313.
Boynton, A.L., McKeehan; Whitfield, J.W., 1982, Ions, Cell Proliferation and Cancer, New York: Acad Press.
Brownlee, C., and Dale, B., 1989, Temporal and spatial correlation of fertilization current, calcium waves and cytoplasmic contraction in eggs of *Ciona intestinalis*, *Proc.R.Soc.B*, London (in press).
Casazza, G., De Santis, R., Pinto, M., 1984, Sperm binding to eggs of *Ciona intestinalis*, *Exp.Cell.Res.*, 155:261.
Chambers, E.L., de Armendi, J., 1979, Membrane potential, action potential and activation potential of eggs of the sea urchin, *Lytechinus variegatus*, Expl.Cell.Res., 122:203.
Cloney, R., and Abbott, L., 1980, The spermatozoa of ascidians: Acrosome and nuclear envelope, *Cell Tissue Res.*, 206:261.
Cotelli, F., De Santis, R., Rosati, F., and Monroy, A., 1980, Acrosome differentiation in the spermatogenesis of *Ciona intestinalis*, *Dev.Growth.Diff.*, 22:561.
Dalcq, A.B., 1932, Etude des localisations germinales dans l'oeuf vierge d'Ascidie par des expériences de mérogonie, *Arch.anat.microscop.*, 28:223.
Dale, B., and De Santis, A., 1981, Maturation and fertilization of the sea urchin oocyte; an electrophysiological study, *Dev.Biol.*, 85:474.
Dale, B., De Felice, L., and Taglietti, V., 1978, Membrane noise and conductance increase during single spermatozoon-egg interactions, *Nature*, 275:217.
Dale, B., and Santella, L., 1985, Sperm-oocyte interaction in the sea-urchin, *J.Cell Sci.*, 74:153.
Dale, B., Hagström, B., and Santella, L., 1989, Partially fertilized sea urchin eggs: An electrophysiological and morphological study, *Dev.Growth Differ.*, 31:165.
Dale, B., Dan-Sohkawa, M., De Santis, A., and Hoshi, M., 1981, Fertilization of the starfish *Astropecten aurantiacus*, *Exp.Cell.Res.*, 132:505.
Dale, B., 1983, "Fertilization in Animals," Edward Arnold, London.
Dale, B., 1989, Fertilization in ascidians, *in:* "Non mammalian Animal Models for Biomedical Research," A.D. Woodhead, ed. CRC Press, Boca Raton.
Dale, B., and De Felice, L., 1984, Sperm activated channels in ascidian oocytes, *Dev.Biol.*, 101:235.

Dale, B., and Monroy, A., 1981, How is polyspermy prevented, *Gamete Res.*, 4:151.

Dale, B., and Talevi, R., 1989, Distribution of ion channels in ascidian eggs and zygotes, *Exp.Cell Res.*, 181:238.

Dale, B., De Santis, A., and Ortolani, G., 1983, Electrical response to fertilization in ascidian oocytes, *Dev.Biol.*, 99:188.

Dale, B., De Felice, L., and Ehrenstein, G., 1985, Injection of a soluble sperm fraction into sea urchin eggs triggers the cortical reaction, *Experientia*, 41:1068.

Dale, B., 1987, Fertilization channels in ascidian eggs are not activated by Ca, *Exp.Cell Res.*, 172:474.

Dale, B., 1988, Primary and secondary messengers in the activation of ascidian eggs, *Exp.Cell Res.*, 205.

Dale, B., 1987, Mechanism of Fertilization, *Nature*, 325:762.

De Felice, L., and Kell, M., 1987, Sperm activated currents in ascidian oocytes, *Dev.Biol.*, 119:123.

De Felice, L., Dale, B., and Talevi, R., 1986, Distribution of fertilization channels in ascidian oocyte membranes, *Proc.R.Soc.B. London*, 229:209.

De Felice, L., and Dale, B., 1979, Voltage response to fertilization and polyspermy in sea urchin eggs and oocytes, *Dev.Biol.*, 72:327.

De Santis, R., Jamunno, G., and Rosati, F., 1980, A study of the chorion and the follicle cells in relation to the sperm egg interaction in the Ascidian *Ciona intestinalis*, *Dev.Biol.*, 74:490.

De Santis, R., Pinto, M., Cotelli, F., Rosati, F., Monroy, A., and D'Alessio, G., 1983, A fucosyl glycoprotein component with sperm receptor and sperm-activating activities from the vitelline coat of *Ciona intestinalis* eggs, *Exp.Cell Res.*, 148:508.

Eckberg, W.R., and Perotti, M.E., 1983, Inhibition of gamete membrane fusion in the sea urchin by Quercitin, *Biol.Bull.mar.biol.Lab.*, *Woods Hole*, 165:154a.

Eisen, A., Kiehart, D., and Reynolds, G., 1984, Temporal sequence and spatial distribution of early events of fertilization in single sea urchin eggs, *J.Cell Biol.*, 99:164.

Elia, V., Rosati, F., Barone, G., Monroy, A., and Liguori, A., 1983, A thermodynamic study of the sperm egg interaction, *EMBO J.*, 2:2053.

Epel, D., Cross, N., and Epel, N., 1973, Flagellar motility is not involved in the incorporation of the sperm into the egg at fertilization, *Dev.Differ.Growth*, 19:15.

Franklin, L., 1965, Morphology of gamete membrane fusion and sperm entry into oocytes of the sea urchin, *J.Cell Biol.*, 25:81.

Franzen, A., 1976, The fine structure of spermatid diferentiation in a tunicate *Corella parallelogramma* (Müller), *Zool.*, 4:115.

Fukumoto, M., 1984, Fertilization in Ascidians: Acrosome fragmentation in *Ciona intestinalis* spermatozoa, *J.Ultra.Res.*, 87:252.

Fukushima, Y., 1982, Blocking kinetics of the anomalous potassium rectifier of tunicate egg studied by single channel recording, *J.Physiol.*, 331:311.

Fukushima, Y., 1981, Single channel potassium currents of the anomalous rectifier, *Nature*, 294:368.

Ginsburg, A., 1987, Egg cortical reaction during fertilization and its role in block to polyspermy,

Sov.Sci.Rev.F.Physiol.Gen.Biol., 1:307.

Hagström, B., and Runnström, J., 1959, Re-fertilization of partially fertilized sea urchin eggs, *Exp.Cell Res.*, 16:309.

Hamaguchi, Y., and Hiramoto, Y., 1981, Activation of sea urchin eggs by micro-injection of calsium buffers, *Exp.Cell Res.*, 134:171.

Hartmann, J.F., 1983, "Mechanism and control of Animal Fertilization," Acad.Press, New York.

Hibbard, H., 1928, Contribution à l'étude de l'ovogenèse de la fécondation et de l'histogenèse chez *Discoglossus pictus*, *Arch.Biol.*, 32:251.

Hirano, T., and Takahashi, K., 1984, Comparison of properties of calcium channels between the differentiated 1-cell embryo and the egg cells of ascidians, *J.Physiol.*, 347:327.

Hirano, T., Takahashi, K., and Yamashita, N., 1984, Determination of excitability types in blastomeres of the cleavage-arrested but differentiated embryos of an ascidian, *J.Physiol.*, 347:301.

Honegger, T., 1986, Fertilization in ascidians: Studies on the egg envelope, sperm and gamete interactions in *Phallusia mammillata*, *Dev.Biol.*, 118:118.

Hoshi, M., De Santis, R., Pinto, M., Cotelli, F., and Rosati, F., 1985, Sperm Glycosidases as mediators of sperm-egg binding in the ascidians, *Zool.Sci.*, 2:65.

Ito, S., and Yoshioka, K., 1973, Effects of various ionic compositions upon the membrane potentials during activation of sea urchin eggs, *Exp.Cell Res.*, 78:191.

Jaffe, L.A., 1976, Fast block to polyspermy in sea urchin eggs is electrically mediated, *Nature*, 261:68.

Kline, D., Simoncini, L., Mandel, G., Maue, R., Kado, R., and Jaffe, L., 1988, Fertilization events induced by neurotransmitters after injection of mRNA in *Xenopus* Eggs, *Science*, 241:464.

Kozuka, K., and Takahashi, K., 1982, Changes in holding and ion channel currents during activation of an ascidian egg under voltage clamp, *J.Physiol.*, 323:207.

Kubo, M., Ishikawa, M., and Numakunai, T., 1978, Differentiation of apical structures during spermiogenesis in the ascidian *Halocynthia roretzi*, *Acta Embryol.Exp.*, 3:283.

Lambert, C., and Epel, D., 1979, Calcium mediated mitochondrial movement in ascidian sperm during fertilization, *Dev.Biol.*, 69:296.

Lambert, C., and Lambert, G., 1984, The role of actin and myosin in ascidian sperm mitochondrial translocation, *Dev.Biol.*, 106:307.

Lambert, C., 1982, The ascidian sperm reaction, *Amer.Zool.*, 22:841.

Lentini, R., 1961, The oxygen uptake of *Ciona intestinalis* eggs during development in normal and experimental conditions, *Acta Embryol.Morphol.Exptl.*, 4:209.

Lillie, R., and Baskerville, M., 1922, The action of ultraviolet rays on *Arbacia* eggs, especially as affecting the response to hypertonic sea-water, *Am.J.Physiol.*, 61:272.

Loeb, J., 1913, "Artificial Parthenogenesis and Fertilization," University Press, Chicago.

Longo, F., Lynn, J., McCulloh, D., and Chambers, E., 1986, Correlative ultrastructural and electrophysiological studies of sperm-egg interactions of the sea urchin

Lytechinus variegatus, Dev.Biol., 118:155.

Longo, F., 1978, Insemination of immature sea urchin *(Arbacia punctulata)* eggs, *Dev.Biol.*, 62:271.

Lynn, J., and Chambers, E., 1984, Voltage clamp studies of fertilization in sea urchin eggs.I. Effect of clamped membrane potential on sperm entry, activation and development, *Dev.Biol.*, 102:98.

Mancuso, V., 1964, The distribution of the ooplasmic components in the unfertilized, fertilized and 16 cells stage of *Ciona intestinalis, Acta Embryol.Morphol.Exp.*, 7:71.

Mazia, D., Schatten, G., and Steinhardt, R., 1975, Turning on of activities in unfertilized sea urchin eggs: correlation with changes of the surface, *Proc.Nat.Acad.Sci. USA*, 72:4469.

McCulloh, D., and Chambers, E., 1987, When does the sperm fuse with the egg, *J.Gen.Physiol.*, 88:38a.

Metz, C., and Monroy, A., 1985, "Biology of Fertilization," Acad.Press, New York.

Miller, R., 1975, Chemotaxis of the spermatozoa of *Ciona intestinalis, Nature*, 254:244.

Minganti, A., 1957, Experiments of the respiration of *Phallusia* eggs and embryos (Ascidians), *Acta Embryol.Morphol. Exptl.*, 1:150.

Miyazaki, S., Takahashi, K., and Tsuda, K., 1974, Electrical excitability in the egg cell membrane of the tunicate, *J.Physiol.*, 238:37.

Monroy, A., and Moscona, A., 1979, "Introductory concepts in developmental Biology," Chicago University Press, Chicago.

Morisawa, S., and Morisawa, M., 1985, Initiation of sperm motility in tunicates, *Zool.Sci.*, 2:91 abs.

Moser, F., 1939, Studies on a cortical layer response to stimulating agents in the Arbacia egg. I: Response to insemination, *J.Exp.Zool.*, 80:423.

Ohmori, H., and Yoshii, M., 1977, Surface potential reflected in both gating and permeation mechanisms of sodium and calcium channels of the tunicate egg cell membrane, *J.Physiol.*, 267:429.

Ohmori, H., 1978, Inactivation kinetics and steady state current noise in the anomalous rectifier of tunicate egg cell membranes, *J.Physiol.*, 281:77.

Ohmori, H., 1981, Unitary current through sodium channel and anomalous rectifier channel estimated from transient current noise in the tunicate egg, *J.Physiol.*, 311:289.

Okamoto, H., Takahashi, K., and Yoshii, M., 1976, Membrane currents of the tunicate egg under the voltage clamp condition, *J.Physiol.*, 254:607.

Okamoto, H., Takahashi, K., and Yoshii, M., 1976, Two components of the calcium current in the egg cell membrane of the tunicate, *J.Physiol.*, 255:527.

Ortolani, G., 1957, Azione della tripsina sul cortex dell'uovo di *Phallusia mammillata, Ric.Sci.*, 27:1175.

Ortolani, G., 1958, Cleavage and development of egg fragments in Ascidians, *Acta Embryol.Morphol.Exptl.*, 1:247.

Ortolani, G., 1955, I movimenti corticali dell'uovo di Ascidie alla fecondazione, *Riv.Biol.*, 47:169.

Ortolani, G., 1973, Modification of the cortex of ascidian eggs after fertilization obtained by means of different methods, *Boll.Zool.*, 40:405.

Ortolani, G., O'Dell, D.S., Mansueto, C., and Monroy, A., 1975, Surface changes and onset of DNA replication in the

Ascidia egg, *Exp.Cell Res.*, 96:122.

Reverberi, G., 1971, Experimental Embryology of Marine and Freshwater Invertebrates, North Holland Press, Amsterdam.

Reverberi, G., 1975, On some effects of cytochalasin B on the eggs and tadpoles of the ascidians, *Acta Embryol.Exp.*, 2:137.

Robertson, T., 1912, Studies on the fertilization of the eggs of a sea urchin *Strongylocentrotus purpuratus* by blood-sera, sperm, sperm extract and other fertilizing agents, *Arch.Entwicklungsmech.*, 35:64.

Rosati, F., and De Santis, R., 1978, Studies on fertilization in the ascidians. I. Self sterility and specific recognition between gametes of *Ciona intestinalis*, *Exp.Cell Res.*, 112:111.

Rosati, F., De Santis, R., and Monroy, A., 1978, Studies on fertilization in the ascidians. II. Lectin binding to the gametes of *Ciona intestinalis*, *Exp.Cell Res.*, 116:419.

Rosati, F., Monroy, A., and De Prisco, P., 1977, Fine structural study of fertilization in the ascidian *Ciona intestinalis*, *J.Ultra.Res.*, 58:261.

Rosati, F., Pinto, M., and Casazza, G., 1985, The acrosomal region of the spermatozoon of *Ciona intestinalis*: Its relationship with the binding to the vitelline coat of the egg, *Gamete Res.*, 11:379.

Rothschild, Lord, and Swann, M., 1952, The fertilization reaction in the sea urchin. The block to polyspermy, *J.Exp.Biol.*, 29:469.

Runnström, J., and Monne, L., 1945, On some properties of the surface layers of immature and mature sea urchin eggs, especially the changes accompanying nuclear and cytoplasmic maturation, *Ark.Zool.*, 36A:1.

Runnström, J., 1963, Sperm induced protrusion in sea urchin oocyte: A study of phase separation and mixing in living cytoplasmic, *Dev.Biol.*, 7:38.

Runnström, J., 1930, Atmungsmechanismus und Entwicklungserregung bei dem Seeigelei, *Protoplasma*, 10:106.

Russo, P., De Santis, A., and Dale, B., 1989, pH during fertilization and activation of ascidian eggs, *J.Exp.Zool.*, 250:329.

Sano, K., Usui, N., Ueki, K., and Mohri, H., 1980, Magnesium ion requiring step in fertilization of sea urchins, *Dev.Growth Differ.*, 22:531.

Sawada, T., and Osanai, K., 1981, The cortical contraction related to the ooplasmic segregation in *Ciona intestinalis* eggs, *W.Roux's Arch.*, 190:208.

Schatten, G., and Hulser, D., 1983, Timing the early events during sea urchin fertilization, *Dev.Biol.*, 100:244.

Schuel, H., 1978, Secretory functions of egg cortical granules in fertilization and development: A critical review, *Gamete Res.*, 1:299.

Speksnijder, J., Corson, D., Jaffe, L., and Sardet, C., 1987, Calcium pulses and waves through ascidian eggs, *Biol.Bull.*, 171:488a.

Speksnijder, J., Corson, D., Qiu, T., and Jaffe, L., 1986, Free calcium pulses during early development of *Ciona* eggs, *Biol.Bull.*, 170:542a.

Steinhardt, R.A., Lundin, L., and Mazia, D., 1971, Biolectric responses of the echinoderm egg to fertilization,

Proc.Nat.Acad.Sci. U.S.A., 68:2426.

Takahashi, K., and Yoshii, M., 1978, Effects of internal free Calcium upon the sodium and calcium channels in the tunicate egg analyzed by the internal perfusion technique, J.Physiol., 279:519.

Talevi, R., and Campanella, C., 1988, Fertilization in Discoglossus pictus (Anura). I. Sperm-egg interactions in distinct regions of the dimple and occurrence of a late stage of sperm penetration, Dev.Biol., 130:524.

Talevi, R., and Dale, B., 1986, Electrical characteristics of ascidian egg fragments, Exp.Cell Res., 162:539.

Talevi, R., Dale, B., and Campanella, C., 1985, Fertilization and activation potentials in Discoglossus pictus (Anura) eggs: A delayed response to activation by pricking, Dev.Biol. 11:316.

Tilney, L.G., and Jaffe, L.A., 1980, Actin, microvilli and the fertilization cone of sea urchin eggs, J.Cell Biol., 87:771.

Tyler, A., and Humason, W., 1937, On the energetics of differentiation. VI. Comparison of the temperature coefficients of the respiratory rates of unfertilized and of fertilized eggs, Biol.Bull., 73:261.

Vacquier, V., 1981, Dynamic changes of the egg cortex, Dev.Biol., 84:1.

Villa, L., and Tripepi, S., 1983, An electron microscope study of spermatogenesis and spermatozoa of Ascidia malaca, Ascidiella aspersa, and Phallusia mammillata (Ascidiacea, Tunicata), Acta Embryol.Morphol.Exp., 4:157.

Villa, L., 1975, Un ultrastructural investigation of normal and irradiated spermatozoa of a tunicate Ascidia malaca, Boll.Zool., 42:95.

Wilson, E., 1895, An Atlas of Fertilization, MacMillan, New York.

Woollacott, R., 1977, Spermatozoa of Ciona intestinalis and analysis of Ascidian fertilization, J.Morphol., 152:77.

Zalokar, M., 1974, Effect of colchicine and cytochalasin B on ooplasmic segregation of ascidian egg, W.Roux's Arch., 175:243.

PATTERNS OF GENE EXPRESSION DURING ASCIDIAN DEVELOPMENT

William R. Jeffery, Rebecca L. Beach
Frederick E. Harrington,[+] Billie J. Swalla
and Mary E. White

Center for Developmental Biology
Department of Zoology
University of Texas
Austin, Texas 78712, USA

[+]Present Address: Department of Biological Sciences
University of Pittsburgh
Pittsburgh, Pennsylvania 15260, USA

INTRODUCTION

Ascidian development has been investigated by embryologists since the latter half of the nineteenth century (see
Venuti and Jeffery, 1989 for a review) due to a number of
desirable features. First, embryonic development is rapid. In
most ascidians, gastrulation occurs only a few hours after
fertilization, and embryogenesis is completed in less than a
day. Second, ascidians are one of the simplest chordates: the
tadpole larva contains only a few thousand cells and about 6
different types of tissue (Berrill, 1935). The ascidian genome
is quite small for a chordate: only about 1.8×10^8 nucleotide
pairs (Mirsky and Ris, 1951; Atkin and Ohno, 1967; Lambert and
Laird, 1971). Third, ascidian embryos are highly mosaic: most
cell fates are established according to a defined cell lineage
(Chabry, 1887; Conklin, 1905a). Fourth, some ascidians have
evolved alternative development modes, which are useful for
examining developmental changes during evolution (Berrill,
1931; 1935). Finally, the eggs of the ascidian *Styela* contain
colored ooplasms (Conklin, 1905b; Berrill, 1929). The most
spectacular of these ooplasms is the yellow crescent or
myoplasm, a unique cytoskeletal domain that segregates to the
future posterior region of the zygote after fertilization
(Conklin, 1905b; Jeffery, 1984). During cleavage, the myoplasm
is distributed to 2 cells of the 2-,4-, and 8-cell embryo, 4
cells of the 16-cell embryo, 6 cells of the 32-cell embryo, 8
cells of the 64-cell embryo, and eventually enters the larval
tail-muscle cells (Fig.1).

Although classical studies usually relied on color for
identifying different blastomeres, molecular markers have been
developed to distinguish the embryonic cell lineages of

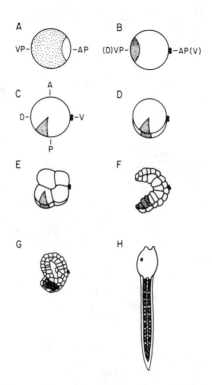

FIG.1. Ascidian development showing the distribution of myoplasm in eggs, different blastomeres of the embryo, and cells of the tadpole larva. A. An unfertilized egg in which the myoplasm (coarsely shaded area) is present throughout the cortex, except at the animal pole (AP). B. A fertilized egg in which myoplasm (finely shaded area) has segregated, forming a cap at the vegetal pole (VP). C. An uncleaved zygote just before first cleavage in which the myoplasm has segregated into a vegetal crescent localized on the future posterior (P) side of the embryo (A is the anterior pole). D. A 2-cell embryo with myoplasm in both cells. E. An 8-cell embryo with myoplasm in 2 vegetal-posterior cells (the primary muscle cell progenitors). F. An early gastrula (shown in section) with primary muscle cells located at the posterior lip of the blastopore. G. A neurula (shown in section) with primary muscle cells located in the future tail region. H. A hatched tadpole larva with muscle cells located in rows within the tail. The solid sphere within the head of the tadpole represents the brain sensory cell. The solid spheres at the animal pole in B-G represent polar bodies. From Jeffery and Bates (1987).

ascidian embryos. For example, endodermal cells show alkaline phosphatase activity (Whittaker, 1977) and brain sensory cells exhibit tyrosinase activity (Whittaker, 1973a). Molecular markers developed for larval muscle cells and their progenitors include acetylcholinesterase (Whittaker, 1973b; Perry and Melton, 1983; Meedel and Whittaker, 1983), myofilaments (Crowther and Whittaker, 1983), myosin heavy chain (Meedel

1983; Nishikata et al., 1987a; Makabe and Satoh, 1989), and α-actin (Tomlinson et al., 1987a; b). Using these markers, it has been established that most larval tail-muscle cells develop autonomously from myoplasm-containing blastomeres (Whittaker et al., 1977; Crowther and Whittaker, 1984; Deno et al., 1984; Nishikata et al., 1987a). These and other embryological experiments (see Venuti and Jeffery, 1989) suggest that larval muscle cell development is caused by intrinsic factors, or determinants, which are localized in the egg myoplasm and segregated into muscle cell precursors during cleavage.

The origin of ascidian larval muscle cells has been investigated by injecting defined blastomeres with horseradish peroxidase (Nishida and Satoh, 1983; 1985; Nishida, 1987). These studies show that most larval tail muscle cells arise from myoplasm-containing blastomeres, which are designated primary muscle cells. A few cells that do not contain significant amounts of myoplasm also contribute to tail muscle; these are known as secondary muscle cells. The secondary muscle cells may be specified by inductive cell interactions rather than localized determinants (Deno et al., 1984; Nishikata et al., 1987a; Meedel et al., 1987). In addition, there must be a third source of ascidian muscle because the primary and secondary muscle cells are destroyed during metamorphosis and new muscle cells form during adult development. The source of the adult muscle cells is unknown.

Relatively little information exists concerning the molecular aspects of ascidian development. Fundamental questions such as the nature and utilization of maternal mRNA, the onset of zygotic transcription, and the temporal and spatial aspects of specific gene expression have received little attention. Because of the existence of different modes of development in closely related species, ascidians provide unique opportunities to examine the relationship between gene expression and evolution. In this paper, we review our studies on the temporal and spatial patterns of gene expression during ascidian development.

ONSET OF GENERAL TRANSCRIPTION

Because ascidians develop rapidly, they present an interesting situation to examine the role of zygotic transcription in embryogenesis. In some animals, transcription continues at low levels throughout early development (sea urchins; see Brandhorst, 1985), while in others it is arrested in the egg and reactivated in the embryo after a specific number of cleavages (amphibians; see Newport and Kirschner, 1982). In all animals studied to date, however, embryogenesis eventually comes under control of the zygotic genome (see Davidson, 1986 for review). It was once believed that zygotic transcription had little or no role in ascidian embryogenesis: embryonic protein synthesis was thought to be mediated entirely by the translation of maternal mRNA. This view was supported by two kinds of experiments. First, when anucleate egg fragments from one ascidian species were fertilized with sperm from another species, the hybrid larvae developed morphological features of the maternal species (Minganti, 1959). Second, new transcription was undetectible by cytochemistry (Cowden and Markert, 1961) or incorporation of radioactive precursors

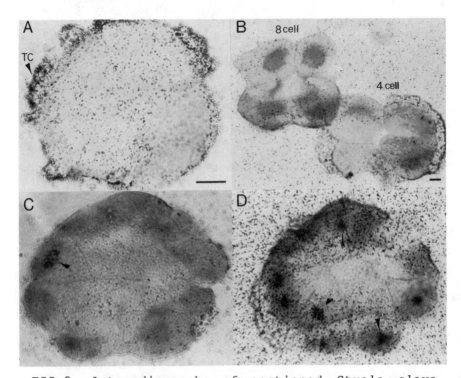

FIG.2. Autoradiographs of sectioned *Styela clava*
embryos showing the incorporation of [3H]-uridine into
RNA. A. A fertilized egg undergoing ooplasmic
segregation showing background labelling throughout
the cytoplasm and labelled test cells (TC) in the
periphery. B. Four-and 8-cell embryos showing no
labelling above background. C. A 16-cell embryo
showing labelling of the nucleus (arrowhead) in a
blastomere. D. A 32-cell embryo showing labelling in
the nuclei of many blastomeres (arrowheads). In this
experiment, unfertilized eggs were preincubated with
20 µCi/ml of [3H]-uridine for 2 hours before insemination. At various times after fertilization, the
developing embryos were fixed with 3:1 ethanol:
acetic acid for 1 hour at 4°C. The fixed embryos were
dehydrated through an ethanol series to absolute
ethanol, cleared in toluene and embedded in para-
plast. The specimens were sectioned at 8µm and
attached to slides. The slides were treated with 5%
trichloroacetic acid for 30 minutes at 4°C to remove
unincorporated radioactive precursors and subjected
to autoradiography. Some slides were treated either
with 20 µg/ml pancreatic RNase or DNase I for 1 hour
at 37°C before autoradiography (data not shown).
After exposure for 2 weeks, the autoradiographs were
developed and stained with Harris hematoxylin. The
scale bars in A and B represent 20 µm (magnification
is the same in A, C and D).

(D'Anna, 1962; Lambert, 1971) until after larval hatching. It is known that actinomycin D treatment blocks embryogenesis before the gastrula stage (Smith, 1967; Bates and Jeffery, 1987) and prevents subsequent expression of AchE (Whittaker, 1973b), tyrosinase (Whittaker, 1973a), and α-actin (Jeffery et al., 1986). Moreover, an increase in translatable AchE mRNA was observed at the gastrula or neurula stage of *Ciona intestinalis* embryos (Meedel and Whittaker, 1983; Perry and Melton, 1983), before the initial appearance of the enzyme. Finally, Meedel and Whittaker (1978) have shown that radioactive precursors are incorporated into poly(A)$^+$RNA as early as the gastrula stage. Although these studies suggest that ascidian development requires zygotic RNA synthesis, the timing of transcriptional initiation has not been elucidated. For instance, Smith (1976) reported that RNA synthesis begins at about the 4-cell stage in *Ascidia nigra*, while Puccia et al.(1967) claim that transcription occurs at all stages of early development in *Ciona intestinalis*.

We have investigated the timing of RNA synthesis during development of the ascidian *Styela clava* by autoradiography of embryos exposed to [^{3}H]-uridine. Unfertilized eggs were incubated with radioactive precursor for 2 hours before insemination to avoid the possibility of changes in isotope uptake (Lambert, 1975). During the interval between addition of the radioactive precursor and insemination, unfertilized eggs did not incorporate [^{3}H]-uridine above background levels, suggesting that they are arrested in transcription. Transcription is probably arrested during or after maturation because sections of immature oocytes showed significant incorporation of [^{3}H]-uridine within the germinal vesicle (data not shown). The incorporation of [^{3}H]-uridine in fertilized eggs and early embryos is shown in Figure 2. There was no significant incorporation in the zygote between fertilization and the 8-cell stage, although the test cells (accessory cells that surround the egg and embryo) were heavily labelled (Fig.2A-B). In contrast, most blastomeres showed nuclear labelling at the 16-cell stage (Fig.2C), indicating that transcription had been initiated. RNA synthesis intensified in the nuclei between the 32-cell stage and gastrulation, and radioactivity also began to accumulate in the cytoplasm (Fig.2D). The lack of labelling in control sections treated with RNase, but not DNase, before autoradiography showed that [^{3}H]-uridine was incorporated into RNA. These results suggest that the onset of general transcription occurs at the 16-cell stage in *Styela* embryos, only 2-3 hours after fertilization.

Further experiments helped determine how the initiation of RNA synthesis is controlled in *S. clava* embryos. First, [^{3}H]-uridine incorporation was examined in artificially activated eggs. Previous studies have shown that the Ca^{+2}-transporting ionophore A23187 activates ascidian eggs, but the eggs do not divide after activation (Steinhardt et al., 1974; Jeffery 1982), probably because cleavage requires a sperm aster. A23187-activated eggs did not initiate transcription (Fig.3A), although they synthesized DNA and underwent nuclear multiplication (Fig.3B). The absence of transcription in activated eggs could be a consequence of incomplete activation by A23187, or it could be due to the absence of cytokinesis. To test the latter possibility, fertilized eggs were treated with cytochalasin B, which blocks cleavage without affecting DNA

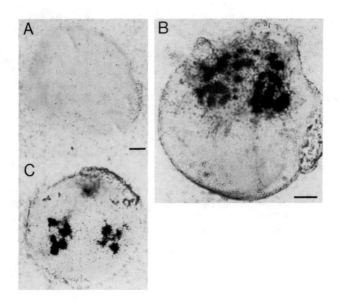

FIG.3. Autoradiographs of sectioned *Styela clava* eggs and embryos. A. An A23187-activated egg exposed to [3H]-uridine for 5 hours. There is no labelling above background. B. An A23187-activated egg exposed to [3H]-thymidine for 5 hours. The multiple nuclei are heavily labelled (dark areas). C. An uncleaved zygote cleavage-arrested by treatment with 2 μg/ml cytochalasin B and exposed to [3H]-uridine for 7 hours. The multiple nuclei (dark areas) and surrounding cytoplasm are labelled. Autoradiographs were prepared as described in Figure 2. The scale bars in A and B represent 20 μm (magnification is the same in A and C).

synthesis or nuclear division (Whittaker, 1973b). The cytochalasin-treated embryos were then incubated with [3H]-uridine until controls reached the tailbud stage. As shown in Figure 3C, treated embryos incorporated [3H]-uridine into RNA, even when cleavage was arrested at the 1-cell stage. The results indicate that the initiation of transcription in *Styela* requires fertilization and is independent of cell division.

In summary, the onset of general transcription occurs at the 16-cell stage in *Styela* embryos. It is also after this stage that different blastomeres begin to divide asynchronously. Thus, the *Styela* 16-cell stage may be analogous to the midblastula transition of amphibian embryos (Newport and Kirschner, 1982).

PATTERNS OF SPECIFIC GENE EXPRESSION

Although the results described above define the beginning of transcription, they do not indicate the nature of the transcribed RNAs or when or where specific genes are expressed. In this section, we describe the expression of genes encoding an α-actin, a β-actin, and an intermediate filament protein.

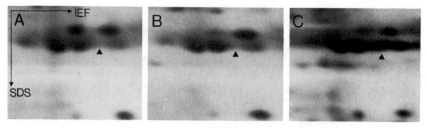

FIG.4. Two-dimensional polyacrylamide gel electrophoresis of proteins extracted from *Styela clava* (A)
unfertilized eggs, (B) gastrulae, and (C) hatched
tadpoles. Only the actin region of the gel is shown
in the frame. The α-actin isoform (arrowhead) is not
detectible in eggs and gastrulae, but accumulates to
substantial levels by the time of larval hatching.
IEF: direction of isoelectric focussing. SDS: direction of electrophoresis in SDS gel. Electrophoresis
and silver staining of gels was as described by
Tomlinson et al. (1987a). From Tomlinson et
al.(1987a).

Multiple Actin Isoforms

There are three major isoforms in adult *Styela* (Tomlinson
et al., 1987a). The two most basic isoforms are present in all
tissues and are likely to be β and γ actins. The most acidic
isoform is restricted to the mantle and branchial sac, which
contain muscle and other mesenchymal tissues, and is probably
an α-actin. As shown by two dimensional gel electrophoresis,
eggs and embryos also contain multiple actin isoforms. However,
while eggs and embryos contain only β- and γ-actins, α-actin
is present in tadpole larvae (Fig.4). Evidence that α-actin is
present in tail muscle cells was obtained from experiments in
which proteins derived from separated tadpole heads and tails

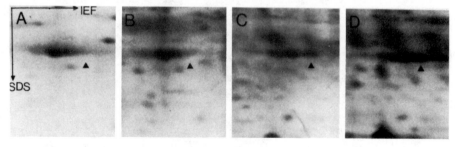

FIG.5. Autoradiographs showing the actin regions of
two-dimensional polyacrylamide gels containing
proteins extracted from (A) unfertilized eggs
labelled with [^{35}S]-methionine for 120 minutes and
embryos labelled with the same precursor for (B) 0-
120, (C) 120-240, and (D) 340-480 minutes after
fertilization. Other details are similar to Figure 4.
Electrophoresis and autoradiography was described by
Tomlinson et al. (1987a). From Tomlinson et al.
(1987a).

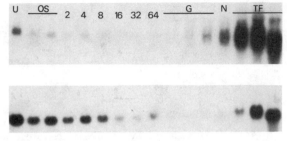

FIG.6. Northern blots showing the accumulation of α-actin mRNA (upper) and a β-actin mRNA (lower) during *Styela clava* embryogenesis. Equal quantities of total RNA isolated from various stages of development was subjected to electrophoresis through agarose-formaldehyde gels. Subsequently, the gels were blotted onto Hybond-N filters, and the filters were hybridized with [32P]-labelled SpMA3C (upper) or ScCA15/*Dde* (lower) probes. The upper and lower frames represent hybridization of the same blot after stripping and rehybridization with a different probe. Further details of the hybridization procedure can be found in Beach and Jeffery (1990). The stages of develoment represented by RNA in each lane are indicated in the upper frame. From left to right: U, unfertilized eggs; OS: stages of oóplasmic segregation (left, 30 minutes after fertilization, and right, 45 minutes after fertilization); 2,4,8,16,32, and 64 represent number of cells in early cleavage stages; G, gastrulae (left, early; middle, mid-; right, late), N, neurulae; TF, tail formation (left, mid-tailbud; middle, late tailbud; right, hatched tadpole). Adapted from Beach and Jeffery (1990).

were compared by two dimensional gel electrophoresis (Tomlinson et al., 1987a). The gels showed that α-actin was concentrated in tails, whereas β- and γ-actin were prevalent in both tails and heads. These results suggest that larval muscle cells and/or their precursors synthesize α-actin during embryogenesis.

Expression of α-Actin Genes during Embryonic Development

Further investigation of embryonic α-actin gene expression was carried out by gel electrophoresis of radioactively-labelled proteins, and by hybridization with a cloned α-actin gene probe. The protein gels are shown in Figure 5. In this experiment, *S. plicata* eggs or embryos were incubated with [35S]-methionine for 2 hour intervals during development, proteins were extracted and separated in two-dimensional gels, and radioactive polypeptides were identified by autoradiograpy. As expected from the previous experiments, β-and γ-actin were synthesized throughout development, but α-actin was synthesized exclusively in embryos. The incorporation of radioactivity into α-actin began during the interval between 2-4 hours after fertilization - or from the 16-cell to the early gastrula stage. A Northern blot of developmental stages is shown in Figure 6. In this experiment, RNA extracted from *S. clava* eggs and embryos was probed with antisense RNA transcribed *in vitro*

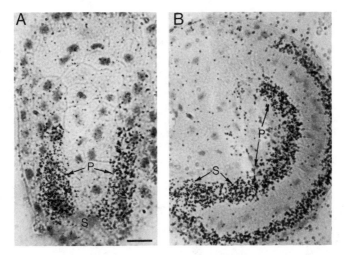

FIG.7. *In situ* hybridization of sectioned tailbud-stage *Styela clava* embryos with SpMAC3 antisense RNA showing the distribution of α-actin mRNA in the primary and secondary muscle cell lineages. A. A frontal section through an early tailbud embryo showing labelling in two bands of primary muscle cell progenitors (P); the secondary muscle cell progenitors (S) are unlabelled. B. A sagittal section through a mid-tailbud embryo showing labelling in two bands of muscle cells formed by primary and secondary muscle cell progenitors. Embryos were fixed and processed for *in situ* hybridization as described by Tomlinson et al. (1987b). The scale bar represents 10 μm. (magnification is the same in A and B). From Tomlinson et al. (1987b).

from a cloned DNA probe, containing the coding region of an *S. plicata* α-actin gene (Tomlinson et al., 1987b). The SpMA3C cDNA originally was isolated from an adult mantle cDNA library. Subsequent studies showed that the corresponding α-actin gene is expressed during adult development, rather than in the embryo (see below), but has sequence homology with embryonic α-actin gene(s) permitting its use as a probe for α-actin mRNA . As shown in Figure 6 (upper), hybridization with SpMA3C revealed a 2kb transcript. Although low levels of this transcript were detected in eggs, cleaving embryos contained no detectable α-actin mRNA (Fig.6; upper), suggesting that the maternal transcripts are degraded after fertilization. The α-actin transcripts were detected again at the early gastrula stage, and accumulated to high levels during subsequent development. The spatial distribution of α-actin mRNA was determined by *in situ* hybridization with SpMA3C (Tomlinson et al., 1987b). As shown in Figure 7, hybridization was restricted to developing muscle cells in the presumptive tail region of the embryo. Other *in situ* hybridization experiments (Tomlinson et al., 1987b) showed that α-actin mRNA began to appear in primary muscle cells at the early gastrula stage. In contrast, secondary muscle cells did not accumulate α-actin mRNA until mid-tailbud stage. The results suggest that the α-actin gene(s) shows differential temporal and spatial expression during embryogenesis.

After the completion of embryogenesis, the tadpole larva hatches and begins to swim. The duration of the free swimming period varies between different species. The free swimming period may last only a few hours in *Molgula citrina* (Grave, 1926), while in *Styela* it can persist for up to two days (Grave, 1944). Eventually, the tadpole settles on a suitable substrate and undergoes metamorphosis (see Berrill, 1947; Cloney, 1978 for reviews). During metamorphosis, the tail of the larva is retracted into the head, and all of the tail tissues (including muscle cells) are phagocytized. The ability of adults to develop in the absence of tail cells was demonstrated by an experiment in which the tails were severed from *Styela* tadpoles after hatching. Without tails, the tadpole heads underwent metamorphosis normally and developed into functional juveniles. Thus, larval tail cells are not necessary to form adult tissues.

Early during metamorphosis, the epidermis forms hollow protrusions called ampullae. Subsequently, these ampullae, which may be respiratory organs, begin to contract and expand (Torrence and Cloney, 1981). Later, a complex morphogenetic process begins which culminates in the formation of a sessile ascidian. The juvenile contains an alimentary tract, a branchial sac and a vascular system, surrounded by a muscular mantle. While little is known about this morphogenetic process, one of the initial events seems to be the migration of mesenchyme cells into spaces within the ampullae and between the endoderm and epidermis. Although the subsequent history of the mesenchyme cells is unclear, they are reported to be precursors of blood cells and vascular tissue (Cowden, 1968). While the larval mesenchyme cells have also been cited as precursors of adult muscle cells (Katz, 1983), there is no direct evidence that they serve this purpose. Instead, our observations suggest that siphon muscle cells originate in the epidermis and migrate to the initial site of muscle formation between the developing siphons.

We have examined α-actin gene expression during adult development in *S. plicata* by hybridization with probes prepared from the α-actin clone SpMA. As described earlier, SpMA3C is a probe derived from the coding region of SpMA. In contrast, SpMA7N is a probe derived from the 3'non-coding region of SpMA (Tomlinson et al., 1987b). Northern blots show that, while SpMA3C hybridizes to transcripts in both embryos and adults, SpMA7N detects only adult α-actin mRNA (data not shown). This suggests that the α-actin gene corresponding to SpMA3 is expressed only in adults. Further information concerning the identity of the SpMA gene was obtained by *in situ* hybridization with SpMA3C and SpMA7N. As shown in Figure 8, SpMA7N hybridized exclusively with transcripts in the mesenchyme cells during adult development, while SpMA3C hybridized with both mesenchyme cells and developing siphon muscle cells. These data suggest that SpMA encodes an α-actin that is expressed primarily in mesenchyme cells and their derivatives, including blood and other vascular tissues. Remarkably, the sequence of the protein coding region of SpMA is virtually identical to that of a vertebrate vascular smooth muscle α-actin (Chang et al., 1984; McHugh and Lessard, 1988). Henceforth, the gene corresponding to SpMA will be referred to as a mesenchymal α-actin gene, and

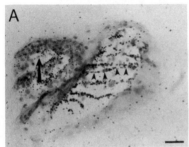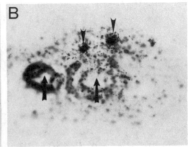

FIG.8. *In situ* hybridization of sectioned *S. plicata* adults after metamorphosis showing different labelling patterns obtained with the SpMA3C and SpMA7N probes. A; A section through the developing siphon muscle area of a 7 day-old adult showing labelling of nascent muscle fibers (arrowheads) with SpMA3C. B. A section through the developing siphon muscle area of a 10 day-old adult showing mesenchyme cells (dark areas) labelled with SpMA7N. Other details are similar to Figure 7. The scale bar represents 20 μm (magnification is the same in A and B).

the α-actin gene(s) expressed in the embryonic muscle will be referred to as a muscle α-actin genes.

The results of our studies on α-actin gene expression during *Styela* development are summarized in Figure 13A. It is concluded that transcription of the α-actin gene(s) begins in different cell lineages at different times during development. Gene expression begins in the primary muscle cells at gastrulation, in the secondary muscle cells during tail formation, and in the mesenchyme cells after metamorphosis.

Expression of a β-Actin Gene during Embryonic Development and in Adults

The pattern of β-actin gene expression was examined by Northern blots and *in situ* hybridization with ScCA15/*Dde*, a probe containing the entire 3' non-coding region of the *S. clava* cDNA clone ScCA15 (Beach and Jeffery, 1990). The sequence of the coding region of this cDNA is similar to vertebrate cytoskeletal β-actin genes (Nudel et al., 1983; Kost et al., 1983). As shown by Northern blot analysis (Fig. 6; lower), a 1.8kb β-actin transcript which is present in *S. clava* eggs and cleaving embryos, disappears before gastrulation. Zygotic β-actin mRNA accumulation begins after neurulation and continues during tail formation. *In situ* hybridization shows that zygotic β-actin mRNA accumulates primarily in epidermis and neural tube (Beach and Jeffery, 1990). These tissues continue to divide after cell division has ceased in other embryonic cells. The β-actin gene is also expressed in specific tissues of the adult: notably the digestive tract and the germinal layers of the testes and ovary, each of which also contain populations of rapidly dividing cells (Ermak, 1975, 1976). Thus, the ascidian β-actin gene corresponding to ScCA15 may function in cell proliferation (Beach and Jeffery, 1990).

FIG.9. A Northern blot showing the temporal expression of IFP mRNA during *S. clava* embryogenesis.
Th blot was hybridized with a random primer labelled
[^{32}P]-DNA probe made from an ScIF insert. Other details are similar to Figure 6. The lanes represent
equal quantities of RNA from unfertilized eggs (U),
1-cell embryos involved in ooplasmic segregation
(OS), 2-cell embryos (2), 4-cell embryos (4), 8-cell
embryos (8), 16-cell embryos (16), 32-cell embryos
(32), 64-cell embryos (64), mid-gastrulae (G), late
gastrulae (LG), neurula (N), and late tailbud (L)
embryos. From White (1989).

Expression of an Intermediate Filament Protein Gene during Embryonic Development and in Adults

Intermediate filaments (IFs) comprise one of the three
major cytoskeletal systems of eukaryotes, and their protein
constituents are encoded by a large multigene family (Steinert
and Parry, 1985). Although IFs are not well characterized in
invertebrates, a monoclonal antibody (anti-IFA) crossreacts
with all classes of vertebrate and invertebrate IFs (Pruss et
al., 1981). To obtain a probe for a *Styela* intermediate
filament protein (IFP) mRNA, we screened an *S. plicata* adult
mantle cDNA library with anti-IFA and isolated a series of
overlapping clones. Sequencing showed that these clones are
homologous to the vertebrate Type III IF family, which includes
desmin, vimentin and glial fibrillary acidic protein. Southern
analysis showed that the cDNAs corresponded to a single-copy
gene, SpIF. The SpIF cDNA was then used to isolate the
orthologous gene (ScIF) from an *S. clava* cDNA library, and an
ScIF probe was prepared. A northern blot of *S. clava* RNA
hybridized with this probe showed a 2.3 kb IFP transcript,
which was absent in eggs and cleaving embryos (Fig.9). The
zygotic IFP mRNA first appeared by the gastrula stage, and
continued to accumulate during the remainder of embryonic
development. *In situ* hybridization (data not shown) showed that
the IFP gene was expressed in epidermis, neural tube,
mesenchyme, and muscle, but not in endoderm and notochord
cells. Similar studies showed that the IFP gene is also
expressed in adult test, mesenchyme and muscle cells. The
results suggest that the IFP gene shows a distinct pattern of
temporal and spatial expression during embryonic development,
and in the adult.

Sequential Gene Activation

The genes we have investigated appear to be transcribed
sequentially during embryogenesis. The muscle α-actin and IFP
genes begin to be transcribed during gastrulation, followed by

the β-actin gene during tail formation, and finally the mesenchymal α-actin gene during adult development. The myosin heavy chain gene, which has been cloned and characterized in *Halocynthia roretzi*, also begins transcription during gastrulation (Makabe and Satoh, 1989), and may be expressed coordinately with the α-actin gene(s) in the primary muscle cell lineage.

ROLE OF CYTOKINESIS IN GENE EXPRESSION

While it is clear that the onset of general transcription at the 16-cell stage is independent of cytokinesis (see Fig. 3C), it is possible that the expression of specific genes may behave differently. This possibility is supported by differences in expression of tissue-specific markers in ascidian embryos. While myosin heavy chain requires several cleavages to be expressed in the muscle cell precursors (Nishikata et al., 1987a), AchE and an epidermal component defined by a monoclonal antibody (Nishikata et al., 1987b) are produced even when embryos are arrested before cleavage.

We have determined the relationship between transcription of specific mRNAs and cytokinesis by northern blots and *in situ* hybridization of cleavage-arrested embryos (Jeffery, 1989). In these experiments, *S. clava* embryos were treated with cytochalasin B at various times in development and incubation was continued until controls reached the tailbud stage. The following results were obtained when northern blots (data not shown) or sections of cleavage-arrested embryos were hybridized with the SpMA3C probe. Embryos arrested before the 8-cell stage did not accumulate α-actin mRNA (Fig. 10A-B); however, this message appeared in some embryos arrested at the 8-cell stage and most embryos arrested at the 16-,32-,and 64-cell stages (Fig.10C-D). In the arrested embryos, α-actin mRNA accumulated only in cells corresponding to the primary muscle cell lineage (i.e. a maximum of 2 cells at the 8-cell stage, 4 cells at the 16-cell stage, 6 cells at the 32-cell stage, and so forth), as expected from the results of similar experiments with other muscle cell markers (Whittaker, 1973b; Nishikata et al., 1987a). Thus, in contrast to general transcription, at least three and usually four cleavages are required for muscle α-actin gene expression.

Similar experiments were conducted to determine the role of cytokinesis on β-actin gene expression (data not shown). In contrast to α-actin mRNA, β-actin mRNA accumulated in embryos arrested beginning at the 4-cell stage. However, there was no accumulation of β-actin mRNA when cleavage was arrested at the 1- or 2-cell stage. Thus, expression of the β-actin gene requires fewer cleavages than α-actin expression.

In contrast to muscle α-actin expression, the appearance of AchE is independent of cleavage (Whittaker, 1973b; Crowther and Whittaker, 1984). Therefore, our results also show that the α-actin and AchE genes, which are normally expressed in the same cell lineage, are affected differently by inhibiting cytokinesis. This difference may be explained if AchE and α-actin transcription are controlled by different regulatory factors. This possibility is supported by experiments showing that AchE and α-actin mRNA can be expressed independently in

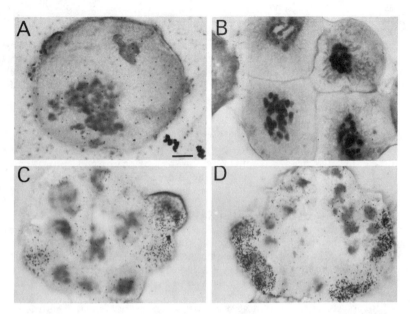

FIG.10. *In situ* hybridization of sectioned cleavage-arrested *S. clava* embryos with SpMA3C showing the relationship between cytokinesis and α-actin mRNA accumulation. A. An unlabelled 1-cell embryo. B. An unlabelled 4-cell embryo. C. A labelled 16-cell embryo with grains in 3 of the primary muscle-cell progenitors in the vegetal-posterior region. D. A labelled 32-cell embryo with grains in 6 of the primary muscle-cell progenitors in the vegetal-posterior region. The darkly-stained spheres in each arrested blastomere represent aggregations of multiple nuclei. From Jeffery (1989).

different muscle lineage cells of the same cleavage arrested embryo (Jeffery, 1989). It is not surprising that AchE and α-actin transcription may be controlled by separate mechanisms. Although α-actin is transcribed exclusively in embryonic muscle cells, AchE is produced in larval muscle (Whittaker, 1973b), mesenchyme (Meedel and Whittaker, 1979), neural (Durante, 1959), and epidermal (Minganti and Falugi, 1980) cells, and eventually in the adult nervous system (Arkett et al., 1989).

At present, we do not understand why specific gene transcription is dependent on cytokinesis. Although a specific number of DNA synthetic cycles is required for the expression of AchE in ascidian embryos (Satoh and Ikegami, 1981; Satoh, 1979), DNA synthesis does not appear to be limiting in cleavage-arrested embryos (Jeffery, 1989). It is also possible that transcription of specific genes requires the attainment of a minimal cytoplasmic-to-nuclear volume ratio. According to this hypothesis, transcription of specific genes would be initiated after this ratio was reduced to a critical value by cleavage. Unfortunately, this hypothesis is insufficient to explain the differences between β- and α-actin gene expression in cleavage-arrested embryos. Since fewer cleavages are required for β-actin mRNA accumulation, expression of the latter would be expected before α-actin during normal development, but instead its expression is initiated several cleavages later during tail formation. Thus, if the attainment of a critical cytoplasmic-to-nuclear volume ratio is actually involved in regulating the timing of gene expression, different thresholds must exist for the transcription of different genes.

GENE EXPRESSION IN ASCIDIANS WITH MODIFIED FORMS OF DEVELOPMENT

The ascidians commonly used for developmental studies - *Ciona*, *Halocynthia* and *Styela* - are divergent phylogenetically, yet exhibit the same basic mode of development. They form a tadpole larva that swims for a day or two before settling on a substrate and undergoing metamorphosis. The studies described above indicate that there is a temporal sequence of α-actin gene expression during *Styela* development (Fig.13A). As described earlier, muscle α-actin genes are first transcribed during gastrulation and mRNA continues to accumulate in tail muscle cells until hatching. During the free swimming period, the number of α-actin transcripts declines, suggesting that transcription is subsequently arrested (Tomlinson et al., 1987b). Later, transcription of the mesenchymal α-actin gene begins during adult development. Finally, muscle α-actin transcription is presumably reactivated by developing adult muscle cells. Below we describe situations in which the pattern of α-actin gene expression is modified in ascidians that depart from the conventional mode of development.

Gene Expression in Ascidians Exhibiting Adultation

Adultation is a heterochronic modification in which metamorphosis is accelerated and/or embryogenesis is retarded so that larval and adult development overlap temporally (Jägersten, 1972). This developmental modification is common in compound ascidians, but difficult to study because these ovoviviparous animals produce small numbers of large yolky eggs (Scott, 1945). In contrast, *Molgula citrina* is an ovoviviparous solitary ascidian that produces a relatively large number of eggs that develop similarly to oviparous Molgulidae (Grave, 1926; Berrill, 1935). In *M. citrina*, preliminary adult features begin to develop in the head region as early as the late tailbud stage. For example, the head endoderm is divided into the pharynx and alimentary tract, the cloacal siphon is formed, and mesenchyme cells begin to migrate into spaces formed between the endodermal regions and epidermis.

To determine whether changes in α-actin gene expression accompany adultation in *M. citrina*, we constructed a cDNA library from adult mantle and screened for actin clones with SpMA3C. Using this approach, a *M. citrina* cDNA (McMA) was isolated corresponding to the *Styela* mesenchymal α-actin gene. Probes for *in situ* hybridization were then prepared containing only the protein coding region (termed McMAC) or the 3'non-coding region (termed McMAN) of McMA. The McMAC probe hybridized to tail muscle cells of tailbud embryos (Fig. 11A), and to mesenchyme cells of late tailbud embryos and juveniles (data not shown). This suggests that muscle α-actin genes are transcribed at the usual time in *M. citrina* embryos, although their embryonic expression period may be abbreviated relative to *Styela*. In contrast, the McMAN probe hybridized only to mesenchyme cells and their descendants beginning in late

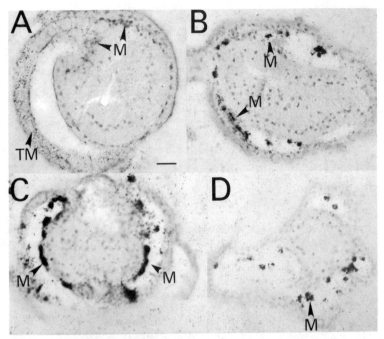

FIG.11. *In situ* hybridization of sectioned *M. citrina*
embryos and developing adults showing the accumulation of α-actin in the tail muscle and mesenchyme
cells. A. A section of a mid-tailbud embryo hybridized with McMAC showing grains in the tail muscle
cells (TM) but not in the mesenchyme cells (M). B. A
sagittal section of a recently hatched tadpole hybridized with McMAN showing labelling in the mesenchyme
cells. Part of the tail can be seen on the far left.
C. A cross-section through the head of a swimming
tadpole hybridized with McMAN showing labelled mesenchyme cells within and lining spaces between the
epidermis and endoderm. D. A section through a
developing adult hybridized with McMAN showing
labelled mesenchyme cells in the space between the
epidermis and endoderm. Other details are similar to
Figure 7. The scale bar in A represents 20 μm
(magnification is the same in A-D).

tailbud embryos and continuing during metamorphosis (Fig. 11B-
D). The results show that mesenchymal α-actin gene expression
in *M. citrina* is shifted forward in development relative to its
expression period in *Styela*. The timing of developmental stages
and α-actin gene expression in *Styela* and *M. citrina* is
compared in Figure 13A-B.

The temporal shift in mesenchymal α-actin gene expression
in *M. citrina* is an example of a molecular heterochrony (Parks
et al., 1988; Wray and McClay, 1989), the first to be described
in ascidians. As described earlier, α-actin expression is
coupled to cell division (Jeffery, 1989). Therefore, precocious
mesenchymal α-actin transcription could be explained by an
increased number of cell divisions. Consistent with this
possibility, in *M. citrina* mesenchyme cells are thought to

proliferate more extensively during the tailbud stage than in Molgulidae showing conventional development (Berrill, 1935).

Gene Expression in Anural Ascidians

Some species in the families Styelidae and Molgulidae are characterized by anural development: they do not form a tailed larva (Lacaze-Duthier, 1874; Damas, 1902; Berrill, 1931; Millar, 1954; 1962; Young et al., 1988). We have investigated anural development in *Molgula occulta*. *M. occulta* inhabits sand flats on the European continental shelf, often in association with a closely related species, *Molgula oculata*. In contrast to *M. occulta*, *M. oculata* exhibits conventional, or urodele, development (Berrill, 1931), and therefore serves as an excellent control for studies of anural development. The timing and mode of development in *M. oculata* and *M. occulta* are compared in Figures 13C-D. *M. oculata* and *M. occulta* develop identically until after the gastrula stage, when *M. oculata* embryos begin to form a tadpole larva, while *M. occulta* embryos remain essentially spherical. *M. occulta* embryos do not show any visible differentiation of tail muscle or notochord cells, and eventually hatch into nonmotile slug-like larvae. The slugs then form ampullae, which signals the beginning of metamorphosis. *M. oculata* tadpoles hatch, and undergo a brief free-swimming period before metamorphosis, which begins about the same time that *M. occulta* start to form ampullae. Since there are modest, if any, changes in developmental timing between these anural and urodele species, anural development in *M. occulta* is not heterochronic. Instead, it is an extreme form of heterotopy (Wray and McClay, 1989), in which presumptive tail cells fail to differentiate into functional tissues.

We have investigated α-actin gene expression in *M. oculata* and *M. occulta* by *in vitro* translation of RNA and *in situ* hybridization. *In vitro* translation indicated that, although α-actin RNA was present in tailbud embryos of *M. oculata*, it was absent from the corresponding stage of *M. occulta* embryos (data not shown). Similar results were obtained by *in situ* hybridization with SpMA3C. In these experiments, *M. oculata* tailbud embryos were mixed with *M. occulta* embryos at the corresponding stage of development, and embryos of both species were processed together for hybridization. *M. oculata* embryos can be distinguished from *M. occulta* embryos in sections because they are smaller and develop a tail. The *M. oculata* embryos showed muscle α-actin mRNA accumulation in tail muscle cell precursors, whereas there was no labelling above background in the corresponding regions of *M. occulta* embryos (Fig. 12A). However, *in vitro* translation and *in situ* hybridization (Fig. 12B) of juvenile *M. occulta* show that α-actin mRNA is transcribed after metamorphosis. These results indicate that muscle α-actin gene expression is suppressed during anural development in *M. occulta*.

The mode of development and patterns of α-actin gene expression during *M. oculata* and *M. occulta* development are summarized in Figure 13C-D. We conclude that anural development may be caused by suppression of the activity of genes required for tail morphogenesis. Although we do not know the mechanism of suppression, it is not likely a reduction in the number of divisions in the tail muscle lineage, since the latter probably divide as many times in *M. occulta* as in *M. oculata*. A more

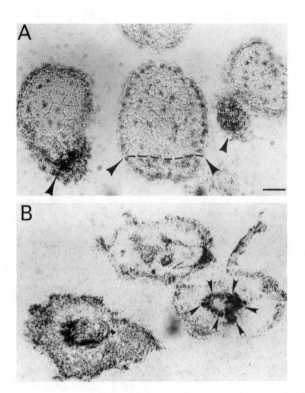

FIG.12. *In situ* hybridization of sections of developing *M. oculata* and *M. occulta* embryos and adults hybridized with SpMA3C showing α-actin mRNA accumulation. A. *M. oculata* tailbud embryos (far right and far left) and an *M. occulta* embryo (middle) at the corresponding stage of development. The tail muscle cells of the *M. oculata* embryos are labelled (arrowheads), but the corresponding region in *M. occulta* (below the dashed line bounded by arrowheads) is unlabelled. B. A section through developing *M. occulta* adults showing labelling within the adult rudiment (arrowheads). The area surrounding the adult rudiment is the developing tunic. Other details are similar to Fig.7. Scale bars 20μm (A), 50μm (B).

likely possibility is that the eggs of anural ascidians may not contain the trans-acting regulatory factors required to initiate transcription of genes involved in urodele development. At present, we are conducting experiments to test this hypothesis.

SUMMARY AND CONCLUSIONS

In this paper, we have reviewed our recent investigations of gene expression during ascidian development. Ascidians are popular and favorable material for embryological investigations, but molecular analysis of their development is just beginning. The incorporation of radioactive precursors into RNA suggests that ascidian embryos are arrested in transcription until the 16-cell stage, when zygotic RNA synthesis is

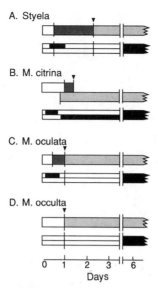

FIG.13. Schematic diagram showing the relationship
between the mode of development and α-actin gene
expression in (A) *Styela*, (B) *Molgula citrina*, (C)
Molgula oculata, and (D) *Molgula occulta*. In A–D, the
upper diagram indicates the mode of development. From
left to right, the open region represents the
embryonic period (fertilization through hatching),
the dark stippled region represents the free-swimming
period (hatching to attachment), and the light
stippled region represents the period of adult
development (following attachment and/or the beginning of ampullar formation). The arrowhead indicates
the beginning of metamorphosis. In A–D, the lower
diagram represents periods of α-actin gene expression
(solid regions) in embryonic and adult muscle cells
(upper row) and in mesenchyme cells and their
descendants (lower row).

simultaneously initiated in each cell lineage. None of the
specific genes that have been examined appear to be transcriptionally activated as early as the 16- cell stage, however.
Thus, the first genes to be expressed during development may
encode other types of structural genes or genes encoding small
nuclear, transfer, or ribosomal RNA. The muscle α-actin, IFP,
and myosin heavy chain (Makabe and Satoh, 1989) genes are
activated during gastrulation, a β-actin gene begins to be
transcribed during tail formation, and a mesenchymal α-actin
gene is activated after metamorphosis. These genes also exhibit
spatial distributions in their expression, both in the embryo
and adult. The muscle α-actin genes are activated independently
in primary and secondary muscle cells during embryogenesis, and
presumably are expressed again in adult muscle cells. The β-
actin gene is expressed in rapidly dividing tissues, which
include epidermis and brain in the embryo and proliferating
cells in adult epithelia. The IFP gene is expressed in
epidermis, brain, muscle and mesenchyme cells of embryos, and
in the mesenchyme and muscle cells of adults. Finally, the
mesenchymal α-actin gene is expressed only in the mesenchyme
cells and their derivatives in adults. Although the onset of

general transcription is independent of cell division, a specific number of cleavages are necessary for muscle α-actin and β-actin expression. The relationship between the initiation of gene expression and cell division is unclear, but may be related to the attainment of a critical cytoplasmic-to-nuclear volume ratio in each cell lineage. The pattern of actin gene expression is altered in ascidian species showing unusual modes of development. In species that exhibit adultation, mesenchymal α-actin transcription is initiated earlier than during conventional development, while the embryo is still elaborating its tail. In ascidians exhibiting anural development, muscle α-actin expression does not occur during embryogenesis, possibly because the appropriate regulatory factors are missing from the egg. These studies show that gene expression in ascidian embryos is differentially regulated in species that have evolved different modes of development.

ACKNOWLEDGEMENTS

These studies were supported by grants from the NIH (HD-13970) and NSF (DCB-8812110) awarded to WRJ. FEH was supported by an NIH post-doctoral fellowship (HD-06854). Dr C.R. Tomlinson participated in some of the earlier aspects of this work. Some of this work was carried out at the Marine Biological Laboratory, Woods Hole; Massachusetts, U.S.A. and the Station Biologique, Roscoff, France.

REFERENCES

Atkin, N.B., and Ohno, S. 1967, DNA values of four primitive chordates. *Chromosoma*, 23:10.

Arkett, S.A., Mackie, G.O., and Singla, C.L. 1989, Neuronal organization of the ascidian (Urochordata) branchial basket revealed by cholinesterase activity, *Cell Tiss. Res.*, 257:285.

Bates, W.R., and Jeffery, W.R. 1987, Alkaline phosphatase expression in ascidian egg fragments and andromerogons, *Dev. Biol.*, 119:383.

Beach, R.L., and Jeffery, W.R., 1990, Temporal and spatial expression of a cytoskeletal actin gene in the ascidian *Styela clava*, *Dev.Genetics* (in press).

Berrill, N.J., 1929, Studies in tunicate development. I. General physiology of development of simple ascidians, *Phil. Trans. Roy.Soc.* London Ser.B, 218:37.

Berrill, N.J., 1931, Studies in tunicate development.II. Abbreviation of development in the Molgulidae, *Phil.Trans.Roy.Soc.* London Ser. B, 219:37.

Berrill, N.J., 1935, Studies in tunicate development. III. Differential retardation and acceleration, *Phil.Trans. Roy.Soc.* London, Ser. B 225:226.

Berrill, N.J., 1947, Metamorphosis in ascidians, *J.Morphol.* 81:249.

Brandhorst, B., 1985, Informational content of the echinoderm egg, *in:* "Developmental Biology: A Comprehensive Synthesis." Volume 1. Oogenesis," L. Browder, ed., Plenum Press, New York.

Chabry, L., 1887, Contribution à l'embryologie normale et tératologique des ascidies simples, *J.Anat.Physiol.*, 23:167.

Chang, K.S., Zimmer, W.E., Bergsma, D.J., Dodgson, J.B., Schwartz, R.J., 1984, Isolation and characterization of six different chicken actin genes, *Mol.Cell. Biol.*, 4:2498.

Cloney, R.A., 1978, Ascidian metamorphosis: review and analysis, *in*: "Settlement and Metamorphosis of Marine Invertebrate Larvae." F. Chia and M.E. Rice, eds, Elsevier, New York.

Conklin, E.G., 1905a, Mosaic development in ascidian eggs, *J.Exp.Zool.*, 2:145.

Conklin, E.G., 1905b, The organization and cell lineage of the ascidian egg, *J.Acad.Nat.Sci.Phila.*, 13:1.

Crowther, R.J., and Whittaker, J.R., 1983, Developmental autonomy of muscle fine structure in muscle lineage cells of ascidian embryos, *Dev.Biol.*, 96:1.

Crowther ,R.J., and Whittaker, J.R., 1984, Differentiation of histospecific ultrastructural features of cleavage arrested early ascidian embryos, *W.Roux's Arch.Dev.Biol.*, 94:87.

Cowden, R.R., 1968, The embryonic origin of blood cells in the tunicate *Clavelina picta*, *Trans.Am.Microsc.Soc.*, 87:521.

Cowden, R.R. and Markert, C.L., 1961, A cytochemical study of the development of *Ascidia nigra*, *Acta Embryol. Morphol. Exp.*, 4:142.

Damas, D., 1902, Recherches sur le développement des Molgules, *Arch.Biol.*, 18:599.

Davidson, E.H., 1986, "Gene Activity in Early Development," Third Edition, Academic Press, New York.

D'Anna, T., 1962, Incorporation of nucleic acid precursors during ascidian development, *Acta Embryol.Morphol.Exp.*, 5:206.

Deno, T., Nishida, H., and Satoh, N., 1984, Autonomous muscle cell differentiation in partial ascidian embryos according to the newly-verified cell lineages, *Dev.Biol.*, 104:322.

Durante, M., 1959, Sulla localizzazione istochimica delle acetilcholinesterase lungo lo sviluppo do alcune Ascidie ed in Appendicularie, *Acta.Embryol.Morphol.Exp.*, 2:234.

Ermak, T.H., 1975, Cell proliferation in the digestive tract of *Styela clava* (Urochordata: Ascidiacea) as revealed by autoradiography with tritiated thymidine, *J.Exp.Zool.*, 194:449.

Ermak, T.H., 1976, Renewal of the gonads in *Styela clava* (Urochordata: Ascidiacea) as revealed by autoradiography with tritiated thymidine, *J.Exp.Zool.*, 194:449.

Grave, C., 1926, Molgula citrina (Alder and Hancock). Activities and structure of the free-swimming larva, *J.Morphol.*, 42:453.

Grave, C., 1944, The larva of *Styela (Cynthia) partita*: structure, activities and duration of life, *J.Morphol.*, 75:453.

Jägersten, G., 1972, "Evolution of the Metazoan Life Cycle," Academic Press, New York.

Jeffery, W.R.,1982, Calcium ionophore polarizes ooplasmic segregation in ascidian eggs, *Science*, 216:545.

Jeffery, W.R., 1984, Pattern formation by ooplasmic segregation in ascidian eggs, *Biol.Bull.*, 166:277.

Jeffery, W.R., 1989, Requirement of cell division for muscle actin expression in the primary muscle cell lineage of ascidian embryos, *Development*, 105:75.

Jeffery, W.R., and Bates, W.R., 1987, Axis determination in ascidian embryos, *in:* "Molecular Biology of Invertebrate Development," J.D.O'Connor, ed.A.R Liss, New York.

Jeffery, W.R., Bates, W.R., Beach, R.L., and Tomlinson, C.R., 1986, Is maternal mRNA a determinant of tissue-specific proteins in ascidian embryos ? *J.Embryol.exp.Morphol.*97, Supplement:1.

Katz, M.J., 1983, Comparative anatomy of the tunicate tadpole, *Ciona intestinalis*, *Biol.Bull.*, 164:1.

Kost, T.A., Theodorakis, N., and Hughes, S.H., 1983, The nucleotide sequence of the chick cytoplasmic β-actin gene. *Nuc.Acids Res.*, 11:8287.

Lacaze-Duthier, F.J.H., 1874, Histoire d'ascidies simples des côtes de France, I. *Arch.Zool.Exp.Gen.*, 3:119.

Lambert, C.C., 1971, Genetic transcription during the development and metamorphosis of the tunicate *Ascidia callosa*, *Exp.Cell.Res.*, 66:401.

Lambert, C.C., 1975, Changes in uridine permiability during the maturation of tunicate eggs, *Dev.Biol.*, 46:40-48.

Lambert, C.C., and Laird, C., 1971, Molecular properties of tunicate DNA, *Biochim.Biophys.Acta*, 240:39.

Makabe, K.W., and Satoh, N., 1989, Temporal expression of myosin heavy chain gene during ascidian embryogenesis, *Dev. Growth Differ.*, 31:71.

McHugh, K.K., and Lessard, J.L., 1988, The nucleotide sequence of a rat vascular smooth muscle α-actin cDNA, *Nuc.Acids Res.*, 16:4167.

Meedel, T.H., 1983, Myosin expression in the developing ascidian embryo, *J.Exp.Zool.*, 227:203.

Meedel, T.H., and Whittaker, J.R., 1978, Messenger RNA synthesis during early ascidian development, *Dev.Biol.*, 66:410.

Meedel, T.H., and Whittaker, J.R., 1979, Development of acetylcholinesterase during embryogenesis of the ascidian *Ciona intestinalis*, *J.Exp.Zool.*, 210:1.

Meedel, T.H., and Whittaker, J.R., 1983, Development of translationally active mRNA for larval muscle acetylcholinesterase during ascidian embryogenesis, *Proc.Nat.Acad.Sci.* U.S.A., 80:4761.

Meedel, T.H., Crowther, R.J., and Whittaker, J.R., 1987, Determinative properties of muscle lineages in ascidian embryos. *Development*, 100:245.

Millar, R.H., 1954, The breeding and development of the ascidian *Pelonaia corrugate* Forbes and Goodsir, *J.Mar. Biol. Assoc.* U.K., 33:681.

Millar, R.H., 1962, The breeding and development of the ascidian *Polycarpa tinctor*, *Quart.J.Microsc.Sci.*, 103:399.

Minganti, A., 1959, Androgenetic hybrids in ascidians. 1. *Ascidia malaca* (♀) x *Phallusia mammillata* (♂). *Acta Embryol.Morphol.Exp.*, 2:244.

Minganti, A., and Falugi, C., 1980, An epthelial localization of acetylcholinesterase in the ascidian *Ciona intestinalis* embryos and larvae, *Acta Embryol. Morphol. Exp.* N.S., 1:143.

Mirsky, A.E., and Ris, H., 1951, The desoxyribonucleic acid content of animal cells and its evolutionary significance, *J.Gen.Physiol.*, 34:451.

Newport, J., and Kirschner, M., 1982, A major developmental transition in early *Xenopus* embryos.I. Characterization and timing of changes at the midblastula stage, *Cell* 30:657.

Nishida, H., 1987, Cell lineage analysis in ascidian embryos by intracellular injection of a tracer enzyme. III. Up to the tissue restricted stage, *Dev.Biol.*, 121:526.

Nishida, H., and Satoh, N., 1983, Cell lineage analysis in ascidian embryos by intracellular injection of a tracer enzyme.I. Up to the 8-cell stage, *Dev.Biol.*, 99:382.

Nishida, H., and Satoh, N., 1985, Cell lineage analysis in ascidian embryos by intracellular injection of a tracer enzyme.II. The 16-and 32-cell stages, *Dev.Biol.*, 110-440.

Nishikata, T., Mita-Miyazawa, I., Deno, T., and Satoh, N., 1987a, Muscle cell differentiation in ascidian embryos analyzed with a tissue-specific monoclonal antibody, *Development*, 99:163.

Nishikata, T., Mita-Miyazawa, I., Deno, T., Takamura, K., and Satoh, N., 1987b, Expression of epidermis-specific antigens during embryogenesis of the ascidian, *Halocynthia roretzi*, *Dev. Biol.*, 121:408.

Nudel, U., Zakut, R., Shani, M., Neumann, S., Levy, Z., and Yaffe, D., 1983, The nucleotide sequence of the rat cytoplasmic β-actin gene, *Nuc.Acids Res.*, 11:1759.

Parks, A.L., Parr, B.A., Chin, J.E., Leaf, D.S., and Raff, R.A., 1988, Molecular analysis of heterochronic changes in the evolution of direct developing sea urchins, *J.Evol.Biol.*, 1:27.

Perry, H.E., and Melton, D.A., 1983, A rapid increase in acetylcholinesterase mRNA during ascidian embryogenesis as demonstrated by microinjection into *Xenopus* oocytes, *Cell Differ.*, 13:233.

Pruss, R.M., Mirsky, R., Raff, M.C., Thorpe, R., Dowding, A.J., and Anderton, B.H., 1981, All classes of intermediate filaments share a common antigenic determinant defined by a monoclonal antibody, *Cell*, 27:419.

Puccia, E., Mansueto-Bonaccorso, C., Farinella-Ferruzza, N., and Morello, R., 1976, Ribonucleic acid synthesis during development of an ascidian *Ciona intestinalis*, *Acta Embryol.Exp.*, 2:167-177.

Satoh, N., 1979, On the "clock" mechanism determining the time of tissue-specific enzyme development during ascidian embryogenesis. I. Acetylcholinesterase development in cleavage-arrested embryos, *J.Embryol.Exp.Morphol.*, 54:131.

Satoh, N., and Ikegami, S., 1981, A definite number of aphidicolin sensitive cell cyclic events are required for acetylcholinesterase development in the presumptive muscle cells of the ascidian embryo, *J.Embryol.Exp. Morphol.*, 61:1

Scott, F.M., 1945, The developmental history of *Amaroecium constellatum*. I. Early embryonic development, *Biol.Bull.*, 88:126.

Smith, K.D., 1967, Genetic control of macromolecular synthesis during development of an ascidian: *Ascidia nigra*, *J.Exp.Zool.*, 164:393.

Steinert, P.M., and Parry, D.A.D., 1985, Intermediate filaments, *Ann.Rev.Cell Biol.*, 1:41.

Steinhardt, R., Epel, D., Carroll, E.J., and Yanagimachi, R., 1974, Is calcium ionophore a universal activator of unfertilized eggs? *Nature*, 252:41.

Tomlinson, C.R., Bates, W.R., and Jeffery, W.R., 1987a, Development of a muscle actin specified by maternal and zygotic mRNA in ascidian embryos, *Dev.Biol.*, 123:471.

Tomlinson, C.R., Beach, R.L., and Jeffery, W.R., 1987b, Differential expression of a muscle actin gene in muscle cell lineages of ascidian embryos, *Development*, 101:751.

Torrence, S.A., and Cloney, R.A., 1981, Rhythmic contractions of the ampullar epidermis during metamorphosis of the ascidian *Molgula occidentalis*, *Cell Tiss.Res.*, 216:293.

Venuti, J.M., and Jeffery, W.R., 1989, Cell lineages and determination of cell fate in ascidian embryos, *Int.J.Dev.Biol.*, 33:197.

White, M.E., 1989, Analysis of the ascidian cytoskeleton: temporal and spatial expression of an invertebrate intermediate filament gene, PhD dissertation, University of Texas, Austin, Texas.

Whittaker, J.R., 1973a, Tyrosinase in the presumptive pigment cells of ascidian embryos: tyrosinase accessibility may initiate melanin synthesis, *Dev.Biol.*, 30:441.

Whittaker, J.R., 1973b, Segregation during ascidian embryogenesis of egg cytoplasmic information for tissue specific enzyme development, *Proc.Nat.Acad.Sci.U.S.A.*, 70:2096.

Whittaker, J.R., Ortolani, G., and Garinella-Ferruzza, N., 1977, Autonomy of acetylcholinesterase differentiation in muscle lineage cells of ascidian embryos, *Dev.Biol.*, 55:196.

Whittaker, J.R., 1977, Segregation during cleavage of a factor determining endodermal alkaline phosphatase development in ascidian embryos, *J.Exp.Zool.*, 20:139.

Wray, G.A., and McClay, D., 1989, Molecular heterochronies and heterotopies in early echinoid development, *Evolution*, 43:803.

Young, C.M., Gowan, R.F., Dalby, J., Pennachetti, C.A., and Gagliardi, D., 1988, Distribution consequences of adhesive eggs and anural development in the ascidian *Molgula pacifica* (Huntsman, 1912), *Biol.Bull.*, 174:39-46.

SOME CONTRIBUTIONS OF RESEARCH ON EARLY TELEOST EMBRYOGENESIS

TO GENERAL PROBLEMS OF DEVELOPMENT

J.P. Trinkaus

Department of Biology
Yale University
New Haven, CT 0651
and
Marine Biological Laboratory
Woods Hole, MA 02543

A number of teleost eggs present outstanding advantages for the study of vertebrate development. Teleosts occur all over the world in both fresh and sea water of all degrees of salinity and often have long spawning seasons. Indeed, some species, such as the zebrafish (*Brachydanio rerio*), the medaka (*Oryzias latipes*), and the rosy barb (*Barbus conchonius*), can be induced to spawn year-round in the laboratory. Moreover, the eggs and embryos of teleosts are often unusually resistant to small environmental changes and thus will withstand much experimental manipulation. Although removal of the chorion is difficult in certain species (*like Fundulus heteroclitus*), it is easy in many others, such as the zebrafish, rosy barb, blennies, and gobies. Further, many species produce eggs of striking lucidity, so that cytokinesis, cell movement and form changes of individual cells can be observed directly and followed in the living embryo. And now, with new powerful means of marking cells by injecting non-toxic fluorescent macro-molecules, the lineage of cells may also be followed readily during early embryogenesis in these transparent embryos. Finally, because of the ease of propagation of some fish embryos throughout the year and their rapidity of development, sophisticated genetic studies of development can be pursued.

It goes without saying that I am discussing mainly the advantages of demersal teleost eggs, those whose specific gravity is greater than that of water. Pelagic eggs, though often of striking optical clarity, pose frustrating problems for the experimentalist.

Cleavage and the Beginning of Cell Movement

Although cleavage can be readily observed and studied in teleost embryos, this in itself does not present a particular advantage. Opaque eggs like those of amphibians can also give valuable information, at least as far as the surface blasto-meres are concerned. What is especially useful about teleost

Experimental Embryology in Aquatic Plants and Animals
Edited by H.-J. Marthy, Plenum Press, New York, 1990

embryos is that, in contrast to those of most vertebrates, many are transparent, which gives one the capacity to observe directly the cleavage of internal blastomeres as well, by optical sectioning (e.g. Kimmel and Law, 1985a). This has also made possible direct study of the time of commencement of cell surface activity leading to cell movement and of cell movement itself relative to the cessation of cleavage. In the *Fundulus* embryo, cleavage is regular and synchronous up to the 11th cleavage. Then, during the 11th cleavage there is both a decrease in synchrony and completeness of cleavage. Not all blastomeres cleave. The 12th cleavage is exceedingly irregular; there is virtually no synchrony and many blastomeres do not cleave at all. Indeed, in some eggs, the 12th cleavage does not occur (Trinkaus, unpublished) and the 11th cleavage is the last. Significantly, blebbing of the blastomere surface, i.e. motile activity, which is totally absent during the early cleavages, is first evident on the surface of some non-cleaving blastomeres during the 11th cleavage, is frequent during the 12th and last cleavage, and seems to involve all or almost all blastomeres after that. Blebbing is actually preceded by undulating waves of deformation passing slowly over the cell surface. But these undulations are quickly succeeded by blebs (Trinkaus, 1973; see also Wourms, 1972). These blebs are often involved in circus movements that involve half or more of the cell surface and, bit by bit, come to be used as organs of locomotion. We call this "blebbing locomotion". Blebs propagate partially around the cell surface, adhere to a substratum, spread on it slightly, and, then, the protoplasm of the rest of the cell pours forward. With this, the whole cell advances (Trinkaus and Erickson, 1983; Fink and Trinkaus, 1988). They move like leukocytes, both *in vitro* (Ramsey, 1972) and *in vivo* (Shure, 1980). All of this motility seems to be restricted to deep cells. Cells of the monolayered epithelial enveloping layer (EVL) at the surface of the blastoderm are not involved. Interestingly, deep cell motility seems to be entirely random at this stage and takes place well before the directional movements of gastrulation. These occur after the beginning of epiboly in teleosts and involve primarily cells of the germ ring and the embryonic shield, out of which the embryo is fashioned. Similar pregastrula motile activity can also be observed in certain echinoderm embryos, again because of their transparency. Primary mesenchyme cells invade the blastocoel well before invagination.

Two important conclusions of general developmental interest can be drawn from these observations. 1) There seems to be an antagonism between cytokinesis and cell movement (Trinkaus, 1980). Motile activity does not begin during embryogenesis until the rapid cytokinesis of cleavage ceases. Also, blebbing ceases when cells go into mitosis, both *in vitro* and *in vivo*, and does not recommence until cytokinesis is complete (Fujinami, 1976, and Trinkaus, 1984a, pp 346-347). 2) Cells begin locomotion per se well before the directional cell movements of gastrulation. It is not known whether this is generally so throughout the Metazoa, for many embryos are too opaque for direct observation of cell movement. But it holds for sea urchins. Perhaps it is generally true, if only we could see. In teleosts, at least, it is as if cells must learn to move before they can move directionally.

Although teleost deep cells begin to move by blebbing

locomotion, soon some cells move by more conventional means - spreading lamellipodia terminated by long, thin filopodia (Trinkaus and Erickson, 1983). And they also leave long, thin, straight retraction fibers in their wake. But, contrary to fibroblasts and neurites moving on plane substrata *in vitro*, these cells moving *in vivo* are always more three - dimensional, less flattened, and give evidence of more protoplasmic flow. This difference, however, is minor. The main point is that close examination of moving deep cells within teleost blastoderms has revealed that they move *in vivo* in basically the same ways as leukocytes or fibroblasts and epithelial cells *in vitro*. Indeed, we can say more than this. SEM micrographs of *Fundulus* deep cells moving on their normal syncytial substratum, the yolk syncytial layer, reveal a leading morphology essentially indistinguishable from the growth cone of neurites extending *in vitro* - a spreading lamellipodium preceded by several filopodia (Trinkaus and Erickson, 1983; Trinkaus, 1985a). Thus, study of teleost embryonic cells moving *in vivo*, made possible by the transparency of the eggs, has led us to a conclusion of major importance. Many tissue cells move by means of the same basic locomotory mechanisms, whether *in vitro* or *in vivo* (Trinkaus, 1985b). In addition, deep cells in annual fish embryos exhibit contact inhibition of cell movement *in vivo*, like many tissue cells *in vitro* (Lesseps et al., 1979; Van Haarlem, 1979).

Another feature common to fibroblasts moving *in vitro* and teleost deep cells moving *in vivo* is persistence of movement. Once a fibroblast begins moving in a certain direction, it continues in that direction for some time in the absence of external directional signals (Gail and Boone, 1970). This is probably due to retraction induced spreading (Chen, 1979; Dunn, 1980). The same persistence occurs in teleost deep cells *in vivo*. Fink and I (1988) have observed that *Fundulus* deep cells move directionally toward a wound in the enveloping layer, a matter of considerable interest in itself but of particular interest in the present context because in the absence of wounding they have an intrinsic tendency to persist moving in whatever direction they started. Thus their movement toward a wound is a combination of natural persistence on their part and some external signal (s) that gives a *particular* direction to the persistence.

A teleost embryo has also provided crucial information on the movement of cell clusters *in vivo*. Epithelial cell clusters move directionally away from the embryo out in the yolk sac on eihter side of the blastoderm in the egg of *Blennius pholis*. Because of the favorable optical qualities of the embryo and the pigmentation of the clusters, they are easy to see and I have observed them moving in sufficient detail to establish that they move by means of their marginal cells, which extend lamellipodia that invariably terminate in fine filopodia (Trinkaus, 1988a). It is important to point out that in this study a teleost embryo has provided the sole unequivocal example of the movement of cell clusters *in vivo* during embryo-genesis. We all have had much reason to suspect cluster movement in several embryonic situations from fixed material, but until the *Blennius* work it had never been observed directly and unambiguously in the living embryo. Because of their ready visibility in the yolk sac, I have also been able to study the rate and directionality of the movement of these cell clusters, their spacing in the yolk sac, the wave of transformation of the epithelial clusters into clusters of dendritic mesenchymal melanocytes and the dissociation of these clusters into individual melanocytes, which then move directionally toward and into the pectoral fin bud (Trinkaus, 1988b). Moreover, here, because of the pigmentation of the cells and their optically clear background, it could be established that the directional movement of these cells is 100% efficient. They all move into the pectoral fin bud.

Gastrulation

Teleost embryos have also provided crucial evidence on cell movement during gastrulation from direct observation of living embryos. Both Thorogood and Wood (1987) and Wood and Timmerman (1988), using the embryo of the rosy barb, and Warga and Kimmel (1989), using the zebrafish embryo, have observed marginal deep cells turning over the edge of the blastoderm (beneath the enveloping layer) in a massive movement of involution, which results in their forming the mesoderm and endoderm of the developing gastrula. The overlying deep cells that are left behind form the ectoderm. These separate studies are confirmatory in two interesting ways. 1) The same basic result was obtained in two separate species of teleosts. 2) Two different techniques were used, both taking advantage of the transparency of each egg. The rosy barb work depended primarily on direct observation of moving cells with DIC optics and time-lapse cinemicrography. The zebrafish work involved injecting deep cells prior to and during gastrulation with a fluorescent macromolecule and following the fate of the cells and their progeny with UV epi-illumination. Cells of the enveloping layer were not observed to undergo involution, confirming Ballard (1966a) and Betchaku and Trinkaus (1978). These observations of involution in transparent teleost eggs are important, because before them it was thought that there is no involution during gastrulation of teleost embryos (e.g. Trinkaus, 1984a), a conclusion based of the marking studies of Ballard on embryos of the trout (Ballard, 1966a, b; 1981). It was therefore proposed that gastrulation in teleosts differs fundamentally from that in amphibians. However, Ballard's observations were flawed because of the opacity of the trout egg and the lack at that time of fluorescent markers. All the movements now described closely resemble their counterparts in *Xenopus*, namely epiboly, involution and convergent extension (compare Warga and Kimmel, 1989, with Keller, 1986). The fate map of the late blastula of a zebrafish is similar to that of an equivalent stage of the amphibian embryo (Kimmel et al., 1989). This is an important conclusion from the point of view of comparative embryology. Since teleost gastrulation now seems not to be qualitatively different from that of amphibia and since amphibian gastrulation shares much with that of reptiles, mammals and birds, we are led to believe that there is more evolutionary uniformity during early development of the vertebrates than previously thought. The forces leading to involution and ingression during gastrulation seem highly conserved in the vertebrates. We can now look forward to more details on gastrulation and on the subsequent fate of the cells from ongoing studies taking place in several laboratories, as at the University of Southampton, the Zoological Institute in Freiburg (Fleig et al., 1990), the Agricultural University of Wageningen, and the University of Oregon.

It should be noted that, although the only modern studies of *directional* cell movement during teleost gastrulation are the ones I have discussed, teleost gastrulation has fascinated embryologists for a long time. Notable among earlier studies are those of Wilson (1891), Morgan (1895), Pasteels (1936) and Oppenheimer (1936). In all these studies, however, (both old and new) certain details of cell activity such as variability in the directionality of movement of individual cells, the rate of movement, its relation to cytokinesis and to contacts with other cells have not been given concerted attention. R.D. Fink, M. Trinkaus and I are currently in the midst of just such a study in *Fundulus*.

Finally, it should be emphasized that all of these deep cell movements I have been discussing are of cells moving as individuals, in small clusters or jostling cell streams. No cohesive cell sheets are involved, at least during early gastrulation. Perhaps many other cell movements of early morphogenesis in other organisms are also by cells moving as individuals or in small groups. This would be difficult to determine in fixed material or in opaque embryos, but recent advances in the analysis of amphibian gastrulation indicate that there too cell streams with extensive cellular inter-calation are also involved (Keller, 1986).

As already indicated, cell surface undulations and blebbing in *Fundulus* commence abruptly after the cessation of cleavage. This suggests the same kind of "mid-blastula transition" (Gerhart, 1980) that occurs in *Xenopus* embryos (Newport and Kirschner, 1982a, b). At any rate, a marked change in cell motile behavior occurs upon cessation of cleavage in both organisms. It now would be of great interest to determine whether there is the same increase in mRNA production observed in *Xenopus*. Recent unpublished work in Kimmel's laboratory suggests that there is in the zebrafish.

Epiboly

Although I have not yet dealt with it, the most spec-tacular feature of gastrulation in teleost embryos is epiboly. During epiboly of a medium sized egg such as that of *Fundulus*, for example, the blastoderm expands twelve fold. The amount of expansion is less in smaller eggs, like that of the zebrafish, and more in larger eggs, like that of the trout (see Trinkaus, 1984b). Analysis of the mechanism of epiboly has attracted a great deal of our attention through the years and some lessons of general developmental interest have emerged from the results. In the first place, it is due entirely to expansion of the enveloping layer (EVL), a highly cohesive, monolayered, epithelial sheet at the surface of the blastoderm, and of the yolk syncytial layer (YSL), at the surface of the yolk beneath the blastoderm. Deep cells are not involved, except that their movements are correlated with the rate of epiboly as they undergo convergence and involution and fill the space between the EVL and the YSL during their epibolic expansion. Although the EVL expands at the same rate as the YSL (Stockard, 1915), it appears not to be the motive force. Much evidence supports the hypothesis that the autonomously expanding YSL, particularly its marginal region, is the prime mover (Trinkaus, 1951; Betchaku and Trinkaus, 1978; and Trinkaus, 1984b; see also Devillers, 1961). Thus, although cells of the EVL actively rearrange during epiboly (see below), the spreading of the layer as a whole seems to be passive. This is the most impressive example I know where the expansion of one layer is apparently solely due to its attachment to another. Therein lies an important lesson. Perhaps passive movements that depend on the attachment of cells and cell layers to actively moving other cells or cell layers are more common during morphogenesis than generally realized (Trinkaus, 1982).

Marking experiments by Long (1980a) suggest that the YSL in *Salmo* and *Catostoma* may play an inductive role as well. It undergoes convergent movements that coincide with the convergent movements of the deep cells in the blastoderm toward the embryonic shield during gastrulation.

Since the enveloping layer does not engage in involution or contribute to organogenesis, its morphogenetic significance rests solely on its role in epiboly. In addition to this, however, it has a very important physiological function. It covers the blastoderm throughout early development up to closure of the yolk plug at the end of gastrulation and after this it covers the entire egg. This covering function is of great significance, for the EVL of *Fundulus* has extremely low permeability (Bennett and Trinkaus, 1970) and therefore serves to shield the developing embryo from fluctuations in the salinity of the estuarine waters that are the everyday environment of this fish. It is really a kind of periderm. In sum, the EVL is a morphogenetic and physiological organ, totally lacking organogenetic significance.

Even though the expansion of the EVL in epiboly seems to depend primarily on its firm marginal attachment to the actively expanding YSL beneath, cells within the EVL constantly rearrange, moving actively relative to one another in the plane of the layer throughout epiboly, as suggested by fixed material (Kageyama, 1982) and demonstrated in the living by Keller and Trinkaus (1987). Cell rearrangement in the expansion or the change in form of an epithelial cell sheet is by no means unique for teleosts (for references, see Fristrom, 1988); however, since it occurs on the surface of the teleost egg, as it does during *Xenopus* gastrulation (Keller, 1978), it can be readily monitored with time-lapse cinemicrography of living cells. Moreover, because of our detailed knowledge of *Fundulus* epiboly, certain thought provoking correlations emerge. One of these, of course, is that these cellular rearrangements take place without disrupting the permeability barrier. How this occurs is not understood. No disruption of the circumferential tight junctions that connect each EVL cell to its nearest neighbors is apparent in electron micrographs (Lentz and Trinkaus, 1971; Bennett and Gilula, 1974). Further, these rearrangements take place without disruption of the electrical coupling between cells of the EVL, which in turn is probably mediated by gap junctions (Lentz and Trinkaus, 1971; Bennett and Trinkaus, 1970). These facts raise a fascinating and important question: how do these occluding junctions and gap junctions preserve their appearance in TEM and freeze fracture electron microscopy during these rearrangements ? It is not known. But the occurrence of cell rearrangement during *Fundulus* epiboly does tell us something important. Cell junctions (tight junctions, gap junctions, desmosomes) are surely far more dynamic that we ever dreamed they might be from simple examination of static electron micrographs (Fristrom, 1988). On the basis of the facts provided by our detailed observations (Keller and Trinkaus, 1987), Weliky and Oster (1990) have very recently constructed a computer model that proposes that cell rearrangements within the *Fundulus* enveloping layer during epiboly can be accounted for by calculating the balance of elastic and pressure forces at operation in the constituent cells during the process. If this model holds for *Fundulus*, it could well help explain epithelial cell rearrangements everywhere.

Another discovery arising out of the analysis of teleost epiboly, that may have important general implications is programmed endocytosis. Betchaku and I (1986) were forced to look for it because we were driven by a need to find a answer to a concrete question: what is the fate of the surface of the cytoplasmic layer covering the yolk, the so-called yolk cyto-plasmic layer (YCL), as it is replaced in epiboly by the surface of the YSL ? Marking showed that it disappears in the vicinity of the meeting of these two parts of the yolk cell in the region of the external YSL (E-YSL). Immersion of normal *Fundulus* gastrulae during full epiboly in the fluorescent dye lucifer yellow gave a quick answer, again because of the optical lucidity of the egg. Numerous endocytic vesicles are clearly visible in the E-YSL after a few minutes immersion in the dye, but nowhere else on the surface of the egg. Since this endocytosis takes place in the absence of macromolecules in the medium, it cannot be receptor mediated, as by coated pits. It must be programmed. But why is it confined to the narrow circumferential band of the E-YSL ? The answer seems to be in the unique surface activity of this restricted region of the egg surface. The E-YSL is higly folded and ultrastructural studies of it after exposure of the egg to the electron-dense molecule ferritin show that the ferritin is endocytosed just there and that the resulting endocytic vesicles have the size of the valleys between the folds. Since we have established that the narrowing of the early E-YSL, when its surface becomes folded, is due to its active contraction (Trinkaus, 1984b), it would appear that this contractile mechanism lies at the basis of the localized endocytosis and hence of the disappearance of the surface of the YCL as it is replaced in epiboly. It seems probable that this highly localized programmed endocytosis in *Fundulus* is an invariable accompaniment of epiboly in other teleosts, but this has not yet been checked. A more exciting possibility is that programmed endocytosis operates as a morphogenetic mechanism elsewhere in the animal kingdom, wherever there is a developmental need to dispose of extra cell surface or where there is surface folding due to contraction of cortical cytoplasm. This could be readily investigated in the folding of all sheets, but nowhere as easily as in the more lucid embryos, like those of some teleosts, where one can more readily detect uptake of fluorescent dye in living material.

Formation of the Yolk Syncytial Layer

Because of its fundamental importance as the probable driving force in epiboly of the EVL (and hence of the entire blastoderm), I have recently paid considerable attention to the origin and formation of the yolk syncytial layer in *Fundulus* (Trinkaus, in preparation). Study of this syncytium in *Fundulus* is of course greatly facilitated by the fact that it takes place at the surface of a transparent egg. First of all, I have confirmed the old observations of Agassiz and Whitman (1884), Wilson (1891), Stockard (1915) and others and the recent observations of Kageyama (1983) and Kimmel and Law (1985b) that the first nuclei of the YSL originate from open marginal blastomeres of the blastoderm, whose cytoplasm is confluent with the cytoplasm of the yolk cell beneath and peripheral to them. In *Fundulus*, this occurs both by collapse of marginal blastomeres and by oriented mitosis, with the more peripheral daughter nuclei deposited in the YSL cytoplasm. This escape of nuclei from the blastoderm takes place sporadically in *Fundulus* all around the margin of the blastoderm during the 8th through the 11th cleavages, but mostly at the 9th cleavage. Once nuclei have entered the YSL cytoplasm, they remain there and divide in approximate synchrony with cleavages in the blastoderm (see also Long, 1980b).

There are four features of these divisions that are of particular interest because of their possible general significance. 1) The first nuclei to enter divide 5 times - no more, no less. This reminds one of the early syncytial *Drosophila* embryo, in which the nuclei also divide a precise number of times. Those that enter the YSL cytoplasm of *Fundulus* later divide with the first nuclei and cease dividing at the same time as the first nuclei. Hence nuclei entering at the 9th cleavage divide 4 times, etc. All nuclei cease dividing at the same time. These facts suggest that the signal (s) for mitosis lies in the cytoplasm. 2) With each succeeding division, some daughter nuclei are located further away from the margin of the blastoderm, so that when the divisions cease the YSL is populated by over 1000 nuclei spread in a wide band around the periphery of the blastoderm. This would be predicted if the spindles were oriented at random, as they apparently are. 3) E-YSL nuclei of *Fundulus*, as well as those of *Oryzias* (Kageyama, 1986), begin mitosis in waves, which move parallel to the margin of the blastoderm. Nuclear divisions are therefore not strictly synchronous. They are metachronous, as indeed are nuclear divisions during early syncytial *Drosophila* development (Foe and Alberts, 1983). The presence of metachrony of nuclear divisions in such widely separate species could well depend in each case on the absence of intervening cell membranes (but see Newport and Kirschner, 1982a). 4) The duration of all five mitosis is about the same, but the duration of the interphases between mitosis III and mitosis IV and between mitosis IV and V is distinctly longer than the previous two interphases, in particular the last interphase, which is uniformly almost twice as long. Moreover, mitosis V is often slightly incomplete; not all nuclei divide. Again, the situation is basically the same in *Drosophila*, where the last interphase is distinctly longer in duration (Zalokar and Erk, 1976), and in *Xenopus* as well, where the last interphases before the cessation of cleavage are also longer (Newport and Kirschner, 1982a). It seems as if the factor (s) making for these divisions diminishes in strength at or toward the end of the series of mitotic cycles. What is fascinating about these three examples is that in each case the last mitosis is succeeded by a new and important develomental event. In *Fundulus*, contraction of the external YSL, which marks the beginning of blastoderm epiboly (Betchaku and Trinkaus, 1978; Trinkaus, 1984b), begins about an hour and a half after tne last mitosis. In *Drosophila*, membranes form between the nuclei after the last mitosis, making the embryo cellular, and gastrulation begins immediately thereafter (Zalokar and Erk, 1976). In *Xenopus*, as noted above, cell motility begins and the syntheses of mRNA is greatly accelerated (Newport and Kirschner, 1982a, b). In each case, we seem to have a kind of "mid-blastula transition". In *Fundulus* there appear to be two midblastula transitions - one for the cellular blastoderm (see above) and one for the yolk syncytial layer. This is clearly a very important phase of development. Incidentally, in *Fundulus* and *Oryzias* (Kageyama, 1983), these YSL nuclei cease dividing after the fifth division, in contrast to deep cells of the blastoderm (but see Long, 1980b), which continue dividing throughout gastrulation and beyond. I suspect that this is true of all teleosts.

Cell Lineage

Again because of their optical clarity, certain fish embryos have proved to be admirable material for studying cell lineage during early development. The lineage of cells labeled with fluorescent, non-toxic macromolecules that remain confined to the injected cell and its progeny can be followed in such embryos with far greater ease than in more opaque embryos. Kimmel and his associates (in particular Warga) have taken advantage of these favorable properties to give a picture of cell lineage in zebrafish development that is the most comprehensive for any vertebrate (for references see Kimmel and Warga, 1988). In brief, they have established that cell fate is not established prior to the mid-blastula stage. Blastomeres injected with dye during cleavage and early blastula stages produce clones whose cells become dispersed and whose tissue end products are likewise dispersed, both in the positions of the descendant cells and in the range of cell types produced. When this result is coupled with the observation that the pattern of cleavage of normally developing embryos may vary in important ways (Kimmel and Warga, 1987), the conclusion is inescapable that early development in the zebrafish is indeterminate. The position in the embryo that cells come to occupy later in development is the crucial factor in their differentiation. It seems possible that this indeterminate situation at the beginning of development could also be due in part to the rather random mixing of cells of the blastoderm revealed by this lineage study and by time-lapse observations of the movements of deep cells before the onset of the ordered movements of gastrulation (Trinkaus, 1973).

In contrast, when dye is injected into cells just before and during the gastrula stage, the labeled cells give rise only to certain tissues. Their lineage has become restricted. Of course, these labeling studies, like all labeling studies, only indicate what tissues a cell's clonal descendants will form during normal development. They indicate developmental fate, not developmental potency. Indeed, it is distinctly possible that some of these cells are not irrevocably commited to the tissue - specific fates they normally express. Oppenheimer (1938) showed by transplantation experiments in *Fundulus* that gastrula cells of this teleost can still change from their normal histogenetic destination. Apparently, such experiments have not yet been carried out in zebrafish embryos.

Some teleosts are also excellent organisms for studying how genes control development in a vertebrate. In contrast to many other vertebrates, the generation time of the zebrafish, for example, is only 3-4 months and females produce several hundred small transparent eggs every few days, which develop rapidly and synchronously outside the mother. Thus, mutations causing developmental changes can often be readily detected and the afflicted embryos relatively easily studied. Developmental genetic research on fish is moving apace at all levels; but, since it has been reviewed very recently (Kimmel, 1989; Powers, 1989), I will not attempt a summary.

ACKNOWLEDGEMENTS

Research in the author's laboratory has been supported through the years by the National Science Foundation and by the National Cancer Institute of the National Institutes of Health of the U.S. Public Health Service.

REFERENCES

Agassiz, A., and Whitman, C.O., 1884, On the development of some pelagic fish eggs. Preliminary notice, *Proc.Amer.Acad.Arts Sci.*, 20:22-76.

Ballard, W.W., 1966a, The role of the cellular envelope in the morphogenetic movements of teleost embryos, *J.Exp.Zool.*, 161:193-200.

Ballard, W.W., 1966b, Origin of the hypoblast in *Salmo*. I. Does the blastodisc edge turn inward ? *J.Exp.Zool.*, 161:201-210.

Ballard, W.W.,1981, Morphogenetic movements and fate maps of vertebrates, *Am.Zool.*, 21:391-399.

Bennett, M.V.L., and Gilula, N.B., 1974, Membranes and junctions in developing *Fundulus* embryos: freeze-fracture and electrophysiology, *J.Cell Biol.*, 63:21a (Abstract).

Bennett, M.V.L., and Trinkaus, J.P., 1970, Electrical coupling between embryonic cell by way of extracellular space and specialized junctions, *J.Cell Biol.*, 44:592-610.

Betchaku, T., and Trinkaus, J.P., 1978, Contact relations, surface activity, and cortical microfilaments of marginal cells of the enveloping layer and of the yolk syncytial and yolk cytoplasmic layers of *Fundulus* before and during epiboly, *J.Exp.Zool.*, 206:381-426.

Betchaku, T., and Trinkaus, J.P., 1986, Programmed endocytosis during epiboly of *Fundulus heteroclitus*, *Amer.Zool.*, 26:193-199.

Chen, W.T., 1979, Induction of spreading during fibroblast movement, *J.Cell Biol.*, 81:684-691.

Devillers, C., 1961, Structural and dynamic aspects of the development of the teleostean egg, Advances in morphogenesis, vol.1, pp 379-428.

Dunn, G.A., 1980, Mechanisms of fibroblast locomotion. *In:* Cell Adhesion and Motility, eds A.S.G. Curtis & J.D. Pitts, Cambridge University, Cambridge, pp 409-423.

Fink, R.D., and Trinkaus, J.P., 1988, *Fundulus* deep cells:

Directional migration in response to epithelial wounding, *Dev.Biol.*, 129:179-190.

Fleig, R., Vollmar, H., and Sander, K., 1990, Gastrulation cells, differentiation of the germ layers, and the formation of the body axis in the zebrafish *Brachydanio rerio* (Teleostei), *Exp.Embryol.Aquatic Plants and Animals* (Abstract).

Foe, V.E., and Alberts, B.M., 1983, Studies of nuclear and cytoplasmic behaviour during the five mitotic cycles that precede gastrulation in *Drosophila* embryogenesis, *J.Cell Sci.*, 61:31-70.

Fristrom, D., 1988, The cellular basis of epithelial morphogenesis. A review, *Tissue & Cell*, 20 (5) 645-690.

Fujinami, N., 1976, Studies on the mechanism of circus movement in dissociated embryonic cells of a teleost, *Oryzias latipes*: fine-structural observations, *J.Cell Sci.*, 22:133-147.

Gail, M.H., and Boone, C.W., 1970, The locomotion of mouse fibroblasts in tissue culture, *J. Biophys.*, 10:980-993.

Gerhart, J.G., 1980, Mechanisms regulating pattern formation in the amphibian egg and early embryo, *in:* Biological Regulation and Development, 2, R.F. Goldberger, ed. Plenum Press, New York.

Kageyama, T., 1982, Cellular basis of epiboly of the enveloping layer in the embryo of the medaka, *Oryzias latipes*. II. Evidence for cell rearrangement, *J.Exp.Zool.*, 219:241-256.

Kageyama, T., 1983, Origin of yolk syncytium and mitotic pattern in the syncytium and blastomeres in *Oryzias latipes*, *Zool.Mag.* (Abstract), 92:485.

Kageyama, T., 1986, Mitotic wave in the yolk syncytial layer of embryos of Oryzias latipes originates in the amplification of mitotic desychrony in early blastomeres, *Zool.Sci.* (Abstract), 3:1046.

Keller, R.E., 1978, Time-lapse cinemicrographic analysis of superficial cell behavior during and prior to gastrulation in *Xenopus laevis*, *J.Morphol.*, 157:223-248.

Keller, R.E., 1986, The cellular basis fo amphibian gastrulation. *In:* Developmental Biology: A Comprehensive Synthesis, Vol.2. The Cellular Basis of Morphogenesis, ed. L. Browder, pp 241-327.

Keller, R.E., and Trinkaus, J.P., 1987, Rearrangement of enveloping layer cells without disruption of the epithelial permeability barrier as a factor in *Fundulus* epiboly, *Dev.Biol.*, 120:12-24.

Kimmel, C.B., 1989, Genetics and early development of zebrafish. *Trends in Genetics*, 5:283-288.

Kimmel, C.B., and Law, R.D., 1985a, Cell lineage of zebrafish blastomeres. I. Cleavage pattern and cytoplasmic bridges between cells, *Dev.Biol.*, 108:78-85.

Kimmel, C.B., and Law, R.D., 1985b, Cell lineage of zebrafish blastomeres. II. Formation of the yolk syncytial layer, *Dev.Biol.*, 108:86-93.

Kimmel, C.B., and Warga, R.M., 1987, Indeterminate cell lineage of the zebrafish embryo, *Dev.Biol.*, 124:269-280.

Kimmel, C.B., and Warga, R.M., 1988, Cell lineage and developmental potential of cells in the zebrafish embryo, *Trends in Genetics*, 4:68-74.

Kimmel, C.B., and Warga, R.M., 1989, Origin of tissue-restricted cell lineages in zebrafish, *Development* (in press).

Kimmel, C.B., Warga, R.M., and Schilling, T., 1989, A fate map for the zebrafish, *Development* (in press).

Lentz, T.L., and Trinkaus, J.P., 1971, Differentiation of the junctional complex of surface cells in the developing *Fundulus* blastoderm, *J.Cell Biol.*, 48:455-472.

Lesseps, R.J., Hall, M., and Murnane, M.B., 1979, Contact inhibition of cell movement in living embryos of an annual fish *Nothobranchius korthausae*: Its role in the switch from persistent to ransom cell motility, *J.Exp.Zool.*, 207:459-469.

Long, W.L., 1980a, Analysis of yolk syncytium behavior in *Salmo* and *Catostomus*, *J.Exp.Zool.*, 214:323-331.

Long, W.L., 1980b, Proliferation, growth, and migration of nuclei in the yolk syncytium of *Salmo* and *Catostomus*, *J.Exp.Zool.*, 214:333-343.

Morgan, T.H., 1895, The formation of the fish embryo, *J.Morphol.*, 10:419-472.

Newport, J., and Kirschner, M.W., 1982a, A major developmental transition in early *Xenopus* embryos: I. Characterization and timing of cellular changes at the midblastula stage, *Cell*, 30:675-686.

Newport, J., and Kirschner, M.W., 1982b, A major developmental transition in early *Xenopus* embryos: II. Control of the onset of transcription, *Cell*, 30:687-696.

Oppenheimer, J.M., 1936, Processes of localization in developing *Fundulus*, *J.Exp.Zool.*, 73:405-444.

Oppenheimer, J.M., 1938, Potencies for differentiation in the teleostean germ ring, *J.Exp.Zool.*, 79:185-212.

Pasteels, J., 1936, Etudes sur la gastrulation des vertébrés méroblastiques. I. Téléostéens, *Arch.de Biologie*, 47:206-308.

Powers, D.A., 1989, Fish as model systems, *Science*, 246:352-358.

Ramsey, W.S., 1972, Locomotion of human polymorphonuclear leukocytes, *Exp.Cell Res.*, 72:489-501.

Shure, M.S., 1980, *In vivo* analysis of leukocyte movement in larvae of *Xenopus* laevis, *J.Cell Biol.* (Abstract), 87:89a.

Stockard, C.R., 1915, A study of wandering mesenchymal cells on the living yolk-sac and their developmental products: chromatophores, vascular epithelium and blood cells, *Amer.J.Anat.*, 18:525-594.

Thorogood, P., and Wood, A., 1987, Analysis of *in vivo* cell movement using transparent tissue systems, *J.Cell Sci.*, Suppl., 8:395-413.

Trinkaus, J.P., 1951, A study of the mechanism of epiboly in the egg of *Fundulus heteroclitus*, *J.Exp.Zool.*, 118:269-320.

Trinkaus, J.P., 1973, Surface activity and locomotion of *Fundulus* deep cells during blastula and gastrula stages, *Dev.Biol.*, 30:68-103.

Trinkaus, J.P., 1980, Formation of protrusions of the cell surface during tissue cell movement. *In:* "Tumor Cell Surfaces and Malignancy", R.O. Hynes and C.F. Fox, eds, Progress in Clinical and Biological Research, 41:887-906.

Trinkaus, J.P., 1982, Some thoughts on directional cell movements during morphogenesis, "Cell Social Behaviour", ed. A.S.G. Curtis, G. Dunn, and R. Bellairs, Cambridge University Press, 471-498.

Trinkaus, J.P., 1984a, Cells into Organs. The Forces that Shape

the Embryo. Second Revised Edition, Prentice-Hall, Inc.
Englewodds Cliffs, New Jersey, 543 pp.

Trinkaus, J.P., 1984b, Mechanism of *Fundulus* epiboly - a
current view, *Amer.Zool.*, 24:673-688.

Trinkaus, J.P., 1985a, Further thoughts on directional cell
movement during morphogenesis, *J.Neurosci.Research*,
13:1-19.

Trinkaus,J.P., 1985b, Protrusive activity of the cell surface
and the initiation of cell movement during
morphogenesis, *In:* G. Haemmerli and P. Sträuli eds. Cell
Traffic in the Developing and Adult Organism. Series in
Exp.Biol. & Med., Karger, Basel, 10:130-173.

Trinkaus, J.P., 1988a, Directional cell movement during early
development of the teleost *Blennius pholis*. I. Formation
of epithelial cell clusters and their pattern and
mechanism of movement, *J.Exp.Zool.*, 245:157-186.

Trinkaus, J.P., 1988b, Directional cell movement during early
development of the teleost *Blennius pholis*. II.
Transformation of the cells of epithelial clusters into
dendritic melanocytes, their dissociation from each
other and their migration to and invasion of the
pectoral fin buds, *J.Exp.Zool.*, 248:55-72.

Trinkaus, J.P., and Erickson, C.A., 1983, Protrusive activity,
mode and rate of locomotion, and pattern adhesion of
Fundulus deep cells during gastrulation, *J.Exp.Zool.*,
228:41-70.

Van Haarlem, R., 1979, Contact inhibition of overlapping: one
of the factors involved in deep cell epiboly of
Nothobranchius korthausae, *Dev.Biol.*, 70:171-179.

Warga, R.M., and Kimmel, C.B., 1989, Cell movements during
epiboly and gastrulation in zebrafish, *Development*, in
press.

Weliky, M., and Oster, G., 1990, The mechanical basis of cell
rearrangement. I. Epithelial morphogenesis during
Fundulus epiboly, (in press).

Wilson, H.V., 1891, The embryology of the sea bass *(Serranus
atrarius)*; *Bulletin of the US fish commission*, 9:209-
277.

Wood, A., and Timmermans, L.P.M., 1988, Teleost epiboly: a
reassessment of deep cell movement in the germ ring,
Development, 102:575-585.

Wourms, J.P., 1972, The developmental biology of annual fishes.
II. Naturally occurring dispersion and reaggregation of
blastomeres during the development of annual fish eggs,
J.Exp.Zool., 182:169-200.

Zalokar, M., and Erk, I., 1976, Division and migration of
nuclei during early embryogenesis of *Drosophila
melanogaster*, *J.Microscopie Biol.Cell*, 25:97-106.

GASTRULATION IN THE ZEBRAFISH *BRACHYDANIO RERIO* (TELEOSTEI)

AS SEEN IN THE SCANNING ELECTRON MICROSCOPE

R.Fleig

Institut für Biologie I (Zoologie)
Albertstrasse 21a
D-7800 Freiburg

INTRODUCTION

Teleost gastrulation has been studied for a long time, albeit with rather controversial results (Oppenheimer, 1936; Pasteels, 1936; Hisaoka and Battle, 1958; Hisaoka and Firlit, 1960; Hamano, 1964; Ballard, 1973 a,b,c; Sander et al., 1984). The separation of mesoderm and endoderm and the cell movements involved in the further development of these layers in teleosts have been described in salmonids, but conflicting conclusions were drawn (Pasteels, 1936; Ballard, 1973b). In the zebrafish, the cells of the future inner germ layers derive from cells involuting along the blastodisc rim (Kimmel, 1989), starting from about mid-epiboly. Their initial movements are incompletely known, but while Hamano (1960) described a strong convergence movement in the germ ring towards the future body axis, Sander et al. (1984) observed only cell movements perpendicular to the blastodisc rim, i.e. towards the animal pole rather than the future body axis (*). The latter authors at first drew the conclusion that these cells move directly underneath the enveloping layer which covers the blastodisc surface (Sander et al., 1984). A later study using radial instead of tangential focal planes (K. Sander and H. Vollmar, pers.comm.) and my SEM-studies showed however that these cells move between the yolk surface and the epiblast as has been described for the rosy barb (Wood and Timmermanns, 1988). In the present report I reconstruct from SEM-preparations the movements of these cells from their segregation at the germ disc margin until the time when the notochord anlage becomes visible.

(*)By a printers error, the average speed of their movement was given as 12 µm/h instead of 120 µm/h.

MATERIAL AND METHODS

Collection and cultivation of eggs were done as described by Baumann and Sander (1984). For scanning electron microscopy the eggs were fixed on ice for one hour in PBS containing 2%

Experimental Embryology in Aquatic Plants and Animals
Edited by H.-J. Marthy, Plenum Press, New York, 1990

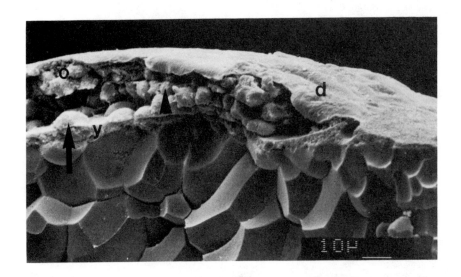

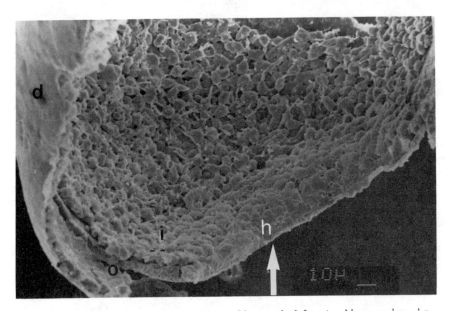

FIG.1. Fraction through yolk and blastodisc rim in the germ ring region during deep cell invagination. Note that inner deep cells attach (arrow) to yolk syncytial layer (y) or (arrowhead) to the outer deep cell layer (o); enveloping layer (d). Animal pole to the left.

FIG.2. Fraction through blastodisc during gastrulation, yolk mass removed (see Fig.3). Blastodisc rim marked by arrow. Meridional fracture (left) shows enveloping layer (d) and outer (o) as well as inner (i) deep cells. Note crowding of inner deep cells near the rim (h) and their wider spacing towards the animal pole (upwards).

glutaraldehyde and 1% osmiumtetroxide. The fixed embryos were dehydrated in an ethanol series (30%, 50%, 70%, 90%, 100%, 15 min. each). Critical point drying, mounting, and gold sputtering followed as described in Baumann and Sander (1984). For observations on fracture faces, both embryo and yolk can be broken apart or separated from each other while in the ethanol or after drying.

RESULTS

For early development including epiboly in teleosts see the contribution of Trinkaus to this volume. A short overview for these stages in the zebrafish is shown in Fig.9. During epiboly both enveloping layer and deep cells expand over the yolk surface towards the vegetal pole in the manner described for *Fundulus heteroclitus* (Betchaku and Trinkaus, 1978, 1986; Keller and Trinkaus, 1987). In the zebrafish this movement slows down briefly when the blastodisc rim is about to reach the equatorial region (Sander et al., 1984). Now the blastodisc rim thickens slightly and thus forms the germ ring described by Hamano (1964). Timelapse films kindly provided by H. Vollmar (Freiburg) show that the margin speeds up again, and now marginal deep cells in the germ ring turn inward and move in the cleft between the submarginal deep cells and the surface of the yolk syncytial layer; thereby the germ ring looses in thickness. Cell inwheeling at the blastodisc rim continues until almost the end of epiboly, while the remaining deep cells (constituting the epiblast) continue progressing towards the vegetal pole. Zebrafish gastrulation thus represents a segregation of two cell populations one of which turns inward and moves back in the direction of the animal pole while the other continues the epibolic movement towards the vegetal pole.

The SEM preparations show internalized deep cells behind the germ ring around its whole circumference. These cells at first are as closely packed as those in the outer layer, but those farther distant from the germ ring loose contacts (Fig.2). The moving cells develop pseudopodia by which they attach to the surface of the yolk syncytial layer or to the inner face of the epiblast (Fig.1,2,3). In the beginning of their migration these cells are of rather globular shape and appear as a uniform aggregate (Fig.3) but soon they separate into 2 distinct populations which differ by cell shape and attachment preferences. The larger population consists of lens-shaped cells sticking to the inner face of the closely packed epiblastic deep cell layer (Fig.4,6). The smaller population consists of rather flat cells that apparently migrate along the surface of the yolk syncytial layer (Fig.5). As far as can be ascertained from a staged series of fixed embryos, the population on the yolk surface will give rise to the endoderm while the larger population attached to the epiblastic deep cells represents the mesoderm. The epiblastic deep cells that at the completion of epiboly are still remaining in the outer layer represent the ectoderm.

The cells turning inward start moving away from the blastodisc rim at right angles, i.e. on meridional trajectories towards the animal pole (Sander et al. 1984) but sooner or later their movement must include a latitudinal component carrying them towards the future body axis. This convergence

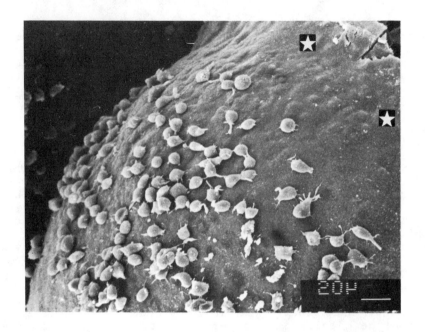

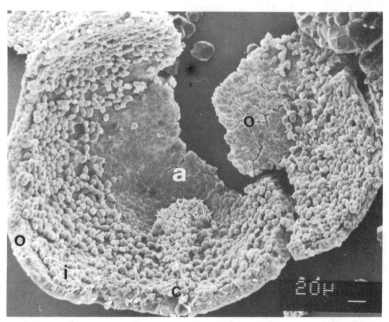

FIG.3. Surface of the yolk syncytial layer after removal of the gastrulation blastodisc (see Fig.2). The former position of the germ ring is marked by asterisks. Note globular internalized deep cells attached to the yolk surface with pseudopodia. Animal pole to the left.

FIG.4. Inner deep cells during notochord formation, towards the end of epiboly and gastrulation. The notochord with the prechordal plate at its anterior end (c) is oriented perpendicular to the germ ring and arises from internalized cells which migrate

movement far above the germ ring has not yet been observed in time-lapse films, perhaps because the developing axis turns out of focus (H.Vollmar, pers.comm.), but its consequences become apparent in SEM preparations made some time after mid-epiboly. In these preparations, the body axis is visible as a strandlike aggregation of mesodermal cells oriented perpendicular to the epiboly margin. This is the anlage of prechordal plate and notochord. Its thick anterior part soon starts extending towards, and ultimately beyond, the animal pole (Fig.4). The mesoderm cells arriving later at the future body axis concentrate along both sides of the developing notochord. Here they will give rise to somites and other mesodermal structures. Below the ventral face of the notochord, the surface of the yolk syncytial layer forms a groove that is also visible in living embryos. Some time after formation of the notochord anlage, both mesodermal and endodermal cells have vanished from the more distant regions. The mesoderm now forms a wide ribbon on either side of the notochord, and the endoderm covers a comparable stripe of yolk surface underneath the mesoderm and notochord; outside these ribbons, the yolk surface and the inner face of the ectoderm are free from loose cells.

The ectodermal deep cell population has become single-layered by the time when the blastodisc rim is approaching the vegetal pole while earlier, until some time after the onset of cell inwheeling, the (epiblastic) deep cell layer of the expanding blastodisc is three to four cells thick. When the notochord anlage becomes first visible, the overlaying ectoderm shows no trace as yet of increasing in thickness (Fig.7). It is only after the separation of the notochord anlage from the remainder of the mesoderm that the adjacent ectoderm starts thickening to give rise to the neural strand (Fig.8).

DISCUSSION

The inwheeling movement of marginal deep cells during the second half of epiboly can be termed gastrulation since it is the process establishing the three germ layers and the cells that invaginate at the germ disc margin represent mesoderm and endoderm. Kimmel (1989) also reports involution of marginal deep cells during gastrulation in the zebrafish comparing the blastodisc rim with the blastophore of tetrapods.

In *Fundulus* the germ ring develops earlier during epiboly and is also much more prominent than in *Brachydanio*; and the same holds true for the embryonic shield (Fleig, unpubl. observations). In *Fundulus* (Oppenheimer, 1936) and in *Salmo* (Ballard, 1973 a,b,c,) the cells of the innermost part of the germ ring, the hypoblast, migrate tangentially along the germ ring so as to converge from both sides on the region where they give rise to the embryonic shield while the blastodisc rim continues moving towards the vegetal pole. This was also described for *Brachydanio* (Hisaoka and Battle, 1958; Hisaoka

---

along the innner face of the outer (epiblastic) deep cells. The anterior part of the notochord anlage will grow towards the animal pole (a) which at the time of fixation was not yet covered by mesodermal cells.

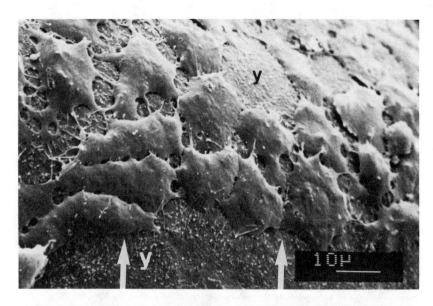

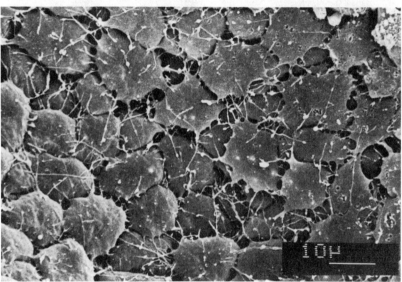

FIG.5. Putative future endoderm cells attached to the
yolk syncytial layer (y). Blastodisc with mesodermal
and ectodermal layers and the enveloping layer (see
Fig.6) are removed. The cells cover a stripe of yolk
surface underneath the developing notochord and
mesoderm; one lateral margin of this stripe is marked
by arrows.

FIG.6. Putative future mesoderm cells after gastrulation attached to the inner surface of the outer
deep cell layer (future ectoderm). Yolk and endoderm
cells (see Fig.5) are removed. The mesoderm forms in
this stage a ribbon on either side of the developing
notochord matching the stripe of endoderm.

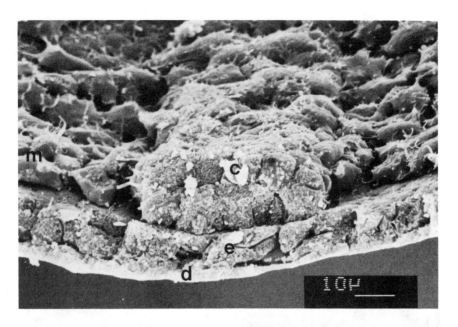

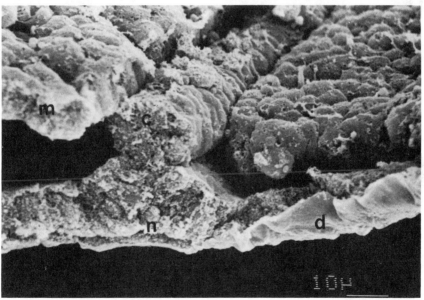

FIG.7. Early notochord anlage (c) flanked by mesoderm (m) and covered by ectoderm (e) and enveloping layer (d). This transverse fracture shows that the ectoderm still maintains a uniform thickness when the notochord anlage is already quite thick.

FIG.8. Preparation similar to Fig.7 but slightly older. Next to the notochord (c) the ectoderm has now thickened to form the neural strand (n). The mesoderm (m) starts separating into somites on either side of the notochord.

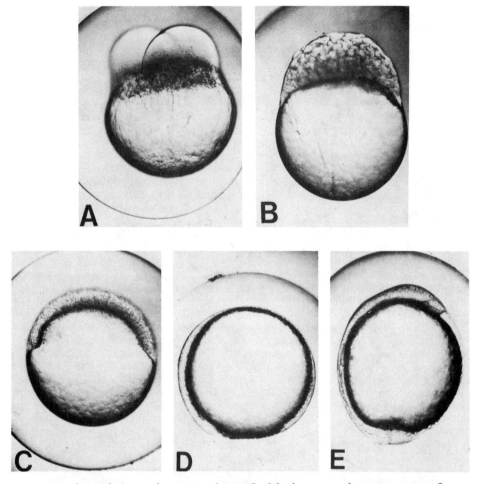

FIG.9. Light micrographs of living early stages of
zebrafish development (26°C), courtesy of M. Baumann
(Freiburg). A: Two-cell stage (0,5h), B: High blastodisc (2,5h), C: Blastodisc during epiboly but before
the onset of inwheeling of marginal cells (6h), D:
Late epiboly, beginning of axis formation at the left
(9h), E: Embryonic axis complete, forehead region at
the animal pole (top), tail bud about to form at the
vegetal pole (bottom), incipient somites seen at the
left (12h).

and Firlit, 1960; Hamano, 1964). However, according to Sander
et al. (1984 and pers.comm.) and to my SEM preparations,
invaginating deep cells leave the germ ring probably on its
entire circumference and migrate perpendicular to it towards
the animal pole; especially in the beginning of gastrulation
this movement is quite strikingly visible in time-lapse films.
I think it is only after migration towards the animal pole for
some distance that the migrating inner cells change their
direction and converge towards a meridional line which will
become the longitudinal axis of the embryo.

Scanning electron microscopy of these stages shows
pseudopodial activity of the internalized cells in all
directions without any evident preference. Shape and pseudopodia of these migrating cells are as described for ameboid
migrating cells in *Fundulus heteroclitus* (Trinkaus and
Erickson, 1983). In the cephalopod *Loligo vulgaris* (Marthy,
1985) and in the insect *Apis mellifera* (Fleig and Sander, 1988)
similar cell shapes of migrating mesoderm and endoderm cells
have been observed during comparable stages.

The first sign of the longitudinal axis of the embryo is
called embryonic shield (Oppenheimer, 1936; Pasteels, 1936;
Hisaoka and Battle, 1958; Hamano, 1964). My preparations show
that in *Brachydanio* the embryonic shield is prominent only due
to the prechordal plate and notochord, i.e. consists mainly of
mesodermal cells. The neural ectoderm thickens only some time
later. That notochord and neural strand are separated from each
other from the beginning, i.e. do not originate from a uniform
axial strand, was also indicated by their independent development after teratogen treatment during epiboly (Baumann and
Sander, 1984). The notochord anlage is formed by mesodermal
cells, endodermal cells are apparently not involved. This is
also observed in some amphibian species whereas in others the
notochord is said to derive from endoderm cells (Brun and
Garson, 1984; Keller et al., 1989).

ACKNOWLEDGEMENT

I wish to thank H. Vollmar for providing unpublished data
and K. Sander for comments and critical reading of the
manuscript.

REFERENCES

Ballard, W.W., 1973a, Normal embryonic stages for salmonid
    fish, based on *Salmo gairdneri R.* and *Salvelinus
    fontinalis M.*, *J.Exp.Zool.*, 184:7-26.
Ballard, W.W., 1973b, Morphogenetic movements in *Salmo
    gairdneri R.*, *J.Exp.Zool.*, 184:27-48.
Ballard, W.W., 1973c, A new fate map for *Salmo gairdneri*,
    J.Exp.Zool., 184:49-74.
Baumann, M., and Sander, K., 1984, Bipartite axiation follows
    incomplete epiboly in zebrafish embryos treated with
    chemical teratogens, *J.Exp.Zool.*, 230:363-376.
Betchaku, T., and Trinkaus, J.P.,1978, Contact relations,
    surface activity, and cortical microfilaments of
    marginal cells of the enveloping layer and of the yolk
    syncytial and yolk cytoplasmic layers of *Fundulus* before
    and during epiboly, *J.Exp.Zool.*, 206:381-426.
Betchaku, T., and Trinkaus, J.P., 1986, Programmed endocytosis
    during epiboly of *Fundulus heteroclitus*, *Amer.Zool.*,
    26:193-199.
Brun, R.B., and Garson, J.A., 1984, Notochord formation in the
    mexican salamander *(Ambystoma mexicanum)* is different
    from notochord formation in *Xenopus laevis*, *J.Exp.Zool.*,
    229:235-240.
Fleig, R., and Sander, K., 1988, Honeybee morphogenesis:
    embryonic cell movement that shape the larval body,
    Development, 103:525-534.

Hisaoka, K.K., and Battle, H.I., 1958, The normal developmental stages of the zebrafish, *Brachydanio rerio* (Hamilton-Buchanan), *J.Morphol.*, 102:311-328.

Hisaoka, K.K., and Firlit, C.F., 1960, Further studies on the embryonic development of the zebrafish, *Brachydanio rerio* (Hamilton-Buchanan), *J.Morphol.*, 107:205-227.

Hamano, S., 1964, A time-lapse cinematographic study on gastrulation in the zebrafish, *Acta Embr.Morph.Exp.*, 7:42-48.

Keller, R.E., and Trinkaus, J.P., 1987, Rearrangement of enveloping layer cells without disruption of the epithelial permeability barrier as a factor in *Fundulus* epiboly, *Dev.Biol.*, 120:12-24.

Keller, R.E., Cooper, M.S., Danilchik, M., Tibbetts, P., Wilson, P.A., 1989, Cell intercalation during notochord development in *Xenopus laevis*, *J.Exp.Zool.*, 251:134-154.

Kimmel, C.B., 1989, Genetics and early development of zebrafish, *Trends Genet.*, 5:283-288.

Marthy, H.J., 1985, Morphological bases for cell-to-cell and cell-to-substrate interaction studies in cephalopod embryos, *in*: "Cellular and molecular control of direct cell interactions," H.J. Marthy, ed. Plenum Press, London.

Oppenheimer, J.M., 1936, Processes of localization in developing *Fundulus*, J.Exp.Zool., 73:405-444.

Pasteels, J., 1936, Etudes sur la gastrulation des vertébrés méroblastiques, I. Téléostéens, *Arch.Biol.*, 47:205-308.

Sander, K., Dollmetsch, K., and Vollmar, H., 1984, Zebrafish epiboly: wheeling movement of deep cells at the blastodisc rim, *JEEM*, 82 suppl.:214.

Trinkaus, J.P., and Erickson, C.A.,1983, Protrusive activity, mode and rate of locomotion, and pattern of adhesion of *Fundulus* deep cells during gastrulation, *J.Exp.Zool.*, 228:41-70.

Wood, A., and Timmermans, L.P.M., 1988, Teleost epiboly: a reassessment of deep cell movement in the germ ring, *Development*, 102:575-585.

SECTION III

HISTORICAL AND CONCEPTUAL ASPECTS
OF "CAUSAL EMBRYOLOGY"

L'EPIGENESE ET LA PREFORMATION A L'EPOQUE

DE L'EMBRYOLOGIE CAUSALE

J.L. Fischer

C.N.R.S.
Centre d'Histoire des Sciences
9 rue Malher
75004 Paris, France

Préformation ou Epigenèse ?

"Zeit und Streitfragen der Biologie. Praeformation oder Epigenese ?" telle était la question que O. Hertwig posait à la communauté scientifique de 1894. Si O. Hertwig posait cette question, c'est que l'antagonisme préformation / épigenèse se trouvait être au coeur des débats, qui étaient entretenus par les nouveaux embryologistes à la suite de leurs résultats expérimentaux. En effet, nul ne pouvait, mieux que les embryologistes, prendre conscience de la puissance que possède la matière vivante à se transformer. Les embryologistes, qui opèrent comme de simples observateurs ou comme des expérimentateurs, sont les perpétuels témoins du déroulement des modelages successifs par lesquels passe l'embryon, ainsi que des adaptations et régulations morphogénétiques que le geste expérimental impose au développement embryonnaire.Il y avait aussi, dans ce contexte embryologique, le développement des théories microméristes (Y. Delage): par exemple la théorie des micelles et de l'idioplasma de Naegeli (1884); celle de la pangenèse intracellulaire de De Vries (1889) et la théorie des déterminants de Weismann (1892). Mais ces dernières théories étaient spéculatives, alors que les embryologistes s'appuyaient sur les faits concrets de l'expérience, qu'ils interprétaient dans l'idée générale, qu'ils pouvaient se faire d'une théorie du vivant. Cette idée elle-même prenait naissance, non seulement dans le fait scientifique, mais aussi dans une idéologie. L'expérimentateur / théoricien, s'il est avant tout un homme de science est aussi un homme social.

Toutefois, l'embryon n'exprime que les formes qui lui sont imposées par l'espèce. D'où, à notre échelle temporelle, le paradoxe que nous pouvons exprimer de cette façon: l'embryon est un organisme, qui évoque d'une façon spectaculaire à la fois une *évolution* des organismes, en mimant des types morphologiques embryonnaires ancestraux, et une *fixité* spécifique dans la précision de la répétition des évènements morphogénétiques qui conduisent, par exemple, invariablement un oeuf de poule à produire un poulet.

Experimental Embryology in Aquatic Plants and Animals
Edited by H.-J. Marthy, Plenum Press, New York, 1990

De plus, soumis à l'expérimentation, les oeufs en phase de développement peuvent différer profondément dans leur réponse suivant les espèces ou les genres systématiques: les résultats ont engendré ces conceptions apparemment contradictoires, dans les notions d'oeufs mosaïques et d'oeufs à régulation.

Les aspects théoriques relevant de l'embryologie sont évoqués par les mots préformation, évolution et épigenèse. Ces théories n'ont pas pris naissance avec l'embryologie expérimentale dans les années 1880: c'est la raison pour laquelle les termes néo-préformation néo-évolution et néo-épigenèse seront forgés. L'emploi de ces termes est particulièrement intéressant pour l'historien, car nous pouvons nous demander dans quelle mesure la synonymie qui a été faite entre la néo-préformation et la néo-évolution peut être justifiée ? En effet, si certains scientifiques, comme O. Hertwig, parlent de préformation et d'épigenèse, d'autres, comme Samassa (1896) ou F. von Wagner (1898) parlent d'évolution et d'épigenèse. Dans les deux cas il est clair que évolution et préformation s'opposent à épigenèse. Mais, historiquement, évolution et préformation sont des termes qui ont une connotation différente. D'abord il ne faut pas confondre la théorie de l'évolution, qui se rattache à l'évolution des espèces (transformisme), avec la théorie de l'évolution telle qu'on la connaissait au 18e siècle, et qui correspond à la théorie de la préexistence des germes. Sans retracer dans les détails, l'histoire de la génération au 18e siècle, il nous paraît nécessaire de rappeler les grandes lignes, qui jalonnent l'histoire de ces trois théories de la génération que sont la préformation, la préexistence des germes ou évolution et l'épigenèse, ne serait-ce que pour répondre à notre question.

De la préexistence des germes à l'épigenèse (1668-1820)

La définition du terme "évolution" par Littré peut nous servir de point de départ: "Evolution organique, système physiologique dont les partisans supposent, à tort, que le nouvel être qui résulte de l'acte de la génération préexistait à cet acte; ce système est opposé à l'épigenèse." Tant de faits divers que j'ai rassemblés dans cet ouvrage en faveur de l'évolution, prouvent assez que les corps organisés ne sont point proprement engendrés, mais qu'ils préexistaient originairement en petit" (C. Bonnet).

Nous posons ce problème car on ne peut, en effet, prendre la préexistence des germes pour la préformation, comme cela a été déjà dit par J. Roger, même si les limites n'apparaissent pas clairement entre ces deux théories qui se confondent parfois chez Bonnet (1778) en raison de l'accumulation des faits d'observation qui influent sur le raisonnement théorique. Il est certain que la préexistence des germes et la préformation ont, au 18e siècle, des rapports d'idées. Ce qui est certain aussi c'est que la préformation n'est pas incompatible avec l'épigenèse, alors que la préexistence des germes, telle qu'elle a été conçue à la fin du 17e siècle ne peut, en aucune manière, être rattachée à une théorie de l'épigenèse.

Si au début du 19e siècle; des auteurs comme Et. et I. Geoffroy Saint-Hilaire, E.R.A. Serres et Virey etc...parlent de préexistence des germes et non pas de préformation ce n'est pas sans raison.

Le système de la préexistence veut que les germes existent avant d'être, avant la fécondation, et qu'ils sont, depuis la création, emboîtés les uns dans les autres. C'est un système qui est avant tout un système fondé sur des notions théologiques et politiques. D'où l'importance que prenait cette doctrine dans un système monarchique, qui défendait les privilèges de l'aristocratie. Bernardin de Saint-Pierre, qui rêvait d'une république idéale, écrivait en 1797: "C'est dependant sur cette opinion si réfutée par l'expérience, que les aristocraties fondent leur prérogative. Dans nos écoles qui ont flatté toutes les tyrannies; on les soutient par des raisonnements subtils. Tous les hommes, y dit-on, ont été contenus de père en fils, dans le premier homme comme des gobelets renfermés les uns dans les autres". De même, E.R.A. Serres notait que la préexistence des germes et leur emboîtement "s'étaient imposés despotiquement" (1859).

La préexistence des germes correspond à un système qui bénéficia, dès son début, d'une "mauvaise" interprétation qui lui permit d'avoir un semblant de caution scientifique. En définitive, on sera avant tout partisan de cette doctrine d'obédience théologique, non pas pour des raisons scientifiques, mais en raison d'une idéologie philosophique ou politique.

Une preuve particulièrement démonstrative nous est fournie par M. Malpighi en 1672, qui apporte à la préexistence un appui "scientifique" en présentant une science du développement qui n'avait rien à envier, par ses observations, à celles que publia G.F. Wolff en 1759.

Néanmoins, c'est bien à Malpighi que nous devons ces phrases: "Dans des ouefs frais et qui n'avaient point encore été couvés, suivant la remarque que je fis le mois d'août passé dans un temps fort chaud...",il observe "une petite bourse" dans laquelle il "découvre" le "foetus"..."C'est pourquoi, conclut-il, il faut avouer que les premières ébauches préexistent dans l'oeuf, et qu'elles y jettent même des racines profondes de la même manière qu'on remarque dans les oeufs des plantes...".

En fait, comme l'ont très bien remarqué C. Dareste en 1876 et M. Duval en 1878, Malpighi observa dans un oeuf non incubé, un embryon au stade de la ligne primitive, en raison d'un début d'embryogenèse dû à la forte chaleur ambiante du mois d'août (une embryogenèse abortive peut se produire chez le poulet à 28°): d'où l'erreur d'interprétation de Malpighi. Mathias Duval écrivait à ce propos: "Malpighi qui faisait ses observations au mois d'août par une grande chaleur, paraît avoir observé la ligne primitive sur des oeufs pondus depuis 24 h non incubés. Il nomme ce premier rudiment de l'embryon la quille ou carène (pulli carina). C'est cette quille, dit-il, qui donne naissance au système nerveux central, c'est à dire à la moelle épinière et à l'encéphale et Malpighi observe très nettement la formation des vésicules cérébrales...".

Le naturaliste italien fit des observations précises, et non dénuées de sens, sur les stades successifs du développement embryonnaire de poulet. Les observations de C.F. Wolff de 1759, qui marquent, historiquement le début de l'épigenèse scientifique, ne seront que plus détaillées dans les dessins des stades embryonnaires, en raison du matériel optique d'observation qui s'était quelque peu amélioré depuis 1672. Nous sommes en présence de deux "savants", Malpighi et Wolff, qui font les mêmes observations, qui publient les mêmes dessins, mais qui, en s'appuyant sur les mêmes faits qu'ils présentent, défendent des théories opposées.

La préexistence des germes a une histoire: il y a un commencement vers 1660 et une fin vers 1820.

Le commencement se situe en 1668/1669 avec Cl. Perrault, mais surtout avec Swammerdam (1669) qui, rejetant les phénomèmes de la métamorphose, voyait le papillon dans la chrysalide, puis dans la chenille et il en déduisait qu'il devait être également présent en totalité dans l'oeuf, par analogie avec la graine des végétaux qui contient virtuellement la plante visible à l'oeil nu. C'est ce que Malebranche (1674-1712), à qui nous devons la diffusion de la doctrine de la préexistence au 18e siècle, exprimait en ces termes: "On voit dans le germe de l'oignon d'une tulipe une tulipe entière. On voit aussi dans le germe d'une oeuf frais, et qui n'a point été couvé, un poulet qui est peut-être entièrement formé. On voit des grenouilles, et on verra encore d'autres animaux dans leur germe, lorqu'on aura assez d'adresse et d'expérience pour le découvrir".La suite de cette citation de Malebranche mérite toute notre attention, car elle montre la raison et la démarche intellectuelle de la spécifité de la préexistence des germes: "Mais il ne faut pas que l'esprit s'arrête avec les yeux: car la vue de l'esprit a bien plus d'étendue que la vue du corps. Nous devons donc penser outre cela, que tous les corps des hommes et des animaux, qui naîtront jusqu'à la consommation des siècles, ont peut-être été produits dès la création du monde; je veux dire, que les femelles des premiers animaux ont peut-être été créées, avec tous ceux de même espèce qu'ils ont engendrés, et qui devaient s'engendrer dans la suite des temps". Il y a le fait, mais au-delà du fait il y a l'homme qui interprète, et cette interprétation ne peut que correspondre à la tendance philosophique qu'il défend.

La doctrine de la préexistence des germes stipule que chaque homme, chaque animal, ou chaque plante, issus d'un "oeuf" d'une graine ou d'un "oignon", possèdent des oeufs dans lesquels préexistent l'homme, l'animal ou la plante, dans une quantité de générations déterminées depuis la création. C'est la théorie de l'emboîtement des germes, dont le concept se trouve dans la citation de Malebranche: les germes étant emboîtés les uns dans les autres, soit dans un oeuf, pour les ovistes, ou dans le spermatozoïde pour les animalculistes. Si les "vers spermatiques" font l'objet d'une attention particulière depuis les années 1677-1678, à la suite des observations de Ham, Leeuwenhoek et Hartsoeker, au début du 18e siècle, de nombreux savants sont déjà convaincus de l'existence des oeufs chez les mammifères, même si cet oeuf, préssenti par Harvey au milieu du 17e siècle, presque découvert par Sténon et Régnier de Graaf en 1668, n'est identifié qu'en 1827 par von Baer.

La théorie de la préexistence des germes, telle que la voyaient Swammerdam ou Malebranche, ne correspond pas tout à fait à celle défendue par Malpighi, car l'interprétation des observations est différente. Malpighi qui défend la préexistence fait une "science" de l'épigenèse: ce qui prouve que le savant se présentait comme un partisan de cette doctrine pour des raisons qui dépassaient la simple description de l'objet naturel. Bonnet, qui se recommande de Malpighi, défend la préexistence des germes pour des raisons idéologiques et philosophiques, et ces raisons témoignent de l'impuissance de la science à produire des faits concrets qui offriraient un autre choix au savant: "La philosophie, écrit Bonnet, ayant compris l'impossibilité où elle était d'expliquer mécaniquement la formation des Etres organisés, a imaginé heureusement qu'ils existaient déjà en petit, sous la forme de Germes ou de Corpuscules organiques".

On croit en la préexistence des germes comme on croit en Dieu, et c'est principalement au nom d'une religion, et non d'une science, que sera défendue cette doctrine. La remarque de Bernardin de Saint-Pierre à ce sujet montre bien aussi l'intérêt que pouvait trouver l'aristocratie dans la défense d'une telle doctrine. L'embryon roi était roi depuis la création par la volonté divine, comme l'embryon de noble ne pouvait être que noble, et l'embryon de routurier ne pouvait prétendre à une autre condition sociale que celle à laquelle la préexistence le destinait.

L'histoire de la préexistence des germes s'achève vers les années 1820. En effet, nous pouvons encore lire en 1817 ces phrases de G. Cuvier: "La vie ne peut s'allumer donc dans des organisations toutes préparées, et les méditations des plus profondes comme les observations les plus délicates n'aboutissent qu'au mystère de la préexistence des germes". La même année J.J. Virey notait: "Cette opinion (la préexistence des germes) aujourd'hui la plus suivie, n'est pas pourtant à l'abri de toute difficulté...".

C'est aussi en 1817 que l'embryologiste allemand Pander publie son premier mémoire d'embryologie descriptive (feuillets embryonnaires) qui seront à la base de la fondation de l'embryologie scientifique, et d'un renouveau de l'épigenèse. Parallèlement aux travaux de l'école embryologique allemande, Et. Geoffroy Saint-Hilaire, qui ignore cette embryologie scientifique, défend dans le contexte de l'anatomie transcendante une épigenèse contre la préexistence: c'est ce qu'il explique, en 1828, à la suite de ses tentatives de tératologie expérimentale: "Cependant le but secret de mes recherches, que je ne crains plus d'avouer dans ces temps de meilleurs jours, fut l'examen d'un pricipe qui dominait les plus hautes questions de l'organisation animale: je veux parler de la théorie philosophique connue sous le nom de préexistence des germes". Là encore, chez Et. Geoffroy Saint-Hilaire, ce sont ses convictions de saint-simonien et d'anatomiste, désirant élaborer une théorie générale pour expliquer tous les phénomènes du monde vivant, qui ont compté, beaucoup plus que ses "résultats expérimentaux" et ses observations anatomiques pour asseoir une théorie de l'épigenèse. Toutefois, l'épigenèse d'Et. Geoffroy Saint-Hilaire ou de E.R.A. Serres diffère, dans le fond, de l'épigenèse, qui sera défendue dans le contexte de l'embryologie scientifique, puisque l'un et l'autre évoquent une embryologie spéculative dans laquelle l'embryon se "développe" par des interactions entre une force centripète et une force centrifuge.

Quant à la théorie de la préformation, ou du moins le concept, elle se trouve déjà chez les Anciens, dans les notions de "matière", de "semence", de "molécules" etc. et ce n'est pas la forme toute entière qui préexiste; la forme est contenue et répartie dans la "matière", la "semence" ou les "molécules" contenues chez l'homme et la femme et qui, lors de la fécondation, se mélangent et participent à la formation du nouvel être. Dans le contexte scientifique contemporain, une théorie de la préformation se retrouve dans la génétique qui a défini une "prédétermination" des caractères dans les gènes de l'individu, de l'espèce, du genre etc.

Historiquement, la théorie de la préformation s'élabore, suivant J. Roger, dans le courant du 17e siècle autour de l'oeuvre de F. Liceti. Mais la percée de la préformation sera discrète en raison de la naissance de la préexistence des germes, qui va bénéficier, pour sa gloire, de la découverte des "spermatozoïdes" et des "oeufs" chez les mammifères. Puis, à la fin du 19e siècle il y a un fondement expérimental à la théorie de la préformation avec la découverte des oeufs mosaïques et, au 20e siècle, avec la génétique.

Si la préformation connaît un début, elle ne connaît pas de fin, à la différence de la préexistence des germes. A la rigueur, nous pouvons dire que la doctrine de la préexistence des germes et leur emboîtement peut être considérée comme un accident idéologique dans une théorie générale de la préformation

Le triomphe de l'épigenèse

Dans les premières années du 19e siècle, de J.F. Meckel (traducteur de C.F. Wolff) à E.R.A. Serres, en passant par d'autres auteurs dont Et. Geoffroy Saint-Hilaire, on s'est plu à comparer les stades embryonnaires aux stades adultes des séries animales. Ainsi, la cicatricule de l'oeuf de poulet a été considérée comme pouvant représenter un stade infusoire; puis certains stades du développement de l'embryon des Vertébrés pouvaient être assimilés à des Invertébrés. C'est ce qu'exprime A. Duméril en 1846, qui s'inspire de Serres: "... à une certaine époque de sa vie, l'embryon représentera un infusoire, puis un mollusque, puis un poisson, et enfin un reptile, non pas au point de vue physiologique, mais sous le rapport anatomique, ou en d'autres termes, relativement à la forme de certains organes".

Cette anatomie comparée que l'on désigne, dans ces années 1820/1840, par l'expression "anatomie transcendante", servait à élaborer le principe de l'unité de plan et de l'unité de composition organique: les organismes vivants sont construits d'après une structure anatomique unique, qui variait dans ses formes; tous les organismes devaient pouvoir se réduire à une structure anatomique unique. Les anatomistes qui pratiquent cette anatomie transcendante ne sont pas spécialement matérialistes, et c'est Dieu qui a créé ce modèle anatomique unique à partir duquel tous les êtres vivants sont construits. Cette anatomie, qui s'appuie non seulement sur des formes adultes, mais aussi sur des formes embryonnaires, s'est forgée dans un contexte épigénétique, dans lequel l'embryon passe par des formes successives; et parmi ces formes, les formes primitives qu'il revêt ne pouvaient, toutefois, en rien évoquer le morphe achevé de l'être fini, mais évoquer seulement ses possibles anatomiques. En fait, cette épigenèse est attachée à une théorie de la préformation, en ce sens que l'embryon ne peut développer que les structures prévues, préformées dans le plan. A partir de l'instant où les formes résultent d'un projet contenu dans le plan - ou dans le programme - nous nous trouvons dans un système de la préformation, qui n'exclut pas l'épigenèse. Les différences tiendront au dosage entre les rôles joués par la préformation et par l'épigenèse dans la formation du vivant.

Théoricien de l'épigenèse, dans le cadre de l'anatomie transcendante, et technicien de l'anatomie comparée et embryonnaire, E.R.A. Serres opposait par des termes le système de la préexistence des germes ou "théorie de l'évolution", qui n'était qu'une manière d'envisager la nature, à l'épigenèse ou "métamorphogénie" ou l'étude du développement des corps organisés:

Préexistence des germes	Epigenèse
Pas de "vraies métamorphoses"	"Tout est métamorphose"
"Fixité absolue"	"Mouvement"
"Immuabilité"	"Changement"
C'est la "Mort"	C'est la "Vie"
"Ancien testament des sciences naturelles"	"Nouveau testament des sciences naturelles"
"Méthode de fixité"	"Méthode de variation"
"Développement des organismes par extension et continuité"	"Développement des organismes par additions successives de matériaux organiques homogèges"

Enfin, la préexistence, "C'est aussi la doctrine de l'hérédité absolue des races, et de la solidarité des enfants dans les pères", tandis que l'épigenèse, "C'est la liberté humaine et le droit de propre personnalité". La préexistence est essentiellement une doctrine de contraintes, alors que l'épigenèse s'ouvre sur les libertés.

Serres, qui dans son oeuvre défend inlassablement l'épigenèse, n'a pas omis de reconnaître en Malpighi un "homme à part", un "géant" de l'embryogénie: Serres et Malpighi ont observé les mêmes phénomènes, et la divergence de leur système de pensée ne pouvait, en rien, entraver la vérité qui se dégageait de leurs observations.

Certes, la lecture de Serres, partisan d'*une* théorie de l'épigenèse, ne sera pas celle de Bonnet, qui penche pour *une* théorie de la préexistence des germes. Toutefois chez Bonnet comme chez Serres, les corps restaient des corps organisés, mais dans un cas on contemplait la nature, Bonnet écrit *Les contemplations de la nature* en 1764, tandis que dans l'autre cas on étudiait des principes, Serres édite ses *Principes d'embryogénie, d'organogénie, de zoogénie et de tératogénie* en 1859.

Serres nous dit qu'il a abordé le problème de l'épigenèse "expérimentalement". L'expérimentation de Serres correspond à l'observation du matériel qui lui permis de construire son univers scientifique. C'est une méthode statique. Aussi, devons-nous porter de l'intérêt à Etienne Geoffroy Saint-Hilaire, ami de Serres, qui élabore une méthode expérimentale dynamique que nous pourrions prendre comme le point de départ de l'expérimentation en embryologie, si Et. Geoffroy Saint-Hilaire avait connu (ou reconnu) l'embryologie scientifique. Geoffroy Saint-Hilaire et Serres ne pouvaient la reconnaître, car elle était fondée sur des concepts qui ne corespondaient pas à ceux de l'anatomie transcendante.

L'embryologie scientifique recherche l'origine des organes sans préjugé d'un plan organique unique, véritable lit de Procuste, dans lequel tout système organique devait pouvoir entrer. De plus, l'anatomie transcendante est un système "préformationniste" dans le sens ou tout est prévu, et la nature, dans ce système, ne peut innover, ce qui fait que la recherche des origines n'est pas la préoccupation de ces anatomistes proches de la "philosophie de la nature" allemande. L'origine des formes est censée être connue, elle est dans cet être abstrait d'essence divine, qui est le modèle idéal de toutes les formes vivantes qui peuplent la terre. On remarque que ce système fondé sur une préformation, n'est pas incompatible avec une théorie de l'épigenèse, car les organismes sont libres de choisir, parmi les possibles anatomiques, la structure organique qui leur sera la plus favorable pour leur permettre de vivre dans un milieu déterminé.

Dans les années 1820, Geoffroy Saint-Hilaire fait des expériences sur l'oeuf de poule pour démontrer le bien fondé des lois tératologiques qu'il vient de créer (arrêt de développement, adhésion des membranes embryonnaires comme cause unique de la monstruosité), mais aussi pour démontrer, dans le cadre d'une épigenèse, la transformation des formes organiques sous l'influence des conditions du milieu (anoxie, hypothermie): fidèle à son principe, il n'aurait pas été surpris de trouver dans ses oeufs de poule soumis à l'expérimentation des formes reptiliennes.

Si les résultats expérimentaux obtenus par l'auteur de la *Philosophie anatomique* n'ont pas été ceux-là même qu'il a prétendu. Geoffroy Saint-Hilaire employait pour ces expériences des poules mutantes du type "poule de padoue" à hernie céphalique, aussi quand il ouvrait les oeufs soumis à l'expérience il notait des "déformations" au niveau de l'encéphale qui étaient normales pour ces mutants. Il soupçonna toutefois cette cause d'erreur dans ses interprétations, mais il ne put s'empêcher, toutefois, de penser que sa méthode expérimentale ne devait pas être sans effet sur la production de ces défauts. Il n'en reste pas moins que pour défendre une théorie de l'épigenèse, c'est sa conviction d'anatomiste et de saint-simonien, qui a compté beaucoup plus que ses résultats expérimentaux.

Si cette première pratique expérimentale est restée timide, elle va connaître un succès au-delà des années 1850 avec Camille Dareste, qui puise ses sources chez Geoffroy Saint-Hilaire. Contrairement à Geoffroy Saint-Hilaire et à Serres, Dareste s'appuie sur l'embryologie scientifique développée par l'école allemande depuis les années 1820.

Pour Dareste, l'épigenèse, dans le contexte de l'embryologie et dans celui de l'anatomie transcendante, devait conduire à élaborer un transformisme expérimental.

Dareste marque son époque par un travail important sur la tératologie expérimentale. Pour des raisons conceptuelles il emploie une méthode expérimentale indirecte. C'est à dire qu'il fait agir sur l'oeuf entier des agents succeptibles de modifier le déroulement normal du développement embryonnaire. Sa méthode expérimentale permit quelques progrès en embryologie: il découvre la dualité primitive du coeur chez l'embryon, à la suite de ses études sur les embryons diplocardes. La préoccupation principale de Dareste étant le transformisme, il ne se concentra pas spécialement sur ces problèmes d'embryogénie.

En 1884-1885, Dareste entre en polémique avec deux physiologiste Suisses, H. Fol et S. Warynski. Ces derniers auteurs, qui s'inspirent des travaux de Dareste, ont pratiqué une méthode expérimentale directe qui ne pouvait-être prise en compte par le créateur de la tératogénie. Fol et Warynski ont osé le geste expérimental direct sur l'embryon, en détruisant, à l'aide d'un thermocautère, une ébauche embryonnaire dans les 20/30 premières heures de l'incubation. Cette méthode "originale et nouvelle", et qui "diffère de tout ce qui a été fait jusqu'à ce jour", a été inaugurée par Fol et Warynski dans le but de rechercher "certains facteurs organogéniques": les intentions et les moyens des physiologistes Suisses diffèrent profondément de ceux prônés par Dareste.

Fol et Warynski désiraient expliquer une mécanique du défaut pour mieux comprendre le développement normal, et la méthode expérimentale directe permettait, à l'expérimentateur, de reproduire régulièrement une malformation précise, alors que la méthode indirecte employée par Dareste fournissait des résultats variables, imprévisibles. Dareste justifiait ainsi sa position: "Lorsque je commençai, il y a longtemps, mes recherches sur la tératogénie, je me proposais de trouver des procédés pour modifier l'évolution des êtres, et pour appliquer la méthode expérimentale à l'étude du transformisme" (1884).

Profondément épigéniste, Dareste s'élevait contre l'emploi d'une méthode expérimentale directe, car non seulement elle ne pouvait être reconnue comme moyen pour une recherche causale de la transformation des espèces et des races, mais, surtout, cette méthode avait dans sa finalité quelques affinités "préformationnistes" en raison de la prévisibilités des résultats.

Avec la méthode directe il devenait possible de suivre les évènements d'une façon relativement précise, puisque le résultat finale était prévu par l'expérimentateur. Cette méthode directe allait faire ses preuves, contrairement à ce qu'affirmait encore Dareste en 1891, qui jugeait cette méthode sans avenir, et c'est la raison pour laquelle il restera étranger aux travaux de l'embryologie causale, et au nouveau débat épigenèse / préformation.

L'épigenèse semblait être au début des années 1880 un acquis dans une théorie du développement. Point n'était besoin de longs discours sur une théorie qui paraissait l'évidence même, d'autant plus que de nombreux résultats expérimentaux parlaient en sa faveur.

La remise en question de l'épigenèse

C'est également vers les années 1880 que la question de l'épigenèse est, dans ce contexte, de nouveau posé, non seulement avec W. Roux (1885) mais aussi avec L. Chabry (1887), qui reconnaît en Dareste, tout comme en Fol et Warynski ses inspirateurs. Chabry qui aborde, sous la direction de G. Pouchet, au laboratoire maritime de Concarneau, une étude de "mécanique" cellulaire, par l'étude de l'embryologie des Ascidies, va être à l'origine d'une prise de conscience, de la part des scientifiques, d'un renouveau théorique de la préformation, dans ce contexte de l'embryologie expérimentale.

Si avec Dareste, Fol et Warynski on expérimentait non pas pour prouver le bien fondé d'une théorie de la génération ou de l'hérédité, l'une des préoccupations de l'école d'embryologie causale sera essentiellement axée sur la remise en question de ces deux théories fondamentales en biologie que sont l'épigenèse et la préformation.

C'est par l'emploi d'une technique particulièrement fine que Chabry démontrait que l'oeuf d'Ascidie était du type mosaïque ou anisotrope suivant la définition de E. Pflüger (1882), qui emploie le langage des physiciens, par opposition aux oeufs isotropes ou à régulation. Déjà W. Roux, à qui nous devons la théorie de la mosaïque, écrivait en 1885: "Le but de la segmentation est de séparer les matériaux qualitativement différents contenus dans le noyau".

En revanche, les expériences de Driesch sur l'oursin (1892-1893), de Morgan sur les poissons (1893), de Loeb sur l'oursin (1894), de Wilson sur l'Amphioxus (1892), et de Roux sur les Amphibiens (1888), démontraient que l'oeuf peut réguler.

Si les résultats expérimentaux prouvent que l'oeuf est isotrope ou anisotrope, cette preuve ne parait pas une condition suffisante pour que s'expérimentateur adopte la théorie qui correspond à ses résultats. Ainsi Chabry, qui montre que les deux premiers blastomères, chez *Ascidia aspera*, sont chacun déjà prédéterminés à fournir certaines structures organiques et non la totalité de l'individu, rejette la théorie de la préformation, que l'on pouvait tirer de ses expériences: "La méthode du traumatisme cellulaire ne doit pas, en effet, conduire toujours aux mêmes résultats et tandis que plusieurs personnes pourraient voir dans mes expériences la preuve décisive que l'animal est préformé dans l'oeuf, et chaque partie de l'animal préformée dans une partie de l'oeuf, je tiens à éloigner cette conclusion trop absolue". De même, quand

Roux expérimente sur l'oeuf d'Amphibien, et observe qu'un blastomère isolé produit une larve parfaite, ce qui était contraire à une théorie de la mosaïque (préformation), il imagine une théorie de la postgénération pour sauver son système.

Entre les "savants" observateurs du 18e siècle et les embryologistes expérimentateurs de la fin du 19e siècle, le fait scientifique, qu'il provienne de l'observation ou de l'expérimentation, n'est pas toujours suffisant pour déclencher le réflexe théorique correspondant chez le chercheur qui se trouve face à l'objet de son étude.

Ce "nouvel avatar", suivant la formule de F. Houssay (1908), de l'ancienne thèse de la "préformation", prend parfois le nom de "prédétermination". Cette synonymie entre les termes préformation et prédétermination, souligne la relation conceptuelle entre une science du développement et une science de l'hérédité.

Si de nombreux résultats expérimentaux démontraient que l'oeuf régule, les vérifications des expériences de Chabry confirmaient que l'oeuf d'Ascidie ne régule pas. E.C. Conklin écrivait à ce propos (1905): "The development of the ascidian eggs is a mosaic work because individual blastomeres are composed of different kinds of ooplasmic material; this mosaic work is not merely a cleavage mosaic but also a mosaic of germinal substance, several of which are recognizable before cleavage begins".

En 1932, l'embryologiste Belge, en expérimentant sur l'oeuf d'Ascidie, qui était historiquement l'oeuf type pour la démonstration de la théorie de la préformation, découvrait que cet oeuf peut réguler, dans certaines conditions particulières. Mais, Dalcq ne considérait pas, pour autant, que cet oeuf soit du type "régulatif": "Ainsi donc, il ne suffit pas de constater la formation d'un têtard entier aux dépens d'un fragment d'oeuf d'Ascidie pour considérer celui-ci comme un oeuf à régulation. Mes observations montrent au contraire que les localisations sont parfaitement définies dans l'oeuf vierge mais avec une disposition qui leur confère néanmoins quelque souplesse".

Les embryologistes de la fin de 19e siècle et du début du 20e siècle sont confrontés à deux théories du développement qui paraissaient antagonistes, d'autant plus que la néo-préformation avait des affinités avec le néo-darwinisme, et la néo-épigenèse avec le néo-lamarckisme. La question d'O. Hertwig, reflétait bien ce débat, qui avait été engendré par l'embryologie expérimentale et par la recherche de théories qui devaient expliquer l'hérédité.

Maintenant, nous pouvons donner raison à O. Hertwig, d'opposer épigenèse à préformation, et tort à Wagner, d'opposer épigenèse à évolution. L'emploi du terme évolution ou néo-évolution est, en effet, injustifié puisque si nous devions établir une synonymie avec ce terme il faudrait le faire avec l'expression "néo-préexistence des germes". La préexistence des germes, ou théorie de l'évolution, étant un dogme qui connu sa fin vers 1820/1830, son utilisation dans les années 1890 ne pouvait correspondre au contenu conceptuel qu'évoquait ce terme: du reste, les embryologistes l'abandonneront pour conserver celui de préformation, d'autant plus que le terme "évolution" était désormais utilisé pour désigner le transformisme, et de plus spécialement le transformisme de la théorie darwinienne.

Le choix que devait faire le "savant" entre une néo-préformation et une néo-épigenèse, était non seulement fondé sur les résultats expérimentaux, mais aussi sur une idéologie. Sans que cela soit une règle applicable à tous ceux qui dévoilent leur affinité pour une théorie, il n'est pas inintéressant de remarquer que Chabry, qui démontre une préformation de l'oeuf, et qui refuse d'adopter une telle théorie, est un guédiste engagé, qui combat les inégalités sociales: c'est un homme de gauche, qui milite pour le mouvement ouvrier. Alors que Weismann, comme le soulignent ses biographes P. Huard et M. Montagné, descendait "de protestants rigides et comptait parmi ses aïeux un martyr de la foi (Vienne XVIe siècle). Cette ascendence a dû exercer sur lui une très grande influence. Le fondateur de la doctrine de l'hérédité biologique pensait que la destinée humaine découle de la qualité des ancêtres et du milieu où cette hérédité ancestrale a été placée".

Certes, dans la période 1880/1920 tous les scientifiques de droite n'étaient pas forcément pour la néo-préformation, et ceux de gauche pour la néo-épigenèse. Toutefois, nous pouvons seulement remarquer que pendant cette période, il y a une tendance idéologique, politique, qui fait que les rationnalistes, les anti-religieux (cf Y. Delage, Et. Rabaud), les sympathisants des mouvements qui prônaient l'égalité sociale, ont défendu une néo-épigenèse et un néo-lamarckisme. Ce n'est pas non plus par hasard, si c'est en URSS, que Lyssenko connu un tel succès: dans ce cas extrème où la science fut bafouée, c'est pour des raisons essentiellement politiques, et non plus "scientifiques", que l'on identifia le néo-darwinisme au capitalisme et à une science bourgeoise de droite, qu'il fallait combattre en lui opposant un néo-lamarckisme. Mais ce néo-lamarckisme n'avait plus rien à voir avec celui de Y. Delage du début du siècle, ni avec celui de P. Wintrebert des années 1950-1960, sur lequel Delage exerça "une influence considérable".

Néo-épigenèse ou néo-préformation ?

Entre le choix d'une néo-préformation ou d'une néo-épigenèse, il y avait une autre possibilité, qui était celle de concilier ces deux théories. Si ce compromis était déjà contenu dans les allusions que faisait Chabry à propos de ses résultats expérimentaux, c'est W. Roux, par nécessité scientifique, qui parle avec précision d'une conciliation entre préformation et épigenèse. C'est dans son travail "Ueber die bei der Vererbung von Variation anzunehmenden Vorgänge, nebst einer Einschaltung über die Hauptarten des Entwicklungsgeschehens" (1913), que Roux expose des idées sur la part qui peut revenir à la préformation et celle qui revient à l'épigenèse dans la formation de l'être vivant: Roux en était arrivé à ce compromis théorique, car il ne pouvait abandonner les deux théories qu'il avait formulées, celle de la "mosaïque", inspirée par les résultats expérimentaux, et celle de "l'excitation fonctionnelle", qu'il déduisait de l'observation de faits scientifiques et de son intime conviction de chercheur et de créateur. Mais il est vrai, qu'en 1905, E.G. Conklin, concrétisait sa pensée, dans ces phrases qui ne manquent pas de force idéologique: "Bien des gens qui ont réfléchi à ces questions ont senti, apparemment, qu'il n'y a pas de juste milieu entre le libre-arbitre absolu et le déterminisme absolu; l'homme est tantôt "libre" et tantôt un simple automate; il est absolument libre ou absolument esclave, complètement indéterminé ou complètement déterminé. Mais ces opinions extrêmes sont inexactes, non scientifiques et insoutenables, car elles sont contredites par des faits d'expériences. L'expérience nous donne l'assurance que nous ne sommes ni absolument libres ni absolument esclaves, mais que nous sommes en partie libres et en parties esclaves; les alternatives ne sont pas la liberté *ou* le déterminisme, mais plutôt la liberté *et* le déterminisme".

En conclusion, nous donnons une série de citations de textes que nous pouvons lire comme autant de messages, formulés par des hommes de science contemporains, qui ont eu conscience que les questions posées par l'épigenèse et la préformation restent d'actualité.

L'embryologiste A. Dalcq écrivait en 1935:" Tout en admettant l'importance de l'épigenèse, elle souligne la nécessité d'un minimum de préformation". Que Dalq écrive une telle phrase, n'est pas pour nous surprendre, puisqu'il a été le premier à montrer que l'oeuf mosaïque par excellence, celui d'Ascidie, peut réguler dans certaines conditions. De même, pour Waddington: " Un système entièrement prédéterminé dans l'ADN quoique à la mode aujourd'hui est inacceptable pour l'embryologie". Un autre embryologiste, L. Gallien (1958), prend aussi une position favorable au compromis théorique: "Ces deux théories ne s'opposent pas en réalité. En fait, elles sont complémentaires". Quant à J. Piaget (1967), qui transposait le couple épigenèse / préformation de "l'embryologie organique" à "l'embryologie mentale", il remarquait qu'avec "le flux et le reflux habituel des modes historiques, la tendance de bien des auteurs contemporains est un retour à la préformation plus ou moins stricte, étant donné que la structure en chaîne ou en hélice de la molécule d'ADN ... prête à une combinatoire quant à l'arrangement de ses éléments et qu'une combinatoire couvre par définition l'ensemble des possibles".

A partir de 1970, le problème prend une autre dimension. Peut-être avec J. Monod qui donne sa définition de l'épigenèse, terme qu'il emploie "..pour qualifier, sans référence à aucune théorie, tout processus de développement structural et fonctionnel"; et après avoir disserté sur la notion de plan et d'information, il écrit: "La construction épigénétique d'une structure n'est pas une création c'est une révélation". Ce terme de "révélation" est bien significatif d'une contrainte: c'est la révélation d'une information, d'un plan, ou d'un programme, ce qui revient à masquer un concept préformationniste. Mais Monod s'est expliqué à ce propos en se dégageant de toute référence historiques se rapportant à l'épigenèse. C'est bien l'interprétation du fait scientifique, contenu dans la génétique moléculaire qui, dans un langage de l'informatique, a conduit à étayer une "théorie" de la préformation".

F. Jacob, également en 1970, s'exprimait ainsi: "Tout le plan de croissance, toute la série des opérations à effectuer, l'ordre et le lieu des synthèses, leur coordination, tout cela est inscrit dans le message nucléique. Et dans l'exécution du plan, il y a peu de ratés: à la rareté des avortements et des monstres se mesure la fidélité du système". Dans un tout autre contexte scientifique que celui dans lequel évoluait E. Geoffroy Saint-Hilaire, nous retrouvons un système de contrainte. L'anatomie transcendante et la biologie moléculaire, nous enseignent la perfection du système, qui ne peut faire des "écarts" ni créer, car la nature est limitée dans des manifestations: dans un cas comme dans l'autre l'organisme ne peut répondre aux facteurs externes que "dans les limites permises par les instructions contenues dans le programme". A cette date, "Le vivant créateur de son évolution" et "Le développement du vivant par lui-même" (P. Wintrebert, 1962-1963), ne paraissent plus concevables.

Cependant, en biologie, rien n'est jamais définitif. En effet, P. Brien, qui se trouve être dans la tradition Belge du néo-lamarckisme, répond, en 1974, à l'offensive des molécularistes: "Le vivant, en s'édifiant de lui même, n'accomplit pas une programmation préétablie, prévue, inscrite en son germe sous quelque forme que ce soit. Il n'y a pas préformisme. Le vivant se fait en se faisant, par épigenèse".

P. Brien, tout comme F. Jacob, s'appuie, pour étayer son argumentation sur les faits scientifiques que la nature dévoile au biologiste expérimentateur et observateur. Mais les faits scientifiques, qui servent d'exemple à Brien, ne sont pas ceux que Jacob produit pour la défense de sa thèse. Alors, il faut bien constater que *La logique du vivant* n'est pas la même pour tout le monde. Au-delà du conflit épigenèse / préformation, se trouve une conception du vivant dans un système globaliste ou réductionniste.

L'objet même de la biologie est profondément dualiste, et le choix strict d'un système engendre des conflits, qui reflètent les tendances des uns et des autres dans leur interprétation du vivant, mais aussi leur sensibilité d'homme de science.

"Aucune découverte n'est une fin, c'est toujours un début renouvelé, un moyen pour toujours mieux nous situer en tant qu'Homme" (Boris Rybak, 1973). Cette phrase situe bien cette éternelle remise en question de la pensée cognitive, et le combat que l'homme de science mène face à la vie qu'il interroge et aux idéologies auxquelles il se trouve sans cesse confronté.

BIBLIOGRAPHIE

(Nous ne présentons pas une bibliographie complète, mais un choix de publications à partir desquel il est possible d'avoir des compléments bibliographiques).

Bernardi, W., 1986, Le metafisiche dell'embrione, scienze della vita e filosofia da Malpighi a Spallanzani (1672-1793), Firenze, L.S. Olschki.
Bernardin de Saint-Pierre, Préambule de la chaumière indienne, *in*: Etudes de la Nature, Bâle, nouvelle édition, 1797, t.V; cité *in:* G. Canguilhem, G. Lapassade, J. Piquemal

et J. Ulmann *in*: Du développement à l'évolution au XIXe siècle, *Thalès*, 1960.

Bowler, P.J. 1971, Preformation and preexistence in the 17th century, a bief analysis, *J.Hist.Biol.*, 4:221-244.

Brien, P., 1974, Propos d'un zoologiste, le vivant, épigenèse, évolution épigénétique, Bruxelles, EDUB.

Chabry, L., 1887, Embryologie normale et tératologique des Ascidies, Félix Alcan, Paris, 154 p.

Cuvier, G., 1817, Le règne animal, Paris, t.1.

Dalcq, A., 1932, Etude des localisatîons germinales dans l'oeuf vierge d'Ascidie par des expériences de mérogonie, *Arch.Anat.Microscop.*, 28:223-333.

Dalcq, A., 1941, L'oeuf et son dynamisme organisateur, Albin Michel, Paris.

Dalcq, A., 1956, Développement et hérédité, Revue de l'Université de Bruxelles, Janvier-février.

Dalcq, A., 1935, La régulation dans le germe et son interprétation, Société de Biologie, réunion plénière, 7-8 juin 1935; et C.R. des séances de la Soc.Biol., 119, n° 28.

Dareste, C., 1891, Recherches sur la production artificielle des monstruosités ou essais de tératogénie expérimantale, Reinwald, Paris, (1ère éd. 1877).

Delage, Y., 1903, L'hérédité et les grands problèmes de la biologie générale, Reinwald et Schleicher, Paris.

Delage, Y., et Goldsmith, M., 1909, Les théories de l'évolution, Flammarion (3e éd. 1918), Paris.

Duval, M., 1878, Etudes sur la ligne primitive de l'embryon du poulet, *Ann.Sc.Nat.*, n° 17, 48 p.

Dumeril, A., 1846, L'évolution du foetus, De Fain et Thunot, Paris.

Fischer, J.L., 1986, De la genèse fabuleuse à la morphogenèse des monstres, Société Française d'Histoire des Sciences et des Techniques, diffusion Berlin, 150 p., Paris.

Fischer, J.L., Chabry and french embryology *in*: "A conceptual History of Modern Embryology," Plenum Publishing Corporation, New York, (à paraître).

Fischer, J.L., and Smith, J., 1984, French embryology and the "mechanics of development" from 1887-1910: L. Chabry, Y. Delage & E. Bataillon, *History and philosophy of live sciences*, 1:25-39.

Gallien, L., 1967, Problèmes et concepts de l'embryologie expérimentale, Gallimard, Paris.

Geoffroy Saint-Hilaire, 1828, Où l'on se propose se rechercher dans quels rapports de structure organique et de parenté, sont entre eux les animaux des âges historiques, et vivants actuellement, et les espèces antédiluviennes et perdues, *Mémoires du Muséum national d'histoire naturelle*, t. 17.

Hertwig, O., 1894, Zeit und Streitfragen der Biologie, Heft I., Praeformation oder Epigenese ? Jena.

Horder, T.J., Witowski, J.A., and Wylie, C.C., 1986, A History of Embryology, Cambridge University Press, 477 p.

Houssay, F., 1908, Nature et sciences naturelles, Flammarion, Paris.

Huard, P., Montagné, M., 1949, August Weismann (1834-1914), *L'extrème Orient médical*, vol. 1:289-304.

Jacob, F., 1970, La Logique de vivant, Gallimard, Paris.

Oppenheimer, J., 1967, Essays in the History of Embryology and Biology, The M.I.T. Press.

Malpighi, M., 1672, De la manière dont se forme le poulet.

Monod, J., 1970, Le hasard et la nécessité, Seuil, Paris.

Roe, S., 1981, Matter, Life, and Generation, Cambridge University Press.

Roger, J., 1971, Les sciences de la vie dans la pensée française du XVIIIe siècle, Arnaud Colin, (1ère éd. 1963), 848 p., Paris.

Samasa, 1896, Ueber die Begriffe Evolution und Epigenese, *Biol.Zentralbl.*, 16:368-371.

Wilkie, J.S., 1967, Preformation and Epigenesis a new historical treatment, *History of Science*, 6:138-150.

Rey, R., 1989, Hérédité et science de l'homme, in: "L'ordre des caractères, aspects de l'hérédité dans l'histoire des sciences de l'homme", Vrin, Paris.

Rybak, B., 1973, Explorations circulatoires, Gauthier-Villars, Paris.

Serres, E.R.A., 1859, Anatomie comparée transcendante, pricipes d'embryogénie, de zoogénie et de tératogénie, Paris.

Weismann, August (1834-1914), und die theoretische Biologie des 19.Jahrhunderts, Herausgegeben von Klaus Sander, *Freiburger Universitätsblätter*, Juli 1985, Heft 87/88.

Pour un complément bibliographique touchant les théories biologiques et l'embryologie expérimentale, consulter *L'année biologique*, à partir de 1895.

SECTION IV

CONTRIBUTIONS OF GENERAL VALUE
TO EMBRYOLOGICAL RESEARCH

THE ROLE OF RETINOIC ACID IN VERTEBRATE LIMB MORPHOGENESIS

Gregor Eichele and Christina Thaller

Harvard Medical School
Department of Cellular and Molecular Physiology
25 Shattuck Street
Boston MA 02115, USA

In my possession are two little embryos in spirit, whose names I have omitted to attach, and at present I am quite unable to say to what class they belong. They may be lizards or small birds, or very young mammalia, so complete is the similarity in the mode of formation of the head and trunk in these animals. The extremities, however, are still absent in these embryos. But even if they had existed in the earliest stages of their development we should learn nothing, for the feet of lizards and mammals, the wings and feet of birds, no less than the hands and feet of man, all arise from the same fundamental form.

K. von Baer, quoted in Darwin (1859)

INTRODUCTION

How an organism develops from a fertilized egg is one of the most challenging questions in biology, and accordingly, has interested biologists for a very long time. Recent advances in molecular and cellular techniques have provided useful tools that are now applied to many of the basic questions of embryology. For example, how do cells during embryogenesis form the intricate *spatial pattern* of tissues characteristic for an organism, and how does the broad spectrum of *differentiated cell* types arise during embryonic development? It is widely appreciated that pattern formation and cell differentiation depend on a concerted expression of specific genes and in many cases also on cell-cell interactions. For example, in *Caenorhabditis elegans* two genes that specify cell fate (*lin-12* and *glp-1*) encode receptor-like transmembrane proteins whose extracellular domains share structural similarities with a diffusible ligand such as epidermal growth factor (for a review see Greenwald, 1989). In *Drosophila*, there is also good evidence that intercellular communication is operative in pattern formation e.g. of the epidermis (reviewed by Arias, 1989) and of the retina (reviewed by Rubin, 1989).

Experimental Embryology in Aquatic Plants and Animals
Edited by H.-J. Marthy, Plenum Press, New York, 1990

Understanding vertebrate development at the level of molecules, and single cells has been less forthcoming. Nevertheless, important advances in vertebrate embryology have been made in recent years. For example, screens of vertebrate libraries with *Drosophila* homeobox probes have led to the identification of homeobox-containing genes in vertebrates (McGinnis et al., 1984; reviewed e.g. in Gehring, 1987; Holland and Hogan, 1988 and Wright et al., 1989), differential cloning techniques have revealed gene products that are unevenly distributed in the early embryo (Weeks and Melton, 1987; Rosa, 1989), and an increasing number of studies document the importance of growth factor-related polypeptides in mesoderm induction (see Smith 1989, for a review).

THE CHICK LIMB SYSTEM

One system that has long been used to study morphogenesis in vertebrates is the developing chick limb (for reviews that discuss various aspects of limb development see e.g. Hinchliffe and Johnson, 1980; Tickle, 1980; Newman, 1988; Eichele, 1989; Smith et al., 1989). In many respects, during limb morphogenesis the same type of processes take place as in the whole embryo, but a limb is obviously less complicated than a whole embryo. For example, developing limbs exhibit ectodermal-mesenchymal interactions (reviewed e.g. in Kelley and Fallon, 1981; Fallon et al., 1983), long-range signalling (Tickle et al., 1975, Cooke and Summerbell, 1980) and programmed cell death (Saunders et al., 1962). Furthermore, limbs consist of a broad range of cell types that arise during development from limb mesenchyme (e.g. Sasse et al., 1984; Stripe and Goetnick, 1989; Sassoon et al., 1989), and thus the developing limb is also a system in which to study cellular differentiation. Connective tissue in the limb derives from lateral plate mesoderm. By contrast, striated muscles in limbs derive from somitic cells that migrate into the limb region (Gumpel-Pinot, 1974; Christ et al. 1977). Hence the developing limb offers an opportunity to study mechanisms of cell migration and of 'lineage'. Finally, studies in the limb system have also lead to novel insights regarding axonal guidance in embryonic tissues (e.g. Tosney et al., 1986 and references therein). In short, the experimentally well accessible chick limb system can help to elucidate processes central to vertebrate morphogenesis.

Vertebrate limbs develop from small buds that protrude from the embryonic flank (see Fig. 1 A to D). In chick, the limb buds are well visible by Hamburger-Hamilton stage 20 (day 3.25 of development, Fig. 1 A; see Hamburger-Hamilton, 1951, for stages). At this stage, the limb rudiments consist of apparently undifferentiated mesenchymal cells that are enclosed in an ectodermal hull. The ectoderm extending along the limb bud margin is thickened, forming the so-called apical ecto-dermal ridge (AER). The region of the mesenchyme that is located beneath the AER is known as the progress zone. Initially, the AER extends around the entire bud and therefore almost all of the limb mesenchyme is part of the progress zone. As the limb rudiment grows out distally, the AER and progress zone are gradually restricted to the tip of the limb rudiment. Around day 4 to 4.5 (stage 22/23) the mesenchyme proximal to the progress zone begins to terminally differentiate to

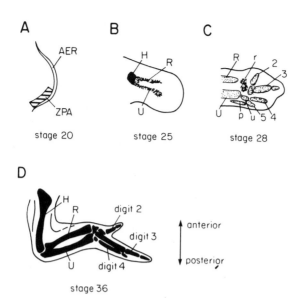

FIG.1: Representative stages of chick wing development. A. Schematic drawing of a Hamburger-Hamilton
stage 20 wing bud (3.25 days). At this stage the wing
buds are about 1 mm wide and consists of
histologically uniform mesenchyme enclosed in an
ectodermal hull that is thickened at the bud's rim
forming the apical ectodermal ridge. The mesenchymal
tissue along the posterior margin is known as the
zone of polarizing activity or polarizing region. B.
Wing rudiment at stage 25 (4.75 days). The emerging
cartilage for humerus, radius, and ulna are
indicated. C. Distal portion of a stage 28 wing bud
(5.75 days). The scheme illustrates the formation of
digits *2,3,4*, and *5*. Note, digit *5* will remain very
small. D. At stage 36 (10 days), the wing pattern is
fully established. Abbreviations: AER, apical
ectodermal ridge; H, humerus; p, pisiform; R, radius;
r, radiale, U, ulna; u, ulnare; ZPA, zone of polarizing activity; 2,3,4,5, digits. Fig. 1 C was drawn
after Hinchliffe and Johnson, 1980.

cartilage, bone, muscle etc. By day 6 (stage 28) all skeletal
elements have formed in at least a rudimentary form (Fig. 1 C).
The product of limb morphogenesis is an intricate pattern that
is fully distinct by day 10 (stage 36) of development. The
wing, for example, consists of humerus, radius and ulna and
three distinguishable digits (see Fig.1 D).

Vertebrate limbs arose about 350 million years ago,
presumably from the 'paddle' of crossopterygian fishes (see
Hinchliffe and Johnson, 1980, for a review). In the course of
time, limbs have become very diversified and specialized, yet a
more in-depth analysis of the structure of limbs of present-day
vertebrates readily reveals a common plan. The reason is that
the limbs of birds, rodents (e.g. Kochhar, 1977; Zeller at al.,
1989), humans (O'Rahilly and Gardener, 1975) and even reptiles
(Raynaud, 1985) all develop in a very similar fashion. This
probably means that the molecular and cellular basis of limb

morphogenesis is evolutionarily conserved. For all these reasons, the understanding gained in the chick limb system is likely to be valid for other limbs as well.

This review is primarily concerned with the mechanisms that underlie pattern formation along the anteroposterior limb axis (Fig. 1 D). How the proximodistal axis (extending between shoulder and fingertips) is generated is less well studied. It appears that the amount of time a cell spends in the progress zone determines its proximodistal fate (for details see e.g. Summerbell et al., 1973; Lewis, 1975). Even less is known about the formation of the dorsoventral axis. Patou's experiments (1977) suggest that the limb bud ectoderm is polarized along the D/V axis and is able to determine the dorsoventral axis in the mesodermal tissue at a time when the mesoderm is still undifferentiated.

It is obvious, that describing pattern formation in terms of three separate, perpendicular axis is somewhat arbitrary. Other investigators prefer to use a polar coordinate system when describing limb formation and especially limb regeneration (see e.g. Bryant et al., 1981; Bryant and Muneoka, 1986). It is surprising though, that a difference of choice of the coordinate system has lead to quite different interpretations of a transplantation experiment that will be discussed in the next section. This rivalry between different 'models' that try to explain the same set of observations, indicates that our present understanding of the limb system is incomplete.

THE ZPA AND THE ESTABLISHMENT OF THE PATTERN ALONG THE ANTEROPOSTERIOR LIMB AXIS

An early limb bud consists of undifferentiated mesenchymal cells. To form a limb with its distinct pattern, these cells must acquire different fates to form, for example, different kinds of digits. Promising insights into the specification of the pattern along the anteroposterior limb axis has come from a tissue transplantation experiment (Fig.2) which is in many ways reminiscent of the organizer grafts of Spemann and Mangold (1924). The experiment goes as follows (see top of Fig. 2): posterior limb bud tissue (the so-called zone of polarizing activity, ZPA) is transplanted to an anterior site in a host limb bud. There the ZPA will induce an extra set of digits (Saunders and Gasseling, 1968; reviewed by Tickle, 1980). As can be seen on the right in Fig. 2, these additional digits (marked by an asterisk) are arranged in a mirror symmetrical fashion to those derived from the host. The ZPA is evolutionarily conserved, since posterior limb bud tissue of all amniote limb buds so far examined is competent to induce duplications when grafted into chick wing- or leg buds (see Tickle 1980 for references and Honig, 1984).

What do the ZPA grafting experiments reveal about normal development? (The reader will undoubtedly realize that drawing conclusions about normal development from observations made in experimentally manipulated systems deserves some caution.) Based on a broad body of experimental work, Wolpert and colleagues (see e.g. Tickle et al., 1975 and Tickle, 1980) have suggested that the ZPA releases a morphogen (i.e. a locally generated diffusible signalling molecule that mediates the

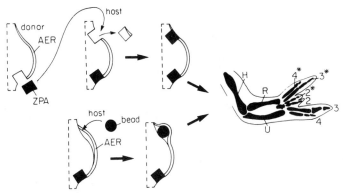

FIG.2: Induction of additional digits by ZPA grafting
(top) or local release of retinoic acid from a bead
implant (bottom). Grafting ZPA tissue from a donor
chick limb bud to the anterior margin of a host wing
bud results in the formation of additional digits.
Note, the ZPA is histologically indistinguishable
from the surrounding mesenchymal tissue, and is
defined operationally by this grafting experiment.
The digit pattern shown on the right is a *432234*
pattern with additional digits *2*, *3*, and *4* (marked
with an asterisk). Morphologically identical duplications are obtained by locally releasing retinoic
acid from an anteriorly implanted ion exchange resin
bead. To hold the bead in place, it is tucked underneath the apical ectodermal ridge. Within a few
hours, ectoderm grows around the bead. For abbreviations see Fig. 1.

formation of patterns of cellular differentiation) that spreads
out into the limb mesenchyme and thereby forms a concentration
gradient (see Fig. 3). By definition, the concentration of
morphogen in such a gradient diminishes with increasing
distance from the source (ZPA). Therefore, cells near the ZPA
will be exposed to high levels of morphogen, while those
further away will perceive progressively less morphogen. The
model also assumes that limb bud cells have a way to measure
the morphogen concentration, presumably with the help of a
specific receptor protein. By virtue of having sensed different
levels of morphogen, cells acquire different fates and later
form e.g. different digits.

    How can a 'smooth' gradient of morphogen generate the
discrete pattern of digits? One possibility is that limb
mesenchymal cells possess built-in thresholds for each type of
digit. The three horizontal lines in Fig. 3 illustrate such
thresholds. Let us assume that the threshold level for digit *4*
is ≥30 nM, that of digit *3* is ≥15 nM and that of digit *2* is
≥8 nM. Accordingly, a digit *4* will develop where the morphogen
concentration is ≥30 nM (region r4). Digit *3* will arise in
region r3, where the morphogen level is ≥15 nM. Digit *2* will
develop in r2, since the level of morphogen there is ≥8 nM.

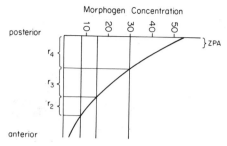

FIG.3: Gradient model of pattern formation applied to the the limb system. The ZPA which is located at the posterior side (left of graph) releases a morphogen (M) that diffuses into the limb bud tissue and forms a gradient. Cells along the anteroposterior axis will therefore be exposed to different concentrations of M. It is assumed that cells have a way to measure the concentration of M and furthermore that a particular threshold concentration of M (horizontal lines) will determine the type of digit formed. In the case illustrated here, the thresholds are 30 nM for digit 4, 15 nM for digit 3 and 8 nM for digit 2. This means that a digit 4 will develop in region r4, since in r4 [M] ≥30 nM. Likewise, a digit 3 will form in r3, since 15 nM ≤ [M] ≥ 30 nM. Finally, digit 2 will develop in r2 (8 nM ≤ [M] ≥ 15 nM).

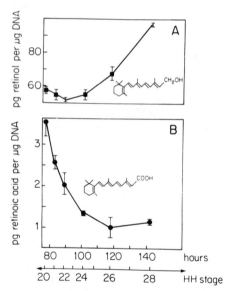

FIG.4: Concentration of retinol (A) and retinoic acid (B) in the limb bud as a function of development. The concentration was plotted on the ordinate and is expressed as pg retinoid per μg DNA. The time axis is given in hours; for reference, the developmental stages (Hamburger and Hamilton, 1951) are provided underneath. The figure also displays next to each curve, the structural formula of retinol and of retinoic acid, respectively.

RETINOIC ACID MIMICS THE ZPA

The crucial unknown in the concentration gradient model is the chemical nature of the postulated morphogen. Tickle et al. (1982) and Summerbell (1983) have reported that locally applied retinoic acid, the biologically active form of vitamin A (see Fig.4 for structures), will induce pattern duplications identical to those obtained by ZPA grafting. To generate duplications with retinoic acid, the compound is first absorbed onto an ion-exchange bead which then is implanted at the anterior wing bud margin (Fig.2, bottom). The bead will slowly release the absorbed retinoic acid into the wing rudiment.

By applying radiolabeled retinoic acid from bead implants it was shown that a retinoic acid concentration in the range of a few nM in the limb bud tissue is required to induce a pattern with an additional digit 2. Approximately 10 nM retinoic acid in the tissue will lead to a pattern with additional digits 2 and 3. At a concentration of around 30 nM retinoic acid, a 432234 or a 43234 will usually develop (Tickle et al., 1985; Eichele unpublished observations). This dose-dependence can be rationalized in terms of the morphogen concentration gradient model (Fig.3) whose central aspect is that the concentration of morphogen determines the character of a digit. If this is the case, one expects that to form the digit sequence 234, retinoic acid should be distributed in the form of a concentration gradient. It was indeed found that local application of retinoids results in a steady-state concentration gradient (Tickle et al., 1985; Eichele and Thaller, 1987). In addition, it was noticed that a high dose of retinoid produces a steep and far reaching gradient which results in a full set of extra digits. By contrast, low doses set up a shallow, short-range gradient and the resulting pattern has just an extra digit 2. Hence the shape of the gradient of applied retinoic acid does relate to the pattern, just as the model predicts.

THE INDUCTION OF ADDITIONAL DIGITS REQUIRES A PROLONGED TREATMENT WITH RETINOIC ACID

In the initial series of experiments conducted by Tickle et al. (1982, 1985) and Summerbell (1983), retinoic acid was applied continuously. Hence, these experiments could not reveal whether a short or a prolonged treatment is necessary to induce pattern duplications. By removing the retinoic acid discharging bead at defined times after implantation it was found that the induction of additional digits is a relatively slow, biphasic process (Eichele et al. 1985). Specifically, treatment for up to 10 hours resulted in normal limbs. Longer application times lead to progressively more complete duplications. The maximal response, that is the competence of the tissue to form additional digits 2, 3 and 4, was reached after approximately 17 hours of retinoic acid application. This indicates that the processes underlying pattern formation are slow. It is possible that retinoic acid triggers a series of reactions, each one with its own time constant. In addition, retinoic acid, once released from the bead, will have to diffuse into the surrounding tissue. Order of magnitude calculations (see Eichele and Thaller, 1987) indicate that it requires about 3 hours for retinoic acid to transverse the entire limb bud.

CHICK LIMB BUDS CONTAIN ENDOGENOUS RETINOIC ACID

That grafted ZPA and applied retinoic acid have such a similar effect and that retinoic acid acts so specifically suggests that it could be the postulated ZPA morphogen. To find out whether limb buds contain endogenous retinoic acid, Thaller and Eichele (1987) extracted homogenates of limb buds with a mixture of organic solvents. These extracts were fractionated and analyzed by high performance liquid chromatography (HPLC). These investigations clearly demonstrated that limb buds contain all-*trans*-retinoic acid, all-*trans*-retinal and all-*trans*-retinol. It was found that a limb bud at Hamburger-Hamilton stage 21, a stage when applied retinoic acid induces extra digits, contains about 6.5 pg of endogenous retinoic acid, corresponding to a mean tissue concentration of 25 nM. This is close to the concentration needed in the bud tissue to induce a full set of additional digits (30 nM). Satre and Kochhar (1989) have determined the concentration of retinoic acid in mouse limb buds of day 11 embryos as 300 pg per mg protein. Their value is in the same range as for chick limbs. A stage 21 chick limb bud contains 6.5 pg retinoic acid and 30 mg protein (protein content measured by C. Thaller, unpublished). These figures result in a retinoic acid to protein ratio of 220 pg/mg.

If retinoic acid serves as a signalling substance for defining the pattern along the anteroposterior limb axis, one would expect to see an elevated level of it during early limb morphogenesis. To find out, extracts of limb rudiments of Hamburger-Hamilton stage 20, 21, 22, 24, 26 and 28 embryos were prepared and the amount of retinoic acid and retinol was determined by HPLC. It was found (Fig. 4 A) that the concentration of retinol in the limb bud of stage 20 to 23 embryos is about 55 pg/µg DNA, and then gradually increases during subsequent development. By contrast, the concentration of retinoic acid declines rapidly between stages 21 and 23 (Fig. 4 B). At stage 20, when the limb consists of uniform, undifferentiated mesenchyme, and exogenously applied retinoic acid will induce duplications, the concentration of endogenous retinoic acid is 3.53 ± 0.3 pg/µg DNA. This figure drops to 1.33 ± 0.06 pg/µg DNA by stage 24, whenovert terminal differentiation of the limb has begun (Fig. 1 B) and when applied retinoic acid is no longer effective (Summerbell, 1983). Beyond that stage, the concentration of retinoic acid stabilizes at about 1 pg/µg DNA. We can draw two conclusions from these data. First, the concentration of retinoic acid is significantly higher during the stages when the pattern is specified. Second, the concentration of retinoic acid and that of its biologically inactive precursor retinol follow an opposite time course. It is thus possible that the enzyme(s) that convert retinol to retinoic acid is developmentally regulated.

RETINOIC ACID IS ENRICHED IN THE ZPA

If retinoic acid is the active agent of the ZPA, one would expect it to be enriched in the posterior region of the limb bud. Hence, limb buds were dissected into a smaller posterior portion containing the ZPA and a larger ZPA-free anterior piece (see Fig. 5). The mean concentration of retinoic acid in each

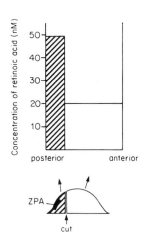

FIG.5: Endogenous retinoic acid is enriched in the posterior, ZPA-containing region of the limb bud. As indicated in the scheme, stage 21 limb buds were dissected into a smaller posterior block that includes the ZPA, and a larger ZPA-free anterior block. The tissue (about 1000 limb bud parts per analysis) was extracted with organic solvent, and the amount of retinoic acid in each region was quantified by high performance liquid chromatography. To obtain concentrations (nM), the quantity (pg) of retinoic acid in each fragment was normalized to the fragment's volume. Moreover, to reflect the different size of the two blocks, the width of the two rectangles was drawn proportional to the volume of each block.

of the two pieces was determined by HPLC and is shown in Fig. 5 (Thaller and Eichele, 1987). It amounts to 50 nM posteriorly, and 20 nM anteriorly. Hence there is 2.5 times more RA in the ZPA than in non-ZPA tissue. For obvious reasons, retinoic acid will not be distributed in a step-wise fashion, but will be spread across the limb bud in the form of a smooth gradient.

It is important to realize that the concentration displayed in Fig. 5 is the total retinoic acid concentration that represents the sum of free and protein-bound retinoic acid. In the cell, a substantial fraction of retinoic acid is specifically bound to cellular retinoic-acid-binding protein (CRABP; for a review see Chytil and Ong, 1984). Extraction with organic solvents will denature CRABP and the hydrophobic ligand will partition into the organic phase. Maden et al. (1988) reported that CRABP is not uniformly distributed across the chick limb bud but forms a 3 fold gradient in opposite direction to that of retinoic acid. These authors point out that a CRABP gradient antiparallel to that of total ligand shown in Fig. 5, will steepen the gradient of free retinoic acid that can bind to the nuclear retinoic acid receptor (see below). Order of magnitude calculations (Smith et al. 1989) indicate that a mere 3 fold CRABP gradient in the opposite direction of e.g. a 5 fold gradient of total retinoic acid, will result in a 20 fold gradient of free retinoic acid. This implies that cells in the limb bud would have to sense concentration differences in that range. That they are capable of doing this can be deduced from the dose-response analyses. It was found that to generate a pattern with a full set of additional digits requires only about 5 to 10 times more retinoid than is needed to form a pattern with just an extra digit *2* (Tickle et al. 1985; Eichele and Thaller, 1987).

LIMB BUDS CAN PRODUCE RETINOIC ACID IN SITU FROM RETINOL

Vertebrates cannot synthesize retinoic acid *de novo* but have to generate it by oxidation from retinol via the intermediate retinal (Dowling and Wald, 1960). Retinol (vitamin A, Fig. 4 A) derives from food intake and is provided to the embryo through maternal blood circulation. In non-mammalian vertebrates, retinol is derived from the egg yolk. Limb buds contain substantial amounts of retinol (Fig. 4 A). This raises the possibility that retinoic acid is generated from retinol directly *in situ*. To find out, radioactive retinol was discharged into wing buds of stage 20 embryos and after 3 hours of incubation *in ovo*, the bead was removed and the metabolites that had formed were fractionated and identified by high performance liquid chromatography (Thaller and Eichele, 1988). These analyses revealed that limb buds can generate a series of metabolites from retinol. Amongst them are all-*trans*-retinal and all-*trans*-retinoic acid. Order of magnitude calculations suggest that the rate of retinoic acid production can account for the concentration of endogenous retinoic acid present in the limb bud. The pattern of metabolites formed in the limb bud is quite complex and it is not yet clear, whether the rate of conversion of retinol to retinoic acid is different in the posterior and anterior region of the limb bud. In principle, differential metabolic rates could generate a gradient. To find out which cells in the bud are capable of retinoic acid production, efforts are underway to purify the responsible enzyme(s), raise antibodies against them and use these for immunohistochemical localization. These studies will not only identify the site(s) of retinoic acid synthesis in the limb bud but also in the embryo as a whole.

RETINOIC ACID BINDS TO NUCLEAR RECEPTOR PROTEINS

Retinoic acid is a small molecule. It is likely that its highly specific effects are mediated by a receptor. It was thought until quite recently that cellular retinoic acid binding protein (CRABP) could be the retinoic acid receptor. It was unclear, though, why e.g. HL 60 cells (a promyelocytic line) are induced to terminally differentiate by retinoic acid, despite the fact that they lack CRABP (Douer and Koeffler, 1982). In 1987, the groups of Chambon and Evans simultaneously reported the discovery of a gene that encodes a nuclear protein which binds retinoic acid with high affinity (Giguère et al. 1987; Petkovich et al. 1987). The strategy by which retinoic acid receptor (RAR) was discovered and identified was quite remarkable and is worth a summary (for a review see also Brockes, 1989).

It had become apparent from sequence comparisons of various steroid hormone receptors and of the thyroid hormone receptor that these proteins are members of a hormone receptor superfamily (Yamamoto, 1985; Evans, 1988; Beato, 1989; Brockes, 1989). These hormone receptors are multidomain proteins,

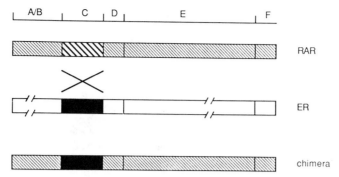

FIG.6: Structure of nuclear hormone receptors and domain swapping experiment between estrogen receptor (ER) and retinoic acid receptor (RAR) resulting in a chimeric receptor. The top diagram shows that hormone receptors can be divided into five regions (A/B, C, D, E, and F region). Displayed underneath are a diagram of RAR and ER. The C region (binds to DNA) of RAR is highlighted with bold hatching. The C region of ER is shown in black. Replacing the C region of RAR with that of ER converts the RAR into a chimeric receptor (bottom) that will now bind to an estrogen responsive element and hence transactivate the downstream gene in the presence not of estrogen but of retinoic acid. For practical aspects of these experiments the reader should consult e.g. Evans, 1988 or other reviews quoted in the Text.

consisting in essence of a transcriptional activation region (A/B region), a zinc finger containing DNA binding domain (C region) and hormone binding domain (E region) (see Fig. 6, top). In the presence of hormone, the receptor will undergo conformational rearrangements (reviewed by Green and Chambon, 1988) and bind to specific DNA sequences referred to as hormone responsive elements (HREs). HREs are located in the regulatory region of hormone-activated genes and act as enhancer sequences. Binding of the hormone/receptor complex to the HRE will activate transcription of the down-stream hormone responsive gene. Because of this mechanism of action these hormone receptors are referred to as ligand-regulated transcription factors.

The kinship between the different hormone receptors is most striking in the C region. For example, the amino acid sequences of the DNA binding domains of glucocorticoid receptor and of progesterone receptor are 90 % identical. Screens of cDNA libraries with oligonucleotide probes corresponding to the most conserved parts of the DNA binding domain resulted in a series of clones (Petkovich et al. 1987). One of them turned out to encode a receptor for retinoic acid. To confirm this, the DNA region that codes for the DNA binding domain (C region) of the estrogen receptor was swapped with the corresponding C region of the putative RAR cDNA (see Fig. 6). Transient transfection assays then revealed that the chimeric estrogen/retinoic acid receptor will function as transcriptional activator in the presence of retinoic acid (Petkovich et al. 1987).

Meanwhile two additional retinoic acid receptors were discovered (Benbrook et al. 1988; Brand et al. 1988, Krust et al., 1989, Zelent et al., 1989; Ragsdale et al., 1989). The three receptors are now known as RARα, RARβ and RARγ, and each of them is encoded by a separate gene. Northern blotting demonstrated that each gene gives rise to several transcripts (see e.g. Benbrook et al. 1988; Zelent et al., 1989; de The et al. 1989). A more detailed investigation of the transcripts of human RARγ cDNAs revealed that these transcript differ in their 5' region (Krust et al. 1989). Hence, RARγ probably exists in multiple forms that differ in their A domain. Analysis of RARβ mRNAs isolated from chick embryos suggest that the RARβ gene also gives rise to multiple transcripts that differ in the 5' region (Smith and Eichele, in preparation).

RNA blots show that the members of the RAR family are expressed in a wide variety of mammalian cell types (Benbrook et al. 1988; Zelent et al., 1989; de The et al. 1989) and also amphibian limb blastemas (Giguère et al. 1989). In situ hybridization experiments with chick embryos revealed that RARβ is expressed in several embryonic tissues including the developing limb, the spinal cord, and the developing heart and face (Smith and Eichele, in preparation). In other words, in addition to a fairly complex gene organization, the RARs also exhibit an intricate spatial pattern of expression.

PERSPECTIVES

A complex gene organization and spatial expression pattern is not unprecedented for developmentally important molecules. For example, the engrailed locus (Kuner et al. 1985), the decapentaplegic complex (Gelbart et al. 1985) and the bithorax complex (see Peifer et al. 1987) have sizable regulatory regions which account for the elaborate pattern of expression of these loci.

How will one be able to define the function of each of the RAR transcripts? It is difficult to give a general answer to this question. As a first step, it will be important to characterize the spatio-temporal expression pattern of each RAR mRNA and of each receptor protein. This will require in situ hybridization studies employing transcript-specific probes complemented by immunocytochemistry using antibodies that are specific for each receptor form. The next level of understanding will require a knock-out of specific transcripts by homologous recombination (see Jaenisch, 1988). Such efforts have succeeded in cultured mammalian cells (e.g. Kuehn et al., 1987; Hooper et al., 1987; Thompson et al., 1989) and Schwartzberg et al. (1989) have recently introduced a mutated gene into the germ-line of mice and obtained mutant offsprings. It is, of course, conceivable that different receptor isoforms (i.e. receptors that derive from the same gene) could, to some extent, substitute for each other. This would make the system redundant and thus less sensitive to outside disturbances. However, should such a redundancy exist, then gene disruption experiments will not be as clear-cut as one might hope. Overexpression or ectopic expression of specific RAR transcripts are easier to come by than homologous recombination (e.g. Balling et al., 1989; McMahon and Moon, 1989), but the results are perhaps less straightforward to interpret.

To sum up: it will require considerable efforts to define the role of retinoic acid in morphogenesis in molecular and cellular terms. It will be important to choose a suitable developmental system that depends on retinoic acid, but is not too complex. The findings summarized in this review suggest that the developing vertebrate limb is such a system.

ACKNOWLEDGMENTS

We wish to thank Kevin Pang for reading and commenting on the manuscript. Work from the author's laboratory was supported by grant HD 20209 from the National Institutes of Health an NP 630 from the American Cancer Society.

REFERENCES

Arias, A.M., 1989, A cellular basis for pattern formation in the insect epidermis, *Trends Genet.*, 5:262.

Balling, R., Mutter, G., Gruss, P., and Kessel, M., 1989, Craniofacial abnormalities induced by ectopic expression of homeobox gene Hox-1.1 in transgenic mice, *Cell*, 58:337.

Beato, M., 1989, Gene regulation by steroid hormone, *Cell*, 56:335.

Benbrook, D., Lernhardt, E., and Pfahl, M., 1988, A new retinoic acid receptor identified from rat hepatocellular carcinoma, *Nature (Lond.)*, 333: 669.

Brand, N.J., Petkovich, M., Krust, A. and Chambon, P., de Thé, H., Marchio, A, Tiollais, P., and Dejean, A., 1988, Identification of a second human retinoic acid receptor, *Nature*, 332:850.

Brockes, J.P., 1989, Retinoids, homeobox genes, and limb morphogenesis, *Neuron*, 2:1285.

Bryant, S.V., French, V., Bryant, P.J., 1981, Distal regeneration and symmetry, *Science*, 212:993.

Bryant, S.,V., and Muneoka, K., 1986, Views of limb development and regeneration, *Trends Genet.*, 2:153.

Christ, B., Jacob, H.J., and Jacob, M., 1977, Experimental analysis of the origin of the wing musculature in avian embryos, *Anat.Embryol.*, 150:171.

Chytil, F., and Ong, D.E., 1984, Cellular Retinoid-binding Proteins in: "The Retinoids," M.B. Sporn, A.B. Roberts, and D.S. Goodman, eds., Academic Press, Orlando, (vol.2), pp. 89-123

Cooke, J. and Summerbell, D., 1980, Cell cycle and experimental pattern duplication in the chick wing during embryonic development, *Nature (Lond.)* , 287:697.

Darwin, C., 1859, "On The Origin of Species by Means of Natural Selection, or the Preservation of Favored Races in the Struggle for Life," Murray, London.

de The, H., Marchio, A., Tiollais, P., and Dejean, A., 1989, Differential expression and ligand regulation of the retinoic acid receptor alpha and beta genes, *EMBO J.*, 8:429.

Douer, D, and Koeffler, H.P., 1982, Inhibition of clonal growth of human myeloid leukemia cells, *J.Clin.Invest.*, 69:277.

Dowling, J.E., and Wald, G., 1960, The biological function of vitamin A acid, *Proc.Natl.Acad.Sci.*, 46:587.

Eichele, G., 1989, Retinoids and vertebrate limb pattern formation, *Trends Genet.*, 5:246.

Eichele, G., Tickle, C., and Alberts, B.M., 1985, Studies on
    the mechanism of retinoid-induced pattern duplications
    in the early chick limb bud: temporal and spatial
    aspects, *J.Cell Biol.*, 101:1913.
Eichele, G., and Thaller, C., 1987, Characterization of
    concentration gradients of a morphogenetically active
    retinoid in the chick limb bud, *J.Cell Biol.* , 105:1917.
Evans, R.M., 1988, The steroid and thyroid hormone receptor
    super-family, *Science*, 240:889.
Fallon, J.F., Rowe, D.A., Frederick, J.M., and Simandl, B.K.,
    1983, Studies on epithelial-mesenchymal interactions
    during limb development *in:* " Epithelial-mesenchymal
    Interactions in Development," R.H. Sawyer and J.F.
    Fallon, eds., Praeger Scientific, New York, pp. 3-25.
Gehring, W.J., 1987, Homeo boxes in the study of development,
    Science, 236:1245.
Gelbart, W.M., Irish, V.F., St., Johnston, R.D., Hoffmann,
    F.M., Blackman, R.K., Segal, D., Posakony, L.M., and
    Grimalia, R., 1985, The decapentaplegic gene complex in
    Drosophila melanogaster, *Cold Spring Habor Symp.Quant.
    Biol.*, 50:119.
Giguère, V., Ong, E.S., Segui, P., and Evans, R.M., 1987,
    Identification of a receptor for the morphogen retinoic
    acid, *Nature (Lond.)*, 330:624.
Giguère, V., Ong, E.S., Evans, R.M., and Tabin, C., 1989,
    Spatial and temporal expression of the retinoic acid
    receptor in the regenerating amphibian limb, Nature
    (Lond.), 337:714.
Green, S., and Chambon, P., (1988), Nuclar receptors enhance
    our understanding of transcriptional regulation, *Trends
    Genet.*, 4:309.
Greenwald, I., 1989, Cell-cell interactions that specify cell
    fates in C. elegans in development, *Trends Genet.*,
    5:237.
Gumpel-Pinot, M., 1974, Contribution du mésoderme somitique à
    la genèse du membre chez l'embryon d'oiseau, *C.r.hebd.
    Séanc.Acad.Sci.Paris D*, 279:1305.
Hamburger, V., and Hamilton, H., 1951, A series of normal
    stages in the development of the chick embryo, *J.Morph.*,
    88:49.
Hinchliffe, J.R., and Johnson, D.R., 1980, "The Development of
    the Vertebrate Limb," Clarendon Press, Oxford.
Holland P. W. H., and Hogan, B. L. M., 1988, Expression of
    homeobox genes during mouse development: a review, *Genes
    Dev.*, 2:773.
Hooper, M., Hardy, K., Handyside, A., Hunter, S., and Monk, M.,
    1987, HPRT-deficient (Lesch-Nyhan) mouse embryos derived
    from germ line colonization by cultured cells, *Nature
    (Lond.)*, 326: 292.
Honig, L.S., 1984, Pattern formation during development of the
    amniote limb *in:* "The Structure, Development and
    Evolution of Reptiles," M.W.J. Ferguson, ed., Academic
    Press, London, pp. 197-221.
Jaenisch, R., 1988, Transgenic animals, *Science*, 240:1468.
Kelley, R.O., and Fallon, J.F., 1981, The developing limb: an
    analysis of interacting cells and tissues in a model
    morphogenetic system *in:* "Morphogenesis and Pattern
    Formation," T.G. Connelly et al., eds., Raven Press, New
    York, pp. 49-85.
Kochhar, D.M., 1977, Abnormal organogenesis in the limb in:

"Handbook of Teratology," J.G. Wilson, and F.C. Fraser, eds., Plenum Press, New York, pp. 453-479.

Krust, A., Kastner, P., Petkovich, M., Zelent , A., and Chambon, P., 1989, A third human retinoic acid receptor, hRARγ, *Proc.Natl.Acad.Sci.*, 86:5310.

Kuehn, M.R., Bradley, A., Robertson, E.J., and Evans, M.J., 1987, A potential animal model for Lesch-Nyhan syndrome trough introduction of HPRT mutations into mice, *Nature*, 326:295.

Kuner, J.M., Nakanishi, M., Ali, Z., Drees, B., Gustavson, E., Theis, J., Kauvar, L., Kornberg, T., and O'Farrell, P.H., 1985, Molecular cloning of engrailed: A gene involved in development of pattern in *Drosophila melanogaster*, *Cell*, 42:309.

Lewis, J.H., 1975, Fate maps and the attern of cell division: a calculation for the chick wing bud, *J.Embryol,exp. Morph.*, 33:419.

Maden, M., Ong, D.E., Summerbell, D., and Chytil, F., 1988, Spatial distribution of cellular protein binding to retinoic acid in the chick limb bud, *Nature (Lond.)*, 335:733.

McGinnis, W., Garber, R.L., Wirz, J., Kuroiwa, A., and Gehring, W., 1984, A homologous protein coding sequence in Drosophila homeotic genes and its conservation in other metazoans, *Cell*, 37:403.

McMahon, A.P., and Moon, R.T., 1989, Ectopic expression of the proto-oncogene int-1 in Xenopus embryos leads to duplication of the embryonic axis, *Cell*, 58:1075.

Newman, S.A., 1988, Lineage and pattern in the developing vertebrate limb, *Trends Genet.*, 4:329.

O'Rahilly, R., and Gardener, E., 1975, The timing and sequence of the limbs in the human embryo, *Anat.Embryol.*, 148:1.

Patou, M.P., 1977, Dorso-ventral axis determination of chick limb bud development *in:* "Vertebrate Limb and Somite Morphogenesis," D.A. Ede, J.R. Hinchliffe, and M. Balls, eds., University Press, Cambridge, pp. 257-266.

Peifer, M., Krach, F., and Bender, W., 1988, The bithorax complex: control and segmental identity, *Genes Dev.*, 1:891.

Petkovich, M., Brand, N.J., Krust, A., and Chambon, P., 1987, A human retinoic acid receptor which belongs to the family of nuclear receptors, *Nature (Lond.)*, 330:444.

Ragsdale, C.W., Petkovich, M., Gates, P.B., Chambon, P., and Brokes, J.P., 1989, Indentification of a novel retinoic acid receptor in regenerative tissues of the newt, *Nature (Lond.)*, 341:654.

Raynaud, A., 1985, Development of limbs and embryonic limb reduction *in:* "Biology of Reptilia," C. Gans and F. Billett, eds., Wiley & Sons, New York, pp. 60-148.

Rosa, F.M., 1989, *Mix.1* a homeobox mRNA inducible by mesoderm inducers, is expressed mostly in the presumptive endodermal cells of Xenopus embryos, *Cell*, 57:965.

Rubin, G.M., 1989, Development of Drosophila retina: inductive events studied at single cell resolution, *Cell*, 57:519.

Sasse, J. Horwitz, A., Pacifici, M., and Holtzer, H., 1984, Separation of precursor myogenic and chondrogenic cells in early limb bud mesenchyme by a monoclonal antibody, *J.Cell Biol.*, 99:1856.

Sassoon, D., Lyons, G., Wright, W.E., Lin, V., Lassar, A., Weintraub, H., and Buckingham, M., 1989, Expression of two myogenic regulator factors myogenin and MyoD1 during mouse embryogenesis, *Nature (Lond.)*, 341:303.

Satre, M.A., and D.M. Kochhar, 1989, Elevations in the endogenous levels of the putative morphogen retinoic acid in embryonic mouse limb buds associated with limb dysmorphogenesis, Dev. Biol., 133:529.

Saunders, J.W., Gasseling, M.T., and Saunders, L.C., 1962, Cellular death in morphogenesis in the avian wing, *Dev. Biol.*, 5:147.

Saunders J.W. , and Gasseling, M.T., 1968, Ectodermal-mesenchymal interactions in the origin of wing symmetry *in:* "Epithelial-mesenchymal Interactions," R. Fleischmajer, and R.E. Billingham, eds., Williams and Wilkins, Baltimore, pp. 78-97.

Schwartzberg, P.L., Goff, S.P., and Robertson, E.J., 1989, Germ-line transmission of a c-abl mutation produced by targeted gene disruption in ES cells, *Science*, 246:799.

Smith, J.C., 1989, Mesoderm induction and mesoderm-inducing factors in early amphibian development, *Development*, 105:665.

Smith, S.M., Pang,K., Sundin, O., Wedden, S. E., Thaller, C., and Eichele, G., 1989, Molecular Approaches to Vertebrate Limb Morphogenesis, *Development*, in press

Spemann,H., and Mangold, H., 1924, Ueber Induktion von Embryonalanlagen durch Implantation artfremder Organisatoren, *Wihelm Roux Arch.*, 100:599.

Stripe, N.S., and Goetnick, P.F. 1989, Gene regulation during cartilage differentiation: temporal and spatial expression of linkprotein and cartilage matrix protein in the developing limb, *Development*, 107:23.

Summerbell, D., 1983, The effects of local application of retinoic acid to the anterior margin of the developing chick limb, *J.Embryol.Exp.Morphol.*, 78:269.

Summerbell, L., Lewis, J.H., and Wolpert, L., 1973, Positional information in chick limb morphogenesis, *Nature (Lond.)*, 224:492.

Thaller, C., and Eichele, G., 1987, Identification and spatial distribution of retinoids in the developing chick limb bud, *Nature (Lond.)*,327:625.

Thaller, C., and Eichele, G., 1988, Characterization of retinoid metabolism in the developing chick limb bud, *Development*, 103:473.

Thompson, S., Clarke, A.R., Pow, A.M., Hooper, M.L., and Melton, D.W., 1989, Germ line transmission and expression of a corrected HPRT gene produced by gene targeting in embryonic stem cells, *Cell*, 56:313.

Tickle, C., 1980, The polarizing region and limb development *in:* "Development in Mammals," M.H. Johnson, ed., Elsevier/ North-Holland Biomedical Press, Amsterdam, (vol.4) pp. 101-136.

Tickle, C., Lee, J., and Eichele, G., 1985, A quantitative analysis of the effect of all-trans-retinoic acid on the pattern of chick wing development, *Dev.Biol.*, 109:82.

Tickle, C., Alberts, B.M., Wolpert, L., and Lee, J., 1982, Local application of retinoic acid to the limb bud mimics the action of the polarizing region, *Nature (Lond.)*, 296:564.

Tickle, C., Summerbell, D., and Wolpert, L., 1975, Positional signalling and specification of digits in chick limb morphogenesis, *Nature (Lond.)* , 254:199.

Tosney, K.W., Watanabe, M., Landmesser, L., and Rutishauser,

U., 1986, The distribution of NCAM in the chick hindlimb during axon outgrowth and synaptogenesis, *Dev.Biol.*, 114:437.

Weeks, D.L., and Melton, D.A., 1987, A maternal mRNA localized to the vegetal hemisphere in Xenopus eggs codes for a groth factor related to TGF-β, *Cell*, 51:861.

Wright, C.V.E., Cho, K.W.Y., Oliver, G., and DeRobertis, E.M., 1989, Vertebrate homeodomain proteins: families of region-specific transcription factors, *Trends Biochem. Sci.*, 1:52.

Yamamoto, K.R., 1985, Steroid receptor regulated transcription of specific genes and gene networks, *Ann.Rev.Genet.*, 19:209.

Zelent, A., Krust, A., Petkovich, M., Kastner, P., and Chambon, P. 1989, Cloning of murine α and β retinoic acid receptors and a novel receptor g predominantly expressed in skin, *Nature (Lond.)*, 339:714.

Zeller, R., Jackson-Grusby, L., and Leder, P., 1989, The limb deformity gene is required for apical ectodermal ridge differentiation and anteroposterior limb pattern formation, *Genes Dev.*, 3:1481.

PHYSIOLOGICAL APPROACH TO THE EARLY EMBRYOGENESIS

Pavel Kucera

Institute of Physiology, Medical
Faculty of the University of Lausanne
Rue du Bugnon 7, CH-1005 Lausanne, Switzerland

INTRODUCTORY REMARKS

The earliest period in metazoan ontogenesis, is characterized by intense proliferation of cells which, as they occupy the allocated space, progressively acquire specialized form and function. The evolving of a complex cell community is a highly dynamical process in which each embryonic cell develops in a given epigenetic context, i.e., interacts with its environment and thus obtains its positional information (Wolpert, 1969).

The interactions underlying the exchange of information (fig.1, left) are realized by means of exchanges of matter and energy between the cell and its immediate vicinity, i.e., the neighbouring cells and extracellular milieu (fig.1, right). The extracellular fluid serves at the same time as a source of substrates or messengers which modulate cell activity as well as a sink for cell products, i.e., catabolites or secretions. However, because the space is limited, and, because the molecules can diffuse through the extracellular fluid, the local microenvironment of a given cell also depends on conditions existing in more distant regions of the embryo.

It is important to recognize the possible regulatory character of such cell-milieu interactions. The regulatory loop may be imagined as follows: a higher cell activity in a given region leads to more complex 3-dimensional configurations of the tissue and extracellular space. These modifications influence the pathways of diffusion,and thus facilitate (or limit) the cell-milieu exchanges. This results in local modifications of concentration of metabolites or signalling molecules which, finally, may potentiate (or inhibit) cell functions in the very same region or in its neighborhood. Thus the differentiation of embryonic cells (expression of genome) and the differentiation of extracellular milieu (epigenetic information) may proceed in parallel and interact with each other.

On one hand, the experimental embryology using a rather "invasive" strategy (cuts, removals, transplants etc.) has

Experimental Embryology in Aquatic Plants and Animals
Edited by H.-J. Marthy, Plenum Press, New York, 1990

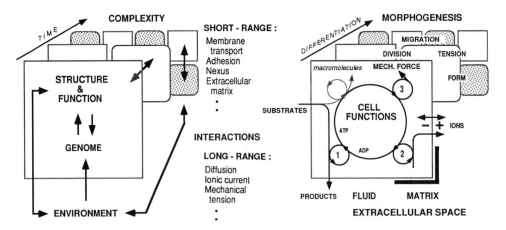

FIG. 1. Schematic representation of cell communications in the early embryogenesis
The complexity in a multicellular cell society evolves through cell-cell, cell-milieu communications (left). These exchanges of information controlling the embryogenesis are not directly identifiable but may be inferred from *in situ* studies of exchanges of matter and energy (right) between cells and their environment (1,2,3).

clearly demonstrated the importance of these interactions in the progressive committement of embryonic cells. On the other hand, the cell physiology has defined several ways whereby the expression of cell genome (and ultimately the cell form and function) may be modulated by extracellular factors. However, studies of real cell-milieu interactions as they happen *in situ*, within a developing cell society such as the whole embryo, calls for a more holistic and physiological approach.

Indeed, the physiological approach to small cell assemblies without as yet specialized functions has needed itself to be developed. Such an approach should avoid reductionism and invasive methods and be able to record the activities of cells with respect to their position. Among the animal embryos, very few offer the possibility to respect this condition. However, organisms with meroblastic cleavage are especially suitable because their very early development unrolls mostly in two dimensions. When explanted *in vitro*, their blastoderms are almost transparent and make thus possible to study the behavior of cell subpopulations under controlled conditions.

In our laboratory, we have extensively used the chick blastoderm and developed several non-invasive methods with high sensitivity and spatial resolution allowing to study the cellular metabolism, transports and mechanical activities and also the modifications of extracellular fluid and matrix (fig.1). These studies will be briefly summarized in this paper.

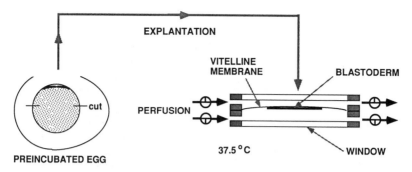

FIG. 2.Culture of the chick blastoderm under
controlled conditions
The blastoderm attached to the vitelline membrane is
excised from the egg and placed in a perfused
transparent chamber. The development of such a "2-
dimensional" complete cell society and the concomitant changes in the surrounding media are studied
by using physiological techniques.

THE CHICK BLASTODERM IN ARTIFICIAL EGG

The chick blastoderms from the stage of early blastulation
to the stage of neurulation have been studied. The intrauterine
stages (VI-X, Eyal-Giladi & Kochav, 1976) were obtained by
manual abortion of hens, the post-laid stages (3-6, Hamburger &
Hamilton, 1951) were obtained from preincubated eggs.

In the older stages, the vitelline membrane was cut and
removed together with the attached blastoderm from the yolk
(fig.2). In younger stages, the membrane and blastoderm were
explanted separately. The vitelline membrane and blastoderm
were mounted in a transparent chamber, perfused with defined
media and stabilized at the incubation temperature. Under these
conditions, the development of blastoderms can continue for 2-3
additional days and is, with a slight delay, comparable to the
development *in ovo* (Kucera and Burnand, 1987a). The development
of blastoderms submitted to physiological experiments was
systematically controlled under the microscope (fig.3).

EXPERIMENTS

Three physiological domains were investigated in the whole
chick blastoderms developing *in vitro*, namely, 1) the energy
metabolism, 2) ionic transports and 3) mechanical behaviour
(cf. fig.1:right and fig.3). In addition, studies of extracellular matrix were also conducted using optical and electron
microscopy.

The table 1 summarizes the parameters studied and
principles of the used methods. It shows that we have mostly
recorded optical or electrical signals originating from the
cells or from the adjacent extracellular fluid. The metabolic
fluxes and ionic transports were determined in the whole
blastoderm, in the embryonic area pellucida and extraembryonic

379

Table 1. THE PHENOMENA STUDIED AND THE METHODOLOGY USED IN THE
BLASTODERM

	PARAMETER:	METHOD:	REF.:
1	GLUCOSE UPTAKE	H^3-2-DEOXYGLUCOSE: SCINTILLATION COUNTING	(1)
		AUTORADIOGRAPHY	(2)
	OXYGEN UPTAKE	HAEMOGLOBIN AS O2 DONNOR / INDICATOR:	
		SCAN. SPECTROPHOTOMETRY	(9)
	CO$_2$ PRODUCTION	TRAPPING AS BaCO$_3$: CONDUCTOMETRY	(22)
		GROWTH OF CRYSTALS	(23)
	LACTATE PRODUCTION	LDH -> GPT COUPLED REACTIONS:	
		NADH SPECTROPHOTOMETRY	(1)
2	IONIC TRANSPORTS	VOLTAGE CLAMP: ION REPLACEMENTS AND DRUGS	(15)
		ACTING ON CHANNELS/CARRIERS	(15)
	EXTRACEL. CURRENTS	VIBRATING PROBE: COMPUTER-CONTROLLED	
		SCANNING ELECTRODE	(16)
3	MECHANICAL TENSION	ANALYSIS OF DEFORMATIONS:	
		REAL-TIME VIDEOPROCESSING	(13)
	MIGRATIONS	TRACING OF IDENTIFIED CELLS:	
		REAL-TIME VIDEOPROCESSING	(13)
	TISSUE VISCOSITY	DAMPING OF INDUCED MECHANICAL OSCILLATIONS:	
		VIBRATING NEEDLE	(10)

The principles and realizations of the used
techniques have been described in detail in the
listed references. Compare also with figures 1 and 3.

area opaca, or locally in small cell groups. The latter
recordings were achieved by using scanning devices or a real-
time video-image analysis system (fig.3). These two approaches
may be briefly explained in two examples, i.e., the mapping of
oxygen consumption and measurements of mechanical tensions
within the blastoderm.

In the first case, the chamber is superfused with
solution of oxyhemoglobin from which the embryonic cells take
up the oxygen. The concomitant spectral change of hemoglobin is
detected from a narrow beam of monochromatic light passing
through the chamber. The measurements are synchronized with
programmed displacements of the preparation so that the
calculated values of the oxygen uptake may be plotted with
respect to spatial coordinates and with resolution of 100 μm
(Kucera and Raddatz, 1980; Raddatz and Kucera, 1983).

In the second case, the preparation does not move but the
image of the blastoderm (or its region) is taken by a TV
camera, digitized and memorized. Such a reference image is then
continuously subtracted from the following images (fig.3). As
result of the subtraction, an image of difference is obtained
in which appear in real time only the changes which have
happened in the preparation, e.g., changes resulting from
mechanical events such as cell contractions or movements
(Kucera and Burnand, 1987b).

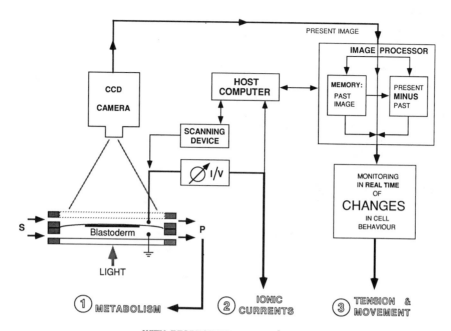

FIG. 3.Recording of cell activities *in situ*
1: The metabolic activity is derived from analysis of
uptake and production of metabolites (S,P) and from
optical signals originating in the cells or adjacent
perfusate. 2: The ionic transports across the
blastoderm are studied by using voltage/current clamp
technique, the ionic currents around the blastoderm
are mapped by a scanning vibrating electrode. 3: The
mechanical behavior of cells is recorded and analysed
on-line by using a video-image processing (compare
with table 1).

REVIEW OF RESULTS

1. Energy metabolism in the blastoderm

Temporal evolution

The most important energy substrate in the early stages is
the glucose. Post-laying blastoderms become increasingly
dependent on exogenous glucose (Baroffio, 1985).

Until the beginning of gastrulation, the main catabolic
pathway of glucose is the aerobic glycolysis but from the
gastrulation onward the metabolism becomes progressively more
oxidative (Kucera et al., 1984).

Insulin at concentration comparable to that found in the
egg increases the glucose uptake and lactate production
especially during the gastrulation-neurulation period (Baroffio
et al., 1986).

During the first day of incubation, the oxygen consumption
per blastoderm increases 40 times and the ATP production

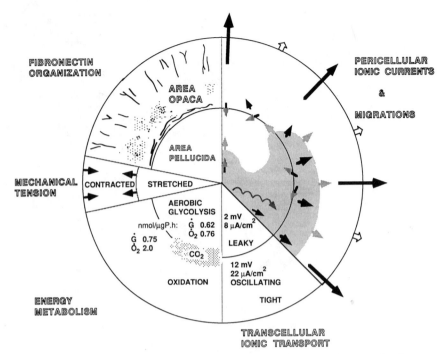

FIG. 4. Differentiation of cell activities and their
extracellular correlates in the one-day chick blastoderm

The results of in situ physiological studies are
summarized as projected onto the ventral face of the
blastoderm. *Lower left*: The extraembryonic area opaca
(AO) shows higher and more oxidative metabolism of
glucose (G) than the embryonic area pellucida (AP).
This probably leads to an uneven distribution of
protons (lactate, CO_2) in the extracellular fluid.
Lower right: The AO also generates a higher dorsoventral sodium flux and transectodermal electro-
chemical potential. *Upper right*: These metabolic and
ionic gradients are dissipated by pericellular
diffusion and ionic currents. The currents leave the
ventral face of the AO, diverge radially and turn
around the margin of blastoderm to its dorsal face
(long black arrows). Some also converge to and pass
through the anterior part of AP (hatched
arrowheads).Such an organized electrochemical field
might carry information for cell migrations (*upper
right:* mesoderm migrations: stippled arrows, edge
cell migrations: white arrows), for cell contractions
(*left*: small arrows) and for oriented assembly of
extracellular matrix (*upper left*: circular and radial
fibers).

reaches 7-10 nmol/µg.protein/h: a value comparable with those
of the most active mammalian differentiated cells (Raddatz and
Kucera, 1983; Kucera et al., 1984; Raddatz et al., 1987).

The production of carbon dioxide in pregastrular stages is
not linked to mitochondrial activity. During the first day of
incubation, the respiratory exchange ratio falls from 3 to 1

and the CO_2 production becomes dependent of exogenous glucose (Raddatz and Kucera, 1988).

The glucose and oxygen uptakes and CO_2 production fall by about 50% when the blastoderm is loosened from the vitelline membrane and left to develop in absence of mechanical tension (Baroffio, 1985; Raddatz and Kucera, 1988).

Spatial evolution

The extraembryonic area opaca is metabolically more active and also more oxidative than the embryonic area pellucida in which the aerobic glycolysis prevails (fig.4, lower left)(Raddatz and Kucera, 1983; Baroffio, 1985)

The metabolic activity is distributed within the blastoderm quite unevenly according to patterns characteristic for each stage. These patterns, radially symmetrical for intrauterine stages, later become bilaterally symmetrical and show also antero-posterior gradients (Kucera and de Ribaupierre, 1980; Raddatz and Kucera, 1983, 1988; Raddatz et al., 1987).

2. Ionic transports in the blastoderm

Transblastodermic transports

The early ectoderm generates a net flux of positive charges in the dorsoventral direction. The short circuit current is mostly due to sodium transport (apical entry sensitive to amiloride, phlorizin, and SITS, basal extrusion sensitive to ouabaine).

The transectodermal short circuit current, open circuit potential and resistance are much higher in the area opaca than in the area pellucida (fig.4, lower right).

The short circuit current shows regular oscillations with 3-5 min period. These oscillations, especially well expressed in the area opaca, are not related to transectodermal conductance but depend on presence of glucose, bicarbonate and chloride (Kucera and Katz, 1988).

Periblastodermic currents

The uneven electrophysiological properties of the areas opaca and pellucida result in extracellular electrical currents presenting a characteristic distribution in space (fig.4, upper right).

These currents originate from the ventral face and close on the dorsal face of the area opaca. The main current loops are radially oriented and traverse the vitelline membrane outside the margin of blastoderm. These currents also show periodicity of about 5 min. Less intense currents converge from the area opaca antero-medially and pass ventro-dorsally through the area pellucida.

During the development, the intensity of extracellular currents and their spatial distribution become more complex (Kucera and de Ribaupierre, 1989).

3. Mechanical behavior of cells in the blastoderm

Stationary motility

The early development of the blastoderm takes place under mechanical tension generated by a sustained contraction of cells in the area opaca. This peripheral contraction results in a stretching of the central area pellucida (fig. 4, left). Such a mechanical equilibrium between active and passive regions is critical for the normal development and depends on energy-dependent microfilament-myosin interactions (Kucera and Burnand, 1987b). A high anti-myosin immunoreactivity is found in the innermost cells of area opaca just surrounding the area pellucida (Monnet-Tschudi and Kucera, 1988).

Brief local extracellular electrical stimuli evoke in the area opaca additional but transient cell contractions detectable by image analysis as well as by measurements of tissue viscosity (Kucera and de Ribaupierre, 1982).

A strong, generalized and reversible contraction of area opaca is also produced by antibodies against fibronectin (Kucera and Monnet-Tschudi, 1987).

Translocating motility

In the area pellucida, the migrating mesenchymal cells move in periodical saccades lasting about 5 min (fig.4, center right) and the tissue viscosity seems to fluctuate with the same periodicity. Brief electrical pulse applied repetitively each 5 min leads to ectopic migration and accumulation of cells (Kucera and Burnand, 1987b; Kucera and de Ribaupierre, 1982)

4. Organization of the extracellular matrix

Period of blastulation

Relatively small amounts of extracellular matrix and associated fibronectin are formed by the epiblast during the intrauterine development.

In the area pellucida, peaks of transient high density of fibronectin-rich extracellular matrix are found at the front of the expanding hypoblast and in the marginal zone where the epiblastic and deeper cell layers are in close contacts and intense rearrangements.

In the area opaca, fibronectin is almost absent at the beginning of incubation but its density steadily increases during the first day of development (Raddatz et al., in press).

Period from gastrulation to neurulation

The fibronectin-rich extracellular matrix form the basement membrane which progressively develops a remarkable spatial organization. This is especially seen when the fibronectin immunoreactivity is examined in whole transparent mounts of the area opaca (Monnet-Tschudi et al.,1985). The fibronectin forms a fine supracellular fibrillar network the pattern of which changes characteristically from dense fibers parallel with the border of area pellucida to long radially oriented fibers at the periphery of the area opaca (fig.4, upper left).

Cells actively migrating upon this fibrillar web show fibronectin immunoreactivity around their surface and also internalized. *In vivo* modifications of extracellular matrix (e.g., by antisera against fibronectin) can modify the activity of adjacent cells (e.g., their contraction state, Kucera and Monnet-Tschudi, 1987).

FUNCTIONAL DIFFERENTIATION IN THE BLASTODERM

Phenomenology

The data mentioned above show that the early chick blasto- derm is a cell society which develops a remarkable degree of complexity in a relatively short time interval and in "two dimensional" space (Kucera and Monnet-Tschudi, 1987). The quantitative and qualitative signs as well as the temporal and spatial aspects of this differentiation are illustrated by the following summary:
The *cells* in the blastoderm are characterized by:
- continuous and rapid increase in metabolic activity,
- increasing dependency on extracellular sources of energy,
- improvement of metabolic efficiency,
- evolving of specific vectorially organized and sometimes periodically oscillating functions
- functional specialization in the embryonic and extraembryonic areas
The adjacent *extracellular fluid* is characterized by:
- increasing depletion of substrates and accumulation of products,
- inhomogenous distribution of substrates, products and ions,
- complex diffusion patterns, such as ionic currents resulting from the two latter conditions.
The adjacent *extracellular matrix* is characterized by:
- increasing content of fibronectin,
- inhomogenous distribution of fibronectin,
- formation of supracellular region-specific webworks,
- possibility to transmit its modifications to the adjacent cells.

Correlations

The data suggest that at least three of the listed phenomena might be interrelated, namely, the pattern of extracellular ionic currents, the distribution of mechanical forces and the supracellular organization of extracellular matrix (see fig.4). Thus, where the ionic currents flow in parallel to the blastoderm, the ectodermal cells contract along these currents (cf. fig.4, black arrows), and, the extracellular matrix secreted by these cells assembles in fibers oriented along the same directions!

The importance of extracellular matrix in cell attachment and migration has been widely recognized and, as far as the chick blastoderm is concerned, recently discussed in some detail (Harrison et al., 1988). A great amount of information has been accumulated about the chemical nature of the matrix but it has become imperative to understand also how is controlled the supracellular assembly of the matrix (Timpl, 1989).

Causality ?

The presented data rise the question whether there is also any causal relationship between the patterns of extracellular matrix on the one hand, and the vectorially oriented cell functions and/or patterns of extracellular diffusion on the other hand (Kucera and Monnet-Tschudi, 1987; Kucera and de Ribaupierre, 1989). The morphological observations in the area opaca show that the polarity of ectodermal cells (and hence transectodermal ionic currents) appears before the formation of a conspicuous basement membrane (Raddatz et al., in press). Furthermore, the radial pattern of extracellular currents is present already at the stage 3 HH and thus seems to preceed the radial arrangement of the matrix fully developed at the stage 4-5 HH (Kucera and de Ribaupierre, 1989; Monnet-Tschudi, 1985).

These two indications allow us to formulate the hypothesis that the matrix precursors secreted by ectodermal cells into the extracellular space might assemble according to the electrochemical field generated by transectodermal and periectodermal ionic transports. The segment of causal sequence covered by the presented data would then be the following:
-> uneven distribution and/or activity of polarized ectodermal cells -> uneven efficiency of transcellular electro-chemical transports -> creation and maintain of uneven electro-chemical gradients across and along the blastoderm -> dissipation of these gradients by passive fluxes through the extracellular space -> assembly of the matrix in the electro-chemical field into an organized network -> use of the matrix network as guiding support by migrating cells ->.

SUMMARY

The early chick blastoderm allows to study the differentiation of embryonic cells within the whole living organism, i.e., in their natural *in situ* context. In this system, the knowledge about the information exchanges controlling the embryogenesis can be derived from physiological studies of material exchanges between the cells and environment. Such a physiological approach has indicated that one of the informations directing the cell migrations, namely the supracellular organization of extracellular matrix, might result from early spatio-temporal differentiation of cell metabolism and transports.

ACKNOWLEDGMENTS

This study was supported by Grants 3.243-0.82 and 3.418-0.86 from the Swiss National Science Foundation.

REFERENCES

1. A. Baroffio, "Etude du métabolisme du glucose pendant le développement précoce de l'embryon de poulet à l'aide d'une adaptation de la méthode du 2-désoxyglucose," *Thèse*

Sci., Univ. Lausanne, 121 ff (1985).

2. A. Baroffio, and P. Kucera, The deoxyglucose method adapted for studies of glucose metabolism in the early chick embryo, *J.Cell Physiol.*, 123:111-116 (1985).

3. A. Baroffio, E. Raddatz, M. Markert, and P. Kucera, Transient stimulation of glucose metabolism by insulin in the 1-day chick embryo, *J.Cell Physiol.*, 127:288-292.(1986).

4. K.S. Cole, 1949, Dynamic electrical characteristics of the squid axon membrane, *Arch.Sci.physiol.*, 3:253-258 (1949).

5. H. Eyal-Giladi, and S. Kochav, From cleavage to primitive streak formation: a complementary normal table and a new look at the first stages of development of the chick, *Dev.Biol.*, 49:321-337 (1976).

6. V. Hamburger, and H.L. Hamilton, A series of normal stages in the development of the chick embryo, *J.Morphol.*, 88:49-92 (1951).

7. F. Harrisson, L. Andries, L. and Vakaet, The chicken blastoderm: current views on cell biological guiding intercellular comunication, *Cell Differentiation*, 22:83-106 (1988).

8. L.F. Jaffe, and R. Nuccitelli, An ultrasensitive vibrating probe for measuring steady extracellular currents, *J.Cell.Biol.*, 63:614-628 (1974).

9. P. Kucera, and E. Raddatz, Spatio-temporal micromeasurements of the oxygen uptake in the developing chick embryo, *Respir.Physiol.*, 39:199-215 (1980).

10. P. Kucera, and Y. de Ribaupierre, *In situ* recording of the mechanical behaviour of cells in the chick embryo, *in:* "Embryonic Development, part B: Cellular Aspects," M.M. Burger, R. Weber, eds, Alan R. Liss, New York, pp. 433-444 (1982).

11. P. Kucera, E. Raddatz, and A. Baroffio, Oxygen and glucose uptakes in the early chick embryo, *in:* "Respiration and Metabolism of Embryonic Vertebrates," R.S. Seymour, ed., Dr. W. Junk Publ., Dordrecht, Boston, London, pp. 299-309 (1984).

12. P. Kucera, and M.-B. Burnand, Routine teratogenicity test that uses chick embryos in vitro, *Terat.Carcinogen. Mutagen.*, 7:427-447 (1987a).

13. P. Kucera, and M.-B. Burnand, Mechanical tension and movement in the chick blastoderm as studied by real-time image analysis, *J.Exp.Zool.* Suppl. 1:329-339 (1987b).

14. P. Kucera, and F. Monnet-Tschudi, Early functional differentiation in the chick embryonic disc: interaction between mechanical activity and extracellular matrix, *J. Cell Sci.* Suppl. 8:415-431 (1987).

15. P. Kucera, and de Y. Ribaupierre, Extracellular electrical currents in the chick blastoderm, *Biol.Bull.*, 176 (S):118-122 (1989).

16. G. Marmont, Studies on the axon membrane, *J.cell.comp. Physiol.*, 34:351-382 (1949).

17. F. Monnet-Tschudi, P. Favrod, M.-B. Burnand, C. Verdan, and P. Kucera, Fibronectin in the area opaca of the young chick embryo, *Cell Tissue Res.* 241:85-92 (1985).

18. F. Monnet-Tschudi, and P. Kucera, Myosin, tubulin and laminin immunoreactivity in the ectoderm of the growing area opaca of the chick embryo, *Anat. Embryol.*, 179:157-164 (1988).

19. E. Raddatz, and P. Kucera, Mapping of the oxygen consumption in the gastrulating chick embryo, *Respir.*

Physiol., 51:153–166 (1983).

20. E. Raddatz, H. Eyal-Giladi, and P. Kucera, Patterns of oxygen consumption during establishment of cephalo-caudal polarity in the early chick embryo, *J.Exp.Zool.* Suppl. 1:213–218 (1987a).

21. E. Raddatz, P. Kucera, and Y. de Ribaupierre, Micro-measurement of total and regional CO_2 productions in the one-day-old chick embryo, *Respir.Physiol.*, 70:1–11 (1987b).

22. E. Raddatz, and P. Kucera, CO_2 production of the chick embryo during the first day of post-laying development, *Respir.Physiol.*, 71:133–145 (1988).

23. E. Raddatz, F. Monnet-Tschudi, C. Verdan, and P. Kucera, Fibronectin distribution in the blastulating chick embryo, submitted (1990).

24. R. Timpl, Structure and biological activity of basement membrane proteins, *Eur.J.Biochem.*, 180:487–502 (1989).

25. H.H. Ussing, and K. Zerahn, Active transport of sodium as the source of electric current in the short circuited isolated frog skin, *Acta Physiol.Scand.*, 23:109–127 (1951).

26. L. Wolpert, Positional information and spatial pattern of cellular differentiation, *J.Theor.Biol.*, 25:1–47.

ENVIRONMENTAL POLLUTION AND EMBRYONIC DEVELOPMENT:

RELEVANCE OF STANDARDIZED TOXICOLOGICAL TESTS

Pavel Kucera and Eric Raddatz

Institute of Physiology
Medical Faculty of the University of Lausanne
Switzerland

During the last decades, all industrial countries have become progressively aware of many deleterious effects which the modern style of life causes to the natural environment and finally to man himself. Quite serious disruptions of large ecosystems already happened that resulted from ill-controlled industrial and agricultural activities and, also, dramatic unforeseen effects were experienced with new chemicals developed in order to improve our comfort or maintain our health. Such catastrophes pushed the governments to consider seriously the ecological aspects of human activities and to control the disposal of waste as well as the inocuity of products to be absorbed by living organisms.

The toxicological control of new compounds with a potential use in the human and veterinary medicine mostly use biological tests in vivo and *in vitro* which now systematically include also the evaluation of embryotoxicity and teratogenicity. This is necessary as the period of early embryonic development is characterized by absence of differentiated detoxication mechanisms and consequently by a high sensitivity to xenobiotics. Toxic compounds present in the embryonic environment either directly kill the life at its very beginning or modify the construction of the organism and thus compromize the quality of the postnatal life. The tests of embryotoxicity and teratogenicity of new drugs accepted by authorities are usually done on pregnant mammalian females. However, serious efforts have been recently made to develop alternatives to animal experiments (see e.g. the special issue of Experientia 44/10, 1988).

In our laboratory, we have been doing for many years physiological studies in the chick blastoderm cultured *in vitro* (see Kucera, in this volume). Three years ago, we adapted this preparation for a routine test of embryotoxicity and teratogenicity and obtained convincing and reproducible results. This positive experience with the chick embryo leads us to propose the use of embryos of other, especially aquatic species in order to monitor the environmental pollution.

Experimental Embryology in Aquatic Plants and Animals
Edited by H.-J. Marthy, Plenum Press, New York, 1990

In the following, we would like to point out the most important conditions that are to be respected whenever a routine test of embryotoxicity is to be developed and briefly summarize the results obtained with the chick embryo.

The choice of the embryo for in vitro tests

The living embryo selected for an embryotoxicity test must be *easy to obtain* (if possible without intervention on parents) and *well characterized* as far as its development is concerned. In the case of avian embryos, eggs of excellent and comparable biological quality can be obtained provided a careful choice of the paternal strain, good housing and controlled nutrition of the animals. As the parental age and seasonal variations influence the degree of fertilization, the viability and normality as well as the development *in ovo* must be systematically controlled during the whole reproduction period. This allows to plan the replacements of animals and thus maintain an optimized quality and hence a minimized variability of eggs. A great amount of information about the composition and development of the avian egg is available (Lillie 1908; Hamburger and Hamilton 1951; Romanoff 1967, 1972; Freeman and Vince 1974; Burley and Vadehra 1989) which facilitates the determination of culture conditions and interpretation of results.

The definition of the test

The method selected must allow to run the test under *well-controlled physical and chemical conditions*. In the case of the chick embryo, this requirement is respected only when the blastoderm is explanted *in vitro* and cultured in a defined medium to which a known amount of the tested compound is added.

The method should be *simple and economical*. In our case, the embryo is explanted in an "artificial egg" , i.e., a transparent silicone chamber (see Kucera in this volume), reincubated, and examined under the microscope after 24, 44 and 66 hours. Four to five concentrations of the tested drug and the control medium are run in parallel, 10-15 embryos being necessary for each condition. Twelve cultures are easily made by one trained person in a half-a-day and the complete evaluation of one compound including statistical tests takes about one month.

The method should ask relevant questions. In this respect, it is important to select simple, meaningful, well-defined qualitative and quantitative developmental criteria and to evaluate systematically all of them. In our case, the morphological and physiological criteria (e.g., growth parameters, presence of important features, functional blood circulation) figure in a standardized pre-printed document which, once completely filled with answers, represents the "*curriculum vitae*" of each preparation and allows to classify the embryo as live normal, live abnormal or dying.

The method should give *reproducible and relevant results*. The first condition is easy to test, the second one calls for comparisons with results obtained in other systems. Such comparisons are essential for the validation of the test.

The methodological aspects of the test using the chick blastoderm have been described in all details elsewhere (Kucera and Burnand 1987, 1988) and the culture was also demonstrated and realized during the practical part of this NATO ASI course by the participants themselves.

The results which were obtained and which may be expected

In a previous study, eight compounds of relatively known effects on embryonic development were tested. The dose-response curves for growth and survival were obtained with a good precision and specific compound-depending anomalies were unambiguously discriminated. These data allowed us to classify the compounds according to their toxic or teratogenic potency (see the table). Most importantly, these results were similar to those obtained with the same compounds in tests *in vivo* as well as in tests using *in vitro* cultures of the rat embryo and aggregates of embryonic nervous cells (see discussion in Kucera and Burnand 1987, 1988; Cicurel and Schmid 1988; Honegger and Werfeli 1988). In order to strengthen the validation of these three *in vitro* tests systems, a new study using 24 coded chemicals has been started recently under the supervision of the Swiss National Science Foundation. The results obtained so far with 12 unknown compounds have again given very comparable data (to be published).

These results are encouraging and show that well-defined tests systems using embryos *in vitro* may be routinely used in screening of chemicals expected to produce embryotoxic or teratogenic effects. They also show that such tests can yield data which may be extrapolated from one species to another.

These studies led us to the following considerations. The first one is, that the reactions found in embryonic mammals and birds should be, at least in principle, also reproducible in embryos of lower vertebrates and invertebrates. Indeed, as the life of all species is based on the same molecular interactions and as the fundamental laws of early morphogenesis are rather comparable in all species, it may be expected that embryos of lower species will react as well to xenobiotics with good sensitivity and specificity. The second one is, that if an embryo can be used to detect harmful effects of a given drug, it can equally be used to monitor the presence or absence of any *a priori* unknown harmful chemicals in its environment.

Let us recall, that most of the early embryos, invertebrate as well as vertebrate, develop in an aqueous environment. Also, they contain themselves a high amount of water and show intense exchanges between the external and embryonic fluids. These exchanges participate in the differentiation of the embryonic *milieu interieur*, which is an undissociable characteristic of multicellularity. The quality of the ambient medium is thus of paramount importance for the normal development. This might be especially true for the embryos exposed more directly (i.e., without specialized barriers) to the external medium such as those living in sea waters. Consequently, these embryos would probably be very sensitive to contaminants polluting the water.

Let us consider, for example, the problem of hypoxic or anoxic waters (Widdows et al., 1989). Indeed, large variations

Concentrations (in mol·l^{-1}) affecting the development of the chick embryo in vitro

Substance	Normal survival up to	Anomalies Malform. in 50%	Perturbation extraemb.memb.	Growth embryo	Mortality LC50	LC100
Dexamethasone	10^{-10}	10^{-7}	10^{-8}	10^{-6}	$3 \cdot 10^{-4}$	10^{-3}
Methotrexate	10^{-8}	$2 \cdot 10^{-7}$	10^{-7}↑	$2 \cdot 10^{-7}$	$2 \cdot 10^{-7}$	10^{-6}
Cadmium Cl	10^{-7}	$4 \cdot 10^{-7}$	10^{-6}	10^{-5}	$2.5 \cdot 10^{-5}$	10^{-4}
Diphenylhydantoin	$5 \cdot 10^{-5}$	10^{-4}	10^{-4}	10^{-4}	$6 \cdot 10^{-4}$	10^{-3}
Phenobarbital	10^{-4}	$5 \cdot 10^{-4}$	$2.5 \cdot 10^{-3}$	$5 \cdot 10^{-3}$	$8 \cdot 10^{-3}$	10^{-2}
Caffeine	10^{-4}	$7 \cdot 10^{-4}$	10^{-3}	$5 \cdot 10^{-3}$	$4 \cdot 10^{-3}$	$5 \cdot 10^{-3}$
Aspirin	10^{-4}	$5 \cdot 10^{-4}$	NS+	NS+	NS+	NS+
Saccharin	$5 \cdot 10^{-4}$	$2.5 \cdot 10^{-3}$	NS++	NS++	NS++	NS++

↑ increase in dimensions; NS no significant effect; + max.concentration tested 10^{-3}; ++ max. concentration tested 10^{-2}.

Reproduced, with permission, from Experientia 44:829 (1988)

of oxygen concentration are observed in polluted waters. Besides natural fluctuations of oxygen concentration due to seasonal or climatic variations (higher temperature, lower solubility), an abnormal decrease in oxygen content might be due to the overdevelopment of algae triggered by pollution (eutrophication), due to warming up of water near atomic plants or due to draining and drying procedures (higher salinity, lower solubility). Such a complex degradation of the quality of water, resulting essentially from progressive accumulation of industrial and agricultural waste is not always easy to detect instrumentally but might influence very early the metabolism and development of embryonic organisms living in the adverse water environment.

As the aquatic organisms represent a major part of the biomass, even slight modifications of water reserves may have considerable biological and economical implications (e.g. all consequences of a break in the food chain). Therefore, a systematic and severe control of the quality of water is of capital importance and should be done with the same seriousness as that applied, for instance, in toxicological tests of pharmaceutical products.

On the basis of our own experience with the embryotoxic tests, we propose that such ecotoxicological controls could be realized relatively simply by using standardized cultures of aquatic invertebrate embryos which are readily obtainable and the development of which is well documented (e.g., coelenterates, molluscs, echinoderms). Such cultures, grown in samples of (possibly contaminated) water could be able to detect embryotoxic and teratogenic effects of factors as diverse as temperature, acidity, salinity, oxygenation, ionizing agents and chemical compounds.

Such tests would need to be defined in preliminary studies and this paper has been written to stimulate such an ecotoxicological aspect of research in the embryology of aquatic organisms.

ACKNOWLEDGMENTS

The studies using the chick embryo were supported by the Grants 4.790.0.84.17 and 4.091.0.88.17 from the Swiss National Science Foundation and by the Grant 15-G29/88 from the Foundation Finanz-Pool 3R.

REFERENCES

Alternatives to animal experimentation, 1988, Follath, F. ed. *Experientia*, 44:805-877.
Cicurel, L., and Schmid, B.P., 1988, Postimplantation embryo culture for the assessment of the teratogenic potential and potency of compounds, *Experientia*, 44:833-840.
Burley, R.W., and Vadehra, D.V. 1989, The avian egg. Chemistry and biology, J. Wiley, New York.
Freeman, B.M., and Vince, M.A., 1974, Development of the Avian embryo. A behavioural and physiological study, Chapman and Hall, London.
Hamburger, V., and Hamilton, H.L., 1951, A series of normal

stages in the development of the chick embryo,
J.Morphol., 88:49-92.

Honegger, P., and Werfeli, P., 1988, Use of aggregating cell
cultures for toxicological studies, *Experientia*, 44:817-823.

Kucera, P., and Burnand, M.-B., 1987, Routine teratogenicity
test that uses chick embryos *in vitro*, *Terat.
Carcinogen.Mutagen.*, 7:427-447.

Kucera, P., and Burnand, M.-B., 1988, Teratogenicity screening
in standardized chick embryo culture: Effects of
dexamethasone and diphenylhydantoin, *Experientia*,
44:827-833.

Lillie, F.R., 1908, .The development of the chick, H. Holt and
comp., New York.

Romanoff, A.L., 1967, Biochemistry of the avian embryo. A
quantitative analysis of orenatal development, J.Wiley,
New York.

Romanoff, A.L., 1972, Pathogenesis of the avian embryo. An
analysis of causes of malformations and prenatal death,
J. Wiley, New York.

Widdows, J., Newell, R.I.E., and Mann, R., 1989, Effects of
hypoxia and anoxia on survival, energy metabolism and
feeding of oyster larvae (Crassostrea virginica,
Gmelin),.*Biol.Bull.* 177:154-166.

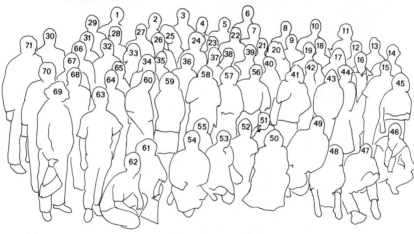

1 Meijer, L. (France) 2 Myers, R. (Canada) 3 Davidov, P. (USSR) 4
Burke, R. (Canada) 5 Cordes, V. (FRG) 6 Schierenberg, E. (FRG) 7
Fischer, J.L. (France) 8 Baxter, E. (UK-Scotland) 9 Meyran, J.C.
(France) 10 Dictus, W. (Netherlands) 11 Lehmann, A. (FRG) 12
Focarelli, R. (Italy) 13 Saint-Jeannet, J.P. (France) 14 Plickert, G.
(Switzerland) 15 Marthy, H.-J. (France) 16 Kucera, P. (Switzerland)
17 Falk-Petersen, I.B. (Norway) 18 Bryce, G. (UK-Scotland) 19 Sardet,
C. (France) 20 Silió, M. (Spain) 21 Berger, S. (FRG) 22 Jeffery, W.
(USA) 23 Gevers, P. (Netherlands) 24 Maleszewski, M. (Poland) 25
Gabel, A. (FRG) 26 Arnold, J. (USA) 27 Piferrer Circuns, F. (Spain)
28 Dorresteijn, A. (FRG) 29 Eichele, G. (USA) 30 Kluge, B. (FRG) 31
Manzanares, M. (Spain) 32 Van den Biggelaar, J. (Netherlands) 33
Leask, K. (Canada) 34 Moné, H. (France) 35 Thompson, J. (UK-Great
Britain) 36 Zernicka-Goetz, M. (Poland) 37 Koussoulakos, S. (Greece)
38 Fleig, R. (FRG) 39 Richelle, E. (Belgium) 40 Schioppa, M. (Italy)
41 Santella, L. (Italy) 42 Gillot, I. (France) 43 McCain, E. (USA)
44 Florent, I. (USA) 45 Blackshaw, S. (UK-Scotland) 46 Gualtieri, R.
(Italy) 47 Brandstätter, R. (Austria) 48 Lehmann, M. (FRG) 49
Bischoff, A. (FRG) 50 Clara, N. (France) 51 d'Aniello, A. (Italy) 52
Paulij, W. (Netherlands) 53 Boardman, K. (UK-Scotland) 54 Ozgunes, H.
(Turkey) 55 Mouahid, A. (France) 56 Simoncini, L. (USA) 57 Castriota
Scanderbeg, M. (Italy) 58 Norel, R. (Israel) 59 Emir, N. (Turkey) 60
Kocamaz, E. (Turkey) 61 Marthy, U. (France) 62 Ugarkovic, D. (FRG)
63 Nishikata, T. (Japan) 64 Coombs-Hahn, J. (USA) 65 Rupp, B.
(Switzerland) 66 Baguñà, J. (Spain) 67 Trinkaus, J.P. (USA) 68
Damen, P. (Netherlands) 69 Nardi, G. (Italy) 70 Sundermann, G. (FRG)
71 Poole, T. (USA); not present on photo: Dale, B (Italy) Métivier, C.
(France) Picard, A. (France) Quatrano, R. (USA)

AUTHOR INDEX

Auladell, C.
Baguñà, J.
Beach, R.L.
Berger, S.
Blackshaw, S.
Boyer, B.C.
Bueno, D.
Burgaya, F.
Burke, R.D.
Carré, D.
Collet, J.
Dale, B.
Dillard, W.L.
Dorresteijn, A.W.C.
Eichele, G.
Fleig, R.
Fischer, J.L.
García-Fernàndez, J.
Harrington, F.E.
Jeffery, W.R.
Kluge, B.
Kucera, P.
Marthy, H.-J.
Meijer, L.
Plickert, G.
Quatrano, R.S.
Raddatz, E.
Ribas, M.
Riutort, M.
Romero, R.
Rouvière, Ch.
Saló, E.
Santella, L.
Sardet, Ch.
Schierenberg, E.
Serras, F.
Swalla, B.J.
Thaller, Ch.
Trinkaus, J.P.
Van den Biggelaar, J.A.M.
White, M.E.

SUBJECT INDEX

Acetabularia,3,14,24,28,29,34,
    37,41
  major, 3
  mediterranea, 14
  pusilla, 3
Acetylcholinesterase, 292, 303
Acicularia schenckii, 14
Acid
  all-trans-retinal, 366, 368
  all-trans-retinol,366
  all-trans-retinoic, 366
Acoela, 100, 105, 111, 114,
    124
Acotylea, 104
Acrosome reaction, 279
Actin, 51, 264, 278
  α-actin, 296, 300
  β-actin, 296
  isoforms, 297
Actinomycin D, 295
Adultation, 305
Aequorea aequorea, 64
Agglutination, 44
Agglutinin, 44
Aging, 165
Alginate, 43
Allometry, 135
Alteromonas, 64
Amphibians, 100
Amphisbetia, 62
Amphitrite, 202
Ampullae, 300
Ancestry, 219
Anlagen, 108
Annelids, 116, 211
Anthozoa, 62
Antibody
  Lan 3-14, 237
  Laz 1-1', 237
Antigens, 237
Antimyosin immunreactivity,
    384
Aphidicolin, 171, 260
Apical constriction, 261
Apical ectodermal ridge, 360
Apical lamina, 265

Apis mellifera, 337
Apothosis, 133
Arabidopsis thaliana, 124, 149
Archenteron elongation, 257,
    259
Area
  opaca, 383
  pellucida, 383
Artificial egg, 379, 390
Ascaris, 164
Ascidia
  malaca, 284
  nigra, 295
Ascidians, 275, 278
Ascophyllum, 42
Axial polarity, 123
Axis
  animal-vegetal, 119, 120
  anteroposterior limb 362
  body, 119, 329
  embryonic, 113
  fixation, 47, 48, 49
  formation, 47, 90
  polar, 47, 49, 51, 62
  stabilizing complex, (ASC),
    48

Barbus conchonius, 315
Basal lamina, 180, 265, 268
Batophora, 4, 14
Bdellocephala punctata, 129
β-amino-proprionitrite, 267
β-galactosidase, 140
β-xyloside, 267
Blastema cells
  formation, 139
  origin of, 138
Blastoderm, 193, 194, 195,
    322, 385
Blastodisc rim, 329
Blastomeren-anarchie, 105, 108
Blastomeres, 112, 115, 117,
    168, 180, 187, 197,
    206, 262, 291, 295,
    316, 322
  fate, 199

Cells (continued)
  totipotent, 140
  yolk, 110, 117
Cellular analysis
  quantitative, 135
Cellular determination, 174
Cellular development, 164
Cellular specification, 172
Cellulose, 43
Cestus, 85
Chaetopterus variopedatus,
    200, 202
Chick
  blastoderm, 379
  limb system, 360
Chimeras, 145
Chlamydomonas, 27, 44
Chloroplast, 27, 28, 37
  genome, 13, 14
  membrane proteins, 15
  replication, 29
  ribosome proteins, 15
  ultrastructure, 29
Cholchicine, 264
Cilia formation, 202
Ciliation, 183
Ciona, 305
  intestinalis, 278, 279, 280,
      282, 295
  savigny, 278
Cleavage, 92, 103, 119, 199,
  early, 185, 187, 211
  equal, 116
  patterning, 114, 179, 21D4
      315,
  plane, 202
  rhythm of, 179
  ring, 32
  spiral, 111, 114, 116
  succession of, 178
  type of, 168
  unequal, 116, 179
Clepsine marginata, 197
Clonal analysis, 144
Clonogenic assays, 153
Clytia, 70
Cnidaria, 61
Collagen, 267
Colonial hydroids, 68
Communication unit, 181
Cordylophora, 68
Cortex, 92, 202
Cortical reaction, 203, 255
Cosmid library, 165
Cotylea, 104
Crepidula, 188
Cross fertilization, 95, 130
Ctenophores, 83, 89
Cyclic AMP, 142
Cyclins, 247, 248, 249
Cysts, 7

Cytochalasin B, 30, 31, 205,
    207, 262, 281, 295
Cytokinesis, 315, 316
Cytoplasmic components, 203
Cytoplasmic determinants, 100,
    112, 113, 114
  localisation of, 214
Cytoplasmic factors, 179, 186
Cytoplasmic filaments, 30
Cytoplasmic rearrangement, 205
Cytoplasmic segregation, 281
Cytoplasmic streaming, 28, 30,
    37
Cytoplasmic structure (P
    granules), 168
Cytoplasmic-to-nuclear volume
    ratio, 304, 310
Cytoskeleton, 89, 205

Dasycladaceae, 3, 21
Dedetermination, 139
Deep cells, 317, 323, 331
  motility of, 316
Dedifferentiation, 139
  theory, 138
Degrowth, 131, 132, 137, 144,
    149, 152
Demersal teleost egg, 315
Dendrocoelum lacteum, 130, 158
Depolarization, 275
Determination, 172, 199, 257
  histotypical, 117
  of polarity, 24
  territorial, 149
Development
  anural, 307
  of ascidians, 291
  of ctenophores, 86
  determinative, 112
  early, 163, 377
  eye, 112
  genetic analysis of, 124
  genetic control of, 124
  mosaic, 171, 197
  of nervous system, 233
  of spiralian, 197
  of teleost, 315, 329
  of vertebrates, 359
Developmental fate, 199, 207,
    219, 323
Developmental pathway, 113
Developmental potency, 323
Developmental potential, 202
Differentiation, 21
  histotypical, 122
  of nerve cells, 67
  potential, 169
  programme, 171
Dimple, 278
Diploneura, 130
Directed movement, 89

Polarity (continued)
  of rhizoid and thallus, 48
Polarization, 62
Pollution, 389
Polycelis
  felina, 130
  nigra, 130
Polychaetes, 116, 197, 199
Polycladida, polyclads, 100,
      101, 111, 115, 118,
      121, 123
Polyp, 60, 61, 67
  branching, 68
  budding, 68
  formation, 72
Polypeptides, 148
Polyspermy, 88
  "fast" block, 43
  "slow" block, 43
Pomatoceros, 199
Positional differences, 156
Positional information, 59,
      219
Positional memory, 157
Positive phototaxis, 22, 23
Post-blastema, 140
Preformation, 341
Primary electrical event, 276
Proboscidactyila flavicirrata,
      64
Progress zone, 360
Proliferation, 110, 132, 134,
      135, 140, 166
  of blastomeres, 119
  signal, 189
  stimulating factor, 184
  teloblastic mode of, 117
Pronucleus
  female, 89
  male, 89
Proportion activating factor
      (PAF), 136
Proseriata, 106, 116
Protein kinase, 245
Protostome, 110, 111, 114
Pseudostylochus, 115

Quercetin, 277

RAR transcripts, 370
Receptor isoforms, 370
Recognition
  species-specific, 42
Regeneration, 34, 122, 131,
      138, 144, 149, 152
  of head structures, 143
Regionalization, 114
Rejuvenation, 157
Reporter gene constructs, 151
Reproductive system, 130
Retinal, 368

Retinoic acid, 67, 359, 364,
      365
  binding protein (CRABP),
      368, 369, 370
Retinol, 366
Retroviral insertion, 123
Retroviral transfection, 140
Retroviruses, 123
Rhabdocoela, rhabdocoels, 106,
      116
Rhizoid, 7
Rhodamine, 92, 123
Rhodomorphin, 46
Ribosome, 29
  accumulation, 29
  transport, 29
RNA synthesis
  timing of, 285

Sabellaria
  alveolata, 200
  cementaria, 200
Saccharomyces cerevisiae, 245
Salmo, 320, 333
Sarsia tubulosa, 64
Schizosaccharomyces pombe, 245
Scyphozoa, 62
Sea urchins, 100, 243, 245,
      257
Sea water, 390
Secondary elongation, 262
Segmentation, 217
Segregation, 117, 122, 199
Self fertilization, 88
  block to, 88
Semelparous species, 158
Senescence, 157
Serotonin, 237
Signal
  transduction, 65
  transmission, 66
Signalling molecules, 362, 377
Sinefungine, 70
Sodium, 383
Somatoblast, 116
Spacing control, 69
Spantide, 142
Sperm
  activation, 279
  binding, 279
  egg fusion, 280
  entry sites, 280
  motility, 279
  recognition, 279
Spermatogenesis, 86
Spermatozoon, 274
Spiralia, spiralians, 113
  higher, 117, 121
Squid, 193, 195
Src-oncogene, 151
Starfish, 245

Starvation, 132, 134
Stathmokinetic method, 133
Stem cells, *see* cells
Stenostomum incandatum, 157, 158
Stigma, 22
Stolon, 68
Strongylocentrotus purpuratus, 258, 261, 264, 265
Styela, 291, 305, 306
  clava, 294, 295, 296, 297, 298, 303
  plicata, 298, 299, 300
Substance
  A, 36
  K, 142
  P, 142
  X, 36
Sulphorhodamine, 101, 237
Symmetry
  bilateral, 110, 171
  embryonic, 112
System
  headed streaming band, 30
  second messenger, 185
  thin filament, 30

Taxol, 205
Teleost, 315
Teloblast, 216, 234, 236
Teloplasm, 214
Teratogenicity, 389
Theromyzon
  rude, 224
  tessulatum, 224
Three quarter larvae, 112
Thymidine kinase, 13
Tip
  body, 28
  formation, 72
Tissue lineage, 108, 110
Tonoplast, 31
Toxicological tests, 389
Tracer molecules, 214
Transcellular voltage gradient, 34
Transcription, 184
Transdetermination, 139
Transdifferentiation, 60, 134
Transduction, 65
Tricladida, triclads, 99, 100, 108, 129

Trigonelline, 70
Trisodium salt, 237
Trochoblast, 183, 197
Trochus, 188
Trout, 319
Tubularia, 68, 70, 116
Tunicamycin, 267
Turbellaria, turbellarians, 95, 110, 114, 117, 120, 123, 125, 129
Two dimensional electrophoresis, 124

Universal intracellular inducer, 248

Vital dyes, 144, 195
Vitality, 158
Vitamin A, 365
Vitellaria, 130, 155
Vitelline membrane, 274
Volvox, 45, 47, 51, 52

Wall assembly, 43
Water quality, 393
Wound
  area, 138, 140, 144
  epithelium, 138

Xenoprorhyncus steinboecki, 116, 117
Xenopus, 183, 184, 245, 248, 249, 318, 322

Yeast, 51, 245
Yolk
  cells, *see* cells
  cytoplasmic layer, 321
  syncytial layer, 319, 321, 329
  syncytium, 194
  rich embryos, 120

Zebrafish, 315, 319, 323, 329
Zone of polarizing activity (ZPA)
Zygote, 22, 24, 25, 43, 48, 50, 168
Zygotic transcription, 293